INVESTIGATING THE Social World

4th Edition

PINE FORGE PRESS TITLES OF RELATED INTEREST IN RESEARCH METHODS AND STATISTICS

Making Sense of the Social World: Methods of Investigation, by Daniel F. Chambliss and Russell K. Schutt

The Practice of Research in Criminology and Criminal Justice, Second Edition, by Ronet Bachman and Russell K. Schutt

Social Statistics for a Diverse Society, Third Edition, by Chava Frankfort-Nachmias and Anna Leon-Guerrero

Social Statistics for a Diverse Society, Third Edition, With Student Version of SPSS v.11.0, by Chava Frankfort-Nachmias and Anna Leon-Guerrero

Adventures in Social Research: Data Analysis Using SPSS for Windows, Fifth Edition, by Earl Babbie, Fred Halley, and Jeanne Zaino

Adventures in Social Research: Data Analysis Using SPSS for Windows, Fifth Edition, With Student Version of SPSS v.11.0, by Earl Babbie, Fred Halley, and Jeanne Zaino

Adventures in Criminal Justice Research: Data Analysis for Windows Using SPSS Versions 11.0/11.5, or Higher, Third Edition, by George W. Dowdall, Kim A. Logio, Earl Babbie, and Fred Halley

Theory-Based Data Analysis for the Social Sciences, by Carol Anashensel

Multiple Regression: A Primer, by Paul Allison

A Guide to Field Research, by Carol A. Bailey

Designing Surveys: A Guide to Decisions and Procedures, by Ronald F. Czaja and Johnny Blair

Experimental Design and the Analysis of Variance, by Robert K. Leik

How Sampling Works, by Richard Maisel and Caroline Hodges Persell

Exploring Social Issues: Using SPSS for Windows 95, by Joseph Healey, John Boli, Earl Babbie, and Fred Halley

Constructing Social Research: The Unity and Diversity of Method, by Charles C. Ragin

INVESTIGATING THE Social World

4th Edition

The Process and Practice of Research

RUSSELL K. SCHUTT

University of Massachusetts, Boston

PINE FORGE PRESS
An Imprint of Sage Publications, Inc.
Thousand Oaks • London • New Delhi

For information:

Pine Forge Press
An imprint of Sage Publications, Inc.
2455 Teller Road
Thousand Oaks, California 91320
E-mail: order@sagepub.com

Sage Publications Ltd.
6 Bonhill Street
London EC2A 4PU
United Kingdom

Sage Publications India Pvt. Ltd.
B-42, Panchsheel Enclave
Post Box 4109
New Delhi 110 017 India

Printed in the United States of America

Library of Congress Cataloging-in-Publication Data

Schutt, Russell K.
Investigating the social world: The process and practice of research / by Russell K. Schutt.-4th ed.
    p. cm.
Includes bibliographical references and index.
ISBN 0-7619-2928-2 (paper)
    1. Social problems-Research. 2. Social sciences-Research. I. Title.
HN29.S34 2003
361.1′072—dc21

                                                      2003009022

03   04   10   9   8   7   6   5   4   3   2   1

Acquiring Editor:	Jerry Westby
Associate Editor:	Benjamin Penner
Editorial Assistant:	Vonessa Vondera
Developmental Editor:	Denise Simon
Production Editor:	Diana E. Axelsen
Copy Editor:	Toni Zuccarini Ackley
Typesetter:	C&M Digitals (P) Ltd.
Indexer:	Mary Mortensen
Cover Designer:	Michelle Kenny
Production Artist:	Sandra Ng Sauvajot
Student Resources	
CD Production:	Eclectic Multimedia

BRIEF CONTENTS

About the Author   xviii

Preface   xix

Acknowledgments   xxiv

1. Science, Society, and Social Research   1

2. The Process and Problems of Social Research   27

3. Theories and Philosophies for Social Research   62

4. Conceptualization and Measurement   85

5. Sampling   127

6. Causation and Research Design   165

7. Experiments   194

8. Survey Research   227

9. Qualitative Methods: Observing, Participating, Listening   276

10. Evaluation Research   310

11. Historical and Comparative Research   337

12. Data Analysis   367

13. Qualitative Data Analysis and Content Analysis   414

14. Reporting Research   450

Appendix A: Summaries of Frequently Cited Research Articles   A-1

Appendix B: Questions to Ask About a Research Article   B-1

Appendix C: How to Read a Research Article   C-1

Appendix D: Finding Information   D-1

Appendix E: Table of Random Numbers   E-1

Appendix F: How to Use a Statistical Package   F-1

Appendix G: How to Use a Qualitative Analysis Package   G-1

Appendix H: Annotated List of Web Sites   H-1

References   R-1

Index   I-1

DETAILED CONTENTS

About the Author   xviii

Preface   xix

Acknowledgments   xxiv

1. Science, Society, and Social Research   1

   Learning About the Social World   2
     Observing   5
     Generalizing   6
     Reasoning   6
     Reevaluating   7
   The Social Science Approach   8
     Motives for Social Research   8
     Types of Social Research   9
       Description: How Often Do People Use the Internet?   11
       Exploration: Can Online Interaction Create
        a Virtual Community?   12
       Explanation: What Effect Does Internet Use Have
        on Social Relations?   13
       Evaluation: Does High-Speed Internet Access Change
        Community Life?   14
     Quantitative and Qualitative Orientations   14
   Social Research Goals   16
     Measurement Validity   17
     Generalizability   17
     Causal Validity   20
     Authenticity   20
   Strengths and Limitations of Social Research   21
   Conclusions   23

     KEY TERMS   24
     HIGHLIGHTS   24
     DISCUSSION QUESTIONS   25
     PRACTICE EXERCISES   25
     WEB EXERCISES   25

SPSS EXERCISES   26
DEVELOPING A RESEARCH PROPOSAL   26

2. The Process and Problems of Social Research   27

Social Research Questions   28
  Identifying Social Research Questions   28
  Refining Social Research Questions   29
  Evaluating Social Research Questions   29
    Feasibility   30
    Social Importance   30
    Scientific Relevance   30
Social Research Foundations   31
  Finding Information   31
    Searching the Literature   31
    Searching the Web   34
  Reviewing Research   37
    A Single-Article Review: Formal and Informal Deterrents
      to Domestic Violence   38
    An Integrated Literature Review: Do Fair Procedures Matter?   40
Social Research Strategies   41
  The Role of Social Theory   41
  The Deductive/Inductive Cycle   44
    Deductive Research   44
    Domestic Violence and the Research Circle   47
    Inductive Research   49
  Exploratory Research: Victim Responses to Police Intervention   50
  Descriptive Research   51
Social Research Ethics   51
  Honesty and Openness   52
  The Uses of Science   52
  Research on People   53
Social Research Proposals, Part I   56
Conclusions   57

  KEY TERMS   58
  HIGHLIGHTS   58
  DISCUSSION QUESTIONS   59
  PRACTICE EXERCISES   59
  WEB EXERCISES   59
  SPSS EXERCISES   60
  DEVELOPING A RESEARCH PROPOSAL   60

3. Theories and Philosophies for Social Research   62

The Origins of Social Science   63
Theoretical Perspectives in Social Science   64
  Functionalism   64
  Conflict Theory   66
  Rational Choice   67

    Symbolic Interactionism   68
    Using Social Theory   70
        The Relationship Between Research and Theory   70
        Paradigm Change   71
  Social Research Philosophies   72
    Positivism and Postpositivism   72
        Positivist Research Guidelines   73
        A Positivist Research Goal: Advancing Knowledge   75
    Interpretivism and Constructivism   75
        Interpretivist Research Guidelines   77
        An Interpretivist Research Goal: Creating Change   78
    An Integrated Philosophy   78
  Extending Social Science Investigations   80
    Social Context   80
        Case Study: Juvenile Justice   81
    The Natural World   81
        Case Study: Adolescent Sexuality   81
  Conclusions   82
    KEY TERMS   82
    HIGHLIGHTS   82
    DISCUSSION QUESTIONS   83
    PRACTICE EXERCISES   83
    WEB EXERCISES   84
    SPSS EXERCISES   84
    DEVELOPING A RESEARCH PROPOSAL   84

4. Conceptualization and Measurement   85
  Concepts   86
    Conceptualization in Practice   87
        Substance Abuse   87
        Alcohol Effects   88
        Poverty   88
    From Concepts to Observations   89
  Measurement Operations   91
    Using Available Data   93
    Constructing Questions   94
        Single Questions   95
        Question Sets   97
        Indexes and Scales   97
    Making Observations   102
    Collecting Unobtrusive Measures   103
    Combining Measurement Operations   104
  Levels of Measurement   106
    Nominal Level of Measurement   107
    Ordinal Level of Measurement   108
    Interval Level of Measurement   109
    Ratio Level of Measurement   110

The Case of Dichotomies   111
Comparison of Levels of Measurement   111
Evaluating Measures   112
Measurement Validity   112
   Face Validity   113
   Content Validity   113
   Criterion Validity   113
   Construct Validity   114
Reliability   115
   Test-Retest Reliability   116
   Interitem Reliability (Internal Consistency) 116
   Alternate-Forms Reliability   117
   Interobserver Reliability   117
Ways to Improve Reliability and Validity   117
Measurement in Qualitative Research   121
Conclusions   121
   KEY TERMS   122
   HIGHLIGHTS   122
   DISCUSSION QUESTIONS   123
   PRACTICE EXERCISES   124
   WEB EXERCISES   125
   SPSS EXERCISES   126
   DEVELOPING A RESEARCH PROPOSAL   126

5. Sampling   127
Sample Planning   128
Define Sample Components and the Population   128
Evaluate Generalizability   131
Assess the Diversity of the Population   132
Consider a Census   134
Sampling Methods   135
Probability Sampling Methods   136
   Simple Random Sampling   139
   Systematic Random Sampling   140
   Stratified Random Sampling   141
   Cluster Sampling   144
Nonprobability Sampling Methods   146
   Availability Sampling   147
   Quota Sampling   148
   Purposive Sampling   150
   Snowball Sampling   151
Lessons About Sample Quality   152
Generalizability in Qualitative Research   154
Sampling Distributions   154
Estimating Sampling Error   155
Determining Sample Size   159
Conclusions   160

KEY TERMS   160
HIGHLIGHTS   161
DISCUSSION QUESTIONS   162
PRACTICE EXERCISES   162
WEB EXERCISES   163
SPSS EXERCISES   163
DEVELOPING A RESEARCH PROPOSAL   164

6. Causation and Research Design   165
Time Order and Research Design   166
    Cross-Sectional Designs   166
    Longitudinal Designs   169
        Repeated Cross-Sectional Designs   169
        Fixed-Sample Panel Designs   171
        Event-Based Designs   173
Units of Analysis and Errors in Causal Reasoning   174
    Individual and Group Units of Analysis   174
    The Ecological Fallacy and Reductionism   175
The Meaning of Explanation   177
    Nomothetic Causal Explanation   177
    Idiographic Causal Explanation   179
    Case-Oriented Understanding   180
Research Designs and Criteria for Causal Explanation   181
    Association   183
    Time Order   183
    Nonspuriousness   184
    Mechanism   186
    Context   188
Conclusions   189
KEY TERMS   190
HIGHLIGHTS   190
DISCUSSION QUESTIONS   191
PRACTICE EXERCISES   192
WEB EXERCISES   192
SPSS EXERCISES   192
DEVELOPING A RESEARCH PROPOSAL   193

7. Experiments   194
True Experiments   195
    Experimental and Comparison Groups   195
    Pretest and Posttest Measures   197
    Randomization   198
    Limitations of True Experimental Designs   201
    Summary: Causality in True Experiments   202
Quasi-Experiments   203
    Nonequivalent Control Group Designs   204
    Before-and-After Designs   206
    Summary: Causality in Quasi-Experiments   208

Nonexperiments   208
   Ex Post Facto Control Group Designs   208
   One-Shot Case Studies and Longitudinal Designs   210
   Summary: Causality in Nonexperiments   211
Validity in Experiments   211
   Causal (Internal) Validity   211
      Selection Bias   212
      Endogenous Change   213
      External Events   213
      Contamination   214
      Treatment Misidentification   214
   Generalizability   215
      Sample Generalizability   215
      External Validity   216
      Interaction of Testing and Treatment   216
Combining Methods   217
   Process Analysis   217
      Case Study: Obedience to Authority   218
   Conducting Factorial Surveys   218
      Case Study: Neighborhood Composition and Racial Segregation 219
Ethical Issues in Experimental Research   220
   Deception   220
   Selective Distribution of Benefits   221
Conclusions   222

   KEY TERMS   222
   HIGHLIGHTS   223
   DISCUSSION QUESTIONS   224
   PRACTICE EXERCISES   224
   WEB EXERCISES   225
   SPSS EXERCISES   225
   DEVELOPING A RESEARCH PROPOSAL   225

8. Survey Research   227
Survey Research in the Social Sciences   228
   Attractions of Survey Research   228
      Versatility   228
      Efficiency   229
      Generalizability   229
   The Omnibus Survey   229
   Errors in Survey Research   230
Writing Questions   231
   Avoid Confusing Phrasing   232
   Minimize the Risk of Bias   234
   Avoid Making Either Disagreement or Agreement Disagreeable   235
   Minimize Fence-Sitting and Floating   236
   Maximize the Utility of Response Categories   238

Designing Questionnaires 240
   Build on Existing Instruments 240
   Refine and Test Questions 241
   Add Interpretive Questions 242
   Maintain Consistent Focus 244
   Order the Questions 244
   Make the Questionnaire Attractive 245
Organizing Surveys 247
   Mailed, Self-Administered Surveys 248
   Group-Administered Surveys 252
   Telephone Surveys 252
      Reaching Sample Units 253
      Maximizing Response to Phone Surveys 256
   In-Person Interviews 258
      Balancing Rapport and Control 258
      Maximizing Response to Interviews 260
   Electronic Surveys 261
   Mixed-Mode Surveys 264
   A Comparison of Survey Designs 264
Combining Methods 267
   Adding Qualitative Data 267
      Case Study: Juvenile Court Records 267
      Case Study: Mental Health System 268
Ethical Issues in Survey Research 268
Conclusions 269

   KEY TERMS 270
   HIGHLIGHTS 270
   DISCUSSION QUESTIONS 271
   PRACTICE EXERCISES 273
   WEB EXERCISES 274
   SPSS EXERCISES 274
   DEVELOPING A RESEARCH PROPOSAL 275

9. Qualitative Methods: Observing, Participating, Listening 276
Fundamentals of Qualitative Methods 276
   Origins of Qualitative Research 280
   Case Study: Making Gray Gold 280
Participant Observation 282
   Choosing a Role 283
      Complete Observation 284
      Participation and Observation 284
      Covert Participation 285
   Entering the Field 287
   Developing and Maintaining Relationships 288
   Sampling People and Events 290
   Taking Notes 293
   Managing the Personal Dimensions 295

Systematic Observation 296
   Case Study: Systematic Observation of Public Spaces 297
Intensive Interviewing 297
   Establishing and Maintaining a Partnership 299
   Asking Questions and Recording Answers 300
   Combining Participant Observation and Intensive Interviewing 301
Focus Groups 302
Ethical Issues in Qualitative Research 303
Conclusions 305

   KEY TERMS 306
   HIGHLIGHTS 306
   DISCUSSION QUESTIONS 307
   PRACTICE EXERCISES 307
   WEB EXERCISES 308
   SPSS EXERCISES 308
   DEVELOPING A RESEARCH PROPOSAL 309

10. Evaluation Research 310
History of Evaluation Research 311
Evaluation Basics 313
Questions for Evaluation Research 315
   Needs Assessment 315
   Evaluability Assessment 317
   Process Evaluation 317
   Impact Analysis 320
   Efficiency Analysis 323
Design Alternatives 324
   Black Box Evaluation or Program Theory? 325
   Researcher or Stakeholder Orientation 326
   Quantitative or Qualitative Methods 328
   Simple or Complex Outcomes 329
Ethics in Evaluation 331
Conclusions 333

   KEY TERMS 334
   HIGHLIGHTS 334
   DISCUSSION QUESTIONS 335
   PRACTICE EXERCISES 335
   WEB EXERCISES 335
   SPSS EXERCISES 335
   DEVELOPING A RESEARCH PROPOSAL 336

11. Historical and Comparative Research 337
Overview of Unobtrusive Methods for
   Historical and Comparative Research 338
Historical Social Science Methods 339
   Historical Events Research 340
      Event-Structure Analysis 341

Oral History	343
Historical Process Research	343
Comparative Social Science Methods	346
Cross-Sectional Comparative Research	346
Comparative Historical Research	347
Secondary Data	348
Secondary Data Sources	350
U.S. Bureau of the Census	350
Integrated Public Use Microdata Series	351
Bureau of Labor Statistics (BLS)	352
Other U.S. Government Sources	352
International Data Sources	352
Survey Datasets	353
Challenges for Secondary Data Analyses	353
Demographic Analysis	355
Methodological Complications	357
Measuring Across Contexts	357
Sampling Across Time and Place	358
Identifying Causes	359
Ethical Issues in Historical and Comparative Research	360
Conclusions	361
KEY TERMS	361
HIGHLIGHTS	362
DISCUSSION QUESTIONS	362
PRACTICE EXERCISES	363
WEB EXERCISES	363
SPSS EXERCISES	365
DEVELOPING A RESEARCH PROPOSAL	366
12. Data Analysis	367
Introducing Statistics	368
Case Study: The Likelihood of Voting	368
Preparing Data for Analysis	370
Displaying Univariate Distributions	372
Graphs	373
Frequency Distributions	377
Ungrouped Data	378
Grouped Data	378
Combined and Compressed Distributions	380
Summarizing Univariate Distributions	382
Measures of Central Tendency	382
Mode	382
Median	383
Mean	383
Median or Mean?	384
Measures of Variation	387
Range	387

Interquartile Range 388
Variance 389
Standard Deviation 390
Analyzing Data Ethically: How Not to Lie With Statistics 391
Crosstabulating Variables 391
Graphing Association 395
Describing Association 396
Evaluating Association 397
Controlling for a Third Variable 399
Intervening Variables 399
Extraneous Variables 401
Specification 403
Regressing Variables 405
Analyzing Data Ethically: How Not to
Lie About Relationships 407
Conclusions 408

KEY TERMS 408
HIGHLIGHTS 409
DISCUSSION QUESTIONS 410
PRACTICE EXERCISES 410
WEB EXERCISES 412
SPSS EXERCISES 412
DEVELOPING A RESEARCH PROPOSAL 413

13. Qualitative Data Analysis and Content Analysis 414
Features of Qualitative Data Analysis 415
Qualitative Data Analysis as an Art 417
Research Questions for Qualitative Data Analysis 418
The Case Study 420
Techniques of Qualitative Data Analysis 421
Documentation 422
Conceptualization, Coding, and Categorizing 423
Examining Relationships and Displaying Data 425
Authenticating Conclusions 427
Reflexivity 429
Alternatives in Qualitative Data Analysis 430
Traditional Ethnography 431
Qualitative Comparative Analysis 432
Narrative Analysis 434
Grounded Theory 436
Computer Assisted Qualitative Data Analysis 437
Content Analysis 440
Ethics in Qualitative Data Analysis 442
Conclusions 443

KEY TERMS 448
HIGHLIGHTS 448

DISCUSSION QUESTIONS 448
PRACTICE EXERCISES 448
WEB EXERCISES 449
HYPERRESEARCH EXERCISES 449
DEVELOPING A RESEARCH PROPOSAL 449

14. Reporting Research 450
Social Research Proposals, Part II 450
    Case Study: Treating Substance Abuse 451
Comparing Research Designs 451
    Performing Meta-Analyses 459
        Case Study: Broken Homes and Delinquency 460
Writing Research 462
Reporting Research 464
    Journal Articles 464
    Applied Research Reports 465
Ethics, Politics, and Research Reports 468
Conclusions 471

KEY TERMS 472
HIGHLIGHTS 472
DISCUSSION QUESTIONS 472
PRACTICE EXERCISES 473
WEB EXERCISES 473
SPSS EXERCISES 473
DEVELOPING A RESEARCH PROPOSAL 474

References R-1

Appendix A: Summaries of Frequently Cited Research Articles A-1

Appendix B: Questions to Ask About a Research Article B-1

Appendix C: How to Read a Research Article C-1

Appendix D: Finding Information D-1

Appendix E: Table of Random Numbers E-1

Appendix F: How to Use a Statistical Package F-1

Appendix G: How to Use a Qualitative Analysis Package G-1

Appendix H: Annotated List of Web Sites H-1

References R-1

Index I-1

ABOUT THE AUTHOR

Russell K. Schutt, Ph.D. is Professor of Sociology and Director of the Graduate Program in Applied Sociology at the University of Massachusetts, Boston, and Lecturer on Sociology in the Department of Psychiatry at the Harvard Medical School. He completed his B.A., M.A., and Ph.D. degrees at the University of Illinois at Chicago and was a Postdoctoral Fellow in the Sociology of Social Control Training Program at Yale University. In addition to four editions of *Investigating the Social World: The Process and Practice of Research,* he has coauthored (with Ronet Bachman) two editions of *The Practice of Research in Criminology and Criminal Justice* and (with Dan Chambliss) a brief version of this text, *Making Sense of the Social World: Methods of Investigation.* He is also author of *Organization in a Changing Environment,* coeditor (with Stephanie Hartwell) of *The Organizational Response to Social Problems*, and coauthor (with Gerald Garrett) of *Responding to the Homeless: Policy and Practice.* He has authored and coauthored numerous journal articles and book chapters on homelessness, mental health, organizations, law, and teaching research methods. His current research focuses on the impact of housing, vocational, and service options for severely mentally ill persons and on the service preferences and recommendations of homeless persons and service personnel. He has also studied influences on well-being, satisfaction, and cognitive functioning; processes of organizational change; decision making in juvenile justice and in union admissions; political participation; media representations of mental illness; and HIV/AIDS prevention.

PREFACE

The terrorist attacks of September 11, 2001 brought enormous personal tragedy to thousands of people in the eastern United States, but other effects began immediately to radiate through the social fabric of American society and into the political culture of other nations. Within the next week, 44% of American adults reported one or more substantial stress symptoms, while over the next two months, 11% of the population of New York City reported symptoms of posttraumatic stress disorder (Schuster et al., 2001; Silver et al., 2002). Lawyers began to report that heightened public fears had made impartial juries almost impossible to find (Cambanis, 2002). Americans' trust in government and in people of other races shot upward, although civic behavior changed little (Skocpol, 2002). Meanwhile, in many other nations, feelings toward the United States grew more negative (Clymer, 2002).

It is through social science research methods that we can extend our vision beyond the tragedies, victories, and everyday events that we experience directly and see the larger picture and ask the broader questions. How has 9/11 affected psychological health? What has been its impact on political processes? Has it changed neighborliness, crime rates, or attitudes toward immigrants? We cannot rely on our own limited perceptions to answer questions like these, nor can we trust a particular journalist or politician to tell us more than what they think we want to hear. We need methods for investigating our social world that enable us to chart our course through the raging passions of the moment and beyond the limitations of our own perceptions.

Consider the study by William Schlenger and his colleagues (2002) of psychological reactions to the terrorist attacks. They surveyed a nationally representative sample of 2,273 adults within 1 to 2 months following the attacks. Each survey assessed mental health and symptoms of stress with standard inventories so that all responses could be compared and combined. Their methods allowed them to identify variation in stress levels across the country and to determine that it was only within New York City that distress levels were substantially elevated. They also found that amount of TV viewing of the attacks as well as some other characteristics, like gender, were associated with stress reactions. It is a comprehensive picture that we can obtain only with the methods that you will study in this text.

TEACHING AND LEARNING GOALS

If you see the importance of pursuing answers to questions about the social world the way Schlenger and his colleagues did, you can understand the importance of investigating the social world. One purpose of this book is to introduce you to social science research methods like the ones Schlenger used and show how they improve on everyday methods of answering questions. Each chapter integrates instruction in research methods with investigation of interesting aspects of the social world: the Internet and social relations, domestic violence, substance abuse, crime, work organizations, stress, gender roles, democratization, and others.

Another purpose of this book is to give you the critical skills necessary to evaluate research. Just "doing research" is not enough. Just reading that some conclusions are "based on a research study" is not sufficient. You must learn to ask many questions before concluding that research-based conclusions are appropriate. What did the researchers set out to investigate? How were people selected for study? What information was collected, and how was it analyzed? Throughout this book, you will learn what questions to ask when critiquing a research study and how to evaluate the answers. You can begin to sharpen your critical teeth on the illustrative studies throughout the book.

Another goal of this book is to train you to actually do research. Substantive examples will help you see how methods are used in practice. Exercises at the end of each chapter give you ways to try different methods alone or in a group. A checklist for research proposals will chart a course for you when you plan more ambitious studies. But research methods cannot be learned by rote and applied mechanically. Thus you will learn the benefits and liabilities of each major approach to research and why employing a combination of them is often preferable. You will come to appreciate why the results of particular research studies must always be interpreted within the context of prior research and through the lens of social theory.

ORGANIZATION OF THE BOOK

The way the book is organized reflects my beliefs in making research methods interesting, teaching students how to critique research, and viewing specific research techniques as parts of an integrated research strategy. The first three chapters introduce the why and how of research in general. Chapter 1 shows how research has helped us understand the effect of the Internet on social relations. Chapter 2 illustrates the basic stages of research with a series of experiments on the police response to domestic violence. Chapter 3 reviews the social science theories that we draw on to guide research and the research philosophies that shape our procedures. The next three chapters discuss how to evaluate the way researchers design their measures, draw their samples, and justify their statements about causal connections. As you learn about these procedures, you will also read about research on substance abuse, homelessness, and the causes of violence.

Chapters 7, 8, and 9 present the three most important primary methods of data collection: experiments, surveys, and qualitative methods (including participant observation, intensive interviews, and focus groups). The substantive studies in these chapters show how these methods have been used to improve our understanding of psychological well-being, as well as social interactions at work, in nursing homes, and on school playgrounds.

Chapters 10 and 11 present methodologies that can combine the primary methods reviewed in the preceding three chapters. Evaluation research, the focus of Chapter 10, can employ experiments, surveys, or qualitative methods to learn about the effects of and need for social and other types of programs. We begin this chapter with an overview of evaluation research on drug abuse prevention programs. Chapter 11 focuses on historical and comparative methodologies, which can use data obtained with one or more of the primary methods to study processes at the regional and societal level over time and between units. We focus on research about political democratization in this chapter

Chapter 12 presents the basic statistical methods that are used to analyze the results of quantitative studies. We will work through an analysis of voting patterns in the 1996 presidential election in order to see how these statistics are used to answer an actual research question. Chapter 13 then shifts our focus to qualitative data analysis techniques, which involve a markedly different approach to analysis, but sometimes overlap in some respects with quantitative methods. In that chapter we also touch on content analysis, a quantitative technique for textual analysis. Our examples in this chapter come from studies of schools and homeless social movements. We finish up in Chapter 14 with an overview of the process of and techniques for reporting research results, a second examination of the development of research proposals, and an introduction to meta-analysis—a special tool for studying prior research.

DISTINCTIVE FEATURES OF THE FOURTH EDITION

The success of this book has been due in no small measure to the feedback I receive from methods instructors and their students. It also results from the availability in the research literature of so many excellent examples of how social scientists investigate interesting and important questions about the social world. You will find all of this reflected in innovations in approach, coverage, and organization:

Examples of social research as it occurs in real-world settings. Interesting studies of social relations, domestic violence, crime, and other pressing social issues have been updated and extended from the third edition. They demonstrate that the exigencies and complexities of real life shape the application of research methods. This book also acknowledges the cross-pressures resulting from the conflicting requirements of different methods.

Greater coverage of social theory and social research philosophy. The foundations for social research are carefully laid in a new chapter (Chapter 3) that helps students to see how theory can be integrated into the research process and to understand the philosophies that shape research procedures and preferences.

Increased attention to qualitative methods. Qualitative and quantitative methods are contrasted in Chapter 1, and most other chapters include a special section on qualitative approaches. Chapter 9 now focuses solely on the logic and design of qualitative research, while a new chapter, Chapter 13, provides much more information about qualitative data analysis. The value of multiple methods of investigation is now illustrated with examples and procedural discussions in many chapters.

Ethical concerns and ethical decision making. Every step in the research process raises ethical concerns, so ethics should be treated in tandem with the study of specific methods. You will find ethics introduced in Chapter 2 and reviewed in the context of each method of data collection, data analysis, and reporting.

Useful instructional software. The enclosed CD-ROM has been enhanced extensively so that there are now interactive exercises to accompany each chapter. You should spend enough time with these lessons to become very comfortable with the basic research concepts presented.

End-of-chapter exercises. In addition to individual and group projects, each chapter includes exercises to give you experience in data analysis using SPSS, the Statistical Package for the Social Sciences, and the 2000 General Social Survey (which is included on the CD-ROM). If you complete these exercises, you will gain some insight into the determinants of support for capital punishment and other issues. End-of-chapter Web exercises have been updated. A new section has been added to each chapter to guide you through preparation of a research proposal. A copy of the HyperRESEARCH program for qualitative analysis has been included on the CD-ROM, together with several datasets, so that students can carry out the fascinating qualitative analyses described in Appendix G and in the exercises for Chapter 13.

Aids to effective study. Lists of main points and key terms provide quick summaries at the end of each chapter. In addition, key terms are highlighted in boldface type when first introduced and defined in the text. Definitions for them can be found in the glossary/index at the end of the book. The Pine Forge Press Web site includes online exercises for the text (click on the Study Sites tab at www.pineforge.com). The instructor's manual on CD-ROM includes more exercises that have been especially designed for collaborative group work in and outside of class. Appendix D, "Finding Information," provides up-to-date information about using the Internet, and basic procedures for searching the literature and the Web have been incorporated directly into Chapter 2. Appendix H presents an annotated list of useful Web sites.

Supplementary books on important topics. Procedural details often obscure important research concepts and principles. So, unlike other methods textbooks, this one does not try to provide detailed advice on every method. Instructors and students who would like more specific help can turn to several Sage and Pine Forge Press books on research methods and statistics, dealing with such important topics as sampling, survey design, field research, and data analysis.

It is, quite honestly, a privilege to be able to share with so many students the results of excellent social science investigations of the social world. If *Investigating the Social World* communicates the excitement of social research and the importance of evaluating carefully the methods we use in that research, then I have succeeded in representing fairly what social scientists do. If this book conveys accurately the latest developments in research methods, it demonstrates simply that social scientists are themselves committed to evaluating and improving their own methods of investigation. I think it is fair to say that we practice what we preach.

Now you're the judge. I hope that you and your instructor enjoy learning how to investigate the social world and perhaps do some investigating along the way. And I hope you find that the knowledge and (dare I say it?) enthusiasm you develop for social research in this course will serve you well throughout your education, in your career, and in your community.

A NOTE ABOUT USING SPSS

To carry out the SPSS exercises at the end of each chapter and in Appendix F, you must already have SPSS on your computer. The exercises use a subset of the 2000 General Social

Survey dataset (included on the disk). This dataset includes variables on topics such as work, family, gender roles, government institutions, race relations, and politics. Appendix F will get you up and running with SPSS for Windows, and you can then spend as much time as you like exploring characteristics and attitudes of Americans. Just start SPSS on your PC, open the GSS2000mini file, and begin with the first SPSS exercise in Chapter 1. If you have the full version of SPSS, you can also work with the complete GSS2000 dataset. Of course, I've included that on your CD-ROM as well. You can also carry out analyses of the GSS data at the University of California–Berkeley Web site: http://csa.berkeley.edu:7502/archive.htm.

ACKNOWLEDGMENTS

My thanks first to Jerry Westby, senior editor for Pine Forge Press. His consistent support made it possible for this project to flourish. Also contributing vitally to the success of the book project were other exceptional members of the Pine Forge Press and Sage Publications team: Denise Simon, Diana Axelsen, Toni Zuccarini Ackley, Vonessa Vondera, Kristin Snow, and Ben Penner.

I also am indebted to the first-rate social scientists recruited by Jerry Westby to critique this edition, and to Robert A. Dentler, for comments on Chapter 10.

Marina A. Adler, University of Maryland, Baltimore

Diane C. Bates, Sam Houston State University

Andrew E. Behrendt, University of Pennsylvania

David H. Folz, University of Tennessee

Christine A. Johnson, Oklahoma State University

Carolyn Liebler, University of Washington

Carol D. Miller, University of Wisconsin-La Crosse

Dan Olson, Indiana University, South Bend

Brian J. Stults, University of Florida

John R. Warren, University of Washington

Ken Wilson, East Carolina University

Third edition reviewers were:

Emmanuel N. Amadi, Mississippi Valley State University

Doug Anderson, University of Southern Maine

Robert B. Arundale, University of Alaska, Fairbanks

Hee-Je Bak, University of Wisconsin, Madison

Marit Berntson, University of Minnesota

Deborah Bhattacharyya, Wittenbert University

Karen Bradley, Central Missouri State University

Cynthia J. Buckley, The University of Texas, Austin

J. P. Burnham, Cumberland College

Gerald Charbonneau, Madonna University

Hugh G. Clark, Texas Women's University

Mark E. Comadena, Illinois State University

John Constantelos, Grand Valley State University

Mary T. Corrigan, Binghamton University

John Eck, University of Cincinnati

Kristin Espinosa, University of Wisconsin, Milwaukee
Kimberly Faust, Fitchburg State College
Kenneth Fidel, DePaul University
Jane Hood, University of New Mexico
Christine Johnson, Oklahoma State University
Joseph Jones, Taylor University
Sean Keenan, Utah State University
Debra Kelley, Longwood College
Kurt Kent, University of Florida
Jan Leighley, Texas A&M University
Joel Lieberman, University of Nevada, Las Vegas
Randall MacIntosh, California State University, Sacramento
Peter J. May, University of Washington
Michael McQuestion, University of Wisconsin, Madison
Bruce Mork, University of Minnesota
Jennifer R. Myhre, University of California, Davis

Zeynep Özgen, Arizona State University
Norah Peters-Davis, Beaver College
Ronald Ramke, High Point University
Adinah Raskas, University of Missouri
Akos Rona-Tas, University of California, San Diego
Pamela J. Shoemaker, Syracuse University
Therese Seibert, Keene State College
Mark A. Shibley, Southern Oregon University
Herbert L. Smith, University of Pennsylvania
Paul C. Smith, Alverno College
Glenna Spitze, State University of New York, Albany
Beverly L. Stiles, Midwestern State University
Caroline Tolbert, Kent State University
Tim Wadsworth, University of Washington
Charles Webb, Freed-Hardeman University
Adam Weinberg, Colgate University

Special thanks to Barbara Costello, University of Rhode Island; Nancy B. Miller, University of Akron; and Gi-Wook Shin, University of California, Los Angeles, for their contributions to the third edition.

Second edition reviewers were:

Nasrin Abdolali, Long Island University, C. W. Post
Lynda Ames, SUNY, Plattsburgh
Matthew Archibald, University of Washington
Karen Baird, State University of New York, Purchase
Kelly Damphousse, Sam Houston State University
Ray Darville, Stephen F. Austin State University
Jana Everett, University of Colorado, Denver
Virginia S. Fink, University of Colorado, Colorado Springs
Jay Hertzog, Valdosta State University
Lin Huff-Corzine, University of Central Florida

Gary Hytrek, University of California, Los Angeles
Debra S. Kelley, Longwood College
Manfred Kuechler, Hunter College (CUNY)
Thomas Linneman, College of William & Mary
Andrew London, Kent State University
Stephanie Luce, University of Wisconsin, Madison
Ronald J. McAllister, Elizabethtown College
Kelly Moore, Barnard College, Columbia University
Kristen Myers, Northern Illinois University
Michael R. Norris, University of Texas, El Paso
Jeffrey Prager, University of California, Los Angeles

Liesl Riddle, University of Texas, Austin
Janet Ruane, Montclair State University
Josephine A. Ruggiero, Providence College
Mary Ann Schwartz, Northeastern Illinois University
Gi-Wook Shin, University of California, Los Angeles
Howard Stine, University of Washington

William J. Swart, The University of Kansas
Guang-zhen Wang, Russell Sage College
Shernaaz M. Webster, University of Nevada, Reno
Karin Wilkins, University of Texas, Austin
Keith Yanner, Central College

And special thanks to Mildred A. Schwartz for comments on Chapter 11 in this edition. First edition reviewers were:

Catherine Berheide, Skidmore College
Terry Besser, University of Kentucky
Lisa Callahan, Russell Sage College
Herbert L. Costner, formerly of University of Washington
Jack Dison, Arkansas State University
Sandra K. Gill, Gettysburg College
Gary Goreham, North Dakota State University
Barbara Keating, Mankato State University
Bebe Lavin, Kent State University
Scott Long, Indiana University

Elizabeth Morrissey, Frostburg State University
Chandra Muller, University of Texas
G. Nanjundappa, California State University, Fullerton
Josephine Ruggiero, Providence College
Valerie Schwebach, Rice University
Judith Stull, Temple University
Robbyn Wacker, University of Northern Colorado
Daniel S. Ward, Rice University
Greg Weiss, Roanoke College
DeeAnn Wenk, University of Oklahoma

A special note of thanks for the comments of Kathy Crittenden on the first three editions and for those of Herbert L. Costner and Richard Campbell on the first edition. Most importantly, my deep appreciation to Steve Rutter for the vision and enthusiasm that guided the text through its first three editions.

The interactive exercises on the CD-ROM that accompanies this book began with a series of exercises that I developed in a project at the University of Massachusetts–Boston. They were expanded for the 2nd edition by Tom Linneman and a team of graduate students he directed at the University of Washington—Mark Edwards, Lorella Palazzo, and Tim Wadsworth—and tested by Gary Hytrek and Gi-Wook Shin at UCLA. My format changes in the exercises for the 3rd edition were tested by my daughter, Julia Schutt. With the help of two outstanding graduate students at the University of Massachusetts–Boston, Heather Albertson and Kathryn Stoeckert, I have substantially expanded the exercises for this 4th edition. Matt Philbin designed the Visual Basic interface for the software. I am grateful to them all for their fine work.

Tracey Newman at the University of Massachusetts–Boston provided important and timely assistance with editing. The current edition of the instructor's manual was designed by Diane Bates. Matthew Archibald helped to revise material for an earlier workbook. I also thank Judith Richlin-Klonsky for her assistance in revising the examples in Chapter 9, for the 3rd edition.

Several faculty and graduate students in Boston made important contributions to earlier editions: Heather Johnson, Chris Gillespie, Ra'eda Al-Zubi, Anne Foxx, Bob Dentler, and students in his 1993–1994 graduate research methods class at the University of Massachusetts–Boston. I continue to be indebted to the many students I have had an opportunity to teach and mentor, at both the undergraduate and graduate levels. In many respects, this book could not have been so successful without the ongoing teaching experiences we have shared.

No scholarly book project can succeed without good library resources, and for these I continue to incur a profound debt to the Harvard University library staff and their extraordinary collection. I also have benefited from the resources maintained by the University of Massachusetts Boston librarians.

Again, most important, I thank my wife for her love and support (and for Appendix D, and for her contributions to Chapter 2, and for her assistance with editing) and our daughter for all the joy she brings to our lives.

—Russell K. Schutt
Lexington, Maasachusetts

To Julia Ellen Schutt

Chapter 1

Science, Society, and Social Research

Learning About the Social World

Errors to Avoid
Observing
Generalizing
Reasoning
Reevaluating

The Social Science Approach
Motives for Social Research
Types of Social Research
  Description: How Often Do People
    Use the Internet?
  Exploration: Can Online Interaction
    Create a Virtual Community?

Explanation: What Effect Does Internet
  Use Have on Social Relations?
Evaluation: Does High-Speed Internet
  Access Change Community Life?
Quantitative and Qualitative Orientations

Social Research Goals
Measurement Validity
Generalizability
Causal Validity
Authenticity

Strengths and Limitations of Social Research

Conclusions

Netville[1] is a development of about 120 single-family homes in a suburb of Toronto. In 1997, the three- and four-bedroom homes cost about $171,000 (U.S.), 13% less than the average for new homes in metropolitan Toronto (Hampton & Wellman, 1999). Residents work in such occupations as technician, police officer, teacher, and small business owner. It is a typical new suburban neighborhood in all respects except one: The homes were connected free of charge with a cable network allowing high-speed access to the Internet and free use of such features as electronic mail, videophones, online health services, and local discussion forums.

1. The name "Netville" is fictitious, but the community is real.

Netville residents agreed to participate in a social experiment meant to answer a pressing research question: How do online connections affect the development of community?

It's hard to escape this question as computer-based connections extend and replace direct human contact in so many areas of our social world. Have you thought about it yourself, as you communicate with friends or family through e-mail? When you spend a late night searching for information, and perhaps companionship, on the World Wide Web? When you shop alone online rather than at the mall with your friends? When a classmate exchanges e-mail rather than listening to the lecture? Or when you hear that people used the Web to help a family in need? Have you become optimistic or pessimistic about the effects of the Internet?

The Netville study is one of the first systematic social science investigations of the Internet's impact on social relations. In the rest of this chapter, you will learn how the Netville study and other recent investigations are helping to answer questions about the social effects of computers and the Internet. By the chapter's end, you should know what is "scientific" in social science and appreciate how the methods of science can help us understand the problems of society.

LEARNING ABOUT THE SOCIAL WORLD

Just one research question about the Internet raises so many more questions about the social world. Let's think about several. Take a few minutes to read each of the following questions and jot down your answers. Don't ruminate about the questions or worry about your responses: *This is not a test;* there are no "wrong" answers.

1. Do you use the Internet?

2. How have you learned about Internet usage?

3. What percentage of households are connected to the Internet?

4. How much does Internet use vary across social groups defined by age, gender, income, or race? Is there a "digital divide" between some social groups?

5. Does Internet use increase or decrease social relationships?

6. Do you think the government should be doing more to encourage Internet use?

I'll bet you didn't have any trouble answering the first two questions, about your own experiences, but what about the others? These four questions concern "the social world"— the experiences and orientations of people in addition to ourselves. Usually, when we answer such questions we combine information from many different sources and times in our lives. If we're on our toes, we also recognize that our answers to the last four questions will be shaped by our answers to the first two—that is, what we think about the social world will be shaped by our own experiences and by the ways we have learned about the experiences of others. Of course, this means that other people, with different experiences, will often come up with different answers to the same questions. Studying research methods will help you learn what criteria to apply when evaluating these different answers and what methods to use when seeking to develop your own answers.

Exhibit 1.1   Internet Use Anywhere by Educational Attainment, Percentage of Persons Age 25+

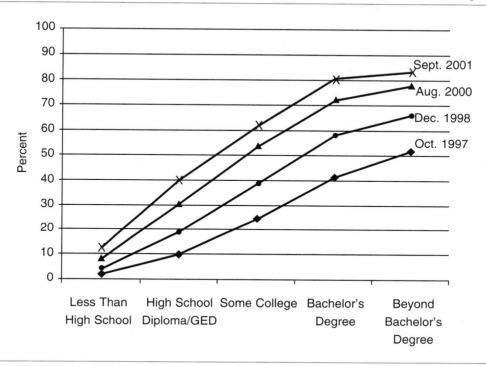

Source: NTIA and ESA, U.S. Department of Commerce, using U.S. Census Bureau Current Population Survey Supplements.

Are you convinced? Take a bit of time in class and share your answers to the six Internet questions. Why do your answers differ? Now, let's compare your answers to questions 3 through 6 to the findings of researchers using social science methods.

3. The U.S. Census Bureau's Current Population Survey (U.S. Department of Commerce, 2002) found in September 2001 that 50.5% of U.S. households were connected to the Internet, with 2 million more people connecting each month.

4. The same survey identified differences in rates of connection by age, income, and race, but not by gender. As indicated in Exhibit 1.1, differences in education level have been diminishing. Does this mean there is less of a "digital divide"?

5. The UCLA Internet Project (UCLA Center for Communication Policy, 2001) found that Internet users spend more time than nonusers socializing with friends, and almost as much time socializing with family members.

6. Only one in five Internet users believes that Internet use helps give them more say about what the government does. However, this doesn't really tell us whether the government should do more to encourage Internet use.

How do these answers compare with the opinions you recorded earlier? Do you think your personal experiences have led you to different estimates than others might have given? A Stanford survey (Nie & Erbring, 2000) revealed that people under the age of 25 use the Internet and Internet chat rooms much more than people over 65. College-educated people also use the Internet more than those with less education. Do these factors regarding Internet use lead you to be cautious about using your own experience as a guide? Were your classmates' opinions about the effect of Internet use on social relations related to the way in which they use the Internet? (question 4) Did you differ in your conceptions of what a "digital divide" is? (question 5) Can we find an answer to a question about our values (question 6) in survey data? Do you see how different people can come to such different conclusions about social issues?

We cannot avoid asking questions about our complex social world, or trying to make sense of our position in it. In fact, the more that you begin to "think like a social scientist," the more such questions will come to mind. But as you've just seen, in our everyday reasoning about the social world, our own prior experiences and orientations can have a major influence on what we perceive and how we interpret these perceptions. As a result, one person may see a devoted Internet user as being on the cutting edge of social change, another person may see the same individual as socially withdrawn, and there will be others who overlook the Internet user entirely.

ERRORS TO AVOID

There are four common errors in reasoning that occur in the nonscientific, unreflective discourse about the social world that we hear on a daily basis. My favorite examples of these "everyday errors in reasoning" come from a letter to Ann Landers. The letter was written by someone who had just moved with her two cats from the city to a house in the country. In the city she had not let her cats outside and felt guilty about confining them. When they arrived in the country, she threw her back door open. Her two cats cautiously went to the door and looked outside for a while, then returned to the living room and lay down. Her conclusion was that people shouldn't feel guilty about keeping their cats indoors—even when they have the chance, cats don't really want to play outside.

Do you see this person's errors in reasoning in her approach to

- *Observing.* She observed the cats at the outside door only once.
- *Generalizing.* She observed only two cats, both of which previously were confined indoors.
- *Reasoning.* She assumed that others feel guilty about keeping their cats indoors and that cats are motivated by feelings about opportunities to play.
- *Reevaluating.* She was quick to conclude that she had no need to change her approach to the cats.

You don't have to be a scientist or use sophisticated research techniques to avoid these four errors in reasoning. If you recognize these errors for what they are and make a conscious effort to avoid them, you can improve your own reasoning. In the process, you will also be implementing the admonishments of your parents (or minister, teacher, or other adviser) not to stereotype people, to avoid jumping to conclusions, and to look at the big picture. These are the same errors that the methods of social science are designed to help us avoid.

Exhibit 1.2   The Difference Between Overgeneralization and Selective Observation

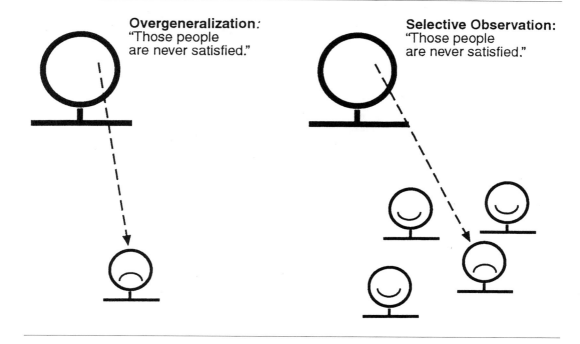

Observing

One common mistake in learning about the social world is **selective observation**—choosing to look only at things that are in line with our preferences or beliefs. When we are inclined to criticize individuals or institutions, it is all too easy to notice their every failing. For example, if we are convinced in advance that all heavy Internet users are antisocial, we can find many confirming instances. But what about elderly people who serve as Internet pen pals for grade school children; doctors who exchange views on medical developments; or therapists who deliver online counseling? If we acknowledge only the instances that confirm our predispositions, we are victims of our own selective observation. Exhibit 1.2 depicts the difference between selective observation and a related error in reasoning, overgeneralization.

Our observations can also simply be inaccurate. If a woman says she is "hungry" and we think she said she is "hunted," we have made an **inaccurate observation.** If we think five people are standing on a street corner when seven actually are, we have made an inaccurate observation.

Such errors occur often in casual conversation and in everyday observation of the world around us. In fact, our perceptions do not provide a direct window onto the world around us, for what we think we have sensed is not necessarily what we have seen (or heard, smelled, felt, or tasted). Even when our senses are functioning fully, our minds have to interpret what

Exhibit 1.3   An Optical Illusion

we have sensed (Humphrey, 1992). The optical illusion in Exhibit 1.3, which can be viewed as either two faces or a vase, should help you realize that perceptions involve interpretations. Different observers may perceive the same situation differently because they interpret it differently.

Generalizing

Overgeneralization occurs when we conclude that what we have observed or what we know to be true for some cases is true for all or most cases (Exhibit 1.2). We are always drawing conclusions about people and social processes from our own interactions with them, but sometimes we forget that our experiences are limited. The social (and natural) world is, after all, a complex place. We have the ability (and inclination) to interact with just a small fraction of the individuals who inhabit the social world, especially in a limited span of time. One heavy Internet user found that his online friendships were "much deeper and have better quality" than his other friendships (Parks & Floyd, 1996). Would his experiences generalize to yours? To others?

Reasoning

When we prematurely jump to conclusions or argue on the basis of invalid assumptions, we are using **illogical reasoning.** For example, it is not reasonable to propose that individuals who are not connected to the Internet don't want to participate in the "information revolution" if evidence indicates that they lack the financial resources to buy a computer or maintain an online account. On the other hand, an unquestioned assumption that everyone should be connected to the Internet overlooks some important considerations, such as the energy required for Internet usage and its impact on traditional stores (Tenner, 1999). Logic that seems impeccable to one person can seem twisted to another—the problem usually is reasoning from different assumptions rather than just failing to "think straight."

Reevaluating

Resistance to change, the reluctance to reevaluate our ideas in light of new information, may occur for several reasons:

Ego-based commitments. We all learn to greet with some skepticism the claims by leaders of companies, schools, agencies, and so on that people in their organization are happy, that revenues are growing, and that services are being delivered in the best possible way. We know how tempting it is to make statements about the social world that conform to our own needs rather than to the observable facts. It can also be difficult to admit that we were wrong once we have staked out a position on an issue. And it even happens in higher education! A number of universities in the late 1990s developed special units to deliver online education through the Web, convinced that this was the wave of the future: "If universities don't adapt, they're educational road kill" (De Ritis, 2001). But it turned out that some university presidents had "got swept up" in Internet enthusiasm and "now the groves of academe are littered with the detritus of failed e-learning start-ups" (Hafner, 2002).

Excessive devotion to tradition. Some degree of devotion to tradition is necessary for the predictable functioning of society. Social life can be richer and more meaningful if it is allowed to flow along the paths charted by those who have preceded us. Some skepticism about the potential for online learning can be a healthy antidote to unrealistic expectations of widespread student enthusiasm (Bray, 1999). But too much devotion to tradition can stifle adaptation to changing circumstances. When we distort our observations or alter our reasoning so that we can maintain beliefs that "were good enough for my grandfather, so they're good enough for me," we hinder our ability to accept new findings and develop new knowledge. The consequences can be deadly, as residents of Hamburg, Germany, might have realized in 1892 (Freedman, 1991). Until the last part of the 19th century, people believed that cholera, a potentially lethal disease, was caused by minute, inanimate, airborne poison particles ("miasmas"). In 1850, English researcher John Snow demonstrated that cholera was, in fact, spread by contaminated water. When a cholera epidemic hit Hamburg in 1892, the authorities did what tradition deemed appropriate: digging up and carting away animal carcasses to prevent the generation of more miasmas. Despite their efforts, thousands died. New York City adopted a new approach based on Snow's discovery, which included boiling drinking water and disinfecting sewage. As a result, the death rate in New York City dropped to a tenth of what the death rate had been in a previous cholera epidemic.

Uncritical agreement with authority. If we do not have the courage to evaluate critically the ideas of those in positions of authority, we will have little basis for complaint if they exercise their authority over us in ways we don't like. And if we do not allow new discoveries to call our beliefs into question, our understanding of the social world will remain limited. An extreme example of this problem was the refusal of leaders in formerly communist countries to acknowledge the decaying social and environmental fabric of their societies while they encouraged their followers to pay homage to the wisdom of Comrades Mao, Lenin, and Stalin. But we don't have to go so far afield to recognize that people often accept the beliefs of those in positions of authority without question. Was it in part uncritical agreement with computer industry authorities that led so many universities to rush too quickly, and mistakenly, toward the goal of "true distance learning on a scale unlike anything before" (Applebome, 1999:26)?

Now take just a minute to reexamine the opinions about Internet use that you recorded earlier. Did you grasp at a simple explanation even though reality is far more complex? Were your beliefs influenced by your own ego and feelings about your similarities to or differences from Internet users or nonusers? Are your beliefs perhaps based on high school stories about "geeks"? Did you weigh carefully the opinions of political authorities who promote Internet use or just accept or reject those opinions out of hand? Could knowledge of research methods help to improve your own understanding of the social world? Do you see some of the challenges faced by social science?

THE SOCIAL SCIENCE APPROACH

The **social science** approach to answering questions about the social world is designed to reduce greatly these potential sources of error in everyday reasoning. **Science** relies on logical and systematic methods to answer questions, and it does so in a way that allows others to inspect and evaluate its methods. In the realm of social research, these methods are not so unusual. After all, they involve asking questions, observing social groups, and counting people, which we often do in our everyday lives. However, social scientists develop, refine, apply, and report their understanding of the social world more systematically, or "scientifically," than Joanna Q. Public does:

- Social science research methods can reduce the likelihood of overgeneralization by using systematic procedures for selecting individuals or groups to study that are representative of the individuals or groups to which we wish to generalize.
- To avoid illogical reasoning, social researchers use explicit criteria for identifying causes and for determining whether these criteria are met in a particular instance.
- Social science methods can reduce the risk of selective or inaccurate observation by requiring that we measure and sample phenomena systematically.
- Because they require that we base our beliefs on evidence that can be examined and critiqued by others, scientific methods lessen the tendency to develop answers about the social world from ego-based commitments, excessive devotion to tradition, and/or unquestioning respect for authority.

Science A set of logical, systematic, documented methods for investigating nature and natural processes; the knowledge produced by these investigations.

Social science The use of scientific methods to investigate individuals, societies, and social processes; the knowledge produced by these investigations.

Motives for Social Research

Like you, social scientists use the Internet, observe other persons using it, and try to make sense of what they experience and observe. For most, that's the end of it. But for some social scientists, the impact of the Internet on social life has become a major research focus. What motivates selection of this or any other particular research focus? Usually it's one or more of the following reasons:

Policy motivations. Many government agencies, elected officials, and private organizations seek better descriptions of Internet users so they can identify unmet computer needs or marketing opportunities. School officials may need information for planning distance learning programs. Law enforcement agencies may seek to track the activities of hate groups or the ploys used by pedophiles. Community planners may try to forecast the impact of public Internet access sites. These policy guidance and program management needs can stimulate numerous research projects. As Cooper and Victory (2002) said in their foreword to a U.S. Department of Commerce report on the Census Bureau's survey of Internet use,

> This information will be useful to a wide variety of policymakers and service providers . . . help all of us determine how we can reach Americans more effectively and take maximum advantage of the opportunities available through new information technologies.

Academic motivations. Questions about changing social relations have stimulated much academic social science. One hundred years ago, Emile Durkheim (1951) linked social processes stemming from urbanization and industrialization to a higher rate of suicide. Fifty years ago, David Reisman (1950/1969) considered whether the growing role of the mass media, among other changes, was leading Americans to become a "lonely crowd." Like this earlier research, contemporary investigations of the effect of computers and the Internet are often motivated by a desire to understand influences on the strength and meaning of social bonds. Does a "virtual community" in cyberspace perform the same functions as face-to-face social relationships? The desire to better understand how the social world works is motivation enough for many social scientists (Hampton & Wellman, 2001:477, 479):

> It is time to move from speculation to evidence. . . . The growth of computer-mediated communication (CMC) introduces a new means of social contact with the potential to affect many aspects of personal communities. . . . This article examines . . . how this technology affected contact and support.

Personal motivations. Some social scientists who conduct research on the impact of computers and the Internet feel that by doing so they can help to improve the quality of social relations, the effectiveness of schooling, or the conditions of institutionalized groups in their communities or countries. Social scientists may become interested in the social effects of the Internet as a result of helping their children become effective users or after developing social relations while online themselves. Exhibit 1.4 is a picture of researchers at a 1994 conference on the organizational impact of telecommunications, sponsored by the European Association for Telematic Applications. Do you get the impression that these researchers might have a personal as well as a professional interest in how well people work together?

Types of Social Research

Whatever the motives, there are four types of social research projects. This section illustrates each type with projects from the rapidly growing body of social research about the Internet:

Exhibit 1.4   Organizational Impact of Telecommunications Conference

Source: http://archimedes.teipir.gr/eata/1994%20Netties%20.htm, 4/12/03

Descriptive research. Defining and describing social phenomena of interest is a part of almost any research investigation, but **descriptive research** is often the primary focus of the first research about some issue. Some of the central descriptive questions asked in research on the Internet have been: How has Internet usage varied over time and by social group? (U.S. Department of Commerce, 2002). What do users do on the Internet? (Nie & Erbring, 2000). Measurement (the topic of Chapter 4) and sampling (Chapter 5) are central concerns in descriptive research. Survey research (Chapter 8) is often used for descriptive purposes. Some comparative research also has a descriptive purpose (Chapter 11).

Exploratory research. **Exploratory research** seeks to find out how people get along in the setting under question, what meanings they give to their actions, and what issues concern them. The goal is to learn "What is going on here?" and to investigate social phenomena without explicit expectations. This purpose is associated with the use of methods that capture large amounts of relatively unstructured information. For example, researchers investigating Internet usage have had to reexamine the meaning of "community," asking whether cyberspace interactions can constitute a community that is seen as "real and essential" to participants (Fox & Roberts, 1999:644). "How is identity—true or counterfeit—established in on-line communities?" asked Peter Kollock and Marc Smith (1999:9). How do people with diabetes use an Internet Usenet group for support? (Loader et al., 2002). Exploratory research like this frequently involves qualitative methods, which are the focus of Chapters 9 and 13, as well as special sections in many other chapters.

Explanatory research. Many consider explanation the premier goal of any science. **Explanatory research** seeks to identify causes and effects of social phenomena, and to predict how one phenomenon will change or vary in response to variation in some other phenomenon. Internet researchers adopted explanation as a goal when they began to ask such questions as, "Does the Internet increase, decrease, or supplement social capital?" (Wellman, Haase, Witte, & Hampton, 2001). Do students who meet through Internet interaction ". . . like each other more than those who met face to face"? (Bargh, McKenna, & Fitzsimons, 2002:41). And "How [does] the Internet affect the role and use of the traditional media?" (Nie & Erbring, 2000). I focus on ways of identifying causal effects in Chapter 6. Explanatory research often involves experiments (see Chapter 7) or surveys (see Chapter 8), both of which are most likely to use quantitative methods.

Evaluation research. Seeking to determine the effects of a social program or other type of intervention is a type of explanatory research, because it deals with cause and effect. However, **evaluation research** differs from other forms of explanatory research because evaluation research considers the implementation and effects of social policies and programs. These issues may not be relevant in other types of explanatory research. Concern over the social implications of the Internet, as well as its potential for enhancing real estate values, provided the impetus for the Netville study. Chapter 10 introduces evaluation research.

I'll now summarize four actual research projects that represent these four types.

Description: How Often Do People Use the Internet?

The National Geographic Society (2000) began one of the most intriguing descriptive Internet studies, "Survey 2000," in fall 1998. Its goal was to describe Internet users around the world and to identify differences among countries. The survey was administered on the Internet itself, in cooperation with schools, libraries, and community centers. Eventually, 80,012 individuals from 178 countries and territories spent an average of 44 minutes answering the survey questions. (Appendix A summarizes the design of this study and the other studies discussed in detail in this book.)

Survey 2000 questions ranged from feelings about respondents' communities and frequency of moving to frequency of Internet usage and preferences in food, music, and authors. The questionnaire was interactive, so that the questions asked varied according to the answers to earlier questions. A resident of the United States would answer questions tailored to their state, whereas residents from other countries would be asked about the spread of American influence. Internet veterans were asked how often they joined chat rooms, but first-time users were not. There was a special survey for children under 16 and supplementary sections that were answered by 71% of the U.S. and Canadian respondents.

Survey responses suggested that the Internet supplemented, but did not displace, community ties. E-mail was used frequently by many people, and just over half of the respondents reported that the Internet made their extended families feel closer. When social scientists

Exhibit 1.5   E-Mail Use by Mean Annual Communication Within 30 Miles (50 km)

E-Mail Use	Family					Friends				
	F2F	Phone	Letters	E-Mail	Total	F2F	Phone	Letters	E-Mail	Total
Never	77	117	6	1	201	104	136	6	1	247
Rarely	65	116	6	5	192	84	112	8	5	209
Monthly	61	113	6	7	187	74	98	5	9	186
Weekly	62	121	6	13	202	76	99	7	20	202
Few times per week	63	115	7	24	209	83	113	7	37	240
Daily	60	118	8	52	238	92	126	9	118	345
Total	61	117	7	39	224	88	120	9	86	303

Source: Wellman et al., 2001: 445.

Barry Wellman, Anabel Quan Haase, James Witte, and Keith Hampton (2001) analyzed responses from the 39,211 United States and Canadian respondents, they found that e-mail had become more popular than letters and phone calls for keeping in touch with family and particularly friends outside of the local area, but was much less popular than phone and face-to-face contact for family within the local area (Exhibit 1.5). Wellman and his colleagues (2001:450) concluded that "the Internet is increasing interpersonal connectivity and organizational involvement."

Exploration: Can Online Interaction Create a Virtual Community?

The Internet provides a "space where disparate individuals can find mutual solace and exchange information within a common community of interest" (Loader et al., 2002:53). It is easy to understand why these features of the Internet "space" have made it a popular medium for individuals seeking help for health problems. Internet Usenet groups on health care have become an increasingly important component of the self-help movement in health care.

Impressed by the vitality of the medical self-help movement and wondering about the quality of the help it provided, British social scientists Brian Loader, Steve Muncer, Roger Burrows, Nicolas Pleace, and Sarah Nettleton (2002) decided to explore computer-mediated social support for people with diabetes. Because many lifestyle changes are required to manage diabetes effectively, it is a condition that is particularly well suited to a self-help approach. On the Internet (or Usenet), conversational newsgroups provide opportunities for persons with diabetes anywhere in the world to share information about the value of such activities as exercise and diet and to provide support to others.

Loader and his colleagues selected for analysis all interactions (postings) on a diabetes newsgroup in 1 week in 1998. Each of 149 different "threads" (chains of interrelated messages on a topic) was categorized for the type of social support it provided. For example, in a message classified as "self-esteem support," the contributor responded to a message by someone complaining, "I am sick of this disease!"

Boy, I am sick of it, too! Your words could have been mine almost exactly. We all get really depressed over it from time to time. And some of us, like me, get really angry about it, too. . . . It controls what I eat, when I eat, when I exercise and for how long. So I think of it as "adjusting" to my diabetes. . . . Hang in! (Loader et al., 2002:58)

In general, the diabetes newsgroup seemed to be "a reasonably active network of people with diabetes, who find value in sharing their experiences and lay knowledge of living with their condition in an informal virtual self-help forum" (Loader et al., 2002:64). The messages they exchanged were primarily supportive, informational, and not misleading—although participants did not accept informational postings uncritically. The participants did not reject evidence-based clinical advice, but used the newsgroup as "a secure space where such information can be assimilated and reflexively shaped to inform lifestyle choices" (Loader et al., 2002:64). The newsgroup was a supplement to professional medical care, not an alternative to it.

Explanation: What Effect Does Internet Use Have on Social Relations?

Norman H. Nie and Lutz Erbring (2000), political scientists at the Stanford Institute for the Quantitative Study of Society, designed a large, innovative survey of Americans to answer this and other questions. They drew a random sample of 4,113 adults in 2,689 households across the United States and then gave every member of the sample a free Web TV, which was then connected to the Internet, also for free. The survey was conducted on the Internet, with respondents answering questions directly on their Web TVs.

The first study report focused on survey respondents who had already been using the Internet when they were contacted for the study. These respondents were questioned about their Internet usage, their personal characteristics and orientations, and the impact of Internet usage on their lives. Their answers suggested adverse effects of Internet use on social relations. The more time people spent using the Internet, the less time they spent with other social activities, even talking on the phone to friends and family. The heavier Internet users also reported an increase in time spent working both at home and at the office. Nie and Erbring also found what some might view as positive effects: less time watching TV, shopping in stores, and commuting in traffic.

Nie and Erbring (2000:19) were troubled by the results:

E-mail is a way to stay in touch, but you can't share a coffee or a beer with somebody on e-mail or give them a hug. . . . The Internet could be the ultimate isolating technology that further reduces our participation in communities even more than television did before it.

But more research evidence on Internet use is accumulating and social patterns are changing. The latest surveys indicate that the Internet seems to be "a catalyst for creating and maintaining friendships and family relationships" (UCLA Center for Communication Policy, 2001:8) and a favored source for information at work, but not a useful tool for resolving workplace social problems (Fallows, 2002).

Evaluation: Does High-Speed Internet Access Change Community Life?

Netville's developers connected all homes in this new suburban Toronto community with a high-speed cable and appropriate devices for Internet access. Sociologists Barry Wellman and Keith Hampton (1999) used this arrangement to evaluate the impact of Internet access on social relations. They surveyed Netville residents who were connected to the Internet and compared them to residents who had not activated their computer connections. Hampton actually lived in Netville for 2 years, participating in community events and taking notes on social interaction.

It proved to be difficult to begin research in a rapidly developing community (Hampton & Wellman, 1999). The researchers wanted to interview new community members several months before they moved in, but were unable to develop the necessary arrangements. Many community members had difficulty completing an online questionnaire, so in-person interviews were substituted. Unexpected early termination of the network arrangements by the service provider prevented the researchers from conducting a later survey to identify changes over time. Nonetheless, the combination of household surveys and participant observation, supplemented by analysis of postings to the community e-mail list and special group discussions (focus groups), resulted in a comprehensive investigation of the role of the computer network in community social life (Hampton & Wellman, 2000).

Wellman and Hampton found that Internet access increased social relations of residents ("Ego" in Exhibit 1.6) with other households, resulting in a larger and less geographically concentrated circle of friends. E-mail was used to set up face-to-face social events rather than as a substitute for them. Information about home repair and other personal and community topics and residents' service needs were exchanged over the Internet. Sensitive personal topics, however, were discussed offline. They also found that being wired into the computer network enabled residents to maintain more effectively their relations with friends and relatives elsewhere. Overall, community ties were enriched and extra-community social ties were strengthened (Hampton & Wellman, 2001).

Quantitative and Qualitative Orientations

Did you notice the difference between the types of data the studies used? The primary data collected in the descriptive National Geographic Society (2000) survey were counts of the number of people using the Internet and of many other behaviors and attitudes. These data were numerical, so we say that this study used **quantitative methods.** The Bureau of the Census survey (U.S. Department of Commerce, 2002), the UCLA (2001) survey, Nie and Erbring's (2000) survey, and the ongoing Pew survey research (e.g., Fallows, 2002) also used quantitative methods; they reported their findings as percents and other statistics that summarized the relationship between Internet usage and various aspects of social relations. By contrast, Loader et al. (2002) studied written comments—original text—in their exploration of the persons with diabetes using the online newsgroup. Because they focused on actual text, not on counts or other quantities, we say that this study used **qualitative methods.**

Quantitative methods Methods such as surveys and experiments that record variation in social life in terms of categories that vary in amount. Data that are treated as quantitative are either numbers or attributes that can be ordered in terms of magnitude.

Exhibit 1.6   The Development of Social Ties in New Wired and Nonwired Neighborhoods

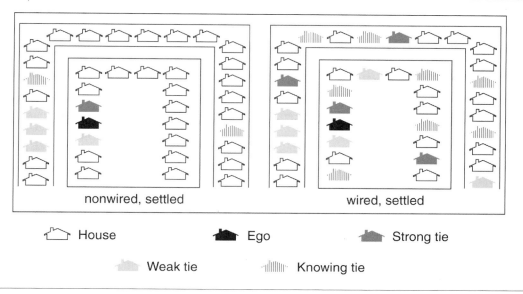

Source: Hampton & Wellman, 2000. Reprinted with permission.

Qualitative methods   Methods such as participant observation, intensive interviewing, and focus groups that are designed to capture social life as participants experience it, rather than in categories predetermined by the researcher. Data that are treated as qualitative are mostly written or spoken words or observations that do not have a direct numerical interpretation.

The distinction between quantitative and qualitative methods involves more than just the type of data collected. Quantitative methods are most often used when the motives for research are explanation, description, or evaluation. Exploration is most often the motive for using qualitative methods, although researchers also use these methods for descriptive, explanatory, and evaluative purposes. I'll highlight several other differences between quantitative and qualitative methods in the next two chapters. Chapters 9 and 13 present qualitative methods in much more detail, and most other chapters include some comparison of quantitative and qualitative approaches.

Important as it is, I don't want to place too much emphasis on the distinction between quantitative and qualitative orientations or methods. Social scientists often combine these methods in order to enrich their research. For example, Hampton and Wellman (2000) used surveys to generate counts of community network usage and other behaviors in Netville, but to help interpret these behaviors, they also observed social interaction and recorded spoken comments. In this way, qualitative data about social settings can be used to better understand patterns in quantitative data (Campbell & Russo, 1999:141).

The use of multiple methods to study one research question is called **triangulation.** The term suggests that a researcher can get a clearer picture of the social reality being studied by viewing it from several different perspectives. Each will have some liabilities in a specific research application and all can benefit from combination with one or more other methods (Brewer & Hunter, 1989; Sechrest & Sidani, 1995).

Triangulation   The use of multiple methods to study one research question.

The distinction between quantitative and qualitative data is not always sharp. Qualitative data can be converted to quantitative data, when we count the frequency of particular words or phrases in a text or measure the time elapsed between different observed behaviors. Surveys that collect primarily quantitative data may also include questions asking for written responses, and these responses may be used in a qualitative, textual analysis. Qualitative researchers may test explicit explanations of social phenomena using textual or observational data. We'll examine such "mixed method" possibilities in Chapters 7 through 11, when we review specific methods of data collection.

SOCIAL RESEARCH GOALS

Social science research can improve our understanding of empirical reality—the reality we encounter firsthand. We have reached the goal of **validity** when our statements or conclusions about this empirical reality are correct. I look out my window and observe that it is raining— a valid observation, if my eyes and ears are to be trusted. I pick up the newspaper and read that the rate of violence may be climbing after several years of decline. I am less certain of the validity of this statement, based as it is on an interpretation of some trends in crime indicators obtained through some process that isn't explained. As you will see in Chapter 12, many political scientists believe that higher social status is associated with a greater probability of voting, because a great many studies in a variety of contexts and countries have convinced them of the validity of this generalization.

If validity sounds desirable to you, you're a good candidate for becoming a social scientist. If you recognize that validity is often a difficult goal to achieve, you may be tough enough for social research. In any case, the goal of social science is not to come up with conclusions that people will like or conclusions that suit our own personal preferences. The goal is to figure out how and why the social world—some aspect of it, that is—operates as it does. In *Investigating the Social World,* we will be concerned with three aspects of validity: **measurement validity**, **generalizability**, and **causal validity** (also known as internal validity). We will learn that invalid measures, invalid generalizations, or invalid causal inferences will result in invalid conclusions. We will also consider the goal of **authenticity**, which some qualitative researchers consider to be a distinct research goal.

Measurement validity   Exists when a measure measures what we think it measures.

Generalizability   Exists when a conclusion holds true for the population, group, setting, or event that we say it does, given the conditions that we specify.

> *Causal validity (internal validity)*   Exists when a conclusion that A leads to or results in B is correct.
>
> *Authenticity*   When the understanding of a social process or social setting is one that reflects fairly the various perspectives of participants in that setting.

Measurement Validity

Measurement validity is our first concern in establishing the validity of research results, because without having measured what we think we measured, we really don't know what we're talking about. Measurement validity is the focus of Chapter 4.

Problems with measurement validity can result for many reasons. In studies of Internet forums, researchers have found that participants may use fictitious identities, even pretending to be a different gender (Donath, 1999). Therefore, researchers could not rely on gender disclosed in the forums when identifying differences in usage patterns between men and women. The Pew Internet & American Life Project (2000) surveyed 3,533 adults residing in the continental United States in March 2000. Among more than 64 survey questions, respondents were asked, "How much, if at all, has the Internet improved connection to members of your family?" Can we assume that these retrospective self-reports were accurate?

Suffice it to say that we must be very careful in designing our measures and in subsequently evaluating how well they have performed. Some researchers use beepers to capture reliably the daily activities of individuals they are studying (participants record their activities when they are beeped). Others question people about their activities over a period of time in order to avoid inaccuracies that can occur when respondents are asked to recall what they did at some time in the past. We cannot just *assume* that measures are valid.

Generalizability

The generalizability of a study is the extent to which it can be used to inform us about persons, places, or events that were not studied. Generalizability is the focus of Chapter 5.

The Internet studies provide some interesting examples of different approaches to establishing generalizability. The Pew project (2000) surveyed a large sample of all adult residents of the continental United States, without regard to whether they used the Internet or not. Nie and Erbring's (2000) study of Internet use was designed with a Web-based survey approach; individuals without an Internet connection could not participate. However, because about two-thirds of Americans were not connected to the Internet in 1999, this approach would have resulted in a survey sample whose characteristics could not be generalized to the American population as a whole. In order to avoid such an unrepresentative sample, Nie and Erbring's research grant funded the purchase of Web TVs for every survey respondent. All individuals who had not been connected previously would then be able to complete the online questionnaire, so it was possible for Nie and Erbring to survey a large, representative sample of the United States population.

The National Geographic Society (2000) international survey of Internet users did not avoid this problem. Only people who were connected to the Internet, who heard about the survey, and who chose to participate were included in the sample. This meant that many more respondents came from more-developed countries that had higher rates of computer and Internet use than from less-developed countries. South Africa was the only African nation in which more than 100 citizens participated. However, the inclusion of individuals from 178 countries and territories does allow some interesting comparisons among countries. Although we cannot be confident that the sample in any country is representative of that country's population or even of its Internet users, the results provide a basis for posing many questions about international differences to be studied more systematically in future research.

It can be very hard to draw large, representative samples across many different types of social or cultural contexts. Studies like the Netville research, which involve special experimental arrangements, would be prohibitively expensive if conducted in a number of communities. Nie and Erbring (2000) received corporate funding for their innovative Internet study that placed Web TVs in thousands of homes, but only because they agreed that this system would also be used for marketing research. Academic and business needs do not always overlap so much. Collection of data in qualitative studies like that of Loader et al. (2002) can also require a great deal of time, thus limiting the size and number of samples that can be studied.

If every person or community we study were like every other one, generalizations based on observations of a small number would be valid. But that's not the case. We are on solid ground if we question the generalizability of statements about Internet effects based on the results of a survey in just one community or among a restricted sample of the population.

Generalizability has two aspects. **Sample generalizability** refers to the ability to generalize from a sample, or subset, of a larger population to that population itself. This is the most common meaning of generalizability. **Cross-population generalizability** refers to the ability to generalize from findings about one group, population, or setting to other groups, populations, or settings (see Exhibit 1.7). Cross-population generalizability can also be termed *external* validity. (Some social scientists equate the term *external validity* with *generalizability,* but in this book I restrict its use to the more limited notion of cross-population generalizability.)

Sample generalizability   Exists when a conclusion based on a sample, or subset, of a larger population holds true for that population.

Cross-population generalizability   Exists when findings about one group, population, or setting hold true for other groups, populations, or settings. Also called *external validity.*

Sample generalizability is a key concern in survey research. Political pollsters may study a sample of likely voters, for example, and then generalize their findings to the entire population of likely voters. No one would be interested in the results of political polls if they represented only the relatively tiny sample that actually was surveyed rather than the entire population.

Cross-population generalizability occurs to the extent that the results of a study hold true for multiple populations; these populations may not all have been sampled, or they

Exhibit 1.7   Sample and Cross-Population Generalizability

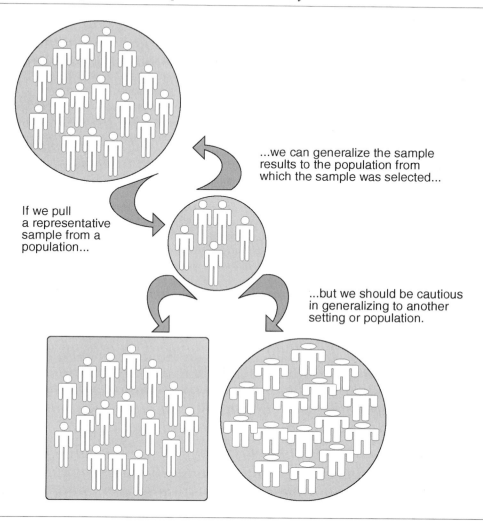

If we pull a representative sample from a population...

...we can generalize the sample results to the population from which the sample was selected...

...but we should be cautious in generalizing to another setting or population.

may be represented as subgroups within the sample studied. We can only wonder about the cross-population generalizability of the Netville results. Are middle-class individuals living in suburban Toronto likely to respond to computer-based communication opportunities in a way that is similar to the responses of other populations in Canada? In other countries? Do persons with diabetes use Internet newsgroups in the same way as those with other issues?

Generalizability is a key concern in research design. We rarely have the resources to study the entire population that is of interest to us, so we have to select cases to study that will allow our findings to be generalized to the population of interest. Nonetheless, since we can never be sure that our findings will hold under all conditions, we should be cautious in generalizing to populations that we did not actually sample.

Causal Validity

Causal validity, also known as **internal validity,** refers to the truthfulness of an assertion that A causes B. It is the focus of Chapter 6.

Most research seeks to determine what causes what, so social scientists frequently must be concerned with causal validity. Much recent research on the Internet is concerned with the effect of the Internet on social relations. For example, Barry Wellman and his coauthors analyzed the National Geographic Society survey data to answer the question, "Does the Internet increase, decrease, or supplement social capital?" John Bargh, Katelyn McKenna, and Grainne Fitzsimons (2002) designed an experiment to test whether college students who communicated through the Internet would be more likely to express their true selves, including parts of themselves not usually expressed, than those who interacted face to face.

The undergraduates who participated in the Bargh experiment first filled out a form that revealed their "true" and "actual" (usually expressed) self-conceptions. Next, they were introduced to a partner of the opposite sex and given 40 minutes to get to know the partner. Half the students interacted on the Internet and half interacted face to face. After this experience, all participants listed the traits they believed their partner possessed. As you can see in Exhibit 1.8, the students who had interacted over the Internet perceived their partners as more like their partners' more complete, "true" selves than did those who had interacted face to face. So, computer-mediated communication actually facilitated projection of one's true self — the "real me"—to another person. Surprised?

Establishing causal validity can be quite difficult. You will learn in more detail in subsequent chapters how experimental designs and statistics can help us evaluate causal propositions, but the solutions are neither easy nor perfect: We always have to consider critically the validity of causal statements that we hear or read.

Authenticity

In order to accept validity as the goal of social research, researchers must believe that it is possible to develop understandings that represent correctly empirical social reality. If you, as a social researcher, did not believe that there is an empirical social reality, or if you believed that it is not possible to discover what that empirical social reality is, it would not make sense for you to accept validity, as it is commonly defined, as the goal for your research. This is the problem that some qualitative researchers have with the goal of validity, and it has led them to suggest alternative research goals.

Authenticity is one of these suggested alternatives. An authentic understanding of a social process or social setting is one that reflects fairly the various perspectives of participants in that setting (Gubrium & Holstein, 1997). Authenticity is only one of several different standards proposed for qualitative research, but it reflects the belief underlying several such standards that those who study the social world can hope to understand only how others view that social world. From this perspective, every observer sees the social world from his or her own vantage point; there is no basis for determining that one perspective is the "valid" one. "The conception of knowledge as a mirror of reality is replaced by knowledge as a linguistic and social construction of reality" (Kvale, 2002:306).

Exhibit 1.8   Success of Self-Presentation Over the Internet Versus Face to Face

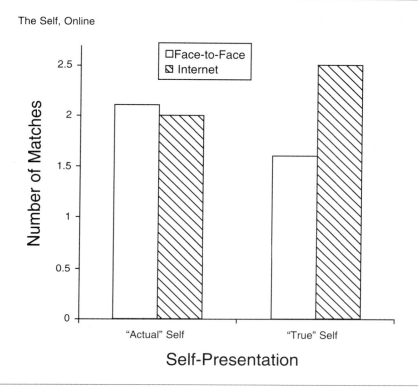

Source: Bargh et al., 2002: 43. Reprinted with permission from Blackwell Publishing, Ltd.

STRENGTHS AND LIMITATIONS OF SOCIAL RESEARCH

Using social scientific research methods to develop answers to questions about the social world reduces the likelihood of making everyday errors in reasoning. The various projects that we have reviewed in this chapter illustrate this point:

- The clear definition of the population of interest in each study and the selection of a broad, representative sample of that population (as done, for example, by Nie and Erbring and the U.S. Department of Commerce) increased the researchers' ability to draw conclusions without overgeneralizing findings to groups to which they did not apply. Although the National Geographic Society study was limited to self-selected Internet users, its international scope facilitates cross-national checks on generalizability of findings.
- The use of surveys in which each respondent was asked the same set of questions reduced the risk of selective or inaccurate observation, as did systematic review of Usenet postings by the researchers participating in the study of diabetes support group members.

- The risk of illogical reasoning was reduced by carefully describing each stage of the research, clearly presenting the findings, and carefully testing the basis for cause-and-effect conclusions.
- Resistance to change was reduced by explicitly encouraging involvement in the research projects in Netville and among the Usenet members. The National Geographic Society, Pew, and Stanford researchers have posted their methods and findings on the Web to help inform the general public.

Nevertheless, I would be less than honest if I implied that we enter the realm of truth and light when we conduct social research or when we rely solely on the best available social research. Research always has some limitations and some flaws (as does any human endeavor), and our findings are always subject to differing interpretations. Social research permits us to see more, to observe with fewer distortions, and to describe more clearly to others what our opinions are based on, but it will not settle all arguments. Others will always have differing opinions, and some of those others will be social scientists who have conducted their own studies and drawn different conclusions.

Although Nie and Erbring (2000) concluded that use of the Internet diminished social relations, their study at Stanford was soon followed by the Pew Internet and American Life Project (2000) and another Internet survey by the UCLA Center for Communication Policy (2000). These two later studies also used survey research methods, but their findings suggested that use of the Internet does *not* diminish social relations. Psychologist Robert Kraut's early research suggested that Internet use was isolating, but his own more recent research indicates more positive effects (Kraut et al., 2002). To what extent are different conclusions due to differences in research methods, to different perspectives on similar findings, or to rapid changes in the population of Internet users?

It's not so easy to answer such questions, so one research study often leads to another, and another, each one improving on previous research or examining a research question from a somewhat different angle. Part of becoming a good social researcher is learning that we have to evaluate critically each research study and weigh carefully the entire body of research about a research question before coming to a conclusion. And we have to keep an open mind about alternative interpretations and the possibility of new discoveries. The social phenomena we study are often complex, so we must take this complexity into account when we choose methods to study social phenomena and when we interpret the results of these studies.

But even in areas of research that are fraught with controversy, where social scientists differ in their interpretations of the evidence, the quest for new and more sophisticated research has value. What is most important for improving understanding of the social world is not the result of any particular study but the accumulation of evidence from different studies of related issues. By designing new studies that focus on the weak points or controversial conclusions of prior research, social scientists contribute to a body of findings that gradually expands our knowledge about the social world and resolves some of the disagreements about it.

Whether you plan to conduct your own research projects, read others' research reports, or just think about and act in the social world, knowing about research methods has many benefits. This knowledge will give you greater confidence in your own opinions; improve your ability to evaluate others' opinions; and encourage you to refine your questions, answers, and methods of inquiry about the social world.

CONCLUSIONS

I hope this first chapter has given you an idea of what to expect in the rest of the book. My aim is to introduce you to social research methods by describing what social scientists have learned about the social world as well as how they have learned it. The substance of social science inevitably is more interesting than its methods, but the methods become more interesting when they're linked to substantive investigations. I have focused attention on Internet research in this chapter; in subsequent chapters I will introduce research examples from other areas.

Chapter 2 continues to build the foundation for our study of social research by reviewing how social scientists select research questions for investigation, how they can find information about prior research on those questions, what process they must use to answer these research questions, and what ethical problems they must strive to avoid. I also introduce the process of writing research proposals, which is then continued in special end-of-chapter exercises throughout the book. Several studies of domestic violence illustrate the research process. Chapter 3 is the last "foundations" chapter. I introduce you to alternative theoretical perspectives that can stimulate social research questions, as well as to the alternative philosophies that shape researchers' strategies.

Then I return to the subject of validity. Chapters 4, 5, and 6 discuss the three aspects of validity and the specific techniques used to maximize the validity of our measures, our generalizations, and our causal assertions. Research about the measurement of substance abuse, sampling of homeless persons, and the causes of violence is highlighted.

Chapters 7, 8, and 9 introduce the three primary methods of data collection. Experimental studies, the subject of Chapter 7, are favored by many psychologists, social psychologists, and policy evaluation researchers. Survey research is the most common method of data collection in sociology, so in Chapter 8 I devote a lot of attention to the different types of surveys. Qualitative methods have long been the method of choice in anthropology, but they also have a long tradition in American sociology and a growing number of adherents around the world. Chapter 9 shows how qualitative techniques can uncover aspects of the social world that we are likely to miss in experiments and surveys, and can sometimes result in a different perspective on social processes. In these chapters, you will learn about research on work organizations, psychological distress, and gender roles and aging.

Chapters 10 and 11 both introduce data collection approaches that can involve several methods. Evaluation research, the subject of Chapter 10, is conducted to identify the impact of social programs or to clarify social processes involving such programs. Evaluation research often uses experimental methods, as was the case in research we will review on drug abuse prevention programs, but survey research and qualitative methods can also be helpful for evaluation researchers. Historical and comparative methods, the subject of Chapter 11, may involve either quantitative or qualitative methods that are used to compare societies and groups at one point in time and to analyze their development over time. We will see how these different approaches have been used to learn about political change in transitional societies.

Chapter 12 is not a substitute for an entire course in statistics, but it gives you a good idea of how to use statistics when analyzing research data and reporting or reviewing research results. I walk you through an analysis of quantitative data on voting. In Chapter 13, we examine in some detail the logic and procedures of qualitative data analysis and content analysis. Content analysis is primarily a quantitative approach, but you will be struck by the differences between the other qualitative data analysis techniques and the quantitative data analysis techniques you learned about in Chapter 12.

Plan to read Chapter 14 very carefully, because our research efforts are really only as good as the attention given to our research reports. I compare and contrast several different studies, point out some of the consequences of particular research strategies, and introduce meta-analysis as a statistical technique for assessing a body of research. I also finish the discussion of research proposals that I started in Chapter 2. Most of the chapter is devoted to the skills, approaches, and standards useful in reporting research. By the end of the chapter, you should have a broader perspective on how much research methods have helped to improve understanding of the social world (as well as an appreciation for how much remains to be done).

Each chapter ends with several helpful learning tools. Lists of key terms and chapter highlights will help you to review. Discussion questions and practice exercises will help you to apply and deepen your knowledge. Special exercises guide you in developing your first research proposal, finding information on the World Wide Web, and conducting statistical analyses of survey data. The CD-ROM that accompanies this book provides interactive exercises for reviewing key concepts, as well as programs for analyzing data and datasets for both qualitative and quantitative analyses.

KEY TERMS

Authenticity

Causal validity

Cross-population generalizability

Descriptive research

Evaluation research

Explanatory research

Exploratory research

External validity

Generalizability

Illogical reasoning

Inaccurate observation

Internal validity

Measurement validity

Overgeneralization

Qualitative methods

Quantitative methods

Resistance to change

Sample generalizability

Science

Selective observation

Social science

Triangulation

Validity

HIGHLIGHTS

- Empirical data are obtained in social science investigations from either direct experience or others' statements.
- Four common errors in reasoning are overgeneralization, selective or inaccurate observation, illogical reasoning, and resistance to change. These errors result from the complexity of the social world, subjective processes that affect the reasoning of researchers and those they study, researchers' self-interestedness, and unquestioning acceptance of tradition or of those in positions of authority.
- Social science is the use of logical, systematic, documented methods to investigate individuals, societies, and social processes, as well as the knowledge produced by these investigations.
- Social research cannot resolve value questions or provide permanent, universally accepted answers.

- Social research can be motivated by policy guidance and program management needs, academic concerns, and charitable impulses.

- Social research can be descriptive, exploratory, explanatory, or evaluative—or some combination of these.

- Valid knowledge is the central concern of scientific research. The three components of validity are measurement validity, generalizability (both from the sample to the population from which it was selected and from the sample to other populations), and causal (internal) validity. Authenticity can also be a concern for qualitative researchers.

- Quantitative and qualitative methods structure research in different ways and are differentially appropriate for diverse research situations.

DISCUSSION QUESTIONS

1. Select a social issue that interests you, like Internet use or crime. List at least four of your beliefs about this phenomenon. Try to identify the sources of each of these beliefs.

2. Find a report of social science research in an article in a daily newspaper. What were the major findings? How much evidence is given about the measurement validity, generalizability, and causal validity of the findings? What additional design features might have helped to improve the study's validity?

3. From the news, record statements of politicians or other leaders that concern some social phenomenon. Which statements do you think are likely to be in error? What evidence might improve the validity of these statements?

PRACTICE EXERCISES

1. Read the abstracts (initial summaries) of each article in a recent issue of a major social science journal. (Ask your instructor for some good journal titles.) On the basis of the abstract only, classify each research project represented in the articles as primarily descriptive, exploratory, explanatory, or evaluative. Note any indications that the research focused on other types of research questions.

2. Review letters to the editor and opinion pieces in your local newspaper. Identify any errors in reasoning: overgeneralization, selective or inaccurate observation, illogical reasoning, or resistance to change.

3. Review Types of Research with the Interactive Exercises lesson on the CD-ROM.

WEB EXERCISES

1. Prepare a 5- to 10-minute class presentation on the National Geographic Society's Survey 2000. Go to the National Geographic Web site at http://survey2000.nationalgeographic.com to view some of the results. Write up a brief outline for your presentation including information on study design, questions asked, and major findings.

2. Is the National Geographic Society's perspective representative of other researchers? Check out the reports of the Stanford Institute for the Quantitative Study of Society's Internet survey at http://www.stanford.edu/group/siqss/ and of the Pew Internet Project at http://www.pewinternet.org, as well as the UCLA Center for Communication Policy site at http://www.ccp.ucla.edu/index.asp. Write up some information regarding the surveys and their goals, methods, and major findings. What do the researchers conclude about the impact of the Internet on social life in the United States? How do these conclusions compare to each other and to those of the National Geographic Society researchers? What

aspects of the methods, questions, or findings might explain differences in their conclusions? Do you think the researchers approached their studies with different perspectives at the outset? If so, what might these perspectives have been?

SPSS EXERCISES

As explained in the Preface, the SPSS Exercises at the end of each chapter focus on support for the death penalty. A portion of the GSS2000 survey data is included on the CD-ROM packaged with this book. You will need a copy of the 2000 General Social Survey to carry out these exercises. You will begin your empirical investigation by thinking a bit about the topic and the data you have available for study.

1. What personal motivation might you have for studying support for the death penalty? What might motivate other people to conduct research on this topic? What about policy and academic motives?

2. Read an article that reviews some of the current concerns about the death penalty. You should find many newspaper articles on this issue because of the ongoing controversy over mistaken convictions. Alternatively, you can read an interesting journal article on this topic by Herb Haines (1992). Can you add any more motives to your list in Question 1?

3. Open the GSS2000mini file containing the 2000 General Social Survey data. In the SPSS menu, click on File, then Open and Data, and then on the name of the data file on the CD-ROM drive, or on the C: drive if GSS2000mini was copied there. How many respondents are there in this subset of the complete GSS file? (Scroll down to the bottom of the dataset.) How many variables were measured? (Scroll down to the bottom of the "variable view" in SPSS v. 10 or 11, or click on Utilities, then Variable List in earlier versions.)

4. What would you estimate as the level of support for capital punishment in the United States in 2000? Now for your first real research experience (in this text): Describe the distribution of support for capital punishment. Obtaining the relevant data is as simple as "a, b, c, d, e."

   a. Click on *Graphs.*
   b. Click on *Bar,* then *Simple* and *Summaries for groups of cases,* and then *Define.*
   c. Click on *Bars represent . . . % of cases,* scroll down the variable list and highlight CAPPUN, and then click on the arrow by *Category Axis.*
   d. Click on *Options* and then click off *Display groups defined by missing values.*
   e. Click on *Continue* and then on *OK.* Inspect the graph.

Now describe the distribution of support for capital punishment. What percentage of the population supported capital punishment in the United States in 2000?

DEVELOPING A RESEARCH PROPOSAL

Will you develop a research proposal in this course? If so, you should begin to consider your alternatives.

1. What topic would you focus on if you could design a social research project without any concern for costs? What are your motives for studying this topic?

2. Develop four questions that you might investigate about the topic you just selected. Each question should reflect a different research motive: description, exploration, explanation, or evaluation. Be specific.

3. Which question most interests you? Would you prefer to attempt to answer that question with quantitative or qualitative methods? Why?

Chapter 2

THE PROCESS AND PROBLEMS OF SOCIAL RESEARCH

Social Research Questions

Identifying Social Research Questions
Refining Social Research Questions
Evaluating Social Research
    Questions
    Feasibility
    Social Importance
    Scientific Relevance

Social Research Foundations

Finding Information
    Searching the Literature
    Searching the Web
Reviewing Research
    A Single-Article Review: Formal and
    Informal Deterrents to Domestic
    Violence
    An Integrated Literature Review: Do
    Fair Procedures Matter?

Social Research Strategies

The Role of Social Theory
The Deductive/Inductive Cycle
    Deductive Research
    Domestic Violence and the
        Research Circle
    Inductive Research
Exploratory Research: Victim Responses
    to Police Intervention
Descriptive Research

Social Research Ethics

Honesty and Openness
The Uses of Science
Research on People

Social Research Proposals, Part I

Conclusions

Domestic violence is a major problem in our society, with police responding to between 2 million and 8 million complaints of assault by a spouse or lover yearly (Sherman, 1992:6). What can be done to reduce this problem? In 1981, the Police Foundation and the Minneapolis Police Department began an experiment to determine whether arresting accused spouse abusers on the spot would deter repeat incidents. The study's results, which were widely publicized, indicated that arrest did have a deterrent effect. In part because of this, the percentage of urban police departments that made arrest the preferred response to complaints of domestic violence rose from 10% in 1984 to 90% in 1988 (Sherman, 1992:14). Six other cities then hosted studies like the Minneapolis experiment in order to determine whether changing the location or other features of the experiment would result in different outcomes (Sherman, 1992; Sherman & Berk, 1984). The Minneapolis Domestic Violence Experiment, the studies modeled after it, and the related controversies will provide good examples for our systematic overview of the social research process.

We will examine in this chapter different social research strategies. We will also consider in some detail the techniques required to begin the research process: formulating research questions, finding information, reviewing prior research, and writing a research proposal. Appendixes B, C, and D provide more details. I will use the Minneapolis experiment and related research to illustrate the different research strategies and some of the related techniques. The chapter also introduces ethical guidelines that should be adhered to no matter what the research strategy. By the chapter's end, you should be ready to formulate a research question, design a general strategy for answering this question, critique previous studies that addressed this question, and begin a proposal for additional research on the question. You can think of Chapter 1 as having introduced the "why" of social research; Chapter 2 introduces the "how."

SOCIAL RESEARCH QUESTIONS

A **social research question** is a question about the social world that you seek to answer through the collection and analysis of firsthand, verifiable, empirical data. It is not a question about who did what to whom but a question about people in groups, about general social processes, or about tendencies in community change. What distinguishes Internet users from other persons? Does community policing reduce the crime rate? What influences the likelihood of spouse abuse? How do people react to social isolation? So many research questions are possible that it is more of a challenge to specify what does *not* qualify as a social research question than to specify what does.

But that doesn't mean it is easy to specify a research question. In fact, formulating a good research question can be surprisingly difficult. We can break the process into three stages: identifying one or more questions for study, refining the questions, and then evaluating the questions.

Identifying Social Research Questions

Social research questions may emerge from your own experience—from your "personal troubles," as C. Wright Mills (1959) put it. One experience might be membership in a church, another could be victimization by crime, and yet another might be moving from a dorm to a sorority house. You may find yourself asking a question like "In what ways do people tend to benefit from church membership?" or "Does victimization change a person's trust in others?" or "How do initiation procedures influence group commitment?" Can you think of other possible research questions that flow from your own experiences in the social world?

The research literature is often the best source for research questions. Every article or book will bring new questions to mind. Even if you're not feeling too creative when you read the literature, most research articles highlight unresolved issues and end with suggestions for additional research. For example, Lawrence Sherman and Douglas Smith, with their colleagues, concluded an article on some of the replications of the Minneapolis experiment on police responses to spouse abuse by suggesting that "deterrence may be effective for a substantial segment of the offender population. . . . [H]owever, the underlying mechanisms remain obscure" (1992:706). A new study could focus on these mechanisms: Why does the arrest of offenders deter some of them from future criminal acts? Any research article in a journal in your field is likely to have comments that point toward unresolved issues.

Many social scientists find the source of their research questions in social theory. Some researchers spend much of their careers conducting research intended to refine an answer to one research question that is critical for a particular social theory. For example, you may find rational choice theory to be a useful approach to understanding diverse forms of social behavior, because you feel that people do seem to make decisions on the basis of personal cost–benefit calculations. So you may ask whether rational choice theory can explain consumer behavior in stores and then whether it can explain shoplifting, spouse abuse, or other forms of deviance.

Finally, some research questions have very pragmatic sources. You may focus on a research question posed by someone else because it seems to be to your advantage to do so. Some social scientists conduct research on specific questions posed by a funding source in what is termed an RFP, a request for proposals. (Sometimes the acronym RFA is used, meaning request for applications.) Or you may learn that the social workers in the homeless shelter where you volunteer need help with a survey to learn about client needs, which becomes the basis for another research question.

Refining Social Research Questions

The problem is not so much coming up with interesting questions for research as it is focusing on a problem of manageable size. We are often interested in much more than we can reasonably investigate with limited time and resources. Researchers may worry about staking a research project (and thereby a grant or a grade) on a particular problem, and so address several research questions at once, often in a jumbled fashion. It might also seem risky to focus on a research question that may lead to results discrepant with our own cherished assumptions about the social world. The prospective commitment of time and effort for some research questions may seem overwhelming, resulting in a certain degree of paralysis.

The best way to avoid these problems is to develop the research question one bit at a time. Don't keep hoping that the perfect research question will just spring forth from your pen. Instead, develop a list of possible research questions as you go along. At the appropriate time, you can look through this list for the research questions that appear more than once. Narrow your list to the most interesting, most workable candidates. Repeat this process as long as it helps to improve your research questions.

Evaluating Social Research Questions

In the third stage of selecting a research question, we evaluate the best candidate against the criteria for good social research questions: feasibility given the time and resources available, social importance, and scientific relevance (King, Keohane, & Verba, 1994).

Feasibility

We must be able to conduct any study within the time and given the resources we have. If time is short, questions that involve long-term change may not be feasible. Another issue is what people or groups we can expect to gain access to. Observing social interaction in corporate boardrooms may be taboo. Then we must consider whether we will have any additional resources, such as other researchers to collaborate with or research funds. Remember that there are severe limits on what one person can accomplish. On the other hand, we may be able to piggyback our research onto a larger research project. We also must take into account the constraints we face due to our schedules and other commitments and our skill level.

The Minneapolis Domestic Violence Experiment shows how ambitious social research questions can be when a team of seasoned researchers secures the backing of influential groups. The project required hundreds of thousands of dollars, the collaboration of many social scientists and criminal justice personnel, and the volunteer efforts of 41 Minneapolis police officers. Of course, for this reason the Sherman and Berk (1984) question would not be a feasible question for a student project. You might instead ask the question "Do students think punishment deters spouse abuse?" Or perhaps you could work out an arrangement with a local police department to study the question "How satisfied are the police with their treatment of domestic violence cases?"

Social Importance

Social research is not a simple undertaking, so it's hard to justify the expenditure of effort and resources unless we focus on a substantive area that is important. Besides, you need to feel motivated to carry out the study. "Importance" is relative, so for a class assignment student reactions to dormitory rules or something like that might be important enough.

But for real research undertakings we should consider whether the research question is important to other people. Will an answer to the research question make a difference for society, for social relations? Again, the Minneapolis Domestic Violence Experiment is an exemplary case. But the social sciences are not wanting for important research questions. The April 1984 issue of the *American Sociological Review,* which contained the first academic article on the Minneapolis experiment, also included articles reporting research on elections, school tracking, discrimination, work commitment, school grades, organizational change, and homicide. All of these articles addressed research questions about important social issues, and all raised new questions for additional research.

Scientific Relevance

Every research question should be grounded in the social science literature. Whether we formulate a research question because we have been stimulated by an academic article or because we want to investigate a current social problem, we must turn to the social science literature to find out what has already been learned about this question. You can be sure that some prior study is relevant to almost any research question you can think of.

The Minneapolis experiment was built on a substantial body of contradictory theorizing about the impact of punishment on criminality (Sherman & Berk, 1984). Deterrence theory predicted that arrest would deter individuals from repeat offenses; labeling theory predicted that arrest would make repeat offenses more likely. One prior experimental study of this issue was about juveniles; studies among adults had yielded inconsistent findings. Clearly, the Minneapolis researchers had good reason for another study. Any new research question should be connected in this way to past research.

SOCIAL RESEARCH FOUNDATIONS

How do we find prior research and theory? You may already know some of the relevant material from prior coursework or your independent reading, but that won't be enough. New research results about many questions appear continually in scholarly journals and books, in research reports from government agencies and other organizations, and on Web sites all over the world. Conducting a thorough search of these sources and then reviewing critically what you have found is an essential foundation for any research project. Fortunately, most of this information can be identified online, without leaving your desktop, and an increasing fraction of published journal articles can be downloaded directly to your own computer (depending on your particular access privileges).

Finding Information

Searching the published research literature is an essential step for serious researchers, but every year the World Wide Web also offers more and more useful material. Everything from copies of particular rating scales to reports from research in progress to forums on related topics can be found on the Web. We will review in this section the basic procedures for finding relevant research information in both the published literature and on the Web. Appendix D provides more detailed instructions.

Searching the Literature

The social science literature should be consulted at the beginning and end of an investigation. Even while an investigation is in progress, consultations with the literature may help to resolve methodological problems or facilitate supplementary explorations. Unlike the largely unregulated Web, research published in social science journals has been subject to a relatively rigorous review process (although standards vary by journal). No matter how tempting it is to rely on the materials more readily available on the Web, you must search the published research literature.

Preparing the Search. Formulate a research question before you begin to search, even though the question may change after that. Identify the question's parts and subparts and any related issues that you think might play an important role in the research. List the authors of relevant studies you are aware of, possible keywords that might specify the subject for your search, and perhaps the most important journals that deal with your topic. For example, if your research question is "What is the effect of informal social control on crime rates?" you might consider searching the literature electronically for studies that mentioned "informal social control" or just "social control" as well as "crime" or "crime rate." You might also search for works by authors such as Robert Sampson, a prominent researcher on this topic, and Donald

Black, who is a major theorist of social control. You might plan to check prominent journals like the *American Sociological Review, American Journal of Sociology, Criminology,* and the *American Journal of Criminology.*

Conducting the Search. Now you are ready to begin searching the literature. You should check for relevant books in your library and perhaps in the other college libraries in your area. This usually means conducting a search of an online catalog using a list of subject terms. But most scientific research is published in journal articles, so the primary focus of your search should be the journal literature.

Searching a computerized bibliographic database is by far the most efficient search strategy, although some libraries still carry paper indexes. The specifics of a database search will vary among libraries and according to your own computer resources (check with your librarian for help). Most academic libraries provide access to online databases like *Sociological Abstracts (Sociofile), Psychological Abstracts (PsychINFO)* and, less often, the *Social Science Citation Index.*

After you have accessed the chosen index, you can locate the published articles pertaining to topics identified by your subject terms. Choose your subject terms very carefully. A good rule is to cast a net wide enough to catch most of the relevant articles with your key terms but not so wide that it identifies many useless citations. For example, a search for "informal social control" would be more successful than a search for "control." Give most attention to articles published in the leading journals in the field, but be prepared to spend a fair amount of time whittling down the list of citations if you are searching for a popular topic.

Exhibit 2.1 shows the results of a search for articles on "informal social control" in *Sociological Abstracts Online.* The search resulted in 64 English language documents.

The sheer number of references you find can be a problem. For example, searching for "social capital" resulted in 484 citations in *Sociological Abstracts, 1986–2000.* Depending on the database you are working with and the purposes of your search, you may want to limit your search to English language publications, to journal articles rather than conference papers or dissertations (both of which are more difficult to acquire), and to materials published in recent years. It's often a good idea to narrow down your search by requiring that abstracts contain combinations of words or phrases.

Checking the Results. Check the titles and read the abstracts and identify articles that appear to be relevant. You may even be able to click on these article titles and generate a list of their references. Now it is time to find the full text of the articles of interest. If you're lucky, some of the journals you need will be available to patrons of your library in online versions and you'll be able to link to the full text of articles in those journals just by clicking on the "full text" link. But many journals are available only in print.

You may be tempted to write up a "review" of the literature based on reading the abstracts or using only those articles available online, but you will be selling yourself short. Many crucial details about methods, findings, and theoretical implications will be found only in the body of the article, and many important articles will not be available online. To understand, critique, and really learn from previous research studies, you must read the important articles, no matter how you have to retrieve them. And don't stop with the articles you identified in your initial search of the *Abstracts* or other index. Always check the bibliographies of the articles that you read for additional relevant sources and then expand your literature search by

Exhibit 2.1   A Search in *Sociological Abstracts* on Informal Control

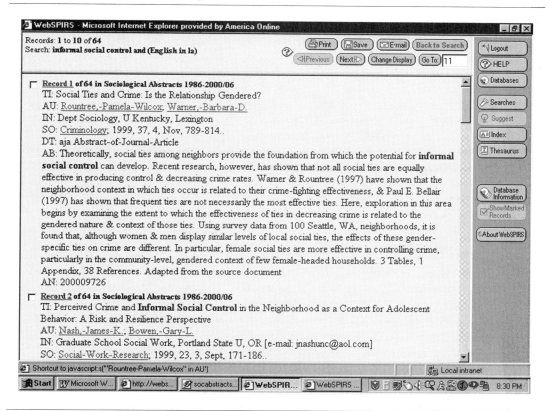

reading those articles and books. Continue this process as long as it identifies new and useful sources. You will be surprised (I always am) at how many important articles your initial online search missed.

If you have done your job well, you will now have more than enough literature as background for your own research, unless it is on a very obscure topic. (Of course, your search will be limited by library holdings you have access to and perhaps by the time required to order copies of conference papers and dissertations you find in your search.) At this point, your main concern is to construct a coherent framework in which to develop your research question, drawing as many lessons as you can from previous research. You may use the literature to identify a useful theory and hypotheses to be reexamined, to find inadequately studied specific research questions, to explicate the disputes about your research question, to summarize the major findings of prior research, and to suggest appropriate methods of investigation. Be sure to take notes on each article you read, organizing your notes into standard sections: theory, methods, findings, conclusions. In any case, write the literature review so that it contributes to your study in some concrete way; don't feel compelled to discuss an article just because you have read it. Be judicious. You are conducting only one study of one issue; it will only obscure the value of your study if you try to relate it to every tangential point in related research.

Don't think of searching the literature as a one-time-only venture—something that you leave behind as you move on to your *real* research. You may encounter new questions or unanticipated problems as you conduct your research or as you burrow deeper into the literature. Searching the literature again to determine what others have found in response to these questions or what steps they have taken to resolve these problems can yield substantial improvements in your own research. There is so much literature on so many topics that it often is not possible to figure out in advance every subject you should search the literature for or what type of search will be most beneficial.

Another reason to make searching the literature an ongoing project is that the literature is always growing. During the course of one research study, whether it takes only one semester or several years, new findings will be published and relevant questions will be debated. Staying attuned to the literature and checking it at least when you are writing up your findings may save your study from being outdated.

Searching the Web

The World Wide Web provides access to vast amounts of information of many different sorts (O'Dochartaigh, 2002). You can search the holdings of other libraries and download the complete text of government reports, some conference papers, and newspaper articles. You can find policies of local governments, descriptions of individual social scientists and particular research projects, and postings of advocacy groups. It's also hard to avoid finding a lot of information in which you have no interest, such as commercial advertisements, third-grade homework assignments, or college course syllabi. Back in 1999, there were already about 800 million publicly available pages of information on the Web (Davis, 1999). Today there may be as many as 15 billion pages on the Web (Novak, 2003).

After you are connected to the Web with a browser like Microsoft Internet Explorer or Netscape Navigator, you can use three basic strategies for finding information: direct addressing, browsing, and searching. For some purposes, you will need to use only one strategy; for other purposes, you will want to use all three. Appendix D contains additional information on all three methods.

Direct Addressing. Every Web information source is identified by an address (a uniform resource locator, or URL). If you know the URL of the information source you want to use, you can instruct your browser to go directly to that source. The end-of-chapter Web exercises, Appendix H, and the CD-ROM for this text list many URLs relevant to social science research.

Browsing Subject Directories. Many Web sites maintain lists of URLs that pertain to their site and, hopefully, have been selected because of their relevance and quality. When you visit one of these sites, you can browse its list of related URLs and then go directly to these sites. Many government agencies, professional organizations, academic departments, and even individuals maintain URL lists as part of their Web sites.

Searching. Search engines are programs that index Web pages on an ongoing basis and let you search the resulting database for pages on topics of interest. A few of the popular search engines available today are Google, AltaVista, and Infoseek. (Yahoo is often thought of as a search engine, but it is actually a subject directory. See Appendix D for more information on the distinction.) When using search engines, keep in mind that not all search engines are the same.

- Search engines vary in size.
- Search engines crawl different sites on the Web and so will yield different results.
- Search engines use their own procedures for identifying and indexing Web resources and vary in what type of information is included. For example, some include newspapers, whereas others do not.
- Search engines have their own searching syntax and relevance ranking system. You can't jump from one engine to another and expect each to work in the same way.
- No single search engine covers more than one-third of the pages on the Web, and it takes most search engines 6 months or more to find new Web pages (Davis, 1999).

Appendix H includes the URLs for InFoPeople and Search Engine Watch, two helpful sites for information on search engines.

When you want the words you're looking for to be next to each other, such as when looking for a concept or a person's name, you do phrase searching. Most search engines perform phrase searching by requiring the search terms to be put in quotation marks. This is a very effective way to narrow your focus and reduce the number of documents you retrieve. Searching for "informal social control" on Google produced 1,990 sites, compared to the 821,000 sites retrieved when Google searched "informal" *and* "social" *and* "control." When searching for names you have to remember to search in both normal and inverted order (i.e., "Russell K. Schutt" and "Schutt, Russell K."). Including or omitting a middle initial will also affect your search results. Exhibit 2.2 shows the results from a search performed on the Web for "informal social control."

Exhibit 2.2 illustrates the first problem that you may encounter when searching the Web: the sheer quantity of resources that are available. It is a much bigger problem than when searching bibliographic databases. On the Web, less is usually more. Limit your inspection of Web sites to the first few pages that turn up in your list (they're ranked by relevance). See what those first pages contain and then try to narrow your search by including some additional terms.

Remember the following warnings when you conduct searches on the Web:

- *Clarify your goals.* Before you begin the search, jot down the terms that you think you need to search for and a statement of what you want to accomplish with your search. Then you will have a sense of what to look for and what to ignore.
- *Quality is not guaranteed.* Anyone can post almost anything, so the accuracy and adequacy of the information you find are always suspect. There's no journal editor or librarian to evaluate quality and relevance.
- *Anticipate change.* Web sites that are not maintained by stable organizations can come and go very quickly. Any search will result in attempts to link to some URLs that no longer exist.
- *One size does not fit all.* Different search engines use different procedures for indexing Web sites. Some attempt to be all-inclusive whereas others aim to be selective. As a

Exhibit 2.2   Google Search Results for "Informal Social Control"

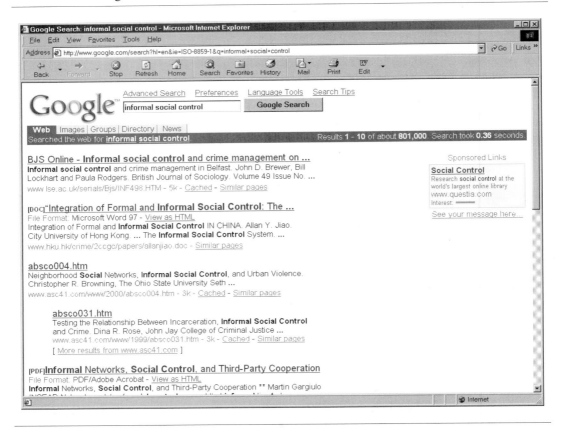

result, you can get different results from different search engines even though you are searching for exactly the same terms.

- *Be concerned about generalizability.* You might be tempted to characterize police department policies by summarizing the documents you find at police department Web sites. But how many police departments are there? How many have posted their policies on the Web? Are these policies representative of all police departments? In order to answer all these questions, you would have to conduct a research project just on the Web sites themselves.

- *Evaluate the sites.* There's a lot of stuff out there, so how do you know what's good? Some Web sites contain excellent advice and pointers on how to differentiate the good from the bad. I have included one such site in Appendix H.

- *Avoid Web addiction.* Another danger of the extraordinary quantity of information available on the Web is that one search will lead to another and to another and. . . . There are always more possibilities to explore and one more interesting source to check. Establish boundaries of time and effort to avoid the risk of losing all sense of proportion.

- *Cite your sources.* Using text or images from Web sources without attribution is plagiarism. It is the same as copying someone else's work from a book or article and pretending that it is your own. Record the Web address (URL), the name of the information provider, and the date on which you obtain material from the site. Include this information in a footnote to the material that you use in a paper. Appendix H includes the URL for "Online!," a guide to citing electronic information.

Reviewing Research

Effective review of the prior research you find is an essential step in building the foundation for new research. You must assess carefully the quality of each research study, consider the implications of each article for your own plans, and expand your thinking about your research question to take account of new perspectives and alternative arguments. It is through reviewing the literature and using it to extend and sharpen your own ideas and methods that you become a part of the social science community. Instead of being just one individual studying an issue that interests you, you are then building on an ever growing body of knowledge that is being constructed by the entire community of scholars.

The research information you find at various Web sites comes in a wide range of formats and represents a variety of sources. *Caveat emptor* (buyer beware) is the watchword when you search the Web; following review guidelines like those I have listed will minimize, but not eliminate, the risk of being led astray. By contrast, the published scholarly journal literature that you find in databases like *Sociological Abstracts* and *Psychological Abstracts* follows a much more standard format and has been subject to a careful review process. There is some variability—some journals publish book reviews, comments on prior articles, and even solicited reviews of the literature about particular research questions—and the major databases of research article abstracts also include references to dissertation abstracts, book reviews, conference papers, and brief reports on innovative service programs. However, most literature you will find on a research topic in these databases represents articles reporting analyses of data collected in a research project. These are the sources on which you should focus. This section concentrates on the procedures you should use for reviewing these articles. These procedures can also be applied to reviews of research monographs— books that provide much more information from a research project than that which can be contained in a journal article.

Reviewing the literature is really a two-stage process. In the first stage, you must assess each article separately. This assessment should follow a standard format like that represented by the "Questions to Ask About a Research Article" in Appendix B. However, you should keep in mind that you can't adequately understand a research study if you just treat it as a series of discrete steps, involving a marriage of convenience among separate techniques. Any research project is an integrated whole, so you must be concerned with how each component of the research design influenced the others—for example, how the measurement approach might have affected the causal validity of the researcher's conclusions and how the sampling strategy might have altered the quality of measures.

The second stage of the review process is to compare your separate article reviews, to assess the implications of the entire set of articles (and other materials) for the relevant aspects of your research question and procedures, and then to write an integrated review for your own article or research proposal. Although you can find literature reviews that consist simply of assessments of one published article after another—that never get beyond stage one in the review process—your understanding of the literature and the quality of your own work will be much improved if you make the effort to write an integrated review.

In the next two sections, I will show how you might answer many of the questions in Appendix B as I review a research article about domestic violence. I will then show how the review of a single article can be used within an integrated review of the body of prior research on this research question. Because at this early point in the text you won't be familiar with all the terminology used in the article review, you might want to read through the more elaborate article review in Appendix C later in the course.

A Single-Article Review: Formal and Informal Deterrents to Domestic Violence

Antony Pate and Edwin Hamilton at the national Police Foundation designed one of the studies that was funded by the U.S. Department of Justice to replicate the Minneapolis Domestic Violence Experiment. In this section we will examine the article that resulted from that replication, which was published in the *American Sociological Review* (Pate & Hamilton, 1992). The numbers in brackets refer to the article review questions in Appendix B.

The Research Question. Like Sherman and Berk's (1984) original Minneapolis study, Pate and Hamilton's (1992) Metro-Dade Spouse Assault Experiment sought to test the deterrent effect of arrest in domestic violence cases, but with an additional focus on the role of informal social control [1]. The purpose of the study was explanatory, because the goal was to explain variation in the propensity to commit spouse abuse [2]. Deterrence theory provided the theoretical framework for the study, but this framework was broadened to include the proposition by Williams and Hawkins (1986) that informal sanctions like stigma and the loss of valued relationships augment the effect of formal sanctions like arrest [4]. Pate and Hamilton's (1992) literature review referred, appropriately, to the original Sherman and Berk (1984) research, to the other studies that attempted to replicate the original findings, and to research on informal social control [3].

There is no explicit discussion of ethical guidelines in the article, although reference is made to a more complete unpublished report [6]. Clearly, important ethical issues had to be considered, given the experimental intervention in the police response to serious assaults, but the adherence to standard criminal justice procedures suggests attention to the welfare of victims as well as the rights of suspects. We will consider these issues in more detail later in this chapter.

The Research Design. Developed as a follow-up to the original Minneapolis experiment, the Metro-Dade experiment exemplified the guidelines for scientific research that will be presented in Chapter 3 [5]. It was designed systematically, with careful attention to specification of terms and clarification of assumptions, and focused on the possibility of different outcomes rather than certainty about one preferred outcome. The major concepts in the study, formal and informal deterrence, were defined clearly [9] and then measured with straightforward indicators—arrest or nonarrest for formal deterrence and marital status and employment status for informal deterrence. However, the specific measurement procedures for marital and

Exhibit 2.3   Percent of Suspects With a Subsequent Assault by Employment Status and Arrest Status

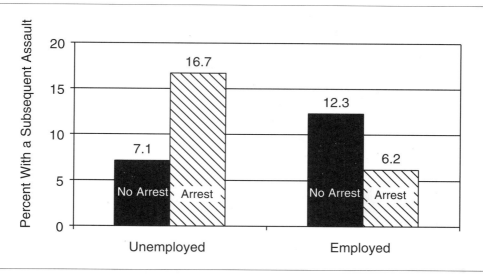

Source: Pate & Hamilton, 1992:695. Reprinted with permission.

employment status were not discussed, and no attempt was made to determine whether they captured adequately the concept of informal social control [9, 10].

Three hypotheses were stated and are related to the larger theoretical framework and prior research [7]. The study design focused on the behavior of individuals [13] and collected data over time, including records indicating subsequent assault up to 6 months after the initial arrest [14]. The project's experimental design was used appropriately to test for the causal effect of arrest on recidivism [15, 17]. The research project involved all eligible cases, rather than a sample of cases, but there were a number of eligibility criteria that narrow the ability to generalize these results to the entire population of domestic assault cases in the Metro-Dade area or elsewhere [11]. There is a brief discussion of the 92 eligible cases that were not given the treatment to which they were assigned, but it does not clarify the reasons for the misassignment [15].

The Research Findings and Conclusion. Pate and Hamilton's (1992) analysis of the Metro-Dade experiment was motivated by concern with the effect of social context, because the replications in other cities of the original Minneapolis domestic violence experiment had not had consistent results [19]. Their analysis gave strong support to the expectation that informal social control processes are important: As they had hypothesized, arrest had a deterrent effect on suspects who were employed, but not on those who were unemployed (Exhibit 2.3). However, marital status had no such effect [20]. The subsequent discussion of these findings gives no attention to the implications of the lack of support for the effect of marital status [21], but the study represents an important improvement over earlier research that had not examined informal sanctions [22]. The importance of the findings for social policy and the need for additional research are highlighted, although more specific suggestions could have been made [23]. If arrest deters only those who have something to lose (e.g., a job), that fact must be taken into account when policies are established (Pate & Hamilton, 1992:695).

Overall, the Pate and Hamilton (1992) study represents an important contribution to understanding how informal social control processes influence the effectiveness of formal sanctions like arrest. Although the use of a population of actual spouse assault cases precluded the use of very sophisticated measures of informal social control, the experimental design of the study and the researchers' ability to interpret the results in the context of several other comparable experiments distinguishes this research as exceptionally worthwhile. It is not hard to understand why these studies continue to stimulate further research and ongoing policy discussions.

An Integrated Literature Review: Do Fair Procedures Matter?

The goal of the second stage of the literature review process is to integrate the results of the separate article reviews and develop an overall assessment of the implications of prior research. At this point you should add to your independent article reviews some judgment of the relative credibility of each article. Consider each of the following questions (Locke, Silverman, & Spirduso, 1998:37–44):

How was the report reviewed prior to its publication or release? Articles published in academic journals go through a very rigorous, usually anonymous, process of review, criticism, and, usually, further revision that takes account of the criticisms. Top "refereed" journals may accept only 5% of the articles submitted to them, so they can be very selective. Less prestigious journals may have somewhat less exacting standards. Dissertations have gone through a lengthy process of criticism and revision by a few members of the dissertation writer's home institution, but are not reviewed anonymously by a wider group. A report released directly by a research organization is likely to have had only a limited review, although major research organizations may have a rigorous internal review process. Papers presented at professional meetings may have been reviewed by one person prior to their acceptance, but many professional associations accept papers for presentation based only on their abstracts. Needless to say, more confidence can be placed in research results that have been subject to a more rigorous review.

What is the author's reputation? Reports by an author or team of authors who have published other work on the research question should be given somewhat greater credibility at the outset. You should have encountered the work of these researchers during the literature review, so you should already have an idea of the quality of their usual work.

Who funded and sponsored the research? Major federal funding agencies and private foundations fund only research that has been highly ranked after an extremely rigorous review process conducted by a panel of experts. They also often monitor closely the progress of the research to make sure that the project is carried out as proposed and, when adaptations are required, that these changes are reasonable. This does not guarantee that every such project report or article is good, but it goes a long way toward ensuring some worthwhile products. On the other hand, research that is funded by organizations that have a preference for a particular outcome should be given particularly close scrutiny.

After you have reviewed the individual articles and developed at least a crude ranking of their likely credibility, you are ready to develop your integrated review. A good example is provided by another article based on the replication in Milwaukee of the Minneapolis Domestic Violence Experiment. For this article, Ray Paternoster, Robert Brame, Ronet Bachman, and Lawrence Sherman (1997) sought to determine whether police officers' use of fair procedures when arresting assault suspects would lessen the rate of subsequent domestic violence.

Paternoster et al. (1997:164) begin their integrated literature review by noting:

> Even at the end of some seven experiments and millions of dollars, then, there is a great deal of ambiguity surrounding the question of how arrest impacts future spouse assault.

They then note that each of the seven experiments focused on the effect of arrest itself, but ignored the possibility that "particular kinds of police *procedure* might inhibit the recurrence of spouse assault" (Paternoster et al., 1997:165).

So Paternoster and his colleagues set out to ground their new analysis in the literature on procedural justice. Their integrated review of this literature presents "the critical components of procedural justice and why we think fair procedures may be important in securing compliance" (Paternoster et al., 1997:166). In a section on "The Elements of Procedural Justice," they canvass the literature and identify six components of procedural justice: representation, consistency, impartiality, accuracy, correctability, and ethicality. One paragraph then summarizes the relevant research about each of these components. Another section in their literature review, "Why Should Fair Procedures Matter," reviews arguments and findings from theoretical pieces and research articles that provide "supporting evidence." The literature review concludes by spelling out what is unique about the Paternoster et al. (1997:172) study with respect to the body of previous research: "It is the first study to examine the effect of fairness judgments regarding a punitive criminal sanction (arrest) on serious criminal behavior (assaulting one's partner)."

Now, when you go on to write your own literature reviews, you should be thinking in terms of an overarching framework and what each prior study contributes within that framework. Try to avoid just a serial review of one study after another.

SOCIAL RESEARCH STRATEGIES

When we conduct social research, we are attempting to connect theory with empirical data—the evidence we obtain from the social world. Researchers may make this connection by starting with a social theory and then testing some of its implications with data. This is the process of deductive research; it is most often the strategy used in quantitative methods. Alternatively, researchers may develop a connection between social theory and data by first collecting the data and then developing a theory that explains patterns in the data (see Exhibit 2.4). This inductive research process is more often the strategy used in qualitative methods. As you'll see, a research project can draw upon both deductive and inductive strategies.

The Role of Social Theory

I have already pointed out that social theory can be a source of research questions and that it plays an important role in literature reviews. What deserves more attention at this point is

Exhibit 2.4   The Links Between Theory and Data

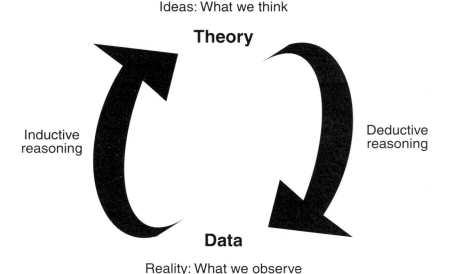

Ideas: What we think

Theory

Inductive
reasoning

Deductive
reasoning

Data

Reality: What we observe

the larger role of social theory in research. **Theories** help us make sense of many interrelated phenomena and predict behavior or attitudes that are likely to occur when certain conditions are met; they help social scientists to know what to look for in a study and to specify the implications of their findings for other research. Building and evaluating theory is therefore one of the most important objectives of social science.

> ***Theory***   A logically interrelated set of propositions about empirical reality. Examples of social theories include structural functionalism, conflict theory, and symbolic interactionism.

Most social research is guided by some theory, although the theory may be only partially developed in a particular study or may even be unrecognized by the researcher. When researchers are involved in conducting a research project or engrossed in writing a research report, they may easily lose sight of the larger picture. It is easy to focus on accumulating or clarifying particular findings rather than considering how the study's findings fit into a more general understanding of the social world.

Social theories do not provide the answers to the questions we pose as topics for research. Instead, social theories suggest the areas on which we should focus and the propositions that we should consider for a test. For example, Lawrence Sherman and Richard Berk's (1984) original domestic violence experiment was actually a test of predictions that they derived from two alternative theories of the impact of punishment on crime.

Deterrence theory expects punishment to deter crime in two ways. General deterrence occurs when people see that crime results in undesirable punishments, that "crime doesn't pay." The persons who are punished serve as examples of what awaits those who engage in proscribed acts. Specific deterrence occurs when persons who are punished decide not to commit another offense so they can avoid further punishment (Lempert & Sanders, 1986:86–87). Deterrence theory leads to the prediction that arresting spouse abusers will lessen their likelihood of reoffending.

Labeling theory distinguishes between primary deviance, the acts of individuals that lead to public sanction, and secondary deviance, the deviance that occurs in response to public sanction (Hagan, 1994:33). Arrest or some other public sanction for misdeeds labels the offender as deviant in the eyes of others. Once the offender is labeled, others will treat the offender as a deviant, and he or she is then more likely to act in a way that is consistent with the deviant label. Ironically, the act of punishment stimulates more of the very behavior that it was intended to eliminate. This theory suggests that persons arrested for domestic assault are more likely to reoffend than those who are not punished, which is the reverse of the deterrence theory prediction.

Theorizing about the logic behind punishment can also help us draw connections to more general theories about social processes. Deterrence theory reflects the assumptions of *rational choice theory,* which assumes that people's behavior is shaped by practical calculations: People break the law if the benefits of doing so exceed the costs. If crime is a rational choice for some people, then increasing the certainty or severity of punishment for crime should shift the cost–benefit balance away from criminal behavior. Labeling theory is rooted in *symbolic interactionism,* which focuses on the symbolic meanings that people give to behavior (Hagan, 1994:40). Instead of assuming that some forms of behavior are deviant in and of themselves (Scull, 1988:678), symbolic interactionists view deviance as a consequence of the application of rules and sanctions to an "offender" (Becker, 1963:9).

Exhibit 2.5 summarizes how these general theories relate to the question of whether or not to arrest spouse abusers. We will discuss such general theories at more length in Chapter 3.

Does either deterrence theory or labeling theory make sense to you as an explanation for the impact of punishment? Do they seem consistent with your observations of social life? As you have already seen, Raymond Paternoster, Robert Brame, Ronet Bachman, and Lawrence Sherman (1997) concluded that something was missing in these theories. Procedural justice theory explains law-abidingness as resulting from a sense of duty or morality, and predicts that people will obey the law from a sense of obligation that flows from seeing legal authorities as moral and legitimate (Tyler, 1990). From this perspective, individuals who are arrested will be less likely to reoffend if they are treated fairly, irrespective of the outcome of their case, because fair treatment will enhance their view of legal authorities as moral and legitimate. Procedural justice theory expands our view of the punishment process by focusing attention on *how* authorities treat subjects, rather than just on *what* decisions they make.

Are you now less certain about the likely effect of arrest for intimate partner violence? Will arrest decrease abuse because abusers do not wish to suffer from legal sanctions again? Will it increase abuse because abusers feel stigmatized by being arrested and thus are more likely to act like criminals? Or will arrest reduce abuse only if the abusers feel they have been treated fairly by the legal authorities? By suggesting such questions, social theory makes us much more sensitive to the possibilities and so helps us to design better research and draw out

Exhibit 2.5   Two Social Theories and Their Predictions About the Effect of Arrest for Domestic Assault

	Rational choice theory	**Symbolic interactionism**
Theoretical assumption	People's behavior is shaped by calculations of the costs and benefits of their actions.	People give symbolic meanings to objects, behaviors, and other people.
	⬇	⬇
Criminological component	Deterrence theory: People break the law if the benefits of doing so outweigh the costs.	Labeling theory: People label offenders as deviant, promoting further deviance.
	⬇	⬇
Prediction (effect of arrest for domestic assault)	Abusing spouse, having seen the costs of abuse (namely, arrest), decides not to abuse again.	Abusing spouse, having been labeled as "an abuser," abuses more often.

the implications of our results. Before, during, and after a research investigation, we need to keep thinking theoretically.

The Deductive/Inductive Cycle

The process of conducting research using a deductive research strategy involves moving from theory to data and then back to theory. This process can be characterized with a **research circle** (Exhibit 2.6).

Deductive Research

As Exhibit 2.6 shows, in **deductive research** a specific expectation is deduced from a general theoretical premise and then tested with data that have been collected for this purpose. A **hypothesis** is a specific expectation deduced from the more general theory. Researchers actually test a hypothesis, not the complete theory itself. A hypothesis proposes a relationship between two or more **variables**—characteristics or properties that can vary. Variation in one variable is proposed to predict, influence, or cause variation in the other variable. The proposed influence is the **independent variable;** its effect or consequence is the **dependent variable.** After the researchers formulate one or more hypotheses and develop research procedures, they collect data with which to test the hypothesis.

Exhibit 2.6   The Research Circle

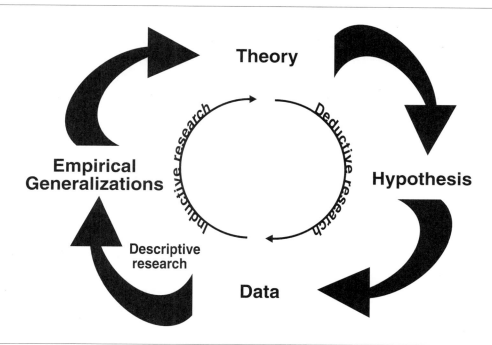

___

Hypothesis   A tentative statement about empirical reality, involving a relationship between two or more variables.

Example of a hypothesis: The higher the poverty rate in a community, the higher the percentage of community residents who are homeless.

Variable   A characteristic or property that can vary (take on different values or attributes).

Example of a variable: The degree of honesty in verbal statements.

Independent variable   A variable that is hypothesized to cause, or lead to, variation in another variable.

Example of an independent variable: Poverty rate.

Dependent variable   A variable that is hypothesized to vary depending on or under the influence of another variable.

Example of a dependent variable: Percentage of community residents who are homeless.

Exhibit 2.7   Examples of Hypotheses

Original Hypothesis	Independent Variable	Dependent Variable	IF-THEN Hypothesis	Direction Of Association
1. The greater the use of internet, the greater the strength of distant family lies.	Level of Internet use	Strength of distant family ties	IF internet use is greater, THEN the strength of distant family ties is greater.	+
2. The risk of property theft decreases as income increases.	Income	Risk of property theft	IF income is higher, THEN the risk of property theft is less.	−
3. If years of education decrease, income decreases.	Years of education	Income	IF years of education decrease, THEN income decreases.	+
4. Political conservatism increases with income.	Income	Political conservatism	IF income increases, THEN political conservatism increases.	+
5. Property crime is higher in urban areas than in suburban or rural areas.	Type of community	Rate of property crime	IF areas are urban, THEN property crime is higher compared to crime in suburban or rural areas.	NA

Hypotheses can be worded in several different ways, and identifying the independent and dependent variables is sometimes difficult. When in doubt, try to rephrase the hypothesis as an "if-then" statement: "*If* the independent variable increases (or decreases), *then* the dependent variable increases (or decreases)." Exhibit 2.7 presents several hypotheses with their independent and dependent variables and their "if-then" equivalents.

Exhibit 2.7 demonstrates another feature of hypotheses: **direction of association.** When researchers hypothesize that one variable increases as the other variable increases, the direction of association is positive (Hypotheses 1 and 4). When one variable decreases as the other variable decreases, the direction of association is also positive (Hypothesis 3). But when one variable increases as the other decreases, or vice versa, the direction of association is negative, or inverse (Hypothesis 2). Hypothesis 5 is a special case, in which the independent variable is qualitative: It cannot be said to increase or decrease. In this case, the concept of direction of association does not apply, and the hypothesis simply states that one category of the independent variable is associated with higher values on the dependent variable.

Both explanatory and evaluative studies are types of deductive research. The original Minneapolis Domestic Violence Experiment was an evaluative study, because Sherman and Berk (1984) sought to explain what sort of response by the authorities might keep a spouse abuser from repeating the offense. The researchers deduced from deterrence theory the expectation that arrest would deter domestic violence. They then collected data to test this expectation.

In both explanatory and evaluative research, the statement of expectations for the findings and the design of the research to test these expectations strengthen the confidence we can place in the test. The deductive researcher shows her hand or states her expectations in advance and then designs a fair test of those expectations. Then "the chips fall where they may"—in other words, the researcher accepts the resulting data as a more or less objective picture of reality.

Domestic Violence and the Research Circle

The Sherman and Berk (1984) study of domestic violence provides our first example of how the research circle works. In an attempt to determine ways to prevent the recurrence of spouse abuse, the researchers repeatedly linked theory and data, developing both hypotheses and empirical generalizations.

The first phase of Sherman and Berk's study was designed to test a hypothesis. According to deterrence theory, punishment will reduce recidivism, or the propensity to commit further crimes. From this theory, Sherman and Berk deduced a specific hypothesis: "Arrest for spouse abuse reduces the risk of repeat offenses." In this hypothesis, arrest is the independent variable, and the risk of repeat offenses is the dependent variable (it is hypothesized to depend on arrest).

Of course, in another study arrest might be the dependent variable in relation to some other independent variable. For example, in the hypothesis "The greater the rate of layoffs in a community, the higher the frequency of arrest," the dependent variable is frequency of arrest. Only within the context of a hypothesis, or a relationship between variables, does it make sense to refer to one variable as dependent and the other as independent.

Sherman and Berk tested their hypothesis by setting up an experiment in which the police responded to complaints of spouse abuse in one of three ways: arresting the offender, separating the spouses without making an arrest, or simply warning the offender. When the researchers examined their data (police records for the persons in their experiment), they found that of those arrested for assaulting their spouse, only 13% repeated the offense, compared to a 26% recidivism rate for those who were separated from their spouse by the police without any arrest. This pattern in the data, or **empirical generalization,** was consistent with the hypothesis that the researchers deduced from deterrence theory. The theory thus received support from the experiment (see Exhibit 2.8).

Because of their doubts about the generalizability of their results, Sherman, Berk, and other researchers began to journey around the research circle again, with funding from the National Institute of Justice for **replications** (repetitions) of the experiment in six more cities.

Exhibit 2.8   The Research Circle: Minneapolis Domestic Violence Experiment

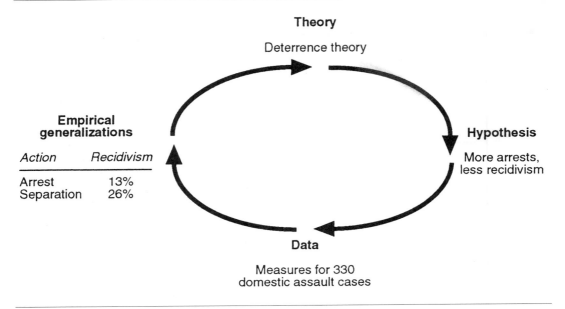

Source: Data from Sherman & Berk, 1984:267.

These replications used the same basic research approach but with some improvements. The random assignment process was tightened up in most of the cities so that police officers would be less likely to replace the assigned treatment with a treatment of their own choice. In addition, data were collected about repeat violence against other victims as well as against the original complainant. Some of the replications also examined different aspects of the arrest process, to see whether professional counseling helped and whether the length of time spent in jail after arrest mattered at all.

By the time results were reported from five of the cities in the new study, a problem was apparent. In three of the cities—Omaha, Nebraska; Charlotte, North Carolina; and Milwaukee, Wisconsin—researchers were finding long-term increases in domestic violence incidents among arrestees. But in two—Colorado Springs, Colorado, and Dade County, Florida—the predicted deterrent effects seemed to be occurring (Sherman et al., 1992).

Sherman and his colleagues had now traversed the research circle twice in an attempt to answer the original research question, first in Minneapolis and then in six other cities. But rather than leading to more confidence in deterrence theory, the research results were calling it into question. Deterrence theory now seemed inadequate to explain empirical reality, at least as the researchers had measured this reality. So the researchers began to reanalyze the follow-up data from several cities to try to explain the discrepant results, thereby starting around the research circle once again (Berk, Campbell, Klap, & Western, 1992; Pate & Hamilton, 1992; Sherman et al., 1992).

Inductive Research

In contrast to deductive research, **inductive research** begins with specific data, which are then used to develop (induce) a general explanation (a theory) to account for the data. One way to think of this process is in terms of the research circle: rather than starting at the top of the circle with a theory, the researcher starts at the bottom of the circle with data and then develops the theory. Researchers most committed to an inductive approach even put off formulating a research question before they begin to collect data—the idea is to let the question emerge from the situation itself (Brewer & Hunter, 1989:54–58).

Research can be designed from the start using an inductive approach, like the exploratory study of the diabetes newsgroup described in Chapter 1 (Loader et al., 2002). Inductive reasoning also enters into deductive research when we find unexpected patterns in the data we have collected for testing a hypothesis. We may call these patterns **serendipitous findings** or **anomalous findings.** Whether we begin by doing inductive research or add an inductive element later, the result of the inductive process can be new insights and provocative questions. But the adequacy of an explanation formulated after the fact is necessarily less certain than an explanation presented prior to the collection of data. Every phenomenon can always be explained in *some* way. Inductive explanations are thus more trustworthy if they are tested subsequently with deductive research.

An Inductive Approach to Explaining Domestic Violence. The domestic violence research took an inductive turn when Sherman and the other researchers began trying to make sense of the differing patterns in the data collected in the different cities. Could systematic differences in the samples or in the implementation of arrest policies explain the differing outcomes? Or was the problem an inadequacy in the theoretical basis of their research? Was deterrence theory really the best way to explain the patterns in the data they were collecting?

As you learned in my review of the Pate and Hamilton (1992) study, the researchers had found that individuals who were married and employed were deterred from repeat offenses by arrest, but individuals who were unmarried and unemployed were actually more likely to commit repeat offenses if they were arrested. What could explain this empirical pattern? The researchers turned to *control theory,* which predicts that having a "stake in conformity" (resulting from inclusion in social networks at work or in the community) decreases a person's likelihood of committing crimes (Toby, 1957). The implication is that people who are employed and married are more likely to be deterred by the threat of arrest than those without such stakes in conformity. And this is indeed what the data revealed.

Now the researchers had traversed the research circle almost three times, a process perhaps better described as a spiral (see Exhibit 2.9). The first two times the researchers had traversed the research circle in a deductive, hypothesis-testing way. They started with theory and then deduced and tested hypotheses. The third time they were more inductive: They started with empirical generalizations from the data they had already obtained and then turned to a new theory to account for the unexpected patterns in the data. At this point they believed that deterrence theory made correct predictions given certain conditions and that another theory, control theory, might specify what these conditions were.

This last inductive step in their research made for a more complex but also conceptually richer picture of the impact of arrest on domestic violence. The researchers seemed to have

Exhibit 2.9   The Research Spiral: Domestic Violence Experiment

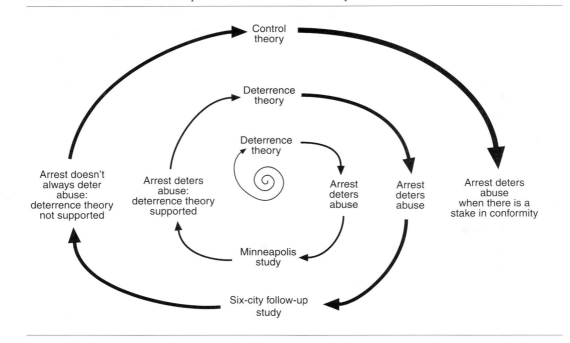

come closer to understanding how to inhibit domestic violence. But they cautioned us that their initial question—the research problem—was still not completely answered. Employment status and marital status do not solely measure the strength of social attachments; they also are related to how much people earn and the social standing of victims in court. So maybe social ties are not really what make arrest an effective deterrent to domestic violence. The real deterrent may be cost–benefit calculations ("If I have a higher income, jail is more costly to me") or perceptions about the actions of authorities ("If I am a married woman, judges will treat my complaint more seriously"). Additional research was needed (Berk et al., 1992).

Exploratory Research:
Victim Responses to Police Intervention

Qualitative research is often exploratory and, hence, inductive: The researchers begin by observing social interaction or interviewing social actors in depth and then developing an explanation for what has been found. The researchers often ask questions like "What is going on here?" "How do people interpret these experiences?" or "Why do people do what they do?" Rather than testing a hypothesis, the researchers are trying to make sense of some social phenomenon. Lauren Bennett, Lisa Goodman, and Mary Ann Dutton (1999) used this approach to investigate one of the problems that emerge when police arrest domestic batterers: The victims often decide not to press charges. Bennett et al. (1999:762) did not set out to test hypotheses with qualitative interviews (there was another, hypothesis-testing component in their research), but sought, inductively, to "add the voice of the victim to the discussion" and present "themes that emerged from [the] interviews."

Research assistants interviewed 49 victims of domestic violence in one court; Lauren Bennett also worked in the same court as a victim advocate. The researchers were able to cull from their qualitative data four reasons why victims became reluctant to press charges. Some were confused by the court procedures, others were frustrated by the delay, some were paralyzed by fear of retribution, and others did not want to send the batterer to jail.

Explanations developed inductively from qualitative research can feel authentic because we have heard what people have to say "in their own words" and we have tried to see the social world "as they see it." One victim interviewed by Bennett felt that she "was doing time instead of the defendant"; another expressed her fear by saying that she would like "to keep him out of jail if that's what it takes to keep my kids safe" (Bennett et al., 1999:768–769). Explanations derived from qualitative research will be richer and more finely textured than they often are in quantitative research, but they are likely to be based on fewer cases from a limited area. We cannot assume that the people studied in this setting are like others or that other researchers would develop explanations similar to ours to make sense of what was observed or heard. Because we do not initially set up a test of a hypothesis according to some specific rules, another researcher cannot come along and conduct just the same test.

Descriptive Research

You learned in Chapter 1 that some social research is purely descriptive. Such research does not involve connecting theory and data, but it is still a part of the research circle—it begins with data and proceeds only to the stage of making empirical generalizations based on those data (refer to Exhibit 2.6, p. 45).

Valid description is important in its own right—in fact, it is a necessary component of all investigations. Much important research for the government and public and private organizations is primarily descriptive: How many poor people live in this community? Is the health of the elderly improving? How frequently do convicted criminals return to crime? Simply put, good description of data is the cornerstone of the scientific research process and an essential component for understanding the social world.

Good descriptive research can also stimulate more ambitious deductive and inductive research. The Minneapolis Domestic Violence Experiment was motivated in part by a growing body of descriptive research indicating that spouse abuse is very common: 572,000 cases of women victimized by a violent partner each year; 1.5 million women (and 500,000 men) requiring medical attention each year due to a domestic assault (Buzawa & Buzawa, 1996:1–3). You may recall from Chapter 1 that much of the research on the Internet and social relations has also been descriptive; however, by identifying the prevalence of Internet use and current levels of social isolation, this research has helped to establish priorities for both public policy and additional research.

SOCIAL RESEARCH ETHICS

Our foundation for social research is not complete until it includes a sensitivity to research ethics. Every scientific investigation, whether in the natural or social sciences, has an ethical dimension to it. First and foremost, the scientific concern with validity requires that scientists be honest and reveal their methods. (How can we otherwise determine if the requirement of honesty has been met?) Scientists also have to consider the uses to which their findings will be put. In addition, because social science is concerned with society and the human beings in that society, social researchers have some unique ethical concerns.

Honesty and Openness

Research distorted by political or personal pressures to find particular outcomes or to achieve the most marketable results is unlikely to be carried out in an honest and open fashion, but distinguishing between unintentional error and deliberate fraud can be very difficult. For example, a 1963 report of the U.S. Senate's Subcommittee on Problems of the Aged and Aging concluded that a study of elderly persons' health needs, publicized by the American Medical Association, was a "supposedly objective, scientific, academic study" that was really a "pseudo-scientific half-effort" (Cain, 1967:78–79). The researchers were accused of having an upper-class bias in the design of their sample and of using some questions that underestimated elders' health needs. Yet the researchers were convinced that they had adhered to scientific guidelines.

It is not clear in this case, nor in many others, whether the research was designed to favor particular findings or to adapt to unavoidable constraints. Error, committed without any intent to defraud, is inevitable. Social scientists who do not do their best to minimize error skirt the boundaries of fraud, but the discovery of errors in a study should not in itself be taken as an indication of dishonesty.

Openness about research procedures and results goes hand in hand with honesty in research design. Openness is also essential if researchers are to learn from the work of others. In spite of this need for openness, some researchers may hesitate to disclose their procedures or results to prevent others from building on their ideas and taking some of the credit. You may have heard of the long legal battle between a U.S. researcher and a French researcher about how credit for discovering the AIDS virus should be allocated. Although such public disputes are unusual, concerns with priority of discovery are common. Scientists are like other people in their desire to be first. Enforcing standards of honesty and encouraging openness about research is the best solution for these problems.

The Uses of Science

Scientists must also consider the uses to which their research is put. Although many scientists believe that personal values should be left outside the laboratory, some feel that it is proper for scientists in their role as citizens to attempt to influence the way their research is used. Social scientists who identify with a more "critical" tradition question the possibility of setting our values aside and instead urge researchers to use research to achieve goals that they believe are worthy.

The Sherman and Berk research provides an interesting cautionary tale about the uses of science. Sherman and Berk explicitly cautioned police departments not to adopt mandatory arrest policies based solely on their findings in Minneapolis (Sherman, 1993), but Sherman did publicize the research results in the mass media (Binder & Meeker, 1993; Lempert, 1989). Some social scientists were very critical of this decision. In part, the question was whether basing policy on partial information was preferable to waiting until the information was more complete. Although we now know that the original finding of a deterrent effect of arrest did not hold up in each replication, Sherman (1992:150–153) later suggested that implementing mandatory arrest policies might have prevented some subsequent cases of spouse abuse. In particular, in the Omaha follow-up study, arrest warrants reduced repeat offenses among spouse abusers who had already left the scene when police arrived. However, this Omaha finding was not publicized, so it could not be used to improve police policies. So how much publicity is warranted and at what point in the research should it occur?

Social scientists who conduct research on behalf of specific organizations may face additional difficulties when the organization, instead of the researcher, controls the final report and the publicity it receives. If organizational leaders decide that particular research results are unwelcome, the researcher's desire to have findings used appropriately and reported fully can conflict with contractual obligations. Researchers can often anticipate such dilemmas in advance and resolve them when the contract for research is negotiated—or simply decline a particular research opportunity altogether. But often such problems only come up after a report has been drafted or the problems are ignored by a researcher who needs to have a job or to maintain particular personal relationships. These possibilities cannot be avoided entirely, but because of them it is always important to acknowledge the source of research funding in reports and to consider carefully the sources of funding for research reports written by others.

Research on People

In physics or chemistry, research subjects (objects and substances) may be treated to extreme conditions and then discarded when they are no longer useful. However, social (and medical) scientists must concern themselves with the way their human subjects are treated in the course of research (much could also be said about research on animals, but this isn't the place for that). Procedures that raise ethical concerns may involve manipulations in laboratory experiments, sensitive questions in survey research, observations in field studies, or analyses of personal data. Here I will review briefly current ethical standards for the treatment of human subjects and identify some of the issues in their application. In the later chapters on data collection, I will examine specific ethical problems that may arise in the course of using particular research methods.

The federal government, professional associations, university review boards, and ethics committees in other organizations all set standards for the treatment of human subjects. Federal regulations require that every institution that seeks federal funding for biomedical or behavioral research on human subjects have an **institutional review board (IRB)** that reviews research proposals. IRBs at universities and other agencies apply ethics standards that are set by federal regulations but can be expanded or specified by the IRB itself (Sieber, 1992:5, 10). To promote adequate review of ethical issues, the regulations require that IRBs include members with diverse backgrounds. The Office for Protection from Research Risks in the National Institutes of Health monitors IRBs, with the exception of research involving drugs (which is the responsibility of the Federal Food and Drug Administration). The American Sociological Association (ASA), like other professional social science organizations, has adopted for practicing sociologists ethics guidelines that are more specific than the federal regulations. Professional organizations may also review complaints of unethical practices when asked.

The code of ethics of the American Sociological Association (1997) is available in print and is posted on the ASA Web site (http://www.asanet.org/members/ecoderev.html). Its standards concerning the treatment of human subjects include federal regulations and ethics guidelines emphasized by most professional social science organizations:

- Research should cause no harm to subjects.
- Participation in research should be voluntary, and therefore subjects must give their informed consent to participate in the research.
- Researchers should fully disclose their identity.
- Anonymity or confidentiality must be maintained for individual research participants unless it is voluntarily and explicitly waived.
- The benefits of a research project should outweigh any foreseeable risks.

As simple as these guidelines may seem, they are difficult to interpret in specific cases and harder yet to define in a way agreeable to all social scientists. For example, how should "no harm to subjects" be interpreted? Does it mean that subjects should not be at all harmed psychologically as well as physically? That they should feel no anxiety or distress whatever during the study, or only after their involvement ends? Should the possibility of any harm, no matter how remote, deter research?

Consider the question of possible harm to the subjects of a well-known prison simulation study (Haney, Banks, & Zimbardo, 1973). The study was designed to investigate the impact of social position on behavior—specifically, the impact of being either a guard or a prisoner in a prison, a "total institution." The researchers selected apparently stable and mature young male volunteers and asked them to sign a contract to work for 2 weeks as a guard or a prisoner in a simulated prison. Within the first 2 days after the prisoners were incarcerated by the "guards" in a makeshift basement prison, the prisoners began to be passive and disorganized, while the guards became verbally and physically aggressive. Five "prisoners" were soon released for depression, uncontrollable crying, fits of rage, and in one case a psychosomatic rash; on the sixth day the researchers terminated the experiment. Through discussions in special postexperiment encounter sessions, feelings of stress among the participants who played the role of prisoner seemed to be relieved; follow-up during the next year indicated no lasting negative effects on the participants and some benefits in the form of greater insight.

Would you ban such experiments because of the potential for harm to subjects? Does the fact that the experiment yielded significant insights into the effect of a situation on human behavior—insights that could be used to improve prisons—make any difference (Reynolds, 1979:133–139)? Do you believe that this benefit outweighed the foreseeable risks?

The requirement of informed consent is also more difficult to define than it first appears. To be informed, consent must be given by persons who are competent to consent, have consented voluntarily, are fully informed about the research, and have comprehended what they have been told (Reynolds, 1979). The researcher's actions and body language must help to convey his verbal assurance that consent is voluntary. Children cannot legally give consent to participate in research, but they must have the opportunity to give or withhold their *assent* to participate in research to which their legal guardians have consented (Sieber, 1992). Can prisoners give informed consent? Can students who are asked to participate in research by their professor? Can participants in covert experiments? These situations require extra care.

Fully informed consent may also reduce participation in research and, because signing consent forms prior to participation may change participants' responses, produce biased results (Larson, 1993:114). Experimental researchers whose research design requires some type of subject deception try to get around this problem by withholding some information before the experiment begins but then debriefing subjects at the end. In the **debriefing,** the researcher explains to the subject what happened in the experiment and why and responds to questions (Sieber, 1992:39–41). However, even though debriefing can be viewed as a substitute in some cases for securing fully informed consent prior to the experiment, if the debriefed subjects disclose the nature of the experiment to other participants, subsequent results may still be contaminated (Adair, Dushenko, & Lindsay, 1985).

Well-intentioned researchers may also fail to foresee all the potential problems. In the prison simulation, all the participants signed consent forms, but how could they have been fully informed in advance? The researchers themselves did not realize that the study participants would experience so much stress so quickly, that some prisoners would have to be released for severe negative reactions within the first few days, or that even those who were not severely stressed would soon be begging to be released from the mock prison. If this risk was not foreseeable, was it acceptable for the researchers to presume in advance that the benefits would outweigh the risks?

Maintaining confidentiality is another key ethical obligation; a statement should be included in the informed consent agreement about how each subject's privacy will be protected (Sieber, 1992). Procedures such as locking records and creating special identifying codes must be created to minimize the risk of access by unauthorized persons. However, statements about confidentiality should be realistic: Laws allow research records to be subpoenaed and may require reporting child abuse; a researcher may feel compelled to release information if a health- or life-threatening situation arises and participants need to be alerted. Also, the standard of confidentiality does not apply to observation in public places and information available in public records.

The potential of withholding a beneficial treatment from some subjects is also cause for ethical concern. The Sherman and Berk experiment required the random assignment of subjects to treatment conditions and thus had the potential of causing harm to the victims of domestic violence whose batterers were not arrested. The justification for the study design, however, is quite persuasive: The researchers didn't know prior to the experiment which response to a domestic violence complaint would be most likely to deter future incidents (Sherman, 1992). The experiment provided clear evidence about the value of arrest, so it can be argued that the benefits outweighed the risks.

The extent to which ethical issues are a problem for researchers and their subjects varies dramatically with the type of research design. Survey research, in particular, creates few ethical problems. In fact, researchers from Michigan's Institute for Survey Research interviewed a representative national sample of adults and found that 68% of those who had participated in a survey were somewhat or very interested in participating in another; the more times respondents had been interviewed, the more willing they were to participate again. Presumably they would have felt differently if they had been treated unethically (Reynolds, 1979:56–57). On the other hand, some experimental studies in the social sciences that have put people in uncomfortable or embarrassing situations have generated vociferous complaints and years of debate about ethics (Reynolds, 1979; Sjoberg, 1967).

The evaluation of ethical issues in a research project should be based on a realistic assessment of the overall potential for harm and benefit to research subjects rather than an apparent inconsistency between any particular aspect of a research plan and a specific ethical guideline. For example, full disclosure of "what is really going on" in an experimental study is unnecessary if subjects are unlikely to be harmed. Nevertheless, researchers should make every effort to foresee all possible risks and to weigh the possible benefits of the research against these risks. They should consult with individuals with different perspectives to develop a realistic risk/benefit assessment, and they should try to maximize the benefits to subjects of the research, as well as minimize the risks (Sieber, 1992:75–108).

SOCIAL RESEARCH PROPOSALS, PART I

Be grateful for those people or groups who require you to write a formal research proposal (as hard as that seems)—and even more for those who give you constructive feedback. Whether your proposal is written for a professor, a thesis committee, an organization seeking practical advice, or a government agency that funds basic research, the proposal will force you to set out a problem statement and a research plan. Too many research projects begin without a clear problem statement or with only the barest of notions about which variables must be measured or what the analysis should look like. Such projects often wander along, lurching from side to side, until they collapse entirely or just peter out with a report that is ignored—and should be. So even in circumstances when a proposal is not required, you should prepare one and present it to others for feedback. Just writing your ideas down will help you to see how they can be improved, and feedback in almost any form will help you to refine your plans.

Each chapter in this book includes "Developing a Research Proposal" exercises that will guide you through the process of proposal writing. This section presents an overview of the process of proposal writing that also serves as an introduction to these special end-of-chapter exercises. The last chapter in the text contains a wrap-up discussion of the entire proposal-preparation process.

Every research proposal should have at least six sections (Locke, Spirduso, & Silverman, 2000):

- *An introductory statement of the research problem,* in which you clarify what it is that you are interested in studying.
- *A literature review,* in which you explain how your problem and plans build on what has already been reported in the literature on this topic.
- *A methodological plan,* detailing just how you will respond to the particular mix of opportunities and constraints you face.
- *A budget,* presenting a careful listing of the anticipated costs.
- *An ethics statement,* identifying human subjects issues in the research and how you will respond to them in an ethical fashion.
- *A statement of limitations,* reviewing weaknesses of the proposed research and presenting plans for minimizing their consequences.

If your research proposal will be reviewed competitively, it must present a compelling rationale for funding. It is not possible to overstate the importance of the research problem that you propose to study (see the first section of this chapter). If you propose to test a hypothesis, be sure that it is one for which there are plausible alternatives. You want to avoid focusing on a "boring hypothesis"—one that has no credible alternatives, even though it is likely to be correct (Dawes, 1995:93).

A research proposal can also be strengthened considerably by presenting results from a pilot study of the research question. This might have involved administering the proposed questionnaire to a small sample, conducting a preliminary version of the proposed experiment with a group of students, or making observations over a limited period of time in a setting like that proposed for a qualitative study. Careful presentation of the methods used in the pilot study and the problems that were encountered will impress anyone who reviews the proposal.

You have learned in this chapter how to formulate a research question, review relevant literature, consider ethical issues, and identify some possible research limitations, so you are now ready to begin proposing new research. If you plan to do so, you can use the proposal exercises at the end of each of the subsequent chapters to incorporate more systematically the research elements discussed in those chapters. By the book's end, in Chapter 14, you will have attained a much firmer grasp of the various research components. At that point, we will return to the process of proposal writing.

CONCLUSIONS

Selecting a worthy research question does not guarantee a worthwhile research project. The simplicity of the research circle presented in this chapter belies the complexity of the social research process. In the next chapter, we will examine different philosophical approaches to social research and some of the social theories that can guide our research. In the following chapters, I will focus on particular aspects of the research process. Chapter 4 examines the interrelated processes of conceptualization and measurement, arguably the most important part of research. Measurement validity is the foundation for the other two aspects of validity. Chapter 5 reviews the meaning of generalizability and the sampling strategies that help us to achieve this goal. Chapter 6 introduces causal validity and illustrates different methods for achieving it. The next five chapters then introduce different approaches to data collection— experiments, surveys, qualitative research, evaluation research, and comparative historical research—that help us, in different ways, to achieve results that are valid.

Of course, our answers to research questions will never be complete or entirely certain. Thus, when we complete a research project, we should point out how the research could be extended and evaluate the confidence we have in our conclusions. Recall how the elaboration of knowledge about deterrence of domestic violence required sensitivity to research difficulties, careful weighing of the evidence, and identification of unanswered questions by several research teams.

Ethical issues also should be considered when evaluating research proposals and completed research studies. As the preceding examples show, ethical issues in social research are no less complex than the other issues that researchers confront. And it is inexcusable to jump into research on people without any attention to ethical considerations.

Owning a large social science toolkit is no guarantee of making the right decisions about which tools to use and how to use them in the investigation of particular research problems, but you are now forewarned about, and thus hopefully forearmed against, some of the problems that social scientists face in their work. I hope that you will return often to this chapter as you read the subsequent chapters, when you criticize the research literature, and when you design your own research projects. To be conscientious, thoughtful, and responsible—this is the mandate of every social scientist. If you formulate a feasible research problem, ask the right questions in advance, try to adhere to the research guidelines, and steer clear of the most common difficulties, you will be well along the road to fulfilling this mandate.

KEY TERMS

Anomalous finding
Debriefing
Deductive research
Dependent variable
Direction of association
Empirical generalization
Hypothesis
Independent variable

Inductive research
Institutional review board (IRB)
Replication
Research circle
Serendipitous finding
Social research question
Theory
Variable

HIGHLIGHTS

• Research questions should be feasible (within the time and resources available), socially important, and scientifically relevant.

• Building social theory is a major objective of social science research. Investigate relevant theories before starting social research projects, and draw out the theoretical implications of research findings.

• The type of reasoning in most research can be described as primarily deductive or inductive. Research based on deductive reasoning proceeds from general ideas, deduces specific expectations from these ideas, and then tests the ideas with empirical data. Research based on inductive reasoning begins with specific data and then develops general ideas or theories to explain patterns in the data.

• It may be possible to explain unanticipated research findings after the fact, but such explanations have less credibility than those that have been tested with data collected for the purpose of the study.

• The scientific process can be represented as circular, with a path from theory to hypotheses, to data, and then to empirical generalizations. Research investigations may begin at different points along the research circle and traverse different portions of it. Deductive research begins at the point of theory; inductive research begins with data but ends with theory; and descriptive research begins with data and ends with empirical generalizations.

• Replications of a study are essential to establish its generalizability in other situations. An ongoing line of research stemming from a particular research question should include a series of studies that, collectively, traverse the research circle multiple times.

• Scientific research should be conducted and reported in an honest and open fashion. Contemporary ethical standards also require that social research cause no harm to subjects, that participation be voluntary as expressed in informed consent, that researchers fully disclose their identity, that benefits to subjects outweigh any foreseeable risks, and that anonymity or confidentiality be maintained for participants unless it is voluntarily and explicitly waived.

• Writing a research proposal is an important part of preparing for research.

DISCUSSION QUESTIONS

1. Find a research journal article that is cited in another source. Compare the cited source to what was said about it in the original article. Was the discussion of it accurate? How well did the authors of both articles summarize their work in their abstracts? What important points would you have missed if you had relied only on the abstracts?

2. Classify five research projects you have read about, either in previous exercises or in other courses, as primarily inductive or deductive. Did you notice any inductive components in the primarily deductive projects? How much descriptive research was involved? Did the findings have any implications that you think should be investigated in a new study? What new hypotheses are implied by the findings?

3. Using a research project on which you focused in Exercise 2, identify the stages of the research project corresponding to the points on the research circle. Did the research cover all four stages? Identify the theories and hypotheses underlying the study. What data were collected? What were the findings (empirical generalizations)?

4. Search the journal literature for three studies concerning some social program or organizational policy. Several possibilities are research on Project Head Start, on the effects of welfare payments, on boot camps or other criminal justice policies, and on jury size. Would you characterize the findings as largely consistent or inconsistent? How would you explain discrepant findings?

5. Evaluate one of the studies you found in Exercise 2 or 4 for its adherence to each of the ethical guidelines for research on people. How would you weigh the study's contribution to knowledge and social policy against its potential risks to human subjects?

PRACTICE EXERCISES

1. Pair up with one other student and select one of the research articles you have reviewed for other exercises. Criticize the research in terms of its adherence to each of the five ethical guidelines for research on human subjects, as well as for the authors' apparent honesty, openness, and consideration of social consequences. Be generally negative but not unreasonable in your criticisms. The student with whom you are working should critique the article in the same way but from a generally positive standpoint, defending its adherence to the five guidelines but without ignoring the study's weak points. Together, write a summary of the study's strong and weak points, or conduct a debate in class.

2. Research problems posed for explanatory studies must specify variables and hypotheses, which need to be stated properly and need to correctly imply any hypothesized causal relationship. The "Variables and Hypotheses" lessons on the CD-ROM distributed with your textbook will help you learn how to do this.

To use these lessons, choose one of the four "Variables and Hypotheses" exercises from the opening menu. About 10 hypotheses are presented in the lesson. After reading each hypothesis, you must name the dependent and independent variables and state the direction (positive or negative) of the relationship between them. The program will evaluate your answers. If an answer is correct, the program will present its version of the correct answer and go on to the next question. If you have made an error, the program will explain the error to you and give you another chance to respond. If your answer is unrecognizable, the program will instruct you to check your spelling and try again.

WEB EXERCISES

1. You can brush up on a wide range of social theories at http://www.digeratiweb.com/sociorealm. Pick a theorist and read some of what you find. What social phenomena does this theorist focus on?

What hypotheses seem consistent with his or her theorizing? Describe a hypothetical research project to test one of these hypotheses.

2. You've been assigned to write a paper on domestic violence and the law. To start, you would like to find out what the American Bar Association's stance is on the issue. Go to the American Bar Association Commission on Domestic Violence's Web site at http://www.abanet.org/domviol/ mrdv/identify.html. What is the American Bar Association's definition of domestic violence? How do they suggest one can identify a person as a victim of domestic violence? What do they identify as "basic warning signs"? Write your answers in a one to two page report.

SPSS EXERCISES

1. Formulate four research questions about support for capital punishment—one question per research purpose: exploratory, descriptive, explanatory, and evaluative. You should be able to answer two of these questions with the GSS2000mini data. Highlight these two.

2. Now to develop some foundation from the literature. Check the bibliography of this book for the following articles that drew on the General Social Survey: Aguirre & Baker, 1993; Barkan & Cohn, 1994; Borg, 1997, 1998; Warr, 1995; Young, 1992. How have social scientists used social theory to explain support for capital punishment? What potential influences on capital punishment have been tested? What influences could you test again with the 2000 GSS?

3. State four hypotheses in which support for capital punishment (CAPPUN) is the dependent variable and another variable in the GSS2000mini is the independent variable. Justify each hypothesis in a sentence or two.

4. Test at least one hypothesis. Marian Borg (1997) suggests that region might be expected to influence support for the death penalty. Test this as follows (after opening the GSS2000mini file, as explained in Chapter 1, SPSS Exercise 3):
   a. Click on *Analyze|Descriptive Statistics|Crosstabs.*
   b. Highlight CAPPUN and click on the arrow so that it moves into the Rows box; highlight REGION and click on the arrow to move it into the Columns box.
   c. Click on *Cells,* click off *Counts-Observed,* and click on *Percentages-Column.*
   d. Click *Continue* and then *OK.* Inspect the table.

Does support for capital punishment vary by region? Scroll down to the percentage table (in which regions appear across the top) and compare the percents in the Favor row for each region. Describe what you have found.

Now you can go on to test your other hypotheses in the same way, if you have the time. I don't have space here to give you more guidance, but I will warn you that there could be some problems at this point (for example, if your independent variable has lots of values). Proceed with caution!

DEVELOPING A RESEARCH PROPOSAL

Now it's time to start writing the proposal. These next exercises are very critical first steps.

1. State a problem for research. If you have not already identified a problem for study, or if you need to evaluate whether your research problem is doable, a few suggestions should help to get the ball rolling and keep it on course:
   a. Jot down questions that have puzzled you in some area having to do with people and social relations, perhaps questions that have come to mind while reading textbooks or research articles or even while hearing news stories. Don't hesitate to jot down many questions, and don't bore yourself—try to identify questions that really interest you.

b. Now take stock of your interests, your opportunities, and the work of others. Which of your research questions no longer seem feasible or interesting? What additional research questions come to mind? Pick out a question that is of interest and seems feasible and that your other coursework suggests has been the focus of some prior research or theorizing.

c. Write out your research question in one sentence, and elaborate on it in one paragraph. List at least three reasons why it is a good research question for you to investigate. Then present your proposal to your classmates and instructor for discussion and feedback.

2. Search the literature (and the Web) on the research question you identified. Refer to Appendix D for more guidance on conducting the search. Copy down at least 10 citations to articles (with abstracts from *Soc Abstracts* or *Psych Abstracts*) and five Web sites reporting research that seems highly relevant to your research question; then look up at least five of these articles and three of the sites. Inspect the article bibliographies and the links in the Web site and identify at least one more relevant article and Web site from each source.

Write a brief description of each article and Web site you consulted and evaluate its relevance to your research question. What additions or changes to your thoughts about the research question are suggested by the sources?

3. Propose at least two hypotheses that pertain to your research question. Justify these hypotheses in terms of the literature you have read.

4. Which standards for the protection of human subjects might pose the most difficulty for researchers on your proposed topic? Explain your answers and suggest appropriate protection procedures for human subjects.

Chapter 3

THEORIES AND PHILOSOPHIES FOR SOCIAL RESEARCH

The Origins of Social Science

Theoretical Perspectives in Social Science

Functionalism
Conflict Theory
Rational Choice
Symbolic Interactionism
Using Social Theory
   The Relationship Between Research and Theory
   Paradigm Change

Social Research Philosophies

Positivism and Postpositivism

Positivist Research Guidelines
A Positivist Research Goal: Advancing Knowledge
Interpretivism
   Interpretivist Research Guidelines
   An Interpretivist Research Goal: Creating Change
An Integrated Philosophy

Extending Social Science Investigations

Social Context
   Case Study: Juvenile Justice
The Natural World
   Case Study: Adolescent Sexuality

Conclusions

The numbers are staggering. Since 1950, the processing power of computers has *increased* by a factor of 10 billion, and the size of the individual transistors within them has *decreased* by a factor of about 7 million (Kaku, 1997:28). And this power is being put to use, as about 533 million Internet users communicate worldwide—149 million in the United States alone (Netcraft, 2002). As a result, trade between nations, migration between continents, communication among family and friends, and even methods of college teaching are being transformed. You will learn in this book that these technological innovations are also changing the practice of social research, through such techniques as Web-based surveys, computer-aided textual analysis, and massive computer-accessible data archives.

I begin this chapter, however, not with the future of social research, but with its past. I locate the origins of modern social science in an earlier period of rapid technological and social change and review the major social theories that emerged from this change. I then demonstrate how these theories provide a foundation for investigating the social world. I will also connect these theories to alternative philosophies about investigating the social world.

You can think of this as the "big picture" chapter. It's here that you'll see how research becomes much more valuable when we connect it to social theory. It's also here that you'll learn that researchers' preferences for quantitative or qualitative methodologies can reflect different philosophies about what social reality is. In the chapter's last section, I'll ask you to consider two other aspects of the big picture: How social processes can vary between social contexts and be affected by the natural world. You'll find that these are good points to keep in mind when you review or design any social investigation.

THE ORIGINS OF SOCIAL SCIENCE

Sociology was first conceived as a distinct social science during the Industrial Revolution in Europe. This period of technological innovation and social change exceeded in scope the changes that have occurred so far with our current information technology revolution. Between 1781 and 1802 in England, imports of raw cotton climbed from 5 million to 60 million pounds as a result of new technologies. Coal production grew ten-fold in just 40 years, and pig iron production doubled, from 68,000 tons (in 1788) to 1,347,000 tons (in 1839) (Heilbroner, 1970:74–75). New power-driven machines made one weaver 20 times more productive and one spinning machine 200 times more productive (Laslett, 1973).

The social world was dislocated, rearranged, and reconsidered. Millions of peasants displaced by changes in agricultural technology began to work in the rapidly expanding factories (Laslett, 1973). The English population increased four-fold during the 19th century, and its gross national product (GNP) soared fourteen-fold (Laslett, 1973). In 40 years, Manchester, England, grew from being "a mere village" to an industrial city with a hundred cotton mills and many other factories (Heilbroner, 1970:75). The certainties of village life and its traditions were replaced by the experience of social disruption and the expectation of social change.

Sociologists often describe this social transformation as a shift in the basis of social organization from community, in which people knew each other intimately, to society, in which people knew many others only through business relations or other specialized social roles. German sociologist Ferdinand Tönnies called this a shift from **gemeinschaft** to **gesellschaft**.

Gemeinschaft societies   Societies, based on community, that are homogeneous, with social relations based on kinship and, often, a common religion.

Gesellschaft societies   Societies, based on association, that are individualistic and competitive, with a developed division of labor.

This pulling apart of the individual from the community and the resulting exposure to a broader range of people and social arrangements highlighted the importance of social bonds and the value of understanding their impact. Because the natural sciences had made such great strides in understanding and controlling the natural world, it seemed possible that a social science could now do the same with respect to the social world.

THEORETICAL PERSPECTIVES IN SOCIAL SCIENCE

Although the early social scientists shared a focus on the impact of societal change, they came to understand this impact in quite different ways (Collins, 1994). French sociologist Emile Durkheim, a functionalist, believed that new forms of solidarity could replace weakened traditional bonds. In contrast, German economist Karl Marx, a conflict theorist, argued that conflicts between social classes would become increasingly severe. English economist Adam Smith proclaimed that the new economic order would free individuals to achieve their own goals—to make rational choices. Some of the early American sociologists, known as *symbolic interactionists,* focused attention on how individuals make sense of the social interaction in which they participate.

What questions are important to ask about the social world? What concepts should we consider and which variables should we measure? What hypotheses are important for understanding society, and which are merely trivial pursuits?

We use social theory to answer questions like these and thus to stimulate our investigations. You have already seen the value of social theory in guiding the Sherman and Berk research on domestic violence (Chapter 2). Here, I will review the four general theoretical perspectives I have just introduced and give some examples of more specific theories and related research.

Functionalism

What were the consequences of weakening social bonds? Emile Durkheim (1966) examined variation in suicide across France and found that provinces with higher suicide rates were more likely to be Protestant than Catholic, to be urban than rural, and to have lower marital rates. Each of these suicide-prone characteristics indicated greater movement toward a more modern, less traditional society characterized by weaker social bonds.

Was there anything that could replace the power of traditional social bonds in a modern society? In *The Division of Labor in Society,* Durkheim (1984) argued that traditional social bonds were based on likeness—on similarity of background and outlook between people; he termed this *mechanical solidarity.* This form of solidarity was weakened in modern society by the growing division of labor, which distinguished people in many different roles. But Durkheim suggested that it was precisely the division of labor that created a new form of social solidarity that would maintain the strength of social bonds. He termed this other form *organic solidarity,* and explained it as the product of interdependence between people who perform different work roles but need each other in order for the society or work organization as a whole to function. Differentiation creates interdependence and so strengthens social bonds.

We could also say that organic solidarity served the *function* of bonding together people in a society that has a developed division of labor, hence the term **functionalism.** Although Durkheim was concerned about weakened social bonds in modern society, his functionalist theory explained how society would restore these bonds. From this perspective, there was no

Exhibit 3.1   Causal Model Involving the Division of Labor

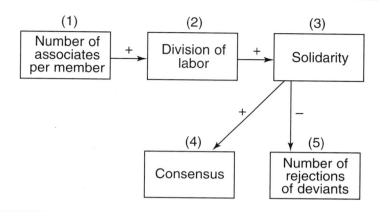

Source: Blalock, 1969, p. 19. Reprinted with permission from Pearson Education, Inc., Upper Saddle River, NJ.

fundamental conflict between the interests of the individual and the interests of society, or among different social groups—they fit together as part of an organic whole.

> ***Functionalism***   A social theory that explains social patterns in terms of their consequences for society as a whole and emphasizes the interdependence of social institutions and their common interest in maintaining the social order.

You can see in this synopsis some of the key concepts in Durkheim's theory: division of labor, forms of solidarity, strength of social bonds, propensity to commit suicide, and societal functions. Perhaps you can also deduce propositions that would link these concepts and form the basis for testable Durkheimian hypotheses. The causal model in Exhibit 3.1 charts the relationships among five concepts according to Durkheim's predictions (Blalock, 1969:19). The number of associates of individuals (population density) results in an increase in the division of labor, which in turn increases the level of solidarity, which in turn increases social consensus and decreases the rejection of deviants (Zetterberg, 1965:159–160).

Do these concepts interest you? Do the propositions strike you as reasonable? If so, you might join a long list of researchers who have attempted to test, extend, and modify various aspects of Durkheim's functionalist theory.

In one example, Robert J. Sampson, Jeffrey D. Morenoff, and Felton Earls (1999) focused on social bonds in a study of neighborhoods and child development. They investigated whether the amount of interaction between children and neighborhood adults differed for children of different racial groups. As you can see in Exhibit 3.2, black children were particularly disadvantaged in this respect. Sampson, Morenoff, and Earls (1999) concluded that these children were more socially vulnerable and experienced less effective social control in their neighborhoods than did children in other neighborhoods.

Exhibit 3.2   Proportion of Neighborhoods by Spatial Typology and Race/Ethnicity:
Child-Centered Social Control, Chicago, 1995

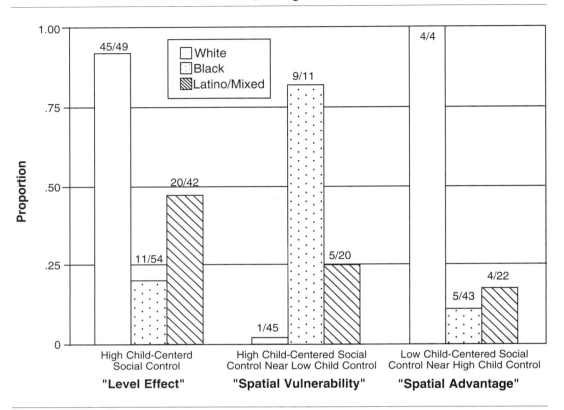

Source: Sampson, Morenoff, & Earls, 1999: 653. Reprinted with permission.

Conflict Theory

The most direct way to introduce Karl Marx's **conflict theory** is with these famous lines
from his and Friedrich Engels's (1961:13–16) *Communist Manifesto:*

> The history of all hitherto existing society is the history of class struggles. . . . Society as
> a whole is more and more splitting up into two great hostile camps, facing each other:
> bourgeoisie and proletariat. . . . The bourgeoisie has torn away from the family its senti-
> mental veil and has reduced the family relation to a mere money relation.

There you have it. For Marx and Engels, social classes were the key groupings in society
and conflict between them was not only the norm, but also the "engine" of social change. But
of course there was much more to it than this. Marx's conflict theory was materialist—it presumed that social change could be explained in terms of the material conditions in society,

most importantly the level of technology. In a similar vein, it treated the economic system of a society as its primary structure, and the educational, political, religious, and cultural institutions as the "superstructure" that helped to acclimate people to economic conditions. Thus, the economic system was the "independent variable" that shaped ideas and other social processes.

Conflict theory   Identifies conflict between social groups as the primary force in society; understanding the bases and consequences of conflict is the key to understanding social processes.

Max Weber, another "classical" German sociologist, can also be considered a conflict theorist, but his version of conflict theory was very different from that of Marx and Engels. In his *The Protestant Ethic and the Spirit of Capitalism,* Weber explained that the rise of the capitalist economic system was due in part to the Protestant Reformation and the ideas associated with it: "unremitting labor was . . . the way of life ordained by God in which every man must prove himself" (Bendix, 1962:62). For Max Weber, then, ideas were the "independent variable" that shaped the economic system.

Weber and Marx also differed in their concept of social stratification. Marx considered economic class to be the primary basis of social stratification, but Weber identified social status and political power as equally important stratification dimensions.

Do conflict theory's concepts strike a responsive chord with you? Can you think of instances when conflict theory propositions might help to explain social change? *Global Inequalities,* by York W. Bradshaw and Michael Wallace (1996) is an example of research motivated by conflict theory. Bradshaw and Wallace present data on corporate sales and national gross domestic products that show the great economic power of multinational corporations relative to countries in less-developed areas of the world. (see Exhibit 3.3).

Rational Choice

Rational choice theory also has its roots in the Industrial Revolution. In *An Inquiry into the Causes of the Wealth of Nations*, first published in 1776, English economist Adam Smith argued that in a capitalist system, rational individual action results in a larger social good:

> . . . he intends only his own gain, . . . led by an invisible hand to promote an end which was no part of his intention. (Smith, 1937:423)

Rational choice theorists in sociology, like those in economics, explain individual behavior in terms of rational cost/benefit calculations: "the actor chooses the action which will maximize utility" (Coleman, 1990:14). Why do people choose the schools they do? Because the expected value of attending exceeds the cost of doing so. Why do people work rather than only pursue leisure activities? Because the rewards exceed the costs. You get the idea.

Rational choice theory   Explains social processes in terms of rational cost/benefit calculations that shape individual behavior.

Exhibit 3.3   The Fifty Richest Economic Entities in the World*

Entity	Millions of U.S. Dollars (1992)	Entity	Millions of U.S. Dollars (1992)
1. China	$506,075	25. SAMSUNG	$51,345
2. Russian Federated Rep.	$387,476	26. PHILIP MORRIS	$50,621
3. India	$214,598	27. IRI	$50,488
4. GENERAL MOTORS	$133,622	28. SIEMENS	$50,381
5. Indonesia	$126,364	29. Colombia	$48,583
6. Thailand	$110,337	30. VOLKSWAGEN	$46,312
7. Iran, Islamic Rep.	$110,258	31. CHRYSLER	$43,600
8. FORD MOTOR	$108,521	32. Pakistan	$41,904
9. Turkey	$99,696	33. UNILEVER	$41,843
10. EXXON	$97,825	34. Chile	$41,203
11. ROYAL DUTCH/ SHELL GROUP	$95,134	35. NESTLE	$38,895
		36. Myanmar	$37,749
12. Ukraine	$94,831	37. ELF AQUITAINE	$37,016
13. TOYOTA MOTOR	$85,283	38. HONDA MOTOR	$35,798
14. Poland	$83,823	39. Algeria	$35,674
15. HITACHI	$68,581	40. ENI	$34,791
16. INTERNATIONAL BUSINESS MACHINES	$62,716	41. FIAT	$34,707
17. MATSUSHITA ELECTRIC IND.	$61,385	42. SONY	$34,603
		43. TEXACO	$34,359
18. GENERAL ELECTRIC	$60,823	44. Egypt, Arab Republic	$33,553
19. DAIMLER-BENZ	$59,102	45. NEC	$33,176
20. Malaysia	$57,568	46. E.I. DU PONT DE NEM	$32,621
21. MOBIL	$56,576	47. CHEVRON	$32,123
22. NISSAN MOTOR	$53,760	49. DAEWOO	$30,893
23. BRITISH PETROLEUM	$52,485	48. PHILLIPS ELECTRONICS	$31,666
24. Philippines	$52,462	50. PROCTOR & GAMBLE	$30,433

Source: Multinational sales data from Haight, 1994; GDP data from World Bank, 1994. Cited in Bradshaw, York W. and Michael Wallace. 1996. *Global Inequalities.* Thousand Oaks, CA: Sage, 49.

*Excludes the richest countries.

If you would like to try your hand at investigating predictions of rational choice theory, a good example to review is the research by Michael R. Gottfredson and Don M. Gottfredson (1988:25) on responses to crime. Exhibit 3.4 presents one piece of their evidence for the value of rational choice theory: the difference in likelihood of reporting thefts to the police varies dramatically depending on whether the victim had theft insurance. The rational calculation is apparently that if reporting a theft doesn't result in financial benefit, it isn't worth the bother.

Symbolic Interactionism

Several early American sociologists attempted to understand social bonds by looking inward, at the meaning people attach to their interactions, rather than outward to larger

Exhibit 3.4 Robbery Victimizations Reported and Not Reported to the Police, by Insurance Coverage, United States, 1973–1977

Theft insurance[a]	Reported to police	
	No[b]	Yes
No	49% (1,163,564)	51% (1,810,863)
Yes	15% (53,705)	85% (304,347)

Source: Analysis of data tapes from the National Crime Survey, Household Portion. 1973–1977. (U.S. Department of Justice, 1977). Cited in Gottfredson, Michael R. and Don M. Gottfredson. 1988. *Decision Making in Criminal Justice: Toward the Rational Exercise of Discretion,* 2nd ed. New York: Plenum, 25.

[a] Excludes victims who responded "Don't know" to the question, "Was there any insurance against theft?"
[b] Includes victims who responded "No" and "Don't know" to the question, "Were the police informed of this incident in any way?"

social structures. They focused on the symbolic nature of social interaction—how social interaction conveys meaning and promotes socialization. For example, Charles Horton Cooley (1962) argued that the self cannot be understood as something apart from interaction with others:

> In general, then, most of our reflective consciousness, of our wide-awake state of mind, is social consciousness . . . self and society are twin-born, we know one as immediately as we know the other, and the notion of a separate and independent ego is an illusion. (Cooley, 1962:5)

George Herbert Mead (1934), another early American sociologist, also focused on the impact of others on the development of the self. Mead (1934:158) believed that the self is only fully developed when it becomes "an individual reflection of the general systematic pattern of social or group behavior in which it and the others are all involved." Geoffrey R. Skoll's (1992:136–137) ethnographic study of a drug abuse treatment facility conveys the flavor of work guided by **symbolic interaction theory:**

> An unstated, but important, goal of the program is to domesticate the female residents. Treatment plans for women are always directed toward making them "good homemakers" and mothers. . . . While the rule against sexual or romantic conduct applies equally to men and women, the essence of women's sexuality is treated and constructed differently. (Skoll, 1992:136, 137)

Do you find yourself thinking of interesting new research questions when you read about Skoll's study? If so, you should consider developing your knowledge of the concepts of symbolic interaction theory.

> ***Symbolic interaction theory*** Focuses on the symbolic nature of social interaction—how social interaction conveys meaning and promotes socialization.

Using Social Theory

Are you ready to choose one of these general theoretical perspectives to guide your research? I suspect not. For now, think of the four theoretical perspectives as tour guides waiting to help you explore a new city. A tour guide gives us an overview of a city and how it operates, points out key landmarks, and suggests where to go for particular types of experiences. But different tour guides will give very different impressions of the same city. The functionalist tour guide points out that in each city neighborhood, from classy Swanktown to shabby Roadside, children go to school, employees go to work, congregants go to church, and the newspapers get delivered. The different parts of the city function together to create the larger whole.

But the conflict tour guide will emphasize social differences: We will see the neighborhoods of the rich and then the ghettos and barrios of the poor. We may stop along the way to visit striking workers outside a factory and then have lunch in a corporate boardroom. We will be impressed by the many bases of conflict between social groups.

The rational choice tour will be a bit more down to earth, but also somewhat repetitious. At every stop we will see transactions in process. We may spend a "day in the life" of a community member who hunts for bargains in shops, decides whether to send her son to a private or public school, calculates the potential benefits from electing a politician who campaigns on a "no new taxes" pledge, and evaluates the tradeoffs between asking for a promotion and seeking a new job.

It is the hardier tourists who will appreciate the symbolic interactionist guide. He will ignore the usual landmarks, make no special effort to show us contrasting neighborhoods, and skip the tourist shops. Instead, the interactionist will have us hang around a street corner with local gang members, sit in the back and listen to the gossip at a PTA meeting, and question local residents at a coffee shop. There will be no fixed itinerary; we will go where things look interesting and appreciate what people say. At the end of the day, our tour guide assures us, we will understand the city by seeing it and hearing about it through the eyes and ears of its residents.

Would you like to sign up for more than one tour? If so, do you think you will end up wondering whether you are in the same city when you tour with different guides? Or do you expect to marvel at the greater understanding that emerges from multiple tours? Do you regret that there isn't one guide who can show you what the city is "really" like?

That's the state of social theory in the early years of the 21st century: general theoretical perspectives that provide alternative frames of reference and encourage us to pose different questions about the social world, but no single approach around which most social scientists have rallied. As a social researcher, you may work within one of these perspectives, seeking to extend it, challenge it, or specify it. You may test alternative implications of the different theoretical perspectives against each other. If you're really feeling ambitious, you may even seek to combine some aspects of the different perspectives. Maybe you'll come up with a different theoretical perspective altogether.

The Relationship Between Research and Theory

If you are like most social scientists, you will focus your attention on a specific theory derived from one of these four perspectives, develop some testable hypotheses, and get on with your research. You have seen how Sherman and Berk (1984) deduced from deterrence theory the hypothesis that arrest would lower the risk of recidivism among people accused of domestic violence and then found some support for that hypothesis. They noted that deterrence theory reflects the rational choice theoretical perspective, but the evidence they found for their hypothesis in itself provided only a little bit more evidence for rational choice theory.

We may feel some greater affinity for one perspective rather than another—appreciate the view provided by its "tour"—but our primary concern in everyday research is likely to be what Robert Merton (1954) called "middle-range theories." You've just seen how middle-range theories like those of Sampson and colleagues (1999) on neighborhood social bonds, Gottredson and Gottfredson (1988) on responses to crime, and Skoll (1992) on social roles in drug treatment facilities can stimulate fascinating research.

Social theory and research findings always influence one another. You now know the primary form that this relationship takes: the testing of specific hypotheses deduced from a theory, with the goal of evaluating the empirical support for the theory's implications. But research can shape the development of theory in more subtle ways, as when unanticipated findings stimulate a search for alternatives to current theory (Merton, 1957:102–117).

Paradigm Change

The process of testing specific hypotheses deduced from a theory adds gradually to the body of scientific knowledge and represents the nuts and bolts of science. In *The Structure of Scientific Revolutions,* Thomas S. Kuhn (1970) called this gradual, incremental work of most scientists "**normal science.**" Research like this operates within a general theoretical perspective, which Kuhn termed a **scientific paradigm,** and does not challenge the basic assumptions of that perspective. Scientists operating within a particular scientific paradigm share a host of major concepts and specific theories, research findings, and presuppositions about the world. The dominant scientific paradigm at any point in time represents the prevailing wisdom in that field—its entire body of knowledge.

The dominant scientific paradigm can change, but only after a large body of contrary evidence accumulates and an alternative perspective appears. This isn't just a matter of one more study that fails to support deterrence theory; instead, it is something like Copernicus's heliocentric view of the solar system replacing the previous prevailing presumption that the earth was the center of the solar system. It took more than 100 years for this **paradigm shift** to occur, but once it did it completely changed prevailing beliefs. Kuhn termed such an abrupt transition from one theoretical paradigm to another a **scientific revolution.** Such revolutions are uncommon, but when they occur they affect many areas of research. Even established scientists begin to accept the new way of thinking.

Scientific paradigm   A set of beliefs that guide scientific work in an area, including unquestioned presuppositions, accepted theories, and exemplary research findings.

Examples: Structural-functional theory; Marxism; Freudian theory.

Have we had any scientific revolutions in sociology or the other social sciences? Not really, because we have had no single widely accepted paradigm that could be overturned by an alternative. But we can think of the four broad theoretical perspectives in this chapter as alternative paradigms that have different implications for how we think about the social world. And when you find yourself feeling very confident about current beliefs about the social world, remember Kuhn's concept of paradigm shifts. Ask yourself whether there is some basis for challenging current beliefs. Consider whether recent research suggests a new theoretical direction .

SOCIAL RESEARCH PHILOSOPHIES

When you set out to investigate the social world, a theoretical perspective will help steer you toward appropriate research questions, hypotheses, and literature. It will help you chart a route that takes you to the places you need to visit. But your investigation also will be shaped by your assumptions about how the social world can best be investigated—by your social research philosophy.

The early social scientists shared with natural scientists a **positivist** research philosophy—a belief that there is a reality that is external to us that we can understand through empirical research. But all the empirical data we collect comes to us through our own senses and must be interpreted with our own minds. To some philosophers, this suggests that we can never be sure that we have understood reality properly, or that we ever can, or that our own understandings can really be judged more valid than someone else's. Concerns like this have begun to appear in many areas of social science and have begun to shape some research methods. In this section, we will focus on two general alternative research philosophies and examine some of their implications for research methods. We will review research guidelines and objectives that are consistent with both philosophies.

Positivism and Postpositivism

A researcher's philosophical perspective on reality and on the appropriate role of the researcher will also shape her methodological preferences. Researchers with a positivist philosophy believe that there is an objective reality that exists apart from the perceptions of those who observe it, and that the goal of science is to better understand this reality.

> Whatever nature "really" is, we assume that it presents itself in precisely the same way to the same human observer standing at different points in time and space. . . . We assume that it also presents itself in precisely the same way across different human observers standing at the same point in time and space. (Wallace, 1983:461)

This philosophy lies behind the research circle (Chapter 2), with its assumption that we can test theoretically based predictions with data collected from the real, objective world. It is the philosophy traditionally associated with science (Weber, 1949:72), with the expectation that there are universal laws of human behavior, and with the belief that scientists must be objective and unbiased in order to see reality clearly. Positivists believe that a well-designed test of a theoretically based hypothesis—like the test of the prediction that arrest will reduce domestic violence—can move us closer to understanding actual social processes.

Postpositivism is a philosophy of reality that is closely related to positivism. Postpositivists believe that there is an external, objective reality, but they are very sensitive to the complexity of this reality and to the limitations and biases of the scientists who study it (Guba & Lincoln, 1994:109–111). As a result, they do not think we can ever be sure that scientific methods allow us to perceive objective reality. Instead, postpositivists believe that the goal of science is to achieve **intersubjective agreement** among scientists about the nature of reality (Wallace, 1983:461).

For example, postpositivists may worry that researchers' predispositions bias them in favor of deterrence theory. Therefore, they remain skeptical of research results that support deterrence theory until a number of researchers report such evidence. A postpositivist has much more confidence in the community of social researchers than in any individual social scientist (Campbell & Russo, 1999:144).

Positivism The belief, shared by most scientists, that there is a reality that exists quite apart from our own perception of it, that it can be understood through observation, and that it follows general laws.

Postpositivism The belief that there is an empirical reality, but that our understanding of it is limited by its complexity and by the biases and other limitations of researchers.

Intersubjective agreement An agreement by different observers on what is happening in the natural or social world.

Positivist Research Guidelines

In order to achieve an accurate, or valid, understanding of the social world, the researcher operating within the positivist or postpositivist tradition must adhere to some basic guidelines about how to conduct research:

1. *Test ideas against empirical reality without becoming too personally invested in a particular outcome.* This guideline requires a commitment to "testing," as opposed to just reacting to events as they happen or looking for what we want to see (Kincaid, 1996:51–54).

2. *Plan and carry out investigations systematically.* Social researchers have little hope of conducting a careful test of their ideas if they do not think through in advance how they should go about the test and then proceed accordingly. But a systematic approach is not always easy. For example, Sherman and Berk (1984) needed to ensure that spouse abusers were assigned to be arrested or not on a random basis rather than on the basis of the police officers' personal preferences. They devised a systematic procedure using different color report sheets, in random order, but then found that police officers sometimes deviated from this procedure due to their feelings about particular cases. Subsequently, in some replications of the study, the researchers ensured compliance with their research procedures by requiring police officers to call in to a central number to receive the experimentally determined treatment.

3. *Document all procedures and disclose them publicly.* Social researchers should disclose the methods on which their conclusions are based so that others can evaluate for

themselves the likely soundness of these conclusions. Such disclosure is a key feature of science. It is the community of researchers, reacting to each others' work, that provides the best guarantee against purely self-interested conclusions (Kincaid, 1996). Sherman and Berk (1984) provide a compelling example. After describing the formal research plan in their research report, they discuss the apparent "slippage" from this plan when some police officers avoided implementing the random assignment procedure.

4. *Clarify assumptions.* No investigation is complete unto itself; whatever the researcher's method, the research rests on some background assumptions. For example, research to determine whether arrest has a deterrent effect assumes that potential law violators think rationally, and that they calculate potential costs and benefits prior to committing crimes. When a researcher conducts an election poll, the assumption is that people actually vote for the candidate they say they will vote for. By definition, research assumptions are not tested, so we do not know for sure whether they are correct. By taking the time to think about and disclose their assumptions, researchers provide important information for those who seek to evaluate the validity of research conclusions.

5. *Specify the meaning of all terms.* Words often have multiple or unclear meanings. "Alienation," "depression," "cold," "crowded," and so on can mean different things to different people. In scientific research, all terms must be defined explicitly and used consistently. For example, Sherman and Berk (1984) identified their focus as misdemeanor domestic assault, not just "wife beating." They specified that their work concerned those cases of spouse assault in which severe injury was not involved and both partners were present when police arrived.

6. *Maintain a skeptical stance toward current knowledge.* The results of any particular investigation must be examined critically, although confidence about interpretations of the social or natural world increases after repeated investigations yield similar results. A general skepticism about current knowledge stimulates researchers to improve the validity of current research results and expand the frontier of knowledge. For example, in response to questions raised about the Sherman and Berk study, Lawrence Sherman and Ellen Cohn (1989) pointed out 13 problems in the Minneapolis Domestic Violence Experiment and weighed carefully the extent to which these problems might have undermined the experiment's validity.

7. *Replicate research and build social theory.* No one study is definitive by itself. We can't fully understand a single study's results apart from the larger body of knowledge to which it is related, and we can't place much confidence in these results until the study has been replicated. Theories organize the knowledge accumulated by numerous investigations into a coherent whole and serve as a guide to future inquiries. Sherman and his colleagues (1992) recognized this as they developed their plans on the basis of prior research and theory and when they called for replications of their research.

8. *Search for regularities or patterns.* Positivist and postpositivist scientists assume that the natural world has some underlying order of relationships, so that unique events and individuals can be understood at least in part in terms of general principles (Grinnell, 1992:27–29). Sherman (1992:162–164), for example, described the abuse histories of

two men to provide greater insight into why arrest could have different effects for different people. The goal is to understand social patterns that characterize many individuals, not just to understand individual cases.

Real investigations by social scientists do not always include much attention to theory, specific definitions of all terms, and so forth. But it behooves any social researcher to study these guidelines and to consider the consequences of not following any with which they do not agree.

A Positivist Research Goal: Advancing Knowledge

The goal of the traditional positivist scientific approach is to advance scientific knowledge. This goal is achieved when research results are published in academic journals or presented at academic conferences.

The positivist approach considers value considerations to be beyond the scope of science: "An empirical science cannot tell anyone what he should do—but rather what he can do—and under certain circumstances—what he wishes to do" (Weber, 1949:54). The idea is that developing valid knowledge about how society *is* organized, or how we live our lives, does not tell us how society *should* be organized or how we *should* live our lives. The determination of empirical facts should be a separate process from the evaluation of these facts as satisfactory or unsatisfactory (Weber, 1949:11).

The idea is not to ignore value considerations, because they are viewed as a legitimate basis for selecting a research problem to investigate. In addition, many scientists also consider it acceptable to encourage government officials or private organizations to act on the basis of a study's findings, after the research is over. During a research project, however, value considerations are to be held in abeyance.

Interpretivism and Constructivism

Qualitative research is often guided by a different, **interpretivist** philosophy. Interpretive social scientists believe that social reality is socially constructed and that the goal of social scientists is to understand what meanings people give to reality, not to determine how reality works apart from these interpretations. This philosophy rejects the positivist belief that there is a concrete, objective reality that scientific methods help us to understand (Lynch & Bogen, 1997); instead, interpretivists believe that scientists construct an image of reality based on their own preferences and prejudices and their interactions with others. From this standpoint, the goal of validity becomes misleading: "Truth is a matter of the best-informed and most sophisticated construction on which there is consensus at a given time" (Schwandt, 1994:128).

Searching for universally applicable social laws can distract from learning what people know and how they understand their lives. The interpretive social researcher examines meanings that have been socially constructed. . . . There is not one reality out there to be measured; objects and events are understood by different people differently, and those perceptions are the reality—or realities—that social science should focus on. (Rubin & Rubin, 1995:35)

The **constructivist paradigm** extends interpretivist philosophy by emphasizing the importance of exploring how different stakeholders in a social setting construct their beliefs (Guba & Lincoln, 1989:44–45). It gives particular attention to the different goals of researchers and other participants in a research setting and seeks to develop a consensus among participants about how to understand the focus of inquiry. The constructivist research report will highlight different views of the social program or other issue and explain how a consensus can be reached among participants.

Interpretivism   The belief that reality is socially constructed and that the goal of social scientists is to understand what meanings people give to that reality. Max Weber termed the goal of interpretivist research *verstehen*, or "understanding."

Constructivist paradigm   A perspective that emphasizes how different stakeholders in social settings construct their beliefs.

Constructivist inquiry uses an interactive research process, in which a researcher begins an evaluation in some social setting by identifying the different interest groups in that setting. The researcher goes on to learn what each group thinks, and then gradually tries to develop a shared perspective on the problem being evaluated (Guba & Lincoln, 1989:42).

These steps are diagrammed as a circular process in Exhibit 3.5. In this process, called a **hermeneutic circle**,

the constructions of a variety of individuals—deliberately chosen so as to uncover widely variable viewpoints—are elicited, challenged, and exposed to new information and new, more sophisticated ways of interpretation, until some level of consensus is reached (although there may be more than one focus for consensus). (Guba & Lincoln, 1989:180–181)

The researcher conducts an open-ended interview with the first respondent (R_1) to learn about her thoughts and feelings on the subject of inquiry—her "construction" (C_1). The researcher then asks this respondent to nominate a second respondent (R_2), who feels very differently. The second respondent is then interviewed in the same way, but also is asked to comment on the themes raised by the previous respondent. The process continues until all major perspectives are represented, and then may be repeated again with the same set of respondents.

The final product is a "case report."

A case report is very unlike the technical reports we are accustomed to seeing in positivist inquiries. It is not a depiction of a "true" or "real" state of affairs. . . . It does not culminate in judgments, conclusions, or recommendations except insofar as these are concurred on by relevant respondents.

The case report helps the reader come to a realization (in the sense of making real) not only of the states of affairs that are believed by constructors [research respondents] to exist but also of the underlying motives, feelings, and rationales leading to those beliefs. The

Exhibit 3.5   The Hermeneutic Circle

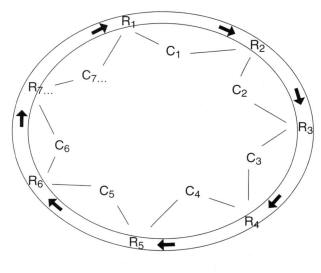

KEY: R = Respondent
C = Construction

Source: Adapted from Guba & Lincoln, 1989:152. Reprinted with permission.

case report is characterized by a thick description that not only clarifies the all-important context, but that makes it possible for the reader vicariously to experience it. (Guba & Lincoln, 1989:180–181)

Interpretivist Research Guidelines

Researchers guided by an interpretivist philosophy reject some of the guidelines to which positivist researchers seek to adhere. In fact, there are a wide variety of specific approaches that can be termed "interpretivist," and each has some guidelines that it highlights. For those working within the constructivist perspective, Guba and Lincoln (1989:42) suggest four key steps for researchers, each of which may be repeated many times in a given study:

1. Identify stakeholders and solicit their "claims, concerns, and issues."

2. Introduce the claims, concerns, and issues of each stakeholder group to the other stakeholder groups and ask for their reactions.

3. Focus further information collection on claims, concerns, and issues about which there is disagreement among stakeholder groups.

4. Negotiate with stakeholder groups about the information collected and attempt to reach consensus on the issues about which there is disagreement.

An Interpretivist Research Goal: Creating Change

Social researchers with an interpretivist or constructivist orientation often reject explicitly the traditional positivist distinction between facts and values (Sjoberg & Nett, 1968). Robert Bellah and his *Habits of the Heart* coauthors (1985) have instead proposed a model of "social science as public philosophy." In this model, social scientists focus explicit attention on achieving a more just society:

> Social science makes assumptions about the nature of persons, the nature of society, and the relation between persons and society. It also, whether it admits it or not, makes assumptions about good persons and a good society and considers how far these conceptions are embodied in our actual society.
>
> Social science as public philosophy, by breaking through the iron curtain between the social sciences and the humanities, becomes a form of social self-understanding or self-interpretation. . . . By probing the past as well as the present, by looking at "values" as much as at "facts," such a social science is able to make connections that are not obvious and to ask difficult questions. (Bellah et al., 1985:301)

William Foote Whyte (1991) proposed a more activist approach to research called **participatory action research.** As the name implies, this approach encourages social researchers to get "out of the academic rut" and bring values into the research process (Whyte, 1991:285).

In participatory action research, the researcher involves as active participants some members of the setting studied. Both the organizational members and the researcher are assumed to want to develop valid conclusions, to bring unique insights, and to desire change, but Whyte believed these objectives were more likely to be obtained if the researcher collaborated actively with the persons he studied. For example, many academic studies have found that employee participation is associated with job satisfaction, but not with employee productivity. After some discussions about this finding with employees and managers, Whyte (1991:278–279) realized that researchers had been using a general concept of employee participation that did not distinguish those aspects of participation that were most likely to influence productivity. For example, occasional employee participation in company meetings had not been distinguished from ongoing employee participation in and control of production decisions. When these and other concepts were defined more precisely, it became clear that employee participation in production decisions had substantially increased overall productivity, whereas simple meeting attendance had not. This discovery would not have occurred without the active involvement of company employees in planning the research.

An Integrated Philosophy

It is tempting to think of positivism and postpositivism as representing an opposing research philosophy to interpretivism and constructivism. Then it seems that we should choose the one philosophy that seems closest to our own preferences and condemn the other as "unscientific," "uncaring," or perhaps just "unrealistic." But there are good reasons to prefer a research philosophy that integrates some of the differences between these philosophies (Smith, 1991).

Society is a product of human action that in turn shapes how people act and think. The "sociology of knowledge" studies this process by which people make themselves as they construct society (Berger & Luckmann, 1966). Individuals internalize the social order through the process of socialization, so that their own beliefs and actions are not entirely of their own making, but instead reflect the social order of which they are a part. This means that we should be very careful to consider how our research approaches and interpretations are shaped by our own social background—just as we are cautioned to do by interpretivist researchers.

When we peer below the surface of standardized research procedures, we also discover the importance of taking into account people's feelings and the meanings that they attach to these feelings. For example, Danielle Lavin and Douglas Maynard (2001) investigated how different survey research centers handle laughter by respondents during telephone surveys. The dilemma for the centers is this: When respondents laugh during an interview, it usually is an attempt to increase rapport with the interviewer, so turning down the "invitation" to laugh can make the interviewer seem unsympathetic. However, accepting this "invitation" to laugh injects an uncontrolled source of bias into what is supposed to be a standardized interview.

> As interviewers manage laughter in the interview, they artfully maneuver through the dilemma of adhering to standardization protocols while maintaining rapport with respondents that retains participation and continues to elicit answers. (Lavin & Maynard, 2001:473)

As a result, what appear to be standardized interviews in fact vary in ways that are not apparent in the answers recorded by the interviewer. Recognition of this interpretive process can improve survey research conducted in the positivist tradition.

Recent research on cognitive functioning (how the brain works) suggests there are neurological reasons to expect that people's feelings shape their perceptions in ways that are often not apparent (Seidman, 1997). Emotional responses to external stimuli travel a shorter circuit in the brain, through a small structure called the amygdala, than do reasoned responses (see Exhibit 3.6). The result, according to some cognitive scientists, is that "what something reminds us of can be far more important than what it is" (Goleman, 1995: 294–295). Our emotions can influence us even before we begin to reason about what we have observed.

So researchers can't ignore the subjective aspects of human experience or expunge it entirely from the data collection process. This helps to explain why the debate continues between positivist and interpretivist philosophies and why research can often be improved by drawing on insights from both.

And what about the important positivist distinction between facts and values in social research? Here, too, there is evidence that neither the "value-free" presumption of positivists nor the constructivist critique of this position is entirely correct. For example, Joachim L. Savelsberg, Ryan King, and Lara Cleveland (2002) examined influences on the focus and findings of published criminal justice scholarship. They found that criminal justice research was more likely to be oriented to topics and theories suggested by the state when it was funded by government agencies. This reflects a political influence on scholarship. However, government funding did not have any bearing on the researchers' conclusions about the criminal justice processes they examined. This suggests that scientific procedures can insulate the research process itself from political pressure.

Exhibit 3.6   Anatomy of an Emotional Hijacking

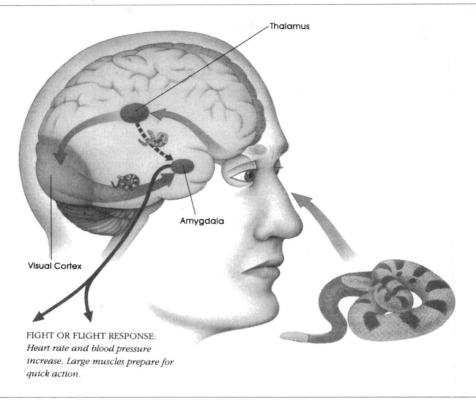

FIGHT OR FLIGHT RESPONSE:
Heart rate and blood pressure
increase. Large muscles prepare for
quick action.

Source: Goleman, 1995:19. Copyright 1995 by Daniel Goleman. Used by permission of Bantam Books, a division of Random House, Inc.

EXTENDING SOCIAL SCIENCE INVESTIGATIONS

Using multiple methods in a single study can lessen the risk of arriving at mistaken conclusions, but it is also important to consider the larger picture. Focusing on people and processes in just one setting can obscure or distort important social processes. Concluding, on the basis of one study, that arrest deters spouse abuse is very different from concluding, after several studies, that arrest deters spouse abuse *only* if the abuser is employed. Taking social context into account will improve our understanding of important concepts and causal processes and identify the limits to our generalizations. We also need to consider the possibility of influence from the natural world in which social life takes place. Are there biological processes or ecological relationships that influence particular social processes?

Social Context

Do the processes in which we are interested vary across neighborhoods? Among organizations? Across regions? These are the types of questions we seek to answer by taking social context into account. When relationships among variables differ across geographic units like counties or across other contexts, researchers say there is a **contextual effect.**

Case Study: Juvenile Justice

Robert Sampson and John Laub (1993) drew a large sample of 538,000 juvenile justice cases from 322 counties across the United States. They then matched these case data from official records with census data on county social characteristics. They hypothesized that juvenile justice would be harsher in areas characterized by racial poverty and a large underclass. Statistical analysis of their data supported the hypothesis: In counties having a relatively large underclass and poverty concentrated among minorities, juvenile cases were more likely to be treated harshly. These relationships occurred for both African American and white juveniles, but were particularly strong for African Americans. Racial polarization and underclass poverty, not the overall affluence of the county, shaped juvenile justice case processing.

The results of this research suggest the importance of taking social context into account when examining criminal justice processes. Studies limited to one social context would not be generalizable to the entire country and would seriously misrepresent the role of race and other factors (Dannefer & Schutt, 1982; Schutt & Dannefer, 1988). Awareness of contextual differences helps to make sense of the discrepant findings from local studies of juvenile justice case processing.

The Natural World

Although the social world is sufficiently complex to challenge the most able researcher, features of the natural world must also be taken into account in order to explain some social phenomena. The natural environment in which people live and the biology of the human body interact with social processes in many ways.

Case Study: Adolescent Sexuality

J. Richard Udry's (1988) study of adolescent sexuality is a methodologically ambitious effort to evaluate biological influences on social processes. Udry studied 8th-, 9th-, and 10th-grade public school students in a southern U.S. city. After signing a consent form (their parents also had to sign a consent form), the students completed a questionnaire about their sexual behavior and attitudes and gave blood samples. Udry then identified effects of both social environment and hormone levels in the blood on sexual behavior and attitudes. Such social variables as church attendance, best (same-sex) friend's attitude toward sexual permissiveness, and the permissiveness of the respondent's own sexual attitudes were related to sexual behavior, but so were levels of testosterone and other hormones.

Tracing the relationship between biological and social processes only begins to identify the many ways in which the natural world influences social life. Microorganisms that spread disease, pollutants that stunt growth, and rivers that power electric generators all shape social life. Keeping possible connections between the natural world and the social world in mind can often result in more interesting research questions and more powerful research designs (Fremont & Bird, 1999; Janesick, 1994:215).

CONCLUSIONS

It is no exaggeration to say that the physical and natural sciences have forever changed the course of human society through such technological innovations as computers, airplanes, nuclear power, brain-imaging devices, and genetic engineering, to name just a few. Social science has not had this much impact, but it does influence many aspects of social life, from the design of social programs and the electoral strategies of politicians to the selection of jurors and the strategies of business. Most important, social science research continues to shape our understanding of the social world. The social theories that we develop and refine through research help us to see who we are and what we can become.

KEY TERMS

Conflict theory
Constructivist paradigm
Contextual effect
Functionalism
Gemeinschaft
Gesellschaft
Hermeneutic circle
Interpretivism
Intersubjective agreement
Normal science

Paradigm shift
Participatory action research
Positivism
Postpositivism
Rational choice theory
Scientific paradigm
Scientific revolution
Symbolic interaction theory
Verstehen

HIGHLIGHTS

- Social science emerged during Europe's Industrial Revolution as community-based social bonds weakened and individual social roles became more fragmented.

- Functionalist theory focuses attention on the ways that individuals and social groups help to maintain society and explains social phenomena in terms of these social consequences.

- Conflict theory focuses attention on the bases of conflict between social groups and uses these conflicts to explain most social phenomena.

- Rational choice theory focuses attention on the rational bases for social exchange and explains most social phenomena in terms of these motives.

- Symbolic interactionist theory focuses attention on the meanings that people attach to and gain from social interaction and explains most social phenomena in terms of these meanings.

- Positivism and postpositivism are research philosophies that emphasize the goal of understanding the real world; these philosophies guide most quantitative researchers. Interpretivism is a research philosophy that emphasizes understanding the meaning people attach to their experiences; it guides many qualitative researchers.

- The constructivist paradigm reflects an interpretivist philosophy. It emphasizes the importance of exploring and representing the ways in which different stakeholders in a social setting construct their beliefs. Constructivists interact with research subjects to gradually develop a shared perspective on the issue being studied.

- Responsible social researchers must be sensitive to the ways in which social and emotional processes can influence problem formulation, data collection, and conclusions.

- Social scientists, like all scientists, should structure their research so that their own ideas can be proved wrong, should disclose their methods for others to critique, and should recognize the possibility of error. Eight specific guidelines are recommended here.

- Some researchers reject the separation of facts from values in the research process and instead urge using research to achieve valued objectives. In one such approach, participatory action research, researchers collaborate actively with those whom they study.

- Social processes can vary with social context and with biological and physical factors. Social researchers should consider carefully whether to take either into account in a specific research project.

DISCUSSION QUESTIONS

1. You read in Chapter 2 about Sherman and Berk's study of the police response to domestic violence. They tested a prediction derived from rational choice theory. Propose hypotheses about the response to domestic violence that are consistent with functionalist, conflict, and symbolic interactionist theories. Which theory seems to you to provide the best framework for understanding domestic violence and how to respond to it?

2. Do you have a theoretical preference? What seem to you to be the strong and weak points of the four theoretical perspectives we have studied? How can you explain your preference for a "tour guide" in terms of your own background, either intellectual or personal?

3. Continue the debate between positivism and interpretivism with an in-class debate. Be sure to review the guidelines for these research philosophies and the associated goals. You might also consider whether an integrated philosophy is preferable.

4. Do social research methods provide a firm foundation for understanding the social world? Discuss the pro and con arguments focusing on the variability of social research findings across different social contexts and the difficulty of understanding human subjectivity.

PRACTICE EXERCISES

1. Defend your favorite theory! Review a social science book or journal article that uses social theory to explain some social phenomenon. Prepare a short presentation in which you describe the theory, give some background about it, and explain why it was appropriate for this study. Ask the class for comments at the end of your presentation and be prepared to defend yourself.

2. What is the state of the debate between positivist and interpretivist research philosophies? Search *Sociological Abstracts* for articles that used the terms "positivism" or "interpretivism" (and perhaps "postpositivism" and "constructivism"). Based on the abstracts, list points that are made in support of and in opposition to both perspectives.

3. Outline your own research philosophy. You can base your outline primarily on your reactions to the points you have read in this chapter, but try also to think seriously about which perspective seems more reasonable to you.

4. Pair up with one other student and select one of the research articles you have reviewed for other exercises. Criticize the research in terms of its adherence to each of the eight positivist guidelines for social research, being generally negative but not unreasonable in your criticisms. The student with whom you are working should critique the article in the same way but from a generally positive standpoint,

defending its adherence to the eight guidelines but without ignoring the study's weak points. Together, write a summary of the study's strong and weak points, or conduct a debate in class.

5. Criticize one of the research articles you have reviewed for other exercises in terms of its adherence to each of the eight positivist guidelines for social research. Discuss the extent to which the study adhered to each guideline and indicate what problem or problems might have occurred in the research as a result of deviation from the guidelines.

WEB EXERCISES

1. You can read a brief summary of three of the four theoretical perspectives introduced in this chapter at http://ryoung001.homestead.com/AssessingTheory.html. Which description do you find most appealing? Can you find other sites that take more partisan positions in favor of one theory?

2. There are many interesting Web sites that discuss philosophy of science issues. Read the summary of the difference between positivism and interpretivism at http://www.suite101.com/article.cfm/374/11517. What does this article add to your understanding of the philosophical alternatives?

SPSS EXERCISES

1. To what extent does the American population interpret social issues in a way that is consistent with conflict theory? Examine the distribution of responses to the questions about the labor movement, subjective class, and feelings about the job:
    a. Click on *Analyze\Descriptive Statistics\Frequencies.*
    b. Highlight the following variables and click them into the *Variable*(s) box:
        CONLABOR, CLASS, JOBLOSE, SATJOB, SATFIN.
    c. Examine the Valid Percents and then write a brief description of American attitudes related to class.
    d. Write a conclusion in which you explain how your findings might be viewed as relevant for conflict theory.

2. Repeat the process in Exercise 1 for the other three theoretical perspectives. Feel free to substitute other variables that you think are relevant to each theory. Here are some suggestions, but realize that you'll have to be a bit creative in linking the theories to these variables:
    Functionalism: RELIG, ATTEND, RELITEN. (Remember Durkheim on suicide and social bonds?)
    Symbolic interactionism: SOCFREND, SOCREL, SOCCOMMUN, FEAR, EMAILHR.
    Rational choice: NOGOVT, WLTHPOV, CHOICE, CNTRLIFE.

DEVELOPING A RESEARCH PROPOSAL

1. Which general theoretical perspective do you believe is most appropriate to guide your proposed research? Write two paragraphs in which you: (1) summarize the major tenets of the theoretical perspective you choose; and (2) explain the relevance of this perspective to your research problem.

2. What middle range theory (or theories) could be used to develop specific hypotheses for your research? You may need to search the literature to answer this question.

3. Which research philosophy is most appropriate for your project? Write a paragraph in which you explain your choice. Start the paragraph with the following statement: "My research approach will reflect a [*your choice*] perspective. I believe this perspective is most appropriate for my investigation because . . ."

Chapter 4

CONCEPTUALIZATION AND MEASUREMENT

Concepts

Conceptualization in Practice
  Substance Abuse
  Alcohol Effects
  Poverty
From Concepts to Observations

Measurement Operations

Using Available Data
Constructing Questions
  Single Questions
  Question Sets
  Indexes and Scales
Making Observations
Collecting Unobtrusive Measures
Combining Measurement Operations

Levels of Measurement

Nominal Level of Measurement
Ordinal Level of Measurement

Interval Level of Measurement
Ratio Level of Measurement
The Case of Dichotomies
Comparison of Levels of Measurement

Evaluating Measures

Measurement Validity
  Face Validity
  Content Validity
  Criterion Validity
  Construct Validity
Reliability
  Test-Retest Reliability
  *Interitem Reliability (Internal
    Consistency)*
  Alternate-Forms Reliability
  Interobserver Reliability
Ways to Improve Reliability and Validity
Measurement in Qualitative Research

Conclusions

Substance abuse is a social problem of remarkable proportions, both on and off campus. Alcohol is involved in about half of all fatal traffic crashes and more than 1 million arrests are made annually for driving under the influence. Four in ten college students binge drink (Wechsler, Lee, Kuo, Seibring, Nelson, & Lee, 2002), and about one in three could be diagnosed as alcohol abusers (Knight, Wechsler, Kuo, Seibring, Weitzman, & Schuckit, 2002).

Drinking is a factor in as many as two-thirds of on-campus sexual assaults (National Institute of Alcohol Abuse and Alcoholism [NIAAA], 1995). All told, the annual costs of prevention and treatment for alcohol and drug abuse exceed $4 billion (Gruenewald, Treno, Taff, & Klitzner, 1997).

Whether your goal is to learn how society works, to deliver useful services, to design effective social policies, or simply to try to protect yourself and your peers, at some point you might decide to read some of the research literature on substance abuse. Perhaps you will even attempt to design your own study of it. Every time you begin to review or design relevant research, you will have to answer two questions: "What is meant by 'substance abuse' in this research?" (the conceptualization issue) and "How was substance abuse measured?" (the operationalization issue). Both types of questions must be answered when we evaluate prior research and both types of questions must be kept in the forefront when we design new research. It is only when we conclude that a study used valid measures of its key concepts that we can have some hope that its conclusions are valid.

In this chapter, I first address the issue of conceptualization, using substance abuse and related concepts as examples. I then focus on measurement, reviewing first how measures of substance abuse have been constructed using such operations as available data, questions, observations, and less direct and obtrusive measures. I then discuss the different possible levels of measurement and methods for assessing the validity and reliability of measures. The final topic is to consider the unique insights that qualitative methods can add to the measurement process. By the chapter's end, you should have a good understanding of measurement, the first of the three legs on which a research project's validity rests.

CONCEPTS

Although the drinking statistics sound scary, we need to be clear about what they mean before we march off to a Temperance Society meeting. What, after all, is binge drinking? The definition that Wechsler et al. (2002:205) used is "heavy episodic drinking." More specifically, "[w]e defined binge drinking as the consumption of at least 5 drinks in a row for men or 4 drinks in a row for women during the 2 weeks before completion of the questionnaire."

Is this what you call "binge drinking"? This definition is widely accepted among social researchers, so when they use the term they can understand each other. So "binge drinking" is a **concept**—a mental image that summarizes a set of similar observations, feelings, or ideas. In order to make that concept useful in research (and even in ordinary discourse), we have to define it.

Concept   A mental image that summarizes a set of similar observations, feelings, or ideas.

This may seem obvious, but only until you realize that many concepts are used without consistent definition, that definitions are themselves often the object of intense debate, and that the meanings of concepts may change over time. For example, when a *New York Times* article (Stille, 2000) announced a rise in the "social health" of the United States, after a precipitous decline in the 1970s and 1980s, we don't know whether we should feel relieved or disinterested. In fact, the authorities on the subject didn't even agree about what the term meant: lessening of social and economic inequalities (Marc Miringoff) or clear moral values (William J. Bennett). Most agreed that "social health" has to do with "things that are not measured in the gross national product" and that it is "a more subtle and more meaningful way of measuring what's important to [people]" (Stille, 2000:A19), but the sparks flew over whose **conceptualization** of social health would prevail.

Conceptualization   The process of specifying what we mean by a term. In deductive research, conceptualization helps to translate portions of an abstract theory into specific variables that can be used in testable hypotheses. In inductive research, conceptualization is an important part of the process used to make sense of related observations.

"Prejudice" is an interesting example of a concept whose meaning has changed over time. As presented in a widely cited book by Harvard psychologist Gordon Allport (1954), during the 1950s many people conceptualized prejudice as referring to "faulty generalizations" about other groups. The idea was that these cognitive "errors in reasoning" could be improved with better education. But by the end of the 1960s, this one-size-fits-all concept was replaced with more specific terms like racism, sexism, and anti-Semitism that were conceptualized as referring to negative dispositions about specific groups that "ran too deep to be accessible to cursory introspection" (Nunberg, 2002). The "isms" were conceived as both more serious and less easily acknowledged than "prejudice."

Concepts like "social health," "prejudice," and even "binge drinking" require an explicit definition before they are used in research because we cannot be certain that all readers will share a particular definition or that the current meaning of the concept is the same as it was when previous research was published. It is especially important to define clearly concepts that are abstract or unfamiliar. When we refer to concepts like "social control," "anomie," or "social health," we cannot count on others knowing exactly what we mean. Even experts may disagree about the meaning of frequently used concepts if they base their conceptualizations on different theories. That's OK. The point is not that there can be only one definition of a concept, but that we have to specify clearly what we mean when we use a concept and we must expect others to do the same.

Conceptualization in Practice

If we are to do an adequate job of conceptualizing, we must do more than just think up some definition, any definition, for our concepts. We have to turn to social theory and prior research to review appropriate definitions. We may need to distinguish subconcepts, or dimensions, of the concept. We should understand how the definition we choose fits within the theoretical framework guiding the research and what assumptions underlie this framework.

Substance Abuse

What observations or images should we associate with the concept "substance abuse"? Someone leaning against a building with a liquor bottle, barely able to speak coherently?

College students drinking heavily at a party? Someone in an Alcoholics Anonymous group drinking one beer? A 10-year-old boy drinking a small glass of wine in an alley? A 10-year-old boy drinking a small glass of wine at the dinner table in France? Do all of these images share something in common that we should define as substance abuse for the purposes of a particular research study? Do some of them? Should we take into account cultural differences? Social situations? Physical tolerance for alcohol? Individual standards?

Many researchers now use the definition of substance abuse contained in the *Diagnostic and Statistical Manual, IV (DSM-IV)* of the American Psychiatric Association (Mueser et al., 1990:33): "repeated use of a substance to the extent that it interferes with adequate social, vocational, or self-care functioning." But in spite of its popularity among professionals, we cannot judge the *DSM-IV* definition of substance abuse as "correct" or "incorrect." Each researcher has the right to conceptualize as he or she sees fit. However, we can say that the *DSM-IV* definition of substance abuse is useful, in part because it has been very widely adopted. It also is stated in clear and precise language that should minimize differences in interpretation and maximize understanding.

This clarity should not prevent us from recognizing that the definition reflects a particular theoretical orientation. *DSM-IV* applies a medical "disease model" to mental illness (which is conceptualized, in *DSM-IV*, to include substance abuse). This theoretical model emphasizes behavioral and biological criteria, instead of the social expectations that are emphasized in a social model of substance abuse. How we conceptualize reflects how we theorize.

And just as we can connect concepts to theory, we can connect them to other concepts. What this means is that the definition of any one concept rests on a shared understanding of the other terms used in the definition. So if our audience does not already have a shared understanding of terms like "adequate social functioning," "self-care functioning," and "repeated use," we must also define these terms before we are finished with the process of defining substance abuse.

Alcohol Effects

Many concepts have multiple dimensions, bringing together several related concepts under a larger conceptual umbrella. We can think of alcohol abuse and drug abuse as subconcepts, or dimensions, of the larger concept of substance abuse. What about the effects of alcohol? Do you think they are all similar, or have you observed both positive and negative effects (or experienced them yourself)? D. J. Rohsenow (1983) focused on the concept of the effects people expected alcohol to have. Based on earlier work by S. A. Brown and his colleagues (1980), he identified seven different types of effects: global positive effects, social and physical pleasure, sexual enhancement, power and aggression, social expressiveness, relaxation and tension reduction, cognitive and physical impairment, and careless unconcern. With this multidimensional conception of the effects of alcohol, Rohsenow and colleagues (1984; 1992) developed a more precise understanding of the role of the perceived effects of alcohol on individual behavior than would have been possible if they had used a unidimensional conceptualization.

Poverty

Decisions about how to define a concept reflect the theoretical framework that guides the researchers. For example, the concept "poverty" has always been somewhat controversial, because different conceptualizations of what poverty is lead to different estimates of its prevalence and different social policies for responding to it.

Most of the statistics that you see in the newspaper about the poverty rate reflect a conception of poverty that was formalized by Mollie Orshansky of the Social Security Administration in 1965 and subsequently adopted by the federal government and many researchers (Putnam, 1977). She defined poverty in terms of what is called an *absolute* standard, based on the amount of money required to purchase an emergency diet that is estimated to be nutritionally adequate for about 2 months. The idea is that people are truly poor if they can barely purchase the food they need and other essential goods. This poverty standard is adjusted for household size and composition (number of children and adults), and the minimal amount needed for food is multiplied by three because a 1955 survey indicated that poor families spend about one-third of their incomes on food (Orshansky, 1977).

Some social scientists disagree with the absolute standard and have instead urged adoption of a *relative* poverty standard. They identify the poor as those in the lowest 5th or 10th of the income distribution or as those having some fraction of the average income. The idea behind this relative conception is that poverty should be defined in terms of what is normal in a given society at a particular time.

Some social scientists prefer yet another conception of poverty. With the *subjective* approach, poverty is defined as what people think would be the minimal income they need to make ends meet. Of course, many have argued that this approach is influenced too much by the different standards that people use to estimate what they "need" (Ruggles, 1990:20–23).

More recently, some social scientists have proposed increasing the absolute standard for poverty so that it reflects what a low-income family must spend to maintain a "socially acceptable standard of living" that allows for a telephone, house repairs, and decent clothes (Uchitelle, 1999).

Which do you think is a more reasonable approach to defining poverty—an absolute standard, a relative standard, a subjective standard, or a higher standard? Our understanding of the concept of poverty is sharpened when we consider the theoretical ramifications of these alternative definitions.

From Concepts to Observations

Identifying the concepts we will study, specifying dimensions of these concepts, and defining their meaning only begins the process of connecting our ideas to concrete observations. If we are to conduct empirical research involving a concept, we must be able to distinguish it in the world around us and determine how it may change over time or differ between persons or locations. **Operationalization** is the process of connecting concepts to observations. You can think of it as the empirical counterpart of the process of conceptualization. When we conceptualize, we specify what we mean by a term (see Exhibit 4.1). When we operationalize, we identify specific observations that we will take to indicate that concept in empirical reality.

Operationalization   The process of specifying the operations that will indicate the value of cases on a variable.

Exhibit 4.1 Conceptualization and Operationalization of Social Control

Concept	Definition	Types	Possible operational indicators
Social Control	The normative aspect of social life*	Law Etiquette Customs Bureaucracy Psychiatric treatment	Legal rules; punishments; police stops Handbooks Gossip; aphorisms Official conduct rules; promotion procedures Rules for dangerousness; competency hearings

Source: Based on Black, 1976.

*Specifically, "the definition of deviant behavior and the response to it" (p. 2).

Exhibit 4.1 illustrates conceptualization and operationalization by using the concept of "social control," which Donald Black (1984) defines as "all of the processes by which people define and respond to deviant behavior." What observations can indicate this conceptualization of social control? Billboards that condemn drunk driving? Proportion of persons arrested in a community? Average length of sentences for crimes? Types of bystander reactions to public intoxication? Gossiping among neighbors? Some combination of these? Should we distinguish formal social control like laws and police actions from informal types of social control like social stigma? If we are to conduct research on the concept of social control, we must identify empirical indicators that are pertinent to our theoretical concerns.

Concepts vary in their level of abstraction, and this in turn affects how readily we can specify the indicators pertaining to the concept. We may not think twice before we move from a conceptual definition of "age" as time elapsed since birth to the concrete indicator "years since birth." "Binge drinking" is also a relatively concrete concept, but it requires a bit more thought. As you've seen, most researchers define binge drinking conceptually as heavy episodic drinking and operationally as drinking five or more drinks in a row (for men) (Wechsler et al., 2002:205). That's pretty straightforward, although we still need to specify the questions that will be used to determine frequency of drinking. A very abstract concept like social status may have a clear role in social theory but a variety of meanings in different social settings. Indicators that pertain to social status may include level of esteem in a group, extent of influence over others, level of income and education, or number of friends. It is very important to specify what we mean by an abstract concept like social status in a particular study and to choose appropriate indicators to represent this meaning.

You have already learned in Chapter 2 that variables are phenomena that vary (and I hope you have practiced using the language of variables and hypotheses with the interactive exercises on the CD-ROM). Where do variables fit in the continuum from concepts to operational indicators that is represented in Exhibit 4.1? Think of it this way: Usually, the term *variable* is used to refer to some specific aspect of a concept that varies, and for which we then have to select even more concrete indicators. For example, research on the *concept* of social support might focus on the *variable* level of perceived support, and we might then select as our *indicator* the responses to a series of statements about social support, such as this one from Cohen et al.'s (1985:93) "Interpersonal Support Evaluation List": "If I needed a quick emergency loan of $100, there is someone I could get it from." Identifying the variables we will measure is a necessary step on the road to developing our specific measurement procedures. I'll give more examples in the next section.

However, the term *variable* is sometimes used interchangeably with the term **indicator,** so that you might find "crime rate" or "importance of extrinsic rewards" being termed as either variables or indicators. Sometimes the term *variable* is used to refer to phenomena that are more abstract, such as "alienation" or "social capital." You might hear one researcher refer to social support as one of the important concepts in a study, another refer to it as a variable that was measured, and another call it an indicator of group cohesion. The important thing to keep in mind is that we need to define clearly the concepts we use and then develop specific procedures for measuring variation in the variables related to these concepts.

Bear in mind that concepts don't necessarily vary. For example, gender may be an important concept in a study of influences on binge drinking, but it isn't a variable in a study of members of an all-male fraternity. When we explain excessive drinking in the fraternity, we might attach great importance to the all-male fraternity subculture. However, because gender doesn't vary in this setting, we won't be able to study differences in binge drinking between male and female students. So, gender will be a **constant**, not a variable, in this study (unless we expand our sample to include members of both sororities and fraternities, or perhaps the general student population).

How do we know what concepts to consider and then which variables to include in a study? It's very tempting, and all too common, to simply try to "measure everything" by including in a study every variable we can think of that might have something to do with our research question. This haphazard approach will inevitably result in the collection of some data that are useless and the failure to collect some data that are important. Instead, a careful researcher will examine relevant theories to identify key concepts, review prior research to learn how useful different indicators have been, and assess the resources available for measuring adequately variables in the specific setting to be studied.

MEASUREMENT OPERATIONS

After we have defined our concepts in the abstract—that is, after conceptualizing—and after we have identified the specific variables we want to measure or indicate, we must develop our measurement procedures. **Measurement** is a "process of linking abstract concepts to empirical indicants" (Carmines & Zeller, 1979:10). Because the goal is to achieve measurement validity, the measurement **operations** that we devise must actually measure the variables we intend to measure.

Measurement   The process of linking abstract concepts to empirical indicants.

Operation   A procedure for identifying or indicating the value of cases on a variable.

Exhibit 4.2 represents the operationalization process in three studies. The first researcher defines her concept, binge drinking, and chooses one variable—frequency of heavy episodic

Exhibit 4.2   Concepts, Variables, and Indicators

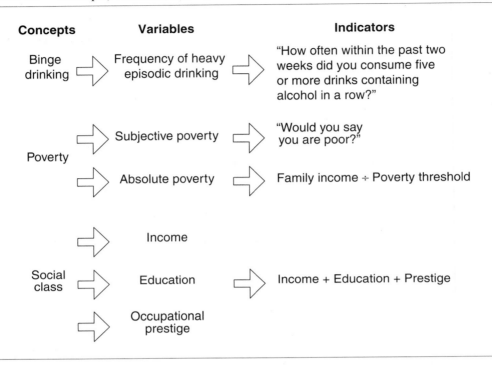

drinking—to represent it. This variable is then measured with responses to a single question, or indicator: "How often within the past two weeks did you consume five or more drinks containing alcohol in a row?" Because "heavy" drinking is defined differently for men and women (relative to their different metabolisms), the question is phrased in terms of "four or more drinks" for women. The second researcher defines her concept, poverty, as having two aspects or dimensions, subjective poverty and absolute poverty. Subjective poverty is measured with responses to a survey question: "Would you say you are poor?" Absolute poverty is measured by comparing family income to the poverty threshold. The third researcher decides that her concept, social class, is defined by a position on three measured variables: income, education, and occupational prestige.

Social researchers have many options for operationalizing concepts. Measures can be based on activities as diverse as asking people questions, reading judicial opinions, observing social interactions, coding words in books, checking census data tapes, enumerating the contents of trash receptacles, or drawing urine and blood samples. Experimental researchers may operationalize a concept by manipulating its value. For example, to operationalize the concept of "exposure to antidrinking messages," some subjects may listen to a talk about binge drinking while others do not. I will focus here on the operations of using published data, asking questions, observing behavior, and using unobtrusive means of measuring people's behavior and attitudes.

The variables and particular measurement operations chosen for a study should be consistent with the research question. If we ask the evaluative research question, "Are self-help groups more effective than hospital-based treatments in reducing drinking among substance abusers?", we may operationalize "form of treatment" in terms of participation in these two types of treatment. However, if we are attempting to answer the explanatory research question, "What influences the success of substance abuse treatment?", we should probably consider what it is about these treatment alternatives that is associated with successful abstinence. Prior theory and research suggest that some of the important variables that differ between these treatment approaches are level of peer support, beliefs about the causes of alcoholism, and financial investment in the treatment.

Time and resource limitations also must be taken into account when we select variables and devise measurement operations. For many sociohistorical questions (such as "How has the poverty rate varied since 1950?"), census data or other published counts must be used. On the other hand, a historical question about the types of social bonds among combat troops in 20th-century wars probably requires retrospective interviews with surviving veterans. The validity of the data is lessened by the unavailability of many veterans from World War I and by problems of recall, but direct observation of their behavior during the war is certainly not an option.

Using Available Data

Government reports are rich and readily accessible sources of social science data. Organizations ranging from nonprofit service groups to private businesses also compile a wealth of figures that may be available to some social scientists for some purposes. In addition, the data collected in many social science surveys are archived and made available for researchers who were not involved in the original survey project.

Before we assume that available data will be useful, we must consider how appropriate they are for our concepts of interest. We may conclude that some other measure would provide a better fit with a concept or that a particular concept simply cannot adequately be operationalized with the available data. For example, law-enforcement and health statistics provide several community-level indicators of substance abuse (Gruenewald et al., 1997). Statistics on arrests for the sale and possession of drugs, drunk driving arrests, and liquor law violations (such as sales to minors) can usually be obtained on an annual basis, and often quarterly, from local police departments or state crime information centers. Health-related indicators of substance abuse at the community level include single-vehicle fatal crashes, the rate of mortality due to alcohol or drug abuse, and the use of alcohol and drug treatment services.

Indicators like these cannot be compared across communities or over time without reviewing carefully how they were constructed. The level of alcohol in the blood that is legally required to establish intoxication can vary among communities, creating the appearance of different rates of substance abuse even though drinking and driving practices may be identical. Enforcement practices can vary among police jurisdictions and over time (Gruenewald et al., 1997:14).

We also cannot assume that available data are accurate, even when they appear to measure the concept in which we are interested in a way that is consistent across communities. "Official" counts of homeless persons have been notoriously unreliable because of the difficulty of locating homeless persons on the streets, and government agencies have at times resorted to "guesstimates" by service providers (Rossi, 1989). Even available data for such seemingly straightforward measures as counts of organizations can contain a surprising amount of error. For example, a 1990 national church directory reported 128 churches in a Midwest county; an intensive search in that county in 1992 located 172 churches (Hadaway, Marler, & Chaves, 1993:744). Perhaps 30% or 40% of death certificates incorrectly identify the cause of death (Altman, 1998).

Government statistics that are generated through a central agency like the U.S. Bureau of the Census are often of high quality, but caution is warranted when using official data collected by local levels of government. For example, the Uniform Crime Reports (UCR) program administered by the FBI imposes standard classification criteria, with explicit guide-lines and regular training at the local level, but data are still inconsistent for many crimes. Consider only a few of the many sources of inconsistency between jurisdictions: variation in the classification of forcible rape cases due to differences in what is considered to be "carnal knowledge of a female;" different decisions about what is considered "more than necessary force" in the definition of "strong-arm" robberies; whether offenses in which threats were made but no physical injury occurred are classified as aggravated or simple assaults. A new National Incident-Based Reporting System (NIBRS) corrects some of the problems with the UCR, but it requires much more training and documentation and has not yet been widely used (Mosher, Miethe, & Phillips, 2002:65–72).

In some cases, problems with an available indicator can be lessened by selecting a more precise indicator. For example, the number of single-vehicle nighttime crashes, whether fatal or not, is a more specific indicator of the frequency of drinking and driving than just the number of single-vehicle fatal accidents (Gruenewald et al., 1997:40–41). Focusing on a different level of aggregation may also improve data quality, because procedures for data collection may dif-fer between cities, counties, states, and so on. (Gruenewald et al., 1997:40–41). It is only after such factors as legal standards, enforcement practices, and measurement procedures have been taken into account that comparisons among communities become credible.

The Inter-University Consortium for Political and Social Research (ICPSR) makes avail-able to university and other researchers extensive archives of government statistics, survey datasets, and other data from social science research. One of its most popular survey datasets is the General Social Survey (GSS). The GSS is administered regularly to a sample of more than 1,500 Americans (annually until 1994, biennially since then). GSS questions vary from year to year, but an unchanging core of questions includes measures of political attitudes, occupation and income, social activities, substance abuse, and many other variables of inter-est to social scientists. However, when researchers use previously collected survey data, they must be sure to consider carefully whether the original questions are sufficiently close to the measures they need for their new research question.

Constructing Questions

Asking people questions is the most common and probably the most versatile operation for measuring social variables. Most concepts about individuals can be defined in such a way that measurement with one or more questions becomes an option. We associate ques-tions with survey research, but questions are also often the basis of measures used in social experiments and in qualitative research. In this section I'll introduce some options for writing single questions, explain why single questions can be inadequate measures of some concepts, and then examine measurement approaches that rely on multiple questions to measure a concept.

Of course, in spite of the fact that questions are, in principle, a straightforward and efficient means to measure individual characteristics, facts about events, level of knowledge, and opinions of any sort, they can easily result in misleading or inappropriate answers. Memories and perceptions of the events about which we might like to ask can be limited and some respondents may intentionally give misleading answers. For these reasons, all questions proposed for a study must be screened carefully for their adherence to basic guidelines and then tested and revised until the researcher feels some confidence that they will be clear to the intended respondents and likely to measure the intended concept (Fowler, 1995). Alternative measurement approaches will be needed when such confidence cannot be achieved.

Specific guidelines for reviewing questions are presented in Chapter 8; here my focus is on the different types of questions used in social research.

Single Questions

Measuring variables with single questions is very popular. Public opinion polls based on answers to single questions are reported frequently in newspaper articles and TV newscasts: "Do you favor or oppose U.S. policy in . . . ?" "If you had to vote today, for which candidate would you vote?" Social science surveys also rely on single questions to measure many variables: "Overall, how satisfied are you with your job?" "How would you rate your current health?"

Single questions can be designed with or without explicit response choices. The question that follows is a **closed-ended question** or **fixed-choice question,** because respondents are offered explicit responses to choose from. It has been selected from the Core Alcohol and Drug Survey distributed by the Core Institute, Southern Illinois University, for the FIPSE Core Analysis Grantee Group (Presley, Meilman, & Lyerla, 1994).

```
Compared to other campuses with which you are familiar, this campus's
use of alcohol is . . . (Mark one)
____ Greater than other campuses
____ Less than other campuses
____ About the same as other campuses
```

Most surveys of a large number of people contain primarily fixed-choice questions, which are easy to process with computers and analyze with statistics. With fixed-choice questions, respondents are also more likely to answer the question that the researcher really wants them to answer. Including the response choices reduces ambiguity and makes it easier for respondents to answer. However, fixed-response choices can obscure what people really think if the choices do not match the range of possible responses to the question; many studies show that some respondents will choose response choices that do not apply to them simply to give some sort of answer (Peterson, 2000:39).

Most important, response choices should be mutually exclusive and exhaustive, so that every respondent can find one and only one choice that applies to him or her (unless the question is of the "Check all that apply" format). To make response choices exhaustive, researchers may need to offer at least one option with room for ambiguity. For example, a questionnaire asking college students to indicate their school status should not use freshman, sophomore, junior, senior, and graduate student as the only response choices. Most campuses also have students in a "special" category, so you might add "Other (please specify)" to the five fixed responses to this question. If respondents do not find a response option that corresponds to their answer to the question, they may skip the question entirely or choose a response option that does not indicate what they are really thinking.

Researchers who study small numbers of people often use **open-ended questions**— questions without explicit response choices, to which respondents write in their answers. The next question is an open-ended version of the earlier fixed-choice question:

> How would you say alcohol use on this campus compares to that on other campuses?

An open-ended format is preferable with questions for which the range of responses cannot adequately be anticipated—namely, questions that have not previously been used in surveys and questions that are asked of new groups. Open-ended questions can also lessen confusion about the meaning of responses involving complex concepts.

Mental illness, for example, is a complex concept that tends to have different meanings for different people. In a survey I conducted in homeless shelters, I asked staff whether they believed that people at the shelter had become homeless due to mental illness (Schutt, 1992). Forty-seven percent chose "Agree" or "Strongly agree" when given fixed-response choices. However, when these same staff members were interviewed in depth, with open-ended questions, it became clear that the meaning of these responses varied among staff. Some believed that mental illness caused homelessness by making people vulnerable in the face of bad luck and insufficient resources:

> Mental illness [is the cause]. Just watching them, my heart goes out to them. Whatever the circumstances were that were in their lives that led them to the streets and being homeless I see it as very sad. . . . Maybe the resources weren't there for them, or maybe they didn't have the capabilities to know when the resources were there. It is misfortune. (Schutt, 1992:7)

Other staff believed that mental illness caused people to reject housing opportunities:

> I believe because of their mental illness that's why they are homeless. So for them to say I would rather live on the street than live in a house and have to pay rent, I mean that to me indicates that they are mentally ill. (Schutt, 1992:7)

Just like fixed-choice questions, open-ended questions should be reviewed carefully for clarity before they are used. For example, if respondents are just asked "When did you move to Boston?" they might respond with a wide range of answers: "In 1944." "After I had my first child." "When I was 10." "20 years ago." Such answers would be very hard to compile. A careful review should identify potential ambiguity. To avoid it, rephrase the question to guide the answer in a certain direction, such as "In what year did you move to Boston?" Or provide explicit response choices (Center for Survey Research, 1987).

Question Sets

Writing single questions that yield usable answers is always a challenge, whether the response format is fixed-choice or open-ended. Simple though they may seem, single questions are prone to problems due to **idiosyncratic variation,** which occurs when individuals' responses vary because of their reactions to particular words or ideas in the question. Differences in respondents' backgrounds, knowledge, and beliefs almost guarantee that they will understand the same question differently. If some respondents do not know some of the words in a question, we will not know what their answers mean—if they answer at all. If a question is too complex, respondents may focus on different parts of the question. If prior experiences or culturally based orientations lead different groups to interpret questions differently, answers will not have a consistent meaning.

In some cases the effect of idiosyncratic variation can be dramatic. For example, when people were asked in a survey whether they would "forbid" public speeches against democracy, 54% agreed. When the question was whether they would "not allow" public speeches against democracy, 75% agreed (Turner & Martin, 1984:ch. 5). Respondents are less likely to respond affirmatively to the question "Did you see *a* broken headlight?" than they are to the question "Did you see *the* broken headlight?" (Turner & Martin, 1984:ch. 9).

If just one question is used to measure a variable, the researcher may not realize that respondents had trouble with a particular word or phrase in the question. One solution is to phrase questions more carefully; the guidelines in Chapter 8 for writing clear questions should help to reduce idiosyncratic variation due to different interpretations of questions. But the best option is to devise multiple rather than single questions to measure concepts.

For example, Henry Wechsler and associates (2000) operationalized binge drinking in terms of both the quantity of alcohol consumed in one episode and the recency of that episode, and they specified different quantities of alcohol for rating men and women as binge drinkers. The result was a set of four questions to assess binge drinking, measuring gender, recency of last drink, and quantity consumed. The quantity question had two versions, one for men and one for women: "Think back over the last two weeks. How many times have you had five or more drinks in a row?" (for men) or "four or more drinks in a row" (for women).

Indexes and Scales

When several questions are used to measure one concept, the responses may be combined by taking the sum or average of responses. A composite measure based on this type of sum or average is termed an **index.** The idea is that idiosyncratic variation in response to particular questions will average out, so that the main influence on the combined measure will be the concept that all the questions focus on. In addition, the index can be considered a more complete measure of the concept than can any one of the component questions.

Creating an index is not just a matter of writing a few questions that seem to focus on a concept. Questions that seem to you to measure a common concept might seem to respondents to concern several different issues. The only way to know that a given set of questions does, in fact, form an index is to administer the questions to people like those you plan to study. If a common concept is being measured, people's responses to the different questions should display some consistency. In other words, responses to the different questions should be correlated. Exhibit 4.3 illustrates an index in which responses to the items are correlated;

Exhibit 4.3   Overlapping Dimensions of a Concept

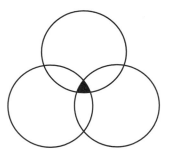

the substantial area of overlap indicates that the questions are measuring a common concept. Special statistics called **reliability measures** help researchers decide whether responses are consistent.

Because of the popularity of survey research, indexes already have been developed to measure many concepts, and some of these indexes have proved to be reliable in a range of studies. It usually is much better to use such an index to measure a concept than to try to devise questions to form a new index. Use of a preexisting index both simplifies the work involved in designing a study and facilitates comparison of findings to those obtained in other studies.

The questions in Exhibit 4.4 are a short form of an index used to measure the concept of depression, the Center for Epidemiologic Studies Depression Index (CES-D). Many researchers in different studies have found that these questions form a reliable index. Note that each question concerns a symptom of depression. People may have idiosyncratic reasons for having a particular symptom without being depressed; for example, persons who have been suffering a physical ailment may report that they have a poor appetite. But by combining the answers to questions about several symptoms, the index score reduces the impact of this idiosyncratic variation.

Another example is an index used to measure student perceptions of tolerance for substance abuse on college campuses (Core Institute, 1994), an excerpt from which is shown in Exhibit 4.5. Alone, no one of these questions would be sufficient to capture the overall tolerance of substance abuse on campus. The totality of a person's responses to these questions is likely to provide a more accurate indication of tolerance for substance abuse than would a single, general question, such as "Do students on this campus feel that drinking or using drugs is OK?"

The advantages of using indexes rather than single questions to measure important concepts are very clear, and so surveys often include sets of multiple-item questions. However, three cautions are in order:

1. *Our presupposition that each component question is indeed measuring the same concept may be mistaken.* Although we may include multiple questions in a survey in order to measure one concept, we may find that answers to the questions are not related to one

Exhibit 4.4 Example of an Index: Short Form of the Center for Epidemiologic Studies Depression Index (CES-D)

At any time during the past week... (Circle one response on each line)	Never	Some of the time	Most of the time
a. Was your appetite so poor that you did not feel like eating?	1	2	3
b. Did you feel so tired and worn out that you could not enjoy anything?	1	2	3
c. Did you feel depressed?	1	2	3
d. Did you feel unhappy about the way your life is going?	1	2	3
e. Did you feel discouraged and worried about your future?	1	2	3
f. Did you feel lonely?	1	2	3

Source: Radloff, 1977:387. Copyright 1977 by West Publishing Company/Applied Psychological Measurement, Inc.; reproduced by permission.

Exhibit 4.5 Example of an Index: Excerpt from the Index of Student Tolerance of Substance Abuse

37. **During the past 30 days, to what extent have you engaged in any of the following behaviors?** *(mark one for each line)*

Response columns: Zero times, One time, Two times, 3–5 times, 6–9 times, 10 or more times

a. Refused an offer of alcohol or other drugs
b. Bragged about your alcohol or other drug use
c. Heard someone else brag about his/her alcohol or other drug use
d. Carried a weapon such as a gun, knife, etc. (do not count hunting situations or weapons used as part of your job)
e. Experienced peer pressure to drink or use drugs
f. Held a drink to have people stop bothering you about why you weren't drinking
g. Thought a sexual partner was not attractive because he/she was drunk
h. Told a sexual partner that he/she was not attractive because he/she was drunk.

Source: Core Institute, 1994:4. Copyright 1994; reprinted with permission.

another and so the index cannot be created. Alternatively, we may find that answers to just a few of the questions are not related to the answers given to most of the others. We may therefore decide to discard these particular questions before computing the average that makes up the index.

2. *Combining responses to specific questions can obscure important differences in meaning among the questions.* My research on the impact of AIDS prevention education in shelters for the homeless provides an example. In this research, I asked a series of questions to ascertain respondents' knowledge about HIV risk factors and about methods of preventing exposure to those risk factors. I then combined these responses into an overall knowledge index. I was somewhat surprised to find that the knowledge index scores were no higher in a shelter with an AIDS education program than in a shelter without such a program. However, further analysis showed that respondents in the shelter with an AIDS education program were more knowledgeable than the other respondents about the specific ways of preventing AIDS, which were in fact the primary focus of the program. Combining responses to these questions with the others about general knowledge of HIV risk factors obscured an important finding (Schutt, Gunston, & O'Brien, 1992).

3. *The questions in an index may cluster together in subsets.* All the questions may be measuring the intended concept, but we may conclude that this concept actually has several different aspects. A **multidimensional index** has then been obtained. This conclusion can in turn help us to refine our understanding of the original concept. For example, Carlo DiClemente and colleagues (1994) sought to determine how confident individuals in treatment for alcoholism were that they could abstain from drinking in different situations that presented typical drinking cues. The 20 situations they presented were of four different types: negative affect, social/positive, physical and other concerns, or withdrawal and urges. The questions used to measure these different dimensions are mixed together in the Alcohol Abstinence Self-Efficacy Scale so that individuals completing the scale may not be aware of them (see Exhibit 4.6). However, the answers to questions representing the particular dimensions tend to be more similar to each other than to answers to questions representing other dimensions—they tend to cluster together. By creating subscales for each of these dimensions, researchers can identify not only the level of confidence in ability to resist drinking cues ("abstinence self-efficacy"), but also the types of drinking cues that are most difficult for individuals to resist.

An index may be designed explicitly to measure multiple conceptual dimensions, but the same dimensions often do not reappear in a subsequent study. The researcher must then try to figure out why: Does the new population studied view issues differently from prior populations surveyed with the index? Were the dimensions found in previous research really just chance associations among the questions making up the larger index? Have sentiments changed since the earlier studies when the multidimensional index was developed? Only after an index has been used in several studies can we begin to have confidence in its ability to represent the concept and subconcepts in which we are interested.

An index score is calculated in one of two ways: (1) as the arithmetic average response to the component questions, so that every question that goes into the index counts equally; or (2) by giving different weights to the responses to different questions before summing or averaging the responses. Such a weighted index is also termed a **scale.** The scaling

Exhibit 4.6   Alcohol Abstinence Self-Efficacy Scale (AASE)

Listed below are a number of situations that lead some people to drink.
We would first like to know:

1. How tempted you may be to drink in each situation.

Circle the number in each column that best describes the feelings of temptation in
each situation at the present time according to the following scale:

1 = Not at all tempted
2 = Not very tempted
3 = Moderately tempted
4 = Very tempted
5 = Extremely tempted

SITUATION			TEMPTED		
	Not at all	Not very	Moderately	Very	Extremely
1. When I am in agony because of stopping or withdrawing from alcohol use	1	2	3	4	5
2. When I have a headache	1	2	3	4	5
3. When I am feeling depressed	1	2	3	4	5
4. When I am on vacation and want to relax	1	2	3	4	5
5. When I am concerned about someone	1	2	3	4	5
6. When I am very worried					
7. When I have the urge to try just one drink to see what happens	1	2	3	4	5
8. When I am being offered a drink in a social situation.	1	2	3	4	5

Source: DiClemente et al., 1994:144. Copyright by Alcohol Research Documentation, Inc., Piscataway, NJ 08854.
Note: This is a partial list of questions.

procedure might be as simple as arbitrarily counting responses to one question as worth
twice or three times as much as responses to another question, but most often the weight
applied to each question is determined through empirical testing. For example, based on
Christopher Mooney and Mei Hsien Lee's (1995) research on abortion law reform, the scoring procedure for a scale of support for abortion might give a "1" to agreement that abortion
should be allowed "when the pregnancy resulted from rape or incest" and a "4" to agreement
with the statement that abortion should be allowed "whenever a woman decided she wanted
one." In other words, agreeing that abortion is allowable in any circumstance is much
stronger support for abortion rights than agreeing that abortion should be allowed in the case
of rape or incest.

Unweighted indexes are much more common than weighted indexes, but several scaling procedures have become popular at times in attitudinal research. Guttman scaling will serve as an example. Responses to a set of questions form a Guttman scale when the likelihood of respondents giving positive answers can be ordered sequentially. For example, Denise Kandel and Kazuo Yamaguchi (1993) reported in the *American Journal of Public Health* that among 12th graders in New York State schools, alcohol or cigarette use tends to precede marijuana use, which in turn tends to precede cocaine and then crack cocaine use. This implies that if we know that a student has used crack, we can assume that she has also used the other substances.

The determination that items form a Guttman scale in this way provides insight into the relationships among the items and could be used to justify a more complex scoring system that takes into account the degree of "difficulty" of each item. However, it is not clear that a more complicated scoring system, using Guttman scale criteria, results in a scale that is better in any respects than a simple summed index (Robinson, 1973). As a result, few researchers actually use this technique to weight responses.

Making Observations

Observations can be used to measure characteristics of individuals, events, and places. The observations may be the primary form of measurement in a study, or they may supplement measures obtained through questioning.

Direct observations can be used as indicators of some concepts. For example, Albert Reiss (1971a) studied police interaction with the public by riding in police squad cars, observing police–citizen interactions and recording their characteristics on a form. Notations on the form indicated such variables as how many police–citizen contacts occurred, who initiated the contacts, how compliant citizens were with police directives, and whether police expressed hostility toward the citizens.

Using a different approach, psychologists Dore Butler and Florence Geis (1990) studied unconscious biases and stereotypes that they thought might hinder the advancement of women and minorities in work organizations. In one experiment, discussion groups of male and female students were observed from behind one-way mirrors as group leaders presented identical talks in each group. The trained observers (who were not told what the study was about) rated the number of frowns, furrowed brows, smiles, and nods of approval as the group leaders spoke. (The leaders themselves did not know what the study was about.) Group participants made disapproving expressions, such as frowns, more often when the group leader was a woman than when the leader was a man. To make matters worse, the more women talked, the less attention they were given. Butler and Geis concluded that there was indeed a basis for unconscious discrimination in these social patterns.

Observations may also supplement data collected in an interview study. This approach was used in a study of homeless persons participating in the Center for Mental Health Services' ACCESS program (Access to Community Care and Effective Services and Supports). After a 47-question interview, interviewers were asked to record observations that would help to indicate whether the respondent was suffering from a major mental illness. For example, the interviewers indicated, on a rating scale from 0 to 4, the degree to which the homeless participants appeared to be responding during the interview to voices or noises that others couldn't hear or to other private experiences (U.S. Department of Health and Human Services, 1995).

Many interviews contain at least a few observational questions. Clinical studies often request a "global," or holistic, interviewer rating of clients, based on observations and responses to questions throughout the interview. One such instrument is called the Global Assessment of Functioning Scale.

Direct observation is often the method of choice for measuring behavior in natural settings, as long as it is possible to make the requisite observations. Direct observation avoids the problems of poor recall and self-serving distortions that can occur with answers to survey questions. It also allows measurement in a context that is more natural than an interview. But observations can be distorted, too. Observers do not see or hear everything, and what they do see is filtered by their own senses and perspectives. Moreover, in some situations the presence of an observer may cause people to act differently from the way they would otherwise (Emerson, 1983). I will discuss these issues in more depth in Chapter 9, but it is important to begin to consider them whenever you read about observational measures.

Collecting Unobtrusive Measures

Unobtrusive measures allow us to collect data about individuals or groups without their direct knowledge or participation. In their classic book (now revised), Eugene Webb and his colleagues (2000) identified four types of unobtrusive measures: physical trace evidence, archives (available data), simple observation, and contrived observation (using hidden recording hardware or manipulation to elicit a response). These measures can provide valuable supplements or alternatives to more standard survey-based measures because they lessen the possibility that subjects will make different statements to an interviewer than when they are not being studied and they are unaffected by an interviewer's appearance or how she asks questions. We have already considered some types of archival data and observational data, so I will focus here on other approaches suggested by Webb and his colleagues (Webb, Campbell, Schwartz, & Sechrest, 2000).

The physical traces of past behavior are one type of unobtrusive measure that is most useful when the behavior of interest cannot be directly observed (perhaps because it is hidden or occurred in the past) and has not been recorded in a source of available data. To measure the prevalence of drinking in college dorms or fraternity houses, we might count the number of empty bottles of alcoholic beverages in the surrounding dumpsters. Student interest in the college courses they are taking might be measured by counting the number of times that books left on reserve as optional reading are checked out or by the number of class handouts left in trash barrels outside a lecture hall. Webb and his colleagues (2000:37) suggested measuring the interest in museum exhibits by the frequency with which tiles in front of the exhibits needed to be replaced.

You can probably see that care must be taken to develop trace measures that are useful for comparative purposes. For instance, comparison of the number of empty bottles in dumpsters outside different dorms could be misleading; you would at least need to take into account the number of residents in the dorms, the time since the last trash collection, and the accessibility of each dumpster to passersby. Counts of usage of books on reserve will only be useful if you take into account how many copies of the books are on reserve for the course, how many students are enrolled in the course, and whether reserve reading is required. Measures of tile erosion in the museum must take into account the nearness of each exhibit to doors, other popular exhibits, and so on (Webb et al., 2000:47–48). Social variables can also be measured by observing clothing, hair length, or people's reactions to such stimuli as dropped letters or jaywalkers.

Unobtrusive measures can also be created from such diverse forms of media as newspaper archives or magazine articles, TV or radio talk shows, legal opinions, historical documents, personal letters, or e-mail messages. Qualitative researchers may read and evaluate text, as Brian Loader and his colleagues (2002) did in their study of computer-mediated social support for people with diabetes (see Chapter 1). Quantitative researchers use content analysis to measure such aspects of media as the frequency of use of particular words or ideas, or the consistency with which authors convey a particular message in their stories. An investigation of the drinking climate on campuses might include a count of the amount of space devoted to ads for alcoholic beverages in a sample of issues of the student newspaper. Campus publications also might be coded to indicate the number of times that statements discouraging substance abuse appear. With this tool, you could measure the frequency of articles reporting substance abuse–related crimes, the degree of approval of drinking expressed in TV shows or songs, or the relationship between region of the country and amount of space devoted in the print media to drug usage.

Combining Measurement Operations

Using available data, asking questions, making observations, and using unobtrusive indicators are interrelated measurement tools, each of which may include or be supplemented by the others. From people's answers to survey questions, the U.S. Bureau of the Census develops widely consulted census reports containing "available data" on people, firms, and geographic units in the United States. Data from employee surveys may be supplemented by information available in company records. Interviewers may record observations about those whom they question. Researchers may use insights gleaned from questioning participants to make sense of the social interaction they have observed. Unobtrusive indicators could be used to evaluate the honesty of survey responses.

The choice of a particular measurement method is often determined by available resources and opportunities, but measurement is improved if this choice also takes into account the particular concept or concepts to be measured. Responses to such questions as "How socially engaged were you at the party?" or "How many days did you use sick leave last year?" are unlikely to provide information as valid as, respectively, direct observation or company records. On the other hand, observations at social gatherings may not answer our questions about why some people do not participate; we may just have to ask people. Or if no record is kept of sick leaves in a company, we may have to ask direct questions.

Questioning can be a particularly poor approach for measuring behaviors that are very socially desirable, such as voting or attending church; or that are socially stigmatized or illegal, such as alcohol or drug abuse. The tendency of people to answer questions in socially approved ways was demonstrated in a study of church attendance in the United States (Hadaway et al., 1993). More than 40% of adult Americans say in surveys that they attend church weekly—a percentage much higher than in Canada, Australia, or Europe. However, a comparison of observed church attendance with self-reported attendance suggested that the actual rate of church attendance was much lower (see Exhibit 4.7). Always consider the possibility of measurement error when only one type of operation has been used. Of course, it is much easier to recognize this possibility than it is to determine the extent of error resulting

Exhibit 4.7   The Inadequacy of Self-Reports Regarding Socially Desirable Behavior: Observed
Versus Self-Reported Church Attendance

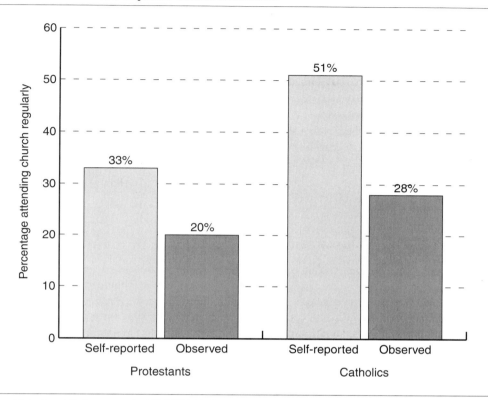

Source: Data from Hadaway et al., 1993:744–746.

from a particular measurement procedure. See the February 1998 issue of the *American
Sociological Review* for a fascinating exchange of views and evidence on the subject of
measuring church attendance.

Triangulation—the use of two or more different measures of the same variable—can
strengthen measurement considerably (Brewer & Hunter, 1989:17). When we achieve similar results with different measures of the same variable, particularly when they are based on
such different methods as survey questions and field-based observations, we can be more
confident in the validity of each measure. If results diverge with different measures, it may
indicate that one or more of these measures are influenced by more measurement error than
we can tolerate. Divergence between measures could also indicate that they actually operationalize different concepts. An interesting example of this interpretation of divergent results
comes from research on crime. Official crime statistics only indicate those crimes that
are reported to and recorded by the police; when surveys are used to measure crimes with
self-reports of victims, many "personal annoyances" are included as if they were crimes
(Levine, 1976).

Exhibit 4.8   Levels of Measurement

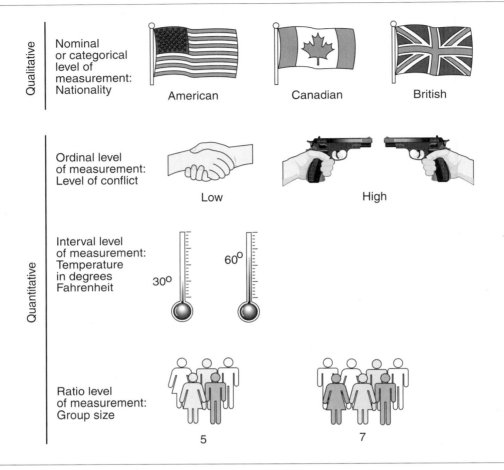

LEVELS OF MEASUREMENT

When we know a variable's **level of measurement,** we can better understand how cases vary on that variable and so understand more fully what we have measured. Level of measurement also has important implications for the type of statistics that can be used with the variable, as you will learn in Chapter 12. There are four levels of measurement: nominal, ordinal, interval, and ratio. Exhibit 4.8 depicts the differences among these four levels.

Level of measurement   The mathematical precision with which the values of a variable can be expressed. The nominal level of measurement, which is qualitative, has no mathematical interpretation; the quantitative levels of measurement—ordinal, interval, and ratio—are progressively more precise mathematically.

Nominal Level of Measurement

The **nominal level of measurement** (also called the categorical or qualitative level) identifies variables whose values have no mathematical interpretation; they vary in kind or quality but not in amount. In fact, it is conventional to refer to the values of nominal variables as "attributes" instead of values. "State" (referring to the United States) is one example. The variable has 50 attributes (or categories or qualities). We might indicate specific states with numbers, so that California might be represented by the value 1 and Oregon with the value 2 and so on, but these numbers do not tell us anything about the difference between the states except that they are different. California is not one unit more of "state" than Oregon, nor is it twice as much "state." Nationality, occupation, religious affiliation, and region of the country are also measured at the nominal level. A person may be Spanish or Portuguese, but one nationality does not represent more nationality than another—just a different nationality (see Exhibit 4.8). A person may be a doctor or a truck driver, but one does not represent three units more occupation than the other. Of course, more people may identify themselves as of one nationality than another, or one occupation may have a higher average income than another; but these are comparisons involving variables other than "nationality" or "occupation" themselves.

Although the attributes of categorical variables do not have a mathematical meaning, they must be assigned to cases with great care. The attributes we use to measure, or categorize, cases must be mutually exclusive and exhaustive:

- A variable's attributes or values are **mutually exclusive** if every case can have only one attribute.
- A variable's attributes or values are **exhaustive** when every case can be classified into one of the categories.

When a variable's attributes are mutually exclusive and exhaustive, every case corresponds to one, and only one, attribute.

I know this sounds pretty straightforward, and oftentimes it is. However, what we think of as mutually exclusive and exhaustive categories may really be so only because of social convention; when these conventions change, or if they differ between the societies in a multi-country study, appropriate classification at the nominal level can become much more complicated.

Consider the concept of race. It is a common variable in social research and has often been treated as a simple nominal-level distinction having four or five categories. But neither the number of categories nor the boundaries between them are absolute. The infamous 1896 U.S. Supreme Court decision in *Plessy v. Ferguson* defined as black any person who had as much as one black ancestor. (Homer Plessy was a Louisiana shoemaker who was told he could not ride in the "whites only" section of the train because even though his skin looked white he had one black ancestor.) Social conventions in Brazil are quite different, as the Brazilian-born director of the Brazilian-American Cultural Institute in Washington explained (Fears, 2002:A3), "'In [the U.S.], . . . if you are not quite white, then you are black.' But in Brazil . . . 'If you are not quite black, then you are white.'"

In the 2000 U.S. Census, 42% of the country's 35 million Latinos classified themselves as "some other race"—neither white nor black. In that same census, 2.4% of Americans identified themselves as multiracial—a new option. But when David Harris and Jeremiah Sim (2002) analyzed responses in a national study of youths, they found that racial self-classification can vary with social context: 6.8% classified themselves as multiracial when asked at school, but only 3.6% did so when asked at home. Even the presence of a parent during the in-home interview had an effect: Youths were less likely to self-identify as multiracial, rather than monoracial, in the presence of a parent.

And as if these operational complexities are not enough to deal with, it's important to note that there has been a highly charged political debate in recent years over these measurement issues. Should people be allowed to choose more than one racial group on the Census? (Some civil rights groups argued no [Holmes, 2001], for fear of diluting political power.) Should the concept of race be replaced with ethnicity? (Sociologist Orlando Patterson [1997] argued that the more specific distinctions associated with the concept of ethnicity were more meaningful.) Issues like these highlight the importance of informed selection of concepts, careful conceptualization of what we mean by a term, and systematic operationalization of the procedures for indicating the attributes of actual cases.

Ordinal Level of Measurement

The first of the three quantitative levels is the **ordinal level of measurement.** At this level, the numbers assigned to cases specify only the order of the cases, permitting "greater than" and "less than" distinctions. The Core Alcohol and Drug Survey (Core Institute, 1994) measures substance abuse with a series of questions that permit ordinal distinctions (see Exhibit 4.9).

Exhibit 4.9   Example of Ordinal Measures: Core Alcohol and Drug Survey

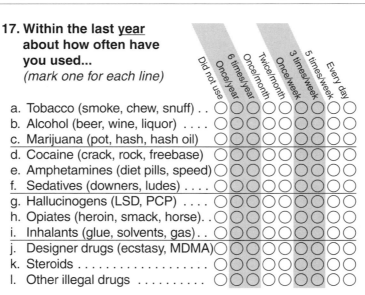

Source: Core Institute, 1994:2. Copyright 1994; reprinted with permission.

The properties of variables measured at the ordinal level are illustrated in Exhibit 4.8 (p. 106) by the contrast between the level of conflict in two groups. The first group, symbolized by two people shaking hands, has a low level of conflict. The second group, symbolized by two persons pointing guns at each other, has a high level of conflict. To measure conflict, we would put the groups "in order" by assigning the number 1 to the low-conflict group and the number 2 to the high-conflict group. The numbers thus indicate only the relative position or order of the cases. Although "low level of conflict" is represented by the number 1, it is not one less unit of conflict than "high level of conflict," which is represented by the number 2.

As with nominal variables, the different values of a variable measured at the ordinal level must be mutually exclusive and exhaustive. They must cover the range of observed values and allow each case to be assigned no more than one value. Often, questions that use an ordinal level of measurement simply ask respondents to rate their response to some question or statement along a continuum like strength of agreement, level of importance, or relative frequency. The numbers assigned to these responses can then be summed or averaged to create a multi-item index, like those in Exhibits 4.4 and 4.5 (p. 99). Sometimes just numbers are offered, without any verbal interpretation. An alternative approach is to ask respondents to rank order a set of items to indicate their agreement or preference.

Of course, an ordinal rating scheme assumes that respondents have similar interpretations of the terms used to designate the ordered responses. This is not always the case, because rankings tend to reflect the range of alternatives with which respondents are familiar (McCarty & Shrum, 2000). For example, a classic experiment shows that a square is judged larger when it is compared to many smaller squares than when it is compared to larger squares. This is particularly a problem if people in the study are from different cultures or from different backgrounds. Also, respondents with more education tend to make finer distinctions between alternatives on a rating scale.

Providing explicit "anchor points" for respondents can improve the comparability of responses to ordinal rating questions. Management faculty John McCarty and L. J. Shrum designed a procedure for rating the importance of items that is simple enough to use in mailed questionnaires. In the first step, respondents are asked to pick the most and least important items from the entire list of items. In the second step, respondents are asked to rate the importance of each item, using the same scale. Just the act of identifying the most and least important items before rating items using terms such as "very important" and "somewhat important" increases the extent to which respondents differentiate between responses.

Interval Level of Measurement

The numbers indicating the values of a variable at the **interval level of measurement** represent fixed measurement units but have no absolute, or fixed, zero point. This level of measurement is represented in Exhibit 4.8 by the difference between two Fahrenheit temperatures. Although 60 degrees is 30 degrees hotter than 30 degrees, 60 in this case is not twice as hot as 30. Why not? Because "heat" does not begin at 0 degrees on the Fahrenheit scale.

An interval-level measure is created by a scale that has fixed measurement units but no absolute, or fixed, zero point. The numbers can therefore be added and subtracted, but ratios are not meaningful. Again, the values must be mutually exclusive and exhaustive.

There are few true interval-level measures in the social sciences, but many social scientists treat indexes created by combining responses to a series of variables measured at the ordinal

Exhibit 4.10   Example of Interval-Level Measures: Core Alcohol and Drug Survey

26. How do you think your close friends feel (or would feel) about you...
(mark one for each line)

	Don't disapprove	Disapprove	Strongly disapprove
a. Trying marijuana once or twice	○	○	○
b. Smoking marijuana occasionally	○	○	○
c. Smoking marijuana regularly	○	○	○
d. Trying cocaine once or twice	○	○	○
e. Taking cocaine regularly	○	○	○
f. Trying LSD once or twice	○	○	○
g. Taking LSD regularly	○	○	○
h. Trying amphetamines once or twice	○	○	○
i. Taking amphetamines regularly	○	○	○
j. Taking one or two drinks of an alcoholic beverage (beer, wine, liquor) nearly every day	○	○	○
k. Taking four or five drinks nearly every day	○	○	○
l. Having five or more drinks in one sitting	○	○	○
m. Taking steroids for body building or improved athletic performance	○	○	○

Source: Core Institute, 1994:3. Copyright 1994; reproduced with permission.

level as interval-level measures. An index of this sort could be created with responses to the Core Institute's questions about friends' disapproval of substance use (see Exhibit 4.10). The survey has 13 questions on the topic, each of which has the same three response choices. If "Don't disapprove" is valued at 1, "Disapprove" is valued at 2, and "Strongly disapprove" is valued at 3, the summed index of disapproval would range from 12 to 36. A score of 20 could be treated as if it were four more units than a score of 16. Or the responses could be averaged to retain the original 1–3 range.

Ratio Level of Measurement

The numbers indicating the values of a variable at the **ratio level of measurement** represent fixed measuring units and an absolute zero point (zero means absolutely no amount of whatever the variable indicates). For most statistical analyses in social science research, the interval and ratio levels of measurement can be treated as equivalent, but there is an important difference: On a ratio scale, 10 is two points higher than 8 and is also two *times* greater than 5. Ratio numbers can be added and subtracted, and because the numbers begin at an absolute zero point, they can be multiplied and divided (so ratios can be formed between the numbers). For example, people's ages can be represented by values ranging from 0 years (or some fraction of a year) to 120 or more. A person who is 30 years old is 15 years older than someone who is 15 years old ($30 - 15 = 15$) and is twice as old as that person ($30/15 = 2$). Of course, the numbers also are mutually exclusive and exhaustive, so that every case can be assigned one and only one value.

Exhibit 4.8 displays an example of a variable measured at the ratio level. The number of people in the first group is 5, and the number in the second group is 7. The ratio of the two groups' sizes is then 1.4, a number that mirrors the relationship between the sizes of the groups. Note that there does not actually have to be any group with a size of 0; what is important is that the numbering scheme begins at an absolute zero—in this case, the absence of any people.

It's tempting to accept the numbers that represent the values of a variable measured at the ratio level at face value, but the precision of the numbers can't make us certain about their accuracy. Income data provided in the U.S. Census is often incomplete (Scott, 2001); the unemployment rate doesn't account for people who have given up looking for work (Zitner, 1996), and the Consumer Price Index (CPI) does not reflect the types of goods that many groups of consumers buy (Uchitelle, 1997). In each of these cases, we have to be sure that the measures that we use reflect adequately the concepts that we intend.

The Case of Dichotomies

Dichotomies, variables having only two values, are a special case from the standpoint of levels of measurement. The values or attributes of a variable such as gender clearly vary in kind or quality, not in amount. Thus the variable is categorical—measured at the nominal level. Yet we can also think of the variable as indicating the presence of the attribute "female" (or "male") or not. Viewed in this way, there is an inherent order: A female has more of the "female" attribute (it is present) than a male (the attribute is not present). So what do you answer to the test question "What is the level of measurement of 'gender'?" Nominal, of course, but you'll find that when a statistical procedure requires that variables be measured at the ordinal (or even interval) level, a dichotomy can be perfectly acceptable.

Comparison of Levels of Measurement

Exhibit 4.11 summarizes the types of comparisons that can be made with different levels of measurement, as well as the mathematical operations that are legitimate. All four levels

Exhibit 4.11 Properties of Measurement Levels

Examples of comparison statements	Appropriate math operations	Nominal	Ordinal	Interval	Ratio
A is equal to (not equal to) *B*	$= (\neq)$	✓	✓	✓	✓
A is greater than (less than) *B*	$> (<)$		✓	✓	✓
A is three more than (less than) *B*	$+ (-)$			✓	✓
A is twice (half) as large as *B*	$\times (\div)$				✓

Relevant level of measurement spans the Nominal, Ordinal, Interval, and Ratio columns.

of measurement allow researchers to assign different values to different cases. All three quantitative measures allow researchers to rank cases in order.

Researchers choose levels of measurement in the process of operationalizing variables; the level of measurement is not inherent in the variable itself. Many variables can be measured at different levels, with different procedures. For example, the Core Alcohol and Drug Survey (Core Institute, 1994) identifies binge drinking by asking students, "Think back over the last two weeks. How many times have you had five or more drinks at a sitting?" You might be ready to classify this as a ratio-level measure, but this would be true only if responses are recorded as the actual number of "times." Instead, the Core Survey treats this as a closed-ended question, and students are asked to indicate their answer by checking "None," "Once," "Twice," "3 to 5 times," "6 to 9 times," or "10 or more times." Use of these categories makes the level of measurement ordinal. The distance between any two cases cannot be clearly determined. A student with a response in the "6 to 9 times" category could have binged just one more time than a student who responded "3 to 5 times." You just can't tell.

It usually is a good idea to try to measure variables at the highest level of measurement possible. The more information available, the more ways we have to compare cases. We also have more possibilities for statistical analysis with quantitative than with qualitative variables. Thus, if doing so does not distort the meaning of the concept that is to be measured, measure at the highest level possible. Even if your primary concern is only to compare teenagers to young adults, measure age in years rather than in categories; you can always combine the ages later into categories corresponding to "teenager" and "young adult."

Be aware, however, that other considerations may preclude measurement at a high level. For example, many people are very reluctant to report their exact incomes, even in anonymous questionnaires. So asking respondents to report their income in categories (such as under $10,000, $10,000–19,999, $20,000–29,999) will result in more responses, and thus more valid data, than asking respondents for their income in dollars.

EVALUATING MEASURES

Do the operations developed to measure our variables actually do so—are they valid? If we have weighed our measurement options, carefully constructed our questions and observational procedures, and selected sensibly from the available data indicators, we should be on the right track. But we cannot have much confidence in a measure until we have empirically evaluated its validity. We must also evaluate the reliability of our measures, because reliability (consistency) is a prerequisite for measurement validity.

Measurement Validity

In Chapter 1 you learned that measurement validity refers to the extent to which measures indicate what they are intended to measure. More technically, a valid measure of a concept is one that is closely related to other apparently valid measures of the concept and to the known or supposed correlates of that concept, but that is not related to measures of unrelated concepts, irrespective of the methods used for the other different measures (adapted from Brewer & Hunter, 1989:134). The extent to which measurement validity has been achieved can be assessed with four different approaches: face validation, content validation, criterion validation, and construct validation. The methods of criterion and construct validation also include subtypes.

Face Validity

Researchers apply the term **face validity** to the confidence gained from careful inspection of a concept to see if it is appropriate "on its face." More precisely, we can say that a measure is face valid if it obviously pertains to the meaning of the concept being measured more than to other concepts (Brewer & Hunter, 1989:131). For example, a count of the number of drinks people had consumed in the past week would be a face valid measure of their alcohol consumption. Political party preference is unlikely on its face to tell us about alcohol consumption, although it would be related to political beliefs and social class.

Although every measure should be inspected in this way, face validation in itself does not provide convincing evidence of measurement validity. The question "How much beer or wine did you have to drink last week?" looks valid on its face as a measure of frequency of drinking, but people who drink heavily tend to underreport the amount they drink. So the question would be an invalid measure, at least in a study of heavy drinkers.

Content Validity

Content validity establishes that the measure covers the full range of the concept's meaning. To determine that range of meaning, the researcher may solicit the opinions of experts and review literature that identifies the different aspects, or dimensions, of the concept.

An example of a measure that covers a wide range of meaning is the Michigan Alcoholism Screening Test (MAST). The MAST includes 24 questions representing the following subscales: recognition of alcohol problems by self and others; legal, social, and work problems; help seeking; marital and family difficulties; and liver pathology (Skinner & Sheu, 1982). Many experts familiar with the direct consequences of substance abuse agree that these dimensions capture the full range of possibilities. Thus the MAST is believed to be valid from the standpoint of content validity.

Criterion Validity

When people drink an alcoholic beverage, the alcohol is absorbed into their blood and then gradually metabolized (broken down into other chemicals) in their liver (NIAAA, 1997). The alcohol that remains in their blood at any point, unmetabolized, impairs both thinking and behavior (NIAAA, 1994). As more alcohol is ingested, cognitive and behavioral consequences multiply. The bases for these biological processes can be identified with direct measures of alcohol concentration in the blood, urine, or breath. Questions about the quantity and frequency of drinking, on the other hand, can be viewed as attempts to measure indirectly what biochemical tests measure directly.

Criterion validity is established when the scores obtained on one measure can be accurately compared to those obtained with a more direct or already validated measure of the same phenomenon (the criterion). A measure of blood-alcohol concentration or a urine test could serve as the criterion for validating a self-report measure of drinking, as long as the questions we ask about drinking refer to the same period. Chemical analysis of hair samples can reveal unacknowledged drug use (Mieczkowski, 1997). Observations made by friends or relatives of substance use could also, in some limited circumstances, serve as a criterion for validating self-report substance use measures.

Criterion validation studies of self-report substance abuse measures have yielded inconsistent results. Self-reports of drug use agreed with urinalysis results for about 85% of the drug users who volunteered for a health study in several cities (Weatherby et al., 1994). On the other hand, the posttreatment drinking behavior self-reported by 100 male alcoholics was substantially less than the drinking behavior observed by the alcoholics' friends or relatives (Watson et al., 1984). Such inconsistent findings can occur because of differences in the adequacy of a measure across settings and populations. We cannot assume that a measure that was validated in one study is also valid in another setting or with a different population.

The criterion that researchers select can be measured either at the same time as the variable to be validated or after that time. **Concurrent validity** exists when a measure yields scores that are closely related to scores on a criterion measured at the same time. A store might validate a test of sales ability by administering it to sales personnel who are already employed and then comparing their test scores to their sales performance. Or a measure of walking speed based on mental counting might be validated concurrently with a stop watch. **Predictive validity** is the ability of a measure to predict scores on a criterion measured in the future. For example, a store might administer a test of sales ability to new sales personnel and then validate the measure by comparing these test scores with the criterion—the subsequent sales performance of the new personnel.

An attempt at criterion validation is well worth the effort because it greatly increases confidence that the measure is measuring what was intended. However, for many concepts of interest to social scientists, no other variable can reasonably be considered a criterion. If we are measuring feelings or beliefs or other subjective states, such as feelings of loneliness, what *direct* indicator could serve as a criterion? Even with variables for which a reasonable criterion exists, the researcher may not be able to gain access to the criterion—as would be the case with a tax return or employer document that we might wish we could use as a criterion for self-reported income.

Construct Validity

Measurement validity can also be established by showing that a measure is related to a variety of other measures as specified in a theory. This validation approach, known as **construct validity,** is commonly used in social research when no clear criterion exists for validation purposes. For example, in one study of the validity of the Addiction Severity Index (ASI), A. Thomas McLellan and his associates (1985) compared subject scores on the ASI to a number of indicators that they felt from prior research should be related to substance abuse: medical problems, employment problems, legal problems, family problems, and psychiatric problems. They could not use a criterion validation approach because they did not have a more direct measure of abuse, such as laboratory test scores or observer reports. However, their extensive research on the subject had given them confidence that these sorts of problems were all related to substance abuse and indeed, they found that individuals with higher ASI ratings tended to have more problems in each of these areas.

Two other approaches to construct validation are termed convergent and discriminant validation. **Convergent validity** is achieved when one measure of a concept is associated with different types of measures of the same concept (this relies on the same type of logic as measurement triangulation). **Discriminant validity** is a complementary approach to construct validation. In this approach, scores on the measure to be validated are compared to scores on measures of different but related concepts. Discriminant validity is achieved if the measure to be validated is not associated strongly with the measures of different concepts. McLellan et al. (1985) found that the ASI passed the tests of convergent and discriminant validity: The ASI's measures of alcohol and drug problems were related more strongly to other measures of alcohol and drug problems than they were to measures of legal problems, family problems, medical problems, and the like.

The distinction between criterion and construct validation is not always clear. Opinions can differ about whether a particular indicator is indeed a criterion for the concept that is to be measured. For example, if you need to validate a question-based measure of sales ability for applicants to a sales position, few would object to using actual sales performance as a criterion. But what if you want to validate a question-based measure of the amount of social support that people receive from their friends? Should you just ask people about the social support they have received? Could friends' reports of the amount of support they provided serve as a criterion? Are verbal accounts of the amount of support provided adequate? What about observations of social support that people receive? Even if you could observe people in the act of counseling or otherwise supporting their friends, can an observer be sure that the interaction is indeed supportive? There isn't really a criterion here, just related concepts that could be used in a construct validation strategy. Even biochemical measures of substance abuse are questionable as criteria for validating self-reported substance use. Urine test results can be altered by ingesting certain substances, and blood tests vary in their sensitivity to the presence of drugs over a particular period.

What both construct and criterion validation have in common is the comparison of scores on one measure to scores on other measures that are predicted to be related. It is not so important that researchers agree that a particular comparison measure is a criterion rather than a related construct. But it is very important to think critically about the quality of the comparison measure and whether it actually represents a different view of the same phenomenon. For example, correspondence between scores on two different self-report measures of alcohol use is a much weaker indicator of measurement validity than the correspondence of a self-report measure with an observer-based measure of substance use.

Reliability

Reliability means that a measurement procedure yields consistent scores when the phenomenon being measured is not changing (or that the measured scores change in direct correspondence to actual changes in the phenomenon). If a measure is reliable, it is affected less by random error, or chance variation, than if it is unreliable. Reliability is a prerequisite for measurement validity: We cannot really measure a phenomenon if the measure we are using gives inconsistent results. In fact, because it usually is easier to assess reliability than validity, you are more likely to see an evaluation of measurement reliability in a research report than an evaluation of measurement validity.

There are four possible indications of unreliability. For example, a test of your knowledge of research methods would be unreliable if every time you took it you received a different score even though your knowledge of research methods had not changed in the interim, not even as a result of taking the test more than once. This is test-retest reliability. Similarly, an index composed of questions to measure knowledge of research methods would be unreliable if respondents' answers to each question were totally independent of their answers to the others. The index has interitem reliability if the component items are closely related. A measure also would be unreliable if slightly different versions of it resulted in markedly different responses (it would not achieve alternate-forms reliability). Finally, an assessment of the level of conflict in social groups would be unreliable if ratings of the level of conflict by two observers were not related to each other (it would then lack interobserver reliability).

Test-Retest Reliability

When researchers measure a phenomenon that does not change between two points separated by an interval of time, the degree to which the two measurements are related to each other is the **test-retest reliability** of the measure. If you take a test of your math ability and then retake the test 2 months later, the test is performing reliably if you receive a similar score both times—presuming that nothing happened during the 2 months to change your math ability. Of course, if events between the test and the retest have changed the variable being measured, then the difference between the test and retest scores should reflect that change.

When ratings by an observer, rather than ratings by the subjects themselves, are being assessed at two or more points in time test-retest reliability is termed **intraobserver reliability** or **intrarater reliability.**

If an observer's ratings of individuals' drinking behavior in bars are similar at two or more points in time, and the behavior has not changed, the observer's ratings of drinking behavior are reliable.

One example of how evidence about test-retest reliability may be developed is a study by Linda Sobell and her associates (1988) of alcohol abusers' past drinking behavior (using the Lifetime Drinking History questionnaire) and life changes (using the Recent Life Changes questionnaire). All 69 subjects in the study were patients in an addiction treatment program. They had not been drinking prior to the interview (determined by a breath test). The two questionnaires were administered by different interviewers about 2 or 3 weeks apart, both times asking the subjects to recall events 8 years prior to the interviews. Reliability was high: 92% of the subjects reported the same life events both times, and at least 81% of the subjects were classified consistently at both interviews as having had an alcohol problem or not. When asked about their inconsistent answers, subjects reported that in the earlier interview they had simply dated an event incorrectly, misunderstood the question, evaluated the importance of an event differently, or forgotten an event. Answers to past drinking questions were less reliable when they were very specific, apparently because the questions exceeded subjects' capacities to remember accurately.

Interitem Reliability (Internal Consistency)

When researchers use multiple items to measure a single concept, they must be concerned with **interitem reliability** (or internal consistency). For example, if we are to have confidence that a set of questions (like those in Exhibit 4.4, p. 99) reliably measures depression, the answers to the questions should be highly associated with one another. The stronger the association among the individual items and the more items that are included, the higher the reliability of the index. **Cronbach's alpha** is a statistic commonly used to measure interitem reliability

Alternate-Forms Reliability

Researchers are testing **alternate-forms reliability** when they compare subjects' answers to slightly different versions of survey questions (Litwin, 1995:13–21). A researcher may reverse the order of the response choices in an index or modify the question wording in minor ways and then readminister that index to subjects. If the two sets of responses are not too different, alternate-forms reliability is established.

A related test of reliability is the **split-halves reliability** approach. A survey sample is divided in two by flipping a coin or using some other random assignment method. These two halves of the sample are then administered the two forms of the questions. If the responses of the two halves of the sample are about the same, the measure's reliability is established.

Interobserver Reliability

When researchers use more than one observer to rate the same people, events, or places, **interobserver reliability** is their goal. If observers are using the same instrument to rate the same thing, their ratings should be very similar. If they are similar, we can have much more confidence that the ratings reflect the phenomenon being assessed rather than the orientations of the observers.

Assessing interobserver reliability is most important when the rating task is complex. Consider a commonly used measure of mental health, the Global Assessment of Functioning Scale (GAFS), a bit of which is shown in Exhibit 4.12. The rating task seems straightforward, with clear descriptions of the subject characteristics that are supposed to lead to high or low GAFS scores. But in fact the judgments that the rater must make while using this scale are very complex. They are affected by a wide range of subject characteristics, attitudes, and behaviors as well as by the rater's reactions. As a result, interobserver agreement is often low on the GAFS, unless the raters are trained carefully.

Ways to Improve Reliability and Validity

Whatever the concept measured or the validation method used, no measure is without some error, nor can we expect it to be valid for all times and places. For example, the reliability and validity of self-report measures of substance abuse vary with such factors as whether the respondents are sober or intoxicated at the time of the interview, whether the measure refers to recent or lifetime abuse, and whether the respondents see their responses as affecting their chances at receiving housing, treatment, or some other desired outcome (Babor, Stephens, & Marlatt, 1987). In addition, persons with severe mental illness are, in general, less likely to respond accurately (Corse, Hirschinger, & Zanis, 1995). We should always be on the lookout for ways in which we can improve the reliability and validity of the measures we use.

Remember that a reliable measure is not necessarily a valid measure, as Exhibit 4.13 illustrates. This discrepancy is a common flaw of self-report measures of substance abuse.

Exhibit 4.12   The Challenge of Interobserver Reliability:
Excerpt from the Global Assessment of Functioning Scale (GAFS)

Consider psychological, social, and occupational functioning on a hypothetical continuum of mental health-illness. Do not include impairment in functioning due to physical (or environmental) limitations.

Code   (**Note:** Use intermediate codes when appropriate, e.g., 45, 68, 72.)

100   **Superior functioning in a wide range of activities, life's problems never seem to get out of hand, is sought by others because of his or her many positive qualities. No**
91   **symptoms.**

90   **Absent or minimal symptoms** (e.g., mild anxiety before an exam), **good functioning in all areas, interested and involved in a wide range of activities, socially effective, generally satisfied with life, no more than everyday problems or concerns** (e.g., an occasional
81   argument with family members).

80   **If symptoms are present, they are transient and expectable reactions to psychosocial stressors** (e.g., difficulty concentrating after family argument); **no more than slight impairment in social, occupational, or school functioning** (e.g., temporarily falling
71   behind in schoolwork).

70   **Some mild symptoms** (e.g., depressive mood and mild insomnia) **OR some difficulty in social, occupational, or school functioning** (e.g., occasional truancy or theft within the household), **but generally functioning pretty well, has some meaningful interpersonal**
61   **relationships.**

60   **Moderate symptoms** (e.g., flat affect and circumstantial speech, occasional panic attacks) **OR moderate difficulty in social, occupational, or school functioning** (e.g., few friends,
51   conflicts with peers or co-workers).

50   **Serious symptoms** (e.g., suicidal ideation, severe obsessional rituals, frequent shoplifting) **OR any serious impairment in social, occupational, or school functioning** (e.g., no
41   friends, unable to keep a job).

40   **Some impairment in reality testing or communication** (e.g., speech is at times illogical, obscure, or irrelevant) **OR major impairment in several areas, such as work or school, family relations, judgment, thinking, or mood** (e.g., depressed man avoids friends, neglects family, and is unable to work, child frequently beats up younger children, is
31   defiant at home, and is failing at school).

30   **Behavior is considerably influenced by delusions or hallucinations OR serious impairment in communication or judgment** (e.g., sometimes incoherent, acts grossly inappropriately, suicidal preoccupation) **OR inability to function in almost all areas** (e.g.,
21   stays in bed all day, no job, home, or friends).

20   **Some danger of hurting self or others** (e.g., suicide attempts without clear expectation of death, frequently violent, manic excitement) **OR occasionally fails to maintain minimal personal hygiene** (e.g., smears feces) **OR gross impairment in communication** (e.g.,
11   largely incoherent or mute).

10   **Persistent danger of severely hurting self or others** (e.g., recurrent violence) **OR persistent inability to maintain minimal personal hygiene OR serious suicidal act with**
1   **clear expectation of death.**

0   Inadequate information.

Source: American Psychiatric Association, 1994:46–47. Copyright 1994 by the American Psychiatric Association; reprinted with permission from the *Diagnostic and Statistical Manual of Mental Disorders,* 4th ed.

Exhibit 4.13   The Difference Between Reliability and Validity: Drinking Behavior

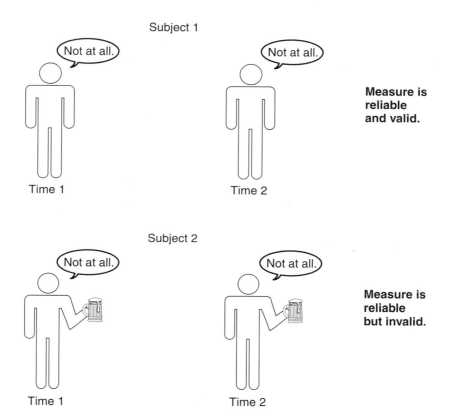

Measure: "How much do you drink?"

Subject 1

Not at all.

Not at all.

**Measure is
reliable
and valid.**

Time 1

Time 2

Subject 2

Not at all.

Not at all.

**Measure is
reliable
but invalid.**

Time 1

Time 2

The multiple questions in self-report indexes of substance abuse are answered by most respondents in a consistent way, so the indexes are reliable. However, a number of respondents will not admit to drinking, even though they drink a lot. Their answers to the questions are consistent, but they are consistently misleading. As a result, some indexes based on self-report are reliable but invalid. Such indexes are not useful and should be improved or discarded. Unfortunately, many measures are judged to be worthwhile on the basis of only a reliability test.

   The reliability and validity of measures in any study must be tested after the fact to assess the quality of the information obtained. But then, if it turns out that a measure cannot be considered reliable and valid, little can be done to save the study. Hence it is supremely important to select in the first place measures that are likely to be reliable and valid. Don't just choose the first measure you find or can think of: Consider the different strengths of different measures and their appropriateness to your study. Conduct a pretest in which you use the measure with a small sample and check its reliability. Provide careful training to ensure a consistent approach if interviewers or observers will administer the measures. In most cases, however, the best strategy is to use measures that have been used before and whose reliability and validity have been established in other contexts. But the selection of "tried and true" measures still does not absolve researchers from the responsibility of testing the reliability and validity of the measure in their own studies.

When the population studied or the measurement context differs from that in previous research, instrument reliability and validity may be affected. So the researchers must take pains with the design of their study. For example, test-retest reliability has proved to be better for several standard measures used to assess substance use among homeless persons when the interview was conducted in a protected setting and when the measures focused on factual information and referred to a recent time interval (Drake, McHugo, & Biesanz, 1995). Subjects who were younger, female, recently homeless, and less severely afflicted with psychiatric problems were also more likely to give reliable answers.

It may be possible to improve the reliability and validity of measures in a study that already has been conducted if multiple measures were used. For example, in our study of housing for homeless mentally ill persons, funded by the National Institute of Mental Health, we assessed substance abuse with several different sets of direct questions as well as with reports from subjects' case managers and others (Goldfinger et al., 1996). We found that the observational reports were often inconsistent with self-reports and that different self-report measures were not always in agreement—hence were unreliable. A more reliable measure was initial reports of lifetime substance abuse problems, which identified all those who subsequently abused substances during the project. We concluded that the lifetime measure was a valid way to identify persons at risk for substance abuse problems. No single measure was adequate to identify substance abusers at a particular point in time during the project. Instead, we constructed a composite of observer and self-report measures that seemed to be a valid indicator of substance abuse over 6-month periods.

If the research focuses on previously unmeasured concepts, new measures will have to be devised. Researchers can use one of three strategies to improve the likelihood that new question-based measures will be reliable and valid (Fowler, 1995):

- *Engage potential respondents in group discussions about the questions to be included in the survey.* This strategy allows researchers to check for consistent understanding of terms and to hear the range of events or experiences that people will report.
- *Conduct cognitive interviews.* Ask people a test question, then probe with follow-up questions about how they understood the question and what their answer meant.
- *Audiotape test interviews during the pretest phase of a survey.* The researchers then review these audiotapes and systematically code them to identify problems in question wording or delivery.

Improved measurement techniques may also result from creativity and insight about the possible strengths and weaknesses of different approaches. For example, psychologists Joshua Correll, Bernadette Park, Charles M. Judd, and Bernd Wittenbrink (2002) sought to identify unconscious biases that could influence behavior in spite of an absence of conscious prejudice. They constructed a test in which individuals played a video game in which they had to make a split-second decision of whether to shoot an image of a person who was holding what was a gun in some pictures and a camera, cell phone, or bottle in others. In this ambiguous situation, white respondents were somewhat more likely to shoot a black man than they were to shoot a white man holding a nonlethal object.

Measurement in Qualitative Research

Qualitative research projects approach measurement in a way that tends to be more inductive and holistic. Instead of deciding in advance which concepts are important for a study, what these concepts mean, and how they should be measured, qualitative researchers begin by recording verbatim what they hear in intensive interviews or what they see during observational sessions. This material is then reviewed in order to identify important concepts and their meaning for participants. Relevant variables may then be identified and procedures developed for indicating variation between participants and settings or variation over time. As an understanding of the participants and social processes develops, the concepts may be refined and the measures modified. Sharp boundaries in quantitative research between developing measures, collecting data with those measures, and evaluating the measures often do not exist.

You will learn more about qualitative research in Chapter 9, but an example here will help you to understand the qualitative measurement approach. For several months, Darin Weinberg (2000) observed participants in three drug abuse treatment programs in southern California. He was puzzled by the apparently contradictory beliefs held by participants in modern drug abuse treatment programs—that drug abuse is a medical disease marked by "loss of control" but that participation in a therapeutic community can be effective treatment. He discovered that treatment participants shared an "ecology of addiction" in which they conceived of being "in" the program as a protected environment, while being in the community was considered being "out there" in a place where drug use was inevitable—in "a space one's addiction compelled one to inhabit."

> I'm doin' real, real bad right now. . . . I'm havin' trouble right now staying clean for more than two days. . . . I hate myself for goin' out and I don't know if there's anything that can save me anymore. . . . I think I'm gonna die out there. (Weinberg, 2000:609)

Conscientiousness while participants were in the program was contrasted to personal dissolution of those out in "the life."

So Weinberg developed the concepts of "in" and "out" inductively, in the course of the research, and identified indicators of these concepts at the same time in the observational text. He continued to refine and evaluate the concept throughout the research. Conceptualization, operationalization, and validation were ongoing and interrelated processes.

CONCLUSIONS

Remember always that measurement validity is a necessary foundation for social research. Gathering data without careful conceptualization or conscientious efforts to operationalize key concepts often is a wasted effort.

The difficulties of achieving valid measurement vary with the concept being operationalized and the circumstances of the particular study. The examples in this chapter of difficulties in achieving valid measures of substance abuse should sensitize you to the need for caution. But don't let these difficulties discourage you: Substance abuse is a relatively diffi-cult concept to operationalize because it involves behavior that is socially stigmatized and often illegal. Most other concepts in social research present fewer difficulties. But even sub-stance abuse can be measured adequately with the proper research design.

Planning ahead is the key to achieving valid measurement in your own research; careful evaluation is the key to sound decisions about the validity of measures in others' research. Statistical tests can help to determine whether a given measure is valid after data have been collected, but if it appears after the fact that a measure is invalid, little can be done to correct the situation. If you cannot tell how key concepts were operationalized when you read a research report, don't trust the findings. And if a researcher does not indicate the results of tests used to establish the reliability and validity of key measures, remain skeptical.

KEY TERMS

Alternate-forms reliability
Closed-ended (fixed-choice) question
Concept
Conceptualization
Concurrent validity
Constant
Construct validity
Content validity
Convergent validity
Criterion validity
Cronbach's alpha
Dichotomy
Discriminant validity
Exhaustive attributes
Face validity
Idiosyncratic variation
Index
Indicator
Interitem reliability
Interobserver reliability

Interval level of measurement
Intrarater (or intraobserver) reliability
Level of measurement
Measurement
Multidimensional index
Mutually exclusive attributes
Nominal level of measurement
Open-ended question
Operation
Operationalization
Ordinal level of measurement
Predictive validity
Ratio level of measurement
Reliability
Reliability measure
Scale
Split-halves reliability
Test-retest reliability
Triangulation
Unobtrusive measure

HIGHLIGHTS

• Conceptualization plays a critical role in research. In deductive research, conceptualization guides the operationalization of specific variables; in inductive research, it guides efforts to make sense of related observations.

• Concepts may refer to either constant or variable phenomena. Concepts that refer to variable phe-nomena may be very similar to the actual variables used in a study, or they may be much more abstract.

• Concepts are operationalized in research by one or more indicators, or measures, which may derive from observation, self-report, available records or statistics, books and other written documents, clinical indicators, discarded materials, or some combination of these.

• Single-question measures may be closed-ended, with fixed-response choices; open-ended; or partially closed, with fixed-response choices and an option to write another response.

- Question sets may be used to operationalize a concept.

- Indexes and scales measure a concept by combining answers to several questions and thus reducing idiosyncratic variation. Several issues should be explored with every intended index: Does each question actually measure the same concept? Does combining items in an index obscure important relationships between individual questions and other variables? Is the index multidimensional?

- If differential weighting is used in the calculation of index scores, then we say that it is a scale.

- Level of measurement indicates the type of information obtained about a variable and the type of statistics that can be used to describe its variation. The four levels of measurement can be ordered by complexity of the mathematical operations they permit: nominal (least complex), ordinal, interval, ratio (most complex). The measurement level of a variable is determined by how the variable is operationalized. Dichotomies, a special case, may be treated as measured at the nominal or ordinal level.

- The validity of measures should always be tested. There are four basic approaches: face validation, content validation, criterion validation (either predictive or concurrent), and construct validation. Criterion validation provides the strongest evidence of measurement validity, but there often is no criterion to use in validating social science measures.

- Measurement reliability is a prerequisite for measurement validity, although reliable measures are not necessarily valid. Reliability can be assessed through a test-retest procedure, in terms of interitem consistency, through a comparison of responses to alternate forms of the test, or in terms of consistency among observers.

DISCUSSION QUESTIONS

1. Are important concepts in social research always defined clearly? Are they defined consistently? Search the literature for six research articles that focus on "substance abuse," "alienation," "poverty," or some other concept suggested by your instructor. Is the concept defined clearly in each article? How similar are the definitions? Write up what you have found in a short report.

2. What are some of the research questions you could attempt to answer with available statistical data? Visit your library and ask for an introduction to the government documents collection. Inspect the volumes from the U.S. Bureau of the Census that report population characteristics by city and state. List five questions you could explore with such data. Identify six variables implied by these research questions that you could operationalize with the available data. What are three factors that might influence variation in these measures, other than the phenomenon of interest? (Hint: Consider how the data are collected.)

3. The questions in Exhibit 4.14 are selected from my survey of shelter staff (Schutt & Fennell, 1992). First, identify the level of measurement for each question. Then, rewrite each question so that it measures the same variable but at a different level. For example, you might change the question that measures seniority at the ratio level (in years, months, and days) to one that measures age at the ordinal level (in categories). Or you might change a variable measured at the ordinal level, such as highest grade in school completed, to one measured at the ratio level. For the variables measured at the nominal level, try to identify at least two underlying quantitative dimensions of variation, and write questions to measure variation along these dimensions. For example, you might change the question asking, "What is your current job title?" to two questions that ask about the pay in their current job and the extent to which their job is satisfying.

What are the advantages and disadvantages of phrasing each question at one level of measurement rather than another? Do you see any limitations on the types of questions for which levels of measurement can be changed?

Exhibit 4.14   Selected Shelter Staff Survey Questions

1. What is your current job title? _____

2. What is your current employment status?
   Paid, full time 1
   Paid, part time (less than 30 hours per week) 2

3. When did you start your current position? _____ / _____ / _____
   Month   Day   Year

4. In the past month, how often did you help guests deal with each of the
   following types of problems? (Circle one response on each line.)

	Very often						Never
Job training/placement	1	2	3	4	5	6	7
Lack of food or bed	1	2	3	4	5	6	7
Drinking problems	1	2	3	4	5	6	7

5. How likely is it that you will leave this shelter within the next year?
   Very likely 1
   Moderately 2
   Not very likely 3
   Not likely at all 4

6. What is the highest grade in school you have completed at this time?
   First through eighth grade 1
   Some high school 2
   High school diploma 3
   Some college 4
   College degree... 5
   Some graduate work 6
   Graduate degree 7

7. Are you a veteran?
   Yes 1
   No 2

Source: Based on Schutt, 1988: 7-10, 15, 16.

PRACTICE EXERCISES

1. Now it's time to try your hand at operationalization with survey-based measures. Formulate a few fixed-choice questions to measure variables pertaining to the concepts you researched for Discussion Question 1, such as perceptions of the level of substance abuse in your community or expectations about future job security. Arrange to interview one or two other students with the questions you have developed. Ask one fixed-choice question at a time, record your interviewee's answer, and then probe for additional comments and clarifications. Your goal is to discover what respondents

take to be the meaning of the concept you used in the question and what additional issues shape their response to it.

When you have finished the interviews, analyze your experience: Did the interviewees interpret the fixed-choice questions and response choices as you intended? Did you learn more about the concepts you were working on? Should your conceptual definition be refined? Should the questions be rewritten, or would more fixed-choice questions be necessary to capture adequately the variation among respondents?

2. Now try index construction. You might begin with some of the questions you wrote for Exercise 1. Try to write about four or five fixed-choice questions that each measures the same concept. Write each question so it has the same response choices. Now conduct a literature search to identify an index that another researcher used to measure your concept or a similar concept. Compare your index to the published index. Which seems preferable to you? Why?

3. Develop a plan for evaluating the validity of a measure. Your instructor will give you a copy of a questionnaire actually used in a study. Pick one question, and define the concept that you believe it is intended to measure. Then develop a construct validation strategy involving other measures in the questionnaire that you think should be related to the question of interest—if it measures what you think it measures.

4. One quick and easy way to check your understanding of levels of measurement, reliability, and validity is with the short quizzes on the CD-ROM. First, select one of the Levels of Measurement options from the main menu, and then read the review information at the start of the lesson. You will then be presented with about 10 variables and response choices and asked to identify the level of measurement for each one. If you make a mistake, the program will give a brief explanation about that level of measurement. After you have reviewed with one to four of these lessons, repeat the process with one or more of the Valid and Reliable Measures lessons.

WEB EXERCISES

1. How would you define "alcoholism"? Write a brief definition. Based on this conceptualization, describe a method of measurement that would be valid for a study of alcoholism (alcoholism as you define it). Now go to the Center of Alcohol Studies (CAS) home page at http://www.rci.rutgers.edu/~cas2. Choose "Library & Information," then "Online Resources." Choose "Other Related Internet Links," followed by "National Council on Alcohol and Drug Dependence." Choose "Facts," then "Medical/Scientific Information," and finally "Definition of Alcoholism."

What is the definition of alcoholism used by the National Council on Alcohol and Drug Dependence (NCADD)? How is "alcoholism" conceptualized? Based on this conceptualization, give an example of one method that would be a valid measurement in a study of alcoholism.

Now look at some of the other related links accessible from the CAS and NCADD Web sites. What are some of the different conceptualizations of alcoholism that you find? How does the chosen conceptualization affect one's choice of methods of measurement?

2. What are the latest findings about student substance abuse from the Harvard School of Public Health? Check out http://www.hsph.harvard.edu/cas/ and write up a brief report.

3. Compare two different measures of substance abuse. A site maintained by the National Institute on Alcoholism and Alcohol Abuse (http://www.niaaa.nih.gov) provides many of the most popular measures. Pick two of them. What concept of substance abuse is reflected in each measure? Is either measure multidimensional? What do you think the relative advantages of each measure might be? What evidence is provided about their reliability and validity? What other test of validity would you suggest?

SPSS EXERCISES

1. View the variable information for the variables AGE, CHILDS, PARTYID, SOCBAR, HHRACE, CONGOVT, and INCOME98. Click on the "variable list" icon or choose *Utilities|Variables* from the menu. Choose PARTYID, then SOCBAR. At which levels (nominal/categorical, ordinal, interval, ratio) are each of these variables measured? (By the way, DK means "Don't Know," NA means "No Answer," and NAP means "Not Applicable.")

2. Review the actual questions used to measure four of the variables in Question 1 or in your hypotheses in Chapter 2's exercises. You can find most GSS questions at the following Web site: http://www.icpsr.umich.edu:8080/GSS/homepage.htm.

Name the variable that you believe each question measures. Discuss the face validity and content validity of each question as a measure of its corresponding variable. Explain why you conclude that each measure is valid or not.

3. CONGOVT is part of an index involving the following question: How much confidence do you have in . . . :

	Complete confidence	A great deal of confidence	Some confidence	Very little confidence	No confidence at all
a. Government departments	1	2	3	4	5
b. United States Supreme Court	1	2	3	4	5
c. Organized labor	1	2	3	4	5

Now answer the following questions:
    a. What is the concept being measured by this index?
    b. Do you agree that each of these variables belongs in the index? Explain.
    c. What additional variables would you like to see included in this index?

DEVELOPING A RESEARCH PROPOSAL

At this point you can begin the processes of conceptualization and operationalization. You'll need to assume that your primary research method will be conducting a survey.

1. List at least 10 variables that will be measured in your research. No more than two of these should be sociodemographic indicators like race or age. The inclusion of each variable should be justified in terms of theory or prior research that suggests it would be an appropriate independent or dependent variable, or will have some relation to either of these.

2. Write a conceptual definition for each variable. Whenever possible, this definition should come from the existing literature—either a book you have read for a course or the research literature that you have been searching. Ask two class members for feedback on your definitions.

3. Develop measurement procedures for each variable. Several measures should be single questions and indexes that were used in prior research (search the Web and the journal literature in *Soc Abstracts* or *Psych Abstracts*). Make up a few questions and one index yourself. Ask classmates to answer these questions and give you feedback on their clarity.

4. Propose tests of reliability and validity for four of the measures.

Chapter 5

SAMPLING

Sample Planning

Define Sample Components and the
    Population
Evaluate Generalizability
Assess the Diversity of the Population
Consider a Census

Sampling Methods

Probability Sampling Methods
    Simple Random Sampling
    Systematic Random Sampling
    Stratified Random Sampling
    Cluster Sampling

Nonprobability Sampling Methods
    Availability Sampling
    Quota Sampling
    Purposive Sampling
    Snowball Sampling
Lessons About Sample Quality
Generalizability in Qualitative Research

Sampling Distributions

Estimating Sampling Error
Determining Sample Size

Conclusions

$\mathbf{A}$ common technique in journalism is to put a "human face" on a story. For instance, a *Boston Globe* reporter (Abel, 2002) interviewed a participant for a story about a substance abuse program at a homeless shelter. "Ron," had ranked seventh in his suburban high school class, played three varsity sports, was president of his college fraternity, married, built himself a three-story Colonial, and seemed ready to take over his father's engineering firm. But his father was an alcoholic, and had moved his family 12 times before Ron was 13. Ron had started drinking at age 10, and after college he drank every day. The alcoholism worsened and extended to drug use. Ron's wife left, his father fired him, and he lost his home. His only goal was "finding his next fix."

It is a tragic story and, together with two other such stories in the article, provides a compelling rationale for the treatment program offered at the shelter, but we don't know whether these three participants are like most program participants, most homeless persons in Boston, or most homeless persons throughout the United States—or whether they are just a few people who caught the eye of this one reporter. In other words, we don't know how generalizable their stories are, and if we don't have confidence in generalizability, then the validity of this account of how program participants became homeless is suspect. Because we don't know whether their situation is widely shared or unique, we cannot really judge what the account tells us about the social world.

In this chapter you will learn about sampling methods, the procedures that primarily determine the generalizability of research findings. I first review the rationale for using sampling in social research and consider two circumstances when sampling is not necessary. The chapter then turns to specific sampling methods and when they are most appropriate, using examples from research on homelessness. This section is followed by a section on sampling distributions, which introduces you to the logic of statistical inference—that is, how to determine how likely it is that our sample statistics represent the population from which the sample was drawn. By the chapter's end, you should understand which questions you need to ask to evaluate the generalizability of a study as well as what choices you need to make when designing a sampling strategy. You should also realize that it is just as important to select the "right people" or objects to study as it is to ask them the right questions.

SAMPLE PLANNING

You have encountered the problem of generalizability in each of the studies you have read about in this book. For example, Keith Hampton and Barry Wellman (1999) discussed their findings in Netville as though they were generalizable to residents of other communities; Norman Nie and Lutz Erbring (2000) generalized their Internet survey findings to the entire American adult population, and the National Geographic Society (2000) Web survey findings were generalized to the entire world. Whether we are designing a sampling strategy or evaluating someone else's findings, we have to understand how and why researchers decide to sample and what the consequences of these decisions are for the generalizability of the study's findings.

Define Sample Components and the Population

Let's say that we are designing a survey about adult homeless persons in one city. We don't have the time or resources to study the entire adult **population** of the city, even though it comprises the set of individuals or other entities to which we wish to be able to generalize our findings. Even the city of Boston, which does conduct an annual census of homeless persons, does not have the resources to actually survey the homeless persons they count. So instead, we resolve to study a **sample,** a subset of this population. The individual members of this sample are called **elements,** or elementary units.

In many studies we sample directly from the elements in the population of interest. We may survey a sample of the entire population of students at a school based on a list obtained from the registrar's office. This list from which the elements of the population are selected is termed the **sampling frame.** The students who are selected and interviewed from that list are the elements.

In some studies, the entities that can easily be reached are not the same as the elements from which we want information, but include those elements. For example, we may have a list of households but not a list of the entire adult population of a town, even though the adults are the elements that we actually want to sample. In this situation, we could draw a sample of households so that we can then identify the adult individuals in these households. The households are termed **enumeration units,** and the adults in the households are the elements (Levy & Lemeshow, 1999:13–14).

Sometimes the individuals or other entities from which we collect information are not actually the elements in our study. For example, a researcher might sample schools for a survey about educational practices and then interview a sample of teachers in each sampled school to obtain the information about educational practices. The schools and the teachers are both termed **sampling units,** because we sample from both (Levy & Lemeshow, 1999:22). The schools are selected in the first stage of the sample, so they are the *primary sampling units* (and in this case they are also the elements in the study). The teachers are *secondary sampling units* (but they are not elements, because they are used to provide information about the entire school) (see Exhibit 5.1).

Population   The entire set of individuals or other entities to which study findings are to be generalized.

Elements   The individual members of the population whose characteristics are to be measured.

Sampling frame   A list of all elements or other units containing the elements in a population.

Enumeration units   Units that contain one or more elements and that are listed in a sampling frame.

Sampling units   Units listed at any stage of a multistage sampling design.

It is important to know exactly what population a sample can represent when you select or evaluate sample components. In a survey of "adult Americans," the general population may reasonably be construed as all residents of the United States who are at least 21 years old. But always be alert to ways in which the population may have been narrowed by the sample selection procedures. For example, perhaps only English-speaking residents of the United States were surveyed. The population for a study is the aggregation of elements that we actually focus on and sample from, not some larger aggregation that we really wish we could have studied.

Some populations, such as the homeless, are not identified by a simple criterion such as a geographic boundary or an organizational membership. Clear definition of such a population is difficult but quite necessary. Anyone should be able to determine just what population was actually studied. However, studies of homeless persons in the early 1980s "did not propose definitions, did not use screening questions to be sure that the people they interviewed were indeed homeless, and did not make major efforts to cover the universe of homeless people." (Perhaps just homeless persons in one shelter were studied.) The result was "a collection of studies that could not be compared" (Burt, 1996:15). Several studies of homeless persons in urban areas addressed the problem by employing a more explicit definition of the population: "People are homeless if they have no home or permanent place to stay of their own (renting or owning) and no regular arrangement to stay at someone else's place" (Burt, 1996).

Even this more explicit definition still leaves some questions unanswered: What is a "regular arrangement"? How permanent does a "permanent place" have to be? In a study of

Exhibit 5.1   Sample Components in a Two-Stage Study

Sample of schools

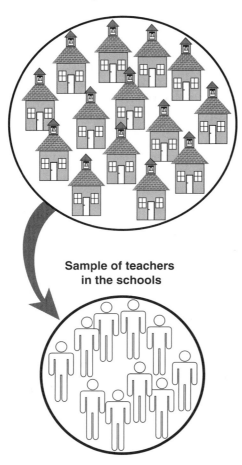

Schools are the elements and
the primary sampling unit.

**Sample of teachers
in the schools**

Teachers are the secondary sampling
units; they provide information
about the schools.

homeless persons in Chicago, Michael Sosin, Paul Colson, and Susan Grossman (1988) answered these questions in their definition of the population of interest:

> We define the homeless as: those current[ly] residing for at least one day but for less than fourteen with a friend or relative, not paying rent, and not sure that the length of stay will surpass fourteen days; those currently residing in a shelter, whether overnight or transitional; those currently without normal, acceptable shelter arrangements and thus sleeping on the street, in doorways, in abandoned buildings, in cars, in subway of bus stations, in alleys, and so forth; those residing in a treatment center for the indigent who have lived at the facility for less than 90 days and who claim that they have no place to go, when released. (p. 22)

This definition reflects accurately Sosin et al.'s concept of homelessness and allows researchers in other locations or at other times to develop procedures for studying a comparable population. The more complete and explicit the definition of the population from which a sample was selected, the more precise our generalizations can be.

Evaluate Generalizability

Once we have defined clearly the population from which we will sample, we need to determine the scope of the generalizations we will seek to make from our sample. Do you recall from Chapter 1 the two different meanings of generalizability?

Can the findings from a sample of the population be generalized to the population from which the sample was selected? Did Nie and Erbring's (2000) findings apply to the United States, National Geographic's (2000) to the entire world, or Wechsler et al.'s (2000) study of binge drinking to all U.S. college students? This type of generalizability was defined as *sample generalizability* in Chapter 1.

Can the findings from a study of one population be generalized to another, somewhat different population? Are e-mail users in Netville similar to those in other Ontario suburbs? In other provinces? In the United States? Are students similar to full-time employees, housewives, or other groups in their drinking patterns? Do findings from a laboratory study about alcohol effects at a small northeastern college differ from those that would be obtained at a college in the Midwest? What is the generalizability of the results from a survey of homeless persons in one city? This type of generalizability question was defined as *cross-population generalizability* in Chapter 1.

This chapter focuses attention primarily on the problem of sample generalizability: Can findings from a sample be generalized to the population from which the sample was drawn? This is really the most basic question to ask about a sample, and social research methods provide many tools with which to address it.

Sample generalizability depends on sample quality, which is determined by the amount of **sampling error**—the difference between the characteristics of a sample and the characteristics of the population from which it was selected. The larger the sampling error, the less representative the sample—and thus the less generalizable the findings. To assess sample quality when you are planning or evaluating a study, ask yourself these questions:

- From what population were the cases selected?
- What method was used to select cases from this population?
- Do the cases that were studied represent, in the aggregate, the population from which they were selected?

Sampling error   Any difference between the characteristics of a sample and the characteristics of the population from which it was drawn. The larger the sampling error, the less representative the sample.

But researchers often project their theories onto groups or populations much larger than, or simply different from, those they have actually studied. The population to which generalizations are made in this way can be termed the **target population**—a set of elements larger than or different from the population that was sampled and to which the researcher would like to generalize any study findings. When we generalize findings to target populations, we must be somewhat speculative. We must carefully consider the validity of claims that the findings can be applied to other groups, geographic areas, cultures, or times.

Because the validity of cross-population generalizations cannot be tested empirically, except by conducting more research in other settings, I will not focus much attention on this problem here. But I'll return to the problem of cross-population generalizability in Chapter 7, which addresses experimental research, and in Chapter 11, which discusses methods for studying different societies.

Assess the Diversity of the Population

Sampling is unnecessary if all the units in the population are identical. Physicists don't need to select a representative sample of atomic particles to learn about basic physical processes. They can study a single atomic particle, because it is identical to every other particle of its type. Similarly, biologists don't need to sample a particular type of plant to determine whether a given chemical has toxic effects on that particular type. The idea is "If you've seen one, you've seen 'em all."

What about people? Certainly all people are not identical (nor are other animals in many respects). Nonetheless, if we are studying physical or psychological processes that are the same among all people, sampling is not needed to achieve generalizable findings. Psychologists and social psychologists often conduct experiments on college students to learn about processes that they think are identical across individuals. They believe that most people would have the same reactions as the college students if they experienced the same experimental conditions. Field researchers who observe group processes in a small community sometimes make the same assumption.

There is a potential problem with this assumption, however: There's no way to know for sure if the processes being studied are identical across all people. In fact, experiments can give different results depending on the type of people who are studied or the conditions for the experiment. Stanley Milgram's (1965) classic experiments on obedience to authority, among the most replicated experiments in the history of social psychological research, illustrate this point very well. The Milgram experiments tested the willingness of male volunteers in New Haven, Connecticut, to comply with the instructions of an authority figure to give "electric shocks" to someone else, even when these shocks seemed to harm the person receiving them. In most cases the volunteers complied. Milgram concluded that people are very obedient to authority.

Were these results generalizable to all men, to men in the United States, or to men in New Haven? The initial experiment was repeated many times to assess the generalizability of the findings. Similar results were obtained in many replications of the Milgram experiments— when the experimental conditions and subjects were similar to those studied by Milgram. Other studies showed that some groups were less likely to react so obediently. Given certain conditions, such as another "subject" in the room who refused to administer the shocks, subjects were likely to resist authority.

Exhibit 5.2   Representative and Unrepresentative Samples

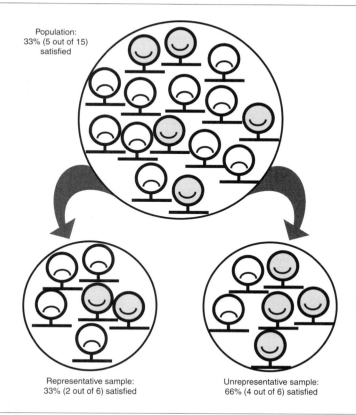

So what do the initial experimental results tell us about how people will react to an authoritarian movement in the real world, when conditions are not so carefully controlled? In the real social world, people may be less likely to react obediently as well. Other individuals may argue against obedience to a particular leader's commands, or people may see on TV the consequences of their actions. But alternatively, people may be even more obedient to authority than the experimental subjects, as they get swept up in mobs or are captivated by ideological fervor. Milgram's initial research and the many replications of it give us great insight into human behavior, in part because they help to identify the types of people and conditions to which the initial findings (lack of resistance to authority) can be generalized. But generalizing the results of single experiments is always risky, because such research often studies a small number of people who are not selected to represent any particular population.

The larger point is that social scientists rarely can skirt the problem of demonstrating the generalizability of their findings. If a small sample has been studied in an experiment or field research project, the study should be replicated in different settings or, preferably, with a **representative sample** of the population to which generalizations are sought (see Exhibit 5.2).

The social world and the people in it are just too diverse to be considered "identical units." Social psychological experiments and small field studies have produced good social science, but they need to be replicated in other settings, with other subjects, to claim any generalizability. Even when we believe that we have uncovered basic social processes in a laboratory experiment or field observation, we should be very concerned with seeking confirmation in other samples and in other research.

Representative sample A sample that "looks like" the population from which it was selected in all respects that are potentially relevant to the study. The distribution of characteristics among the elements of a representative sample is the same as the distribution of those characteristics among the total population. In an unrepresentative sample, some characteristics are overrepresented or underrepresented.

Consider a Census

In some circumstances, it may be feasible to skirt the issue of generalizability by conducting a **census**—studying the entire population of interest—rather than drawing a sample. This is what the federal government tries to do every 10 years with the U.S. Census. Censuses also include studies of all the employees (or students) in small organizations, studies comparing all 50 states, and studies of the entire population of a particular type of organization in some area. However, in comparison to the U.S. Census and similar efforts in other countries, states, and cities, the population that is studied in these other censuses is relatively small.

The reason that social scientists don't often attempt to collect data from all the members of some large population is simply that doing so would be too expensive and time-consuming—and they can do almost as well with a sample. Some social scientists do conduct research with data from the U.S. Census, but it's the government that collects the data and your tax dollars that pay for the effort. In order to conduct the 2000 census, Congress and the President allocated almost $4.5 billion (Prewitt, 2000) and the U.S. Bureau of the Census spent 12 years doing the planning (U.S. Bureau of the Census, 2000a). For the 2010 Census, the Census Bureau is already testing new approaches, including an Internet-based response option (U.S. Bureau of the Census, 2003).

Even if the population of interest for a survey is a small town of 20,000 or students in a university of 10,000, researchers will have to sample. The costs of surveying "just" thousands of individuals exceed by far the budgets for most research projects. In fact, not even the U.S. Bureau of the Census can afford to have everyone answer all the questions that should be covered in the census. So it draws a sample. Every household must complete a short version of the census (it had seven basic questions in 2000), and a sample consisting of one in six households must complete a long form (with 53 additional questions) (Rosenbaum, 2000).

Another costly fact is that it is hard to get people to complete a survey. Even the U.S. Bureau of the Census (1999) must make multiple efforts to increase the rate of response in spite of the federal law requiring all citizens to complete their census questionnaire. After the Census Bureau spent $167 million on publicity (Forero, 2000b), two-thirds of the population returned their census questionnaire in the mail, ending a three-decade decline (U.S. Bureau of the Census, 2000e). However, half a million temporary workers and up to six follow-ups were required to contact the rest of the households that did not respond by mail (U.S. Bureau of the Census, 2000b, 2000c). As the U.S. 2000 census progressed, concerns arose about underrepresentation of minority groups (Kershaw, 2000), impoverished cities (Zielbauer, 2000), well-to-do individuals in gated communities and luxury buildings (Langford, 2000), and even college students (Abel, 2000), so the Bureau conducted an even more intensive sample survey to learn about the characteristics of those who still had not responded (Anderson & Fienberg, 1999; U.S. Bureau of the Census, 2000d). The number of persons missed in the census was still estimated to be between 3.2 and 6.4 million (U.S. Bureau of the Census, 2001) and controversy continued over underrepresentation of some groups (Armas, 2002; Holmes, 2001).

The average survey project has far less legal and financial backing, and so an adequate census is not likely to be possible. Even in Russia, which spent almost $200 million to survey its population of about 145 million, resource shortages after the collapse of the Soviet Union prevented an adequate census (Myers, 2002). The census had to be postponed from 1999 to 2002 due to insufficient funds and had to rely on voluntary participation. In spite of an $8 million advertising campaign, many residents in impoverished regions refused to take part (Tavernise, 2002). In Vladivostok, "many residents, angry about a recent rise in electricity prices, refused to take part. Residents on Russian Island . . . boycotted to protest dilapidated roads" (Tavernise, 2002:A13).

In most survey situations, it is much better to survey only a limited number from the total population so that there are more resources for follow-up procedures that can overcome reluctance or indifference about participation. (I will give more attention to the problem of nonresponse in Chapter 8.)

SAMPLING METHODS

We can now study more systematically the features of samples that make them more or less likely to represent the population from which they are selected. The most important distinction that needs to be made about samples is whether they are based on a probability or a nonprobability sampling method. Sampling methods that allow us to know in advance how likely it is that any element of a population will be selected for the sample are termed **probability sampling methods.** Sampling methods that do not let us know in advance the likelihood of selecting each element are termed **nonprobability sampling methods.**

Probability sampling methods rely on a random, or chance, selection procedure, which is in principle the same as flipping a coin to decide which of two people "wins" and which one "loses." Heads and tails are equally likely to turn up in a coin toss, so both persons have an equal chance to win. That chance, their **probability of selection,** is 1 out of 2, or .5.

Probability of selection The likelihood that an element will be selected from the population for inclusion in the sample. In a census of all the elements of a population, the probability that any particular element will be selected is 1.0. If half the elements in the population are sampled on the basis of chance (say, by tossing a coin), the probability of selection for each element is one-half, or .5. As the size of the sample as a proportion of the population decreases, so does the probability of selection.

Flipping a coin is a fair way to select one of two people because the selection process harbors no systematic bias. You might win or lose the coin toss, but you know that the outcome was due simply to chance, not to bias. For the same reason, a roll of a six-sided die is a fair way to choose one of six possible outcomes (the odds of selection are 1 out of 6, or .17). Dealing out a hand after shuffling a deck of cards is a fair way to allocate sets of cards in a poker game (the odds of each person getting a particular outcome, such as a full house or a flush, are the same). Similarly, state lotteries use a random process to select winning numbers. Thus, the odds of winning a lottery, the probability of selection, are known, even though they are very much smaller (perhaps 1 out of 1 million) than the odds of winning a coin toss.

There is a natural tendency to confuse the concept of **random sampling,** in which cases are selected only on the basis of chance, with a haphazard method of sampling. On first impression, "leaving things up to chance" seems to imply not exerting any control over the sampling method. But to ensure that nothing but chance influences the selection of cases, the researcher must proceed very methodically, leaving nothing to chance except the selection of the cases themselves. The researcher must follow carefully controlled procedures if a purely random process is to occur. In fact, when reading about sampling methods, do not assume that a random sample was obtained just because the researcher used a random selection method at some point in the sampling process. Look for these two particular problems: selecting elements from an incomplete list of the total population and failing to obtain an adequate response rate.

If the sampling frame is incomplete, a sample selected randomly from that list will not really be a random sample of the population. You should always consider the adequacy of the sampling frame. Even for a simple population like a university's student body, the registrar's list is likely to be at least a bit out of date at any given time. For example, some students will have dropped out, but their status will not yet be officially recorded. Although you may judge the amount of error introduced in this particular situation to be negligible, the problems are greatly compounded for a larger population. The sampling frame for a city, state, or nation is always likely to be incomplete, because of constant migration into and out of the area. Even unavoidable omissions from the sampling frame can bias a sample against particular groups within the population.

A very inclusive sampling frame may still yield systematic bias if many sample members cannot be contacted or refuse to participate. Nonresponse is a major hazard in survey research because **nonrespondents** are likely to differ systematically from those who take the time to participate. You should not assume that findings from a randomly selected sample will be generalizable to the population from which the sample was selected if the rate of nonresponse is considerable (certainly not if it is much above 30%).

Probability Sampling Methods

Probability sampling methods are those in which the probability of selection is known and is not zero (so there is some chance of selecting each element). These methods randomly select elements and therefore have no **systematic bias;** nothing but chance determines which elements are included in the sample. This feature of probability samples makes them much more desirable than nonprobability samples when the goal is to generalize to a larger population.

Even though a random sample has no systematic bias, it will certainly have some sampling error due to chance. The probability of selecting a head is .5 in a single toss of a coin and in 20, 30, or however many tosses of a coin you like. But it is perfectly possible to toss a coin twice and get a head both times. The random "sample" of the two sides of the coin is selected in an unbiased fashion, but it still is unrepresentative. Imagine selecting randomly a sample of 10 people from a population comprising 50 men and 50 women. Just by chance, can't you imagine finding that these 10 people include 7 women and only 3 men? Fortunately, we can determine mathematically the likely degree of sampling error in an estimate based on a random sample (as we'll discuss later in this chapter)—assuming that the sample's randomness has not been destroyed by a high rate of nonresponse or by poor control over the selection process.

In general, both the size of the sample and the homogeneity (sameness) of the population affect the degree of error due to chance; the proportion of the population that the sample represents does not. To elaborate:

- *The larger the sample, the more confidence we can have in the sample's representativeness.* If we randomly pick 5 people to represent the entire population of our city, our sample is unlikely to be very representative of the entire population in terms of age, gender, race, attitudes, and so on. But if we randomly pick 100 people, the odds of having a representative sample are much better; with a random sample of 1,000, the odds become very good indeed.
- *The more homogeneous the population, the more confidence we can have in the representativeness of a sample of any particular size.* Let's say we plan to draw samples of 50 from each of two communities to estimate mean family income. One community is very diverse, with family incomes varying from $12,000 to $85,000. In the other, more homogeneous community, family incomes are concentrated in a narrow range, from $41,000 to $64,000. The estimated mean family income based on the sample from the homogeneous community is more likely to be representative than is the estimate based on the sample from the more heterogeneous community. With less variation to represent, fewer cases are needed to represent the homogeneous community.
- *The fraction of the total population that a sample contains does not affect the sample's representativeness, unless that fraction is large.* We can regard any sampling fraction under 2% with about the same degree of confidence (Sudman, 1976:184). In fact, sample representativeness is not likely to increase much until the sampling fraction is quite a bit higher. Other things being equal, a sample of 1,000 from a population of 1 million (with a sampling fraction of 0.001, or 0.1%) is much better than a sample of 100 from a population of 10,000 (although the sampling fraction is 0.01, or 1%, which is 10 times higher). The size of the samples is what makes representativeness more likely, not the proportion of the whole that the sample represents.

Polls to predict presidential election outcomes illustrate both the value of random sampling and the problems that it cannot overcome. In most presidential elections, pollsters have predicted accurately the outcomes of the actual votes by using random sampling and, these days, phone interviewing to learn whom likely voters intend to vote for. Exhibit 5.3 shows how close these sample-based predictions have been in the last 11 contests. The exceptions were the 1980 and 1992 elections, when third-party candidates had an unpredicted effect. Otherwise, the

Exhibit 5.3   Election Outcomes: Predicted[1] and Actual

Winner/Year	Polls	Result
Kennedy (1960)	51%	50%
Johnson (1964)	64%	61%
Nixon (1968)[2]	43%	43%
Nixon (1972)	62%	62%
Carter (1976)	48%	50%
Reagan (1980)[2]	47%	51%
Reagan (1984)	59%	59%
Bush (1988)	56%	54%
Clinton (1992)[2]	49%	43%
Clinton (1996)[2]	52%	50%
Bush, G. W. (2000)[2]	48%	50%

Source: Gallup Poll Accuracy Record, 12/13/00, www.gallup.com/poll/trends/
ptaccuracy.asp. Copyright 2000 by the Gallup Organization. All rights reserved.
Used with permission.

[1]Final Gallup poll prior to the election.
[2]There was also a third-party candidate.

small discrepancies between the votes predicted through random sampling and the actual votes can be attributed to random error.

The Gallup poll did quite well in predicting the result of the remarkable 2000 presidential election. The final Gallup prediction was that George W. Bush would win with 48% (Al Gore was predicted to receive only 46%, while Green Party nominee Ralph Nader was predicted to secure 4%). Although the race turned out much closer, with Gore actually winning the popular vote (before losing in the Electoral College), Gallup accurately noted that there appeared to have been a late-breaking trend in favor of Gore (Newport, 2000).

But election polls have produced some major errors in prediction. The reasons for these errors illustrate some of the ways in which unintentional systematic bias can influence sample results. In 1936, a *Literary Digest* poll predicted that Alfred M. Landon would defeat President Franklin Delano Roosevelt in a landslide, but instead Roosevelt took 63% of the popular vote. The problem? The *Digest* mailed out 10 million mock ballots to people listed in telephone directories, automobile registration records, voter lists, and so on. But in 1936, during the Great Depression, only relatively wealthy people had phones and cars, and they were more likely to be Republican. Furthermore, only 2,376,523 completed ballots were returned, and a response rate of only 24% leaves much room for error. Of course, this poll was not designed as a random sample, so the appearance of systematic bias is not surprising. Gallup was able to predict the 1936 election results accurately with a randomly selected sample of just 3,000 (Bainbridge, 1989:43–44).

In 1948, pollsters mistakenly predicted that Thomas E. Dewey would beat Harry S. Truman, based on the random sampling method that George Gallup had used successfully since 1934. The problem? Pollsters stopped collecting data several weeks before the election, and in those weeks many people changed their minds (Kenney, 1987). So the sample was systematically biased by underrepresenting shifts in voter sentiment just before the election.

Because they do not disproportionately exclude or include particular groups within the population, random samples that are successfully implemented avoid systematic bias. Random error can still be considerable, however, and different types of random samples vary in their ability to minimize it. The four most common methods for drawing random samples are simple random sampling, systematic random sampling, stratified random sampling, and cluster sampling.

Simple Random Sampling

Simple random sampling requires some procedure that generates numbers or otherwise identifies cases strictly on the basis of chance. As you know, flipping a coin and rolling a die both can be used to identify cases strictly on the basis of chance, but these procedures are not very efficient tools for drawing a sample. A **random number table,** like the one in Appendix E, simplifies the process considerably. The researcher numbers all the elements in the sampling frame and then uses a systematic procedure for picking corresponding numbers from the random number table. (Exercise 1 of the Practice Exercises at the end of this chapter explains the process step by step.) Alternatively, a researcher may use a lottery procedure. Each case number is written on a small card, and then the cards are mixed up and the sample selected from the cards.

When a large sample must be generated, these procedures are very cumbersome. Fortunately, a computer program can easily generate a random sample of any size. The researcher must first number all the elements to be sampled (the sampling frame) and then run the computer program to generate a random selection of the numbers within the desired range. The elements represented by these numbers are the sample.

Organizations that conduct phone surveys often draw random samples with another automated procedure, called **random digit dialing.** A machine dials random numbers within the phone prefixes corresponding to the area in which the survey is to be conducted. Random digit dialing is particularly useful when a sampling frame is not available. The researcher simply replaces any inappropriate numbers (those that are no longer in service or that are for businesses, for example) with the next randomly generated phone number.

The probability of selection in a true simple random sample is equal for each element. If a sample of 500 is selected from a population of 17,000 (that is, a sampling frame of 17,000), then the probability of selection for each element is 500/17,000, or .03. Every element has an equal chance of being selected, just like the odds in a toss of a coin (1/2) or a roll of a die (1/6). Thus, simple random sampling is an "equal probability of selection method," or EPSEM.

Simple random sampling can be done either with or without replacement sampling. In **replacement sampling,** each element is returned to the sampling frame after it is selected so that it may be sampled again. In sampling without replacement, each element selected for the sample is then excluded from the sampling frame. In practice it makes no difference whether sampled elements are replaced after selection, as long as the population is large and the sample is to contain only a small fraction of the population. Random sampling with replacement is, in fact, rarely used.

In a study involving simple random sampling, Bruce Link and his associates (1996) used random digit dialing to contact adult household members in the continental United States for an investigation of public attitudes and beliefs about homeless people. Sixty-three percent of the potential interviewees responded. The sample actually obtained was not exactly comparable to the population sampled: Compared to U.S. Census figures, the sample overrepresented women, people ages 25 to 54, married people, and those with more than a high school education; it underrepresented Latinos.

How does this sample strike you? Let's assess sample quality using the questions posed earlier in the chapter:

- *From what population were the cases selected?* There is a clearly defined population: the adult residents of the continental United States (who live in households with phones).
- *What method was used to select cases from this population?* The case selection method is a random selection procedure and there are no systematic biases in the sampling.
- *Do the cases that were studied represent, in the aggregate, the population from which they were selected?* The findings are very likely to represent the population sampled, because there were no biases in the sampling and a very large number of cases was selected. However, 37% of those selected for interviews could not be contacted or chose not to respond. This rate of nonresponse seems to create a small bias in the sample for several characteristics.

We also must consider the issue of cross-population generalizability: Do findings from this sample have implications for any larger group beyond the population from which the sample was selected? Because a representative sample of the entire U.S. adult population was drawn, this question has to do with cross-national generalizations. Link and his colleagues don't make any such generalizations. There's no telling what might occur in other countries with different histories of homelessness and different social policies.

Systematic Random Sampling

Systematic random sampling is a variant of simple random sampling. The first element is selected randomly from a list or from sequential files, and then every *n*th element is selected. This is a convenient method for drawing a random sample when the population elements are arranged sequentially. It is particularly efficient when the elements are not actually printed (that is, there is no sampling frame) but instead are represented by folders in filing cabinets.

Systematic random sampling requires three steps:

1. The total number of cases in the population is divided by the number of cases required for the sample. This division yields the **sampling interval,** the number of cases from one sampled case to another. If 50 cases are to be selected out of 1,000, the sampling interval is 20; every 20th case is selected.

2. A number from 1 to 20 (or whatever the sampling interval is) is selected randomly. This number identifies the first case to be sampled, counting from the first case on the list or in the files.

3. After the first case is selected, every *n*th case is selected for the sample, where *n* is the sampling interval. If the sampling interval is not a whole number, the size of the

Exhibit 5.4   The Effect of Periodicity on Systematic Random Sampling

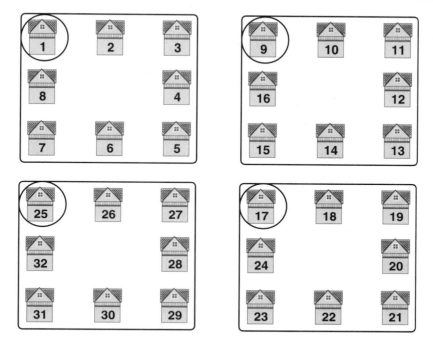

If the sampling interval is 8 for a study in this neighborhood,
every element of the sample will be a house on the northwest
corner—and thus the sample will be biased.

sampling interval is varied systematically to yield the proper number of cases for the sample. For example, if the sampling interval is 30.5, the sampling interval alternates between 30 and 31.

In almost all sampling situations, systematic random sampling yields what is essentially a simple random sample. The exception is a situation in which the sequence of elements is affected by **periodicity**—that is, the sequence varies in some regular, periodic pattern. For example, the houses in a new development with the same number of houses on each block (eight, for example) may be listed by block, starting with the house in the northwest corner of each block and continuing clockwise. If the sampling interval is 8, the same as the periodic pattern, all the cases selected will be in the same position (see Exhibit 5.4). But in reality, periodicity and the sampling interval are rarely the same.

Stratified Random Sampling

Although all probability sampling methods use random sampling, some add steps to the sampling process in order to make sampling more efficient or easier. **Stratified random**

sampling uses information known about the total population prior to sampling to make the sampling process more efficient. First, all elements in the population (that is, in the sampling frame) are distinguished according to their value on some relevant characteristic. That characteristic forms the sampling strata. Next, elements are sampled randomly from within these strata. For example, race may be the basis for distinguishing individuals in some population of interest. Within each racial category, individuals are then sampled randomly. Of course, in order to use this method more information is required prior to sampling than is the case with simple random sampling. It must be possible to categorize each element in one and only one stratum and, for proportionate to size sampling, the size of each stratum in the population must be known.

This method is more efficient than drawing a simple random sample because it ensures appropriate representation of elements across strata. Imagine that you plan to draw a sample of 500 from an ethnically diverse neighborhood. The neighborhood population is 15% black, 10% Hispanic, 5% Asian, and 70% white. If you drew a simple random sample, you might end up with somewhat disproportionate numbers of each group. But if you created sampling strata based on race and ethnicity, you could randomly select cases from each stratum: 75 blacks (15% of the sample), 50 Hispanics (10%), 25 Asians (5%), and 350 whites (70%). By using **proportionate stratified sampling,** you would eliminate any possibility of sampling error in the sample's distribution of ethnicity. Each stratum would be represented exactly in proportion to its size in the population from which the sample was drawn (see Exhibit 5.5).

In **disproportionate stratified sampling,** the proportion of each stratum that is included in the sample is intentionally varied from what it is in the population. In the case of the sample stratified by ethnicity, you might select equal numbers of cases from each racial or ethnic group: 125 blacks (25% of the sample), 125 Hispanics (25%), 125 Asians (25%), and 125 whites (25%). In this type of sample, the probability of selection of every case is known but unequal between strata. You know what the proportions are in the population, and so you can easily adjust your combined sample statistics to reflect these true proportions. For instance, if you want to combine the ethnic groups and estimate the average income of the total population, you would have to "weight" each case in the sample. The weight is a number you multiply by the value of each case based on the stratum it is in. For example, you would multiply the incomes of all blacks in the sample by 0.6 (75/125), the incomes of all Hispanics by 0.4 (50/125), and so on. Weighting in this way reduces the influence of the oversampled strata and increases the influence of the undersampled strata to just what they would have been if pure probability sampling had been used.

Why would anyone select a sample that is so unrepresentative in the first place? The most common reason is to ensure that cases from smaller strata are included in the sample in sufficient numbers to allow separate statistical estimates and to facilitate comparisons between strata. Remember that one of the determinants of sample quality is sample size. The same is true for subgroups within samples. If a key concern in a research project is to describe and compare the incomes of people from different racial and ethnic groups, then it is important that the researchers base the mean income of each group on enough cases to be a valid representation. If few members of a particular minority group are in the population, they need to be oversampled. Such disproportionate sampling may also result in a more efficient sampling design if the costs of data collection differ markedly between strata or if the variability (heterogeneity) of the strata differs.

Exhibit 5.5 Stratified Random Sampling

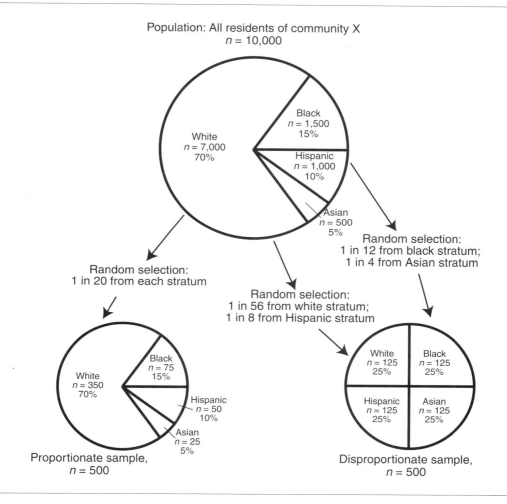

Weighting is also sometimes used to reduce the lack of representativeness of a sample that occurs due to nonresponse. Upon finding that the obtained sample does not represent the population in terms of some known characteristics such as, perhaps, gender or education, the researcher weights the cases in the sample so that it has the same proportions of men and women, or high school graduates and college graduates, as the complete population (see Exhibit 5.6). Keep in mind, though, that this procedure does not solve the problems caused by an unrepresentative sample because you still don't know what the sample composition should have been in terms of the other variables in your study; all you have done is to reduce the sample's unrepresentativeness in terms of the variables used in weighting. This may, in turn, make it more likely that the sample is representative of the population in terms of other characteristics, but you don't really know.

Exhibit 5.6   Weighting an Obtained Sample to Match a Population Proportion

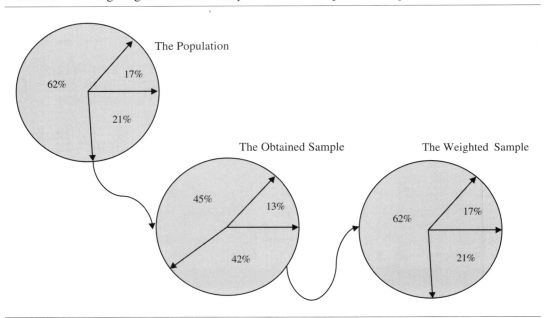

Cluster Sampling

Cluster sampling is useful when a sampling frame of elements is not available, as often is the case for large populations spread out across a wide geographic area or among many different organizations. A **cluster** is a naturally occurring, mixed aggregate of elements of the population, with each element appearing in one and only one cluster. Schools could serve as clusters for sampling students, blocks could serve as clusters for sampling city residents, counties could serve as clusters for sampling the general population, and businesses could serve as clusters for sampling employees.

Drawing a cluster sample is at least a two-stage procedure. First, the researcher draws a random sample of clusters. A list of clusters should be much easier to obtain than a list of all the individuals in each cluster in the population. Next, the researcher draws a random sample of elements within each selected cluster. Because only a fraction of the total clusters are involved, obtaining the sampling frame at this stage should be much easier.

In a cluster sample of city residents, for example, blocks could be the first-stage clusters. A research assistant could walk around each selected block and record the addresses of all occupied dwelling units. Or in a cluster sample of students, a researcher could contact the schools selected in the first stage and make arrangements with the registrar to obtain lists of students at each school. Cluster samples often involve multiple stages (see Exhibit 5.7), with clusters within clusters, as when a national sample of individuals might involve first sampling states, then geographic units within those states, then dwellings within those units, and finally individuals within the dwellings. In multistage cluster

Exhibit 5.7   Multistage Cluster Sampling

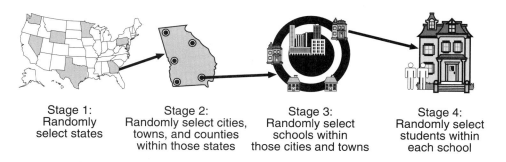

Stage 1:	Stage 2:	Stage 3:	Stage 4:
Randomly	Randomly select cities,	Randomly select	Randomly select
select states	towns, and counties	schools within	students within
	within those states	those cities and towns	each school

sampling, the clusters at the first stage of sampling are termed the *primary sampling units* (Levy & Lemeshow, 1999:228).

How many clusters and how many individuals within clusters should be selected? As a general rule, the set of cases in the sample will be closer to the true population value if the researcher maximizes the number of clusters selected and minimizes the number of individuals within each cluster. Unfortunately, this strategy also maximizes the cost of the sample. The more clusters selected, the higher the travel costs. It also is important to take into account the homogeneity of the individuals within clusters—the more homogeneous the clusters, the fewer cases needed per cluster.

Cluster sampling is a very popular method among survey researchers, but it has one drawback: Sampling error is greater in a cluster sample than in a simple random sample. This error increases as the number of clusters decreases, and it decreases as the homogeneity of cases per cluster increases.

Many professionally designed surveys use combinations of cluster and stratified probability sampling methods. For example, Peter Rossi (1989) drew a disproportionate stratified cluster sample of shelter users for a homelessness study in Chicago (see Exhibit 5.8). The shelter sample was stratified by size, with smaller shelters having a smaller likelihood of selection than larger shelters. In fact, the larger shelters were all selected; they had a probability of selection of 1.0. Within the selected shelters, shelter users were then sampled using a systematic random selection procedure (except in the small shelters, in which all persons were interviewed). Homeless persons living on the streets were also sampled randomly. In the first stage, city blocks were classified in strata based on the likely concentration of homeless persons (estimated by several knowledgeable groups). Blocks were then picked randomly within these strata and, on the survey night between 1 A.M. and 6 A.M., teams of interviewers screened each person found outside on that block for her or his homeless status. Persons identified as homeless were then interviewed (and given $5 for their time). The rate of response for two different samples (fall and winter) in the shelters and on the streets was between 73% and 83%.

How would we evaluate the Chicago homeless sample, using the sample evaluation questions?

Exhibit 5.8 Chicago Shelter Universe and Shelter Samples, Fall and Winter Surveys

A. Shelter Universe and Samples

	Fall	Winter
Eligible shelters in universe	28	45
Universe bed capacities	1,573	2,001
Shelters drawn in sample	22	27

B. Details of Winter Shelter Sample

Shelter Size Classification	Number in Universe	Number in Sample	Occupant Sampling Ratio
Large (37 or more beds)	17	17	0.25
Medium (18-33 beds)	12	6	0.50
Small (under 18 beds)	16	4	1.00

Source: Rossi, 1989:225. Reprinted with permission from the University of Chicago Press.

Note: Shelters were drawn with probabilities proportionate to size, with residents sampled disproportionately within shelters to form a self-weighting sample. Sampling ratios for the phase two sample are given in panel B.

- *From what population were the cases selected?* The population was clearly defined for each cluster.
- *What method was used to select cases from this population?* The random selection method was carefully described.
- *Do the cases that were studied represent, in the aggregate, the population from which they were selected?* The unbiased selection procedures make us reasonably confident in the representativeness of the sample, although we know little about the nonrespondents and therefore may justifiably worry that some types of homeless persons were missed.

Cross-population generalization seems to be reasonable with this sample, because it seems likely that the findings reflect general processes involving homeless persons. Rossi clearly thought so, because his book's title referred to homelessness in America, not just in Chicago.

Nonprobability Sampling Methods

Nonprobability sampling methods are often used in qualitative research; they also are used in quantitative studies when researchers are unable to use probability selection methods. In qualitative research, a focus on one setting or a very small sample allows a more intensive portrait of activities and actors, but it also limits field researchers' ability to generalize and lowers the confidence that others can place in these generalizations. The use of nonprobability sampling methods in quantitative research too often reflects lack of concern with generalizability or lack of understanding of the importance of probability-based sampling.

There are four common nonprobability sampling methods: availability sampling, quota sampling, purposive sampling, and snowball sampling. Because they do not use a random selection procedure, we cannot expect a sample selected with any of these methods to yield a representative sample. They should not be used in quantitative studies if a probability-based method is feasible. Nonetheless, these methods are useful when random sampling is not possible, when a research question calls for an intensive investigation of a small population, or when performing a preliminary, exploratory study.

Availability Sampling

Elements are selected for **availability sampling** because they're available or easy to find. Thus this sampling method is also known as a haphazard, accidental, or convenience sample. There are many ways to select elements for an availability sample: standing on street corners and talking to whoever walks by; asking questions of employees who have time to talk when they pick up their paycheck at a personnel office; approaching particular individuals at opportune times while observing activities in a social setting. You may find yourself interviewing available students at campus hangouts as part of a course assignment. I have occasionally had my methods students learn about survey research by interviewing students who happen to be using the school cafeteria. A participant observation study of a group may require no more sophisticated approach. When Philippe Bourgois, Mark Lettiere, and James Quesada (1997) studied homeless heroin addicts in San Francisco, they immersed themselves in a community of addicts living in a public park. These addicts became the availability sample.

An availability sample is often appropriate in social research—for example, when a field researcher is exploring a new setting and trying to get some sense of prevailing attitudes or when a survey researcher conducts a preliminary test of a new set of questions.

Now I'd like you to use the sample evaluation questions to evaluate person-in-the-street interviews of the homeless. If your answers are something like "The population was unknown," "The method for selecting cases was haphazard," and "The cases studied do not represent the population," you're right! There is no clearly definable population from which the respondents were drawn, and no systematic technique was used to select the respondents. There certainly is not much likelihood that the interviewees represent the distribution of sentiment among homeless persons in the Boston area or of welfare mothers or of impoverished rural migrants or of whatever we imagine the relevant population is.

In a similar vein, perhaps person-in-the-street comments to news reporters suggest something about what homeless persons think. Or maybe they don't; we can't really be sure. But let's give reporters their due: If they just want to have a few quotes to make their story more appealing, nothing is wrong with their sampling method. However, their approach gives us no basis for thinking that we have an overview of community sentiment. The people who happen to be available in any situation are unlikely to be just like those who are unavailable. We can't be at all certain that what we learn can be generalized with any confidence to a larger population of concern.

Availability sampling often masquerades as a more rigorous form of research. Popular magazines periodically survey their readers by printing a questionnaire for readers to fill out and mail in. A follow-up article then appears in the magazine under a title like "What You Think About Intimacy in Marriage." If the magazine's circulation is large, a large sample can be achieved in this way. The problem is that usually only a tiny fraction of readers return the questionnaire, and these respondents are probably unlike other readers who did not have the interest or time to participate. So the survey is based on an availability sample. Even though the follow-up article may be interesting, we have no basis for thinking that the results describe the readership as a whole—much less the population at large.

Do you see now why availability sampling differs so much from random sampling methods, which require that "nothing but chance" affect the actual selection of cases? What makes availability sampling "haphazard" is precisely that a great many things other than chance can affect the selection of cases, ranging from the prejudices of the research staff to the work schedules of potential respondents. In order to truly leave the selection of cases up to chance, we have to design the selection process very carefully so that other factors are not influential. There's nothing "haphazard" about selecting cases randomly.

Quota Sampling

Quota sampling is intended to overcome the most obvious flaw of availability sampling—that the sample will just consist of whoever or whatever is available, without any concern for its similarity to the population of interest. The distinguishing feature of a quota sample is that quotas are set to ensure that the sample represents certain characteristics in proportion to their prevalence in the population.

Suppose that you wish to sample adult residents of a town in a study of support for a tax increase to improve the town's schools. You know from the town's annual report what the proportions of town residents are in terms of gender, race, age, and number of children. You think that each of these characteristics might influence support for new school taxes, so you want to be sure that the sample includes men, women, whites, blacks, Hispanics, Asians, older people, younger people, big families, small families, and childless families in proportion to their numbers in the town population.

This is where quotas come in. Let's say that 48% of the town's adult residents are men and 52% are women, and that 60% are employed, 5% are unemployed, and 35% are out of the labor force. These percentages and the percentages corresponding to the other characteristics become the quotas for the sample. If you plan to include a total of 500 residents in your sample, 240 must be men (48% of 500), 260 must be women, 300 must be employed, and so on. You may even set more refined quotas, such as certain numbers of employed women, employed men, unemployed men, and so on. With the quota list in hand, you (or your research staff) can now go out into the community looking for the right number of people in each quota category. You may go door to door, bar to bar, or just stand on a street corner until you have surveyed 240 men, 260 women, and so on.

The problem is that even when we know that a quota sample is representative of the particular characteristics for which quotas have been set, we have no way of knowing if the sample is representative in terms of any other characteristics. In Exhibit 5.9, for example, quotas have been set for gender only. Under the circumstances, it's no surprise that the sample is representative of the population only in terms of gender, not in terms of race. Interviewers are only human; they may avoid potential respondents with menacing dogs in

Exhibit 5.9 Quota Sampling

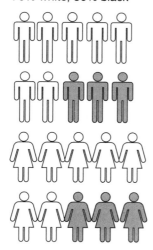

Population
50% male, 50% female
70% white, 30% black

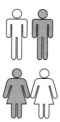

Quota sample
50% male, 50% female

Representative of gender distribution
in population, not representative of
race distribution.

the front yard, or they could seek out respondents who are physically attractive or who look like they'd be easy to interview. Realistically, researchers can set quotas for only a small fraction of the characteristics relevant to a study, so a quota sample is really not much better than an availability sample (although following careful, consistent procedures for selecting cases within the quota limits always helps).

This last point leads me to another limitation of quota sampling: You must know the characteristics of the entire population to set the right quotas. In most cases researchers know what the population looks like in terms of no more than a few of the characteristics relevant to their concerns—and in some cases they have no such information on the entire population. Exhibit 5.10 summarizes the differences between quota sampling and stratified random sampling. The key difference, of course, is quota sampling's lack of random selection.

If you're now feeling skeptical of quota sampling, you've gotten the drift of my remarks. Nonetheless, in some situations, establishing quotas can add rigor to sampling procedures. It's almost always better to maximize possibilities for comparison in research, and quota sampling techniques can help qualitative researchers to do this. For instance, Doug Timmer, Stanley Eitzen, and Kathryn Talley (1993:7) interviewed homeless persons in several cities and other locations for their book on the sources of homelessness. Persons who were available were interviewed, but the researchers paid some attention to generating a diverse sample. They interviewed 20 homeless men who lived on the streets without shelter and 20 mothers who were found in family shelters. About half of those the researchers selected in the street sample were black, and about half were white. Although

Exhibit 5.10   An Unrepresentative Quota Sample Versus a Representative Stratified Sample

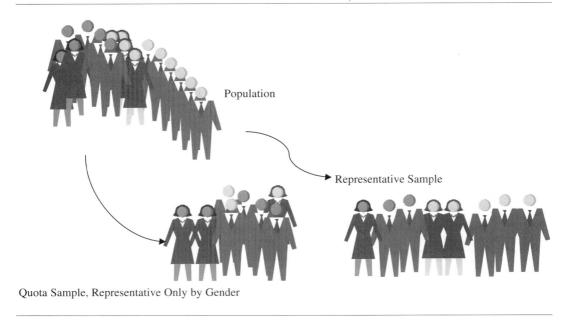

Population

Representative Sample

Quota Sample, Representative Only by Gender

the researchers did not use quotas to try to match the distribution of characteristics among the total homeless population, their informal quotas helped to ensure some diversity in key characteristics.

Purposive Sampling

In **purposive sampling,** each sample element is selected for a purpose, usually because of the unique position of the sample elements. Purposive sampling may involve studying the entire population of some limited group (directors of shelters for homeless adults) or a subset of a population (mid-level managers with a reputation for efficiency). Or a purposive sample may be a "key informant survey," which targets individuals who are particularly knowledgeable about the issues under investigation.

Herbert Rubin and Irene Rubin (1995:66) suggest three guidelines for selecting informants when designing any purposive sampling strategy. Informants should be:

- "Knowledgeable about the cultural arena or situation or experience being studied."
- "Willing to talk."
- "Represent[ative of] the range of points of view."

In addition, Rubin and Rubin suggest continuing to select interviewees until you can pass two tests:

- *Completeness.* "What you hear provides an overall sense of the meaning of a concept, theme, or process" (p. 72).
- *Saturation.* "You gain confidence that you are learning little that is new from subsequent interview[s]" (p. 73).

Adhering to these guidelines will help to ensure that a purposive sample adequately represents the setting or issues studied.

Of course, purposive sampling does not produce a sample that represents some larger population, but it can be exactly what is needed in a case study of an organization, community, or some other clearly defined and relatively limited group. In an intensive organizational case study, a purposive sample of organizational leaders might be complemented with a probability sample of organizational members. Before designing her probability samples of hospital patients and homeless persons, Dee Roth (1990:146–147) interviewed a purposive sample of 164 key informants from organizations that had contact with homeless people in each county she studied.

Snowball Sampling

Snowball sampling is useful for hard-to-reach or hard-to-identify populations for which there is no sampling frame, but the members of which are somewhat interconnected (at least some members of the population know each other). It can be used to sample members of such groups as drug dealers, prostitutes, practicing criminals, participants in Alcoholics Anonymous groups, gang leaders, informal organizational leaders, and homeless persons. It also may be used for charting the relationships among members of some group (a sociometric study), for exploring the population of interest prior to developing a formal sampling plan, and for developing what becomes a census of informal leaders of small organizations or communities. However, researchers using snowball sampling normally cannot be confident that their sample represents the total population of interest, so generalizations must be tentative.

Rob Rosenthal (1994) used snowball sampling to study homeless persons living in Santa Barbara, California:

> I began this process by attending a meeting of homeless people I had heard about through my housing advocate contacts. . . . One homeless woman . . . invited me to . . . where she promised to introduce me around. Thus a process of snowballing began. I gained entree to a group through people I knew, came to know others, and through them gained entree to new circles. (pp. 178, 180)

One problem with this technique is that the initial contacts may shape the entire sample and foreclose access to some members of the population of interest:

> Sat around with [my contact] at the Tree. Other people come by, are friendly, but some regulars, especially the tougher men, don't sit with her. Am I making a mistake by tying myself too closely to her? She lectures them a lot. (Rosenthal, 1994:181)

More systematic versions of snowball sampling can reduce the potential for bias. For example, "respondent-driven sampling" gives financial incentives to respondents to recruit

Exhibit 5.11 Respondent-Driven Sampling

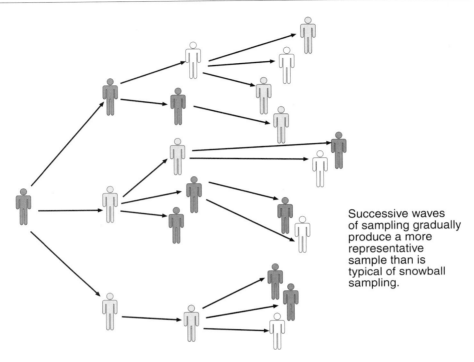

Successive waves of sampling gradually produce a more representative sample than is typical of snowball sampling.

Instructions to respondents:
"We'll pay you $5 each for up to three names, but only one of those names can be somebody from your own town. The others have to be from somewhere else."

peers (Heckathorn, 1997). Limitations on the number of incentives that any one respondent can receive increase the sample's diversity. Targeted incentives can steer the sample to include specific subgroups. When the sampling is repeated through several waves, with new respondents bringing in more peers, the composition of the sample converges on a more representative mix of characteristics than would occur with uncontrolled snowball sampling. Exhibit 5.11 shows how the sample spreads out through successive recruitment waves to an increasingly diverse pool (Heckathorn, 1997:178). Exhibit 5.12 shows that even if the starting point were all white persons, respondent-driven sampling would result in an appropriate ethnic mix from an ethnically diverse population (Heckathorn, 2002:17).

Lessons About Sample Quality

Some lessons are implicit in my evaluations of the samples in this chapter:

- We can't evaluate the quality of a sample if we don't know what population it is supposed to represent. If the population is unspecified because the researchers were

Exhibit 5.12   Convergence of Respondent-Driven Sample to True Ethnic Proportions in Population, After Starting With Only Whites

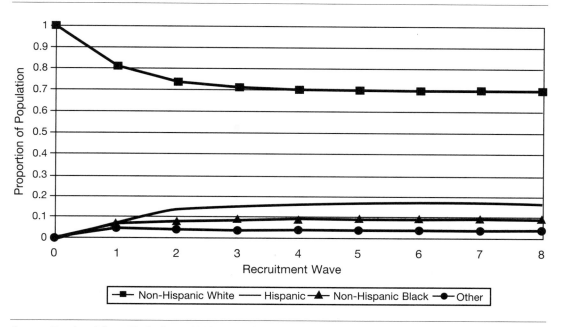

Source: Reprinted from Heckathorn, 2002:11-34, by permission. Copyright 2002 by the Society for the Study of Social Problems.

never clear about just what population they were trying to sample, then we can safely conclude that the sample itself is no good.

- We can't evaluate the quality of a sample if we don't know just how cases in the sample were selected from the population. If the method was specified, we then need to know whether cases were selected in a systematic fashion and on the basis of chance. In any case, we know that a haphazard method of sampling (as in person-on-the-street interviews) undermines generalizability.

- Sample quality is determined by the sample actually obtained, not just by the sampling method itself. If many of the people selected for our sample are nonrespondents or people (or other entities) who do not participate in the study although they have been selected for the sample, the quality of our sample is undermined—even if we chose the sample in the best possible way.

- We need to be aware that even researchers who obtain very good samples may talk about the implications of their findings for some group that is larger than or just different from the population they actually sampled. For example, findings from a representative sample of students in one university often are discussed as if they tell us about university students in general. And maybe they do; we just don't know for sure.

- A sample that allows for comparisons involving theoretically important variables is better than one that does not allow such comparisons. Even when we study people or social processes in depth, it is best to select individuals or settings with an eye to how useful they will be for examining relationships. Limiting an investigation to just one setting or just one type of person will inevitably leave us wondering what it is that makes a difference.

Generalizability in Qualitative Research

You have learned that nonprobability sampling methods are often used in qualitative research because of the difficulty—often impossibility—of selecting cases randomly for observational studies or for intensive interviewing involving hard-to-locate populations. This means that the findings of qualitative research often cannot be generalized to some clearly defined population. Far from seeing this as a limitation of qualitative research, however, researchers who identify with the interpretive tradition turn this limitation into a virtue by rejecting the goal of generalizability altogether. In the words of sociologist Norman Denzin (Schofield, 2002:173),

> The interpretivist rejects generalization as a goal and never aims to draw randomly selected samples of human experience. [E]very instance of social interaction . . . represents a slice from the life world that is the proper subject matter for interpretive inquiry.

But other qualitative researchers maintain a concern with generalizability and have suggested ways to increase the likelihood of achieving it. Among the suggestions of Janet Ward Schofield are the following:

Studying the Typical. Choosing sites on the basis of their fit with a typical situation is far preferable to choosing on the basis of convenience. (Schofield, 2002:181)

Performing Multisite Studies. A finding emerging repeatedly in the study of numerous sites would appear to be more likely to be a good working hypothesis about some as yet unstudied site than a finding emerging from just one or two sites. . . . Generally speaking, a finding emerging from the study of several very heterogeneous sites would be more . . . likely to be useful in understanding various other sites than one emerging from the study of several very similar sites. (Schofield, 2002:184)

So when you evaluate the results of qualitative research, or design qualitative research yourself, you may want first to consider whether you think generalizability is an important goal for that study.

SAMPLING DISTRIBUTIONS

A well-designed probability sample is one that is likely to be representative of the population from which it was selected. But as you've seen, random samples still are subject to sampling error due just to chance. To deal with that problem, social researchers take into account the properties of a sampling distribution, a hypothetical distribution of a statistic across all the random samples that could be drawn from a population. Any single random sample can be thought of as just one of an infinite number of random samples that, in theory, could have been selected from the population. If we had the finances of Gatsby and the patience of Job and were able actually to draw an infinite number of samples, and we calculated the same type of statistic for each of these samples, we would then have a sampling distribution. Understanding sampling distributions is the foundation for understanding how statisticians can estimate sampling error.

What does a sampling distribution look like? Because a sampling distribution is based on some statistic calculated for different samples, we need to choose a statistic. Let's focus on the arithmetic average, or mean. I will explain the calculation of the mean in Chapter 12, but you may already be familiar with it: You add up the values of all the cases and divide by the total number of cases. Let's say you draw a random sample of 500 families and find that their average (mean) family income is $36,239. Imagine that you then draw another random sample. That sample's mean family income might be $31,302. Imagine marking these two means on graph paper and then drawing more random samples and marking their means on the graph. The resulting graph would be a sampling distribution of the mean.

Exhibit 5.13 demonstrates what happened when I did something very similar to what I have just described—not with an infinite number of samples and not from a large population but through the same process using the 1996 General Social Survey (GSS) sample as if it were a population. First, I drew 49 different random samples, each consisting of 30 cases, from the 1996 GSS. (The standard notation for the number of cases in each sample is $n = 30$.) Then I calculated for each random sample the approximate mean family income (approximate because the GSS does not record actual income in dollars). I then graphed the means of the 49 samples. Each bar in Exhibit 5.13 shows how many samples had a particular family income. The mean for the population (the total sample) is $38,249, and you can see that the sampling distribution centers around this value. However, although many of the sample means are close to the population mean, some are quite far from it. If you had calculated the mean from only one sample, it could have been anywhere in this sampling distribution, but it is unlikely to have been far from the population mean—that is, unlikely to have been close to either end (or "tail") of the distribution.

Estimating Sampling Error

We don't actually observe sampling distributions in real research; researchers just draw the best sample they can and then are stuck with the results—one sample, not a distribution of samples. A sampling distribution is a theoretical distribution. However, we can use the properties of sampling distributions to calculate the amount of sampling error that was likely with the random sample used in a study. The tool for calculating sampling error is called **inferential statistics.**

Inferential statistics   A mathematical tool for estimating how likely it is that a statistical result based on data from a random sample is representative of the population from which the sample is assumed to have been selected.

Sampling distributions for many statistics, including the mean, have a "normal" shape. A graph of a normal distribution looks like a bell, with one "hump" in the middle, centered around the population mean, and the number of cases tapering off on both sides of the mean. Note that a normal distribution is symmetric: If you folded it in half at its center

Exhibit 5.13   Partial Sampling Distribution: Mean Family Income

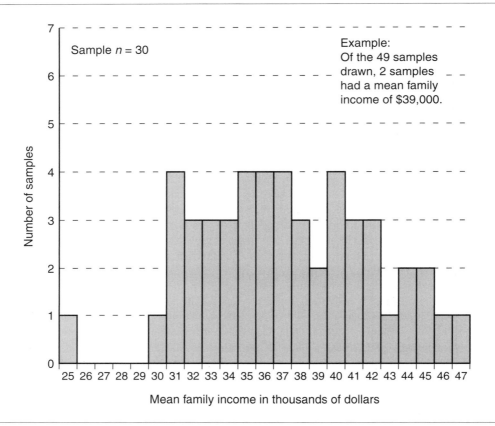

Source: Data from General Social Survey, 1996.

(at the population mean), the two halves would match perfectly. This shape is produced by **random sampling error**—variation due purely to chance. The value of the statistic varies from sample to sample because of chance, so higher and lower values are equally likely.

The partial sampling distribution in Exhibit 5.13 does not have a completely normal shape because it involves only a small number of samples (49), each of which has only 30 cases. Exhibit 5.14 shows what the sampling distribution of family incomes would look like if it formed a perfectly normal distribution—if, rather than 49 random samples, I had selected thousands of random samples.

Random sampling error (chance sampling error)   Differences between the population and the sample that are due only to chance factors (random error), not to systematic sampling error. Random sampling error may or may not result in an unrepresentative sample. The magnitude of sampling error due to chance factors can be estimated statistically.

Exhibit 5.14   Normal Sampling Distribution: Mean Family Income

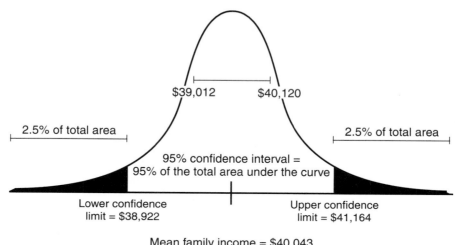

Mean family income = $40,043

The properties of a sampling distribution facilitate the process of statistical inference. In the sampling distribution, the most frequent value of the **sample statistic**—the statistic (such as the mean) computed from sample data—is identical to the **population parameter**—the statistic computed for the entire population. In other words, we can have a lot of confidence that the value at the peak of the bell curve represents the norm for the entire population. A population parameter also may be termed the *true value* for the statistic in that population. A sample statistic is an estimate of a population parameter.

In a normal distribution, a predictable proportion of cases falls within certain ranges. Inferential statistics takes advantage of this feature and allow researchers to estimate how likely it is that, given a particular sample, the true population value will be within some range of the statistic. For example, a statistician might conclude from a sample of 30 families that *we can be 95% confident that the true mean family income in the total population is between $39,012 and $40,120.* The interval from $39,012 to $40,120 would then be called the "95% confidence interval for the mean." The upper ($40,120) and lower ($39,012) bounds of this interval are termed the confidence limits. Exhibit 5.14 marks such confidence limits, indicating the range that encompasses 95% of the area under the normal curve; 95% of all sample means would fall within this range, as does the mean of our hypothetical sample of 30 cases.

Although all normal distributions have these same basic features, they differ in the extent to which they cluster around the mean. A sampling distribution is more compact when it is based on larger samples. Stated another way, we can be more confident in estimates based on larger random samples because we know that a larger sample creates a more compact sampling distribution. Compare the two sampling distributions of mean family income shown in Exhibit 5.15. Both depict the results for about 50 samples. However, in one study each sample comprised 100 families, and in the other study each sample comprised only 5 families. Clearly, the larger samples result in a sampling distribution that is much more tightly

Exhibit 5.15   The Effect of Sample Size on Sampling Distribution

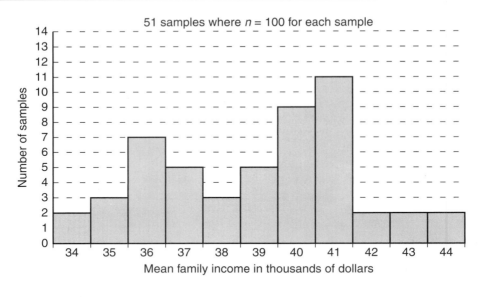

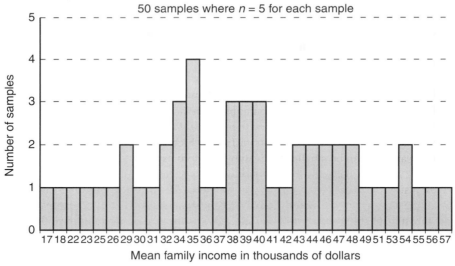

Source: Data from General Social Survey, 1996.

clustered around the mean (range of 34 to 44) than is the case with the smaller samples (range of 17 to 57). The 95% confidence interval for mean family income for the entire 1996 GSS sample of 1,368 cases (the ones that had valid values of family income) was $29,421 to $31,711—an interval only about $2,300 wide. But the 95% confidence interval for the mean family income in one GSS subsample of 100 cases was much wider, with limits of $25,733 and $35,399. And for a subsample of only 5 cases, the 95% confidence interval was very broad: $14,104 to $47,028. Such small samples often result in statistics that actually give us very little useful information about the population.

Other confidence intervals, such as the 99% confidence interval, can be reported. As a matter of convention, statisticians use only the 95%, 99%, and 99.9% confidence limits to estimate the range of values that are likely to contain the true value. These conventional limits reflect the conservatism inherent in classical statistical inference: Don't make an inferential statement unless you are very confident (at least 95% confident) that it is correct.

The less precise an estimate of a particular statistic from a particular sample, the more confident we can be—and the wider the confidence interval. The 95% confidence interval for the entire 1996 GSS sample is $29,421 to $31,711 (a width of $2,290); the 99% confidence interval is $28,814 to $32,318 (a width of $3,504).

I have not explained how to calculate confidence intervals, which is a subject better left to a statistics course. You should, however, now have a sense of how researchers make inferences from a random sample to a population.

Determining Sample Size

You have learned that more confidence can be placed in the generalizability of statistics from larger samples, so you may be eager to work with random samples that are as large as possible. Unfortunately, researchers often cannot afford to sample a very large number of cases. They therefore try to determine during the design phase of their study how large a sample they must have to achieve their purposes. They have to consider the degree of confidence desired, the homogeneity of the population, the complexity of the analysis they plan, and the expected strength of the relationships they will measure:

- The less sampling error desired, the larger the sample size must be.
- Samples of more homogeneous populations can be smaller than samples of more diverse populations. Stratified sampling uses prior information on the population to create more homogeneous population strata from which the sample can be selected, so stratified samples can be smaller than simple random samples.
- If the only analysis planned for a survey sample is to describe the population in terms of a few variables, a smaller sample is required than if a more complex analysis involving sample subgroups is planned. If much of the analysis will focus on estimating the characteristics of subgroups within the sample, it is the size of the subgroups that must be considered, not the size of the total sample (Levy & Lemeshow, 1999:74).
- When the researchers will be testing hypotheses and expect to find very strong relationships among the variables, they will need a smaller sample to detect these relationships than if they expect weaker relationships.

Researchers can make more precise estimates of the sample size required through a method termed "statistical power analysis" (Kraemer & Thiemann, 1987). Statistical power analysis requires a good advance estimate of the strength of the hypothesized relationship in the population. In addition, the math is complicated, so it helps to have some background in mathematics or to be able to consult a statistician. For these reasons, many researchers do not conduct formal power analyses when deciding how many cases to sample.

You can obtain some general guidance about sample sizes from the current practices of social scientists. For professional studies of the national population in which only a simple description is desired, professional social science studies typically have used a sample size of between 1,000 and 1,500 people, with up to 2,500 being included if detailed analyses are planned. Studies of local or regional populations often sample only a few hundred people, in part because these studies lack sufficient funding to draw larger samples. Of course, the sampling error in these smaller studies is considerably larger than in a typical national study (Sudman, 1976:87).

CONCLUSIONS

Sampling is a powerful tool for social science research. Probability sampling methods allow a researcher to use the laws of chance, or probability, to draw samples from which population parameters can be estimated with a high degree of confidence. A sample of just 1,000 or 1,500 individuals can be used to estimate reliably the characteristics of the population of a nation comprising millions of individuals.

But researchers do not come by representative samples easily. Well-designed samples require careful planning, some advance knowledge about the population to be sampled, and adherence to systematic selection procedures—all so that the selection procedures are not biased. And even after the sample data are collected, the researcher's ability to generalize from the sample findings to the population is not completely certain. The best that he or she can do is to perform additional calculations that state the degree of confidence that can be placed in the sample statistic.

The alternatives to random, or probability-based, sampling methods are almost always much less palatable for quantitative studies, even though they typically are much cheaper. Without a method of selecting cases likely to represent the population in which the researcher is interested, research findings will have to be carefully qualified. Qualitative researchers whose goal is to understand a small group or setting in depth may necessarily have to use unrepresentative samples, but they must keep in mind that the generalizability of their findings will not be known. Additional procedures for sampling in qualitative studies will be introduced in Chapter 9.

Social scientists often seek to generalize their conclusions from the population that they studied to some larger target population. The validity of generalizations of this type is necessarily uncertain, because having a representative sample of a particular population does not at all ensure that what we find will hold true in other populations. Nonetheless, as you will see in Chapter 14, the cumulation of findings from studies based on local or otherwise unrepresentative populations can provide important information about broader populations.

KEY TERMS

Availability sampling
Census
Cluster
Cluster sampling
Disproportionate stratified sampling

Element
Enumeration units
Inferential statistics
Nonprobability sampling method
Nonrespondent

Periodicity
Population
Population parameter
Probability of selection
Probability sampling method
Proportionate stratified sampling
Purposive sampling
Quota sampling
Random digit dialing
Random number table
Random sampling
Random sampling error
Replacement sampling

Representative sample
Sample
Sample statistic
Sampling error
Sampling frame
Sampling interval
Sampling unit
Simple random sampling
Snowball sampling
Stratified random sampling
Systematic bias
Systematic random sampling
Target population

HIGHLIGHTS

- Sampling theory focuses on the generalizability of descriptive findings to the population from which the sample was drawn. It also considers whether statements can be generalized from one population to another.

- Sampling is unnecessary when the elements that would be sampled are identical, but the complexity of the social world makes it difficult to argue very often that different elements are identical. Conducting a complete census of a population also eliminates the need for sampling, but the resources required for a complete census of a large population are usually prohibitive.

- Nonresponse undermines sample quality: It is the obtained sample, not the desired sample, that determines sample quality.

- Probability sampling methods rely on a random selection procedure to ensure no systematic bias in the selection of elements. In a probability sample, the odds of selecting elements are known, and the method of selection is carefully controlled.

- A sampling frame (a list of elements in the population) is required in most probability sampling methods. The adequacy of the sampling frame is an important determinant of sample quality.

- Simple random sampling and systematic random sampling are equivalent probability sampling methods in most situations. However, systematic random sampling is inappropriate for sampling from lists of elements that have a regular, periodic structure.

- Stratified random sampling uses prior information about a population to make sampling more efficient. Stratified sampling may be either proportionate or disproportionate. Disproportionate stratified sampling is useful when a research question focuses on a stratum or on strata that make up a small proportion of the population.

- Cluster sampling is less efficient than simple random sampling but is useful when a sampling frame is unavailable. It is also useful for large populations spread out across a wide area or among many organizations.

- Nonprobability sampling methods can be useful when random sampling is not possible, when a research question does not concern a larger population, and when a preliminary exploratory study is appropriate. However, the representativeness of nonprobability samples cannot be determined.

- The likely degree of error in an estimate of a population characteristic based on a probability sample decreases when the size of the sample and the homogeneity of the population from which the sample was selected increases. Sampling error is not affected by the proportion of the population that is sampled, except when that proportion is large. The degree of sampling error affecting a sample statistic can be estimated from the characteristics of the sample and knowledge of the properties of sampling distributions.

DISCUSSION QUESTIONS

1. Locate one or more newspaper articles reporting the results of an opinion poll. What information does the article provide on the sample that was selected? What additional information do you need to determine whether the sample was a representative one?

2. Shere Hite's popular book *Women and Love* (1987) is a good example of the claims that are often made based on an availability sample. In this case, however, the sample didn't necessarily appear to be an availability sample because it consisted of so many people. Hite distributed 100,000 questionnaires to church groups and many other organizations and received back 4.5%; 4,500 women took the time to answer some or all of her 127 essay questions regarding love and sex. Is Hite's sample likely to represent American women in general? Why or why not? You might take a look at the book's empirical generalizations and consider whether they are justified.

3. In professional journals, select five articles that describe research using a sample drawn from some population. Identify the type of sample used in each study, and note any strong and weak points in how the sample was actually drawn. Did the researchers have a problem due to nonresponse? Considering the sample, how confident are you in the validity of generalizations about the population based on the sample? Do you need any additional information to evaluate the sample? Do you think a different sampling strategy would have been preferable? What larger population were the findings generalized to? Do you think these generalizations were warranted? Why or why not?

PRACTICE EXERCISES

1. Select a random sample using the table of random numbers in Appendix E. Compute a statistic based on your sample, and compare it to the corresponding figure for the entire population. Here's how to proceed:
   a. First, select a very small population for which you have a reasonably complete sampling frame. One possibility would be the list of asking prices for houses advertised in your local paper. Another would be the listing of some characteristic of states in a U.S. Census Bureau publication, such as average income or population size.
   b. The next step is to create your sampling frame, a numbered list of all the elements in the population. If you are using a complete listing of all elements, as from a U.S. Census Bureau publication, the sampling frame is the same as the list. Just number the elements (states). If your population is composed of housing ads in the local paper, your sampling frame will be those ads that contain a housing price. Identify these ads, and then number them sequentially, starting with 1.
   c. Decide on a method of picking numbers out of the random number table in Appendix E, such as taking every number in each row, row by row (or you may move down or diagonally across the columns). Use only the first (or last) digit in each number if you need to select 1 to 9 cases or only the first (or last) two digits if you want fewer than 100 cases.
   d. Pick a starting location in the random number table. It's important to pick a starting point in an unbiased way, perhaps by closing your eyes and then pointing to some part of the page.
   e. Record the numbers you encounter as you move from the starting location in the direction you decided on in advance, until you have recorded as many random numbers as the number of cases you need in the sample. If you are selecting states, 10 might be a good number. Ignore numbers

that are too large (or small) for the range of numbers used to identify the elements in the population. Discard duplicate numbers.

f. Calculate the average value in your sample for some variable that was measured—for example, population size in a sample of states or housing price for the housing ads. Calculate the average by adding up the values of all the elements in the sample and dividing by the number of elements in the sample.

g. Go back to the sampling frame and calculate this same average for all the elements in the list. How close is the sample average to the population average?

h. Estimate the range of sample averages that would be likely to include 90% of the possible samples.

2. Draw a snowball sample of people who are involved in bungee jumping or some other uncommon sport that does not involve teams. Ask friends and relatives to locate a first contact, and then call or visit this person and ask for names of others. Stop when you have identified a sample of 10. Review the problems you encountered, and consider how you would proceed if you had to draw a larger sample.

3. Two lesson sets on the CD-ROM will help you to review the terminology involved in "Identifying Sampling Techniques" and the logic of "Assessing Generalizability."

WEB EXERCISES

1. Research on homelessness has been rising in recent years as housing affordability has declined. Search the Web for sites that include the word "homelessness" and see what you find. You might try limiting your search to those that also contain the word "census." Pick a site and write a paragraph about what you learned from it.

2. Check out the "people" section of the U.S. Bureau of the Census Web site: www.census.gov. Based on some of the data you find there, write a brief summary of some aspect of the current characteristics of the American population.

SPSS EXERCISES

1. Take a look again at the distribution of support for capital punishment (CAPPUN), this time with what is called a "frequency distribution."
   a. Click *Analyze|Descriptive Statistics|Frequencies*.
   b. Highlight CAPPUN and click on the arrow that sends it over to the Variables window, then click OK.
   Examine the percentages in the Valid percent column. What percentage of the American population in 2000 favored capital punishment?

2. Now select random samples of the GSS2000mini respondents and see how the distribution of CAPPUN in these subsamples compares to that for the total GSS sample:
   a. Go to the Data Editor window, and select a random sample containing 40 of the respondents. From the menu:
      (1) Click *Data|Select cases|All Cases|OK*.
      (2) Click *Select cases|Random sample of cases|Sample*.
      (3) Select exactly 40 cases from the first 100 cases.
      (4) Click *Continue|OK*. (Before you click OK, be sure that the "Unselected cases are FILTERED" box is checked.)

   b. Determine the percentage of this subsample that favored capital punishment by repeating the steps in SPSS Exercise 1. Record the subsample characteristics and this percentage.

   c. Now repeat Steps 2a and 2b ten times. Each time, add 100 to the "first 100 cases" request (so that on the last step you will be requesting "Exactly 20 cases from the first 1,000 cases").

   d. Select a random sample containing five of the respondents. Now repeat Steps a through c, this time for samples of five.

   e. Plot the results of Steps c and d on separate sheets of graph paper. Each graph's horizontal axis will represent the possible range of percentages (0 to 100, perhaps in increments of 5); the vertical axis will represent the number of samples in each range of percentages (perhaps ranging from 0 to 10). Make an X to indicate this percentage for each sample. If two samples have the same percentage, place the corresponding X's on top of each other. The X for each sample should be one unit high on the vertical axis.

   f. Draw a vertical line corresponding to the point on the horizontal axis that indicates the percentage of the total GSS sample that favors capital punishment.

   g. Describe the shape of both graphs. These are the sampling distributions for the two sets of samples. Compare them to each other. Do the percentages from the larger samples tend to be closer to the mean of the entire sample (as obtained in Exercise 1)? What does this tell you about the relationship between sample size and sampling error?

DEVELOPING A RESEARCH PROPOSAL

Consider the possibilities for sampling.

   1. Propose a sampling design that would be appropriate if you were to survey students on your campus only. Define the population, identify the sampling frame(s), and specify the elements and any other units at different stages. Indicate the exact procedure for selecting people to be included in the sample.

   2. Propose a different sampling design for conducting your survey in a larger population, such as your city, state, or the entire nation.

Chapter 6

CAUSATION AND RESEARCH DESIGN

Time Order and Research Design

Cross-Sectional Designs
Longitudinal Designs
   Repeated Cross-Sectional Designs
   Fixed-Sample Panel Designs
   Event-Based Designs

**Units of Analysis and
   Errors in Causal Reasoning**

Individual and Group Units of Analysis
The Ecological Fallacy and Reductionism

The Meaning of Explanation

Nomothetic Causal Explanation

Idiographic Causal Explanation
Case-Oriented Understanding

**Research Designs and Criteria
   for Causal Explanation**

Association
Time Order
Nonspuriousness
Mechanism
Context

Conclusions

Identifying causes—figuring out why things happen—is the goal of most social science research. Unfortunately, valid explanations of the causes of social phenomena do not come easily. Why have "serious crimes like homicide and robbery . . . risen in the United States for the first time in almost a decade" (Kershaw, 2002:A10)? Is it due to "anger over the Sept. 11 terrorist attack and the economic downturn" (Kershaw, 2002)? The release of hard-core convicts who had been imprisoned during the crime wave of the 1980s and early 1990s? Simply a "crime-drop party is over" phenomenon, as criminologist James Alan Fox has suggested (Lichtblau, 2000:A2)? But then why has the violent crime rate continued its downward trend in New York City? Is it because of Compstat, the city's new computer program that identifies to police where crimes are clustering (Kaplan, 2002:A3)? Or should credit be given to New York's "Safe Streets, Safe Cities" program, which increased the ranks of police officers (Rashbaum, 2002)? What about better emergency room care causing a decline in homicides

(Harris et al., 2002)? In order to determine which of these possibilities could contribute to the increase or decline of serious crime, we must design our research strategies carefully.

This chapter first considers aspects of research design related to determining causality, including types of longitudinal designs and designs using different units of analysis. I then discuss the meaning of causation from different perspectives and review the criteria for achieving causally valid explanations from a nomothetic perspective. I also discuss the ways in which different research designs seek to meet these criteria. By the end of the chapter, you should have a good grasp of the different meanings of causation and be able to ask the right questions to determine whether causal inferences are likely to be valid. And perhaps you will have a better answer about the causes of crime and violence.

TIME ORDER AND RESEARCH DESIGN

Research designs can be either cross-sectional or longitudinal. In a **cross-sectional research design,** all data are collected at one point in time. Identifying the **time order** of effects—what happened first, and so on—is critical for developing a causal analysis, but can be an insurmountable problem with a cross-sectional design. In **longitudinal research designs,** data are collected at two or more points in time, and so identification of the time order of effects can be quite straightforward.

Cross-Sectional Designs

Much of the research you have encountered so far in this text—the surveys of Internet usage in Chapter 1, of binge drinking in Chapter 4, and of homeless persons in Chapter 5—has been cross-sectional. Although each of these surveys took some time to carry out, they measured the actions, attitudes, and characteristics of respondents only at one time.

Robert Sampson and Stephen Raudenbush (1999) used a very ambitious cross-sectional design to study the effect of visible public social and physical disorder on the crime rate in Chicago neighborhoods. Their theoretical framework focused on the concept of informal social control: the ability of residents to regulate social activity in their neighborhoods through their collective efforts according to desired principles. They believed that informal social control would vary between neighborhoods, and they hypothesized that it was the strength of informal social control that would explain variation in crime rates rather than just the visible signs of disorder. In other words, they hypothesized that variation in informal social control created a **spurious relationship** between variation in rates and visible signs of disorder. They contrasted this prediction to the "broken windows" theory: the belief that signs of disorder themselves cause crime. In the theory proposed by Sampson and Raudenbush, both visible disorder and crime were consequences of low levels of informal social control (measured with an index of "collective efficacy"). One did not cause the other (Exhibit 6.1). The crime–visible disorder relationship is hypothesized to be spurious.

Sampson and Raudenbush measured visible disorder through direct observation: Trained observers rode slowly around every street in 196 Chicago census tracts. They also conducted a survey of residents and examined police records. Both survey responses and police records were used to measure crime levels. The level of neighborhood informal social control and other variables were measured with the average resident responses to several survey questions.

Exhibit 6.1   The Effect of Informal Social Control

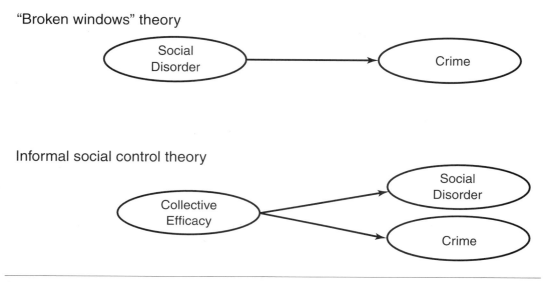

"Broken windows" theory

Informal social control theory

Source: Based on Sampson & Roudenbush, 1999:635.

Both the crime rate and the level of social and physical disorder varied between neighborhoods in relation to the level of informal social control. Informal social control (collective efficacy) was a much more important factor in the neighborhood crime rate than visible social and physical disorder (Exhibit 6.2).

In spite of these compelling findings, Sampson and Raudenbush's cross-sectional design could not establish directly that the variation in the crime rate occurred after variation in informal social control. Maybe it was a high crime rate that led residents to stop trying to exert much control over deviant activities in the neighborhood, perhaps because of fear of crime. It is difficult to discount such a possibility when only cross-sectional data are available.

Although it is risky to draw conclusions about time order on the basis of cross-sectional data, there are four special circumstances when it is reasonable. Because in these special circumstances the data can be ordered in time, they might even be thought of as longitudinal designs (Campbell, 1992):

The independent variable is fixed at some point prior to the variation in the dependent variable. So-called demographic variables that are determined at birth—such as sex, race, and age—are fixed in this way. So are variables like education and marital status, if we know when the value of cases on these variables was established and if we know that the value of cases on the dependent variable was set some time later. For example, say we hypothesize that education influences the type of job individuals have. If we know that respondents completed their education before taking their current jobs, we would satisfy the time order requirement even if we were to measure education at the same time we measure type of job. However, if some

Exhibit 6.2   Effect of Social Disorder and Collective Efficacy on Personal Violent Crimes

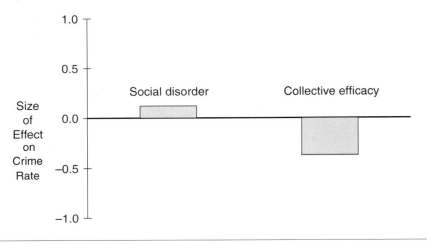

Source: Adapted from Sampson & Raudenbush, 1999.

respondents possibly went back to school as a benefit of their current job, the time order requirement would not be satisfied.

We believe that respondents can give us reliable reports of what happened to them or what they thought at some earlier point in time. Julie Horney, D. Wayne Osgood, and Ineke Haen Marshall (1995) provide an interesting example of the use of such retrospective data. The researchers wanted to identify how criminal activity varies in response to changes in life circumstances. They interviewed 658 newly convicted male offenders sentenced to a Nebraska state prison. In a 45- to 90-minute interview, they recorded each inmate's report of his life circumstances and of his criminal activities for the preceding 2 to 3 years. They then found that criminal involvement was related strongly to adverse changes in life circumstances, such as marital separation or drug use. Retrospective data are often inadequate for measuring variation in past psychological states or behaviors, however, because what we recall about our feelings or actions in the past is likely to be influenced by what we feel in the present. For example, retrospective reports by both adult alcoholics and their parents appear to greatly overestimate the frequency of childhood problems (Vaillant, 1995). People cannot report reliably the frequency and timing of many past events, from hospitalization to hours worked. However, retrospective data tends to be reliable when it concerns major, persistent experiences in the past, such as what type of school someone went to or how a person's family was structured (Campbell, 1992).

Our measures are based on records that contain information on cases in earlier periods. Government, agency, and organizational records are an excellent source of time-ordered data after the fact. However, sloppy record keeping and changes in data-collection policies can lead to inconsistencies, which must be taken into account. Another weakness of such archival data is that they usually contain measures of only a fraction of the variables that we think are important.

We know that cases were equivalent on the dependent variable prior to the treatment. For example, we may hypothesize that a training program (independent variable) improves the English-speaking abilities (dependent variable) of a group of recent immigrants. If we know that none of the immigrants could speak English prior to enrolling in the training program, we can be confident that any subsequent variation in their ability to speak English did not precede exposure to the training program. This is one way that traditional experiments establish time order: Two or more equivalent groups are formed prior to exposing one of them to some treatment.

Longitudinal Designs

In longitudinal research data are collected that can be ordered in time. By measuring the value of cases on an independent variable and a dependent variable at different times, the researcher can determine whether variation in the independent variable precedes variation in the dependent variable.

In some longitudinal designs, the same sample (or panel) is followed over time; in other designs, sample members are rotated or completely replaced. The population from which the sample is selected may be defined broadly, as when a longitudinal survey of the general population is conducted. Or the population may be defined narrowly, as when members of a specific age group are sampled at multiple points in time. The frequency of follow-up measurement can vary, ranging from a before-and-after design with just one follow-up to studies in which various indicators are measured every month for many years.

Certainly it is more difficult to collect data at two or more points in time than at one time. Quite frequently researchers simply cannot, or are unwilling to, delay completion of a study for even 1 year in order to collect follow-up data. But think of the many research questions that really should involve a much longer follow-up period: What is the impact of job training on subsequent employment? How effective is a school-based program in improving parenting skills? Under what conditions do traumatic experiences in childhood result in mental illness? It is safe to say that we will never have enough longitudinal data to answer many important research questions. Nonetheless, the value of longitudinal data is so great that every effort should be made to develop longitudinal research designs when they are appropriate for the research question asked. The following discussion of the three major types of longitudinal designs will give you a sense of the possibilities (see Exhibit 6.3).

Repeated Cross-Sectional Designs

Repeated cross-sectional studies, also known as *trend studies,* have become fixtures of the political arena around election time. Particularly in presidential election years, we have all become accustomed to reading weekly, even daily, reports on the percentage of the population that supports each candidate. Similar polls are conducted to track sentiment on many other social issues. For example, a 1993 poll reported that 52% of adult Americans supported a ban on the possession of handguns, compared to 41% in a similar poll conducted in 1991. According to pollster Louis Harris, this increase indicated a "sea change" in public attitudes (Barringer, 1993). Another researcher said, "It shows that people are responding to their experience [of an increase in handgun-related killings]" (Barringer, 1993:1).

Exhibit 6.3   Three Types of Longitudinal Design

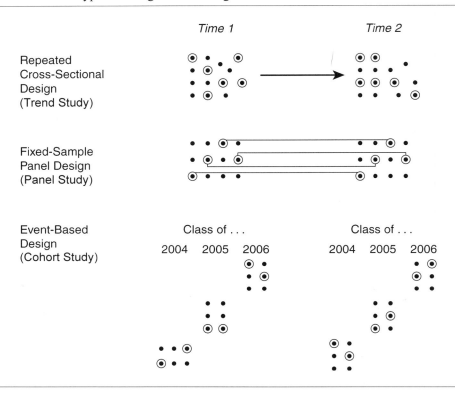

Repeated cross-sectional design (trend study)   A type of longitudinal study in which data are collected at two or more points in time from different samples of the same population.

Repeated cross-sectional surveys are conducted as follows:

1. A sample is drawn from a population at time 1, and data are collected from the sample.

2. As time passes, some people leave the population and others enter it.

3. At time 2, a different sample is drawn from this population.

These features make the repeated cross-sectional design appropriate when the goal is to determine whether a population has changed over time. Has racial tolerance increased among Americans in the past 20 years? Are employers more likely to pay maternity benefits today than they were in the 1950s? These questions concern changes in the population as a whole, not changes in individuals within the population. We want to know whether racial tolerance increased in society, not whether this change was due to migration that brought more racially tolerant people into the country or to individual U.S. citizens becoming more tolerant. We are asking whether employers overall are more likely to pay maternity benefits today than they were yesterday, not whether any such increase was due to recalcitrant employers going out of business or to individual employers changing their maternity benefits. When we do need to know whether individuals in the population changed, we must turn to a panel design.

Fixed-Sample Panel Designs

Panel designs allow us to identify changes in individuals, groups, or whatever we are studying. This is the process for conducting **fixed-sample panel studies:**

1. A sample (called a panel) is drawn from a population at time 1, and data are collected from the sample.

2. As time passes, some panel members become unavailable for follow-up, and the population changes.

3. At time 2, data are collected from the same people as at time 1 (the panel)—except for those people who cannot be located.

Fixed-sample panel design (panel study)   A type of longitudinal study in which data are collected from the same individuals—the panel—at two or more points in time. In another type of panel design, panel members who leave are replaced with new members.

Because a panel design follows the same individuals, it is better than a repeated cross-sectional design for testing causal hypotheses. For example, Sampson and Laub (1990) used a fixed-sample panel design to investigate the effect of childhood deviance on adult crime. They studied a sample of white males in Boston when the subjects were between 10 and 17 years old and then followed up when the subjects were in their adult years. Data were collected from multiple sources, including the subjects themselves and criminal justice records. Sampson and Laub (1990:614) found that children who had been committed to a correctional school for persistent delinquency were much more likely to commit crimes as adults: 61% were arrested between the ages of 25 and 32, compared to 14% of those who had not been in correctional schools as juveniles. In this study, juvenile delinquency unquestionably occurred before adult criminality. If the researchers had used a cross-sectional design to study the past of adults, the juvenile delinquency measure might have been biased by memory lapses, by self-serving recollections about behavior as juveniles, or by loss of agency records.

If you now wonder why every longitudinal study isn't designed as a panel study, you've understood the advantages of panel designs. However, remember that this design does not in itself establish causality. Variation in both the independent variable and the dependent variables may be due to some other variable, even to earlier variation in what is considered the dependent variable. In the example in Exhibit 6.4, there is a hypothesized association between delinquency in the 11th grade and grades obtained in the 12th grade (the dependent variable). The time order is clear. However, both variables are consequences of grades

Exhibit 6.4   Causality in Panel Studies

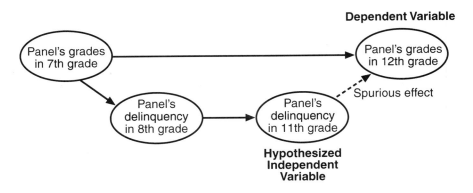

Although delinquency in the 11th grade and grades in the 12th grade
are clearly associated and the time order is clear, causality cannot be
assumed. In reality, grades in the 7th grade also play a role.

obtained in the 7th grade. The apparent effect of 11th-grade delinquency on 12th-grade
grades is spurious because of variation in the dependent variable (grades) at an earlier time.

Panel designs are also a challenge to implement successfully, and often are not even
attempted, because of two major difficulties:

Expense and attrition. It can be difficult, and very expensive, to keep track of individuals over
a long period, and inevitably the proportion of panel members who can be located for follow-
up will decline over time. Panel studies often lose more than one-quarter of their members
through attrition (Miller, 1991:170). However, subject attrition can be reduced substantially if
sufficient staff can be used to keep track of panel members. In their panel study, Sampson and
Laub (1990) lost only 12% of the juveniles in the original sample (8% if you do not count those
who had died). The consequences of a high rate of subject attrition are that the follow-up
sample may no longer be representative of the population from which it was drawn and may
no longer provide a sound basis for estimating change. Subjects who were lost to follow-up
may have been those who changed the most, or the least, over time. It does help to compare
the baseline characteristics of those who are interviewed at follow-up with characteristics of
those lost to follow-up. If these two groups of panel members were not very different at baseline, it is less likely that changes had anything to do with characteristics of the missing panel
members.

Subject fatigue. Panel members may grow weary of repeated interviews and drop out of the
study, or they may become so used to answering the standard questions in the survey that
they start giving stock answers rather than actually thinking about their current feelings
or actions (Campbell, 1992). This is called the problem of **subject fatigue.** Fortunately,
subjects do not often seem to become fatigued in this way, particularly if the research staff

have maintained positive relations with the subjects. For example, at the end of an 18-month-long experimental study of housing alternatives for persons with mental illness who had been homeless, only 3 or 4 individuals (out of 93 who could still be located) refused to participate in the fourth and final round of interviews. The interviews took a total of about 5 hours to complete, and participants received about $50 for their time (Schutt, Goldfinger, & Penk, 1997).

Because panel studies are so useful, social researchers have developed increasingly effective techniques for keeping track of individuals and overcoming subject fatigue. But when resources do not permit use of these techniques to maintain an adequate panel, repeated cross-sectional designs usually can be employed at a cost that is not a great deal higher than that of a one-time-only cross-sectional study. The payoff in explanatory power should be well worth the cost.

Event-Based Designs

In an **event-based design,** often called a *cohort study,* the follow-up samples (at one or more times) are selected from the same **cohort**—people who all have experienced a similar event or a common starting point. Examples include:

- *Birth cohorts*—Those who share a common period of birth (those born in the 1940s, 1950s, 1960s, and so on)
- *Seniority cohorts*—Those who have worked at the same place for about 5 years, about 10 years, and so on
- *School cohorts*—Freshmen, sophomores, juniors, seniors

Event-based design (cohort study) A type of longitudinal study in which data are collected at two or more points in time from individuals in a cohort.

Cohort Individuals or groups with a common starting point. Examples include college class of 1997, people who graduated from high school in the 1980s, General Motors employees who started work between 1990 and the year 2000, and people who were born in the late 1940s or the 1950s (the "baby boom generation").

An event-based design can be a type of repeated cross-sectional design or a type of panel design. In an event-based repeated cross-sectional design, separate samples are drawn from the same cohort at two or more different times. In an event-based panel design, the same individuals from the same cohort are studied at two or more different times.

We can see the value of event-based research in a comparison of two studies that estimated the impact of public and private schooling on high school students' achievement test scores. In a cross-sectional study, James Coleman, Thomas Hoffer, and Sally Kilgore (1982) compared standardized achievement test scores of high school sophomores and seniors in public, Catholic, and other private schools. They found that test scores were higher in the private high schools (both Catholic and other) than in the public high schools. But was this difference a causal effect of private schooling? Perhaps the parents of higher-performing children were choosing to send them to private rather than to public schools. In other words, the higher achievement levels of private-sector students might have been in place before they started high school and not have developed as a consequence of their high school education.

The researchers tried to reduce the impact of this problem by statistically controlling for a range of family background variables: family income, parents' education, race, number of siblings, number of rooms in the home, number of parents present, mother working, and other indicators of a family orientation to education. But some critics pointed out that even with all these controls for family background, the cross-sectional study did not ensure that the students had been comparable in achievement when they started high school.

So James Coleman and Thomas Hoffer (1987) went back to the high schools and studied the test scores of the former sophomores 2 years later, when they were seniors; in other words, the researchers used an event-based panel design. This time they found that the verbal and math achievement test scores of the Catholic school students had increased more over the 2 years than was the case for the public school students (it was not clear whether the scores of the other private school students had increased). Irrespective of students' initial achievement test scores, the Catholic schools seemed to "do more" for their students than did the public schools. This finding continued to be true even when dropouts were studied, too. The researchers' causal conclusion rested on much stronger ground because they used an event-based panel design.

UNITS OF ANALYSIS AND ERRORS IN CAUSAL REASONING

Regardless of the research design, we can easily come to invalid conclusions about causal influences if we do not know what **units of analysis** the measures in our study refer to—that is, the level of social life on which the research question is focused, such as individuals, groups, towns, or nations.

Individual and Group Units of Analysis

In most sociological and psychological studies, the units of analysis are individuals. The researcher may collect survey data from individuals, analyze the data, and then report on, say, how many individuals felt socially isolated and whether substance abuse by individuals was related to their feelings of social isolation.

The units of analysis may instead be groups of some sort, such as families, schools, work organizations, towns, states, or countries. For example, a researcher may collect data from town and police records on the number of accidents in which a driver was intoxicated and the presence or absence of a server liability law in the town. (These laws make those who serve liquor liable for accidents caused by those to whom they served liquor.) The researcher can then analyze the relationship between server liability laws and the frequency of accidents due to drunk driving (perhaps also taking into account town population). Because the data describe the town, towns are the units of analysis.

In some studies, groups are the units of analysis but data are collected from individuals. For example, in their study of influences on violent crime in Chicago neighborhoods, Robert

Sampson, Stephen Raudenbush, and Felton Earls (1997) hypothesized that "collective efficacy" would influence neighborhood crime rates. Collective efficacy was defined conceptually as a characteristic of the neighborhood: the extent to which residents were likely to help other residents and were trusted by other residents. However, they measured this variable in a survey of individuals. The responses of individual residents about their perceptions of their neighbors' helpfulness and trustworthiness were averaged together to create a collective efficacy score for each neighborhood. It was this neighborhood measure of collective efficacy that was used to explain variation in the rate of violent crime between neighborhoods. The data were collected from individuals and were about individuals, but they were combined (aggregated) so as to describe neighborhoods. The units of analysis were thus groups (neighborhoods).

In a study like Sampson's, we can distinguish the concept of units of analysis from the **units of observation.** Data were collected from individuals, the units of observation, and then the data were aggregated and analyzed at the group level. In some studies, the units of observation and the units of analysis are the same. The important point is to know. A conclusion that "crime increases with joblessness" could imply either that individuals who lose their jobs are more likely to commit a crime or that a community with a high unemployment rate is likely to have a high crime rate—or both. Whether we are drawing conclusions from data or interpreting others' conclusions, it is important to be clear about which relationship is being referred to.

We also have to know the units of analysis to interpret statistics appropriately. Measures of association tend to be stronger for group-level than for individual-level data because measurement errors at the individual level tend to cancel out at the group level (Bridges & Weis, 1989:29–31).

The Ecological Fallacy and Reductionism

Researchers should make sure that their causal conclusions reflect the units of analysis in their study. Conclusions about processes at the individual level should be based on individual-level data; conclusions about group-level processes should be based on data collected about groups. In most cases, violation of this rule creates one more reason to suspect the validity of the causal conclusions.

A researcher who draws conclusions about individual-level processes from group-level data could be making what is termed an **ecological fallacy** (see Exhibit 6.5). The conclusions may or may not be correct, but we must recognize that group-level data do not necessarily reflect solely individual-level processes. For example, a researcher may examine factory records and find that the higher the percentage of unskilled workers in factories, the higher the rate of employee sabotage in those factories. But the researcher would commit an ecological fallacy if she then concluded that individual unskilled factory workers are more likely to engage in sabotage. This conclusion is about an individual-level causal process (the relationship between the occupation and criminal propensities of individuals), even though the data describe groups (factories). It could actually be that white-collar workers are the ones more likely to commit sabotage in factories with more unskilled workers, perhaps because the white-collar workers feel they won't be suspected in these settings.

Don't be too quick to reject all conclusions about individual processes based on group-level data; just keep in mind the possibility of an ecological fallacy. If we don't have individual-level data, we can't be sure that patterns at the group level will hold at the individual level.

Exhibit 6.5   Errors in Causal Conclusions

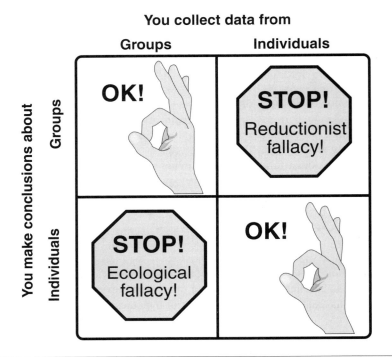

On the other hand, when data about individuals are used to make inferences about group-level processes, a problem occurs that can be thought of as the mirror image of the ecological fallacy: the **reductionist fallacy,** also known as *reductionism,* or the *individualist fallacy* (see Exhibit 6.5). For example, William Julius Wilson (1987:58) notes that we can be misled into concluding from individual-level data that race has a causal effect on violence because there is an association at the individual level between race and the likelihood of arrest for violent crime. However, community-level data reveal that almost 40% of poor blacks lived in extremely poor areas in 1980, compared to only 7% of poor whites. The concentration of African Americans in poverty areas, not the race or other characteristics of the individuals in these areas, may be the cause of higher rates of violence. Explaining violence in this case requires community-level data.

The fact that errors in causal reasoning can be made should not deter you from conducting research with aggregate data nor make you unduly critical of researchers who make inferences about individuals on the basis of aggregate data. When considered broadly, many research questions point to relationships that could be manifested in many ways and on many levels. Sampson's (1987) study of urban violence is a case in point. His analysis involved only aggregate data about cities, and he explained his research approach as in part a response to the failure of other researchers to examine this problem at the structural, aggregate level. Moreover, Sampson argued that the rates of joblessness and family disruption in communities influence community social processes, not just the behavior of the specific individuals who are unemployed or who grew up without two parents. Yet Sampson suggests that the experience of joblessness and poverty is what tends to reduce the propensity of individual men to marry and that the experience of growing up in a home without two parents in turn increases the propensity of individual juveniles to commit crimes. These conclusions about the behavior of individuals seem consistent with the patterns Sampson found in his aggregate, city-level data, so it seems unlikely that he is committing an ecological fallacy when he proposes them.

The solution is to know what the units of analysis and units of observation were in a study and to take these into account in weighing the credibility of the researcher's conclusions. The goal is not to reject out of hand conclusions that refer to a level of analysis different from what was actually studied. Instead, the goal is to consider the likelihood that an ecological fallacy or a reductionist fallacy has been made when estimating the causal validity of the conclusions.

THE MEANING OF EXPLANATION

Now we can get down to the most important business of this chapter—identifying causes. A cause is an explanation for some characteristic, attitude, or behavior of groups, individuals, or other entities (such as families, organizations, or cities) or for events. Most social scientists seek causal explanations that reflect tests of the types of hypotheses with which you are familiar (see Chapter 2): The independent variable is the presumed cause and the dependent variable is the potential effect. For example, the study by Robert Sampson and Stephen Raudenbush (2001) tested whether disorder in urban neighborhoods (the independent variable) leads to crime (the dependent variable). (As you know, they concluded that it didn't, at least not directly.) This type of causal explanation is termed *nomothetic.*

A different type of cause is the focus of some qualitative research (Chapter 9), some historical/comparative research (Chapter 11), and our everyday conversations about causes. In this type of causal explanation, termed *idiographic,* individual events or the behaviors of individuals are explained with a series of related, prior events. For example, you might explain a particular crime as resulting from several incidents in the life of the perpetrator that resulted in a tendency toward violence, coupled with stress resulting from a failed marriage, and a chance meeting.

Some qualitative researchers avoid causal language entirely and seek instead to provide a "thick description" of the ways in which participants made sense of their situation. In this section, I will discuss each type of explanation, but most of the chapter focuses on the aspects of research design that influence our ability to identify nomothetic causes.

Nomothetic Causal Explanation

A **nomothetic causal explanation** is one involving the belief that variation in an independent variable will be followed by variation in the dependent variable, when all other things are equal (*ceteris paribus*). In this perspective, researchers who claim a causal effect have concluded that the value of cases on the dependent variable differs from what their value would have been in the absence of variation in the independent variable. For instance,

Exhibit 6.6   The Counterfactual in Causal Research

Independent variable: Dependent variable:

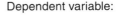

Actual situation:
People who watch violence on TV are more likely to commit violent acts.

Independent variable: Dependent variable:

Counterfactual situation:
The same people watch nonviolent TV shows at the same time, in the same circumstances. They are not more likely to commit violent acts.

researchers might claim that the likelihood of committing violent crimes is higher for individuals who were abused as children than it would be if these same individuals had not been abused as children. Or, researchers might claim that the likelihood of committing violent crimes is higher for individuals exposed to media violence than it would be if these same individuals had not been exposed to media violence. The situation as it would have been in the absence of variation in the independent variable is termed the **counterfactual** (see Exhibit 6.6).

Of course, the fundamental difficulty with this perspective is that we never really know what would have happened at the same time to the same people (or groups, cities, and so on) if the independent variable had not varied—because it did. We can't rerun real-life scenarios (King, Keohane, & Verba, 1994). We could observe the aggressiveness of people's behavior before and after they were exposed to media violence. But this comparison involves an earlier time period, when by definition the people and their circumstances were not exactly the same.

But we do not need to give up hope! Far from it. We can design research to create conditions that are very comparable indeed, so that we can confidently assert our conclusions *ceteris paribus*—other things being equal. We can examine the impact on the dependent variable of variation in the independent variable alone, even though we will not be able to compare the same people at the same time in exactly the same circumstances except for the variation in the independent variable. And by knowing the ideal standard of comparability, we can improve our research designs and strengthen our causal conclusions even when we cannot come so close to living up to the meaning of *ceteris paribus*.

Quantitative researchers seek to test nomothetic causal explanations with either experimental or nonexperimental research designs. However, the way in which experimental and nonexperimental designs attempt to identify causes differs quite a bit. It is very hard to meet some of the criteria for achieving valid nomothetic causal explanations using a nonexperimental design. Most of the rest of this chapter is devoted to a review of these causal criteria and a discussion of how experimental and nonexperimental designs can help to establish them.

Causal effect (nomothetic perspective)   The finding that change in one variable leads to change in another variable, *ceteris paribus* (other things being equal).

Example of a nomothetic causal effect: Individuals arrested for domestic assault tend to commit fewer subsequent assaults than similar individuals who are accused in the same circumstances but not arrested.

Idiographic Causal Explanation

The other meaning of the term *cause* is one that we have in mind very often in everyday speech. This is **idiographic causal explanation:** the concrete, individual sequence of events, thoughts, or actions that resulted in a particular outcome for a particular individual or that led to a particular event (Hage & Meeker, 1988). An idiographic explanation also may be termed an *individualist* or a *historicist explanation.*

Causal effect (idiographic perspective)   The finding that a series of events following an initial set of conditions leads in a progressive manner to a particular event or outcome.

Example of an idiographic causal effect: An individual is neglected by her parents but has a supportive grandparent. She comes to distrust others, has trouble in school, is unable to keep a job, and eventually becomes homeless. She subsequently develops a supportive relationship with a shelter case manager, who helps her find a job and regain her housing (based on Hirsch, 1989).

A causal explanation that is idiographic includes statements of initial conditions and then relates a series of events at different times that led to the outcome, or causal effect. This narrative, or story, is the critical element in an idiographic explanation, which may therefore be classified as narrative reasoning (Richardson, 1995:200–201). Idiographic explanations focus on particular social actors, in particular social places, at particular social times (Abbott, 1992).

Idiographic explanations are also typically very concerned with context—with understanding the particular outcome as part of a larger set of interrelated circumstances. Idiographic explanations thus can be termed holistic.

Idiographic explanation is deterministic, focusing on what caused a particular event to occur or what caused a particular case to change. As in nomothetic explanations, idiographic causal explanations can involve counterfactuals, by trying to identify what would have happened if a different circumstance had occurred. But unlike nomothetic explanations, the notion of a probabilistic relationship, an average effect, does not really apply. A deterministic cause has an effect in every case under consideration.

Elijah Anderson's (1990) field research in a poor urban community produced a narrative account of how drug addiction can result in a downward slide into residential instability and crime:

> When addicts deplete their resources, they may go to those closest to them, drawing them into their schemes. . . . [T]he family may put up with the person for a while. They provide money if they can. . . . They come to realize that the person is on drugs. . . . Slowly the reality sets in more and more completely, and the family becomes drained of both financial and emotional resources. . . . Close relatives lose faith and begin to see the person as untrustworthy and weak. Eventually the addict begins to "mess up" in a variety of ways, taking furniture from the house [and] anything of value. . . . Relatives and friends begin to see the person . . . as "out there" in the streets. . . . One deviant act leads to another. (Anderson, 1990:86–87)

An idiographic explanation like Anderson's pays close attention to time order and causal mechanisms. Nonetheless, it is difficult to make a convincing case that one particular causal narrative should be chosen over an alternative narrative (Abbott, 1992). Does low self-esteem result in vulnerability to the appeals of drug dealers, or does a chance drug encounter precipitate a slide in self-esteem? The prudent causal analyst remains open to alternative explanations.

Case-Oriented Understanding

Case-oriented understanding can be termed phenomenological, because it attempts to understand a phenomenon from the standpoint of the participants. Although it is not explicitly causal, it is a means of explaining social phenomena. For example, Constance Fischer and Fredrick Wertz (2002) constructed a phenomenological analysis of being criminally victimized. They first recounted crime victims' stories, and then identified common themes in these stories.

You can see how an explanation of the effect of crime on its victims is constructed from excerpts that illustrate the response process they identified (Fischer & Wertz, 2002:288–290). The first stage in this process was "living routinely" before the crime: "he/she . . . feels that the defended against crime could never happen to him/her. I said, 'nah, you've got to be kidding.'"

In a second stage, "Being Disrupted," the victim copes with the discovered crime and fears worse outcomes: "You imagine the worst when it's happening. . . . I just kept thinking my baby's upstairs." In a later stage, "Reintegrating," the victim begins to assimilate the violation by taking some protective action: "but I clean out my purse now since then and I leave very little of that kind of stuff in there."

Finally, when the victim is "Going On," he/she reflects on the changes the crime produced: "I don't think it made me stronger. It made me smarter."

Is this a *causal* explanation of the impact of crime on its victims? Not all would agree, but this illustration shows how the effort to "understand" what happened also inevitably gives us a better sense of *why* things happened as they did.

RESEARCH DESIGNS AND CRITERIA FOR CAUSAL EXPLANATION

In order to achieve causally valid nomothetic explanations, research designs must have certain features. In this section I will introduce these features and discuss what makes them so important.

Five criteria must be considered when deciding whether a causal connection exists. Research designs that allow us to establish these criteria require very careful planning, implementation, and analysis. Many times, researchers have to leave one or more of the criteria unmet and therefore are left with some important doubts about the validity of their causal conclusions; or they may avoid even making any causal assertions. The first three of the criteria are generally considered the most important bases for identifying a nomothetic causal effect: empirical association, appropriate time order, and nonspuriousness. Because experimental research designs have several features that are designed to meet these criteria, they are particularly strong designs for testing nomothetic causal explanations.

Evidence that meets the other two criteria—identifying a causal mechanism and specifying the context in which the effect occurs—can considerably strengthen causal explanations. These criteria can be met in different ways by both experimental and nonexperimental designs.

In the following subsections, I will indicate how researchers attempt to meet the five criteria with both experimental and nonexperimental designs. Illustrations of experimental design features will use a 1999 study by Brad Bushman, Roy Baumeister, and Angela Stack on the effect of catharsis on aggression. Most illustrations of nonexperimental design features will be based on the study by Robert Sampson and Stephen Raudenbush (1999) of neighborhood social control, which I have already introduced.

Bushman and his colleagues recruited 707 undergraduate students from introductory psychology courses. The experiment had several stages, but I will focus on only a few (see Exhibit 6.7). First, students were told they were in a study of the accuracy of perceptions in social interactions. They gave their consent to participate and were then asked to read either a statement that endorsed the catharsis effect (on reducing aggression), a statement that disputed the catharsis effect, or no statement. Next, each student wrote a short essay on abortion, which was then evaluated by a student in another room. The evaluations, all of them very negative, were returned to the students. At this point, all the students were invited to hit a punching bag, alone, for 2 minutes. (This was the opportunity for catharsis—getting anger out of your system.)

Now the students were told they were to engage in a competitive reaction-time task. This task consisted of trying to press a button faster than a partner. Each time the student pressed the button faster, they were able to "blast" their competitor with a noise that was as loud and long as they liked (within limits). It turned out that students who had read the procatharsis

Exhibit 6.7   An Experiment to Test the Effect of Media Endorsement of Catharsis on Aggression

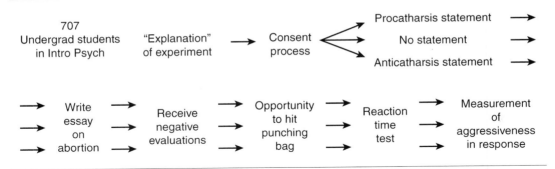

Source: Based on Bushman, Baumeister, & Stack, 1999:370–371.

Exhibit 6.8   Interpersonal Aggression as a Function of Message Content

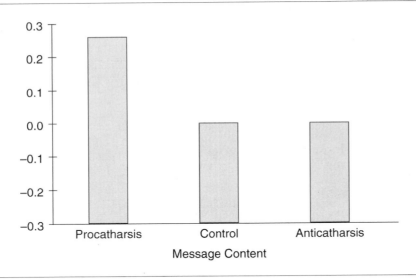

Source: Based on Bushman, Baumeister, & Stack, 1999:372.

message "blasted" their competitors more than did those who had read no message, while those who had read the anticatharsis message blasted their competitors the least (see Exhibit 6.8). Bushman and his colleagues concluded that reading a procartharsis message increased rather than decreased interpersonal aggression.

Was this causal conclusion justified? How confident can we be in its internal validity? What about the conclusion by Sampson and Raudenbush (1999) that social and physical disorder does not directly cause neighborhood crime? I will answer these questions by reviewing how these two studies attempted to meet each of the causal criteria. I will also identify the key features of a "true experiment."

Exhibit 6.9   Experimental Conditions: A "3 × 2" Design

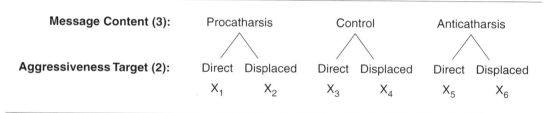

Source: Based on Bushman, Baumeister, & Stack, 1999:371.

Association

We say that there was an **association** between interpersonal aggression and type of message in Bushman's experiment because the level of interpersonal aggression varied according to the type of message. An empirical (or observed) association between the independent and dependent variables is the first criterion for identifying a nomothetic causal effect.

We can determine whether an association exists between the independent and dependent variables in a true experiment because there are two or more groups that differ in terms of their value on the independent variable. One group receives some "treatment," such as reading a cathartic message, that is a manipulation of the value of the independent variable. This group is termed the *experimental group*. In a simple experiment, there may be one other group that does not receive the treatment; it is termed the *control group*. The Bushman study, as I have described it, compared three groups; other experiments may compare more groups that represent multiple values of the independent variable or even combinations of the values of two or more independent variables. In fact, for each of the three groups that differed in terms of message content, Bushman actually compared subgroups that differed in having direct or displaced targets for their aggression (see Exhibit 6.9).

In nonexperimental research, the test for an association between the independent and dependent variables is like that used in experimental research—seeing whether values of cases that differ on the independent variable tend to differ in terms of the dependent variable. The difference with nonexperimental research designs is that the independent variable is not a treatment to which the researcher assigns some individuals. In their nonexperimental study of neighborhood crime, Sampson and Raudenbush (1999) studied the association between the independent variable (level of social and physical disorder) and the crime rate, but they did not assign individuals to live in neighborhoods with low or high levels of disorder.

Time Order

Association is a necessary criterion for establishing a causal effect, but it is not sufficient. We must also ensure that the variation in the dependent variable occurred after the variation in the independent variable. This is the criterion of time order. In a true experiment, the time order is determined by the researcher. Bushman and his colleagues (1999) first exposed the students to the different messages and then measured their level of interpersonal aggression. If we find an association between the types of messages people have read and their aggressiveness outside of an experimental situation, the criterion of time order may not be met.

People who are more inclined to interpersonal aggression may be more likely than others to read messages that encourage displays of aggressiveness. This would result in an association between type of message and interpersonal aggression, but the association would reflect the influence of aggression on type of message rather than the other way around.

You have already seen that in nonexperimental research, time order can be readily established if a longitudinal design is used. Sampson and Raudenbush (1999) could not determine time order unambiguously in their cross-sectional study of the effect of social disorder on crime rates, but Sampson and Laub's (1990) longitudinal study of the effects of childhood deviance on adult crime provided strong evidence of appropriate time order.

Nonspuriousness

Nonspuriousness is another essential criterion for establishing the existence of a causal effect of an independent variable on a dependent variable; in some respects it is the most important criterion. We say that a relationship between two variables is not spurious when it is not due to variation in a third variable. Have you heard the old adage "Correlation does not prove causation"? It is meant to remind us that an association between two variables might be caused by something other than an effect of the presumed independent variable on the dependent variable. If we measure children's shoe sizes and their academic knowledge, for example, we will find a positive association. However, the association results from the fact that older children have larger feet as well as more academic knowledge. Shoe size does not cause knowledge, or vice versa.

Do storks bring babies? If you believe that correlation proves causation, then you might think so. The more storks that appear in certain districts in Holland, the more babies are born. But the association in Holland between number of storks and number of babies is spurious. In fact, both the number of storks and the birth rate are higher in rural districts than in urban districts. The rural or urban character of the districts (the extraneous variable) causes variation in the other two variables

If you think this point is obvious, consider a social science example. Do schools with more resources produce better student outcomes? Before you answer the question, consider the fact that parents with more education and higher income tend to live in neighborhoods that spend more on their schools. These parents are also more likely to have books in the home and provide other advantages for their children. Do the parents cause variation in both school resources and student performance? If so, there would be an association between school resources and student performance that was at least partially spurious.

A true experiment like Bushman's (1999) study of catharsis uses a technique called **randomization** to reduce the risk of spuriousness. Students in Bushman's experiment were asked to select a message to read by drawing a random number out of a bag. That is, the students were assigned randomly to a treatment condition. If students were assigned to only two groups, a coin toss could have been used (see Exhibit 6.10). **Random assignment** ensures that neither students' aggressiveness nor any of their other characteristics or attitudes could influence which of the messages they read. As a result, the different groups are likely to be equivalent in all respects at the outset of the experiment. The greater the number of cases assigned randomly to the groups, the more likely that the groups will be equivalent in all respects. Whatever the preexisting sources of variation among the students, these could not explain why the group that read the procatharsis message became more aggressive, while the others didn't.

Exhibit 6.10 Random Assignment to One of Two Groups

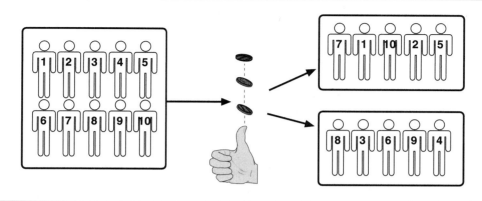

A nonexperimental study like Sampson and Raudenbush's (1999) cannot use random assignment to comparison groups in order to minimize the risk of spurious effects. Even if we wanted to, we couldn't randomly assign people to live in neighborhoods with different levels of informal social control. Instead, nonexperimental researchers commonly use an alternative approach to try to achieve the criterion of nonspuriousness. The technique of **statistical control** allows researchers to determine whether the relationship between the independent and dependent variables still occurs while we hold constant the values of other variables. If it does, the relationship could not be caused by variation in these other variables.

Sampson and Raudenbush designed their study in part to determine whether the apparent effect of visible disorder on crime—the "broken windows" thesis—was spurious due to the effect of informal social control (see Exhibit 6.1, p. 167). Exhibit 6.11 shows how statistical control was used to test this possibility. The data for all neighborhoods show that neighborhoods with much visible disorder had higher crime rates than those with less visible disorder. However, when we examine the relationship between visible disorder and neighborhood crime rate separately for neighborhoods with high and low levels of informal social control (when we statistically control for social control level), we see that the crime rate no longer varies with visible disorder. Therefore, we must conclude that the apparent effect of "broken windows" was spurious due to level of informal social control. Neighborhoods with low levels of social control were more likely to have high levels of visible social and physical disorder, and they were also more likely to have a high crime rate, but the visible disorder itself did not alter the crime rate.

Statistical control   A technique used in nonexperimental research to reduce the risk of spuriousness. The effect of one or more variables are removed, for example, by holding them constant, so that the relationship between the independent and dependent variables can be assessed without the influence of variation in the control variables.

Exhibit 6.11 The Use of Statistical Control to Reduce Spuriousness

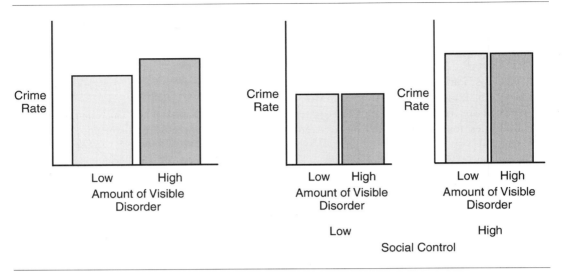

Source: Based on Sampson & Raudenbush, 1999.

> *Example:* In a different study, Sampson (1987) found a relationship between rates
> of family disruption and violent crime. He then classified cities by their level of
> joblessness (the control variable) and found that same relationship between the
> rates of family disruption and violent crime among cities with different levels of
> joblessness. So the rate of joblessness could not have caused the association
> between family disruption and violent crime.

We can strengthen our understanding of nomothetic causal connections, and increase the
likelihood of drawing causally valid conclusions, by considering two additional criteria:
causal mechanism and causal context. These two criteria are emphasized in the definition of
idiographic causal explanation, with its attention to the sequence of events and the context in
which they happen, but here I will limit my discussion of these criteria to research oriented
to nomothetic causal explanations.

Mechanism

A causal **mechanism** is some process that creates the connection between variation in an
independent variable and the variation in the dependent variable it is hypothesized to cause
(Cook & Campbell, 1979:35; Marini & Singer, 1988). Many social scientists (and scientists in
other fields) argue that no nomothetic causal explanation is adequate until a causal mechanism
is identified.

Up to this point, I have described only a portion of Bushman's (1999) experiment about
catharsis. He and his colleagues actually conducted two experiments and measured some

other variables that I haven't described. They tested the effect of reading a procatharsis message on the desire to hit a punching bag; they asked students how much they enjoyed hitting the punching bag; and they compared the aggressiveness of students who had hit the punching bag with those who hadn't. The findings that emerged from these additional study components provided a substantial bit of information about the causal mechanism that linked reading the procatharsis message to aggressive behavior. They concluded that the process went like this: Participants who read a procatharsis message were more likely to want to hit a punching bag; these students were then more likely to enjoy hitting the punching bag, and they were more likely to be aggressive in their actions toward others. When Bushman and his colleagues found that aggressiveness remained high throughout subsequent competitions, they also speculated that there was a "self-defeating prophecy" at work: When participants did not experience a reduction in their anger after expressing it, they became even more frustrated and angry.

Figuring out some aspects of the process by which the independent variable influenced the variation in the dependent variable should increase confidence in our conclusion that there was a causal effect (Costner, 1989). However, there may be many components to the causal mechanism and we cannot hope to identify them all in one study. For example, Bushman and his colleagues (1999:374) acknowledged that they had not identified empirically "the intrapsychic process, or mechanism that mediated effects of the persuasive messages." They did speculate that both anger and diminished self-esteem might be important, but an empirical test was left for another project.

In their study of deterrence of spouse abuse (introduced in Chapter 2), Lawrence Sherman and Richard Berk (1984) designed follow-up experiments to test or control for several causal mechanisms that they wondered about after their first experiment: Did recidivism decrease for those who were arrested for spouse abuse because of the exemplary work of the arresting officers? Did recidivism increase for arrestees as time passed and they experienced more stressors with their spouses? Investigating these and other possible causal mechanisms enriched Sherman and Berk's eventual explanation of how arrest influences recidivism.

Our confidence in causal conclusions based on nonexperimental research also increases with identification of a causal mechanism. Such mechanisms, which are termed **intervening variables** in nonexperimental research, help us to understand how variation in the independent variable results in variation in the dependent variable. For example, in a study that reanalyzed data from Sheldon Glueck and Elenor Glueck's (1950) pathbreaking study of juvenile delinquency, Robert Sampson and John Laub (1994) found that children who grew up with such structural disadvantages as family poverty and geographic mobility were more likely to become juvenile delinquents. Why did this occur? Their analysis indicated that these structural disadvantages led to lower levels of informal social control in the family (less parent–child attachment, less maternal supervision, and more erratic or harsh discipline). Lower levels of informal social control resulted in a higher probability of delinquency (Exhibit 6.12). Informal social control intervened in the relationship between structural context and delinquency.

Of course, identification of one (or two or three) intervening variables does not end the possibilities for clarifying the causal mechanisms. You might ask why structural disadvantage tends to result in lower levels of family social control or how family social control influences delinquency. You could then conduct research to identify the mechanisms that link, for example, family social control and juvenile delinquency. (Perhaps the children feel they're

Exhibit 6.12   Intervening Variables in Nonexperimental Research: Structural Disadvantage and
Juvenile Delinquency

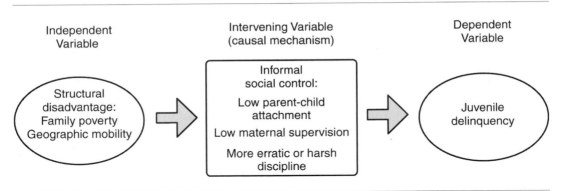

Source: Based on Sampson & Laub, 1994.

not cared for, so they become less concerned with conforming to social expectations.) This
process could go on and on. The point is that identification of a mechanism through which
the independent variable influences the dependent variable increases our confidence in the
conclusion that a causal connection does indeed exist.

When you think about the role of variables in causal relationships, don't confuse variables that cause **spurious relationships** with those that intervene in causal relationships—
even though both are "third variables" that do not appear in the initial hypothesis. In
Exhibit 6.13 the **extraneous variable,** joblessness, creates a spurious relationship. By contrast, in Exhibit 6.12, the intervening variable is part of the process that links the independent variable and the dependent variable; intervening variables help to explain the
relationship between the independent variable (structural disadvantage) and the dependent
variable (juvenile delinquency) (Davis, 1985).

Context

No cause has its effect apart from some larger **context** involving other variables. For
whom and when and in what conditions does this effect occur? A cause is really one among
a set of interrelated factors required for the effect (Hage & Meeker, 1988; Papineau, 1978).
Identification of the context in which a causal effect occurs is not itself a criterion for a valid
causal conclusion and it is not always attempted, but it does help us to understand the causal
relationship.

Bushman and colleagues tested the effect of several contextual factors having to do with
the types of persons reading the messages. They found that people had the same aggressive
response to the cathartic message whether they competed against the person who was actually
the source of their angry feelings (the person who wrote the negative evaluation) or against
an innocent third person. An earlier experiment also showed that being angry was a precondition for the effect of the procatharsis and anticatharsis statements.

Exhibit 6.13   Extraneous Variables in Nonexperimental Research: Parent–Child Attachment and Juvenile Delinquency

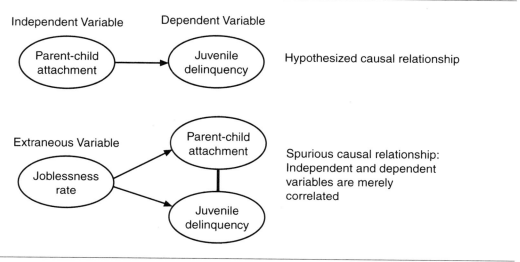

Source: Based on Sampson & Laub, 1994.

Context was also important in Sherman and Berk's research on domestic violence. Arrest was less effective in reducing subsequent domestic violence in cities with high levels of unemployment than in cities with low levels of unemployment. This seemed to be more evidence of the importance of individuals having a "stake in conformity" (Berk et al., 1992).

CONCLUSIONS

Causation and the means for achieving causally valid conclusions in research is the last of the three legs on which the validity of research rests. In this chapter, you have learned about the two main meanings of causation (nomothetic and idiographic), as well as an alternative approach to explanation—case-oriented understanding—that does not involve causal reasoning. You also have learned how to establish the time order of effects in nonexperimental research, and you have been exposed to the problem of spuriousness and the ways that randomization and statistical control deal with it—and you have learned that the use of randomization in experimental designs makes this design preferable for establishing causal validity. Finally, you have studied the five criteria used to evaluate the extent to which particular research designs may achieve causally valid findings.

I should reemphasize that the results of any particular study are part of an always changing body of empirical knowledge about social reality. Thus our understandings of causal relationships are always partial. Researchers always wonder whether they have omitted some relevant variables from their controls, whether their experimental results would differ if the experiment were conducted in another setting, or whether they have overlooked a critical historical event. But by using consistent definitions of terms and maintaining clear standards for establishing the validity of research results—and by expecting the same of others who do research—social researchers can contribute to a growing body of knowledge that can reliably guide social policy and social understanding.

When you read the results of a social scientific study, you should now be able to evaluate critically the validity of the study's findings. If you plan to engage in social research, you should now be able to plan an approach that will lead to valid findings. And with a good understanding of the three dimensions of validity (measurement validity, generalizability, and causal validity) under your belt, and with sensitivity also to the goal of "authenticity" emphasized by some qualitative researchers, you are ready to focus on the major methods of data collection used by social scientists. Each of these methods tends to use a somewhat different approach to achieving validity.

KEY TERMS

Association
Case-oriented understanding
Causal effect (idiographic perspective)
Causal effect (nomothetic perspective)
Ceteris paribus
Cohort
Cohort study
Context
Counterfactual
Cross-sectional research design
Ecological fallacy
Event-based design
Extraneous variable
Fixed-sample panel design
Idiographic causal explanation
Intervening variable

Longitudinal research design
Mechanism
Nomothetic causal explanation
Nonspuriousness
Random assignment
Randomization
Reductionist fallacy (reductionism)
Repeated cross-sectional design
Spurious relationship
Statistical control
Subject fatigue
Time order
Trend study
Units of analysis
Unit of observation

HIGHLIGHTS

• Causation can be defined in either nomothetic or idiographic terms. Nomothetic causal explanations deal with effects on average. Idiographic causal explanations deal with the sequence of events that led to a particular outcome.

• Case-oriented understanding is a form of explanation in which the researcher seeks to understand a phenomenon from the standpoint of the participants.

• The concept of nomothetic causal explanation relies on a comparison. The value of cases on the dependent variable is measured after they have been exposed to variation in an independent variable. This measurement is compared to what the value of cases on the dependent variable would have been if they had not been exposed to the variation in the independent variable (the counterfactual). The validity of nomothetic causal conclusions rests on how closely the comparison group comes to the ideal counterfactual.

• From a nomothetic perspective three criteria are generally viewed as necessary for identifying a causal relationship: association between the variables, proper time order, and nonspuriousness of the association. In addition, the basis for concluding that a causal relationship exists is strengthened by identification of a causal mechanism and the context for the relationship.

- Association between two variables is in itself insufficient evidence of a causal relationship. This point is commonly made with the expression "Correlation does not prove causation."

- Experiments use random assignment to make comparison groups as similar as possible at the outset of an experiment in order to reduce the risk of spurious effects due to extraneous variables.

- Nonexperimental designs use statistical controls to reduce the risk of spuriousness. A variable is controlled when it is held constant so that the association between the independent and dependent variables can be assessed without being influenced by the control variable.

- Ethical and practical constraints often preclude the use of experimental designs.

- Idiographic causal explanations can be difficult to identify, because the starting and ending points of particular events and the determination of which events act as causes in particular sequences may be ambiguous.

- Longitudinal designs are usually preferable to cross-sectional designs for establishing the time order of effects. Longitudinal designs vary in terms of whether the same people are measured at different times, how the population of interest is defined, and how frequently follow-up measurements are taken. Fixed-sample panel designs provide the strongest test for the time order of effects, but they can be difficult to carry out successfully because of their expense, as well as subject attrition and fatigue.

- We do not fully understand the variables in a study until we know what units of analysis—what level of social life—they refer to.

- Invalid conclusions about causality may occur when relationships between variables measured at the group level are assumed to apply at the individual level (the ecological fallacy) and when relationships between variables measured at the level of individuals are assumed to apply at the group level (the reductionist fallacy). Nonetheless, many research questions point to relationships at multiple levels and so may profitably be investigated at multiple units of analysis.

DISCUSSION QUESTIONS

1. Review articles in several newspapers, copying down all causal assertions. These might range from assertions that the stock market declined because of uncertainty in the Middle East to explanations about why a murder was committed or why test scores are declining in U.S. schools. Inspect the articles carefully, noting all evidence used to support the causal assertions. Are the explanations nomothetic, idiographic, or a combination of both? Which criteria for establishing causality in a nomothetic framework are met? How satisfactory are the idiographic explanations? What other potentially important influences on the reported outcome have been overlooked?

2. Select several research articles in professional journals that assert, or imply, that they have identified a causal relationship between two or more variables. Are each of the criteria for establishing the existence of a causal relationship met? Find a study in which subjects were assigned randomly to experimental and comparison groups to reduce the risk of spurious influences on the supposedly causal relationship. How convinced are you by the study?

Find a survey study that makes causal assertions based on the relationships, or correlations, among variables. What variables have been statistically controlled? List other variables that might be influencing the relationship but that have not been controlled. How convinced are you by the study?

3. Search *Sociological Abstracts* or another index to the social science literature for several articles on studies using any type of longitudinal design. You will be searching for article titles that use words

like "longitudinal," "panel," "trend," or "over time." How successful were the researchers in carrying out the design? What steps did the researchers who used a panel design take to minimize panel attrition? How convinced are you by those using repeated cross-sectional designs that they have identified a process of change in individuals? Did any researchers use retrospective questions? How did they defend the validity of these measures?

PRACTICE EXERCISES

1. The CD-ROM contains lessons on units of analysis and the related problems of ecological fallacy and reductionism. Choose the Units of Analysis lesson from the main menu. It describes several research projects and asks you to identify the units of analysis in each. Then it presents several conclusions for particular studies and asks you to determine whether an error has been made.

2. Propose a hypothesis involving variables that could be measured with individuals as the units of analysis. How might this hypothesis be restated so as to involve groups as the units of analysis? Would you expect the hypothesis to be supported at both levels? Why or why not? Repeat the exercise, this time starting with a different hypothesis involving groups as the units of analysis and then restating it so as to involve individuals as the units of analysis.

WEB EXERCISES

1. Go to SocioRealm at http://www.digeratiweb.com/sociorealm. From the links supplied, find information regarding a subject of your choosing related to crime and/or violence (for example, youth violence, corporate crime, rape, etc.). Report on the prevalence and/or extent of the phenomenon you have identified. Propose a causal explanation for variation in this phenomenon. What research design would you propose to test this explanation? Explain.

2. Go to Crime Stoppers International's (CSI) Web site at http://www.c-s-i.org. Check out "About Us" and "Crime Stoppers." How is CSI "fighting crime"? What does CSI's approach assume about the cause of crime? Do you think CSI's approach to fighting crime is based on valid conclusions about causality? Explain.

3. What are the latest trends in crime? Write a short statement after inspecting the FBI's Uniform Crime Reports at www.fbi.gov (go to the "Library and References" section). You will need to use Adobe Acrobat Reader to access some of these reports (those in PDF format). Follow the instructions on the site if you're not familiar with this program.

SPSS EXERCISES

We can use the GSS2000mini data to learn how causal hypotheses can be evaluated with nonexperimental data.

1. Specify four hypotheses in which CAPPUN is the dependent variable and the independent variable is also measured with a question in the GSS2000. The independent variables should have no more than 10 valid values (check the variable list).
   a. Inspect the frequency distributions of each independent variable in your hypotheses. If it appears that any have little valid data or were coded with more than 10 categories, substitute another independent variable.
   b. Generate crosstabulations that show the association between CAPPUN and each of the independent variables. Make sure that CAPPUN is the row variable and that you select "Column Percents."

c. Does support for capital punishment vary across the categories of any of the independent variables? By how much? Would you conclude that there is an association, as hypothesized, for any pairs of variables?

d. Might one of the associations you have just identified be spurious due to the effect of a third variable? What might such an extraneous variable be? Look through the variable list and find a variable that might play this role. If you can't think of any possible extraneous variables, or if you didn't find an association in support of any of your hypotheses, try this: Examine the association between CAPPUN and WRKSTAT2. In the next step, control for sex (gender). The idea is that there is an association between work status and support for capital punishment that might be spurious due to the effect of sex (gender). Proceed with the following steps:

(1) Select *Analyze|Descriptive statistics|Crosstabs.*

(2) In the Crosstabs window, highlight CAPPUN and then click the right arrow to move it into Rows. Move WRKSTAT2 into Columns and SEX into Layer 1 of 1.

(3) Select *Cells|Percentages Column|Continue|OK.*

Is the association between employment status and support for capital punishment affected by gender? Do you conclude that the association between CAPPUN and WRKSTSAT2 seems to be spurious due to the effect of SEX?

2. Does the association between support for capital punishment and any of your independent variables vary with social context? Marian Borg (1997) concluded that it did. Test this by reviewing the association between attitude toward African Americans (RACPUSH2) and CAPPUN. Follow the procedures in Exercise 1d, but click RACPUSH2 into columns and REGION4 into Layer 1 of 1. (You must first return the variables used previously to the variables list.) Take a while to study this complex three-variable table. Does the association between CAPPUN and RACPUSH2 vary with region? How would you interpret this finding?

3. Now, how about the influence of an astrological sign on support for capital punishment? Create a crosstabulation in which ZODIAC is the independent (column) variable and CAPPUN is the dependent (row) variable (with column percents). What do you make of the results?

DEVELOPING A RESEARCH PROPOSAL

How will you try to establish the causal effects you hypothesize?

1. Identify at least one hypothesis involving what you expect is a causal relationship.

2. Identify key variables that should be controlled in your survey design in order to increase your ability to avoid arriving at a spurious conclusion about the hypothesized causal effect. Draw on relevant research literature and social theory to identify these variables.

3. Add a longitudinal component to your research design. Explain why you decided to use this particular longitudinal design.

4. Review the criteria for establishing a nomothetic causal effect and discuss your ability to satisfy each one. Include in your discussion some consideration of how well your design will avoid each of the threats to experimental validity.

Chapter 7

EXPERIMENTS

True Experiments

Experimental and Comparison Groups
Pretest and Posttest Measures
Randomization
Limitations of True Experimental Designs
Summary: Causality in True Experiments

Quasi-Experiments

Nonequivalent Control Group Designs
Before-and-After Designs
Summary: Causality in Quasi-
    Experiments

Nonexperiments

Ex Post Facto Control Group Designs
One-Shot Case Studies and Longitudinal
    Designs
Summary: Causality in
    Nonexperiments

Validity in Experiments

Causal (Internal) Validity

Selection Bias
Endogenous Change
External Events
Contamination
Treatment Misidentification
Generalizability
    Sample Generalizability
    External Validity
    Interaction of Testing and Treatment

Combining Methods

Process Analysis
    Case Study: Obedience to Authority
Conducting Factorial Surveys
    Case Study: Neighborhood
        Composition and Racial Segregation

Ethical Issues in Experimental Research

Deception
Selective Distribution of Benefits

Conclusions

How does the organization of work influence attitudes and behavior? The influence of the workplace has been a central concern of sociologists since the discipline's origins in the 19th century. In the late 1800s, Emile Durkheim (1964) theorized about the impact of the division of labor on social solidarity, Max Weber (1947) identified the attitudes appropriate for employment in rational bureaucratic organizations, and Karl Marx (1967) speculated on the effects of workers' separation from the means of production. In the late 20th century, researchers from all the social science disciplines accumulated a substantial body of research based on investigations in many different types of work organizations. Experimental research, the subject of this chapter, has been used to test some very specific but quite important hypotheses about the impact of work and work-related training.

Experimental research is most appropriate for answering research questions about the effect of a treatment or some other variable whose values can be manipulated by the researcher. Experimental research provides the most powerful design for testing nomothetic causal hypotheses. In Chapter 6, Brad Bushman's (1995) research about the impact of cathartic messages provides a good example of how experiments are used to test causal hypotheses. You have also seen the value of experimental research in Lawrence Sherman and Richard Berk's (1984) research on police response to domestic violence (Chapter 2). This chapter examines experimental methodology in more detail: You will learn to distinguish different types of experimental design (which include true experiments and quasi-experiments) and to contrast them with nonexperimental designs, to evaluate the utility of particular designs for reaching causally valid conclusions, to identify problems of generalizability with experiments, and to consider ethical problems in experimentation.

TRUE EXPERIMENTS

True experiments must have at least three things:

- Two comparison groups (in the simplest case, an experimental and a control group)
- Variation in the independent variable before assessment of change in the dependent variable
- Random assignment to the two (or more) comparison groups

The combination of these features permits us to have much greater confidence in the validity of causal conclusions than is possible in other research designs. As you learned in Chapter 6, our confidence in the validity of an experiment's findings is further enhanced by two more things:

- Identification of the causal mechanism
- Control over the context of an experiment

You will learn more about each of these key features of experimental design as you review three different experimental studies about work and its impact. I will use simple diagrams to help describe and compare the experiments' designs. These diagrams also show at a glance just how well suited any experiment is to identifying causal relationships, by indicating whether the experiment has a comparison group, a pretest and a posttest, and randomization.

Experimental and Comparison Groups

True experiments must have at least one **experimental group** (subjects who receive some treatment) and at least one **comparison group** (subjects to whom the experimental group can be compared). The comparison group differs from the experimental group in terms of one or more independent variables, whose effects are being tested. In other words, the difference between the experimental and comparison groups is determined by variation in the independent variable.

Experimental group   In an experiment, the group of subjects that receives the treatment or experimental manipulation.

Comparison group   The group of subjects that is exposed to a different treatment from the experimental group (or that has a different value on the independent variable).

In many experiments, the independent variable indicates the presence or absence of something, such as receiving a treatment program or not receiving it. In these experiments, the comparison group, consisting of the subjects who do not receive the treatment, is termed a **control group.** You learned in Chapter 6 that an experiment can have more than two groups. There can be several treatment groups, corresponding to different values of the independent variable, and several comparison groups, including a control group that receives no treatment.

Control group   A comparison group that receives no treatment.

An example of the importance of having experimental and comparison groups is provided by Richard Price, Michelle Van Ryn, and Amiram Vinokur (1992). The researchers hypothesized that a job-search program to help newly unemployed persons could reduce the risk of depression among this group. The researchers tested this hypothesis with a sample of unemployed persons who volunteered for job-search help at Michigan Employment Security Commission offices. The unemployed volunteers were randomly assigned either to participate in eight 3-hour group seminars over a 2-week period (the treatment) or to receive self-help information in the mail on how to conduct a job search (the comparison condition). The primary outcome measure was an index of depressive symptoms (see Exhibit 7.1). The researchers found fewer depression symptoms among the subjects who had participated in the group seminars. Price et al. (1992:165), speculating about the causal mechanism underlying the long-term beneficial effects of the job-search seminars, noted that those in the seminars were more likely to obtain jobs, which would naturally decrease their risk of depression.

The Price et al. study is also a good example of why the comparison group in an experiment often is not a true control group. Remember, a control group receives no intervention whatsoever. Compared to conducting a job-search seminar for the experimental group, mailing job-search information to the comparison group seems almost like no intervention. But the mailing was important for two reasons. First, it was probably ethically necessary to provide all study participants with some additional help. Second, the plan to mail the materials allowed the researchers to recruit subjects with the promise that they would receive something for their participation.

Exhibit 7.1   Experimental and Comparison Groups: Job-Search Help and Depression

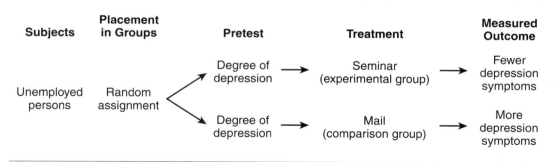

Source: Based on Price et al., 1992.

Price et al. could not carefully control conditions, because the experimental treatment required subjects to attend a series of training sessions over 2 weeks; between sessions, many other events at home and in the community could have influenced the subjects' levels of depression. However, the training sessions as a whole were the experimental treatment, so the researchers had little concern that something other than the treatment would happen during the sessions to affect the results. And because the subjects were randomly assigned to the groups, their home and community environments during the treatment period should have been the same, on average. So even though the conditions for all the subjects were not literally controlled during the experiment, the nature of the treatment and the random composition of the groups made it unlikely that any bias occurred as a result.

Pretest and Posttest Measures

All true experiments have a **posttest**—that is, measurement of the outcome in both groups after the experimental group has received the treatment. Many true experiments also have **pretests** that measure the dependent variable prior to the experimental intervention. A pretest is exactly the same as a posttest, just administered at a different time. Strictly speaking, a true experiment does not require a pretest. When researchers use random assignment, the groups' initial scores on the dependent variable and on all other variables are very likely to be similar. Any difference in outcome between the experimental and comparison groups is therefore likely to be due to the intervention (or to other processes occurring during the experiment), and the likelihood of a difference just on the basis of chance can be calculated. This is fortunate, because the dependent variable in some experiments cannot be measured in a pretest; for example, if you want to test the effect of class size on student reactions to a teacher, you can't measure their reactions to the teacher until they have been exposed to the experimental treatment—the classes of different size.

But, in fact, having pretest scores can be advantageous. They provide a direct measure of how much the experimental and comparison groups changed over time. They allow the researcher to verify that randomization was successful (that chance factors did not lead to an initial difference between the groups). In addition, by identifying subjects' initial scores on the dependent variable, a pretest provides a more complete picture of the conditions in which the intervention had (or didn't have) an effect (Mohr, 1992:46–48). A randomized experimental design with a pretest and posttest is termed a **randomized comparative change design,** or a **pretest-posttest control group design.**

An experiment may have multiple posttests and perhaps even multiple pretests. Multiple posttests can identify just when the treatment has its effect and for how long. They are particularly important for treatments delivered over time (Rossi & Freeman, 1989:289–290).

Randomization

Randomization, or random assignment, is what makes the comparison group in a true experiment such a powerful tool for identifying the effects of the treatment. A randomized comparison group can provide a good estimate of the counterfactual—the outcome that would have occurred if the subjects who were exposed to the treatment actually had not been exposed but otherwise had had the same experiences (Mohr, 1992:3; Rossi & Freeman, 1989:229). If the comparison group differed from the experimental group in any way besides not receiving the treatment (or receiving a different treatment), a researcher would not be able to determine for sure what the unique effects of the treatment were.

Assigning subjects randomly to the experimental and comparison groups ensures that systematic bias does not affect the assignment of subjects to groups. Of course, random assignment cannot guarantee that the groups are perfectly identical at the start of the experiment. Randomization removes bias from the assignment process, but only by relying on chance, which itself can result in some intergroup differences. Fortunately, researchers can use statistical methods to determine the odds of ending up with groups that differ very much on the basis of chance, and these odds are low even for groups of moderate size. The larger the group, the less likely it is that even modest differences will occur on the basis of chance and the more possible it becomes to draw conclusions about causal effects from relatively small differences in the outcome.

Note that the random assignment of subjects to experimental and comparison groups is not the same as random sampling of individuals from some larger population (see Exhibit 7.2). In fact, random assignment (randomization) does not help at all to ensure that the research subjects are representative of some larger population; instead, representativeness is the goal of random sampling. What random assignment does—create two (or more) equivalent groups—is useful for ensuring internal validity, not generalizability.

Matching is another procedure sometimes used to equate experimental and comparison groups, but by itself it is a poor substitute for randomization. Matching of individuals in a treatment group with those in a comparison group might involve pairing persons on the basis of similarity of gender, age, year in school, or some other characteristic. The basic problem is that, as a practical matter, individuals can be matched on only a few characteristics; unmatched differences between the experimental and comparison groups may still influence outcomes. When matching is used as a substitute for random assignment, the research becomes quasi-experimental instead of being a true experiment. However, matching combined with randomization can reduce the possibility of differences due to chance. For example, if individuals are matched in terms of gender and age, and then the members of each matched pair are assigned randomly to the experimental and comparison groups, the possibility of differences due to chance in the gender and age composition of the groups is eliminated (see Exhibit 7.3).

Exhibit 7.2   Random Sampling Versus Random Assignment

Random sampling (a tool for ensuring generalizability):
Individuals are randomly selected from a population to participate in a study.

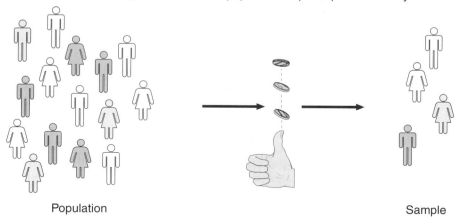

Population   Sample

Random assignment, or randomization (a tool for ensuring internal validity):
Individuals who are to participate in a study are randomly divided into an
experimental group and a comparison group.

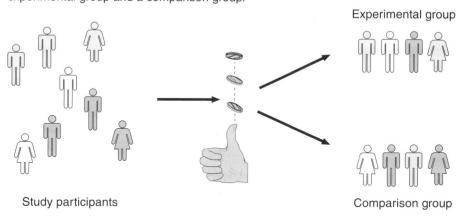

Study participants   Comparison group

Michael W. Morris and Paul C. Moore (2000) used the classic **randomized comparative posttest design,** also termed the *posttest-only control group design,* to test the impact of organizational accountability on learning from experience. Prior research had indicated that people learn from experience, in part by comparing their actual experience to what they imagine might have been and then using this imagined scenario—this "counterfactual comparison"—to shape their actions in the future. But prior research also indicated that counterfactual comparisons could be either "upward" or "downward," and it was only

Exhibit 7.3   Experimental Design Combining Matching and Random Assignment

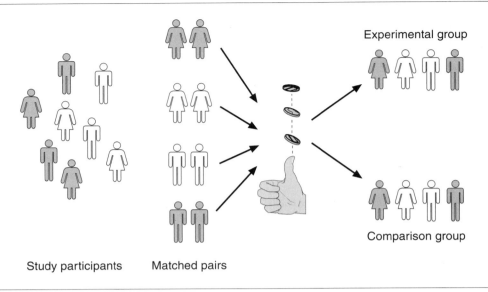

upward comparisons—to an imagined better outcome—that enhanced learning. Morris and Moore hypothesized that (1) upward comparisons would result in more learning from experience; and (2) individuals would be less likely to make these upward comparisons, and hence be less likely to learn from experience, when they were performing under organizational accountability, meaning that they had to account for their performance to a supervisor.

Forty-two Stanford University students were paid to use a flight simulator (Microsoft's Flight Simulator 5.0 and Microsoft's Sidewinder joystick) on which they were given a short lesson on "flying." The students were then told they were either private or commercial "pilots" and asked to land their "plane" under very difficult conditions. After their first landing, students were asked to fill out a flight log and to list the lessons they had learned. In subsequent trials, the researchers measured performance improvement. At the end of this process, the students were paid and debriefed (told what the experiment was about).

The experimental design is depicted in Exhibit 7.4. (The diagram at the top of the exhibit is a standard form of notation for the design of true experiments.)

1. Cases were assigned randomly to the two groups. There was no pretest.

2. One group received the experimental intervention (organizational accountability, by being told they were commercial pilots), and the other received the comparison condition (no organizational accountability, as "private pilots").

3. Students in both groups attempted to land their planes, with all conditions equivalent except for the independent variable (organizational accountability) and several other controlled test factors.

Exhibit 7.4   A Flight Simulation Experiment to Test Counterfactual Thinking

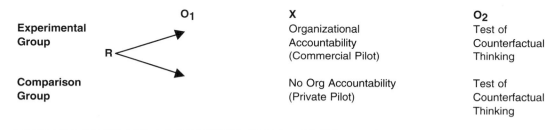

Key: R = Random assignment
       O = Observation (employment status at pretest or posttest)
       X = Experimental treatment

	O_1	X	O_2
Experimental Group	R	Organizational Accountability (Commercial Pilot)	Test of Counterfactual Thinking
Comparison Group		No Org Accountability (Private Pilot)	Test of Counterfactual Thinking

Source: Morris & Moore, 2000:752–753. Copyright 2000; reprinted with permission.

4. The posttest measured whether counterfactual thinking was present in the flight log statement and whether that thinking involved an upward or downward comparison, as well as
   whether it was expressed in terms of the self as the hypothetical pilot or another.

Some of the results are presented in Exhibit 7.5. Student pilots who had been told they were
working for a company were less likely to engage in upward comparisons than were students
who had been told they were private pilots. This supported Morris and Moore's hypothesis.

Limitations of True Experimental Designs

The distinguishing features of true experiments—experimental and comparison groups,
pretests (which are not always used) and posttests, and randomization—do not help researchers
identify the mechanisms by which treatments have their effects. In fact, this question of
causal mechanism often is not addressed in experimental research. The hypothesis test itself
does not require any analysis of mechanism, and if the experiment was conducted under carefully controlled conditions during a limited span of time, the causal effect (if any) may seem
to be quite direct. But attention to causal mechanisms can augment experimental findings. For
example, evaluation researchers often focus attention on the mechanism by which a social
program has its effect (Mohr, 1992:25–27; Scriven, 1972a). The goal is to measure the intermediate steps that lead to the change that is the program's primary focus.

True experimental designs also do not guarantee that the researcher has been able to maintain control over the conditions to which subjects are exposed after they are assigned to the

Exhibit 7.5   Participants' Responses in the Pilot Log

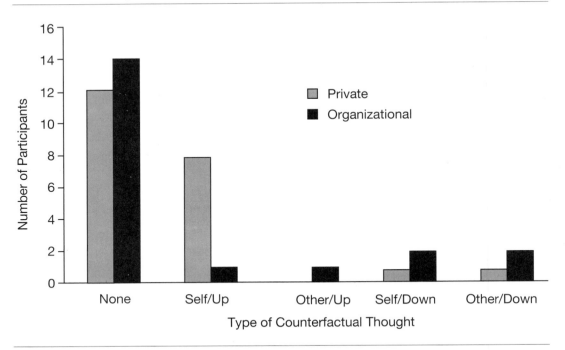

Source: Morris & Moore, 2000:754. Copyright 2000; reprinted with permission.

experimental and comparison groups. If these conditions begin to differ, the variation between the experimental and comparison groups will not be what was intended. Such unintended variation is often not much of a problem in laboratory experiments, where the researcher has almost complete control over the conditions (and can ensure that these conditions are nearly identical for both groups). But control over conditions can become a very big concern for **field experiments,** experimental studies that are conducted in the field, in real-world settings.

Summary: Causality in True Experiments

The two studies reviewed here were true experiments because each had at least one experimental and one comparison group to which subjects were randomly assigned. They also compared variation in the dependent variable after variation in the independent variable, although they differed in number of pretests and posttests. Price et al. (1992) had one pretest and one posttest in their study of job-search help. Morris and Moore (2000) used only a posttest in their study of college students' learning in relation to organizational accountability; Bushman's study of catharsis (Chapter 6) also did not have a pretest. The studies also differed in the extent to which the researchers maintained control over conditions and investigated causal mechanisms. Morris and Moore's and Bushman's laboratory experiments allowed conditions to be carefully controlled, and the researchers systematically considered the causal processes involved. Price et al. could not control conditions in their study of job-search programs for the newly unemployed, but they used subjects selected randomly from different environments. They speculated about causal mechanisms. Control over conditions, investigation of the causal mechanism, and pretesting are not defining features of true experiments, but they are nonetheless important components to evaluate in any experimental design.

Let's examine how well true experiments meet the criteria for identifying a nomothetic cause that were identified in Chapter 6:

Association between the hypothesized independent and dependent variables. As you have seen, experiments can provide unambiguous evidence of association by comparing the experimental and comparison groups on the dependent variable.

Time order of effects of one variable on the others. Unquestionably, arrest for spouse abuse preceded recidivism in the Lawrence Sherman and Richard Berk (1984) study (described in Chapter 2), and the job loss seminars in the Price et al. study preceded the differential rates of depression between the experimental and comparison groups. In experiments with a pretest, time order can be established by comparing posttest to pretest scores. In experiments with random assignment of subjects to the experimental and comparison groups, time order can be established by comparison of posttest scores only.

Nonspurious relationships between variables. Nonspuriousness is difficult—some would say impossible—to establish in nonexperimental designs. The random assignment of subjects to experimental and comparison groups is what makes true experiments such powerful designs for testing causal hypotheses. Randomization controls for the host of possible extraneous influences that can create misleading, spurious relationships in both experimental and non-experimental data. If we determine that a design has used randomization successfully, we can be much more confident in the resulting causal conclusions.

Mechanism that creates the causal effect. The features of a true experiment do not in themselves allow identification of causal mechanisms; as a result there can be some ambiguity about how the independent variable influenced the dependent variable and the resulting causal conclusions. Morris and Moore focused their experiment on processes of counterfactual thinking that they believed served as a causal mechanism that could explain the effect of organizational accountability on learning.

Context in which change occurs. Control over conditions is more feasible in many experimental designs than it is in nonexperimental designs, but it is often difficult to control conditions in field experiments. Later in this chapter, you will see how the lack of control over experimental conditions can threaten internal validity.

QUASI-EXPERIMENTS

Often, testing a hypothesis with a true experimental design is not feasible with the desired subjects and in the desired setting. Such a test may be too costly or take too long to carry out;

it may not be ethical to randomly assign subjects to the different conditions; or it may be too late to do so. Researchers may instead use "quasi-experimental" designs that retain several components of experimental design but differ in important details.

A **quasi-experimental design** is one in which the comparison group is predetermined to be comparable to the treatment group in critical ways, such as being eligible for the same services or being in the same school cohort (Rossi & Freeman, 1989:313). These research designs are only "quasi" experimental because subjects are not randomly assigned to the comparison and experimental groups. As a result, we cannot be as confident in the comparability of the groups as in true experimental designs. Nonetheless, in order to term a research design quasi-experimental, we have to be sure that the comparison groups meet specific criteria.

I will discuss here the two major types of quasi-experimental designs (other types can be found in Cook & Campbell, 1979; Mohr, 1992):

- *Nonequivalent control group designs.* **Nonequivalent control group designs** have experimental and comparison groups that are designated before the treatment occurs and are not created by random assignment.
- *Before-and-after designs.* **Before-and-after designs** have a pretest and posttest but no comparison group. In other words, the subjects exposed to the treatment serve, at an earlier time, as their own controls.

Exhibit 7.6 diagrams these two types of quasi-experiments.

Nonequivalent Control Group Designs

In this type of quasi-experimental design, a comparison group is selected to be as comparable as possible to the treatment group. Two selection methods can be used:

Individual matching. Individual cases in the treatment group are matched with similar individuals in the comparison group. In some situations this can create a comparison group that is very similar to the experimental group, as when Head Start participants were matched with their siblings in order to estimate the effect of participation in Head Start. However, in many studies it may not be possible to match on the most important variables.

Aggregate matching. In most situations when random assignment is not possible, the second method of matching makes more sense: identifying a comparison group that matches the treatment group in the aggregate rather than trying to match individual cases. This means finding a comparison group that has similar distributions on key variables: the same average age, the same percentage female, and so on. For this design to be considered quasi-experimental, however, individuals must not have been able to choose whether to be in the treatment group or the control group.

Ruth Wageman (1995) used a quasi-experimental design to investigate how the way tasks were designed and rewards allotted affected work team functioning. Her research question was whether it was preferable to organize work tasks and work rewards in a way that stressed team interdependence or individual autonomy. Over 800 Xerox service technicians in 152 teams participated in the research. District managers volunteered to let their work teams participate in the study but were able to choose which intervention they would implement. This

Exhibit 7.6   Quasi-Experimental Designs

Quasi-Experimental Designs

Nonequivalent control group design:

Experimental group:	O_1	X_a	O_2
Comparison group 1:	O_1	X_b	O_2
Comparison group 2:	O_1	X_c	O_2

		Pretest	*Treatment*	*Posttest*
Team	Group	Team performance	Independent tasks	Team performance
Interdependence	Hybrid	Team performance	Mixed tasks	Team performance
	Individual	Team performance	Individual tasks	Team performance

---

Before-and-after design:
Soap-opera suicide and actual suicide (Phillips, 1982)

Experimental group:	O_{11}	X_1	O_{21}
	O_{12}	X_2	O_{22}
	O_{13}	X_3	O_{23}
	O_{14}	X_4	O_{24}

Pretest	*Treatment*	*Posttest*
Suicide rate	Soap-opera suicides	Suicide rate

Key: O = Observation (pretest or posttest)
        X = Experimental treatment

---

meant that even though the work teams themselves were not randomized to the different conditions, the team participants still were not able to choose which conditions to work in. Thus, this design met the definition of a nonequivalent control group quasi-experiment. One month prior to the intervention, Wageman collected survey data about group performance. These measures were repeated 4 months after the intervention began. Team performance measures were also collected from archival data (company records).

Surprisingly, team performance was influenced positively by management that stressed either interdependence or autonomy. It was the teams that used a "hybrid" model that performed more poorly. The hybrid teams required technicians to work part of the time as an interdependent team and part of the time as autonomous individuals (Exhibit 7.7). The key to improving performance was how the tasks were organized; team members' attitudes improved when the way in which rewards were distributed (on a group or individual basis) matched the organization of tasks on their team, but this had no independent effect on team performance.

Exhibit 7.7   Work Team Interdependence and Performance

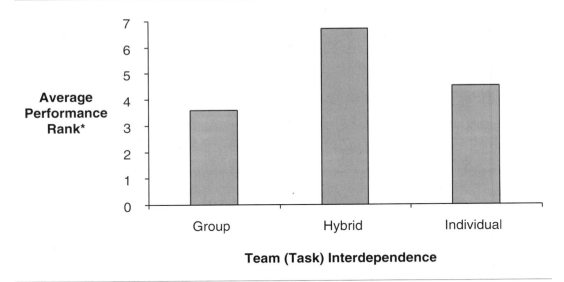

Source: Wageman, 1995:170.

*1 = high rank, 7 = low rank.

Before-and-After Designs

The common feature of before-and-after designs is the absence of a comparison group: All cases are exposed to the experimental treatment. The basis for comparison is instead provided by the pretreatment measures in the experimental group. These designs are thus useful for studies of interventions that are experienced by virtually every case in some population, such as total coverage programs like Social Security or single-organization studies of the effect of a new management strategy.

The simplest type of before-and-after design is the fixed-sample panel design. As you may recall from Chapter 6, a panel design involves only one pretest and one posttest. It does not itself qualify as a quasi-experimental design because comparing subjects to themselves at just one earlier point in time does not provide an adequate comparison group. Many influences other than the experimental treatment may affect a subject following the pretest—basic life experiences for a young subject, for instance.

David P. Phillips's (1982) study of the effect of TV soap-opera suicides on the number of actual suicides in the United States illustrates a more powerful **multiple group before-and-after design.** In this design, several before-and-after comparisons are made involving the same variables but different groups. Phillips identified 13 soap-opera suicides in 1977 and then recorded the U.S. suicide rate in the weeks prior to and following each TV story. In effect, the researcher had 13 different before-and-after studies, one for each suicide story. In 12 of these 13 comparisons, deaths due to suicide increased from the week before each soap-opera suicide to the week after (see Exhibit 7.8). Phillips also found similar increases in

Exhibit 7.8   Real Suicides and Soap-Opera Suicides

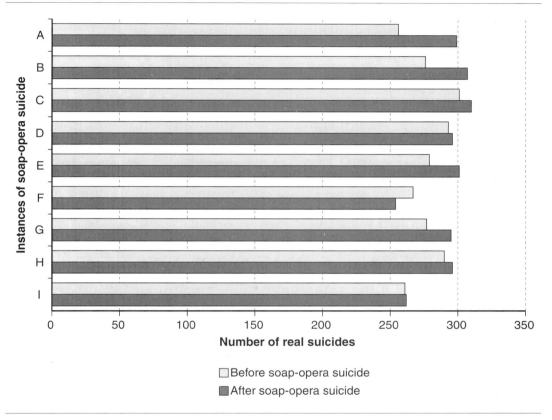

Source: Adapted from Phillips, 1982:1347. Reprinted with permission from the University of Chicago Press.

motor-vehicle deaths and crashes during the same period, some portion of which reflects covert suicide attempts.

Another type of before-and-after design involves multiple pretest and posttest observations of the same group. Most methodologists distinguish between **repeated measures panel designs,** which include several pretest and posttest observations, and **time series designs,** which include many (preferably 30 or more) such observations in both pretest and posttest periods. Repeated measures panel designs are stronger than simple before-and-after panel designs because they allow the researcher to study the process by which an intervention or treatment has an impact over time.

Time series designs are particularly useful for studies of the impact of new laws or social programs that affect everyone and that are readily assessed by some ongoing measurement. For example, we might use a time series design to study the impact of a new seat-belt law on the severity of injuries in automobile accidents, using a monthly state government report on insurance claims. Special statistics are required to analyze time series data, but the basic idea is to identify a trend in the dependent variable up to the date of the intervention or event whose effect is being studied and then to project the trend into the postintervention period. This projected trend is then compared to the actual trend of the dependent variable after the intervention. A substantial disparity between the actual and projected trend is evidence that the intervention or event had an impact (Rossi & Freeman, 1989:260–261, 358–363).

Summary: Causality in Quasi-Experiments

Let's now examine how well quasi-experiments meet the criteria for identifying a nomothetic cause that were identified in Chapter 6:

Association between the hypothesized independent and dependent variables. Quasi-experiments can provide evidence of association between the independent and dependent variables that is as unambiguous as that provided by a true experiment.

Time order of effects of one variable on the others. This is a strength of the various quasi-experimental before-and-after designs, but we cannot be as sure of correctly identifying the time order of effects with nonequivalent control group designs, because we cannot be certain that some features of the groups did not attract individuals to them who differed at the outset.

Nonspurious relationships between variables. We cannot be certain of ruling out all potentially extraneous influences with either type of quasi-experimental design, but it is important to note that the criteria for these designs do give us considerable confidence that most extraneous influences could not have occurred.

Mechanism that creates the causal effect. The features of quasi-experiments do not in themselves allow identification of causal mechanisms; however, the repeated measures design does provide a means for testing hypotheses about causal mechanism.

Context in which change occurs. The quasi-experimental designs that involve multiple groups can provide a great deal of information about the importance of context, as long as the researcher measures contextual variables.

NONEXPERIMENTS

All the other research designs we study are, of course, "nonexperimental." One of these designs, the ex post facto control group design, is often called quasi-experimental, but that's really not correct, as I explain next. Other designs are covered in other chapters under the headings of "cross-sectional" and "longitudinal" designs. Here, I'll briefly contrast these nonexperimental designs with experimental and quasi-experimental designs.

Ex Post Facto Control Group Designs

The **ex post facto control group design** appears to be very similar to the nonequivalent control group design, and is often confused with it, but it does not meet as well the criteria for quasi-experimental designs. Like nonequivalent control group designs, this design has

Exhibit 7.9   Ex Post Facto Control Group Design

**Ex post facto control group design:
Self-managing work teams (Cohen & Ledford)**

Experimental Group	O_1	X	O_2
Comparison Group	O_1		O_2

	O_1	**X**	**O_2**
Experimental group	Pretest: Measures of satisfaction and productivity	Self-managing work team	Posttest: Measures of satisfaction
Comparison group	Pretest: Measures of satisfaction and productivity		Posttest: Measures of satisfaction

Key: R = Random assignment
       O = Observation (pretest or posttest)
       X = Experimental treatment

Source: Based on Cohen & Ledford, 1994.

experimental and comparison groups that are not created by random assignment. But unlike the groups in nonequivalent control group designs, the groups in ex post facto (after the fact) designs are designated after the treatment has occurred. The problem with this is that if the treatment takes any time at all, people with particular characteristics may select themselves for the treatment or avoid it. However, the particulars will vary from study to study; in some circumstances we may conclude that the treatment and control groups are so similar that causal effects can be tested (Rossi & Freeman, 1989:343–344).

Susan Cohen and Gerald Ledford's (1994) study of the effectiveness of self-managing teams used a well-constructed ex post facto design (Exhibit 7.9). They studied a telecommunication company with some work teams that were self-managing and some that were traditionally managed (meaning that a manager was responsible for the team's decisions). Unlike Ruth Wageman's (1995) quasi-experimental study of work teams, Cohen and Ledford studied work teams as they found them; they did not attempt to alter their functioning. Work groups were identified as self-managing if managers and employees agreed that the employees worked as a team, were responsible for making a product or providing a service, and had discretion over key work decisions. Each work group with these characteristics was matched with a traditionally managed work group that produced the same product or service.

Cohen and Ledford found the self-reported quality of work life to be higher in the self-managed groups than in the traditionally managed groups. Job performance also seemed higher in the self-managing groups in clerical and craft functions but not in small business offices. A special review of operations in the small business offices revealed that their work did not lend itself to a team approach. This finding helped to specify the context in which the hypothesized cause would have its effect.

What distinguishes this study design from a quasi-experimental design is the fact that the teams themselves and their managers had some influence on how they were managed. As the researchers noted, "If the groups which were already high performers were the ones selected to be self-managing teams, then the findings could be due to a selection bias rather than any effects of self-management" (Cohen & Ledford, 1994:34). Thus, preexisting characteristics of employees and managers or their team composition might have influenced which "treatment" they received, as well as the outcomes achieved. However, the work histories and demographic characteristics of the two groups were similar, and the members of each group rated one another as similarly proficient. In addition, the dropout rate during the study did not differ between the groups so much as to affect the outcome measures. These additional tests give us more confidence that indeed the difference in management style between the two groups, and not their makeup, led to their difference in posttest performance.

One-Shot Case Studies and Longitudinal Designs

Cross-sectional designs, termed "one-shot case studies" in the experimental design literature, are easily able to establish whether an association exists between two variables, but we cannot be anywhere near as confident in their conclusions about appropriate time order or nonspuriousness as with true experiments or even quasi-experiments. As you learned at the start of Chapter 6, longitudinal designs improve greatly our ability to test the time order of effects, but they are unable to rule out all extraneous influences.

Sigal Barsade, Andrew Ward, Jean Turner, and Jeffrey Sonnenfeld (2000) used a one-shot case study design in their research on "affective diversity"—variation in such positive feelings as cheerfulness and energy. Their goal was to evaluate the effect of affective diversity on the orientations and performance of members of top management teams. They measured both individual and team characteristics in a sample of 62 top U.S. management teams and hypothesized, in part, that "[a]ffectively homogeneous groups will have better group performance than will affectively diverse groups"(Barsade et al., 2000:809). The idea is that employees who work on teams whose members are more similar in their emotions will work better together than employees on more heterogeneous teams.

Although their analysis supported the hypothesis and generated many insights into the functioning of work groups, Barsade et al. (2000:827) noted in their conclusions that, "[w]hen thinking about our results, it is natural to question the causation of the effects between affective team composition and team performance."

Did group performance generate more affectively homogeneous teams, rather than the other way around? It's not possible to be certain. Did some other factor, such as educational level, influence both emotional characteristics of team members and team performance? Although the researchers did statistically control for similarities in some other background characteristics, it is not possible to rule out the influence of all other variables that might have created a spurious relationship.

Summary: Causality in Nonexperiments

How well do nonexperimental designs allow us to meet the criteria for identifying a nomothetic cause that were identified in Chapter 6?

Association between the hypothesized independent and dependent variables. Nonexperiments can provide clear evidence of association between the independent and dependent variables.

Time order of effects of one variable on the others. Cross-sectional designs (one-shot case studies) can establish time order with some confidence, but only in the limited cases identified in Chapter 6. Longitudinal designs, even when nonexperimental, do allow identification of time order.

Nonspurious relationships between variables. This is the Achilles heel of nonexperimental designs. As explained in Chapter 6, statistical controls can increase our confidence that extraneous variables do not confound the relationship between the independent and dependent variables, but it is unlikely that we will be able to control for all potential confounders.

Mechanism that creates the causal effect. Nonexperimental designs have no particular advantages or disadvantages for establishing causal mechanisms, although qualitative research designs facilitate investigations about causal process.

Context in which change occurs. Because they make it easy to survey large numbers of widely dispersed persons or organizations, one-shot case studies facilitate investigation of contextual effects.

VALIDITY IN EXPERIMENTS

Like any research design, experimental designs must be evaluated in terms of their ability to yield valid conclusions. True experiments are particularly well suited to producing valid conclusions about causality (internal validity), but they are likely to fare less well in achieving generalizability. Quasi-experiments may provide more generalizable results than true experiments but are more prone to problems of internal invalidity (although some quasi-experimental designs allow the researcher to rule out almost as many potential sources of internal invalidity as does a true experiment). Measurement validity is also a central concern, but experimental design does not in itself offer any special tools or particular advantages or disadvantages in measurement. In this section you will learn more about the ways in which experiments help (or don't help) to resolve potential problems of internal validity and generalizability.

Causal (Internal) Validity

An experiment's ability to yield valid conclusions about causal effects is determined by the comparability of its experimental and comparison groups. First, of course, a comparison group must be created. Second, this comparison group must be so similar to the experimental group or groups that it shows what the experimental group would be like if it had not received the experimental treatment—if the independent variable had not varied.

There are four basic sources of noncomparability (other than the treatment) between a comparison group and an experimental group. They produce four of the five sources of internal invalidity:

- *Selection bias.* When characteristics of the experimental and comparison group subjects differ.
- *Endogenous change.* When the subjects develop or change during the experiment as part of an ongoing process independent of the experimental treatment.
- *History effects.* When something occurs during the experiment, other than the treatment, which influences outcome scores.
- *Contamination.* When either the experimental group or the comparison group is aware of the other group and is influenced in the posttest as a result (Mohr, 1992).

The fifth source of internal invalidity can be termed **treatment misidentification:** Variation in the independent variable (the treatment) is associated with variation in the observed outcome, but the change occurs through a process that the researcher has not identified.

Selection Bias

You may already realize that the composition of the experimental and comparison groups in a true experiment is unlikely to be affected by **selection bias.** Randomization equates the groups' characteristics, though with some possibility for error due to chance. The likelihood of difference due to chance can be identified with appropriate statistics.

But in field experiments, what has been planned as a random assignment process may deteriorate when it is delegated to front-line program staff. This problem occurred in the Sherman and Berk (1984) domestic violence experiment in Minneapolis. Some police officers sometimes violated the random assignment plan when they thought the circumstances warranted arresting a suspect who had been randomly assigned to receive just a warning. In several of the follow-up studies, the researchers maintained closer control over the assignment process so that randomization could be maintained.

Even when random assignment works as planned, the groups can become different over time because of **differential attrition,** or what can be thought of as "deselection." That is, the groups become different because subjects are more likely to drop out of one of the groups for various reasons. This is not a likely problem in a laboratory experiment that occurs in one session, but some laboratory experiments occur over time, making differential attrition a problem. Subjects who experience the experimental condition may become more motivated than comparison subjects to continue in the experiment.

When subjects are not assigned randomly to treatment and comparison groups, as in nonequivalent control group designs, the threat of selection bias is very great. Even if the researcher selects a comparison group that matches the treatment group on important variables, there is no guarantee that the groups were similar initially in terms of the dependent variable or in terms of some other characteristic that ultimately influences posttest scores. However, a pretest helps the researchers to determine and control for selection bias. Because most variables that might influence outcome scores will also have influenced scores on the pretest, statistically controlling for the pretest scores also serves to control for many of the unmeasured variables that might have influenced the posttest scores.

Endogenous Change

The type of problem subsumed under the label **endogenous change** occurs when natural developments in the subjects, independent of the experimental treatment itself, account for some or all of the observed change between pretest and posttest. Endogenous change includes these three specific threats to internal validity:

- *Testing*. Taking the pretest can in itself influence posttest scores. Subjects may learn something or be sensitized to an issue by the pretest and as a result, respond differently the next time they are asked the same questions, on the posttest.
- *Maturation*. Changes in outcome scores during experiments that involve a lengthy treatment period may be due to maturation. Subjects may age, gain experience, or grow in knowledge all as part of a natural maturational experience and thus respond differently on the posttest than on the pretest.
- *Regression*. People experience cyclical or episodic changes that result in different posttest scores, a phenomenon known as a **regression effect.** Subjects who are chosen for a study because they received very low scores on a test may show improvement in the posttest, on average, simply because some of the low scorers were having a bad day. On the other hand, individuals selected for an experiment because they are suffering from tooth decay will not show improvement in the posttest because a decaying tooth is not likely to improve in the natural course of things. It is hard in many cases to know whether a phenomenon is subject to naturally occurring fluctuations, so the possibility of regression effects should be considered whenever subjects are selected because of their extremely high or low values on the outcome variable (Mohr, 1992:56, 71–79).

Testing, maturation, and regression effects are generally not a problem in true experiments, because they would affect the experimental group and the comparison group equally. However, these effects could explain any change over time in most before-and-after designs, because they do not have a comparison group. Repeated measures panel studies and time series designs are better in this regard because they allow the researcher to trace the pattern of change or stability in the dependent variable up to and after the treatment. Ongoing effects of maturation and regression can thus be identified and taken into account.

External Events

History, or **external events** during the experiment (things that happen outside the experiment), could change subjects' outcome scores. Examples are newsworthy events that have to do with the focus of an experiment and major disasters to which subjects are exposed. This problem is often referred to as a **history effect**—history during the experiment, that is.

Causal conclusions can be invalid in some true and quasi-experiments because of the influence of external events. For example, in an experiment in which subjects go to a special location for the treatment, something in that location unrelated to the treatment could influence these subjects. Experimental and comparison group subjects in the Price et al. (1992) study of job search services differed in whether they attended the special seminars, so external events could have happened to subjects in the experimental group that might not have happened to those in the control group. Perhaps program participants witnessed a robbery outside of the seminar building one day, and their orientations changed as a result. External events are a major concern in evaluation studies that compare programs in different cities or states (Hunt, 1985:276–277).

Contamination

Contamination occurs in an experiment when the comparison group is in some way affected by, or affects, the treatment group. This problem basically arises from failure to control adequately the conditions of the experiment. When comparison group members are aware that they are being denied some advantage, they may as a result increase their efforts to compensate, creating a problem termed **compensatory rivalry,** or the **John Henry effect** (Cook & Campbell, 1979:55). On the other hand, comparison group members may become demoralized if they feel that they have been left out of some valuable treatment and perform worse than expected as a result. Both compensatory rivalry and demoralization thus distort the impact of the experimental treatment.

Contamination is not ruled out by the basic features of experimental and quasi-experimental designs, but careful inspection of the research design can determine how much it is likely to be a problem in a particular experiment. If the experiment is conducted in a laboratory, if members of the experimental group and the comparison group have no contact while the study is in progress, and if the treatment is relatively brief, contamination is not likely to be a problem. To the degree that these conditions are not met, the likelihood of contamination will increase.

Contamination was a potential problem in the field-based unemployment training study by Price et al. (1992), because all participants used the same unemployment offices.

Treatment Misidentification

Treatment misidentification occurs when some process that the researcher is not aware of is responsible for the apparent effect of treatment. The subjects experience something other than, or in addition to, the treatment the researchers believe they have experienced. Treatment misidentification has at least three sources:

Expectancies of experimental staff. Change among experimental subjects may be due to the positive **expectations of the experimental staff** who are delivering the treatment rather than due to the treatment itself. Even well-trained staff may convey their enthusiasm for an experimental program to the subjects in subtle ways. This is a special concern in evaluation research, when program staff and researchers may be biased in favor of the program for which they work and eager to believe that their work is helping clients. Such positive staff expectations thus create a **self-fulfilling prophecy.** However, in experiments on the effects of treatments like medical drugs, **double-blind procedures** can be used: Staff delivering the treatments do not know which subjects are getting the treatment and which are receiving a placebo, something that looks like the treatment but has no effect.

Placebo effect. Treatment misidentification may occur when subjects receive a treatment that they consider likely to be beneficial and improve because of that expectation rather than because of the treatment itself. In medical research, where the placebo is often a chemically inert substance that looks like the experimental drug but actually has no effect, some research has indicated that the **placebo effect** itself produces positive health effects in many patients suffering from relatively mild medical problems (Goleman, 1993a:C3). (It is not clear that these improvements are really any greater than what the patients would have experienced without the placebo [Hrobjartsson & Gotzsche, 2001]). In any case, it is possible for placebo effects to occur in social science research, so, when possible, experimental researchers can reduce this threat to internal validity by treating the comparison group with something that seems similar to what the experimental group receives.

Hawthorne effect. Members of the treatment group may change in terms of the dependent variable because their participation in the study makes them feel special. This problem could occur when treatment group members compare their situation to that of members of the control group, who are not receiving the treatment, in which case it would be a type of contamination effect. But experimental group members could feel special simply because they are in the experiment. This is termed a **Hawthorne effect,** after a famous productivity experiment at the Hawthorne electric plant outside Chicago. No matter what conditions the researchers changed in order to improve or diminish productivity, the workers seemed to work harder simply because they were part of a special experiment. Hawthorne effects are also a concern in evaluation research, particularly when program clients know that the research findings may affect the chances for further program funding.

Generalizability

The need for generalizable findings can be thought of as the Achilles heel of true experimental design. The design components that are essential for a true experiment and that minimize the threats to causal validity make it more difficult to achieve sample generalizability (being able to apply the findings to some clearly defined larger population) and cross-population generalizability (generalizing across subgroups and to other populations and settings).

Sample Generalizability

Subjects who can be recruited for a laboratory experiment, randomly assigned to a group, and kept under carefully controlled conditions for the study's duration are unlikely to be a representative sample of any large population of interest to social scientists. Can they be expected to react to the experimental treatment in the same way as members of the larger population? The generalizability of the treatment and of the setting for the experiment also must be considered (Cook & Campbell, 1979:73–74). The more artificial the experimental arrangements, the greater the problem (Campbell & Stanley, 1966:20–21).

A researcher can take steps both before and after an experiment to increase a study's generalizability. Conducting a field experiment, like Sherman and Berk's (1984) study of arrest in actual domestic violence incidents, is likely to yield more generalizable findings than are laboratory experiments, for which subjects must volunteer. In some field experiments, participants can even be selected randomly from the population of interest, and thus the researchers can achieve results generalizable to that population. For example, some studies of the effects of income supports on the work behavior of poor persons have randomly sampled persons within particular states before randomly assigning them to experimental and comparison groups. When random selection is not feasible, the researchers may be able to increase generalizability by selecting several different experimental sites that offer marked contrasts on key variables (Cook & Campbell, 1979:76–77).

External Validity

Researchers are often interested in determining whether treatment effects identified in an experiment hold true for subgroups of subjects and across different populations, times, or settings. Of course, determining that a relationship between the treatment and the outcome variable holds true for certain subgroups does not establish that the relationship also holds true for these subgroups in the larger population, but it suggests that the relationship might be externally valid.

We have already seen examples of how the existence of treatment effects in particular subgroups of experimental subjects can help us to predict the cross-population generalizability of the findings. For example, Sherman and Berk's research (see Chapter 2) found that arrest did not deter subsequent domestic violence for unemployed individuals; arrest also failed to deter subsequent violence in communities with high levels of unemployment. Price et al. (1992) found that intensive job-search assistance reduced depression among individuals who were at high risk for it because of other psychosocial characteristics; however, the intervention did not influence the rate of depression among individuals at low risk for depression. This is an important interaction effect that limits the generalizability of the treatment, even if Price et al.'s sample was representative of the population of unemployed persons.

There is always an implicit tradeoff in experimental design between maximizing causal validity and generalizability. The more that assignment to treatments is randomized and all experimental conditions are controlled, the less likely it is that the research subjects and setting will be representative of the larger population. College students are easy to recruit and to assign to artificial but controlled manipulations, but both practical and ethical concerns preclude this approach with many groups and with respect to many treatments. However, although we need to be skeptical about the generalizability of the results of a single experimental test of a hypothesis, the body of findings accumulated from many experimental tests with different people in different settings can provide a very solid basis for generalization (Campbell & Russo, 1999:143).

Interaction of Testing and Treatment

A variant on the problem of external validity occurs when the experimental treatment has an effect only when particular conditions created by the experiment occur. One such problem occurs when the treatment has an effect only if subjects have had the pretest. The pretest sensitizes the subjects to some issue, so that when they are exposed to the treatment, they react in a way they would not have reacted if they had not taken the pretest. In other words, testing and treatment interact to produce the outcome. For example, answering questions in a

Exhibit 7.10   Solomon Four-Group Design Testing the Interaction of Pretesting and
Treatment

Experimental group:	R	O_1	X	O_2
Comparison group:	R	O_1		O_2
Experimental group:	R		X	O_2
Comparison group:	R			O_2

Key: R = Random assignment
O = Observation (pretest or posttest)
X = Experimental treatment

pretest about racial prejudice may sensitize subjects so that when they are exposed to the experimental treatment, seeing a film about prejudice, their attitudes are different from what they would have been. In this situation, the treatment truly had an effect, but it would not have had an effect if it were repeated without the sensitizing pretest. This possibility can be evaluated by using the Solomon Four-Group Design to compare groups with and without a pretest (see Exhibit 7.10). If testing and treatment do interact, the difference in outcome scores between the experimental and comparison groups will be different for subjects who took the pretest compared to those who did not.

As you can see, there is no single procedure that establishes the external validity of experimental results. Ultimately, we must base our evaluation of external validity on the success of replications taking place at different times and places and using different forms of the treatment.

COMBINING METHODS

Innovative methodologists can combine elements of two or more research designs to overcome limitations of each. Qualitative methods can help to understand experimental effects, and experimental techniques can be added to survey research projects to allow stronger hypothesis tests.

Process Analysis

Process analysis is a technique for understanding how an experiment affects the dependent variable. It also can be used to avoid mistaken identification of the experimental treatment as the causal influence when in fact some other aspect of the experiment is responsible (Hunt, 1985:272–274). Periodic measures are taken throughout an experiment to assess whether the treatment is being delivered as planned. Process analysis is particularly important in field experiments and will be discussed at greater length in Chapter 10.

Case Study: Obedience to Authority

For an example of process analysis, consider Stanley Milgram's (1965) classic study of obedience to authority. Volunteers were recruited for what they were told was a study of the learning process. The experimenter told the volunteers they were to play the role of "teacher" and to administer an electric shock to a "student" in the next room when the student failed a memory test. Although the shocks were phony (and the students were actors), the volunteers were told the intensity of the shocks increased beyond a lethal level. Many subjects obeyed the authority in the study (the experimenter), even when their obedience involved administering potentially lethal shocks to another person. But did the experimental subjects actually believe that they were harming someone? Observational data suggest they did: "Persons were observed to sweat, tremble, stutter, bite their lips, and groan as they found themselves increasingly implicated in the experimental conflict" (Milgram, 1965:66). And verbatim transcripts of the sessions also clarified what participants were thinking as they disobeyed or complied with the experimenter's instructions:

> "150 volts delivered. You want me to keep going?"
> "165 volts delivered. That guy is hollering in there. There's a lot of them here. He's liable to have a heart condition. You want me to go on?"
> "180 volts delivered. He can't stand it! I'm not going to kill that man in there! You hear him hollering? He's hollering. He can't stand it. . . . I mean who is going to take responsibility if anything happens to that gentleman?"
> *[The experimenter accepts responsibility.]* "All right."
> "195 volts delivered. You see he's hollering. Hear that. Gee, I don't know. *[The experimenter says: The experiment requires that you go on.]* I know it does, sir, but I mean—uhh—he don't know what he's in for. He's up to 195 volts. . . ." (Milgram, 1966:67)

Milgram's analysis of qualitative process data permitted greater confidence in his conclusions through improved understanding of the social processes underlying the treatment effects.

Conducting Factorial Surveys

Factorial surveys combine the features of true experiments that maximize causal validity with the features of surveys that maximize generalizability. In the simplest type of factorial survey, randomly selected subsets of survey respondents are asked different questions. These different questions represent, in effect, different experimental treatments; the goal is to determine the impact of these different questions on answers to other questions. For example, Howard Schuman and Stanley Presser (1981) used factorial surveys to assess how the wording of survey questions influenced respondents' answers. In another type of factorial survey, respondents are asked for their likely responses to one or more vignettes about hypothetical situations. The content of these vignettes is varied randomly among survey respondents so as to create "treatment groups" that differ in terms of particular variables reflected in the vignettes.

Case Study: Neighborhood
Composition and Racial Segregation

Michael O. Emerson, George Yancey, and Karen J. Chai (2001) used a factorial survey design to test the effect of neighborhood racial composition on housing preferences. A national random sample of 1,663 white Americans was surveyed by phone. The factorial experiment began with a description of a hypothetical house-hunting situation:

> Imagine that you are looking for a new house and that you have two school-aged children. You find a house that you like much better than any other house—it has everything that you'd been looking for, it is close to work, and it is within your price range. (Emerson et al., 2001:925)

The variations of this vignette allowed Emerson, Yancey, and Chai to test the effect of neighborhood racial composition as well as of other variables, such as crime rate and property values, that are often given as reasons that whites care about neighborhood racial composition. The values of these several variables were presented in a list. Both the order of the variables and the values presented for each of them were varied randomly.

Checking on the neighborhood, you find that

> The public schools are of [low, medium, high] quality,
> The neighborhood is [5–100%] [Asian, black, Hispanic],
> Property values are [declining, stable, increasing],
> The other homes in the neighborhood are of [lower value than, equal value to, higher value than] the home you are considering,
> And the crime rate is [low, average, high].

> How likely or unlikely do you think it is that you would buy this home? (with responses from very unlikely [1] to very likely [6]). (Emerson et al., 2001:925)

Emerson et al. (2001:931) found that Asian or Hispanic neighborhood composition had no effect on whites' self-assessed likelihood of buying a home that was separate from the other variables, but percent black mattered significantly, even after taking into account the variables like crime rate and property values. In fact, when the percentage of blacks in the neighborhood rose above 15%, whites stated that they would be unlikely to buy the house. The higher the percentage of blacks in the neighborhood, the less likely whites were to buy the house.

The findings indicated that residential segregation is not just a matter of differences in crime rates or property values, real or perceived, between neighborhoods with different percentages black and white (Emerson et al., 2001:932). Most whites simply did not want to live in areas with many blacks, even though they have no such reaction to Asians or Hispanics, once crime rates and property values are controlled.

There is still an important limitation to the generalizability of factorial surveys: They only indicate what respondents *say* they would do in situations that have been described to them. If these individuals had to make decisions in comparable real-life situations, we cannot be sure that they would act in accord with their stated intentions. So factorial surveys do not completely resolve the problems caused by the difficulty of conducting true experiments with representative samples. Nonetheless, by combining some of the advantages of experimental and survey designs, factorial surveys can provide stronger tests of causal hypotheses than surveys and more generalizable findings than experiments.

ETHICAL ISSUES IN EXPERIMENTAL RESEARCH

Social science experiments often involve subject deception. Primarily because of this feature, some experiments have prompted contentious debates about research ethics. Experimental evaluations of social programs also pose ethical dilemmas because they require researchers to withhold possibly beneficial treatment from some of the subjects just on the basis of chance. Such research may also yield sensitive information about program compliance, personal habits, and even illegal activity—information that is protected from legal subpoenas only in some research concerning mental illness or criminal activity (Boruch, 1997). In this section, I will give special attention to the problems of deception and the distribution of benefits in experimental research.

Deception

Deception occurs when subjects are misled about research procedures to determine how they would react to the treatment if they were not research subjects. Deception is a critical component of many social experiments, in part because of the difficulty of simulating real-world stresses and dilemmas in a laboratory setting. Elliot Aronson and Judson Mills (1959), for example, wanted to learn how severity of initiation to real social groups influences liking for those groups. But they could not practically design a field experiment on initiation. Their alternative, which relied on a tape-recorded discussion staged by the researcher, was of course deceptive. In many experiments, if subjects understood what was really happening to them the results would be worthless.

Although the American Sociological Association's *Code of Ethics* (1997) does not discuss experimentation explicitly, the Code highlights the ethical dilemma posed by deceptive research:

12.05 Use of Deception in Research: (a) Sociologists do not use deceptive techniques (1) unless they have determined that their use will not be harmful to research participants; is justified by the study's prospective scientific, educational, or applied value; and that equally effective alternative procedures that do not use deception are not feasible, and (2) unless they have obtained the approval of institutional review boards or, in the absence of such boards, with another authoritative body with expertise on the ethics of research. (b) Sociologists never deceive research participants about significant aspects of the research that would affect their willingness to participate, such as physical risks, discomfort, or unpleasant emotional experiences. (c) When deception is an integral feature of the design and conduct of research, sociologists attempt to correct any misconception that research participants may have no later than at the conclusion of the research. (http://www.asanet.org/members/ecoderev.html, June 8, 2003)

How can the potential for harm be determined? What scientific or educational or applied "value" would make deception justifiable? Who determines whether a non-deceptive alternative is "equally effective"? How much risk, discomfort, or unpleasantness might be seen as affecting willingness to participate? When is an "attempt to correct any misconception" due to deception deemed sufficient? Can you see why an institutional review board, representing a range of perspectives, is an important tool for making reasonable, ethical research decisions when confronted with such ambiguity?

Aronson and Mills's study of severity of initiation (at an all-women's college in the 1950s) is a good example of experimental research that does not pose greater-than-everyday risks to subjects. The students who were randomly assigned to the "severe initiation" experimental condition had to read a list of embarrassing words. I think it's fair to say that even in the 1950s, reading a list of potentially embarrassing words in a laboratory setting and listening to a taped discussion are unlikely to increase the risks to which students are exposed in their everyday lives. Moreover, the researchers informed subjects that they would be expected to talk about sex and could decline to participate in the experiment if this requirement would bother them. None dropped out.

To further ensure that no psychological harm was caused, Aronson and Mills explained the true nature of the experiment to subjects after the experiment. The subjects' reactions were typical:

> None of the Ss expressed any resentment or annoyance at having been misled. In fact, the majority were intrigued by the experiment, and several returned at the end of the academic quarter to ascertain the result. (1959:179)

This procedure is called **debriefing,** and it is usually a good idea. Except for those who are opposed to any degree of deception whatsoever in research (and there are some), the minimal deception in the Aronson and Mills experiment, coupled with the lack of any ascertainable risk to subjects and a debriefing, would meet most standards of ethical research.

Selective Distribution of Benefits

Field experiments conducted to evaluate social programs also can involve issues of informed consent (Hunt, 1985:275–276). One ethical issue that is somewhat unique to field experiments is the **distribution of benefits:** How much are subjects harmed by the way treatments are distributed in the experiment? For example, Sherman and Berk's (1984) experiment, and its successors, required police to make arrests in domestic violence cases largely on the basis of a random process. When arrests were not made, did the subjects' abused spouses suffer? Price et al. (1992) randomly assigned unemployed individuals who had volunteered for job-search help to an intensive program. Were the unemployed volunteers assigned to the comparison group at a big disadvantage?

Is it ethical to give some potentially advantageous or disadvantageous treatment to people on a random basis? Random distribution of benefits is justified when the researchers do not know whether some treatment actually is beneficial or not—and, of course, it is the goal of the experiment to find out. Chance is as reasonable a basis for distributing the treatment as any other. Also, if insufficient resources are available to fully fund a benefit for every eligible person, distribution of the benefit on the basis of chance to equally needy persons is ethically defensible (Boruch, 1997:66–67).

The extent to which participation was voluntary varied in the field studies discussed in this chapter. Potential participants in the Price et al. study signed a detailed consent form in which they agreed to participate in a study involving random assignment to one of two types of job-search help, but researchers only accepted into the study persons who expressed equal preference for the job-search seminar and the mailed job materials (for those in the comparison condition).

Thus, Price et al. avoided the problem of not acceding to subjects' preferences. It therefore doesn't seem at all unethical that the researchers gave treatment to only some of the subjects. As it turned out, subjects did benefit from the experimental treatment (the workshops). Now that the study has been conducted, government bodies will have a basis for expecting that tax dollars spent on job-search workshops for the unemployed will have a beneficial impact. If this knowledge results in more such programs, the benefit of the experiment will have been very considerable indeed.

Unlike Price et al.'s subjects, individuals who were the subjects of domestic violence complaints in the Sherman and Berk study had no choice about being arrested or receiving a warning, nor were they aware that they were in a research study.

Perhaps it seems unreasonable to let a random procedure determine how police resolve cases of domestic violence. And indeed, it would be unreasonable if this procedure were a regular police practice. The Sherman and Berk experiment and its successors do pass ethical muster, however, when seen for what they were: a way of learning how to increase the effectiveness of police responses to this all-too-common crime. The initial Sherman and Berk findings encouraged police departments to make many more arrests for these crimes, and the follow-up studies resulted in a better understanding of when arrests are not likely to be effective. The implications of this research may be complex and difficult to implement, but the research provides a much stronger factual basis for policy development.

CONCLUSIONS

True experiments play two critical roles in social science research. First, they are the best research design for testing nomothetic causal hypotheses. Even when conditions preclude use of a true experimental design, many research designs can be improved by adding some experimental components. Second, true experiments also provide a comparison point for evaluating the ability of other research designs to achieve causally valid results.

In spite of their obvious strengths, true experiments are used infrequently to study many of the research problems that interest social scientists. There are three basic reasons: The experiments required to test many important hypotheses require far more resources than most social scientists have access to; most of the research problems of interest to social scientists simply are not amenable to experimental designs, for reasons ranging from ethical considerations to the limited possibilities for randomly assigning people to different conditions in the real world; and finally, the requirements of experimental design usually preclude large-scale studies and so limit generalizability to a degree that is unacceptable to many social scientists.

Although it may be possible to test a hypothesis with an experiment, it may not always be desirable to do so. When a social program is first being developed and its elements are in flux, it is not a good idea to begin a large evaluation study that cannot possibly succeed unless the program design remains constant. Researchers should wait until the program design stabilizes somewhat. It also does not make sense for evaluation researchers to test the impact of programs that cannot actually be implemented or that are unlikely to be implemented in the real world because of financial or political problems (Rossi & Freeman, 1989:304–307).

Even laboratory experiments are inadvisable when they do not test the real hypothesis of interest but test instead a limited version amenable to laboratory manipulation. The intersecting complexity of societies, social relationships, and social beings—of people and the groups to which they belong—is so great that it often defies reduction to the simplicity of a laboratory or restriction to the requirements of experimental design. Yet the virtues of experimental designs mean that they should always be considered when explanatory research is planned.

KEY TERMS

Before-and-after design
Comparison group
Compensatory rivalry (John Henry effect)
Contamination
Control group
Debriefing
Differential attrition
Distribution of benefits
Double-blind procedure
Endogenous change
Ex post facto control group design
Expectancies of experimental staff
Experimental group
External event
Factorial survey
Field experiment
Hawthorne effect
History effect

Matching
Multiple group before-and-after design
Nonequivalent control group design
Placebo effect
Posttest
Pretest
Pretest-posttest control group design
Process analysis
Quasi-experimental design
Randomized comparative change design
Randomized comparative posttest design
Regression effect
Repeated measures panel design
Selection bias
Self-fulfilling prophecy
Time series design
Treatment misidentification
True experiment

HIGHLIGHTS

• The independent variable in an experiment is represented by a treatment or other intervention. Some subjects receive one type of treatment; others may receive a different treatment or no treatment. In true experiments, subjects are assigned randomly to comparison groups.

• Experimental research designs have three essential components: use of at least two groups of subjects for comparison, measurement of the change that occurs as a result of the experimental treatment, and use of random assignment. In addition, experiments may include identification of a causal mechanism and control over experimental conditions.

• Random assignment of subjects to experimental and comparison groups eliminates systematic bias in group assignment. The odds of a difference between the experimental and comparison groups on the basis of chance can be calculated. They become very small for experiments with at least 30 subjects per group.

• Random assignment and random sampling both rely on a chance selection procedure, but their purposes differ. Random assignment involves placing predesignated subjects into two or more groups on the basis of chance; random sampling involves selecting subjects out of a larger population on the basis of chance. Matching of cases in the experimental and comparison groups is a poor substitute for randomization because identifying in advance all important variables on which to make the match is not possible. However, matching can improve the comparability of groups when it is used to supplement randomization.

• Quasi-experiments include features that maximize the comparability of the control and experimental groups and make it unlikely that self-selection determines group membership. Nonexperiments rely only on naturally occurring groups without any particular criteria to reduce the risk of selection bias.

• Causal conclusions derived from experiments can be invalid because of selection bias, endogenous change, the effects of external events, cross-group contamination, or treatment misidentification.

In true experiments, randomization should eliminate selection bias and bias due to endogenous change. External events, cross-group contamination, and treatment misidentification can threaten the validity of causal conclusions in both true experiments and quasi-experiments.

• Process analysis can be used in experiments to identify how the treatment had (or didn't have) its effect—a matter of particular concern in field experiments. Treatment misidentification is less likely when process analysis is used.

• The generalizability of experimental results declines if the study conditions are artificial and the experimental subjects are unique. Field experiments are likely to produce more generalizable results than experiments conducted in the laboratory.

• The external validity of causal conclusions is determined by the extent to which they apply to different types of individuals and settings. When causal conclusions do not apply to all the subgroups in a study, they are not generalizable to corresponding subgroups in the population—and so they are not externally valid with respect to those subgroups. Causal conclusions can also be considered externally invalid when they occur only under the experimental conditions.

• Subject deception is common in laboratory experiments and poses unique ethical issues. Researchers must weigh the potential harm to subjects and debrief subjects who have been deceived. In field experiments, a common ethical problem is selective distribution of benefits. Random assignment may be the fairest way of allocating treatment when treatment openings are insufficient for all eligible individuals and when the efficacy of the treatment is unknown.

DISCUSSION QUESTIONS

1. Read the original article reporting one of the experiments described in this chapter. Critique the article using as your guide the article review questions presented in Appendix B. Focus on the extent to which experimental conditions were controlled and the causal mechanism was identified. Did inadequate control over conditions or inadequate identification of the causal mechanism make you feel uncertain about the causal conclusions?

2. Select a true experiment, perhaps from the *Journal of Experimental and Social Psychology,* the *Journal of Personality and Social Psychology,* or from sources suggested in class. Diagram the experiment using the exhibits in this chapter as a model. Discuss the extent to which experimental conditions were controlled and the causal mechanism was identified. How confident can you be in the causal conclusions from the study, based on review of the threats to internal validity discussed in this chapter: selection bias, endogenous change, external events, contamination, and treatment misidentification? How generalizable do you think the study's results are to the population from which cases were selected? To specific subgroups in the study? How thoroughly do the researchers discuss these issues?

3. Repeat Exercise 2 with a quasi-experiment.

4. Critique the ethics of one of the experiments presented in this chapter. What specific rules do you think should guide researchers' decisions about subject deception and the selective distribution of benefits?

PRACTICE EXERCISES

1. Arrange with an instructor in a large class to conduct a multiple pretest-posttest study of the impact of watching a regularly scheduled class movie. Design a 10-question questionnaire to measure knowledge about the topics in the film. Administer this questionnaire shortly before and shortly after

the film is shown and then again one week afterward. After scoring the knowledge tests, describe the immediate and long-term impact of the movie.

2. Volunteer for an experiment! Contact the psychology department, and ask about opportunities for participating in laboratory experiments. Discuss the experience with your classmates.

3. Take a few minutes to review "Sources of Internal Invalidity" with the CD-ROM lessons. It will be time well spent.

WEB EXERCISES

1. Go to Sociosite at http://www.pscw.uva.nl/sociosite. Choose "Subject Areas." Choose a socio-logical subject area you are interested in, and find an example of research that has been done in this subject using experimental methods. Explain the experiment. Choose at least five of the "Key Terms" listed at the end of this chapter that are relevant to and incorporated in the research experiment you have located on the Web. Explain how each of the five key terms you have chosen plays a role in the research example you have found on the Web.

2. Try out the process of randomization. Go to the Web site www.randomizer.org. Type numbers into the randomizer for an experiment with 2 groups and 20 individuals per group. Repeat the process for an experiment with 4 groups and 10 individuals per group. Plot the numbers corresponding to each individual in each group. Does the distribution of numbers within each group truly seem to be random?

3. Participate in a social psychology experiment on the Web. Go to http://www.socialpsychology. org/expts.htm. Pick an experiment in which to participate and follow the instructions. After you finish, write up a description of the experiment and evaluate it using the criteria discussed in the chapter.

SPSS EXERCISES

Because the GSS2000mini doesn't provide experimental data to work with, we'll pause in our study of support for capital punishment and examine some relationships involving workplace variables like some of those that were the focus of research reviewed in this chapter.

Do the features of work influence attitudes about the work experience? We can test some hypothetical answers to this question with the GSS2000mini dataset (although not within the context of an experimental design).

1. Describe the feelings of working Americans about their jobs and economic rewards, based on their responses to questions about balancing work and family demands, their satisfaction with their finances, and their job satisfaction. Generate the frequencies as follows:
   a. Click *Analyze|Descriptive statistics|Frequencies.*
   b. Select SATFIN, SATJOB.

How satisfied are working people with their jobs and their pay?

2. Do these feelings vary with work features?
   a. Pose at least three hypotheses in which either SATFIN or SATJOB is the dependent variable and one of the following two variables is the independent variable: earnings or work status. Now test these hypotheses by comparing average scores on the attitudinal variables between categories of the independent variables:
      (1) Click *Analyze|Compare means|Means.*
      (2) Select *Dependent List*: SATFIN, SATJOB
          Independent List: RINC98D, WRKSTAT2

b. Which hypotheses appear to be supported? (Remember to review the distributions of the dependent variables [Q1c] to remind yourself what a higher average score indicates on each variable.)

c. If you already have had a statistics course, you will want to know whether the difference in mean values between the categories of the independent variable is statistically significant. You can test this with the *t*-test procedure, available in the Statistics menu.

DEVELOPING A RESEARCH PROPOSAL

Your work in this section should build on your answers to the proposal development questions in the last chapter.

1. Design a laboratory experiment to test one of your hypotheses, or a related hypothesis. Describe the experimental design, commenting on each component of a true experiment. Specify clearly how the independent variable will be manipulated and how the dependent variable will be measured.

2. Assume that your experiment will be conducted on campus. Formulate recruitment and randomization procedures.

3. Discuss the extent to which each source of internal invalidity is a problem in the study. Propose procedures like process analysis to cope with these sources of invalidity.

4. How generalizable would you expect the study's findings to be? What can be done to increase generalizability?

5. Develop appropriate procedures for the protection of human subjects in your experiment. Include among these procedures a consent form. Give particular attention to any aspects of the study that are likely to raise ethical concerns.

Chapter 8

SURVEY RESEARCH

Survey Research in the Social Sciences

Attractions of Survey Research
Versatility
Efficiency
Generalizability
The Omnibus Survey
Errors in Survey Research

Writing Questions

Avoid Confusing Phrasing
Minimize the Risk of Bias
Avoid Making Either Disagreement or Agreement Disagreeable
Minimize Fence-Sitting and Floating
Maximize the Utility of Response Categories

Designing Questionnaires

Build on Existing Instruments
Refine and Test Questions
Add Interpretive Questions
Maintain Consistent Focus

Order the Questions
Make the Questionnaire Attractive

Organizing Surveys

Mailed, Self-Administered Surveys
Group-Administered Surveys
Telephone Surveys
Reaching Sample Units
Maximizing Response to Phone Surveys
In-Person Interviews
Balancing Rapport and Control
Maximizing Response to Interviews
Electronic Surveys
Mixed-Mode Surveys
A Comparison of Survey Designs

Combining Methods

Adding Qualitative Data
Case Study: Juvenile Court Records
Case Study: Mental Health System

Ethical Issues in Survey Research

Conclusions

The intersection between work and family life has changed considerably during the 20th century. For much of the industrial period, separation of work and family activities and a gender-based division of responsibilities were the norm. But we have seen in recent decades a dramatic increase in the proportion of two-income families, many more single-parent/single-earner families, more telecommuting and other work-at-home arrangements, and some changes in the household division of labor. Social scientists who seek to understand these changes in the social structure have had plenty to keep themselves busy.

Ohio State sociology professor Catherine Ross (1990) wanted to know how these changes shape people's sense of control and, in turn, how their sense of control affects feelings of depression, anxiety, and distress. To answer these questions, she proposed to the National Science Foundation a survey of adult Americans. In this chapter I will use her successful project to illustrate some key features of survey research, after an initial review of the reasons for using survey methods. I explain the major steps in questionnaire design, and then consider the features of four types of surveys, highlighting the unique problems attending each one and suggesting some possible solutions. I discuss ethics issues in the final section. By the chapter's end, you should be well on your way to becoming an informed consumer of survey reports and a knowledgeable developer of survey designs—as well as a more informed student of the relationships among work, family, and well-being.

SURVEY RESEARCH IN THE SOCIAL SCIENCES

Survey research involves the collection of information from a sample of individuals through their responses to questions. Ross (1990) turned to survey research for her study of social structure and well-being because it is an efficient method for systematically collecting data from a broad spectrum of individuals and social settings. As you probably have observed, a great many social scientists—as well as newspaper editors, political pundits, and marketing gurus—make the same methodological choice. In fact, surveys have become such a vital part of our society's social fabric that we cannot assess much of what we read in the newspaper or see on TV without having some understanding of this method of data collection (Converse, 1984). Although survey research is more popular in sociology than in economics or social psychology, it accounts for more than a third of published research articles in all three disciplines.

Attractions of Survey Research

Regardless of its scope, survey research owes its continuing popularity to three features: versatility, efficiency, and generalizability.

Versatility

First and foremost, survey methods are versatile. Although a survey is not the ideal method for testing all hypotheses or learning about every social process, a well-designed survey can enhance our understanding of just about any social issue. Ross's survey covered a range of topics about work and health, and there is hardly any other topic of interest to social scientists that has not been studied at some time with survey methods. Politicians campaigning for election use surveys, as do businesses marketing a product, governments assessing community needs, agencies monitoring program effectiveness, and lawyers seeking to buttress claims of discrimination or select favorable juries. The broad range of measures that can be used in survey research have made it the focus of measurement development work.

Efficiency

Surveys also are popular because data can be collected from many people at relatively low cost and, depending on the survey design, relatively quickly. Catherine Ross contracted with the University of Illinois Survey Research Laboratory (SRL) for her 1990 telephone survey of 2,000 adult Americans. SRL estimated that the survey would incur direct costs of $60,823—only $30.41 per respondent—and take 5 to 6 months to complete. Large mailed surveys cost even less, about $10 to $15 per potential respondent, although the costs can increase greatly when intensive follow-up efforts are made. Surveys of the general population using personal interviews are much more expensive, with costs ranging from about $100 per potential respondent for studies in a limited geographical area to $300 or more when lengthy travel or repeat visits are needed to connect with respondents (Fowler, 1998; see also Dillman, 1982; Groves & Kahn, 1979). As you would expect, phone surveys are the quickest survey method, which accounts for their popularity in political polling.

Surveys also are efficient because many variables can be measured without substantially increasing the time or cost. Mailed questionnaires can include up to 10 pages of questions before respondents begin to balk. In-person interviews can be much longer, taking more than an hour; for example, the 1991 General Social Survey included 196 questions, many with multiple parts, and was 75 pages long. The upper limit for phone surveys seems to be about 45 minutes.

Of course, these efficiencies can be attained only in a place with a reliable communications infrastructure (Labaw, 1980:xiii–xiv). A reliable postal service, which is required for mail surveys, has generally been available in the United States—although residents of the Bronx, New York, have complained that delivery of local first-class mail often takes 2 weeks or more, almost ruling out mail surveys (Purdy, 1994). Phone surveys can be effective in the United States because 95% of households have phones (Czaja & Blair, 1995), and only 4% of persons live in households without a phone (Levy & Lemeshow, 1999:456).

Also important to efficiency are the many survey organizations that provide the trained staff and the proper equipment for conducting high-quality surveys.

Generalizability

Survey methods lend themselves to probability sampling from large populations. Thus, survey research is very appealing when sample generalizability is a central research goal. In fact, survey research is often the only means available for developing a representative picture of the attitudes and characteristics of a large population.

Surveys also are the method of choice when cross-population generalizability is a key concern, because they allow a range of social contexts and subgroups to be sampled. The consistency of relationships can then be examined across the various subgroups.

The Omnibus Survey

An omnibus survey shows just how versatile, efficient, and generalizable a survey can be. An **omnibus survey** covers a range of topics of interest to different social scientists, in contrast to the typical survey that is directed at a specific research question. It has multiple sponsors or is designed to generate data useful to a broad segment of the social science community rather than to answer a particular research question. It is usually directed to a sample of some general population, so the questions about a range of different issues are appropriate to at least some sample members.

One of sociology's most successful omnibus surveys is the General Social Survey (GSS) of the National Opinion Research Center at the University of Chicago. It is a 90-minute interview administered biennially to a probability sample of almost 3,000 Americans, with a wide range of questions and topic areas chosen by a board of overseers. Some questions are asked of only a randomly selected subset of respondents. This **split-ballot design** allows more questions without increasing the survey's cost. It also facilitates experiments on the effect of question wording: Different forms of the same question are included in the split-ballot subsets. The GSS is widely available to universities, instructors, and students (Davis & Smith, 1992; National Opinion Research Center, 1992), as are many other survey datasets archived by the Inter-university Consortium for Political and Social Research (ICPSR) (more details about the ICPSR are in Chapter 10). Catherine Ross contributed her survey dataset to the ICPSR.

Errors in Survey Research

It might be said that surveys are too easy to conduct. Organizations and individuals often decide that a survey would help to solve some important problem because it seems so easy to prepare a form with some questions and send it out. But without careful attention to sampling, measurement, and overall survey design, the effort is likely to be a flop. Such flops are too common for comfort, and the responsible survey researcher must take the time to design surveys properly and to convince sponsoring organizations that this time is worth the effort (Turner & Martin, 1984:68).

In order for a survey to succeed, it must minimize the risk of two types of error: poor measurement of cases that are surveyed (**errors of observation**) and omission of cases that should be surveyed (**errors of nonobservation**) (Groves, 1989). Measurement error was a key concern in Chapter 4, but there is much more to be learned about how to minimize these errors of observation in the survey process. We will consider in this chapter potential problems with the questions we write, the way we present these questions in our questionnaires, the interviewers we may use to ask the questions, and the characteristics of the respondents who answer the questions.

Errors of nonobservation—the omission from the survey of some cases that should be included—are a major problem in survey research. There are three sources of errors of nonobservation:

- Nonresponse can distort the sample when individuals refuse to respond or cannot be contacted.
- Coverage of the population can be inadequate due to a poor sampling frame.
- The process of random sampling can result in "sampling error"—differences between the characteristics of the sample members and the population that arise due to chance.

We considered the importance of a good sampling frame and the procedures for estimating and reducing sampling error in Chapter 5; I will add only a few more points here.

I will give much more attention in this chapter to procedures for reducing nonresponse in surveys.

Nonresponse is a major problem in survey research. Many survey researchers believe that at least a 70% response rate must be achieved in order to be reasonably confident that the survey results will be representative of the population from which the survey sample was selected. However, this goal is often difficult to achieve in mailed surveys, and even that much nonresponse leaves considerable room for a difference between the sample members and the population (Dennis, 1998). Moreover, although nonresponse has always been a concern, it is getting worse. For reasons that are not entirely understood, but that may include growing popular cynicism and distrust of government, nonresponse rates have been growing in the United States and western Europe since the early 1950s (Groves, 1989:145–155; Groves & Couper, 1998:155–189). Just within the last few years, the use of caller ID and reliance on cell phones is making the problem much worse for phone studies. Many people use caller ID to screen out calls from unknown parties, and regulations prohibit unsolicited calls to cell phone numbers because the recipient must pay the cost of the call (Nagourney, 2002).

We can begin to anticipate problems that lead to survey errors and identify possible solutions if we take enough time to think about the issue theoretically. Survey expert Don Dillman (2000:14–15) proposes using social exchange theory to guide our expectations about survey error. This theory asserts that behavior is motivated by the return expected to the individual for the behavior (Blau, 1964). More specifically, expected returns are based on the social rewards that the individual thinks will be received for the behavior, the costs that will be incurred, and the trust that in the long run the rewards will exceed the costs. A well-designed survey will maximize the social rewards and minimize the costs for participating in the survey and establish trust that the rewards will outweigh the costs. Unfortunately, the desire to avoid telemarketers now leads many people simply to ignore calls from unknown callers; the benefit of not dealing with such a call certainly outweighs the negligible cost of checking the caller ID screen.

Using clear and interesting questions and presenting them in a well-organized questionnaire go a long way to reducing the cost of responding carefully to a survey (for those who open their mail, answer the door, or pick up the phone). Question writing will be the focus of the next section, and questionnaire design will be discussed in the section that follows. Other steps for increasing rewards, reducing costs, and maximizing trust in order to reduce nonresponse in each type of survey will be the focus of the last section.

WRITING QUESTIONS

Questions are the centerpiece of survey research. Because the way they are worded can have a great effect on the way they are answered, selecting good questions is the single most important concern for survey researchers. All hope for achieving measurement validity is lost unless the questions in a survey are clear and convey the intended meaning to respondents.

You may be thinking that you ask people questions all the time and have no trouble understanding the answers you receive, but can't you also think of times when you've been confused in casual conversation by misleading or misunderstood questions? Now consider just a few of the differences between everyday conversations and standardized surveys that make writing survey questions much more difficult:

- Survey questions must be asked of many people, not just one.
- The same survey question must be used with each person, not tailored to the specifics of a given conversation.
- Survey questions must be understood in the same way by people who differ in many ways.
- You will not be able to rephrase a survey question if someone doesn't understand it, because that would result in a different question for that person.
- Survey respondents don't know you and so can't be expected to share the nuances of expression that help you and your friends and family to communicate.

Question writing for a particular survey might begin with a brainstorming session or a review of previous surveys. Then, whatever questions are being considered must be systematically evaluated and refined. Although most professionally prepared surveys contain previously used questions as well as some new ones, every question that is considered for inclusion must be reviewed carefully for its clarity and ability to convey the intended meaning. Questions that were clear and meaningful to one population may not be so to another. Nor can you simply assume that a question used in a previously published study was carefully evaluated.

Adherence to a few basic principles will go a long way toward ensuring clear and meaningful questions. Each of these principles summarizes a great deal of the wisdom of experienced survey researchers, although none of them should be viewed as an inflexible mandate. As you will learn in the next section, every question must be considered in terms of its relationship to the other questions in a survey. Moreover, every survey has its own unique requirements and constraints; sometimes violating one principle is necessary in order to achieve others.

Avoid Confusing Phrasing

What's a confusing question? Try this one that I received years ago from The Planetary Society in their "National Priorities Survey, United States Space Program":

```
The Moon may be a place for an eventual scientific base, and even
for engineering resources. Setting up a base or mining experiment
will cost tens of billions of dollars in the next century. Should
the United States pursue further manned and unmanned scientific
research projects on the surface of the Moon?


☐ Yes  ☐ No  ☐ No opinion
```

Does a "yes" response mean that you favor spending tens of billions of dollars for a base or mining experiment? Does " the next century" refer to the 21st century or to the 100 years after the survey (which was distributed in the 1980s)? Could you favor further research projects on the Moon but oppose funding a scientific base or engineering resources? Are engineering resources supposed to have something to do with a mining experiment? Does a mining experiment occur "on the surface of the Moon"? How do you answer if you favor unmanned scientific research projects but not manned projects?

There are several ways to avoid such confusing phrasing. In most cases, a simple direct approach to asking a question minimizes confusion. Use shorter rather than longer words and sentences: "brave" rather than "courageous"; "job concerns" rather than "work-related employment issues" (Dillman, 2000:52). Try to keep the total number of words to 20 or fewer and the number of commas to 3 or fewer (Peterson, 2000:50). On the other hand, questions shouldn't be abbreviated in a way that results in confusion: To ask, "In what city or town do you live?" is to focus attention clearly on a specific geographic unit, a specific time, and a specific person (you); the simple statement,

Residential location: _____

does not do this.

Sometimes, when sensitive topics or past behaviors are the topic, longer questions can provide cues that make the respondent feel comfortable or aid memory (Peterson, 2000:51).

A sure way to muddy the meaning of a question is to use **double negatives:** "Do you *disagree* that there should *not* be a tax increase?" Respondents have a hard time figuring out which response matches their sentiments. Such errors can easily be avoided with minor wording changes, but even experienced survey researchers can make this mistake unintentionally, perhaps while trying to avoid some other wording problem. For instance, in a survey commissioned by the American Jewish Committee, the Roper polling organization wrote a question about the Holocaust that was carefully worded to be neutral and value-free: "Does it seem possible or does it seem impossible to you that the Nazi extermination of the Jews never happened?" Among a representative sample of adult Americans, 22% answered that it was possible the extermination never happened (Kifner, 1994:A12). Many Jewish leaders and politicians were stunned, wondering how one in five Americans could be so misinformed. But a careful reading of the question reveals how confusing it is: Choosing "possible," the seemingly positive response, means that you don't believe the Holocaust happened. In fact, the Gallup organization then rephrased the question to avoid the double negative, giving a brief definition of the Holocaust and then asking, "Do you doubt that the Holocaust actually happened or not?" Only 9% responded that they doubted it happened. When a wider range of response choices was given, only 2.9% said that the Holocaust "definitely" or "probably" did not happen. To be safe, it's best just to avoid using negative words like "don't" and "not" in questions.

So-called **double-barreled questions** are also guaranteed to produce uninterpretable results because they actually ask two questions but allow only one answer. For example, during the Watergate scandal, Gallup poll results indicated that, when the question was "Do you think President Nixon should be impeached and compelled to leave the presidency, or not?" only about a third of Americans supported impeaching President Richard M. Nixon. But when the Gallup organization changed the question to ask respondents if they "think there is enough evidence of possible wrongdoing in the case of President Nixon to bring him to trial before the Senate, or not," over half answered yes. Apparently the first, "double-barreled" version of the question confused support for impeaching Nixon—putting him on trial before the Senate—with concluding that he was guilty before he had had a chance to defend himself (Kagay & Elder, 1992:E5).

It is also important to identify clearly what kind of information each question is to obtain. Some questions focus on attitudes, or what people say they want or how they feel. Some questions focus on beliefs, or what people think is true. Some questions focus on behavior, or what people do. And some questions focus on attributes, or what people are like or have

Exhibit 8.1   Filter Questions and Skip Patterns

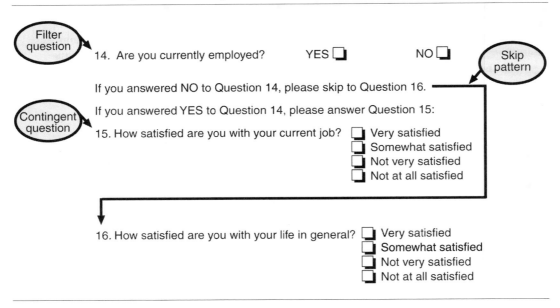

experienced (Dillman, 1978:79–118; Gordon, 1992). Rarely can a single question effectively address more than one of these dimensions at a time.

Whichever type of information a question is designed to obtain, be sure it is asked of only the respondents who may have that information. If you include a question about job satisfaction in a survey of the general population, first ask respondents whether they have a job. These **filter questions** create **skip patterns.** For example, respondents who answer no to one question are directed to skip ahead to another question, but respondents who answer yes go on to the **contingent question.** Skip patterns should be indicated clearly with arrows or other marks in the questionnaire as demonstrated in Exhibit 8.1.

Minimize the Risk of Bias

Specific words in survey questions should not trigger biases, unless that is the researcher's conscious intent. Biased or loaded words and phrases tend to produce misleading answers. For example, a 1974 survey found that 18% of respondents supported sending U.S. troops "if a situation like Vietnam were to develop in another part of the world." But when the question was reworded to mention sending troops to "stop a communist takeover"—"communist takeover" being a loaded phrase—favorable responses rose to 33% (Schuman & Presser, 1981:285).

Answers can also be biased by more subtle problems in phrasing that make certain responses more or less attractive to particular groups. To minimize biased responses, researchers have to test reactions to the phrasing of a question. When Ross (1990) was seeking to determine respondents' interests in household work rather than formal employment, she took special care to phrase her questions in a balanced, unbiased way. For example, she asked, "If you could choose, would you rather do the kind of work people do on jobs or the kind of work that is done around the house?" Her response options were "Jobs," "House," "Both," "Neither," "Don't care," and "Don't know." She could easily have biased the distribution of responses to this question by referring to housework as "the kind of work that women traditionally have done around the house." The explicit gender-typing would probably have made men less likely to choose housework as their preference. Note that, if Ross's purpose had been to find out how men respond to explicitly gender-linked roles, this wording would have been appropriate. Bias can be defined only in terms of the concept that the question is designed to measure.

Responses can also be biased when response alternatives do not reflect the full range of possible sentiment on an issue. When people pick a response choice, they seem to be influenced by where they are placing themselves relative to the other response choices. For example, the Detroit Area Study (Turner & Martin, 1984:252) asked the following question: "People feel differently about making changes in the way our country is run. In order to keep America great, which of these statements do you think is best?" When the only response choices were "We should be very cautious of making changes" and "We should be free to make changes," only 37% said that we should be free to make changes. However, when a response choice was added that suggested we should "constantly" make changes, 24% picked that response and another 32% chose the "free to make changes" response, for a total of 56% who seemed open to making changes in the way our country is run (Turner & Martin, 1984:252). Including the more extreme positive alternative ("constantly" make changes) made the less extreme positive alternative more attractive.

When the response alternatives fall on a continuum from positive to negative sentiment of some type, it is important that the number of positive and negative categories be balanced so that one end of the continuum doesn't seem more attractive (Dillman, 2000:57–58). If you ask respondents, "How satisfied are you with the intramural sports program here?" and include "completely satisfied" as the most positive possible response, then "completely dissatisfied" should be included as the most negative possible response.

Of course, the advice to minimize the risk of bias means nothing to those who conduct surveys to elicit bias. This is the goal of "push polling," a technique that has been used in some political campaigns. In a push poll, the "pollsters" for a candidate call potential voters and ask them a series of questions that convey negative information about the opposing candidate. It's really not a survey at all—just a propaganda effort—but it gives reputable researchers (and ethical political polling firms) a bad name (Connolly & Manning, 2001).

Avoid Making Either Disagreement or Agreement Disagreeable

People often tend to "agree" with a statement just to avoid seeming disagreeable. You can see the impact of this human tendency in a 1974 Michigan Survey Research Center survey that asked who was to blame for crime and lawlessness in the United States (Schuman & Presser, 1981:208). When one question stated that individuals were more to blame than social conditions, 60% of the respondents agreed. But when the question was rephrased so respondents were asked, in a balanced fashion, whether individuals or social conditions were more to blame, only 46% chose individuals.

You can take several steps to reduce the likelihood of agreement bias. As a general rule, you should present both sides of attitude scales in the question itself (Dillman, 2000:61–62): "In general, do you believe that *individuals* or *social conditions* are more to blame for crime and lawlessness in the United States?" The response choices themselves should be phrased to make each one seem as socially approved, as "agreeable," as the others. You should also consider replacing a range of response alternatives that focus on the word "agree" with others. For example, "To what extent do you support or oppose the new health care plan?" (response choices range from "strongly support" to "strongly oppose") is probably a better approach than the question "To what extent do you agree or disagree with the statement: 'The new health care plan is worthy of support'?" (response choices range from "strongly agree" to "strongly disagree").

You may also gain a more realistic assessment of respondents' sentiment by adding to a question a counterargument in favor of one side to balance an argument in favor of the other side. Thus, don't just ask in an employee survey whether employees should be required to join the union; instead, ask whether employees should be required to join the union or be able to make their own decision about joining. In one survey, 10% more respondents said they favored mandatory union membership when the counterargument was left out than when it was included. It is reassuring to know, however, that this approach does not change the distribution of answers to questions about which people have very strong beliefs (Schuman & Presser, 1981:186).

When an illegal or socially disapproved behavior or attitude is the focus, we have to be concerned that some respondents will be reluctant to agree that they have ever done or thought such a thing. In this situation, the goal is to write a question and response choices that make agreement seem more acceptable. For example, Dillman (2000:75) suggests that we ask, "Have you ever taken anything from a store without paying for it?" rather than "Have you ever shoplifted something from a store?" Asking about a variety of behaviors or attitudes that range from socially acceptable to socially unacceptable will also soften the impact of agreeing with those that are socially unacceptable.

Minimize Fence-Sitting and Floating

Two related problems in question writing also stem from people's desire to choose an acceptable answer. There is no uniformly correct solution to these problems; researchers have to weigh the alternatives in light of the concept to be measured and whatever they know about the respondents.

Fence-sitters, people who see themselves as being neutral, may skew the results if you force them to choose between opposites. In most cases, about 10% to 20% of such respondents—those who do not have strong feelings on an issue—will choose an explicit middle, neutral alternative (Schuman & Presser, 1981:161–178). Adding an explicit neutral response option is appropriate when you want to find out who is a fence-sitter.

Even more people can be termed **floaters:** respondents who choose a substantive answer when they really don't know. A third of the public will provide an opinion on a proposed law that they know nothing about if they are asked for their opinion in a closed-ended survey question that does not include "Don't know" as an explicit response choice. However, 90% of these persons will select the "Don't know" response if they are explicitly given that option. On average, offering an explicit response option increases the "Don't know" responses by about a fifth (Schuman & Presser, 1981:113–160).

Exhibit 8.2   The Effect of Floaters on Public Opinion Polls

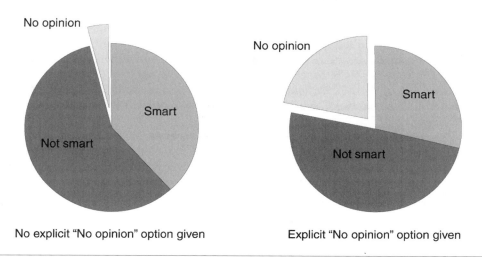

Responses to "Are government leaders smart?"

No explicit "No opinion" option given   Explicit "No opinion" option given

Source: Data from Schuman & Presser, 1981:121.

Exhibit 8.2 depicts the results of one study that tested the effect of giving respondents an explicit "No opinion" option to the question "Are government leaders smart?" Notice how many more people chose "No opinion" when they were given that choice than when their only explicit options were "Smart" and "Not smart."

The "Don't know" option has been a bone of contention for political pollsters. The debate heated up after the 1992 election, in which come-from-behind candidate Bill Clinton raced past President George Bush after the Democratic convention, but then appeared to be losing his lead just before the election. David W. Moore, director of the University of New Hampshire's Survey Center, argued in a *New York Times* article that the last-minute changes showed that the "Undecided" category was being undercounted. Only 10% of the voters were classified as undecided by the major pollsters, but Moore reminded readers that "there are many undecided voters who play our polling game—who specify a candidate they might choose 'if the election were held today' but who have no commitment to that candidate beyond the time of the interview" (Moore, 1992:E15).

It's a good idea to omit the "no opinion" or "don't know" category when you feel that people have an opinion but are reluctant to express it. In fact, most political pollsters use **forced-choice questions** without a "Don't know" option. Just after President Clinton's victory, Frank Newport, editor in chief of the Gallup poll, defended pollsters' efforts to get all prospective voters to declare a preferred candidate:

It would not be very instructive for pollsters . . . to allow large numbers of voters to claim they are undecided all through the election season. We would miss the dynamics of change, we would be unable to tell how well candidates were doing in response to events, and publicly released polls would be out of synchronization with private, campaign polls. (Newport, 1992:A28)

Because there are so many floaters in the typical survey sample, the decision to include an explicit "Don't know" option for a question is important. This decision is particularly important with surveys of less-educated populations because "Don't know" responses are offered more often by those with less education—except for questions that are really impossible to decipher, to which more educated persons are likely to say they don't know (Schuman & Presser, 1981:113–146). Unfortunately, the inclusion of an explicit "Don't know" response choice leads some people who do have a preference to take the easy way out and choose "Don't know."

The likelihood of "floating" also varies with the issue. Many people did not yet know much about what "stem cell research" was in July 2001 (57% in a July 10–11, 2001 Gallup poll), but that did not stop some polling organizations from asking questions about it without giving respondents the option of indicating they didn't know enough about it yet. The usual approach in such a situation is to explain the issue and then ask questions about it, but it is not clear that this results in a good picture of the attitudes that people will have when they learn about the issue in the normal course of events (Clymer, 2001).

There are several ways to phrase questions and response choices to reduce the risk of completely missing fence-sitters and floaters. One good idea is to include an explicit "no opinion" category after all the substantive responses; if neutral sentiment is a possibility, also include a neutral category in the middle of the substantive responses (such as "neither agree nor disagree") (Dillman, 2000:58–60). Adding an open-ended question in which respondents are asked to discuss their opinions (or reasons for having no opinion) can help shed light on why some people choose "Don't know" in response to a particular question (Smith, 1984). And researchers who use in-person or telephone interviews (rather than self-administered questionnaires) may get around the dilemma somewhat by reading the response choices without a middle or "Don't know" alternative but recording a noncommittal response if it is offered. Ross's (1990) questionnaire for her survey on the changing U.S. household included the following example:

```
If you could choose, would you rather do the kind of work people
do on jobs or the kind of work that is done around the house?

     JOBS          1
     HOUSE         2
     BOTH          3
     NEITHER       4
     DON'T CARE    5
     DON'T KNOW    8
```

Maximize the Utility of Response Categories

Questions with fixed response choices must provide one and only one possible response for everyone who is asked the question—that is, the response choices must be exhaustive and mutually exclusive. Ranges of ages, incomes, years of schooling, and so forth should not overlap and should provide a response option for all respondents.

There are two exceptions to this principle: Filter questions may tell some respondents to skip over a question (the response choices do not have to be exhaustive); and respondents may be asked to "check all that apply" (the response choices are not mutually exclusive). Even these exceptions should be kept to a minimum. Respondents to a self-administered questionnaire should not have to do a lot of "skipping around" or they may lose interest in completing carefully all the applicable questions. Some survey respondents react to a "check all that apply" request by just checking enough responses so that they feel they have "done enough" for that question and then ignoring the rest of the choices (Dillman, 2000:63).

Vagueness in the response choices is also to be avoided. Questions about thoughts and feelings will be more reliable if they refer to specific times or events (Turner & Martin, 1984:300). Usually a question like "On how many days did you read the newspaper in the last week?" produces more reliable answers than one like "How often do you read the newspaper? (frequently, sometimes, never)." In her survey, Ross (1990) sensibly asked the question "Do you currently smoke 7 or more cigarettes a week?" rather than the vaguer question "Do you smoke?" Of course, being specific doesn't help if you end up making unreasonable demands of your respondents' memories. One survey asked, "During the past 12 months, about how many times did you see or talk to a medical doctor?" According to their written health records, respondents forgot 60% of their doctor visits (Goleman, 1993b:C11). So limit questions about specific past experiences to, at most, the past month, unless your focus is on major events that are unlikely to have been forgotten.

Sometimes problems with response choices can be corrected by adding questions. For example, if you ask, "How many years of schooling have you completed?" someone who dropped out of high school but completed the requirements for a General Equivalency Diploma might not be sure how to respond. By asking a second question, "What is the highest degree you have received?" you can provide the correct alternative for those with a G.E.D. as well as for those who graduated from high school.

Adding questions may also improve memory about specific past events. This is the approach taken in **cognitive interviewing,** in which a series of questions help to improve memories about the event of real interest (Dillman, 2000:66–67). Imagine the problem you might have identifying the correct response to the question "How often did you receive help from classmates while preparing for exams or completing assignments during the last month? (very often, somewhat often, occasionally, rarely, or never)." Now imagine a series of questions that asks you to identify the exams and assignments you had in the past month and, for each one, inquires whether you received each of several types of help from classmates: study suggestions, study sessions, related examples, general encouragement, and so on. The more specific focus on particular exams and assignments should result in more complete recall (Dykema & Schaeffer, 2000).

How many response categories are desirable? It really depends on the mode of survey administration (phone interviews require fewer categories), respondents' educational levels, and the extent of their knowledge of the issue on which the question focuses. There are no fixed rules, so some type of pretesting is probably a good idea. Pretesting also can help you to decide whether to include a middle (neutral) category and how to label the response categories (Peterson, 2000:63–74).

DESIGNING QUESTIONNAIRES

Survey questions are answered as part of a **questionnaire** (or **interview schedule,** as it's often called in interview-based studies), not in isolation from other questions. The context created by the questionnaire has a major impact on how individual questions are interpreted and whether they are even answered. As a result, survey researchers must give very careful attention to the design of the questionnaire as well as to the individual questions that it includes.

Questionnaire   The survey instrument containing the questions in a self-administered survey.

Interview schedule   The survey instrument containing the questions asked by the interviewer in an in-person or phone survey.

The way a questionnaire should be designed varies with the specific survey method used and with other particulars of a survey project. There can be no precise formula for identifying questionnaire features that reduce error. Nonetheless, some key principles should guide the design of any questionnaire and some systematic procedures should be considered for refining it. I will use Ross's (1990) questionnaire for studying the psychological effects of changes in household structure to illustrate some of these principles and procedures.

Build on Existing Instruments

If another researcher already has designed a set of questions to measure a key concept, and evidence from previous surveys indicates that this measure is reliable and valid, then by all means use that instrument. Resources like Delbert Miller's (1991) *Handbook of Research Design and Social Measurement* can give you many ideas about existing instruments; your literature review at the start of a research project should be an even better source. Catherine Ross (1990) drew many of her measures from an extensive body of prior research (including her own). She measured feelings of distress with the well-established Center for Epidemiologic Studies' Depression scale (see Chapter 4), self-esteem with a measure developed by Morris Rosenberg (1965), and "learned helplessness" with Martin Seligman's (1975) scale.

But there is a trade-off here. Questions used previously may not concern quite the right concept or may not be appropriate in some ways to your population. Ross (1990:8) even used the need to develop new measures for the study of work and family issues as a selling point in her research proposal: "Part of the proposed project will be to refine, modify, and develop measures, in addition to reviewing literature on already developed measures." Together with John Mirowsky (Mirowsky & Ross, 1991), she developed a new measure of the sense of control, the central concept in her 1990 survey. So even though using a previously designed and well-regarded instrument may reassure other social scientists, it may not really be appropriate for your own specific survey. A good rule of thumb is to use a previously designed instrument if it measures the concept of concern to you and if you have no clear reason for thinking it is inappropriate with your survey population. You can always solicit the opinions of other researchers before making a final decision.

Refine and Test Questions

Adhering to the preceding question-writing guidelines will go a long way toward producing a useful questionnaire. However, simply asking what appear to you to be clear questions does not ensure that people have a consistent understanding of what you are asking. You need some external feedback—the more of it the better. This feedback is obtained from some type of pretest (Dillman, 2000:140–147). Pretesting of some sort is an essential step in preparing any survey.

One important form of feedback results from simply discussing the questionnaire content with others. Persons who should be consulted include expert researchers, key figures in the locale or organization to be surveyed (such as elected representatives, company presidents, and community leaders), and some individuals from the population to be sampled. Run your list of variables and specific questions by such figures whenever you have a chance. Reviewing the relevant literature to find results obtained with similar surveys and comparable questions is also an important step to take, if you haven't already conducted such a review before writing your questions. Forming a panel of experts to review the questions can also help: Presser and Blair (1994) recommend a panel of a psychologist, a questionnaire design expert, and a general methodologist (Peterson, 2000:116).

Another increasingly popular form of feedback comes from guided discussions among potential respondents, called focus groups, to check for consistent understanding of terms and to identify the range of events or experiences about which people will be asked to report. By listening to and observing the focus group discussions, researchers can validate their assumptions about what level of vocabulary is appropriate and what people are going to be reporting (Fowler, 1995). (See Chapter 9 for more about this technique.)

Professional survey researchers have also developed a technique for evaluating questions called the cognitive interview (Fowler, 1995). Although the specifics vary, the basic approach is to ask people to "think aloud" as they answer questions. The researcher asks a test question, then probes with follow-up questions to learn how the question was understood and whether its meaning varied for different respondents. This method can identify many potential problems, particularly if the individuals interviewed reflect much of the diversity of the population to be surveyed. A different approach to identifying problems is **behavior coding:** A researcher observes several interviews or listens to taped interviews and codes, according to strict rules, the number of times that difficulties occur with questions. Such difficulties include respondents asking for clarification and interviewers rephrasing questions rather than reading them verbatim (Presser & Blair, 1994:74–75).

Conducting a pilot study is the final stage of questionnaire preparation. Prepare for the pilot study by completing the questionnaire yourself and then revise it. Next, try it out on some colleagues or other friends, and then revise it. For the actual pilot study, draw a small sample of individuals from the population you are studying or one very similar to it (it is best to draw a sample of at least 100 respondents) and carry out the survey procedures with them. This should include as many mailings as you plan for a mailed questionnaire and actual interviews if you are preparing to conduct in-person interviews. You may include in the pretest version of a written questionnaire some space for individuals to add comments on each key question or, with in-person interviews, audiotape the test interviews for later review (a good idea, particularly if you have not previously conducted cognitive interviews).

Review the distribution of responses to each question, listen to the audiotapes, or read all the comments, and then code what you heard or read to identify problems in question wording or delivery. Revise any questions that respondents do not seem to interpret as you had intended or that are not working well for other reasons. If the response rate is relatively low, consider whether it can be improved by some modifications in procedures.

Ross's (1990) survey of U.S. households included limited pretesting, as Johnny Blair noted in a letter to Ross summarizing the procedure to be used:

> Before being used for data collection, the survey questionnaire will be given a pretest consisting of 30 interviews conducted in Illinois. The pretest will be used to evaluate the adequacy of the questionnaire, to try out systematically all the various procedures in the main survey, to establish and evaluate codes for questionnaire responses, and to gauge the length of the interview. Only upon the basis of the diagnostic information obtained in the pretest interviews will the fully refined version of the survey questionnaire be prepared, ready for administration in the full-scale survey. (J. E. Blair, personal communication to C. E. Ross, April 10, 1989)

Which pretesting method is best? Each has some unique advantages and disadvantages. Behavior coding, with its clearly specified rules, is the most reliable method across interviewers and repetitions, whereas pilot studies are the least reliable. However, behavior coding provides no information about the cause of problems with questions; the other methods are better at this. Review of questions by an expert panel is the least expensive method and identifies the greatest number of problems with questions (Presser & Blair, 1994).

Add Interpretive Questions

A survey researcher can also try to understand what respondents mean by their responses after the fact by including additional questions in the survey itself. Adding such **interpretive questions** after key survey questions is always a good idea, but it is of utmost importance when the questions in a survey have not been thoroughly pretested.

An example from a study of people with motor-vehicle driving violations illustrates the importance of interpretive questions:

> When asked whether their emotional state affected their driving at all, respondents would reply that their emotions had very little effect on their driving habits. Then, when asked to describe the circumstances surrounding their last traffic violation, respondents typically replied, "I was mad at my girlfriend," or "I had a quarrel with my wife," or "We had a family quarrel," or "I was angry with my boss." (Labaw, 1980:71)

Were these respondents lying in response to the first question? Probably not. More likely, they simply didn't interpret their own behavior in terms of general concepts like "emotional state." But their responses to the first question were likely to be misinterpreted without the further detail provided by answers to the second.

Consider five issues when you develop interpretive questions—or when you review survey results and need to consider what the answers tell you:

- *What do the respondents know?* Answers to many questions about current events and government policies are almost uninterpretable without also learning what the respondents know. In studies like Ross's (1990), however, which focused on personal experiences and feelings, questions assessing knowledge are not so necessary.

- *What relevant experiences do the respondents have?* Such experiences undoubtedly color the responses. For example, the meaning of opinions about crime and punishment may differ greatly between those who have been crime victims themselves and those who have not. Ross had to begin her survey with a question about the respondent's current employment status, which determined whether many of the work-related questions would be relevant. Similarly, her questions about child care were preceded by questions to determine whether the respondent had children.

- *How consistent are the respondents' attitudes, and do they express some larger perspective or ideology?* An employee who seeks more wages because she believes that all employer profits result from exploitation is expressing a different sentiment from one who seeks more wages because she really wants a more expensive car with which to impress her neighbors.

- *Are respondents' actions consistent with their expressed attitudes?* We probably should interpret differently the meaning of expressed support for gender equality from married men who help with household chores and those who do not. Questions about behavior may also provide a better way to assess orientations than questions about attitudes. Labaw (1980:100) points out that "the respondent's actual purchase of life insurance is a more accurate representation of what he believes about his life insurance needs than anything he might say in response to a direct question" about whether it is important to carry life insurance. In her study, Ross eschewed attitudinal questions about household roles altogether, instead focusing on behaviors in such questions as "What percentage [of the housework] do you do?" and "Who makes decisions in your household?"

- *How strongly are the attitudes held?* The attitudes of those with stronger beliefs are more likely to be translated into action than attitudes that are held less strongly. Just knowing the level of popular support for, say, abortion rights or gun control thus fails to capture the likelihood of people to march or petition their representatives on behalf of the cause; we also need to know what proportion of supporters feel strongly (Schuman & Presser, 1981:ch. 9). Thus, rather than just asking if respondents favored or opposed their spouse having a job, Ross (1990) used the following question and response choices to measure attitude strength in her telephone survey:

```
How do you feel about your (spouse/partner) having a job? (Are
you/Would you be) . . .

    STRONGLY IN FAVOR,              1
    SOMEWHAT IN FAVOR,             2
    SOMEWHAT OPPOSED, OR           3
    STRONGLY OPPOSED?              4
    MIXED                         5
    DOES NOT CARE/UP TO HIM/HER   6
```

Maintain Consistent Focus

A survey (with the exception of an omnibus survey) should be guided by a clear conception of the research problem under investigation and the population to be sampled. Does the study seek to describe some phenomenon in detail, to explain some behavior, or to explore some type of social relationship? Until the research objective is formulated clearly, survey design cannot begin. Throughout the process of questionnaire design, this objective should be the primary basis for making decisions about what to include and exclude and what to emphasize or treat in a cursory fashion. Moreover, the questionnaire should be viewed as an integrated whole, in which each section and every question serves a clear purpose related to the study's objective and is a complement to other sections or questions.

Surveys often include too many irrelevant questions and fail to include questions that, the researchers realize later, are crucial. One way to ensure that possibly relevant questions are asked is to use questions suggested by prior research, theory, experience, or experts (including participants) who are knowledgeable about the setting under investigation. Of course, not even the best researcher can anticipate the relevance of every question. Researchers tend to try to avoid "missing something" by erring on the side of extraneous questions (Labaw, 1980:40).

Order the Questions

The order in which questions are presented will influence how respondents react to the questionnaire as a whole and how they may answer some questions. As a first step, the individual questions should be sorted into broad thematic categories, which then become separate sections in the questionnaire. For example, Ross's (1990) questionnaire contained the following four sections: sociodemographics, social–psychological attitudes, health and well-being, and work and employment. Both the sections and the questions within the sections must then be organized in a logical order that would make sense in a conversation. Throughout the design process, the grouping of variables in sections and the ordering of questions within sections should be adjusted to maximize the questionnaire's overall coherence.

The first question deserves special attention, particularly if the questionnaire is to be self-administered. This question signals to the respondent what the survey is about, whether it will be interesting, and how easy it will be to complete. For these reasons, the first question should be connected to the primary purpose of the survey, it should be interesting, it should be easy, and it should apply to everyone in the sample (Dillman, 2000:92–94).

One or more filter or screening questions may also appear early in the survey in order to identify respondents for whom the questionnaire is not intended or perhaps to determine which sections of a multi-part questionnaire a respondent is to skip (Peterson, 2000:106–107).

Question order can lead to **context effects** when one or more questions influence how subsequent questions are interpreted (Schober, 1999:89–88). For example, when a sample of the general public was asked, "Do you think it should be possible for a pregnant woman to obtain a legal abortion if she is married and does not want any more children?" 58% said yes. However, when this question was preceded by a less permissive question that asked whether the respondent would allow abortion of a defective fetus, only 40% said yes. Asking the question about a defective fetus altered respondents' frame of reference, perhaps by making abortion simply to avoid having more children seem frivolous by comparison

(Turner & Martin, 1984:135). Context effects have also been identified in the measurement of general happiness, in what is termed a **part-whole question effect** (Peterson, 2000:113). Married people tend to report that they are more happy "in general" if the general happiness question is preceded by a question about their happiness with their marriage (Schuman & Presser, 1981:23–77).

Prior questions can influence how questions are comprehended, what beliefs shape responses, and whether comparative judgments are made (Tourangeau, 1999). The potential for context effects is greatest when two or more questions concern the same issue or closely related issues, as in the example of the two questions about abortion. The impact of question order also tends to be greater for general, summary-type questions, as with the example about general happiness.

Context effects can be identified empirically if the question order is reversed on a subset of the questionnaires (the so-called split-ballot design) and the results compared. However, knowing that a context effect occurs does not tell us which order is best. Reviewing the overall survey goals and any other surveys with which comparisons should be made can help to decide on question order. What is most important is to be aware of the potential for problems due to question order and to evaluate carefully the likelihood of context effects in any particular questionnaire. Those who report survey results should mention, at least in a footnote, the order in which key questions were asked when more than one question about a topic was used (Labaw, 1980).

Some questions may be presented in a "matrix" format. Matrix questions are a series of questions that concern a common theme and that have the same response choices. The questions are written so that a common initial phrase applies to each one (Question 49 in Exhibit 8.3). This format shortens the questionnaire by reducing the number of words that must be used for each question. It also emphasizes the common theme among the questions, and so invites answering each question in relation to other questions in the matrix. It is very important to provide an explicit instruction to "Check one response on each line" in a matrix question, because some respondents will think that they have completed the entire matrix after they have responded to just a few of the specific questions.

Make the Questionnaire Attractive

An attractive questionnaire is more likely to be completed and less likely to confuse either the respondent or, in an interview, the interviewer. An attractive questionnaire also should increase the likelihood that different respondents interpret the same questions in the same way.

Printing a multi-page questionnaire in booklet form usually results in the most attractive and simple-to-use questionnaire. Printing on both sides of folded over legal-size paper (8 ½" by 14") is a good approach, although pages can be printed on one side only and stapled in the corner if finances are very tight (Dillman, 2000:80–86). An attractive questionnaire does not look cramped; plenty of "white space"—more between questions than within question components—makes the questionnaire appear easy to complete. Response choices are distinguished clearly and consistently, perhaps by formatting them with light print (while questions are formatted with dark print) and keeping them in the middle of the pages. Response choices are listed vertically rather than horizontally across the page.

The proper path through the questionnaire for each respondent is identified with arrows or other graphics and judicious use of spacing and other aspects of layout. Respondents

Exhibit 8.3 A Page From Ross's Interview Schedule

45. In the past 12 months about how many times have you gone on a diet to lose weight?   v94

> Never 0
>
> Once 1
>
> Twice 2
>
> Three times or more 3
>
> Always on a diet 4

46. What is your height without shoes on?   v95

> _____ ft.   _____ in.

47. What is your weight without clothing?   v96

> _____ lbs.

48a. Do you currently smoke 7 or more cigarettes a week?   v97

> Yes . . . . 1 --> (SKIP TO Q.49)
>
> No 2

48b. Have you ever smoked 7 or more cigarettes a week?   v98

> Yes 1
>
> No 2

49. How much difficulty do you have . . .

		No difficulty,	Some difficulty, or	A great deal of difficulty?	
a.	Going up and down stairs? Would you say 1		2	3	v99
b.	Kneeling or stooping? 1		2	3	v100
c.	Lifting or carrying objects less than 10 pounds, like a bag of groceries? 1		2	3	v101
d.	Using your hands or fingers? .1		2	3	v102
e.	Seeing, even with glasses? 1		2	3	v103
f.	Hearing? 1		2	3	v104
g.	Walking? 1		2	3	v105

Source: Ross, 1990:11–12. Reprinted with kind permission of the author.

should not be confused about where to go next after they are told to skip a question. Instructions should help to route respondents through skip patterns, and such skip patterns should be used infrequently. Instructions should also explain how each type of question is to be answered (such as by circling a number or writing a response)—in a neutral way that isn't likely to influence responses. Some distinctive type of formatting should be used to identify instructions.

Exhibit 8.3 contains portions of the questionnaire Ross (1990) used in her phone survey of contemporary families. This page illustrates three of the features that I have just reviewed: numeric designation of response choices, clear instructions, and an attractive, open layout. Because this questionnaire was read over the phone, rather than being self-administered, there was no need for more explicit instructions about the matrix question (Question 49) or for a more distinctive format for the response choices (Questions 45 and 48).

ORGANIZING SURVEYS

There are five basic social science survey designs: mailed, group-administered, phone, in-person, and electronic. Exhibit 8.4 summarizes the typical features of the five different survey designs. Each design differs from the others in one or more important features.

Manner of administration. The five survey designs differ in the manner in which the questionnaire is administered. Mailed, group, and electronic surveys are completed by the respondents themselves. During phone and in-person interviews, however, the researcher or a staff person asks the questions and records the respondent's answers.

Questionnaire structure. Survey designs also differ in the extent to which the content and order of questions are structured in advance by the researcher. Most mailed, group, phone, and electronic surveys are highly structured, fixing in advance the content and order of questions and response choices. Some of these types of surveys, particularly mailed surveys, may include some open-ended questions (respondents write in their answers rather than checking off one of several response choices). In-person interviews are often highly structured, but they may include many questions without fixed response choices. Moreover, some interviews may proceed from an interview guide rather than a fixed set of questions. In these relatively unstructured interviews, the interviewer covers the same topics with respondents but varies questions according to the respondent's answers to previous questions. Extra questions are added as needed to clarify or explore answers to the most important questions.

Exhibit 8.4   Typical Features of the Five Survey Designs

Design	Manner of Administration	Setting	Questionnaire Structure	Cost
Mailed survey	Self	Individual	Mostly structured	Low
Group survey	Self	Group	Mostly structured	Very low
Phone survey	Professional	Individual	Structured	Moderate
In-person interview	Professional	Individual	Structured or unstructured	High
Electronic survey	Self	Individual	Mostly structured	Very low

Setting. Most surveys are conducted in settings where only one respondent completes the survey at a time; most mail and electronic questionnaires and phone interviews are intended for completion by only one respondent. The same is usually true of in-person interviews, although sometimes researchers interview several family members at once. On the other hand, a variant of the standard survey is a questionnaire distributed simultaneously to a group of respondents, who complete the survey while the researcher (or assistant) waits. Students in classrooms are typically the group involved, although this type of group distribution also occurs in surveys of employees and members of voluntary groups.

Cost. As mentioned earlier, in-person interviews are the most expensive type of survey. Phone interviews are much less expensive, but surveying by mail is cheaper yet. Electronic surveys are now the least expensive method, because there are no interviewer costs, no mailing costs, and, for many designs, almost no costs for data entry. Of course extra staff time and expertise are required to prepare an electronic questionnaire.

Because of their different features, the five designs vary in the types of error to which they are most prone and the situations in which they are most appropriate. The rest of this section focuses on the various designs' unique advantages and disadvantages, and identifies techniques for reducing error within each design.

Mailed, Self-Administered Surveys

A **mailed survey** is conducted by mailing a questionnaire to respondents, who then administer the survey themselves. The central concern in a mailed survey is maximizing the response rate. Even an attractive questionnaire full of clear questions will probably be returned by no more than 30% of a sample unless extra steps are taken to increase the rate of response. It's just too much bother for most potential recipients; in the language of social exchange theory, the costs of responding are perceived to be much higher than any anticipated rewards for doing so. Of course, a response rate of 30% is a disaster; even a response rate of 60% represents so much nonresponse error that it is hard to justify using the resulting data. Fortunately, the conscientious use of a systematic survey design method can be expected to lead to an acceptable 70% or higher rate of response to most mailed surveys (Dillman, 2000).

Sending follow-up mailings to nonrespondents is the single most important requirement for obtaining an adequate response rate to a mailed survey. The follow-up mailings explicitly encourage initial nonrespondents to return a completed questionnaire; implicitly, they convey the importance of the effort. Don Dillman (2000:155–158, 177–188) has demonstrated the effectiveness of a standard procedure for the mailing process:

1. A few days before the questionnaire is to be mailed, send a brief letter to respondents that notifies them of the importance of the survey they are to receive.

2. Send the questionnaire with a well-designed, personalized cover letter (see the next section), a self-addressed stamped return envelope, and, if possible, a token monetary reward. The materials should be inserted in the mail-out envelope so that they will all be pulled out together when the envelope is opened (Dillman, 2000:174–175). There should be no chance that the respondent will miss something.

3. Send a reminder postcard, thanking respondents and reminding nonrespondents, to all sample members 2 weeks after the initial mailing. The postcard should be friendly in tone and must include a phone number for those people who may not have received the questionnaire. It is important that this postcard be sent before most nonrespondents will have discarded their questionnaire, even though this means the postcard will arrive before all those who might have responded to the first mailing have done so.

4. Send a replacement questionnaire with a new cover letter only to nonrespondents 2 to 4 weeks after the initial questionnaire mailing. This cover letter should be a bit shorter and more insistent than the original cover letter. It should note that the recipient has not yet responded, and it should stress the survey's importance. Of course, a self-addressed stamped return envelope must be included.

5. The final step is taken 6 to 8 weeks after the initial survey mailing. This step uses a different mode of delivery (either priority or special delivery) or a different survey design— usually an attempt to administer the questionnaire over the phone. These special procedures emphasize the importance of the survey and encourage people to respond.

The **cover letter** for a mailed questionnaire is critical to the success of a mailed survey. This statement to respondents sets the tone for the entire questionnaire. A carefully prepared cover letter should increase the response rate and result in more honest and complete answers to the survey questions; a poorly prepared cover letter can have the reverse effects.

The cover letter or introductory statement must be:

- *Credible.* The letter should establish that the research is being conducted by a researcher or organization that the respondent is likely to accept as a credible, unbiased authority. Research conducted by government agencies, well-known universities, and recognized research organizations (like Gallup or RAND) is usually credible in this sense, with government surveys getting the most attention. On the other hand, a questionnaire from an animal rights group on the topic of animal rights will probably be viewed as biased.
- *Personalized.* The cover letter should include a personalized salutation (using the respondent's name, not just "Dear Student," for example), close with the researcher's signature (blue ballpoint pen is best, because it makes it clear that the researcher has personally signed), and refer to the respondent in the second person ("Your participation . . . ").
- *Interesting.* The statement should interest the respondent in the contents of the questionnaire. Never make the mistake of assuming that what is of interest to you will also interest your respondents. Try to put yourself in their shoes before composing the statement, and then test your appeal with a variety of potential respondents.
- *Responsible.* Reassure the respondent that the information you obtain will be treated confidentially, and include a phone number to call if the respondent has any questions or would like a summary of the final report. Point out that the respondent's participation is completely voluntary (Dillman, 1978:165–172).

Exhibit 8.5 is an example of a cover letter for a questionnaire.

Exhibit 8.5   Sample Questionnaire Cover Letter

University of Massachusetts at Boston
Department of Sociology
May 24, 2003

Jane Doe
AIDS Coordinator
Shattuck Shelter

Dear Jane:

AIDS is an increasing concern for homeless people and for homeless shelters. The enclosed survey is about the AIDS problem and related issues confronting shelters. It is sponsored by the Life Lines AIDS Prevention Project for the Homeless—a program of the Massachusetts Department of Public Health.

As an AIDS coordinator/shelter director, you have learned about homeless persons' problems and about implementing programs in response to those problems. The Life Lines Project needs to learn from your experience. Your answers to the questions in the enclosed survey will improve substantially the base of information for improving AIDS prevention programs.

Questions in the survey focus on AIDS prevention activities and on related aspects of shelter operations. It should take about 30 minutes to answer all the questions.

Every shelter AIDS coordinator (or shelter director) in Massachusetts is being asked to complete the survey. And every response is vital to the success of the survey: The survey report must represent the full range of experiences.

You may be assured of complete confidentiality. No one outside of the university will have access to the questionnaire you return. (The ID number on the survey will permit us to check with nonrespondents to see if they need a replacement survey or other information.) All information presented in the report to Life Lines will be in aggregate form, with the exception of a list of the number, gender, and family status of each shelter's guests.

Please mail the survey back to us by Monday, June 4, and feel free to call if you have any questions.

Thank you for your assistance.

Yours sincerely,

Russell K. Schutt   *Stephanie Howard*

Russell K. Schutt, Ph.D.   Stephanie Howard
Project Director   Project Assistant

Other steps are necessary to maximize the response rate (Fowler, 1988:99–106; Mangione, 1995:79–82; Miller, 1991:144):

- It is particularly important in self-administered surveys that the individual questions are clear and understandable to all the respondents, because no interviewers will be on hand to clarify the meaning of the questions or to probe for additional details.

- Use no more than a few open-ended questions, because respondents are likely to be put off by the idea of having to write out answers.
- Have a credible research sponsor. According to one investigation, a sponsor known to respondents may increase their rate of response by as much as 17%. Government sponsors tend to elicit high rates of response. The next most credible sponsors are state headquarters of an organization and then other people in a similar field. Publishing firms, students (sorry!), and private associations elicit the lowest response rates.
- Write an identifying number on the questionnaire so you can determine who non-respondents are. This is essential for follow-up efforts. Of course, the identification must be explained in the cover letter.
- Enclosing a token incentive with the survey can help. Even a coupon or ticket worth $1 can increase the response rate, but a $2 or $5 bill seems to be the best incentive. Such an incentive is both a reward for the respondent and an indication of your trust that the respondent will carry out her end of the "bargain." Offering a large monetary reward or some type of lottery ticket only for those who return their questionnaire is actually less effective, apparently because it does not indicate trust in the respondent (Dillman, 2000:167–170).
- Include a stamped, self-addressed return envelope with each copy of the questionnaire. This reduces the cost for responding. The stamp helps to personalize the exchange and is another indication of trust in the respondent (who could use the stamp for something else). Using a stamp rather than metered postage on the mail-out envelope does not seem to influence the response rate, but it is very important to use first class rather than bulk rate postage (Dillman, 2000:171–174).
- Consider presurvey publicity efforts. A vigorous advertising campaign increased considerably the response to the 2000 Census mailed questionnaire; the results were particularly successful among minority groups who had been targeted due to low response rates in the 1990 Census (Holmes, 2000).

If Dillman's procedures are followed, and the guidelines for cover letters and questionnaire design also are adhered to, the response rate is almost certain to approach 70%. One review of studies using Dillman's method to survey the general population indicates that the average response to a first mailing will be about 24%; the response rate will rise to 42% after the postcard follow-up, to 50% after the first replacement questionnaire, and to 72% after a second replacement questionnaire is sent by certified mail (Dillman, Christenson, Carpenter, & Brooks, 1974).

The response rate may be higher with particular populations surveyed on topics of interest to them, and it may be lower with surveys of populations that do not have much interest in the topic. When a survey has many nonrespondents, getting some ideas about their characteristics, by comparing late respondents to early respondents, can help to determine the likelihood of bias due to the low rate of response. If those who returned their questionnaires at an early stage are more educated or more interested in the topic of the questionnaire, the sample may be biased; if the respondents are not more educated or more interested than nonrespondents, the sample will be more credible.

If resources did not permit phone calls to all nonrespondents, a random sample of nonrespondents can be selected and contacted by phone or interviewed in person. It should be possible to secure responses from a substantial majority of these nonrespondents in this way. With appropriate weighting, these new respondents can then be added to the sample of respondents to the initial mailed questionnaire, resulting in a more representative total sample (for more details, see Levy & Lemeshow, 1999:398–402).

Related to the threat of nonresponse in mailed surveys is the hazard of incomplete response. Some respondents may skip some questions or just stop answering questions at some point in the questionnaire. Fortunately, this problem does not occur often with well-designed questionnaires. Potential respondents who have decided to participate in the survey usually complete it. But there are many exceptions to this observation, because questions that are poorly written, too complex, or about sensitive personal issues simply turn off some respondents. The revision or elimination of such questions during the design phase should minimize the problem. When it does not, it may make sense to impute values for the missing data. One imputation procedure would be to substitute the mean (arithmetic average) value of a variable for those cases that have a missing value on the variable (Levy & Lemeshow, 1999:404–416).

Group-Administered Surveys

A **group-administered survey** is completed by individual respondents assembled in a group. The response rate is not usually a major concern in surveys that are distributed and collected in a group setting because most group members will participate. The real difficulty with this method is that it is seldom feasible, because it requires what might be called a captive audience. With the exception of students, employees, members of the armed forces, and some institutionalized populations, most populations cannot be sampled in such a setting.

Whoever is responsible for administering the survey to the group must be careful to minimize comments that might bias answers or that could vary between different groups in the same survey (Dillman, 2000:253–256). A standard introductory statement should be read to the group that expresses appreciation for their participation, describes the steps of the survey, and emphasizes (in classroom surveys) that the survey is not the same as a test. A cover letter like that used in mailed surveys also should be distributed with the questionnaires. In order to emphasize confidentiality, respondents should be given an envelope in which to seal their questionnaire after it is completed.

Another issue of special concern with group-administered surveys is the possibility that respondents will feel coerced to participate and as a result will be less likely to answer questions honestly. Also, because administering a survey in this way requires approval of the powers that be—and this sponsorship is made quite obvious by the fact that the survey is conducted on the organization's premises—respondents may infer that the researcher is not at all independent of the sponsor. No complete solution to this problem exists, but it helps to make an introductory statement emphasizing the researcher's independence and giving participants a chance to ask questions about the survey. The sponsor should also understand the need to keep a low profile and to allow the researcher both control over the data and autonomy in report writing.

Telephone Surveys

In a **phone survey,** interviewers question respondents over the phone and then record respondents' answers. Phone interviewing has become a very popular method of conducting surveys in the United States because almost all families have phones. But two matters may undermine the validity of a phone survey: not reaching the proper sampling units and not getting enough complete responses to make the results generalizable.

Reaching Sample Units

There are three different ways of obtaining a sampling frame of telephone exchanges or numbers: Phone directories provide a useful frame for local studies; a nationwide list of area code-exchange numbers can be obtained from a commercial firm (random digit dialing is used to fill in the last four digits); and commercial firms can provide files based on local directories from around the nation. There are coverage errors with each of these frames: 10%–15% of directory listings will turn out not to still be valid residential numbers; more than 35% of U.S. households with phones have numbers that are unlisted in directories—and the percentage is as high as 60% in some communities; and less than 25% of the area codes and exchanges in the one national comprehensive list (available from Bell Core Research, Inc.) refer to residential units (Levy & Lemeshow, 1999:455–460). Survey planning must consider the advantages and disadvantages of these methods for a particular study and develop means for compensating for the weaknesses of the specific method chosen.

Most telephone surveys use random digit dialing at some point in the sampling process (Lavrakas, 1987). A machine calls random phone numbers within the designated exchanges, whether or not the numbers are published. When the machine reaches an inappropriate household (such as a business in a survey that is directed to the general population), the phone number is simply replaced with another. The University of Illinois Survey Research Laboratory used the following procedures to draw a sample for Ross's (1990) study of social structure and well-being:

> The universe for this study will be all persons 18–65 years of age, in the coterminous United States. A national probability sample designed to yield 2,000 interviews will be generated by the random-digit-dialing technique developed by J. Waksberg. The Waksberg method involves a two-stage sample design in which primary sampling units (PSUs) are selected with probabilities proportionate to size at the first stage and a specified cluster size at the second stage. To achieve 2,000 interviews, approximately 8,400 telephone numbers will be sampled. In order to avoid any potential bias in the sex or age distributions of the sample that might result from simply interviewing the persons who answer the telephone, a further sampling stage is required. For each selected household, one person will be chosen from all adults 18–65 years of age in that household in such a way that each adult has an equal probability of being selected for an interview. (J. E. Blair, personal communication to C. E. Ross, April 10, 1989)

However households are contacted, the interviewers must ask a series of questions at the start of the survey to ensure that they are speaking to the appropriate member of the household. Exhibit 8.6 displays a phone interview schedule, the instrument containing the questions asked by the interviewer. This example shows how appropriate and inappropriate households can be distinguished in a phone survey, so that the interviewer is guided to the correct respondent.

Exhibit 8.6   Phone Interview Procedures for Respondent Designation

PATH COMMUNITY SURVEY   Metro Social Services
CALL RECORD (CR)   Nashville-Davidson County, TN
                                   October 1987

Respondent Household (RH)

_____

Case No. [SEE TOP OF   Call Outcome Codes
_____   INTERVIEW FORM]
                              CI = Completed interview
Date Precontact Letter   PC = Partially completed
Mailed   RI = Refused interview
                              II   = Impossible: language
_____   etc.
                              BN = Business number
                              OC = Number outside county
                              NA = No answer
[TRY REACHING RH ON FIVE   BS = Busy signal
DIFFERENT DAYS BEFORE   LD = Line disconnected
CLOSING OUT CR]   WN= Wrong number
                              UL = Unlisted number
                              ML = Message left on machine
                              NC = Number changed
                              CB = Call back [WRITE DATE]
                                   Date:
                                   Time:
                                   R's First Name:

Call Record: Day/Date   Call No.   Time   Call Outcome

_____

_____

_____   Case No.

Introduction

A. Hello, is this the (_R's last name_) residence?

   * [IF NOT, SAY: The number I was calling is (_R's phone no._) and
   it was for the (_R's first and last name_) residence. IF WRONG
   NUMBER, CODE OUTCOME IN CR AND TERMINATE WITH: I'm sorry to
   have bothered you. Goodbye.]

B. **My name is _____ . I'm calling for Metro Social Services and the Tennessee Department of Human Services. We're conducting a study to find out how local residents feel about the issue of homelessness in our community. Your household has been randomly selected to help us with this important task.**

C. **I don't know if you've seen it yet, but a letter about the study was mailed to your home several days ago. Just to verify our records, your home is located in Davidson County, isn't it?**

*[IF NOT, ASK: What county are you in? WRITE COUNTY ON RH LABEL, CODE OUTCOME IN CR, AND TERMINATE WITH: I'm sorry but only Davidson County residents are eligible for the study. Thanks anyway. Goodbye.]

D. **We need to interview men in some households and women in others so that our results will represent all adults in the county. According to our selection method, I need to interview the   . . .**

DESIGNATED R: youngest / oldest / man / woman

presently living in your household who is at least 18 years of age. May I please speak with him/her?

*[IF PERSON ON PHONE, GO TO E.]

*[IF NO SUCH PERSON, ASK: As a substitute, then, may I please speak with the . . . SUBSTITUTE R: youngest / oldest / man / woman in your household who is at least 18? IF PERSON ON PHONE, GO TO E. IF NOT AVAILABLE, MAKE ARRANGEMENTS TO CALL BACK AND WRITE DATE, TIME, AND R'S FIRST NAME IN CR. CLOSE WITH: Please tell (R's first name) that I will be calling back on (date and time). Thank you].

*[IF DIFFERENT PERSON COMES TO PHONE, REPEAT B AND ADD: You are the adult who's been randomly chosen in your household. GO TO E.]

*[IF NOT AVAILABLE, MAKE ARRANGEMENTS . . . (see above)]

E. **The questions I'd like to ask you are easy to answer and should take only about 15 minutes. Everything you tell me will be kept strictly confidential. If you have any questions about the study, I'll be happy to answer them now or later. Okay?**

Time interview started:

Person actually interviewed:

   1 Designated R
   2 Substitute R

(Continued)

Exhibit 8.6 Continued

I'll be using the word "homeless" to mean not having a permanent address or place to live. Please think about all types of people who fit that description as we go through the interview.

Here's the first question.

1. Right now, how important is homelessness as a public issue in Nashville? Would you say it's . . . [READ 0–2]

0	Not too important	8	DK
1	Somewhat important, or	9	NR
2	Very important?		

Source: Metro Social Services, Nashville-Davidson County, TN, 1987. *PATH Community Survey.*

Maximizing Response to Phone Surveys

Four issues require special attention in phone surveys. First, because people often are not home, multiple call-backs will be needed for many sample members. The failure to call people back was one of the reasons for the discrepancy between poll predictions and actual votes in the 1988 presidential race between George Bush and Michael Dukakis. Andrew Kohut (1988) found that if pollsters in one Gallup poll had stopped attempting to contact unavailable respondents after one call, a 6-percentage-point margin for Bush would have been replaced by a 2-point margin for Dukakis. Those with more money and education are more likely to be away from home, and such persons are also more likely to vote Republican.

The number of call-backs needed to reach respondents by telephone has increased greatly in the last 20 years, with increasing numbers of single-person households, dual-earner families, and out-of-home activities. Survey research organizations have increased the usual number of phone contact attempts from just 4–8 to 20. The growth of telemarketing has created another problem for telephone survey researchers: Individuals have become more accustomed to "just say no" to calls from unknown individuals and organizations or to simply use their answering machines to screen out unwanted calls (Dillman, 2000:8, 28).

Phone surveys also must cope with difficulties due to the impersonal nature of phone contact. Visual aids cannot be used, so the interviewer must be able to convey verbally all information about response choices and skip patterns. Instructions to the interviewer must clarify how to ask each question, and response choices must be short. The Survey Research Laboratory developed the instructions shown in Exhibit 8.7 to clarify procedures for asking and coding a series of questions that Ross (1990) used to measure symptoms of stress within households.

In addition, interviewers must be prepared for distractions as the respondent is interrupted by other household members. Sprinkling interesting questions throughout the questionnaire

Exhibit 8.7   Sample Interviewer Instructions

Question:
41. On how many of the past 7 days have you…

Number of days

    a.   Worried a lot about little things? ....   _____

    b.   Felt tense or anxious? ....   _____

Instructions for interviewers:
Q41 For the series of "On how many of the past 7 days," make sure the respondent gives the numerical answer. If he/she responds with a vague answer like "not too often" or "just a few times," ask again "On how many of the past 7 days would you say?" Do NOT lead the respondent with a number (e.g., "would that be 2 or 3?"). If R says "all of them," verify that the answer is "7."

Question:
45. In the past 12 months about how many times have you gone on a diet to lose weight?

Never 0

Once 1

Twice 2

Three times or more 3

Always on a diet 4

Instructions for interviewers:
Q45 Notice that this question ends with a question mark. That means that you are not to read the answer categories. Rather, wait for R to respond and circle the appropriate number.

Source: Ross, 1990.

may help to maintain respondent interest. In general, rapport between the interviewer and the respondent is likely to be lower with phone surveys than with in-person interviews, and so respondents may tire and refuse to answer all the questions (Miller, 1991:166).

Careful interviewer training is essential for phone surveys. This is how one polling organization describes its training:

> In preparation for data collection, survey interviewers are required to attend a two-part training session. The first part covers general interviewing procedures and techniques as related to the proposed survey. The second entails in-depth training and practice for the survey. This training includes instructions on relevant subject matter, a question-by-question review of the survey instrument and various forms of role-playing and practice interviewing with supervisors and other interviewers. (J. E. Blair, personal communication to C. E. Ross, April 10, 1989)

Procedures can be standardized more effectively, quality control maintained, and processing speed maximized when phone interviewers are assisted by computers using **computer-assisted telephone interviews (CATI):**

> The interviewing will be conducted using "CATI" (Computer-Assisted Telephone Interviewing). . . . The questionnaire is "programmed" into the computer, along with relevant skip patterns throughout the instrument. Only legal entries are allowed. The system incorporates the tasks of interviewing, data entry, and some data cleaning. (J. E. Blair, personal communication to C. E. Ross, April 10, 1989)

Phone surveying is the method of choice for relatively short surveys of the general population. Response rates in phone surveys traditionally have tended to be very high—often above 80%—because few individuals would hang up on a polite caller or refuse to stop answering questions (at least within the first 30 minutes or so). Ross achieved a response rate of 82% over a 3-month period at the end of 1990, resulting in a final sample of 2,031 Americans. However, as I have noted, the refusal rate in phone interviews is rising with the prevalence of telemarketing and answering machines.

In-Person Interviews

What is unique to the **in-person interview,** compared to the other survey designs, is the face-to-face social interaction between interviewer and respondent. If money is no object, in-person interviewing is often the best survey design.

In-person interviewing has several advantages: Response rates are higher than with any other survey design; questionnaires can be much longer than with mailed or phone surveys; the questionnaire can be complex, with both open-ended and closed-ended questions and frequent branching patterns; the order in which questions are read and answered can be controlled by the interviewer; the physical and social circumstances of the interview can be monitored; and respondents' interpretations of questions can be probed and clarified.

But researchers must be alert to some special hazards due to the presence of an interviewer. Respondents should experience the interview process as a personalized interaction with an interviewer who is very interested in the respondent's experiences and opinions. At the same time, however, every respondent should have the same interview experience—asked the same questions in the same way by the same type of person, who reacts similarly to the answers. Therein lies the researcher's challenge—to plan an interview process that will be personal and engaging and yet consistent and nonreactive (and to hire interviewers who can carry out this plan). Careful training and supervision are essential, because small differences in intonation or emphasis on particular words can alter respondents' interpretations of question meaning (Peterson, 2000:24; Groves, 1989:404–406). Without a personalized approach, the rate of response will be lower and answers will be less thoughtful—and potentially less valid. Without a consistent approach, information obtained from different respondents will not be comparable—less reliable and less valid.

Balancing Rapport and Control

Adherence to some basic guidelines for interacting with respondents can help interviewers to maintain an appropriate balance between personalization and standardization:

- Project a professional image in the interview, that of someone who is sympathetic to the respondent but nonetheless has a job to do.

- Establish rapport at the outset by explaining what the interview is about and how it will work and by reading the consent form. Ask the respondent if he or she has any questions or concerns, and respond to these honestly and fully. Emphasize that everything the respondent says is confidential.
- During the interview, ask questions from a distance that is close but not intimate. Stay focused on the respondent and make sure that your posture conveys interest. Maintain eye contact, respond with appropriate facial expressions, and speak in a conversational tone of voice.
- Be sure to maintain a consistent approach; deliver each question as written and in the same tone of voice. Listen empathetically, but avoid self-expression or loaded reactions.
- Repeat questions if the respondent is confused. Use nondirective probes—such as "Can you tell me more about that?"—for open-ended questions.

As with phone interviewing, computers can be used to increase control of the in-person interview. In a **computer-assisted personal interviewing (CAPI)** project, interviewers carry a laptop computer that is programmed to display the interview questions and to process the responses that the interviewer types in, as well as to check that these responses fall within allowed ranges. Interviewers seem to like CAPI, and the data obtained are of at least as good quality as with a noncomputerized interview (Shepherd, Hill, Bristor, & Montalvan, 1996). A CAPI approach also makes it easier for the researcher to develop skip patterns and experiment with different types of questions for different respondents without increasing the risk of interviewer mistakes (Couper et al., 1998).

The presence of an interviewer may make it more difficult for respondents to give honest answers to questions about sensitive personal matters. For this reason, interviewers may hand respondents a separate self-administered questionnaire containing the more sensitive questions. After answering these questions, the respondent seals the separate questionnaire in an envelope so that the interviewer does not know the answers. When this approach was used for the GSS questions about sexual activity, about 21% of men and 13% of women who were married or had been married admitted to having cheated on a spouse ("Survey on Adultery," 1993:A20). You may have heard reports of much higher rates of marital infidelity, but these were from studies using unrepresentative samples.

The degree of rapport becomes a special challenge when survey questions concern issues related to such demographic characteristics as race or gender (Groves, 1989). If the interviewer and respondent are similar on the characteristics at issue, the responses to these questions may differ from those that would be given if the interviewer and respondent differ on these characteristics. For example, a white respondent may not disclose feelings of racial prejudice to a black interviewer that he would admit to a white interviewer.

Although in-person interview procedures are typically designed with the expectation that the interview will involve only the interviewer and the respondent, one or more other household members are often within earshot. In a mental health survey in Los Angeles, for example, almost half the interviews were conducted in the presence of another person (Pollner & Adams, 1994). It is reasonable to worry that this third-party presence will influence responses about sensitive subjects—even more so because the likelihood of a third party being present may correspond with other subject characteristics. For example, in the Los

Angeles survey, another person was present in 36% of the interviews with Anglos, in 47% of the interviews with African Americans, and in 59% of the interviews with Hispanics. However, there is no consistent evidence that respondents change their answers because of the presence of another person. Analysis of this problem with the Los Angeles study found very little difference in reports of mental illness symptoms between respondents who were alone and those who were in the presence of others.

Maximizing Response to Interviews

Even if the right balance has been struck between maintaining control over interviews and achieving good rapport with respondents, in-person interviews can still have a problem. Because of the difficulty of finding all the members of a sample, response rates may suffer. Exhibit 8.8 displays the breakdown of nonrespondents to the 1990 General Social Survey. Of the total original sample of 2,165, only 86% (1,857) were determined to be valid selections of dwelling units with potentially eligible respondents. Among these potentially eligible respondents, the response rate was 74%. The GSS is a well-designed survey using carefully trained and supervised interviewers, so this response rate indicates the difficulty of securing respondents from a sample of the general population even when everything is done "by the book."

Exhibit 8.8   Reasons for Nonresponse in Personal Interviews (1990 General Social Survey)

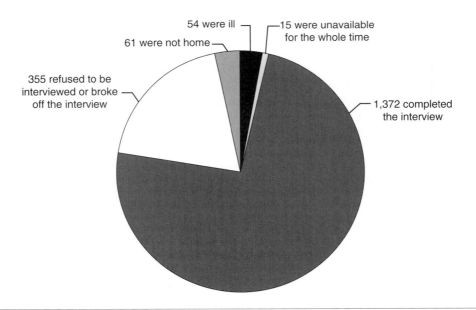

Of 1,857 units in the sample . . .

54 were ill
61 were not home
15 were unavailable for the whole time
355 refused to be interviewed or broke off the interview
1,372 completed the interview

Source: Data from Davis & Smith, 1992:54.

Several factors affect the response rate in interview studies. Contact rates tend to be lower in central cities, in part because of difficulties in finding people at home and gaining access to high-rise apartments and in part because of interviewer reluctance to visit some areas at night, when people are more likely to be home (Fowler, 1988:45–60). Single-person households also are more difficult to reach, whereas households with young children or elderly adults tend to be easier to contact (Groves & Couper, 1998:119–154).

Refusal rates vary with some respondent characteristics. People with less education participate somewhat less in surveys of political issues (perhaps because they are less aware of current political issues). Less education is also associated with higher rates of "don't know" responses (Groves, 1989). High-income persons tend to participate less in surveys about income and economic behavior (perhaps because they are suspicious about why others want to know about their situation). Unusual strains and disillusionment in a society can also undermine the general credibility of research efforts and the ability of interviewers to achieve an acceptable response rate. These problems can be lessened with an advance letter introducing the survey project and by multiple contact attempts throughout the day and evening, but they cannot entirely be avoided (Fowler, 1988:52–53; Groves & Couper, 1998).

Electronic Surveys

The widespread use of personal computers and the growth of the Internet have created new possibilities for survey research. As you learned in Chapter 1, in September 2001 half of American households were connected to the Internet (U.S. Department of Commerce, 2002). This percentage is growing rapidly, so it is not unreasonable to think that use of the Internet will soon become comparable to the use of telephones. You also learned in Chapter 1 that some credible surveys have already been conducted with the Internet. As the proportion of the population that is connected increases, the Internet will become the preferred medium for survey research on many topics.

Electronic surveys can be prepared in two ways (Dillman, 2000:352–354). **E-mail surveys** can be sent as messages to respondent e-mail addresses. Respondents then mark their answers in the message and send them back to the researcher. This approach is easy for researchers to develop and for respondents to use. However, this approach is cumbersome for surveys that are more than four or five pages in length. By contrast, **Web surveys** are designed on a server controlled by the researcher. Respondents are asked by e-mail (or regular mail) to visit the Web site and respond to the Web questionnaire by checking answers. A PIN (personal identification number) can be required for access to the survey. A Web survey requires programming expertise by the researcher or her staff and in many cases more skill on the part of the respondent.

Web surveys are becoming the more popular form of Internet survey because they are so flexible (see Exhibit 8.9). Web surveys can be quite long, with questions that are inapplicable to a given respondent hidden from them so that the survey may actually seem much shorter than it is. The questionnaire's design can feature many graphic and typographic elements. Respondents can view definitions of words or instructions for answering questions by clicking on linked terms. Lengthy sets of response choices can be presented with pull-down menus. Pictures and audio segments can be added when they are useful. Because answers are recorded directly in the researcher's database, data entry errors are almost eliminated and results can be reported quickly.

Exhibit 8.9   SURVEY.NET—Year 2000 Presidential Election Survey

Your source for information, opinions & demographics from the Net Community!

Year 2000 Presidential Election Survey

Take the year 2000 presidential election survey!

1. What is your age?
   No Answer ↕

2. Your Sex:
   No Answer ↕

3. Your highest level of education completed:
   No Answer ↕

4. Your political affiliation:
   No Answer ↕

5. Who did you vote for in 1996?
   No Answer ↕

6. Even though not all of these candidates are necessarily running, if the presidential election were held today, who would you vote for?
   No Answer ↕

7. Of the following TWO potential presidential candidates, who would you vote for?
   No Answer ↕

8. Of the following presidential candidates, who would you vote for?
   No Answer ↕

9. Do you consider yourself...
   No Answer ↕

10. What political concepts do you agree with? *(check all that apply)*

    ☐ - We need less government regulation in general
    ☐ - We need more responsible government regulation
    ☐ - States should have more responsibility than the Federal Gov.

    ☐ - The government should NOT mandate moral standards
    ☐ - The government SHOULD mandate moral standards

    ☐ - Tax breaks are more important than reducing the deficit
    ☐ - Reducing the deficit is more important than tax breaks

    ☐ - Unions are destroying American productivity
    ☐ - Unions protect the worker

    ☐ - The economy is more important than the environment
    ☐ - The environment is more important than the economy

11. In your opinion, what is the worst problem with our society?
    [No Answer ◆]

12. Of those items listed, what should be our next President's highest priority?
    [No Answer ◆]

13. Without turning this into a partisan/rhetorical argument, who do you want to see for president in 2000 and why? (*Limit this to one or two sentences*)
    [_____]

Thanks very much for participating in the survey!

To submit your survey choices, select:
[SUBMIT SURVEY]

or [Reset survey settings]

You can view the latest survey results after you submit your answers.

We hope you will also participate in other surveys online as well. Please note that you should only complete each survey once.

Source: www.survey.net. Copyright ©1994–2001, ICorp (InterCommerce Corporation). All rights reserved worldwide.

The most important drawback to either Internet survey approach is the large fraction of households that are not yet connected to the Internet. For special populations with high rates of Internet use, though, the technology makes possible fast and effective surveys (Dillman, 2000:354–355). To lessen the opposite problem—that individuals who are not in the survey sample find it too easy to participate—researchers can require that respondents enter a PIN in order to gain access to the Web survey (Dillman, 2000:378).

Another problem researchers must try their best to avoid is creating survey formats that are so complicated that some computers cannot read them or would display them in a way that differs from what the researcher intended (Dillman, 2000:353–401).

Computerized **interactive voice response (IVR)** systems already allow the ease of Internet surveys to be achieved with a telephone-based system. In IVR surveys, respondents receive automated calls and answer questions by pressing numbers on their touch-tone phones or speaking numbers that are interpreted by computerized voice recognition software. These surveys can also record verbal responses to open-ended questions for later transcription. Although they present some difficulties when many answer choices must be used or skip patterns must be followed, IVR surveys have been used successfully with short questionnaires and when respondents are highly motivated to participate (Dillman, 2000:402–411). When these conditions are not met, potential respondents may be put off by the impersonality of this computer-driven approach.

Mixed-Mode Surveys

Survey researchers increasingly are combining different survey designs. **Mixed-mode surveys** allow the strengths of one survey design to compensate for the weaknesses of another and can maximize the likelihood of securing data from different types of respondents. For example, a survey may be sent electronically to sample members who have e-mail addresses and mailed to those who don't. Alternatively, nonrespondents in a mailed survey may be interviewed in person or over the phone. As noted previously, an interviewer may use a self-administered questionnaire to present sensitive questions to a respondent.

Mixing survey designs like this makes it possible that respondents will give different answers to different questions because of the mode in which they are asked, rather than because they actually have different opinions. For example, when equivalent samples were asked by phone or mail, "Is the gasoline shortage real or artificial?," many more phone respondents answered that it was "very real" (Peterson, 2000:24).

When responses differ by survey mode, there is often no way to know which responses are more accurate (Peterson, 2000:24). However, use of what Dillman (2000:232–240) calls "unimode design" substantially reduces the likelihood of mode effects. A unimode design uses questions and response choices that are least likely to yield different answers according to the survey mode that is used. Unimode design principles include use of the same question structures, response choices, and skip instructions across modes, as well as using a small number of response choices for each question.

A Comparison of Survey Designs

Which survey design should be used when? Group-administered surveys are similar in most respects to mailed surveys, except that they require the unusual circumstance of having

Exhibit 8.10   Advantages and Disadvantages of the Four Survey Designs

Characteristics of Design	Mail Survey	Phone Survey	In-person Survey	Electronic Survey
Representative sample				
Opportunity for inclusion is known				
For completely listed populations	High	High	High	Medium
For incompletely listed populations	Medium	Medium	High	Low
Selection within sampling units is controlled	Medium	High	High	Low
(e.g., specific family members must respond)				
Respondents are likely to be located				
If samples are heterogeneous	Medium	High	High	Low
If samples are homogeneous and	High	High	High	High
specialized				
Questionnaire construction and question design				
Allowable length of questionnaire	Medium	Medium	High	Medium
Ability to include				
Complex questions	Medium	Low	High	High
Open questions	Low	High	High	Medium
Screening questions	Low	High	High	High
Tedious, boring questions	Low	High	High	Low
Ability to control question sequence	Low	High	High	High
Ability to ensure questionnaire	Medium	High	High	Low
completion				
Distortion of answers				
Odds of avoiding social desirability bias	High	Medium	Low	High
Odds of avoiding interviewer distortion	High	Medium	Low	High
Odds of avoiding contamination by others	Medium	High	Medium	Medium
Administrative goals				
Odds of meeting personnel requirements	High	High	Low	Medium
Odds of implementing quickly	Low	High	Low	High
Odds of keeping costs low	High	Medium	Low	High

Source: Adapted from Dillman, 1978:74–75. *Mail and Telephone Surveys: The Total Design Method.* Copyright © 1978 Don A. Dillman. Reprinted by permission of John Wiley & Sons, Inc.

access to the sample in a group setting. We therefore don't need to consider this survey design by itself; what applies to mailed surveys applies to group-administered survey designs, with the exception of sampling issues. The features of mixed-mode surveys depend on the survey types that are being combined. Thus, we can focus our comparison on the four survey designs that involve the use of a questionnaire with individuals sampled from a larger population: mailed surveys, phone surveys, in-person surveys, and electronic surveys. Exhibit 8.10 summarizes their strong and weak points.

The most important consideration in comparing the advantages and disadvantages of the four methods is the likely response rate they will generate. Because of the great weakness of mailed surveys in this respect, they must be considered the least preferred survey design from a sampling standpoint. However, researchers may still prefer a mailed survey when they have to reach a widely dispersed population and don't have enough financial resources to hire and train an interview staff or to contract with a survey organization that already has an interview staff available in many locations.

Contracting with an established survey research organization for a phone survey is often the best alternative to a mailed survey. The persistent follow-up attempts that are necessary to secure an adequate response rate are much easier over the phone than in person. But the process is not simple:

> Working phone numbers in the sample are called up to 10 times at different times of the day and on different days of the week before the number is recorded as a noncontact. To facilitate contact with households and individuals, telephoning is done in the evening during the week, and during the day over weekends. A final disposition is obtained and recorded for each sample telephone number, i.e., whether an interview, refusal, noncontact, nonworking number, or other disposition. "Control" reports are issued weekly showing progress of the work through various stages of data collection. (J. E. Blair, personal communication to C. E. Ross, April 10, 1989)

In-person surveys are clearly preferable in terms of the possible length and complexity of the questionnaire itself, as well as the researcher's ability to monitor conditions while the questionnaire is being completed. Mailed surveys often are preferable for asking sensitive questions, although this problem can be lessened in an interview by giving respondents a separate sheet to fill out on their own. Although interviewers may themselves distort results, either by changing the wording of questions or by failing to record answers properly, this problem can be lessened by careful training, monitoring, and tape-recording the answers.

A phone survey limits the length and complexity of the questionnaire but offers the possibility of very carefully monitoring interviewers (Dillman, 1978; Fowler, 1988:61–73):

> Supervisors in [one organization's] Telephone Centers work closely with the interviewers, monitor their work, and maintain records of their performance in relation to the time schedule, the quality of their work, and help detect and correct any mistakes in completed interviews prior to data reduction and processing. (J. E. Blair, personal communication to C. E. Ross, April 10, 1989)

The advantages and disadvantages of electronic surveys must be weighed in light of the capabilities at the time that the survey is to be conducted. At this time, too many people lack Internet connections for general use of Internet surveying, and too many people who have computers lack adequate computer capacity for displaying complex Web pages.

These various points about the different survey designs lead to two general conclusions. First, in-person interviews are the strongest design and generally preferable when sufficient resources and a trained interview staff are available; telephone surveys have many of the advantages of in-person interviews at much less cost, but response rates are an increasing problem. Second, a decision about the best survey design for any particular study must take into account the unique features and goals of the study.

COMBINING METHODS

Conducting qualitative interviews can often enhance a research design that uses primarily quantitative measurement techniques. Qualitative data can provide information about the quality of standardized case records and quantitative survey measures, as well as offer some insight into the meaning of particular fixed responses.

Adding Qualitative Data

It makes sense to use official records to study the treatment of juveniles accused of illegal acts because these records document the critical decisions to arrest, to convict, or to release (Dannefer & Schutt, 1982). But research based on official records can be only as good as the records themselves. In contrast to the controlled interview process in a research study, there is little guarantee that officials' acts and decisions were recorded in a careful and unbiased manner.

Case Study: Juvenile Court Records

Research on official records can be strengthened by interviewing officials who create the records or by observing them while they record information. A participant observation study of how probation officers screened cases in two New York juvenile court intake units shows how important such information can be (Needleman, 1981). As indicated in Exhibit 8.11, Carolyn Needleman (1981) found that the concepts most researchers believe they are measuring with official records differ markedly from the meaning attached to these records by probation officers. Researchers assume that sending a juvenile case to court indicates a more severe disposition than retaining a case in the intake unit, but probation officers often diverted cases from court because they thought the court would be too lenient. Researchers assume that probation officers evaluate juveniles as individuals, but in these settings probation officers often based their decisions on juveniles' current social situation (for example, whether they were living in a stable home), without learning anything about the individual juvenile. Perhaps most troubling for research using case records, Needleman (1981) found that probation

Exhibit 8.11   Researchers' and Juvenile Court Workers' Discrepant Assumptions

Researcher Assumptions	Intake Worker Assumptions
• Being sent to court is a harsher sanction than diversion from court	• Being sent to court often results in more lenient and less effective treatment
• Screening involves judgments about individual juveniles	• Screening centers on the juvenile's social situation
• Official records accurately capture case facts	• Records are manipulated to achieve the desired outcome

Source: Needleman, 1981:248–256.

officers decided how to handle cases first and then created an official record that appeared to justify their decisions.

This one example certainly does not call into question all legal records or all other types of official records. It does, however, highlight the value of using multiple methods, particularly when the primary method of data collection is analysis of records generated by **street-level bureaucrats**—officials who serve clients and have a high degree of discretion (Lipsky, 1980). When officials both make decisions and record the bases for their decisions without much supervision, records may diverge considerably from the decisions they are supposed to reflect. More generally, Needleman's (1981) research indicates how important it is to learn how people make sense of the social world when we want to describe their circumstances and explain their behavior (see Chapter 9).

Case Study: Mental Health System

The same observation can be made about the value of supplementing fixed-choice survey questions with more probing, open-ended questions. For example, Renee Anspach (1991) wondered about the use of standard surveys to study the effectiveness of mental health systems. Instead of drawing a large sample and asking a set of closed-ended questions, Anspach used snowball sampling techniques to select some administrators, case managers, clients, and family members in four community mental health systems, and then asked these respondents a series of open-ended questions. When asked whether their programs were effective, the interviewees were likely to respond in the affirmative. Their comments in response to other questions, however, pointed to many program failings. Anspach concluded that the respondents simply wanted the interviewer (and others) to believe in the program's effectiveness, for several reasons: Administrators wanted to maintain funding and employee morale; case managers wanted to ensure cooperation by talking up the program with clients and their families; and case managers also preferred to deflect blame for problems to clients, families, or system constraints.

ETHICAL ISSUES IN SURVEY RESEARCH

Survey research usually poses fewer ethical dilemmas than do experimental or field research designs. Potential respondents to a survey can easily decline to participate, and a cover letter or introductory statement that identifies the sponsors of and motivations for the survey gives them the information required to make this decision. The methods of data collection are quite obvious in a survey, so little is concealed from the respondents. Only in group-administered survey designs might the respondents be, in effect, a captive audience (probably of students or employees), and so they require special attention to ensure that participation is truly voluntary. (Those who do not wish to participate may be told they can just hand in a blank form.)

Confidentiality is most often the primary focus of ethical concern in survey research. Many surveys include some essential questions that might in some way prove damaging to the subjects if their answers were disclosed. To prevent any possibility of harm to subjects due to disclosure of such information, it is critical to preserve subject confidentiality. Nobody but research personnel should have access to information that could be used to link respondents to their responses, and even that access should be limited to what is necessary for specific research purposes. Only numbers should be used to identify respondents on their questionnaires, and the researcher should keep the names that correspond to these numbers in a safe, private location, unavailable to staff and others who might otherwise come across them. Follow-up mailings or contact attempts that require linking the ID numbers with names and addresses should be carried out by trustworthy assistants under close supervision. For electronic surveys, encryption technology should be used to make information provided over the Internet secure from unauthorized persons.

Not many surveys can provide true **anonymity,** so that no identifying information is ever recorded to link respondents with their responses. The main problem with anonymous surveys is that they preclude follow-up attempts to encourage participation by initial non-respondents, and they prevent panel designs, which measure change through repeated surveys of the same individuals. In-person surveys rarely can be anonymous because an interviewer must in almost all cases know the name and address of the interviewee. However, phone surveys that are meant only to sample opinion at one point in time, as in political polls, can safely be completely anonymous. When no future follow-up is desired, group-administered surveys also can be anonymous. To provide anonymity in a mail survey, the researcher should omit identifying codes from the questionnaire but could include a self-addressed, stamped postcard so the respondent can notify the researcher that the questionnaire has been returned without creating any linkage to the questionnaire itself (Mangione, 1995:69).

CONCLUSIONS

Survey research is an exceptionally efficient and productive method for investigating a wide array of social research questions. In 6 months, Catherine Ross's survey produced a unique, comprehensive dataset on work, family, and health issues. These data allowed Ross and her coauthors to investigate the relationships among sex stratification, health lifestyle, and perceived health (Ross & Bird, 1994); between education and health (Ross & Wu, 1995); between physical impairment and income (Mirowsky & Hu, 1996); among gender, parenthood, and anger (Ross & Van Willigen, 1996); and among age, the sense of control, and health (Mirowsky, 1995; Mirowsky & Ross, 1992; Mirowsky & Ross, 1999; Ross & Wu, 1996). As a result, we know much more about how social structure influences health, what might be done to mitigate the negative health consequences of aging and low income, and where social theories of health need to be improved.

In addition to the potential benefits for social science, considerations of time and expense frequently make a survey the preferred data-collection method. One or more of the six survey designs reviewed in this chapter (including mixed-mode) can be applied to almost any research question. It is no wonder that surveys have become the most popular research method in sociology and that they frequently inform discussion and planning about important social and political questions. As use of the Internet increases, survey research should become even more efficient and popular.

The relative ease of conducting at least some types of survey research leads many people to imagine that no particular training or systematic procedures are required. Nothing could be further from the truth. But as a result of this widespread misconception, you will encounter a great many nearly worthless survey results. You must be prepared to examine carefully the procedures used in any survey before accepting its findings as credible. And if you decide to conduct a survey, you must be prepared to invest the time and effort required by proper procedures.

KEY TERMS

Anonymity
Behavior coding
Cognitive interview
Computer-assisted personal interview (CAPI)
Computer-assisted telephone interview (CATI)
Confidentiality
Context effect
Contingent question
Cover letter
Double-barreled question
Double negative
Electronic survey
E-mail survey
Errors of nonobservation
Errors of observation
Fence-sitter
Filter question
Floater

Forced-choice question
Group-administered survey
In-person interview
Interactive voice response (IVR)
Interpretive question
Interview schedule
Mailed survey
Mixed-mode survey
Omnibus survey
Part-whole question effect
Phone survey
Questionnaire
Skip pattern
Split-ballot design
Street-level bureaucrat
Survey research
Web survey

HIGHLIGHTS

- Surveys are the most popular form of social research because of their versatility, efficiency, and generalizability. Many survey datasets, like the General Social Survey, are available for social scientists to use in teaching and research.

- Omnibus surveys cover a range of topics of interest and generate data useful to multiple sponsors.

- Survey designs must minimize the risk of errors of observation (measurement error) and errors of nonobservation (errors due to inadequate coverage, sampling error, and nonresponse). The likelihood of both types of error varies with the survey goals. For example, political polling can produce inconsistent results because of rapid changes in popular sentiment.

- Social exchange theory asserts that behavior is motivated by the return expected to the individual for the behavior. Survey designs must maximize the social rewards, minimize the costs for participating, and establish trust that the rewards will outweigh the costs.

- A survey questionnaire or interview schedule should be designed as an integrated whole, with each question and section serving some clear purpose and complementing the others.

- Questions must be worded carefully to avoid confusing respondents, encouraging a less-than-honest response, or triggering biases. Inclusion of "Don't know" choices and neutral responses may help, but the presence of such options also affects the distribution of answers. Open-ended questions can be used to determine the meaning that respondents attach to their answers. Answers to any survey questions may be affected by the questions that precede them in a questionnaire or interview schedule.

- Questions can be tested and improved through review by experts, focus group discussions, cognitive interviews, behavior coding, and pilot testing. Every questionnaire and interview schedule should be pretested on a small sample that is like the sample to be surveyed.

- Interpretive questions should be used in questionnaires to help clarify the meaning of responses to critical questions.

• The cover letter for a mailed questionnaire should be credible, personalized, interesting, and responsible.

• Response rates in mailed surveys are typically well below 70% unless multiple mailings are made to nonrespondents and the questionnaire and cover letter are attractive, interesting, and carefully planned. Response rates for group-administered surveys are usually much higher.

• Phone interviews using random digit dialing allow fast turnaround and efficient sampling. Multiple call-backs are often required and the rate of nonresponse to phone interviews is rising. Phone interviews should be limited in length to about 30 to 45 minutes.

• In-person interviews have several advantages over other types of surveys: They allow longer and more complex interview schedules, monitoring of the conditions when the questions are answered, probing for respondents' understanding of the questions, and high response rates. However, the interviewer must balance the need to establish rapport with the respondent with the importance of maintaining control over the delivery of the interview questions.

• Electronic surveys may be e-mailed or posted on the Web. Interactive voice response systems using the telephone are another option. At this time, use of the Internet is not sufficiently widespread to allow e-mail or Web surveys of the general population, but these approaches can be fast and efficient for populations with high rates of computer use.

• Mixed-mode surveys allow the strengths of one survey design to compensate for the weaknesses of another. However, questions and procedures must be designed carefully, using "unimode design" principles, to reduce the possibility that responses to the same question will vary as a result of the mode of delivery.

• The decision to use a particular survey design must take into account the unique features and goals of the study. In general, in-person interviews are the strongest but most expensive survey design.

• Most survey research poses few ethical problems because respondents are able to decline to participate—an option that should be stated clearly in the cover letter or introductory statement. Special care must be taken when questionnaires are administered in group settings (to "captive audiences") and when sensitive personal questions are to be asked; subject confidentiality should always be preserved.

DISCUSSION QUESTIONS

1. Read the original article reporting one of the surveys described in this book (check Appendix A or the text of the chapters for ideas). Critique the article using the questions presented in Appendix C as your guide, but focus particular attention on sampling, measurement, and survey design.

2. *Responding to the Homeless: Policy and Practice* (Schutt & Garrett, 1992) includes an appendix that contains an interview schedule for case managers at homeless shelters. Check the book out of your library and critique the form. What are the key concepts in the instrument? Which measures do you think are strong? Weak? Point out the key features of the interview schedule, including sections, response formats, skip patterns, and routing instructions. Do you think the order of the sections and of the questions within sections makes sense? Why or why not? What do you think might be the advantages and disadvantages of having shelter case managers administer this instrument?

3. Each of the following questions was used in a survey that I received at some time in the past. Evaluate each question and its response choices using the guidelines for question writing presented in this chapter. What errors do you find? Try to rewrite each question to avoid such errors and improve question wording.

a. The first question in an *Info World* (computer publication) "product evaluation survey":

```
How interested are you in PostScript Level 2 printers?
____ Very ____ Somewhat ____ Not at all
```

b. From the Greenpeace "National Marine Mammal Survey":

```
Do you support Greenpeace's nonviolent, direct action to intercept whal-
ing ships, tuna fleets and other commercial fishermen in order to stop
their wanton destruction of thousands of magnificent marine mammals?

____ Yes ____ No ____ Undecided
```

c. From a U.S. Department of Education survey of college faculty:

```
How satisfied or dissatisfied are you with each of the following aspects
of your instructional duties at this institution?
```

	Very Dissat.	Somewhat Dissat.	Somewhat Satisf.	Very Satisf.
a. The authority I have to make decisions about what courses I teach	1	2	3	4
b. Time available for working with students as advisor, mentor	1	2	3	4

d. From a survey about affordable housing in a Massachusetts community:

```
    Higher than single-family density is acceptable in order to make
housing affordable.
```

Strongly Agree	Undecided	Disagree	Strongly Agree	Disagree
1	2	3	4	5

e. From a survey of faculty experience with ethical problems in research:

```
Are you reasonably familiar with the codes of ethics of any of the
following professional associations?
```

	Very Familiar	Familiar	Not too Familiar
American Sociological Association	1	2	0
Society for the Study of Social Problems	1	2	0
American Society of Criminology	1	2	0

```
    If you are familiar with any of the above codes of ethics, to what
extent do you agree with them?
```

Strongly Agree   Agree   No opinion   Disagree   Strongly Disagree

```
    Some researchers have avoided using a professional code of ethics as a
guide for the following reason. Which responses, if any, best describe
your reasons for not using all or any of the parts of the codes?
```

	Yes	No
1. Vagueness	1	0
2. Political pressures	1	0
3. Codes protect only individuals, not groups	1	0

f. From a survey of faculty perceptions:

Of the students you have observed while teaching college courses, please indicate the percentage who significantly improve their performance in the following areas.

```
Reading        ____%
Organization   ____%
Abstraction    ____%
```

g. From a University of Massachusetts-Boston student survey:

A person has a responsibility to stop a friend or relative from driving when drunk.

Strongly Agree ___ Agree ___ Disagree ___ Strongly Disagree ___

Even if I wanted to, I would probably not be able to stop most people from driving drunk.

Strongly Agree ___ Agree ___ Disagree ___ Strongly Disagree ___

PRACTICE EXERCISES

1. Consider how you could design a split-ballot experiment to determine the effect of phrasing a question or its response choices in different ways. Check recent issues of the local newspaper for a question used in a survey of attitudes about some social policy or political position. Propose some hypothesis about how the wording of the question or its response choices might have influenced the answers people gave and devise an alternative that differs only in this respect. Distribute these questionnaires to a large class (after your instructor makes the necessary arrangements) to test your hypothesis.

2. I received in my university mailbox some years ago a two-page questionnaire that began with the following "cover letter" at the top of the first page:

Faculty Questionnaire

This survey seeks information on faculty perception of the learning process and student performance in their undergraduate careers. Surveys have been distributed in nine universities in the Northeast, through random deposit in mailboxes of selected departments. This survey is being conducted by graduate students affiliated with the School of Education and the Sociology Department. We greatly appreciate your time and effort in helping us with our study.

Critique this cover letter, and then draft a more persuasive one.

3. *Down and Out in America,* by Peter Rossi (1989), includes an appendix containing an annotated bibliography of survey-based studies of homeless and extremely poor populations. Critique the survey

designs based on Rossi's descriptions. Which designs seem likely to produce more generalizable results? Comment on sample generalizability and cross-population generalizability. Propose a plan to survey either homeless persons or those who provide services to homeless persons in some city in your state. How would you draw a sample? How would you approach potential respondents? What survey design do you think would have the greatest chance of success?

4. In Chapter 7, review the description of the experiment by Richard Price, Michelle Van Ryn, and Amiram Vinokur (1992). Propose a survey design that would test the same hypothesis but with a sample from a larger population. Your survey design can be longitudinal but should remain experimental, not quasi-experimental. Compare your survey design to the original experimental design. What are the advantages and disadvantages of your survey design in terms of causal validity? Generalizability? Measurement validity?

WEB EXERCISES

1. Who does survey research and how do they do it? These questions can be answered through careful inspection of organizations listed at http://www.ukans.edu/cwis/units/coms2/po/index.html. Spend some time reading about some of the different survey research organizations, and write a brief summary of the types of research they conduct, the projects in which they are involved, and the resources they offer on their Web sites. What are the distinctive features of different survey research organizations?

2. Go to the Research Triangle Institute site at http://www.rti.org. Click on "Tools and Methods," then "Surveys," and then "Survey Design and Development." Read about their methods for computer-assisted interviewing (under "Survey Methods") and their cognitive laboratory methods for refining questions (under "Usability Testing"). What does this add to my treatment of these topics in this chapter?

3. Go to The Question Bank at http://qb.soc.surrey.ac.uk/docs/home.htm. Click on the link for one of the listed surveys. Review 10 questions used in the survey and critique them in terms of the principles for question writing that you have learned. Do you find any question features that might be attributed to the use of British English?

4. Go to the "CyClone Project" home page by William Sims Bainbridge at http://mysite.verizon. net/william.bainbridge/system/cyindex.htm. Now examine the "Emotions" section and try converting the items into survey questions, as suggested. How well do the questions capture your own emotion? Would you make any changes in the questions? What would you add, omit, or change? Why?

SPSS EXERCISES

What can we learn from the GSS data about the orientations of people who support capital punishment? Is it related to religion? Reflective of attitudes toward race? What about political views? Is it a guy thing? Do attitudes and behavior concerning guns have some relation to support for capital punishment?

1. To answer these questions, we will use some version of each of the following variables in our analysis: PARTYID3, GUNLAW, BLKSIMP, RACDIF1, FUND, OWNGUN2, and CAPPUN. Check the wording of each of these questions at the University of Michigan's GSS Web site: www.icpsr. umich.edu:8080/GSS/homepage.htm. (This site does not contain questions added in the last few years.)
How well do each of these questions meet the guidelines for writing survey questions? What improvements would you suggest?

2. Now generate crosstabulations to show the relationship between each of these variables, treated as independent variables, and support for capital punishment. A crosstabulation can be used to display the distribution of responses on the dependent variable for each category of the independent variable.

For this purpose, you should substitute several slightly different versions of the variables you just reviewed. From the menu, select *Analyze.* Then, in the Crosstabs window, set:

Rows: CAPPUN

Columns: SEX, PARTYID3, GUNLAW, BLKSIMP, RACDIF1, FUND, OWNGUN2

Cells: column percents

(If you have had a statistics course, you will also want to request the chi-square statistic for each of the above tables.)

Describe the relationships you have found in the tables, noting the difference in the distribution of the dependent (row) variable—support for capital punishment—between the categories of each of the independent (column) variables.

3. Summarize your findings. What attitudes and characteristics are associated strongly with support for the death penalty?

4. What other hypotheses would you like to test? What else do you think needs to be taken into account in order to understand the relationships you have identified? For example, should you take into account the race of the respondents? Why or why not?

5. Let's take a minute to learn about recoding variables. If you generate the frequencies for POLVIEWS and for POLVIEWS3, you'll see how I recoded POLVIEWS3. Why? Because I wanted to use a simple categorization by political party views in the crosstabulation. You can try to replicate my recoding in SPSS. From the menu, click *Transform|Recode|Into different* variables. Identify the old variable name and type in the new one. Type in the appropriate sets of old values and the corresponding new values. You may need to check the numerical codes corresponding to the old values with the variable list pulldown menu (the ladder icon with a question mark).

DEVELOPING A RESEARCH PROPOSAL

1. Write 10 questions for a one-page questionnaire that concerns your proposed research question. Your questions should operationalize at least three of the variables on which you have focused, including at least one independent and one dependent variable (you may have multiple questions to measure some variables). Make all but one of your questions closed-ended. If you completed the "Developing a Research Proposal" exercises in Chapter 4, you can select your questions from the ones you developed for those exercises.

2. Conduct a preliminary pretest of the questionnaire by conducting cognitive interviews with two students or other persons like those to whom the survey is directed. Follow up the closed-ended questions with open-ended probes that ask the students what they meant by each response or what came to mind when they were asked each question. Take account of the feedback you receive when you revise your questions.

3. Polish up the organization and layout of the questionnaire, following the guidelines in this chapter. Prepare a rationale for the order of questions in your questionnaire. Write a cover letter directed to the appropriate population that contains appropriate statements about research ethics (human subjects' issues).

Chapter 9

QUALITATIVE METHODS
Observing, Participating, Listening

Fundamentals of Qualitative Methods

Origins of Qualitative Research
Case Study: *Making Gray Gold*

Participant Observation

Choosing a Role
   Complete Observation
   Participation and Observation
   Covert Participation
Entering the Field
Developing and Maintaining
   Relationships
Sampling People and Events
Taking Notes
Managing the Personal Dimensions

Systematic Observation

Case Study: Systematic Observation of
   Public Spaces

Intensive Interviewing

Establishing and Maintaining a
   Partnership
Asking Questions and Recording
   Answers
Combining Participant Observation and
   Intensive Interviewing

Focus Groups

Ethical Issues in Qualitative Research

Conclusions

"**Y**ou have to look into a patient's eyes as much as you can, and learn to get the signals from there." This suggestion was made by a nurse explaining to future nursing home assistants how they were to deal with a dying patient. One of those future assistants, Timothy Diamond (1992:17), was also a sociologist intent on studying work in nursing homes. For us, the statement he recorded has a dual purpose: It exemplifies qualitative methods, in which sociologists learn by observing as they participate in a natural setting; it also reminds us that some features of the social world are ill suited to investigation with experiments or surveys.

In this chapter you will learn how Tim Diamond (1992) used qualitative methods to illuminate the inside of a nursing home and the attitudes and actions of its staff. You will also see how sociologist Barrie Thorne (1993) observed schoolchildren on a playground as they defined gender-appropriate behavior. Throughout the chapter, you will learn, from a variety of other examples, that some of our greatest insights into social processes can result from what appear to be very ordinary activities: observing, participating, listening, and talking.

But you will also learn that qualitative research is much more than just doing what comes naturally in social situations. Qualitative researchers must observe keenly, take notes systematically, question respondents strategically, and prepare to spend more time and invest more of their whole selves than often occurs with experiments or surveys. Moreover, if we are to have any confidence in the validity of a qualitative study's conclusions, each element of its design must be reviewed as carefully as we would review the elements of an experiment or survey.

The chapter begins with an overview of the major features of qualitative research, as reflected in Diamond's (1992) study of nursing homes. The next section discusses the various approaches to participant observation research, which is the most distinctive qualitative method, and reviews the stages of research using participant observation. I then discuss the method of systematic observation, which is actually a quantitative approach to recording observational data. In the next section, I review in some detail the issues involved in intensive interviewing before briefly explaining focus groups, an increasingly popular qualitative method. The last section covers ethical issues that are of concern in any type of qualitative research project. By the chapter's end, you should appreciate the hard work required to translate "doing what comes naturally" into systematic research, be able to recognize strong and weak points in qualitative studies, and be ready to do some of it yourself.

FUNDAMENTALS OF QUALITATIVE METHODS

Qualitative techniques can often be used to enrich experiments and surveys. **Qualitative methods** also refer to several distinctive research designs: **participant observation, intensive interviewing,** and **focus groups.** Participant observation and intensive interviewing are often used in the same project; focus groups combine some elements of these two approaches into a unique data-collection strategy.

Participant observation   A qualitative method for gathering data that involves developing a sustained relationship with people while they go about their normal activities.

Intensive (depth) interviewing   A qualitative method that involves open-ended, relatively unstructured questioning in which the interviewer seeks in-depth information on the interviewee's feelings, experiences, and perceptions (Lofland & Lofland, 1984:12).

Focus groups   A qualitative method that involves unstructured group interviews in which the focus group leader actively encourages discussion among participants on the topics of interest.

Although these three qualitative designs differ in many respects, they share several features that distinguish them from experimental and survey research designs (Denzin & Lincoln, 1994; Maxwell, 1996; Wolcott, 1995):

Collection primarily of qualitative rather than quantitative data. Any research design may collect both qualitative and quantitative data, but qualitative methods emphasize observations about natural behavior and artifacts that capture social life as it is experienced by the participants rather than in categories predetermined by the researcher.

Exploratory research questions, with a commitment to inductive reasoning. Qualitative researchers typically begin their projects seeking not to test preformulated hypotheses but to discover what people think and how they act, and why, in some social setting. Only after many observations do qualitative researchers try to develop general principles to account for their observations.

A focus on previously unstudied processes and unanticipated phenomena. Previously unstudied attitudes and actions can't adequately be understood with a structured set of questions or within a highly controlled experiment. So qualitative methods have their greatest appeal when we need to explore new issues, investigate hard-to-study groups, or determine the meaning people give to their lives and actions. Diamond (1992:4) asked, "What was life like inside, day in and day out? Who lived in nursing homes, and what did they do there?"

An orientation to social context, to the interconnections between social phenomena rather than to their discrete features. The context of concern may be a program or organization, a "case," or a broader social context. For example:

In this book I begin not with individuals, although they certainly appear in the account, but with *group life*—with social relations, the organization and meanings of social situations, the collective practices through which children and adults create and recreate gender in their daily interactions. . . . [C]hildren's collective activities should weigh more fully in our overall understanding of gender and social life. (Thorne, 1993:4)

A focus on human subjectivity, on the meanings that participants attach to events and that people give to their lives. "Through life stories, people 'account for their lives'. . . . [T]he themes people create are the means by which they interpret and evaluate their life experiences and attempt to integrate these experiences to form a self-concept" (Kaufman, 1986:24–25).

Use of idiographic rather than nomothetic causal explanation. With its focus on particular actors and situations and the processes that connect them, qualitative research tends to identify causes as particular events embedded within an unfolding, interconnected action sequence (Maxwell, 1996:20–21). The language of variables and hypotheses appears only rarely in the qualitative literature.

Reflexive research design, in which the design develops as the research progresses:

Each component of the design may need to be reconsidered or modified in response to new developments or to changes in some other component. . . . The activities of collecting and analyzing data, developing and modifying theory, elaborating or refocusing the research

Exhibit 9.1   Qualitative Research Process

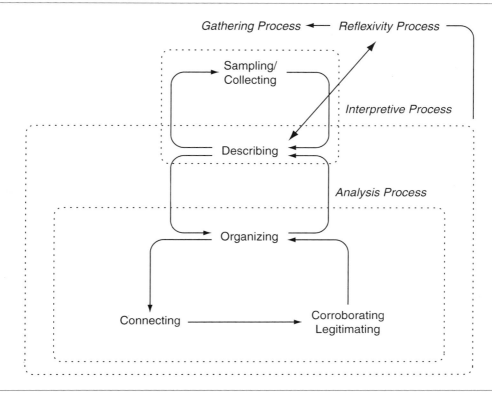

Source: Adapted from Miller & Crabtree, 1999a:16.

questions, and identifying and eliminating validity threats are usually all going on more or less simultaneously, each influencing all of the others. (Maxwell, 1996:2–3)

Sensitivity to the subjective role of the researcher. Little pretense is made of achieving an objective perspective on social phenomena:

> I felt closer to the girls not only through memories of my own past, but also because I knew more about their gender-typed interactions. I had once played games like jump rope and statue buyer, but I had never ridden a skateboard and had barely tried sports like basketball and soccer. . . . Were my moments of remembering, the times when I felt like a ten-year-old girl, a source of distortion or insight? (Thorne, 1993:26)

William Miller and Benjamin Crabtree (1999a:16) capture the entire process of qualitative research in a simple diagram (Exhibit 9.1). In this diagram, qualitative research begins with the qualitative researcher reflecting on the setting and her relation to it and interpretations of it. The researcher then describes the goals and means for the research. This description is followed by *sampling* and *collecting* data, *describing* the data and *organizing* those data. Thus, the *gathering process* and the *analysis process* proceed together, with repeated description and analysis of data as they are collected. As the data are organized, *connections* are identified between different data segments, and efforts are made to *corroborate* the credibility of these connections. This *interpretive process* begins to emerge in a written account that represents what has been done and how the data have been interpreted. Each of these steps in the research process informs the others and is repeated throughout the research process.

Origins of Qualitative Research

Anthropologists and sociologists laid the foundation for modern qualitative methods while doing **field research** in the early decades of the 20th century. Dissatisfied with studies of native peoples that relied on second-hand accounts and inspection of artifacts, anthropologists Franz Boas and Bronislaw Malinowski went to live in or near the communities they studied. Boas visited Native American villages in the American Northwest; Malinowski lived among New Guinea natives. Neither truly participated in the ongoing social life of those they studied (Boas collected artifacts and original texts, and Malinowski reputedly lived as something of a noble among the natives he studied), but both helped to establish the value of intimate familiarity with the community of interest and thus laid the basis for modern anthropology (Emerson, 1983:2–5).

Many of sociology's field research pioneers were former social workers and reformers. Some brought their missionary concern with the spread of civic virtue among new immigrants to the Department of Sociology and Anthropology at the University of Chicago. Their successors continued to focus on sources of community cohesion and urban strain but came to view the city as a social science "laboratory" rather than as a focus for reform. They adapted the fieldwork methods of anthropology to studying the "natural areas" of the city and the social life of small towns (Vidich & Lyman, 1994). By the 1930s, 1940s, and 1950s, qualitative researchers were emphasizing the value of direct participation in community life and sharing in subjects' perceptions and interpretations of events (Emerson, 1983:6–13).

Case Study: *Making Gray Gold*

You can get a better feel for qualitative methods by reading the following excerpts from Timothy Diamond's book about nursing homes, *Making Gray Gold* (Diamond, 1992), and reasoning inductively from his observations. See if you can induce from these particulars some of the general features of field research. Ask yourself, What was the research question? How were the issues of generalizability, measurement, and causation approached? How did social factors influence the research?

Let's begin near the beginning of Diamond's account:

First I went to school for six months in 1982, two evenings a week and all day Saturdays, to obtain the certificate the state required [to work in a nursing home]. Then, after weeks of searching for jobs, I worked in three different nursing homes in Chicago for periods of three to four months each. (Diamond, 1992:5)

As this excerpt indicates, Diamond's research involved becoming a participant in the social setting that was the object of his study. Note how long Diamond spent gathering data: more than a year of full-time work.

Diamond also describes for us the development of his research questions. A medical sociologist, his curiosity about health care for older people was piqued when he happened to become acquainted with Ina Williams and Aileen Crawford in a coffee shop across the street from the nursing home where they worked as assistants. He began to wonder,

> How does the work of caretaking become defined and get reproduced day in and day out as a business? . . . How, in other words, does the everyday world of Ina and Aileen and their co-workers, and that of the people they tend, get turned into a system in which gray can be written about in financial journals as producing gold, a classic metaphor for money? What is the process of making gray gold? (Diamond, 1992:5)

With these exploratory research questions in mind, Diamond explains why he chose participant observation as his research method:

> I wanted to collect stories and to experience situations like those Ina and Aileen had begun to describe. I decided that . . . I would go inside to experience the work myself. (Diamond, 1992:5)

The choice of participant observation precluded random sampling of cases, but Diamond did not ignore the need to generalize his findings. He went to considerable lengths to include three nursing homes that would represent a range of care-giving arrangements:

> These [nursing] homes were situated in widely different neighborhoods of the city. In one of them residents paid for their own care, often with initial help from Medicare. In the other two, most of the residents were supported by Medicaid. . . . In the course of writing, I visited many homes across the United States to validate my observations and to update them in instances where regulatory changes had been instituted. (Diamond, 1992:6)

The data in Diamond's study were notes on the activities of the people as he observed and interacted with them. He did not use structured questionnaires and other formal data-collection instruments, so his data are primarily qualitative rather than quantitative.

As for his method, it was inductive. First he gathered data. Then, as data collection continued, Diamond figured out how to interpret the data—how to make sense of the social situations he was studying. His analytic categories ultimately came not from social theory but from the categories by which people themselves described one another and made sense of their social world. These categories seem to have broad applicability, suggesting the generalizability of the researcher's findings. For instance, one of the teachers Diamond encountered while earning his certificate passed along a unique way of making sense of the caregiver's role in a nursing home:

> The tensions generated by the introductory lecture and . . . ideas of career professionalism were reflected in our conversations as we waited for the second class to get under way. Yet within the next half hour they seemed to dissolve. Mrs. Bonderoid, our teacher,

saw to that. A registered nurse and nurse practitioner, an African American woman of about fifty, she must have understood a lot about classroom jitters and about who was sitting in front of her as well. "What this is going to take," she instructed, "is a lot of mother's wit." "Mother's wit," she said, not "mother wit," which connotes native intelligence irrespective of gender. She was talking about maternal feelings and skills. (Diamond, 1992:17)

Diamond did develop general conclusions about social life from his research. In the nursing home, he argues,

There were two kinds of narratives on caregiving: one formal, written, and shared by the professionals and administrators; another submerged, unwritten, and shared by the people who lived and worked on the floors. (Diamond, 1992:215)

To summarize, Diamond's research began with an exploratory question (to find out what was going on) and proceeded inductively throughout, developing general concepts to make sense of specific observations. Although Diamond, a white man, was something of an outsider in a setting dominated by women of color, he was able to share many participants' experiences and perspectives. His in-depth descriptions and idiographic connections of sequences of events enabled him to construct plausible explanations about what seemed to be a typical group. He thus successfully used field research to explore human experiences in depth, carefully analyzing the social contexts in which they occur.

PARTICIPANT OBSERVATION

Diamond carried out his study through participant observation, termed "fieldwork" in anthropology. It is a method in which natural social processes are studied as they happen (in "the field" rather than in the laboratory) and left relatively undisturbed. It is the seminal field research method—a means for seeing the social world as the research subjects see it, in its totality, and for understanding subjects' interpretations of that world (Wolcott, 1995:66). By observing people and interacting with them in the course of their normal activities, participant observers seek to avoid the artificiality of experimental designs and the unnatural structured questioning of survey research (Koegel, 1987:8). This method encourages consideration of the context in which social interaction occurs, of the complex and interconnected nature of social relations, and of the sequencing of events (Bogdewic, 1999:49).

The term *participant observer* actually represents a continuum of roles (see Exhibit 9.2), ranging from being a complete observer, who does not participate in group activities and is publicly defined as a researcher, to being a covert participant, who acts just like other group members and does not disclose his or her research role. Many field researchers develop a role between these extremes, publicly acknowledging being a researcher but nonetheless participating in group activities. In some settings, it also is possible to observe covertly, without acknowledging being a researcher or participating.

Exhibit 9.2   The Observational Continuum

To study a political activist group...

You could take the role of complete observer:

You could take the role of participant and observer:

You could take the role of covert participant:

Choosing a Role

The first concern of every participant observer is to decide what balance to strike between observing and participating and whether to reveal his or her role as a researcher. These decisions must take into account the specifics of the social situation being studied, the researcher's own background and personality, the larger sociopolitical context, and ethical concerns. Which balance of participating and observing is most appropriate also changes during most projects, often many times. And the researcher's ability to maintain either a covert or an overt role will many times be challenged.

Complete Observation

In **complete observation,** researchers try to see things as they happen, without actively participating in these events. Although there is no fixed formula to guide the observational process, observers try to identify the who, what, when, where, why, and how of activities in the setting. Their observations will usually become more focused over time, as the observer develops a sense of the important categories of people and activities and gradually develops a theory that accounts for what is observed (Bogdewic, 1999:54–56).

Of course, the researcher's very presence as an observer alters the social situation being observed. This is the problem of **reactive effects.** It is not "natural" in most social situations for an observer—someone who will record her or his observations for research and publication purposes—to be present, so individuals may alter their behavior. In social settings involving many people, in which observing while standing or sitting does not attract attention, the complete observer is unlikely to have much effect on social processes. On the other hand, when the social setting involves few people and observing is unlike the usual activities in the setting, or when the observer differs in obvious respects from the participants, the complete observer is more likely to have an impact. For example, some children treated Barrie Thorne (1993:16–17) as a teacher when she was observing them in a school playground—as a regular adult authority figure. No matter what the circumstances are, researchers who act as complete observers must be prepared to experience some pressure to participate (Thorne, 1993:20).

Participation and Observation

Most field researchers adopt a role that involves some active participation in the setting. Usually they inform at least some group members of their research interests, but then they participate in enough group activities to develop rapport with members and to gain a direct sense of what group members experience. This is not an easy balancing act, but

> the key to participant observation as a fieldwork strategy is to take seriously the challenge it poses to participate more, and to play the role of the aloof observer less. Do not think of yourself as someone who needs to wear a white lab coat and carry a clipboard to learn about how humans go about their everyday lives. (Wolcott, 1995:100)

Richard Fenno (1978) provides a good example of the rapport-building function of participation in his study of relationships between members of the U.S. House of Representatives and their constituents:

> Once, for example, I arrived in a district in time to make a Friday night event, only to find the congressman had been unable to leave Washington. . . . I sat down beside someone [at campaign headquarters] and started stamping and sealing a huge stack of envelopes. An hour or two later, someone asked me to help with a telephone poll, which I did. (Fenno, 1978:267)

As a result of his contribution, Fenno was shown the confidential poll results and invited to a campaign strategy meeting the next day.

Participating and observing have two clear ethical advantages as well. Because group members know the researcher's real role in the group, they can choose to keep some information or attitudes hidden. By the same token, the researcher can decline to participate in unethical or dangerous activities without fear of exposing his or her identity.

Most field researchers who opt for disclosure get the feeling that, after they have become known and at least somewhat trusted figures in the group, their presence does not have any palpable effect on members' actions. The major influences on individual actions and attitudes are past experiences, personality, group structure, and so on, so the argument goes, and these continue to exert their influence even when an outside observer is present. The participant observer can presumably be ethical about identity disclosure and still observe the natural social world. Of course, the argument is less persuasive when the behavior to be observed is illegal or stigmatized, so that participants have reason to fear the consequences of disclosure to any outsider.

In practice it can be difficult to maintain a fully open research role even in a setting without these special characteristics:

> During and after the fieldwork the first question many people asked was "Did you tell them?" . . . I had initially hoped to disclose at every phase of the project my dual objective of working as a nursing assistant and writing about these experiences. In some instances it was possible to disclose this dual purpose, in others it was not. I told many nursing assistants and people who lived in the homes that I was both working and investigating. I told some of my nursing supervisors and some administrators. . . . The short answer is that as the study proceeded it was forced increasingly to become a piece of undercover research. (Diamond, 1992:7–8)

Even when researchers maintain a public identity as researchers, ethical dilemmas arising from participation in group activities do not go away. In fact, researchers may have to "prove themselves" to group members by joining in some of their questionable activities. For example, police officers gave John Van Maanen (1982) a nonstandard and technically prohibited pistol to carry on police patrols. Harold Pepinsky (1980) witnessed police harassment of a citizen but did not intervene when the citizen was arrested. Trying to strengthen his ties with a local political figure in his study of a poor Boston community he called Cornerville, William Foote Whyte (1955) illegally voted multiple times in a local election.

Experienced participant observers try to lessen some of the problems of identity disclosure by evaluating both their effect on others in the setting and the effect of others on the observers, writing about these effects throughout the time they are in the field and while they analyze their data. They also are sure while in the field to preserve some physical space and regular time when they can concentrate on their research and schedule occasional meetings with other researchers to review the fieldwork. Participant observers modify their role as circumstances seem to require, perhaps not always disclosing their research role at casual social gatherings or group outings but being sure to inform new members of it.

Covert Participation

To lessen the potential for reactive effects and to gain entry to otherwise inaccessible settings, some field researchers have adopted the role of covert participant, keeping their research secret and trying their best to act like other participants in a social setting or group. **Covert participation** is also known as **complete participation.** Laud Humphreys (1970) served as a "watch queen" so that he could learn about men engaging in homosexual acts in a public restroom. Randall Alfred (1976) joined a group of Satanists to investigate group members and their interaction. Erving Goffman (1961) worked as a state hospital assistant while studying the treatment of psychiatric patients.

Although the role of covert participant lessens some of the reactive effects encountered by the complete observer, covert participants confront other problems:

Covert participants cannot take notes openly or use any obvious recording devices. They must write up notes based solely on memory and must do so at times when it is natural for them to be away from group members.

Covert participants cannot ask questions that will arouse suspicion. Thus they often have trouble clarifying the meaning of other participants' attitudes or actions.

The role of covert participant is difficult to play successfully. Covert participants will not know how regular participants would act in every situation in which the researchers find themselves. Regular participants have entered the situation from different social backgrounds and with different goals from the researchers. Researchers' spontaneous reactions to every event are unlikely to be consistent with those of the regular participants (Mitchell, 1993). Suspicion that researchers are not "one of us" may then have reactive effects, obviating the value of complete participation (Erikson, 1967). In his study of the Satanists, for example, Alfred pretended to be a regular group participant until he completed his research, at which time he informed the group leader of his covert role. Rather than act surprised, the leader told Alfred that he had long considered Alfred to be "strange," not like the others—and we will never know for sure how Alfred's observations were affected. Even Diamond, though an acknowledged researcher in the nursing home, found that simply disclosing the fact that he did not work another job to make ends meet set him apart from other nursing assistants:

> "There's one thing I learned when I came to the States," [said a Haitian nursing assistant]. "Here you can't make it on just one job." She tilted her head, looked at me curiously, then asked, "You know, Tim, there's just one thing I don't understand about you. How do you make it on just one job?" (Diamond, 1992:47–48)

Covert participants need to keep up the act at all times while in the setting under study. Researchers may experience enormous psychological strain, particularly in situations where they are expected to choose sides in intragroup conflict or to participate in criminal or other acts. Of course, some covert observers may become so wrapped up in the role they are playing that they adopt not just the mannerisms, but also the perspectives and goals of the regular participants—they "go native." At this point, they abandon research goals and cease to evaluate critically what they are observing.

Ethical issues have been at the forefront of debate over the strategy of covert participation. Kai Erikson (1967) argues that covert participation is by its very nature unethical and should not be allowed except in public settings. Covert researchers cannot anticipate the unintended consequences of their actions for research subjects, Erikson points out. If others suspect the researcher's identity or if the researcher contributes to, or impedes, group action, these consequences can be adverse. In addition, other social scientists are harmed when covert research is disclosed—either during the research or upon its publication—because distrust of social scientists increases and access to research opportunities may decrease.

But a total ban on covert participation would "kill many a project stone dead" (Punch, 1994:90). Studies of unusual religious or sexual practices and of institutional malpractice would rarely be possible. "The crux of the matter is that some deception, passive or active, enables you to get at data not obtainable by other means" (Punch, 1994:91). Therefore, some field researchers argue that covert participation is legitimate in some settings. If the researcher maintains the confidentiality of others, keeps commitments to others, and does not directly lie to others, some degree of deception may be justified in exchange for the knowledge gained (Punch, 1994:90).

Entering the Field

Entering the field, the setting under investigation, is a critical stage in a participant observation project because it can shape many subsequent experiences. Some background work is necessary before entering the field—at least enough to develop a clear understanding of what the research questions are likely to be and to review one's personal stance toward the people and problems likely to be encountered. With participant observation, researchers must also learn in advance how participants dress and what their typical activities are, so as to avoid being caught completely unprepared. Finding a participant who can make introductions is often critical (Rossman & Rallis, 1998:102–103), and formal permission may be needed in an organizational setting (Bogdewic, 1999:51–53). It can take weeks or even months until entry is possible.

For his study, Diamond tried to enter a nursing home twice, first without finding out about necessary qualifications:

> My first job interview. . . . The administrator of the home had agreed to see me on [the recommendation of two current assistants]. [T]he administrator . . . probed suspiciously, "Now why would a white guy want to work for these kinds of wages?" . . . He continued without pause, "Besides, I couldn't hire you if I wanted to. You're not certified." That, he quickly concluded, was the end of our interview, and he showed me to the door. (Diamond, 1992:8–9)

After taking a course and receiving his certificate, Diamond was able to enter the role of nursing assistant as others did.

Many field researchers avoid systematic study and extensive reading about a setting for fear that it will bias their first impressions, but entering without any sense of the social norms can lead to disaster. Whyte came close to such disaster when he despaired of making any social contacts in Cornerville and decided to try an unconventional entry approach (unconventional for a field researcher, that is). In *Street Corner Society,* the account of his study, Whyte describes what happened when he went to a hotel bar in search of women to talk with:

> I looked around me again and now noticed a threesome: one man and two women. It occurred to me that here was a maldistribution of females which I might be able to

rectify. I approached the group and opened with something like this: "Pardon me. Would you mind if I joined you?" There was a moment of silence while the man stared at me. He then offered to throw me downstairs. I assured him that this would not be necessary and demonstrated as much by walking right out of there without any assistance. (Whyte, 1955:289)

Whyte needed a **gatekeeper** who could grant him access to the setting; he finally found one in "Doc" (Rossman & Rallis, 1998:108–111). A helpful social worker at the local settlement house introduced Whyte to this respected leader, who agreed to help:

Well, any nights you want to see anything, I'll take you around. I can take you to the joints—gambling joints—I can take you around to the street corners. Just remember that you're my friend. That's all they need to know [so they won't bother you]. (Whyte, 1955:291)

When participant observing involves public figures who are used to reporters and researchers, a more direct approach may secure entry into the field. Fenno simply wrote a letter to most of the members of Congress he sought to study, asking for their permission to observe them at work (Fenno, 1978:257). He received only two refusals, attributing this high rate of subject cooperation to such reasons as interest in a change in the daily routine, commitment to making themselves available, a desire for more publicity, the flattery of scholarly attention, and interest in helping to teach others about politics. Other groups have other motivations, but in every case some consideration of these potential motives in advance should help smooth entry into the field.

In short, field researchers must be very sensitive to the impression they make and the ties they establish when entering the field. This stage lays the groundwork for collecting data from people who have different perspectives and for developing relationships that the researcher can use to surmount the problems in data collection that inevitably arise in the field. The researcher should be ready with a rationale for her participation and some sense of the potential benefits to participants. Discussion about these issues with key participants or gatekeepers should be honest and should identify what the participants expect from the research, without necessarily going into detail about the researcher's hypotheses or research questions (Rossman & Rallis, 1998:51–53, 105–108).

Developing and Maintaining Relationships

Researchers must be careful to manage their relationships in the research setting so they can continue to observe and interview diverse members of the social setting throughout the long period typical of participant observation (Maxwell, 1996:66). Every action the researcher takes can develop or undermine this relationship. Interaction early in the research process is particularly sensitive, because participants don't know the researcher and the researcher doesn't know the routines. Thorne (1993:18–19) felt she had gained access to kids' more private world "when kids violated rules in my presence, like swearing or openly blowing bubble gum where these acts were forbidden, or swapping stories about recent acts of shoplifting." On the other hand, Van Maanen found his relationship with police officers undermined by one incident:

Following a family beef call in what was tagged the Little Africa section of town, I once got into what I regarded as a soft but nonetheless heated debate with the officer I was working with that evening on the merits of residential desegregation. My more or less liberal leanings on the matter were bothersome to this officer, who later reported my disturbing thoughts to his friends in the squad. Before long, I was an anathema to this friendship clique and labeled by them undesirable. Members of this group refused to work with me again. (Van Maanen, 1982:110)

So Van Maanen failed to maintain a research (or personal) relationship with this group. Do you think he should have kept his opinions about residential desegregation to himself? How honest should field researchers be about their feelings? Should they "go along to get along"?

Whyte used what in retrospect was a sophisticated two-part strategy to develop and maintain relationships with the Cornerville street-corner men. The first part of Whyte's strategy was to maintain good relations with Doc and, through Doc, to stay on good terms with the others. Doc became a **key informant** in the research setting—a knowledgeable insider who knew the group's culture and was willing to share access and insights with the researcher (Gilchrist & Williams, 1999). The less obvious part of Whyte's strategy was a consequence of his decision to move into Cornerville, a move he decided was necessary to really understand and be accepted in the community. The room he rented in a local family's home became his base of operations. In some respects, this family became an important dimension of Whyte's immersion in the community: He tried to learn Italian by speaking with family members, and they conversed late at night as if Whyte were a real family member. But Whyte recognized that he needed a place to unwind after his days of constant alertness in the field, so he made a conscious decision not to include the family as an object of study. Living in this family's home became a means for Whyte to maintain standing as a community insider without becoming totally immersed in the demands of research (Whyte, 1955:294–297).

Experienced participant observers have developed some sound advice for others seeking to maintain relationships in the field (Bogdewic, 1999:53–54; Rossman & Rallis, 1998:105–108; Whyte, 1955:300–306; Wolcott, 1995:91–95):

- Develop a plausible (and honest) explanation for yourself and your study.
- Maintain the support of key individuals in groups or organizations under study.
- Be unobtrusive and unassuming. Don't "show off" your expertise.
- Don't be too aggressive in questioning others (for example, don't violate implicit norms that preclude discussion of illegal activity with outsiders). Being a researcher requires that you not simultaneously try to be the guardian of law and order. Instead, be a reflective listener.
- Ask very sensitive questions only of informants with whom your relationship is good.
- Be self-revealing, but only up to a point. Let participants learn about you as a person, but without making too much of yourself.
- Don't fake your social similarity with your subjects. Taking a friendly interest in them should be an adequate basis for developing trust.
- Avoid giving or receiving monetary or other tangible gifts but without violating norms of reciprocity. Living with other people, taking others' time for conversations, going

out for a social evening all create expectations and incur social obligations, and you can't be an active participant without occasionally helping others. But you will lose your ability to function as a researcher if you come to be seen as someone who gives away money or other favors. Such small forms of assistance as an occasional ride to the store or advice on applying to college may strike the right balance.

- Be prepared for special difficulties and tensions if multiple groups are involved. It is hard to avoid taking sides or being used in situations of intergroup conflict.

Sampling People and Events

Sampling decisions in qualitative research are guided by the need to study intensively the people, places, or phenomena of interest. In fact, most qualitative researchers limit their focus to just one or a few sites or programs, so that they can focus all their attention on the social dynamics of those settings. This focus on a limited number of cases does not mean that sampling is unimportant. The researcher must be reasonably confident that she can gain access and that the site can provide relevant information. The sample must be appropriate and adequate for the study, even if it is not representative. The qualitative researcher may select a "critical case" that is unusually rich in information pertaining to the research question, a "typical case" precisely because it is judged to be typical, and/or a "deviant case" that provides a useful contrast (Kuzel, 1999). Within a research site, plans may be made to sample different settings, people, events, and artifacts (see Exhibit 9.3).

Studying more than one case or setting almost always strengthens the causal conclusions and makes the findings more generalizable (King, Keohane, & Verba, 1994). To make his conclusions more generalizable, Diamond (1992:5) worked in three different Chicago nursing homes "in widely different neighborhoods" and with different fractions of residents supported by Medicaid. He then "visited many homes across the United States to validate my observations." Thorne (1993:6–7) observed in a public elementary school in California for 8 months and then, 4 years later, in a public elementary school in Michigan for 3 months.

Other approaches to sampling in field research are more systematic. You already learned in Chapter 5 about some of the nonprobability sampling methods that are used in field research. For instance, purposive sampling can be used to identify opinion leaders and representatives of different roles. With snowball sampling, field researchers learn from participants about who represents different subgroups in a setting. Quota sampling also may be employed to ensure the representation of particular categories of participants. Using some type of intentional sampling strategy within a particular setting can allow tests of some hypotheses that would otherwise have to wait until comparative data could be collected from several settings (King, Keohane, & Verba, 1994).

Theoretical sampling is a systematic approach to sampling in participant observation studies (Glaser & Strauss, 1967). When field researchers discover in an investigation that particular processes seem to be important, implying that certain comparisons should be made or that similar instances should be checked, the researchers then choose new settings or individuals that permit these comparisons or checks (Ragin, 1994:98–101) (see Exhibit 9.4). Fenno's strategy for selecting members of Congress to observe in their home districts exemplifies this type of approach:

Exhibit 9.3   Sampling Plan for a Participant Observation Project in Schools

Information Source*	Type of Information to Be Obtained				
	Collegiality	Goals & Community	Action Expectations	Knowledge Orientation	Base
SETTINGS					
Public places (halls, main offices)					
Teachers' lounge	X	X		X	X
Classrooms		X	X	X	X
Meeting rooms	X		X	X	
Gymnasium or locker room		X			
EVENTS					
Faculty meetings	X		X		X
Lunch hour	X				X
Teaching		X	X	X	X
PEOPLE					
Principal		X	X	X	X
Teachers	X	X	X	X	X
Students		X	X	X	
ARTIFACTS					
Newspapers		X	X		X
Decorations		X			

* Selected examples in each category.

Source: Adapted from Marshall & Rossman, 1999:75–76.

Whom should I observe? . . . If I had been certain about what types of representatives and what types of districts to sample, I would already have had answers to a lot of the questions raised in this book. My procedure was slowly to build up the size of the group being observed and constantly to monitor its composition to see what commonly recognized types of members or districts I might be neglecting. Then I would move to remedy any imagined deficiencies. I spent a lot of time trying to figure out a priori what types of members or districts might pose serious tests for, or exceptions to, whatever generalizations seemed to be emerging—with the intent of bringing such members or districts into the group. At one point, I noticed there were too many lawyers; the next two people I chose were nonlawyers. (Fenno, 1978:253)

Exhibit 9.4   Theoretical Sampling

Original cases interviewed in a study of cocaine users:

Realization: Some cocaine users are businesspeople.
Add businesspeople to sample:

Realization: Sample is low on women.
Add women to sample:

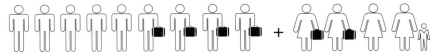

Realization: Some female cocaine users are mothers of young children.
Add mothers to sample:

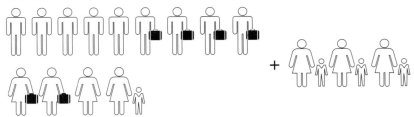

When field studies do not require ongoing, intensive involvement by researchers in the setting, the **experience sampling method (ESM)** can be used. The experiences, thoughts, and feelings of a number of people are sampled randomly as they go about their daily activities. Participants in an ESM study carry an electronic pager and fill out reports when they are beeped. For example, 107 adults carried pagers in Robert Kubey's (1990) ESM study of television habits and family quality of life. Participants' reports indicated that heavy TV viewers were less active during non-TV family activities, although heavy TV viewers also spent more time with their families and felt as positively toward other family members as did those who watched less TV.

Although ESM is a powerful tool for field research, it is still limited by the need to recruit people to carry pagers. Ultimately, the generalizability of ESM findings relies on the representativeness, and reliability, of the persons who cooperate in the research.

Taking Notes

Written notes are the primary means of recording participant observation data (Emerson, Fretz, & Shaw, 1995). Of course, "written" no longer means handwritten; many field researchers jot down partial notes while observing and then retreat to their computer to write up more complete notes on a daily basis. The computerized text can then be inspected and organized after it is printed out, or it can be marked up and organized for analysis using one of several computer programs designed especially for the task.

It is almost always a mistake to try to take comprehensive notes while engaged in the field—the process of writing extensively is just too disruptive. The usual procedure is to jot down brief notes about highlights of the observation period. These brief notes (called **jottings**) can then serve as memory joggers when writing the actual **field notes** at a later session. It will also help to maintain a daily log in which each day's activities are recorded (Bogdewic, 1999:58–67). With the aid of the jottings and some practice, researchers usually remember a great deal of what happened—as long as the comprehensive field notes are written immediately afterward, or at least within the next 24 hours, and before they have been discussed with anyone else.

The following excerpts shed light on the note-taking processes that Diamond and Thorne used while in the field. Taking notes was more of a challenge for Diamond, because many people in the setting did not know that he was a researcher:

> While I was getting to know nursing assistants and residents and experiencing aspects of their daily routines, I would surreptitiously take notes on scraps of paper, in the bathroom or otherwise out of sight, jotting down what someone had said or done. (Diamond, 1992:6–7)

Thorne was able to take notes openly:

> I went through the school days with a small spiral notebook in hand, jotting descriptions that I later expanded into field notes. When I was at the margins of a scene, I took notes on the spot. When I was more fully involved, sitting and talking with kids at a cafeteria table or playing a game of jump rope, I held observations in my memory and recorded them later. (Thorne, 1993:17)

Usually, writing up notes takes much longer—at least three times longer—than the observing did. Field notes must be as complete, detailed, and true to what was observed and heard as possible. Direct quotes should be distinguished clearly from paraphrased quotes and both should be set off from the researcher's observations and reflections. Pauses and interruptions should be indicated. The surrounding context should receive as much attention as possible, and a map of the setting always should be included, with indications of where individuals were at different times.

Careful note-taking yields a big payoff. On page after page, field notes will suggest new concepts, causal connections, and theoretical propositions. Social processes and settings can be described in rich detail, with ample illustrations. Exhibit 9.5, for example, contains field notes recorded by Norma Ware, an anthropologist studying living arrangements for homeless mentally ill persons (Goldfinger et al., 1997). The notes contain observations of the

Exhibit 9.5   Field Notes from an ECH*

I arrive around 4:30 P.M. and walk into a conversation between Jim and somebody else as to what color jeans he should buy. There is quite a lot of joking going on between Jim and Susan. I go out to the kitchen and find Dick about to take his dinner out to the picnic table to eat (his idea?) so I go ask if I can join him. He says yes. In the course of the conversation, I find out that he works 3 days a week in the "prevoc" program at the local day program, Food Services branch, for which he gets $10 per week. Does he think the living situation will work out? Yes. All they need is a plan for things like when somebody buys something and then everybody else uses it. Like he bought a gallon of milk and it was gone in two days, because everyone was using it for their coffee. I ask if he's gone back to the shelter to visit and he says "No. I was glad to get out of there." He came to [the ECH] from [a shelter] through homeless outreach [a Department of Mental Health program]. Had been at [the shelter] since January. Affirms that [the ECH] is a better place to live than the shelter. Why? Because you have your own room and privacy and stuff. How have people been getting along with each other? He says, "Fine."

I return to the living room and sit down on the couch with Jim and Susan. Susan teases Jim and he jokes back. Susan is eating a T.V. dinner with M and M's for dessert. There is joking about working off the calories from the M and M's by doing sit-up's, which she proceeds to demonstrate. This leads to a conversation about exercise during which Jim declares his intention to get back into exercise by doing sports, like basketball.
  Jim seems to have his mind on pulling himself together, which he characterizes as "getting my old self back." When I ask him what he's been doing since I saw him last, he says, "Working on my appearance." And in fact, he has had a haircut, a shave, and washed his clothes. When I ask him what his old self was like, he says, "you mean before I lost everything?" I learn that he used to work two jobs, had "a family" and was into "religion." This seems to have been when he was quite young, around eighteen. He tells me he was on the street for 7–8 years, from 1978–1985, drinking the whole time. I ask him whether he thinks living at [the ECH] will help him to get his "old self back" and he says that it will "help motivate me." I observe that he seems pretty motivated already. He says yes, "but this will motivate me more."

Jim has a warm personality, likes to joke and laugh. He also speaks up—in meetings he is among the first to say what he thinks and he talks among the most. His "team" relationship with Bill is also important to him—"me and Bill, we work together."

Source: Norma Ware, Ph.D., Department of Psychiatry, Harvard Medical School, unpublished ethnographic notes, 1991.

*Evolving Consumer Household.

setting, the questions the anthropologist asked, the answers she received, and her analytic thoughts about one of the residents. What can be learned from just this one page of field notes? The mood of the house at this time is evident, with joking, casual conversation, and close friendships. "Dick" remarks on problems with household financial management, and at the same time we learn a bit about his own activities and personality (a regular worker who appears to like systematic plans). We see how a few questions and a private conversation elicit information about the transition from the shelter to the house, as well as about household operations. The field notes also provide the foundation for a more complete picture of one resident, describing "Jim's" relationships with others, his personal history, his interests and personality, and his orientation to the future. We can see analytic concepts emerge in the notes, such as the concept of "pulling himself together" and of some house members working as a "team." You can imagine how researchers can go on to develop a theoretical framework for understanding the setting and a set of concepts and questions to inform subsequent observations.

Complete field notes must provide even more than a record of what was observed or heard. Notes also should include descriptions of the methodology: where researchers were standing or sitting while they observed, how they chose people for conversation or observation, what counts of people or events they made and why. Sprinkled throughout the notes also should be a record of the researchers' feelings and thoughts while observing: when they were disgusted by some statement or act, when they felt threatened or intimidated, why their attention shifted from one group to another, and what ethical concerns arose. Notes like these provide a foundation for later review of the likelihood of bias or of inattention to some salient features of the situation.

Notes may in some situations be supplemented by still pictures, videotapes, and printed material circulated or posted in the research setting. Such visual material can bring an entirely different qualitative dimension into the analysis and call attention to some features of the social situation and actors within it that were missed in the notes (Grady, 1996). Commentary on this material can be integrated with the written notes (Bogdewic, 1999:67–68).

Managing the Personal Dimensions

Our overview of participant observation would not be complete without considering its personal dimensions. Because field researchers become a part of the social situation they are studying, they cannot help but be affected on a personal, emotional level. At the same time, those being studied react to researchers not just as researchers but as personal acquaintances—often as friends, sometimes as personal rivals. Managing and learning from this personal side of field research is an important part of any project.

The impact of personal issues varies with the depth of researchers' involvement in the setting. The more involved researchers are in multiple aspects of the ongoing social situation, the more important personal issues become and the greater the risk of "going native." Even when researchers acknowledge their role, "increased contact brings sympathy, and sympathy in its turn dulls the edge of criticism" (Fenno, 1978:277). Fenno minimized this problem by returning frequently to the university and by avoiding involvement in the personal lives of the congressional representatives he was studying. To study the social life of "corner boys," however, Whyte could not stay so disengaged. He moved into an apartment with a Cornerville family and lived for about 4 years in the community he was investigating:

The researcher, like his informants, is a social animal. He has a role to play, and he has his own personality needs that must be met in some degree if he is to function successfully. Where the researcher operates out of a university, just going into the field for a few hours at a time, he can keep his personal social life separate from field activity. His problem of role is not quite so complicated. If, on the other hand, the researcher is living for an extended period in the community he is studying, his personal life is inextricably mixed with his research. (Whyte, 1955:279)

The correspondence between researchers' social attributes—age, sex, race, and so on—and those of their subjects also shapes personal relationships, as Diamond noted:

The staff were mostly people of color, residents mostly white. . . . Never before, or since, have I been so acutely aware of being a white American man. At first the people who lived in the homes stared at me, then some approached to get a closer look, saying that I reminded them of a nephew, a son, a grandson, a brother, a doctor. This behavior made more sense as time went on: except for the few male residents and occasional visitors, I was the only white man many would see from one end of the month to the next. (Diamond, 1992:39)

Thorne wondered whether "my moments of remembering, the times when I felt like a ten-year-old girl, [were] a source of distortion or insight?" She concluded they were both: "Memory, like observing, is a way of knowing and can be a rich resource." But "When my own responses, . . . were driven by emotions like envy or aversion, they clearly obscured my ability to grasp the full social situation" (Thorne, 1993:26).

There is no formula for successfully managing the personal dimension of field research. It is much more art than science and flows more from the researcher's own personality and natural approach to other people than from formal training. But novice field researchers often neglect to consider how they will manage personal relationships when they plan and carry out their projects. Then suddenly they find themselves doing something they don't believe they should, just to stay in the good graces of research subjects, or juggling the emotions resulting from conflict within the group. As Whyte noted:

The field worker cannot afford to think only of learning to live with others in the field. He has to continue living with himself. If the participant observer finds himself engaging in behavior that he has learned to think of as immoral, then he is likely to begin to wonder what sort of a person he is after all. Unless the field worker can carry with him a reasonably consistent picture of himself, he is likely to run into difficulties. (Whyte, 1955:317)

If you plan a field research project, follow these guidelines (Whyte, 1955:300–317):

- Take the time to consider how you want to relate to your potential subjects as people.
- Speculate about what personal problems might arise and how you will respond to them.
- Keep in touch with other researchers and personal friends outside the research setting.
- Maintain standards of conduct that make you comfortable as a person and that respect the integrity of your subjects.

When you evaluate participant observers' reports, pay attention to how they defined their role in the setting and dealt with personal problems. Don't place too much confidence in such research unless the report provides this information.

SYSTEMATIC OBSERVATION

Observations can be made in a more systematic, quantitative design that allows systematic comparisons and more confident generalizations. A researcher using systematic observation develops a standard form on which to record variation within the observed setting in terms of variables of interest. Such variables might include the frequency of some behavior(s), the particular people observed, the weather or other environmental conditions, and the number and state of repair of physical structures. In some systematic observation studies, records will be obtained from a random sample of places or times.

Case Study: Systematic Observation of Public Spaces

You first learned about Robert Sampson and Stephen Raudenbush's (1999) study of disorder and crime in urban neighborhoods in Chapter 6. In this section I'll elaborate on their use of the method of systematic social observation of public spaces to learn about these neighborhoods. A **systematic observational** strategy increases the reliability of observational data by using explicit rules that standardize coding practices across observers (Reiss, 1971b). It is a method particularly well suited to overcoming one of the limitations of survey research on crime and disorder: Residents who are fearful of crime perceive more neighborhood disorder than do residents who are less fearful, even though both are observing the same neighborhood (Sampson & Raudenbush, 1999:606).

This ambitious multiple methods investigation combined observational research, survey research, and archival research. The observational component involved a stratified probability (random) sample of 196 Chicago census tracts. A specially equipped sport utility vehicle was driven down each street in these tracts at the rate of 5 miles per hour. Two video recorders taped the blocks on both sides of the street, while two observers peered out the vehicle's windows and recorded their observations in logs. The result was an observational record of 23,816 face blocks (the block on one side of the street is a face block). The observers recorded in their logs codes that indicated land use, traffic, physical conditions, and evidence of physical disorder. The video tapes were sampled and then coded for 126 variables, including housing characteristics, businesses, and social interactions. Physical disorder was measured by counting·such features as cigarettes or cigars in the street, garbage, empty beer bottles, graffiti, condoms, and syringes. Indicators of social disorder included adults loitering, drinking alcohol in public, fighting, and selling drugs. To check for reliability, a different set of coders recoded the videos for 10% of the blocks. The repeat codes achieved 98% agreement with the original codes.

Sampson and Raudenbush also measured crime levels with data from police records, census tract socioeconomic characteristics with census data, and resident attitudes and behavior with a survey. As you learned in Chapter 6, the combination of data from these sources allowed a test of the relative impact on the crime rate of informal social control efforts by residents and of the appearance of social and physical disorder.

This study illustrates both the value of multiple methods and the technique of recording observations in a form from which quantitative data can be obtained.

INTENSIVE INTERVIEWING

Asking questions is part of almost all participant observation (Wolcott, 1995:102–105). However, many qualitative researchers employ intensive or depth interviewing exclusively, without systematic observation of respondents in their natural setting.

Unlike the more structured interviewing that may be used in survey research (discussed in Chapter 8), intensive or depth interviewing relies on open-ended questions. Qualitative researchers do not presume to know the range of answers that respondents might give and seek to hear these answers in the respondents' own words. Rather than asking standard questions in a fixed order, intensive interviewers may allow the specific content and order of questions to vary from one interviewee to another.

What distinguishes intensive interviewing from less structured forms of questioning is consistency and thoroughness. The goal is to develop a comprehensive picture of the interviewee's background, attitudes, and actions, in his or her own terms; to "listen to people as they describe how they understand the worlds in which they live and work" (Rubin & Rubin, 1995:3). For example, Sharon Kaufman (1986:6) sought through intensive interviewing to learn how old people cope with change. She wanted to hear the words of the elderly themselves, for "the voices of individual old people can tell us much about the experience of being old."

Intensive interview studies do not reveal as directly as does participant observation the social context in which action is taken and opinions are formed. But like participant observation studies, intensive interviewing engages researchers more actively with subjects than does standard survey research. The researchers must listen to lengthy explanations, ask follow-up questions tailored to the preceding answers, and seek to learn about interrelated belief systems or personal approaches to things, rather than measure a limited set of variables. As a result, intensive interviews are often much longer than standardized interviews, sometimes as long as 15 hours, conducted in several different sessions. The intensive interview becomes more like a conversation between partners than between a researcher and a subject (Kaufman, 1986:22–23). Some call it "a conversation with a purpose" (Rossman & Rallis, 1998:126).

Intensive interviewers actively try to probe understandings and engage interviewees in a dialogue about what they mean by their comments. To prepare for this active interviewing, the interviewer should learn in advance about the setting to be studied. Preliminary discussion with key informants, inspection of written documents, and even a review of your own feelings about the setting can all help (Miller & Crabtree, 1999c:94–96). Robert Bellah, Richard Madsen, William Sullivan, Ann Swidler, and Steven Tipton (1985) elaborate on this aspect of intensive interviewing in a methodological appendix to their national best-seller about American individualism, *Habits of the Heart:*

> We did not, as in some scientific version of "Candid Camera," seek to capture their beliefs and actions without our subjects being aware of us. Rather, we sought to bring our preconceptions and questions into the conversation and to understand the answers we were receiving not only in terms of the language but also, so far as we could discover, in the lives of those we were talking with. Though we did not seek to impose our ideas on those with whom we talked . . . , we did attempt to uncover assumptions, to make explicit what the person we were talking to might rather have left implicit. The interview as we employed it was active, Socratic. (Bellah et al., 1985:304)

The intensive interview follows a preplanned outline of topics. It may begin with a few simple questions that gather background information while building rapport. These are often followed by a few general **"grand tour" questions** that are meant to elicit lengthy narratives (Miller & Crabtree, 1999c:96–99). Some projects may use relatively structured interviews,

Exhibit 9.6   The Saturation Point in Intensive Interviewing

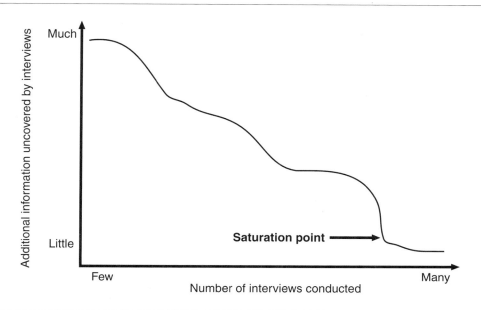

particularly when the focus is on developing knowledge about prior events or some narrowly defined topic. But more exploratory projects, particularly those aiming to learn about interviewees' interpretations of the world, may let each interview flow in a unique direction in response to the interviewee's experiences and interests (Kvale, 1996:3–5; Rubin & Rubin, 1995:6; Wolcott, 1995:113–114). In either case, qualitative interviewers must adapt nimbly throughout the interview, paying attention to nonverbal cues, expressions with symbolic value, and the ebb and flow of the interviewee's feelings and interests. "You have to be free to follow your data where they lead" (Rubin & Rubin, 1995:64).

Random selection is rarely used to select respondents for intensive interviews, but the selection method still must carefully be considered. If interviewees are selected in a haphazard manner, as by speaking just to those who happen to be available at the time that the researcher is on site, the interviews are likely to be of less value than when a more purposive selection strategy is used. Researchers should try to select interviewees who are knowledgeable about the subject of the interview, who are open to talking, and who represent the range of perspectives (Rubin & Rubin, 1995:65–92). Selection of new interviewees should continue, if possible, at least until the **saturation point** is reached, the point when new interviews seem to yield little additional information (see Exhibit 9.6). As new issues are uncovered, additional interviewees may be selected to represent different opinions about these issues.

Establishing and Maintaining a Partnership

Because intensive interviewing does not engage researchers as participants in subjects' daily affairs, the problems of entering the field are much reduced. However, the logistics of arranging long periods for personal interviews can still be pretty complicated. It also is important to establish rapport with subjects by considering in advance how they will react to the interview arrangements and by developing an approach that does not violate their standards for social behavior. Interviewees should be treated with respect, as knowledgeable partners whose time is valued (in other words, avoid coming late for appointments). A commitment to confidentiality should be stated and honored (Rubin & Rubin, 1995).

But the intensive interviewer's relationship with the interviewee is not an equal partnership, because the researcher seeks to gain certain types of information and strategizes throughout to maintain an appropriate relationship (Kvale, 1996:6). In the first few minutes of the interview, the goal is to show interest in the interviewee and to explain clearly what the purpose of the interview is (Kvale, 1996:128). During the interview, the interviewer should maintain an appropriate distance from the interviewee, one that doesn't violate cultural norms; the interviewer should maintain eye contact and not engage in distracting behavior. An appropriate pace is also important; pause to allow the interviewee to reflect, elaborate, and generally not feel rushed (Gordon, 1992). When an interview covers emotional or otherwise stressful topics, the interviewer should give the interviewee an opportunity to unwind at the interview's end (Rubin & Rubin, 1995:138).

Asking Questions and Recording Answers

Intensive interviewers must plan their main questions around an outline of the interview topic. The questions should generally be short and to the point. More details can then be elicited through nondirective probes (such as "Can you tell me more about that?" or "uh-huh," echoing the respondent's comment, or just maintaining a moment of silence). Follow-up questions can then be tailored to answers to the main questions.

Interviewers should strategize throughout an interview about how best to achieve their objectives while taking into account interviewees' answers. *Habits of the Heart* again provides a useful illustration:

[Coinvestigator Steven] Tipton, in interviewing Margaret Oldham [a pseudonym], tried to discover at what point she would take responsibility for another human being:

Q: So what are you responsible for?

A: I'm responsible for my acts and for what I do.

Q: Does that mean you're responsible for others, too?

A: No.

Q: Are you your sister's keeper?

A: No.

Q: Your brother's keeper?

A: No.

Q: Are you responsible for your husband?

A: I'm not. He makes his own decisions. He is his own person. He acts his own acts. I can agree with them, or I can disagree with them. If I ever find them nauseous enough, I have a responsibility to leave and not deal with it any more.

Q: What about children?

A: I . . . I would say I have a legal responsibility for them, but in a sense I think they in turn are responsible for their own acts. (Bellah et al., 1985:304)

Do you see how the interviewer actively encouraged the subject to explain what she meant by "responsibility"? This sort of active questioning undoubtedly did a better job of clarifying her concept of responsibility than a fixed set of questions would have.

Tape recorders commonly are used to record intensive and focus group interviews. Most researchers who have tape recorded interviews (including me) feel that they do not inhibit most interviewees and, in fact, are routinely ignored. The occasional respondent is very concerned with his or her public image and may therefore speak "for the tape recorder," but such individuals are unlikely to speak frankly in any research interview. In any case, constant note-taking during an interview prevents adequate displays of interest and appreciation by the interviewer and hinders the degree of concentration that results in the best interviews.

Of course, there are exceptions to every rule. Fenno presents a compelling argument for avoiding the tape recorder when interviewing public figures who are concerned with their public image:

My belief is that the only chance to get a nonroutine, nonreflexive interview [from many of the members of Congress] is to converse casually, pursuing targets of opportunity without the presence of a recording instrument other than myself. If [worse] comes to worst, they can always deny what they have said in person; on tape they leave themselves no room for escape. I believe they are not unaware of the difference. (Fenno, 1978:280)

Combining Participant Observation and Intensive Interviewing

Eric Hirsch (1990) used a combination of methodologies—including participant observation, intensive interviewing, and a standardized survey—to study the 1985 student movement that attempted to make Columbia University divest its stock in companies dealing with South Africa. The study illustrates the value of combining methods.

One point Hirsch tried to establish in his study was the importance of "consciousness raising" for social movements. Participant observation revealed that

consciousness-raising was done in a variety of small group settings, including dormitory rap sessions, forums, and teach-ins. Coverage of [Coalition for a Free South Africa] activities in the Columbia student newspaper and television reports on the violent repression of the anti-apartheid movement in South Africa increased student consciousness of apartheid and encouraged many students to support divestment. (Hirsch, 1990:247)

Hirsch also found an association between student questionnaire responses indicating "raised consciousness" about apartheid in South Africa and those indicating support for the divestment campaign. Comments from intensive interviews then deepened Hirsch's understanding of how consciousness was raised and the role that it played. Here's one example of a subject's observations:

> I remember in '83 when the [Columbia University Student] Senate voted to divest. I was convinced that students had voiced their opinion and had been able to convince the minority of administrators that what they wanted was a moral thing. It hadn't been a bunch of radical youths taking buildings and burning things down, to destroy. But rather, going through the system, and it seemed to me that for the first time in a really long time the system was going to work. And then I found out that it hadn't worked, and that just reaffirmed my feelings about how the system at Columbia really did work. (Hirsch, 1990:247)

Comments like these, combined with survey responses and Hirsch's own observations, provided a comprehensive picture of students' motivations.

FOCUS GROUPS

Focus groups are groups of unrelated individuals that are formed by a researcher and then led in group discussion of a topic for 1 to 2 hours. The researcher asks specific questions and guides the discussion to ensure that group members address these questions, but the resulting information is qualitative and relatively unstructured. Focus groups do not involve representative samples; instead, a few individuals are recruited for the group who have the time to participate, have some knowledge pertinent to the focus group topic, and share key characteristics with the target population.

Focus groups have their roots in the interviewing techniques developed in the 1930s by sociologists and psychologists who were dissatisfied with traditional surveys. Traditionally, in a questionnaire survey, subjects are directed to consider certain issues and particular response options in a predetermined order. The spontaneous exchange and development of ideas that characterize social life outside the survey situation is lost—and with it, some social scientists feared, the prospects for validity.

Focus groups were used by the military in World War II to investigate morale and then were popularized by the great American sociologist Robert K. Merton and two collaborators, Marjorie Fiske and Patricia Kendall, in *The Focused Interview* (1956). But marketing researchers were the first to adopt focus groups as a widespread methodology. Marketing researchers use focus groups to investigate likely popular reactions to possible advertising themes and techniques. Their success has prompted other social scientists to use focus groups to evaluate social programs and to assess social needs (Krueger, 1988:18–22).

Most focus groups involve 7 to 10 people, a number that facilitates discussion by all in attendance. Participants usually do not know one another, although some studies in organized settings may include friends or coworkers. Opinions differ on the value of using homogeneous versus heterogeneous participants. Homogeneous groups may be more convivial and willing to share feelings, but heterogeneous groups may stimulate more ideas (Brown, 1999:115–117). Of course, the characteristics of individuals that determine their inclusion are based on the researcher's conception of the target population for the study. Focus group leaders must begin the discussion by creating the expectation that all will participate and that the researcher will not favor any particular perspective or participant.

Focus groups are used to collect qualitative data, using open-ended questions posed by the researcher (or group leader). Thus a focused discussion mimics the natural process of forming and expressing opinions—and may give some sense of validity. The researcher, or group moderator, uses an interview guide, but the dynamics of group discussion often require changes in the order and manner in which different topics are addressed (Brown, 1999:120). No formal procedure exists for determining the generalizability of focus group answers, but the careful researcher should conduct at least several focus groups on the same topic and check for consistency in the findings. Some focus group experts advise conducting enough focus groups to reach the point of "saturation," when an additional focus group adds little new information to that which already has been generated (Brown, 1999:118).

Richard Krueger provides a good example of a situation in which focus groups were used effectively:

> [A] University recently launched a $100 million fund drive. The key aspect of the drive was a film depicting science and research efforts. The film was shown in over two dozen focus groups of alumni, with surprising results to University officials. Alumni simply did not like the film and instead were more attracted to supporting undergraduate humanistic education. (Krueger, 1988:33–37)

Focus groups are now used extensively in political campaigns, as a quick means of generating insight into voter preferences and reactions to possible candidate positions. For example, focus groups were used by Michigan Democratic legislators to determine why voters were turning away from them in 1985. Elizabeth Kolbert found that white, middle-class Democrats were shifting to the Republican Party because of their feelings about race:

> These Democratic defectors saw affirmative action as a direct threat to their own livelihoods, and they saw the black-majority city of Detroit as a sinkhole into which their tax dollars were disappearing. . . . [T]he participants listen[ed] to a quotation from Robert Kennedy exhorting whites to honor their "special obligation" to blacks. Virtually every participant in the four groups—37 in all—reacted angrily. (Kolbert, 1992:21)

Focus group methods share with other field research techniques an emphasis on discovering unanticipated findings and exploring hidden meanings. Although they do not provide a means for developing reliable, generalizable results (the traditional strong suits of survey research), focus groups can be an indispensable aid for developing hypotheses and survey questions, for investigating the meaning of survey results, and for quickly assessing the range of opinion about an issue.

ETHICAL ISSUES IN QUALITATIVE RESEARCH

Qualitative research can raise some complex ethical issues. No matter how hard the field researcher strives to study the social world naturally, leaving no traces, the very act of research itself imposes something "unnatural" on the situation. It is up to the researcher to identify and take responsibility for the consequences of her or his involvement. Five main ethical issues arise:

Voluntary participation. Ensuring that subjects are participating in a study voluntarily is not often a problem with intensive interviewing and focus group research, but it is often a point of contention in participant observation studies. Few researchers or institutional review boards are willing to condone covert participation because it offers no way to ensure that participation by the subjects is voluntary. Even when the researcher's role is more open, interpreting the standard of voluntary participation still can be difficult. Practically, much field research would be impossible if the participant observer were required to request permission of everyone having some contact, no matter how minimal, with a group or setting being observed. And should the requirement of voluntary participation apply equally to every member of an organization being observed? What if the manager consents, the workers are ambivalent, and the union says no? Requiring everyone's consent would limit participant observation research to only settings without serious conflicts of interest.

Subject well-being. Every field researcher should consider carefully before beginning a project how to avoid harm to subjects. It is not possible to avoid every theoretical possibility of harm nor to be sure that any project will cause no adverse consequences whatsoever to any individual. Some of the Cornerville men read Whyte's book and felt discomfited by it (others found it enlightening). Some police accused Van Maanen of damaging their reputations with his studies. But such consequences could follow from any research, even from any public discourse. Direct harm to the reputations or feelings of particular individuals is what researchers must carefully avoid. They can do so in part by maintaining the confidentiality of research subjects. They must also avoid adversely affecting the course of events while engaged in a setting. Whyte (1955:335–337) found himself regretting having recommended that a particular politician be allowed to speak to a social club he was observing, because the speech led to serious dissension in the club and strains between Whyte and some club members. These problems are rare in intensive interviewing and focus groups, but even there, researchers should try to identify negative feelings and help distressed subjects cope with their feelings through debriefing or referrals for professional help.

Identity disclosure. We already have considered the problems of identity disclosure, particularly in the case of covert participation. Current ethical standards require informed consent of research subjects and most would argue that this standard cannot be met in any meaningful way if researchers do not disclose fully their identity. But how much disclosure about the study is necessary and how hard should researchers try to make sure that their research purposes are understood? In field research on Codependents Anonymous, Leslie Irvine (1998) found that the emphasis on anonymity and the expectations for group discussion made it difficult to disclose her identity. Less-educated subjects may not readily comprehend what a researcher is or be able to weigh the possible consequences of the research for themselves. Should researchers inform subjects if the study's interests and foci change while it is in progress? Can a balance be struck between the disclosure of critical facts and a coherent research strategy?

Confidentiality. Field researchers normally use fictitious names for the characters in their reports, but doing so does not always guarantee confidentiality to their research subjects. Individuals in the setting studied may be able to identify those whose actions are described and may thus become privy to some knowledge about their colleagues or neighbors that had formerly been kept from them. Researchers should thus make every effort to expunge possible identifying material from published information and to alter unimportant aspects of a description when necessary to prevent identity disclosure. In any case, no field research project should begin if some participants clearly will suffer serious harm by being identified in project publications.

Online research. The large number of discussion groups and bulletin boards on the Internet has stimulated much research. Such research can violate the principles of voluntary participation and identity disclosure when researchers participate in discussions and record and analyze text, but do not identify themselves as researchers (Jesnadum, 2000).

These ethical issues cannot be evaluated independently. The final decision to proceed must be made after weighing the relative benefits and risks to participants. Few qualitative research projects will be barred by consideration of these ethical issues, however, except for those involving covert participation. The more important concern for researchers is to identify the ethically troublesome aspects of their proposed research and resolve them before the project begins and to act on new ethical issues as they come up during the project. Combining methods is often the best strategy.

CONCLUSIONS

Qualitative research allows the careful investigator to obtain a richer and more intimate view of the social world than with more structured methods. It is not hard to understand why so many qualitative studies have become classics in the social science literature. And the emphases in qualitative research on inductive reasoning and incremental understanding help to stimulate and inform other research approaches. Exploratory research to chart the dimensions of previously unstudied social settings and intensive investigations of the subjective meanings that motivate individual action are particularly well served by the techniques of participant observation, intensive interviewing, and focus groups.

The very characteristics that make qualitative research techniques so appealing restrict their use to a limited set of research problems. It is not possible to draw representative samples for study using participant observation, and for this reason the generalizability of any particular field study's results cannot really be known. Only the cumulation of findings from numerous qualitative studies permits confident generalization, but here again the time and effort required to collect and analyze the data make it unlikely that many field research studies will be replicated.

Even if qualitative researchers made more of an effort to replicate key studies, their notion of developing and grounding explanations inductively in the observations made in a particular setting would hamper comparison of findings. Measurement reliability is thereby hindered, as are systematic tests for the validity of key indicators and formal tests for causal connections.

In the final analysis, qualitative research involves a mode of thinking and investigating different from that used in experimental and survey research. Qualitative research is inductive and idiographic; experiments and surveys tend to be conducted in a deductive, quantitative, and nomothetic framework. Both approaches can help social scientists learn about the social world; the proficient researcher must be ready to use either. Qualitative data are often supplemented with counts of characteristics or activities. And as you have already seen, quantitative data are often enriched with written comments and observations, and focus groups have become a common tool of survey researchers seeking to develop their questionnaires. Thus the distinction between qualitative and quantitative research techniques is not always clear-cut, and combining methods is often a good idea.

KEY TERMS

Complete observation	Intensive (depth) interviewing
Complete participation	Jottings
Covert participation	Key informant
Experience sampling method (ESM)	Participant observation
Field notes	Qualitative method
Field research	Reactive effect
Focus group	Saturation point
Gatekeeper	Systematic observation
Grand tour questions	Theoretical sampling

HIGHLIGHTS

• Qualitative methods are most useful in exploring new issues, investigating hard-to-study groups, and determining the meaning people give to their lives and actions. In addition, most social research projects can be improved in some respects by taking advantage of qualitative techniques.

• Qualitative researchers tend to develop ideas inductively, try to understand the social context and sequential nature of attitudes and actions, and explore the subjective meanings that participants attach to events. They rely primarily on participant observation, intensive interviewing, and in recent years, focus groups.

• Participant observers may adopt one of several roles for a particular research project. Each role represents a different balance between observing and participating. Many field researchers prefer a moderate role, participating as well as observing in a group but acknowledging publicly the researcher role. Such a role avoids the ethical issues posed by covert participation while still allowing the insights into the social world derived from participating directly in it. The role that the participant observer chooses should be based on an evaluation of the problems likely to arise from reactive effects and the ethical dilemmas of covert participation.

• Systematic observation techniques quantify the observational process to allow more systematic comparison between cases and greater generalizability.

• Field researchers must develop strategies for entering the field, developing and maintaining relations in the field, sampling, and recording and analyzing data. Selection of sites or other units to study may reflect an emphasis on typical cases, deviant cases, and/or critical cases that can provide more information than others. Sampling techniques commonly used within sites or in selecting interviewees in field research include theoretical sampling, purposive sampling, snowball sampling, quota sampling, and in special circumstances, random selection with the experience sampling method.

• Recording and analyzing notes is a crucial step in field research. Jottings are used as brief reminders about events in the field, while daily logs are useful to chronicle the researcher's activities.

Detailed field notes should be recorded and analyzed daily. Analysis of the notes can guide refinement of methods used in the field and of the concepts, indicators, and models developed to explain what has been observed.

- Intensive interviews involve open-ended questions and follow-up probes, with specific question content and order varying from one interview to another. Intensive interviews can supplement participant observation data.

- Focus groups combine elements of participant observation and intensive interviewing. They can increase the validity of attitude measurement by revealing what people say when presenting their opinions in a group context, instead of the artificial one-on-one interview setting.

- Four ethical issues that should be given particular attention in field research concern voluntary participation, subject well-being, identity disclosure, and confidentiality. Qualitative research conducted online, with discussion groups or e-mail traffic, raises special concerns about voluntary participation and identity disclosure.

DISCUSSION QUESTIONS

1. The April 1992 issue of the *Journal of Contemporary Ethnography* is devoted to a series of essays reevaluating Whyte's classic field study, *Street Corner Society.* A social scientist interviewed some of the people described in Whyte's book and concluded that the researcher had made methodological and ethical errors. Whyte and others offer able rejoinders and further commentary. Reading the entire issue of this journal will improve your appreciation of the issues that field researchers confront.

2. Review the experiments and surveys described in previous chapters. Pick one, and propose a field research design that would focus on the same research question but with participant observation techniques in a local setting. Propose the role that you would play in the setting, along the participant observation continuum, and explain why you would favor this role. Describe the stages of your field research study, including your plans for entering the field, developing and maintaining relationships, sampling, and recording and analyzing data. Then discuss what you would expect your study to add to the findings resulting from the study described in the book.

3. Read and summarize one of the qualitative studies discussed in this chapter, or another classic study recommended by your instructor. Review and critique the study using the article review questions presented in Appendix B. What questions are answered by the study? What questions are raised for further investigation?

4. Write a short critique of the ethics of Whyte's or Van Maanen's study or of some field research that has been challenged as ethically questionable (Alfred, 1976, and Humphreys, 1970, are good choices). Read their books ahead of time to clarify the details, and then focus on four of the ethical guidelines presented in this chapter: voluntary participation, subject well-being, identity disclosure, and confidentiality. Conclude with a statement about the extent to which field researchers should be required to disclose their identities and the circumstances in which they should not be permitted to participate actively in the social life they study.

PRACTICE EXERCISES

1. Conduct a brief observational study in a public location on campus where students congregate. A cafeteria, a building lobby, or a lounge would be ideal. You can sit and observe, taking occasional notes unobtrusively, without violating any expectations of privacy. Observe for 30 minutes. Write up field notes, being sure to include a description of the setting and a commentary on your own behavior and your reactions to what you observed.

2. Develop an interview guide that focuses on a research question addressed in one of the studies in this book. Using this guide, conduct an intensive interview with one person who is involved with the topic in some way. Take only brief notes during the interview, and then write up as complete a record of the interview as you can immediately afterward. Turn in an evaluation of your performance as an interviewer and note-taker, together with your notes.

3. Read about focus groups in one of the references cited in this chapter. Then devise a plan for using a focus group to explore and explain student perspectives on some current event. How would you recruit students for the group? What types of students would you try to include? How would you introduce the topic and the method to the group? What questions would you ask? What problems would you anticipate, such as discord between focus group members or digressions from the chosen topic? How would you respond to these problems?

4. Find the Qualitative Research lesson in the interactive exercises on the CD-ROM. Answer the questions in this lesson in order to review the types of ethical issues that can arise in the course of participant observation research.

WEB EXERCISES

1. Go to the *Annual Review of Sociology*'s Web site by following the publications link at http://AnnualReviews.org. Search for articles that use qualitative methods as the primary method of gathering data on any one of the following subjects: child development/socialization; gender/sex roles; aging/gerontology. Enter "Qualitative AND Methods" in the subject field to begin this search. Review at least five articles and report on the specific method of field research used in each.

2. Go to the Social Science Information Gateway (SOSIG) at http://sosig.esrc.bris.ac.uk. Choose "Social Science General" and then "Social Science Methodology." Now choose three or four interesting sites to find out more about field research. Explore the sites to find out what information they provide regarding field research, what kinds of projects are being done that involve field research, and the purposes that specific field research methods are being used for.

3. You have been asked to do field research on the World Wide Web's impact on the socialization of children in today's world. The first part of the project involves your writing a compare and contrast report on the differences between how you and your generation were socialized as children and the way children today are being socialized. Collect your data by surfing the Web "as if you were a kid." The Web is your field and you are the field researcher.

4. Using any of the major search engines, explore the Web within the "Kids" or "Children" subject heading, keeping field notes on what you observe. Write a brief report based on the data you have collected. How has the Web impacted child socialization in comparison to when you were a child?

SPSS EXERCISES

The crosstabulations you examined in Chapter 8's SPSS exercises highlighted the strength of the association between attitudes related to race and support for capital punishment. In this chapter you will explore related issues.

1. Examine the association between race and support for capital punishment. From the menu, click:

Analyze\Descriptives\Crosstabs

In the Crosstabs window, set
Rows: CAPPUN

Columns: HHRACE
Cells: column percents

2. What is the association between race and support for capital punishment? How would you explain that association?

3. Now consider what might lead to variation in support for capital punishment among whites and blacks. Consider gun ownership (OWNGUN2), religious beliefs (FUND), attitudes about race (RACDIF1), education (EDUCR3), and political party identification (PARTYID3).

4. Generate crosstabs for the association of support for capital punishment with each of these variables, separately for blacks and whites. Follow the same procedures you used in Step 1, substituting the variables mentioned in Step 3 for HHRACE in Step 1. However, you must repeat the crosstabs request for blacks and whites. To do this, before you choose *Analyze,* select black respondents only. From the menu above the Data Editor window, select *Data,* then *Select cases.* Then from the Select cases window, select If condition is satisfied and create this expression:

If . . . HHRACE=1

After you have generated the crosstabs, go back and repeat the data selection procedures, ending with HHRACE=2.

5. Are the bases of support for capital punishment similar among blacks and whites? Discuss your findings.

6. Propose a focus group to explore these issues further. Identify the setting and sample for the study, and describe how you would carry out your focus group.

DEVELOPING A RESEARCH PROPOSAL

Add a qualitative component to your proposed study. You can choose to do this with a participant observation project or intensive interviewing. Pick the method that seems most likely to help answer the research question for the overall survey project.

1. For a participant observation component, propose an observational plan that would complement the overall survey project. Present in your proposal the following information about your plan: (a) choose a site and justify its selection in terms of its likely value for the research; (b) choose a role along the participation-observation continuum and justify your choice; (c) describe access procedures and note any likely problems; (d) discuss how you will develop and maintain relations in the site; (e) review any sampling issues; (f) present an overview of the way in which you will analyze the data you collect.

2. For an intensive interview component, propose a focus for the intensive interviews that you believe will add the most to findings from the survey project. Present in your proposal the following information about your plan: (a) present and justify a method for selecting individuals to interview; (b) write out three introductory biographical questions and five "grand tour" questions for your interview schedule; (c) list at least six different probes you may use; (d) present and justify at least two follow-up questions for one of your grand tour questions; (e) explain what you expect this intensive interview component to add to your overall survey project.

Chapter 10

EVALUATION RESEARCH

History of Evaluation Research

Evaluation Basics

Questions for Evaluation Research
Needs Assessment
Evaluability Assessment
Process Evaluation
Impact Analysis
Efficiency Analysis

Design Alternatives
Black Box Evaluation or Program Theory?
Researcher or Stakeholder Orientation
Quantitative or Qualitative Methods
Simple or Complex Outcomes

Ethics in Evaluation

Conclusions

D.A.R.E.: Drug Abuse Resistance Education. As you probably know, it's offered in elementary schools across America. For parents worried about drug abuse among youth, and for any concerned citizens, the program has immediate appeal. It brings a special police officer into the schools once a week to speak with classes about the hazards of drug abuse and to establish a direct link between local law enforcement and young people. You only have to check out bumper stickers or attend a few P.T.A. meetings to learn that it's a popular program.

And it is appealing. D.A.R.E. seems to improve relations between the schools and law enforcement and to create a positive image of the police in the eyes of students.

> It's a very positive program for kids . . . a way for law enforcement to interact with children in a nonthreatening fashion . . . DARE sponsored a basketball game. The middle school jazz band played . . . We had families there. . . . DARE officers lead activities at the [middle school] . . . Kids do woodworking and produce a play. (Taylor, 1999)

Yet when all is said and done, D.A.R.E. hasn't worked. It doesn't do what it was designed to do—lessen the use of illicit drugs among D.A.R.E. students, either while they are enrolled in the program or, more importantly, after they enter middle or high school. Research designed to evaluate D.A.R.E. using social science methods has repeatedly come to the same conclusion: Students who have participated in D.A.R.E. are no less likely to use illicit drugs than comparable students who have not participated in D.A.R.E. (Ringwalt et al., 1994).

If, like me, you have children who enjoyed D.A.R.E., or were yourself a D.A.R.E. student, this may seem like a depressing way to begin a chapter on **evaluation research.** Nonetheless, it drives home an important point: In order to know whether social programs work, or how they work, we have to evaluate them systematically and fairly, whether we personally like the program or not. And there's actually an optimistic conclusion to this introductory story: Evaluation research can make a difference. A new D.A.R.E. program has been designed to remedy the deficiencies identified by evaluation researchers (Toppo, 2002). This new program brings D.A.R.E. into a wider range of classes and integrates the program with regular instruction. And so, of course, it's now being evaluated, too.

In this chapter, you will read about a variety of social program evaluations as I introduce the evaluation research process, illustrate the different types of evaluation research, highlight alternative approaches, and review ethical concerns.

HISTORY OF EVALUATION RESEARCH

Evaluation research is not a method of data collection, like survey research or experiments, nor is it a unique component of research designs, like sampling or measurement. Instead, evaluation research is social research that is conducted for a distinctive purpose: to investigate social programs (such as substance abuse treatment programs, welfare programs, criminal justice programs, or employment and training programs). For each project, an evaluation researcher must select a research design and method of data collection that are useful for answering the particular research questions posed and appropriate for the particular program investigated.

So you can see why this chapter comes after those on experiments, surveys, and qualitative methods: When you review or plan evaluation research, you have to think about the research process as a whole and how different parts of that process can best be combined.

The development of evaluation research as a major enterprise followed on the heels of the expansion of the federal government during the Great Depression and World War II. Large Depression-era government outlays for social programs stimulated interest in monitoring program output, and the military effort in World War II led to some of the necessary review and contracting procedures for sponsoring evaluation research. In the 1960s, criminal justice researchers began to use experiments to test the value of different policies (Orr, 1999:24). New government social programs of the 1960s often came with evaluation requirements attached, and more than 100 contract research and development firms began operation in the United States between 1965 and 1975 (Dentler, 2002; Rossi & Freeman, 1989:34). The RAND Corporation expanded from its role as a U.S. Air Force planning unit into a major social research firm; SRI International spun off from Stanford University as a private firm; and Abt Associates in Cambridge, Massachusetts, begun in a garage in 1965, grew to employ more than 1,000 staff in 5 offices in the United States, Canada, and Europe. The World Bank and International Monetary Fund (IMF) also began to require evaluation of the programs they funded in other countries (Dentler, 2002:147).

The New Jersey Income Maintenance Experiment was the first large-scale, randomized experiment to test social policy in action. Designed in 1967, the New Jersey Experiment

Exhibit 10.1   Social Experiments Initiated, 1961–1995

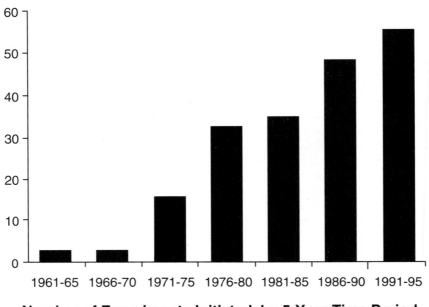

Number of Experiments Initiated, by 5-Year Time Period

Source: Orr, 1999:26, citing Greenberg & Shroder, 1997.

randomly assigned 1,300 families to different income support levels in order to test the impact of cash transfers to the working poor on their work effort. It was soon followed by even larger experiments to test other income maintenance questions, most notably the Seattle-Denver Income Maintenance Experiment (Orr, 1999:24–26). As Exhibit 10.1 illustrates, the number of social experiments like this continued to increase in subsequent years.

In the early 1980s, after this period of rapid growth, many evaluation research firms closed in tandem with the decline of many Great Society programs. However, the demand for evaluation research continues, due in part to government requirements. The Community Mental Health Act Amendments of 1975 (Public Law 94–63) required quality assurance (QA) reviews, which often involve evaluation-like activities (Patton, 2002:147–151), while the Government Performance and Results Act of 1993 required some type of evaluation of all government programs (Office of Management and the Budget, 2002). At century's end, the federal government was spending about $200 million annually on evaluating $400 billion in domestic programs, and the 30 major federal agencies had between them 200 distinct evaluation units (Boruch, 1997). In 1999, the new Governmental Accounting Standards Board urged that more attention be given to "service efforts and accomplishments" in standard government fiscal reports (Campbell, 2002).

The growth of evaluation research is also reflected in the social science community. The American Evaluation Association was founded in 1986 as a professional organization for evaluation researchers (merging two previous associations) and the publisher of an evaluation research journal. In 1999, evaluation researchers founded the Campbell Collaboration in order to publicize and encourage systematic review of evaluation research studies. Their online archive contained 10,449 reports on randomized evaluation studies (Davies, Petrosino, & Chalmers, 1999).

EVALUATION BASICS

Exhibit 10.2 illustrates the process of evaluation research as a simple systems model. First, clients, customers, students or some other persons or units—cases—enter the program as **inputs**. (You'll notice that this model treats programs like machines, with people functioning as raw materials to be processed.) Students may begin a new school program, welfare recipients may enroll in a new job training program, or crime victims may be sent to a victim advocate. Resources and staff required by a program are also program inputs.

Next, some service or treatment is provided to the cases. This may be attendance in a class, assistance with a health problem, residence in new housing, or receipt of special cash benefits. The **program process** may be simple or complicated, short or long, but it is designed to have some impact on the cases.

The direct product of the program's service delivery process is its **output.** Program outputs may include clients served, case managers trained, food parcels delivered, or arrests made. The program outputs may be desirable in themselves, but they primarily serve to indicate that the program is operating.

Program **outcomes** indicate the impact of the program on the cases that have been processed. Outcomes can range from improved test scores or higher rates of job retention to fewer criminal offenses and lower rates of poverty. Any social program is likely to have

Exhibit 10.2 A Model of Evaluation

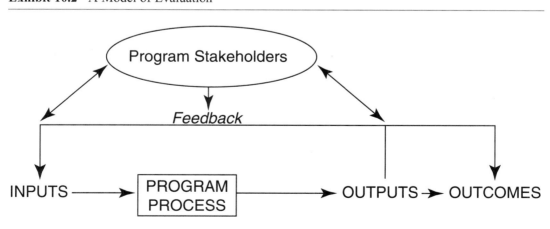

Source: Adapted from Martin, Lawrence L. and Peter M. Kettner. 1996. *Measuring the Performance of Human Service Programs.* Thousand Oaks, CA: Sage. Used with permission.

multiple outcomes, some intended and some unintended, some positive and others that are viewed as negative.

Variation in both outputs and outcomes in turn influence the inputs to the program through a **feedback** process. If not enough clients are being served, recruitment of new clients may increase. If too many negative side effects result from a trial medication, the trials may be limited or terminated. If a program does not appear to lead to improved outcomes, clients may go elsewhere.

Evaluation research is simply a systematic approach to feedback: It strengthens the feedback loop through credible analyses of program operations and outcomes. Evaluation research also broadens this loop to include connections to parties outside of the program itself. A funding agency or political authority may mandate the research, outside experts may be brought in to conduct the research, and the evaluation research findings may be released to the public, or at least funders, in a formal report.

The evaluation process as a whole, and feedback in particular, can be understood only in relation to the interests and perspectives of program stakeholders. **Stakeholders** are those individuals and groups who have some basis of concern with the program. They might be clients, staff, managers, funders, or the public. The board of a program or agency, the parents or spouses of clients, the foundations that award program grants, the auditors who monitor program spending, the members of Congress—each is a potential stakeholder, and each has an interest in the outcome of any program evaluation. Some may fund the evaluation, some may provide research data, and some may review, or even approve, the research report (Martin & Kettner, 1996:3). Who the program stakeholders are and what role they play in the program evaluation will have tremendous consequences for the research.

Inputs   Resources, raw materials, clients, and staff that go into a program.

Program process   The complete treatment or service delivered by the program.

Outputs   The services delivered or new products produced by the program process.

Outcomes   The impact of the program process on the cases processed.

Feedback   Information about service delivery system outputs, outcomes, or operations that is available to any program inputs.

Stakeholders   Individuals and groups who have some basis of concern with the program.

Can you see the difference between evaluation research and traditional social science research (Posavac & Carey, 1997)? Unlike explanatory social science research, evaluation research is not designed to test the implications of a social theory; the basic issue is often, What is the program's impact? Process evaluation, for instance, often uses qualitative methods like traditional social science does, but unlike exploratory research, the goal is not to induce a broad theoretical explanation for what is discovered. Instead, the question is, How does the program do what it does? Unlike social science research, the researchers cannot design evaluation studies simply in accord with the highest scientific standards and the most important research questions; instead, it is program stakeholders who set the agenda. But there is no sharp boundary between the two. In their attempt to explain how and why the program has an impact, and whether the program is needed, evaluation researchers often bring social theories into their projects, but for immediately practical aims.

QUESTIONS FOR EVALUATION RESEARCH

Evaluation projects can focus on several questions related to the operation of social programs and the impact they have:

- Is the program needed?
- Can the program be evaluated?
- How does the program operate?
- What is the program's impact?
- How efficient is the program?

The specific methods used in an evaluation research project depend in part on which of these foci the project has.

Needs Assessment

Is a new program needed or an old one still required? Is there a need at all? A **needs assessment** attempts to answer these questions with systematic, credible evidence. Need may be assessed by social indicators such as the poverty rate or the level of home ownership, by interviews of such local experts as school board members or team captains, by surveys of populations in need, or by focus groups with community residents (Rossi & Freeman, 1989).

It is not as easy as it sounds (Posavac & Carey, 1997). Whose definitions or perceptions should be used to shape our description of the level of need? How will we deal with ignorance of need? How can we understand the level of need without understanding the social context from which that level of need emerges? (Short answer to that one: We can't!) What, after all, does "need" mean in the abstract? We won't really understand what the level of need is until we develop plans for implementing a program in response to the identified needs.

The results of the Boston McKinney Project reveal the importance of taking a multidimensional approach to the investigation of need. The Boston McKinney Project evaluated the merits of providing formerly homeless mentally ill persons with staffed group housing as compared to individual housing (Goldfinger et al., 1997). In a sense, you can think of the whole experiment as involving an attempt to answer the question, What type of housing do these persons "need"? Goldfinger and colleagues (including myself) first examined this question at the start of the project, by asking two clinicians to estimate which of the two housing alternatives would be best for each project participant (Goldfinger & Schutt, 1996) and by asking each participant which type of housing they wanted (Schutt & Goldfinger, 1996).

Exhibit 10.3 displays the findings. Clinicians recommended staffed group housing for 69% of the participants, whereas most of the participants (78%) sought individual housing. In fact, there was no correspondence between the housing recommendations of the clinicians and the

Exhibit 10.3   Type of Residence: Preferred and Recommended

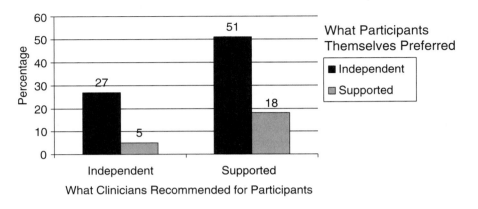

Source: Based on Goldfinger & Schutt, 1996.

housing preferences of the participants (who did not know what the clinicians had recommended for them). So, which perspective reveals the level of "need" for staffed group housing as opposed to individual housing?

Yet another perspective on housing needs is introduced by the project's outcomes. Individuals assigned to the group housing were somewhat more successful in retaining their housing than were those who were assigned to individual housing (Goldfinger et al., 1999). So does this reveal that these homeless mentally ill persons "needed" group housing more than they needed individual housing, in spite of their preferences? What should we make of the fact that participants with the stronger preferences for individual housing were more likely to lose their housing during the project, whereas the participants whom the clinicians had rated as ready for independent living were less likely to lose their housing? And what should we make of the fact that whether or not participants received the type of housing the clinicians recommended or that they themselves preferred made no difference to the likelihood of their losing their housing during the project? Does this mean that neither initial preferences nor clinician recommendations tell us about "need" for one or the other type of housing, only about the risk of losing whatever housing they were assigned to?

The methodological lesson here is that in needs assessment, as in other forms of evaluation research, it is a good idea to use multiple indicators. You can also see that there is no absolute definition of "need" in this situation, nor is there likely to be in any but the most simplistic evaluation projects. A good evaluation researcher will do his or her best to capture different perspectives on need and then to help others make sense of the results.

A wonderful little tale, popular with evaluation researchers, reveals the importance of thinking creatively about what people "need":

The manager of a 20-story office building had received many complaints about the slowness of the elevators. He hired an engineering consultant to propose a solution. The consultant measured traffic flow and elevator features and proposed replacing the old elevators with new ones, which could shave 20 seconds off the average waiting time. The only problem: It cost $100,000. A second consultant proposed adding 2 additional elevators, for a total wait time reduction of 35 seconds and a cost of $150,000. Neither alternative was affordable. A third consultant was brought in. He looked around for a few days and announced that the problem was not really the waiting times, but boredom. For a cost of less than $1000, the manager had large mirrors installed next to the elevators so people could primp and observe themselves while waiting for an elevator. The result: no more complaints. Problem solved. (Witkin & Altschuld, 1995)

Evaluability Assessment

Evaluation research will be pointless if the program itself cannot be evaluated. Yes, some type of study is always possible, but a study specifically to identify the effects of a particular program may not be possible within the available time and resources. So researchers may conduct an **evaluability assessment** to learn this in advance, rather than expend time and effort on a fruitless project.

Why might a social program not be evaluable?

- Management only wants to have its superior performance confirmed and does not really care whether the program is having its intended effects. This is a very common problem.
- Staff are so alienated from the agency that they don't trust any attempt sponsored by management to check on their performance.
- Program personnel are just "helping people" or "putting in time" without any clear sense of what the program is trying to achieve.
- The program is not clearly distinct from other services delivered from the agency, and so can't be evaluated by itself. (Patton, 2002:164)

An evaluability assessment can help to solve the problems identified. Discussion with program managers and staff can result in changes in program operations. The evaluators may use the evaluability assessment to "sell" the evaluation to participants and sensitize them to the importance of clarifying their goals and objectives. Knowledge about the program gleaned through the evaluability assessment can be used to refine evaluation plans.

Because they are preliminary studies to "check things out," evaluability assessments often rely on qualitative methods. Program managers and key staff may be interviewed in depth or program sponsors may be asked about the importance they attach to different goals. These assessments may also have an "action research" aspect, because the researcher presents the findings to program managers and encourages changes in program operations.

Process Evaluation

What actually happens in a social program? In the New Jersey Income Maintenance Experiment, some welfare recipients received higher payments than others (Kershaw & Fair, 1976). Simple enough, and not too difficult to verify that the right people received the intended treatment. In the Minneapolis experiment on the police response to domestic violence (Sherman & Berk, 1984), some individuals accused of assaulting their spouses were arrested, whereas others were just warned. This is a little bit more complicated, because the severity of the warning might have varied between police officers and, to minimize the risk of repeat harm, police officers were allowed to override the experimental assignment. In order to identify the extent of variation from the intended experimental design, the researchers would have had to keep track of the treatments delivered to each accused spouse and collect some information on what officers actually did when they warned an accused spouse. This would be process analysis or **process evaluation**—research to investigate the process of service delivery.

Process evaluation is even more important when more complex programs are evaluated. Many social programs comprise multiple elements and are delivered over an extended period of time, often by different providers in different areas. Due to this complexity, it is quite possible that the program as delivered is not the same for all program recipients, nor consistent with the formal program design.

The evaluation of D.A.R.E. by Research Triangle Institute researchers Christopher Ringwalt and colleagues (1994:7) included a process evaluation with three objectives:

- Assess the organizational structure and operation of representative D.A.R.E. programs nationwide.
- Review and assess factors that contribute to the effective implementation of D.A.R.E. programs nationwide.
- Assess how D.A.R.E. and other school-based drug prevention programs are tailored to meet the needs of specific populations.

The process evaluation (they called it an "implementation assessment") was an ambitious research project in itself, with site visits, informal interviews, discussions, and surveys of D.A.R.E. program coordinators and advisors. These data indicated that D.A.R.E. was operating as designed and was running relatively smoothly. As shown in Exhibit 10.4, drug prevention coordinators in D.A.R.E. school districts rated the program components as much more satisfactory than did coordinators in school districts with other types of alcohol and drug prevention programs.

Process evaluation also can be used to identify the specific aspects of the service delivery process that have an impact. This, in turn, will help to explain why the program has an effect and which conditions are required for these effects. (In Chapter 6, I described this as identifying the causal mechanism.) Implementation problems identified in site visits

Exhibit 10.4   Components of D.A.R.E. and Other Alcohol and Drug Prevention Programs Rated as Very Satisfactory (%)

Components	D.A.R.E. Program (N = 222)	Other AOD Programs (N = 406)
Curriculum	67.5	34.2
Teaching	69.7	29.8
Administrative Requirements	55.7	23.1
Receptivity of Students	76.5	34.6
Effects on Students	63.2	22.8

Source: Ringwalt et al., 1994:58.

included insufficient numbers of officers to carry out the program as planned and a lack of Spanish-language D.A.R.E. books in a largely Hispanic school. Classroom observations indicated engaging presentations and active student participation (Ringwalt et al., 1994:58).

Process evaluation   Evaluation research that investigates the process of service delivery.

Process analysis of this sort can also help to show how apparently unambiguous findings may be incorrect. The apparently disappointing results of the Transitional Aid Research Project (TARP) provide an instructive lesson of this sort. TARP was a social experiment designed to determine whether financial aid during the transition from prison to the community would help released prisoners to find employment and avoid returning to crime. Two thousand participants in Georgia and Texas were randomized to receive a particular level of benefits over a particular period of time, or no benefits (the control group). Initially, it seemed that the payments had no effect: The rate of subsequent arrests for both property and nonproperty crimes weren't affected by TARP treatment condition.

But this wasn't all there was to it. Peter Rossi tested a more elaborate causal model of TARP effects that is summarized in Exhibit 10.5 (Chen, 1990:210). Participants who received TARP payments had more income to begin with, and so had more to lose if they were arrested; therefore they were less likely to commit crimes. However, TARP payments also created a disincentive to work and therefore increased the time available in which to commit crimes. Thus, the positive direct effect of TARP (more to lose) was cancelled out by its negative indirect effect (more free time).

The term **formative evaluation** may be used instead of process evaluation when the evaluation findings are used to help shape and refine the program (Rossi & Freeman, 1989). Formative evaluation procedures that are incorporated into the initial development of

Exhibit 10.5   Model of TARP Effects

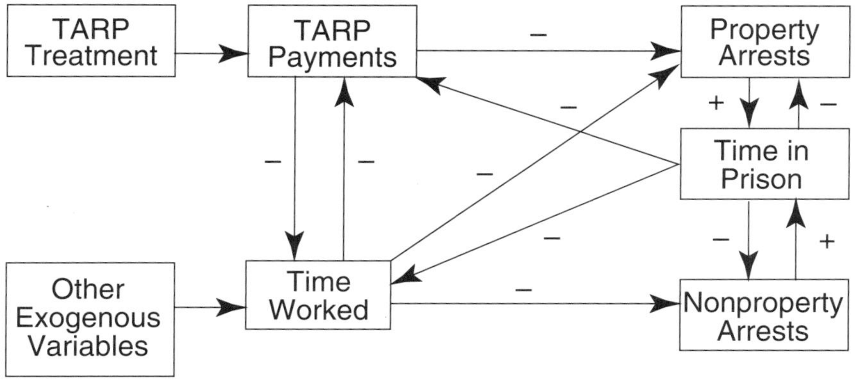

Source: From Chen, Huey-Tsyh, 1990. *Theory-Driven Evaluations.* Thousand Oaks, CA: Sage. Used with permission.

the service program can specify the treatment process and lead to changes in recruitment procedures, program delivery, or measurement tools (Patton, 2002:220).

Formative evaluation   Process evaluation that is used to shape and refine program operations.

You can see the "formative" element in the following government report on the performance of the Health Care Finance Administration (HCFA) (U.S. Government Accounting Office, 2001:7).

> While HCFA's performance report and plan indicate that it is making some progress toward achieving its Medicare program integrity outcome, progress is difficult to measure because of continual goal changes that are sometimes hard to track or that are made with insufficient explanation. Of the five fiscal year 2000 program integrity goals it discussed, HCFA reported that three were met, a fourth unmet goal was revised to reflect a new focus, and performance data for the fifth will not be available until mid-2001. HCFA plans to discontinue three of these goals. Although the federal share of Medicaid is projected to be $124 billion in fiscal year 2001, HCFA had no program integrity goal for Medicaid for fiscal year 2000. HCFA has since added a developmental goal concerning Medicaid payment accuracy.

Process evaluation can employ a wide range of indicators. Program coverage can be monitored through program records, participant surveys, community surveys, or utilizers versus dropouts and ineligibles. Service delivery can be monitored through service records completed by program staff, a management information system maintained by program administrators, or reports by program recipients (Rossi & Freeman, 1989).

Qualitative methods are often a key component of process evaluation studies because they can be used to elucidate and understand internal program dynamics—even those that were not anticipated (Patton, 2002:159; Posavac & Carey, 1997). Qualitative researchers may develop detailed descriptions of how program participants engage with each other, how the program experience varies for different people, and how the program changes and evolves over time.

Impact Analysis

The core questions of evaluation research are, Did the program work? Did it have the intended result? This part of the research is variously called **impact analysis, impact evaluation,** or **summative evaluation.** Formally speaking, impact analysis compares what happened after a program with what would have happened had there been no program.

Impact evaluation (or analysis)   The extent to which a treatment or other service has an effect. Also known as *summative evaluation*.

Think of the program—a new strategy for combating domestic violence, an income supplement, whatever—as an independent variable, and the result it seeks as a dependent variable. The D.A.R.E. program (independent variable), for instance, tries to reduce drug use (dependent variable). When the program is present, we expect less drug use. In a more elaborate study, we might have multiple values of the independent variable; for instance, we might look at "no program," "D.A.R.E. program," and "other drug/alcohol education" conditions, and compare the results of each.

As in other areas of research, an experimental design is the preferred method for maximizing internal validity—that is, for making sure your causal claims about program impact are justified. Cases are assigned randomly to one or more experimental treatment groups and to a control group so that there is no systematic difference between the groups at the outset (see Chapter 7). The goal is to achieve a fair, unbiased test of the program itself, so that the judgment about the program's impact is not influenced by differences between the types of people who are in the different groups. It can be a difficult goal to achieve, because the usual practice in social programs is to let people decide for themselves whether they want to enter a program or not, and also to establish eligibility criteria that ensure that people who enter the program are different from those who do not (Boruch, 1997). In either case, a selection bias is introduced.

Impact analyses that do not use an experimental design can still provide useful information and may be all that is affordable, conceptually feasible, or ethically permissible in many circumstances. But sometimes researchers are able to use true experimental designs in which individuals are assigned randomly to either the program or to some other condition. Robert Drake, Gregory McHugo, Deborah Becker, William Anthony, and Robin Clark (1996) evaluated the impact of two different approaches to providing employment services for people diagnosed with severe mental disorders, using a randomized experimental design. One approach, group skills training (GST), emphasizes pre-employment skills training and uses separate agencies to provide vocational and mental health services. The other approach, individual placement and support (IPS), provides vocational and mental health services in a single program and places people directly into jobs without pre-employment skills training. The researchers hypothesized that GST participants would be more likely to obtain jobs during the 18-month study period than would IPS participants.

Their experimental design is depicted in Exhibit 10.6. Cases were assigned randomly to the two groups, and then:

1. Both groups received a pretest (assessment of employment status).

2. One group received the experimental intervention (GST), and the other received the IPS approach.

3. Both groups received three posttests (about employment status), at 6, 12, and 18 months.

Contrary to the researchers' hypothesis, the IPS participants were twice as likely to obtain a competitive job as the GST participants. The IPS participants also worked more hours and earned more total wages. Although this was not the outcome Drake et al. had anticipated, it was valuable information for policy makers and program planners—and the study was rigorously experimental.

Of course, program impact may also be evaluated with quasi-experimental designs (see Chapter 7) or survey or field research methods, without a randomized experimental design. But if current participants who are already in a program are compared to nonparticipants, it is unlikely that the treatment group will be comparable to the control group. Participants will probably be a selected group, different at the outset from nonparticipants. As a result, causal

Exhibit 10.6 Randomized Comparative Change Design: Employment Services for People With Severe Mental Disorders

Key: R = Random assignment
O = Observation (employment status at pretest or posttest)
X = Experimental treatment

	O_1	X	O_2	O_3	O_4
Experimental Group	Pretest	Preemployment skills training	Posttest at 6 months	Posttest at 12 months	Posttest at 18 months
Comparison Group	Pretest		Posttest at 6 months	Posttest at 12 months	Posttest at 18 months

R (branches to Experimental Group and Comparison Group)

Source: From Drake, McHugo, Becker, Anthony, and Clark, 1996, 64:391–399. Used with permission.

conclusions about program impact will be on much shakier ground. For instance, when a study at New York's maximum-security prison for women found that "Income Education [i.e., classes] Is Found to Lower Risk of New Arrest," the conclusions were immediately suspect: The research design did not ensure that the women who enrolled in the prison classes were the same as those who were not, "leaving open the possibility that the results were due, at least in part, to self-selection, with the women most motivated to avoid reincarceration being the ones who took the college classes" (Lewin, 2001b).

Impact analysis is an important undertaking that fully deserves the attention it has been given in government program funding requirements. However, you should realize that more rigorous evaluation designs are less likely to conclude that a program has the desired effect; as the standard of proof goes up, success is harder to demonstrate. The prevalence of "null findings" (or "we can't be sure it works") has led to a bit of gallows humor among evaluation researchers.

The Output/Outcome/Downstream Impact Blues

Donors often say,
And this is a fact
Get out there and show us
Your impact
You must change people's lives
And help us take the credit
Or next time you want funding
You just might not get it.

So donors wake up
From your impossible dream
You drop in your funding
A long way upstream
The waters they flow,
They mingle, they blend
So how can you take credit
For what comes out in the end?

—Terry Smutylo, Director
Evaluation International Development Research Centre,
Ottawa, Canada
(Reprinted in Patton, 2002:154)

Efficiency Analysis

Whatever the program's benefits, are they sufficient to offset the program's costs? Are the taxpayers getting their money's worth? What resources are required by the program? These efficiency questions can be the primary reason that funders require evaluation of the programs they fund. As a result, **efficiency analysis,** which compares program effects to costs, is often a necessary component of an evaluation research project.

Efficiency analysis   A type of evaluation research that compares program costs to program effects. It can be either a cost-benefit analysis or a cost-effectiveness analysis.

Cost-benefit analysis   A type of evaluation research that compares program costs to the economic value of program benefits.

Cost-effectiveness analysis   A type of evaluation research that compares program costs to actual program outcomes.

A **cost-benefit analysis** must identify the specific costs and benefits that will be studied, which requires in turn that the analyst identify whose perspective will be used in order to determine what can be considered a benefit rather than a cost. Program clients will have a different perspective on these issues than do taxpayers or program staff. Exhibit 10.7 lists factors that can be considered costs or benefits in an employment and training program, from the standpoint of program participants, the rest of society, and the society as a whole (the combination of program participants and the rest of society) (Orr, 1999:224). Note that some anticipated impacts of the program, on welfare benefits and wage subsidies, are considered a cost to one group and a benefit to the other, whereas some are not relevant to one of the groups.

Once potential costs and benefits have been identified, they must be measured. It is a need highlighted in recent government programs (Campbell, 2002:1):

> The Governmental Accounting Standards Board's (GASB) mission is to establish and improve standards of accounting and financial reporting for state and local governments in the United States. In June 1999, the GASB issued a major revision to current reporting requirements ("Statement 34"). The new reporting will provide information that citizens and other users can utilize to gain an understanding of the financial position and cost of programs for a government and a descriptive management's discussion and analysis to assist in understanding a government's financial results.

In addition to measuring services and their associated costs, a cost-benefit analysis must be able to make some type of estimation of how clients benefited from the program. Normally, this will involve a comparison of some indicators of client status before and after clients received program services, or between clients who received program services and a comparable group who did not.

A recent study of therapeutic communities provides a clear illustration. A therapeutic community is a method for treating substance abuse in which abusers participate in an intensive, structured living experience with other addicts who are attempting to stay sober. Because the

Exhibit 10.7 Conceptual Framework for Cost-Benefit Analysis of an Employment and Training Program

Costs/Benefits	Perspective of Program Participants	Perspective of Rest of Society	Perspective of Entire Society*
Costs			
Operational costs of the program	0	–	–
Forgone leisure and home production	–	0	–
Benefits			
Earnings gains	+	0	+
Reduced costs of nonexperimental services	0	+	+
Transfers			
Reduced welfare benefits	–	+	0
Wage subsidies	+	–	0
Net benefits	+/–	+/–	+/–

Key: – = program costs; + = program benefits; +/– = program costs and benefits; 0 = no program costs or benefits. * Entire society = program participants + rest of society.

Source: Orr, 1999:224, Table 6.5.

treatment involves residential support as well as other types of services, it can be quite costly. Are those costs worth it?

Sacks et al. (2002) conducted a cost-benefit analysis of a modified therapeutic community (TC). Three hundred and forty-two homeless mentally ill chemical abusers were randomly assigned to either a TC or a "treatment-as-usual" comparison group. Employment status, criminal activity, and utilization of health care services were each measured for the 3 months prior to entering treatment and the 3 months after treatment. Earnings from employment in each period were adjusted for costs incurred by criminal activity and utilization of health care services.

Was it worth it? The average cost of TC treatment for a client was $20,361. In comparison, the economic benefit (based on earnings) to the average TC client was $305,273, which declined to $273,698 after comparing post- to pre-program earnings, but was still $253,337 even after adjustment for costs. The resulting benefit-cost ratio was 13:1, although this ratio declined to only 5.2:1 after further adjustments (for cases with extreme values). Nonetheless, the TC program studied seems to have had a substantial benefit relative to its costs.

DESIGN ALTERNATIVES

Once we have decided on, or identified, the goal or focus for a program evaluation, there are still important decisions to be made about how to design the specific evaluation project. The most important decisions are the following:

- *Black box or program theory*—Do we care how the program gets results?
- *Researcher or stakeholder orientation*—Whose goals matter most?
- *Quantitative or qualitative methods*—Which methods provide the best answers?
- *Simple or complex outcomes*—How complicated should the findings be?

Black Box Evaluation or Program Theory?

The "meat and potatoes" of most evaluation research involves determining whether a program has the intended effect. If the effect occurred, the program "worked"; if the effect didn't occur, then, some would say, the program should be abandoned or redesigned. In this approach, the process by which a program has an effect on outcomes is often treated as a **black box**—that is, the focus of the evaluation researcher is on whether cases seem to have changed as a result of their exposure to the program, between the time they entered the program as inputs and when they exited the program as outputs (Chen, 1990). The assumption is that program evaluation requires only the test of a simple input/output model, like that shown in Exhibit 10.2. There may be no attempt to open the black box of the program process.

But there is good reason to open the black box and investigate how the process works (or doesn't work). Consider recent research on welfare-to-work programs. The Manpower Demonstration Research Corporation reviewed findings from research on these programs in Florida, Minnesota, and Canada. In each location, adolescents with parents in a welfare-to-work program were compared to a control group of teenagers whose parents were on welfare but were not enrolled in welfare-to-work. In all three locations, teenagers in the welfare-to-work families actually did worse in school than those in the control group—troubling findings.

But why? Why did requiring welfare mothers to work hurt their children's schoolwork? Unfortunately, because the researchers had not investigated program process—had not "opened the black box"—we can't know for sure. Martha Zaslow, an author of the resulting research report, speculated (Lewin, 2001a:A16):

> parents in the programs might have less time and energy to monitor their adolescents' behavior once they were employed. . . . under the stress of working, they might adopt harsher parenting styles . . . the adolescents' assuming more responsibilities at home when parents got jobs was creating too great a burden.

But as Ms. Zaslow admitted (Lewin, 2001a:A16), "We don't know exactly what's causing these effects, so it's really hard to say, at this point, what will be the long-term effects on these kids."

If an investigation of program process is conducted, a **program theory** may be developed. A program theory describes what has been learned about how the program has its effect. When a researcher has sufficient knowledge before the investigation begins, outlining a program theory can help to guide the investigation of program process in the most productive directions. This is termed a **theory-driven evaluation.**

A program theory specifies how the program is expected to operate and identifies which program elements are operational (Chen, 1990:32). In addition, a program theory specifies how a program is to produce its effects and so improves understanding of the relationship between the independent variable (the program) and the dependent variable (the outcome or

Exhibit 10.8   The Program Theory for a Treatment Program for Homeless Alcoholics

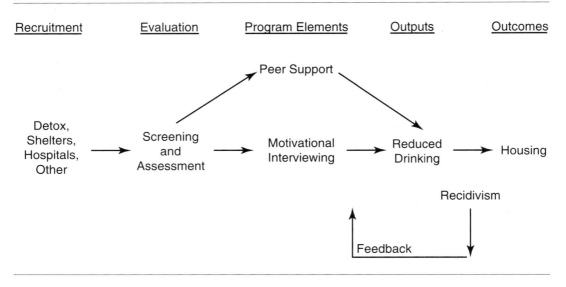

outcomes). For example, Exhibit 10.8 illustrates the theory for an alcoholism treatment program. It shows that persons entering the program are expected to respond to the combination of motivational interviewing and peer support. A program theory can also decrease the risk of failure when the program is transported to other settings, because it will help to identify the conditions required for the program to have its intended effect.

> ***Program theory***   A descriptive or prescriptive model of how a program operates and produces effects.

Program theory can be either descriptive or prescriptive (Chen, 1990). Descriptive theory specifies what impacts are generated and how they occur. It suggests a causal mechanism, including intervening factors, and the necessary context for the effects. Descriptive theories are generally empirically based. On the other hand, prescriptive theory specifies what ought to be done by the program and is not actually tested. Prescriptive theory specifies how to design or implement the treatment, what outcomes should be expected, and how performance should be judged. Comparison of the descriptive and prescriptive theories of the program can help to identify implementation difficulties and incorrect understandings that can be corrected (Patton, 2002:162–164).

Researcher or Stakeholder Orientation

Whose prescriptions specify how the program should operate, what outcomes it should try to achieve, or who it should serve? Most social science research assumes that the researcher specifies the research questions, the applicable theory or theories, and the outcomes to be investigated. Social science research results are most often reported in a professional journal or at professional conferences where scientific standards determine how the research is received. In program evaluation, however, the research question is often set by the program sponsors or the government agency that is responsible for reviewing the program. In consulting projects for businesses, the client—a manager, perhaps, or a division president—decides what question researchers will study. It is to these authorities that research findings are reported. Most often this authority also specifies the outcomes to be investigated. The first evaluator of the evaluation research is the funding agency, then, not the professional social science community. Evaluation research is research for a client, and its results may directly affect the services, treatments, or even punishments (in the case of prison studies, for example) that program users receive. In this case, the person who pays the piper gets to call the tune.

Should the evaluation researcher insist on designing the evaluation project and specifying its goals or should she accept the suggestions and adopt the goals of the funding agency? What role should the preferences of program staff or clients play? What responsibility does the evaluation researcher have to politicians and taxpayers when evaluating government-funded programs? The different answers that various evaluation researchers have given to these questions are reflected in different approaches to evaluation (Chen, 1990:66–68).

Stakeholder approaches encourage researchers to be responsive to program stakeholders. Issues for study are to be based on the views of people involved with the program, and reports are to be made to program participants (Shadish, Cook, & Levitan, 1991:275–276). The program theory is developed by the researcher to clarify and develop the key stakeholders' theory of the program (Shadish, Cook, & Levitan, 1991:254–255). In one stakeholder approach, termed *utilization-focused evaluation,* the evaluator forms a task force of program stakeholders who help to shape the evaluation project so that they are most likely to use its results (Patton, 2002:171–175). In evaluation research termed *action research* or *participatory research,* program participants are engaged with the researchers as co-researchers and help to design, conduct, and report the research. One research approach that has been termed *appreciative inquiry* eliminates the professional researcher altogether in favor of a structured dialogue about needed changes among program participants themselves (Patton, 2002:177–185).

Egon Guba and Yvonna Lincoln (1989:11) argue for evaluations oriented toward stakeholders in their book, *Fourth Generation Evaluation:*

> [T]he stakeholders and others who may be drawn into the evaluation are welcomed as equal partners in every aspect of design, implementation, interpretation, and resulting action of an evaluation—that is, they are accorded a full measure of political parity and control. . . . determining what questions are to be asked and what information is to be collected on the basis of stakeholder inputs.

Social science approaches emphasize the importance of researcher expertise and maintenance of some autonomy in order to develop the most trustworthy, unbiased program evaluation. It is assumed that "evaluators cannot passively accept the values and views of the other stakeholders" (Chen, 1990:78). Evaluators who adopt this approach derive a program theory from information they obtain on how the program operates and extant social science theory and knowledge, not from the views of stakeholders. In one somewhat extreme form of this approach, *goal-free evaluation,* researchers do not even permit themselves to learn what goals the program stakeholders have for the program. Instead, the researcher assesses and then compares the needs of participants to a wide array of program outcomes (Scriven, 1972b). The goal-free evaluator wants to see the unanticipated outcomes and to remove any biases caused by knowing the program goals in advance.

Of course, there are disadvantages to both stakeholder and social science approaches to program evaluation. If stakeholders are ignored, researchers may find that participants are uncooperative, that their reports are unused, and that the next project remains unfunded. On the other hand, if social science procedures are neglected, standards of evidence will be compromised, conclusions about program effects will likely be invalid, and results are unlikely to be generalizable to other settings. These equally undesirable possibilities have led to several attempts to develop more integrated approaches to evaluation research.

Integrative approaches attempt to cover issues of concern to both stakeholders and evaluators, and to include stakeholders in the group from which guidance is routinely sought (Chen & Rossi, 1987:101–102). The emphasis given to either stakeholder or social concerns is expected to vary with the specific project circumstances. Integrative approaches seek to balance the goal of carrying out a project that is responsive to stakeholder concerns with the goal of objective, scientifically trustworthy and generalizable results. When the research is planned, evaluators are expected to communicate and negotiate regularly with key stakeholders and to take stakeholder concerns into account. Findings from preliminary inquiries are reported back to program decision makers so that they can make improvements in the program before it is formally evaluated. When the actual evaluation is conducted, the evaluation research team is expected to operate more autonomously, minimizing intrusions from program stakeholders.

Many evaluation researchers now recognize that they must take account of multiple values in their research and be sensitive to the perspectives of different stakeholders, in addition to maintaining a commitment to the goals of measurement validity, internal validity, and generalizability (Chen, 1990).

Quantitative or Qualitative Methods

Evaluation research that attempts to identify the effects of a social program typically is quantitative: Did the response times of emergency personnel tend to decrease? Did the students' test scores increase? Did housing retention improve? Did substance abuse decline? It's fair to say that when there's an interest in comparing outcomes between an experimental and a control group, or tracking change over time in a systematic manner, quantitative methods are favored.

But qualitative methods can add much to quantitative evaluation research studies, including more depth, detail, nuance, and exemplary case studies (Patton, 2002). Perhaps the greatest contribution qualitative methods can make in many evaluation studies is investigating program process—finding out what is "inside the black box." Although it is possible to track service delivery with quantitative measures like staff contact hours and frequency of complaints, finding out what is happening to clients and how clients experience the program can often best be accomplished by observing program activities and interviewing staff and clients intensively.

For example, Patton (2002:160) describes a study in which process analysis in an evaluation of a prenatal clinic's outreach program led to program changes. The process analysis revealed that the outreach workers were spending a lot of time responding to immediate problems, such as needs for rat control, protection from violence, and access to English classes. As a result, the outreach workers were recruiting fewer community residents for the prenatal clinic. New training and recruitment strategies were adopted to lessen this deviation from program goals.

Another good reason for using qualitative methods in evaluation research is the importance of learning how different individuals react to the treatment. For example, a quantitative evaluation of student reactions to an adult basic skills program for new immigrants relied heavily on the students' initial statements of their goals. However, qualitative interviews revealed that most new immigrants lacked sufficient experience in America to set meaningful goals; their initial goal statements simply reflected their eagerness to agree with their counselors' suggestions (Patton, 2002:177–181).

Qualitative methods can also help in understanding how social programs actually operate. Complex social programs have many different features, and it is not always clear whether it is the combination of those features or some particular features that are responsible for the program's effect—or for the absence of an effect. Lisbeth B.Schorr, director of the Harvard Project on Effective Interventions, and Daniel Yankelovich, president of Public Agenda, put it this way (Schorr & Yankelovich, 2000:A19): "Social programs are sprawling efforts with multiple components requiring constant mid-course corrections, the involvement of committed human beings, and flexible adaptation to local circumstances."

The more complex the social program, the more value that qualitative methods can add to the evaluation process. Schorr and Yankelovich (2000) point to the Ten Point Coalition, an alliance of black ministers that helped to reduce gang warfare in Boston through multiple initiatives, "ranging from neighborhood probation patrols to safe havens for recreation" (p. A19). Qualitative methods would help to describe a complex, multifaced program like this.

Simple or Complex Outcomes

Does the program have only one outcome? Unlikely. How many outcomes are anticipated? How many might be unintended? Which are direct consequences of program action and which are indirect effects that occur as a result of the direct effects (Mohr, 1992)? Do the longer-term outcomes follow directly from the immediate program outputs? Does the output (the increase in test scores at the end of the preparation course) result surely in the desired outcomes (increased rates of college admission)? Due to these and other possibilities, the selection of outcome measures is a critical step in evaluation research.

The decision to focus on one outcome rather than another, on a single outcome or on several, can have enormous implications. When Sherman and Berk (1984) evaluated the impact of an immediate arrest policy in cases of domestic violence in Minneapolis, they focused on recidivism as the key outcome. Similarly, the reduction of recidivism was the single desired outcome of prison "boot camps" opened in the 1990s. Boot camps are military-style programs for prison inmates that provide tough, highly regimented activities and harsh punishment for disciplinary infractions, with the goal of scaring inmates "straight." They were quite the rage in the 1990s, and the researchers who evaluated their impact understandably focused on criminal recidivism.

But these single-purpose programs turned out not to be quite so simple to evaluate. The Minneapolis researchers found that there was no adequate single source for records of recidivism in domestic violence cases, so they had to hunt for evidence from court and police records,

Exhibit 10.9   Outcomes in Project New Hope

Income and Employment (2nd Program year)	New Hope	Control group
Earnings	$6,602	$6,129
Wage subsidies	1,477	862
Welfare income	1,716	1,690
Food stamp income	1,418	1,242
Total income:	11,213	9,915
% above poverty level:	27%	19%
% continuously unemployed for 2 years	6%	13%
Hardships and Stress	New Hope	Control group
% reporting:		
Unmet medical needs	17%	23%
Unmet dental needs	27%	34%
Periods without health insurance	49%	61%
Living in overcrowded conditions	14%	15%
Stressed much or all of the time	45%	50%
Satisfied or very satisfied with standard of living	65%	67%

Source: From DeParle, Jason. 1999. "Project to Rescue Needy Stumbles Against the Persistence of Poverty." *The New York Times,* May 15:A1, A10. Reprinted with permission.

follow-up interviews with victims, and family member reports. More easily measured variables, such as partners' ratings of the accused's subsequent behavior, eventually received more attention. Boot camp research soon concluded that the experience did not reduce recidivism, although some participants felt the study had missed something (Latour, 2002:B7):

> [A staff member] saw things unfold that he had never witnessed among inmates and their caretakers. . . . profoundly affected the drill instructors and their charges . . . graduation ceremonies routinely reduced inmates . . . sometimes even supervisors to tears. . . . Here, it was a totally different experience.

Some now argue that the failure of boot camps to reduce recidivism was due to the lack of post-prison support, rather than to failure of the camps to promote positive change in inmates. Looking only at recidivism rates would ignore some important positive results.

So in spite of the additional difficulties they can introduce, most evaluation researchers attempt to measure multiple outcomes (Mohr, 1992). The result usually is a much more realistic, and richer, understanding of program impact.

Some of the multiple outcomes measured in the evaluation of Project New Hope appear in Exhibit 10.9. Project New Hope was an ambitious experimental evaluation of the impact of guaranteeing jobs to poor persons (DeParle, 1999). It was designed to answer the following question: If low-income adults are given a job at a sufficient wage, above the poverty level, with child care and health care assured, how many would ultimately prosper?

Six hundred and seventy-seven low-income adults in Milwaukee were offered a job involving work for 30 hours a week as well as child care and health care benefits. The outcome? Only 27% stuck with the job long enough to lift themselves out of poverty, and their earnings as a whole were only slightly higher than those of a control group that did not receive guaranteed jobs. Levels of depression were not decreased nor self-esteem increased by the job guarantee. But there were some positive effects: The number of people who never worked at all declined, and rates of health insurance and use of formal child care increased. Perhaps most importantly, the classroom performance and educational hopes of participants' male children increased, with the boys' test scores rising by the equivalent of 100 points on the SAT and their teachers ranking them as better behaved.

So did the New Hope program "work"? Clearly it didn't live up to initial expectations, but it certainly showed that social interventions can have some benefits. Would the boys' gains continue through adolescence? Longer-term outcomes would be needed. Why didn't girls (who were already performing better than the boys) benefit from their parents' enrollment in New Hope just as the boys did? A process analysis would add a great deal to the evaluation design. The long and short of it is that collection of multiple outcomes gave a better picture of program impact.

Of course there is a potential downside to the collection of multiple outcomes. Policy makers may choose to publicize those outcomes that support their own policy preferences and ignore the rest. Often, evaluation researchers themselves have little ability to publicize a more complete story.

In a sense, all of these choices (black box or program theory, researcher or stakeholder interests, and so on) hinge on (1) what your real goals are in doing the project, and (2) how able you will be in a "research for hire" setting to achieve those goals. Not every agency really wants to know if its programs work, especially if the answer is "no." Dealing with such issues, and the choices they require, is part of what makes evaluation research both scientifically and politically fascinating.

ETHICS IN EVALUATION

Evaluation research can make a difference in people's lives while it is in progress, as well as after the results are reported. Job opportunities, welfare requirements, housing options, treatment for substance abuse, training programs—each is a potentially important benefit, and an evaluation research project can change both their type and their availability. This direct impact on research participants and, potentially, their families, heightens the attention that evaluation researchers have to give to human subjects concerns. Although the particular criteria that are at issue and the decisions that are most ethical vary with the type of evaluation research conducted and the specifics of a particular project, there are always serious ethical as well as political concerns for the evaluation researcher (Boruch, 1997:13; Dentler, 2002:166).

Assessing needs, determining evaluability, and examining the process of treatment delivery have few special ethical dimensions. Cost-benefit analyses in themselves also raise few ethical concerns. It is when program impact is the focus that human subjects considerations multiply. What about assigning persons randomly to receive some social program or benefit? One justification given by evaluation researchers has to do with the scarcity of these resources. If not everyone in the population who is eligible for a program can receive it, due to resource limitations, what could be a fairer way to distribute the program benefits than through a lottery? Random assignment also seems like a reasonable way to allocate potential program benefits when a new program is being tested with only some members of the target recipient population. However, when an ongoing entitlement program is being evaluated and experimental subjects would normally be eligible for program participation, it may not be ethical simply to bar some potential participants from the program. Instead, evaluation researchers may test alternative treatments or provide some alternative benefit while the treatment is being denied.

There are many other ethical challenges in evaluation research:

- How can confidentiality be preserved when the data are owned by a government agency or are subject to discovery in a legal proceeding?
- Who decides what level of burden an evaluation project may tolerably impose upon participants?
- Is it legitimate for a research decision to be shaped by political considerations?
- Must evaluation findings be shared with stakeholders, rather than only with policy makers?
- Is the effectiveness of the proposed program improvements really uncertain?
- Will a randomized experiment yield more defensible evidence than the alternatives?
- Will the results actually be used?

The Health Research Extension Act of 1985 (Public Law 99–158) mandated that the Department of Health and Human Services require all research organizations receiving federal funds to have an Institutional Review Board (IRB) to assess all research for adherence to ethical practice guidelines. We have already reviewed the federally mandated criteria (Boruch, 1997:29–33):

- Are risks minimized?
- Are risks reasonable in relation to benefits?
- Is the selection of individuals equitable? (randomization implies this)
- Is informed consent given?
- Are the data monitored?
- Are privacy and confidentiality assured?

Evaluation researchers must consider whether it will be possible to meet each of these criteria long before they even design a study.

The problem of maintaining subject confidentiality is particularly thorny, because researchers, in general, are not legally protected from the requirement that they provide evidence requested in legal proceedings, particularly through the process known as "discovery." However, it is important to be aware that several federal statutes have been passed specifically to protect research data about vulnerable populations from legal disclosure requirements. For example, the Crime Control and Safe Streets Act (28 CFR Part 11) includes the following stipulation (Boruch, 1997:60):

Copies of [research] information [about persons receiving services under the act or the subject of inquiries into criminal behavior] shall be immune from legal process and shall not, without the consent of the persons furnishing such information, be admitted as evidence or used for any purpose in any action, suit, or other judicial or administrative proceedings.

When it appears that it will be difficult to meet the ethical standards in an evaluation project, at least from the perspective of some of the relevant stakeholders, modifications should be considered in the study design. Several steps can be taken to lessen any possibly detrimental program impact (Boruch, 1997:67–68):

- Alter the group allocation ratios to minimize the number in the untreated control group.
- Use the minimum sample size required to be able to adequately test the results.
- Test just parts of new programs, rather than the entire program.
- Compare treatments that vary in intensity (rather than presence or absence).
- Vary treatments between settings, rather than among individuals within a setting.

Essentially, each of these approaches limits the program's impact during the experiment and so lessens any potential adverse effects on human subjects. It is also important to realize that it is costly to society and potentially harmful to participants to maintain ineffective programs. In the long run, at least, it may be more ethical to conduct an evaluation study than to let the status quo remain in place.

CONCLUSIONS

Hopes for evaluation research are high: Society could benefit from the development of programs that work well, that accomplish their goals, and that serve people who genuinely need them. At least that is the hope. Unfortunately, there are many obstacles to realizing this hope:

- Because social programs and the people who use them are complex, evaluation research designs can easily miss important outcomes or aspects of the program process.
- Because the many program stakeholders all have an interest in particular results from the evaluation, researchers can be subjected to an unusual level of cross-pressures and demands.
- Because the need to include program stakeholders in research decisions may undermine adherence to scientific standards, research designs can be weakened.
- Because some program administrators want to believe their programs really work well, researchers may be pressured to avoid null findings or, if they are not responsive, find their research report ignored. Plenty of well-done evaluation research studies wind up in a recycling bin, or hidden away in a file cabinet.
- Because the primary audience for evaluation research reports are program administrators, politicians, or members of the public, evaluation findings may need to be overly simplified, distorting the findings (Posavac & Carey, 1997).

The rewards of evaluation research are often worth the risks, however. Evaluation research can provide social scientists with rare opportunities to study complex social processes, with real consequences, and to contribute to the public good. Although they may face unusual constraints on their research designs, most evaluation projects can result in high-quality analyses and publications in reputable social science journals. In many respects, evaluation research is an idea whose time has come. We may never achieve Donald Campbell's (Campbell & Russo, 1999) vision of an "experimenting society," in which research is consistently used to evaluate new programs and to suggest constructive changes, but we are close enough to continue trying.

KEY TERMS

Black box evaluation
Cost-benefit analysis
Cost-effectiveness analysis
Efficiency analysis
Evaluability assessment
Evaluation research
Feedback
Formative evaluation
Impact evaluation (or analysis)
Inputs
Integrative approach

Needs assessment
Outcomes
Outputs
Process evaluation
Program process
Program theory
Social science approach
Stakeholder approach
Stakeholders
Summative evaluation
Theory-driven evaluation

HIGHLIGHTS

• Evaluation research is social research that is conducted for a distinctive purpose: to investigate social programs.

• The development of evaluation research as a major enterprise followed on the heels of the expansion of the federal government during the Great Depression and World War II.

• The evaluation process can be modeled as a feedback system, with inputs entering the program, which generates outputs and then outcomes, which feed back to program stakeholders and affect program inputs.

• The evaluation process as a whole, and the feedback process in particular, can be understood only in relation to the interests and perspectives of program stakeholders.

• The process by which a program has an effect on outcomes is often treated as a "black box," but there is good reason to open the black box and investigate the process by which the program operates and produces, or fails to produce, an effect.

• A program theory may be developed before or after an investigation of program process is completed. It may be either descriptive or prescriptive.

• Evaluation research is done for a client, and its results may directly affect the services, treatments, or punishments that program users receive. Evaluation researchers differ in the extent to which they attempt to orient their evaluations to program stakeholders.

• Qualitative methods are useful in describing the process of program delivery.

• Multiple outcomes are often necessary to understand program effects.

- There are five primary types of program evaluation: needs assessment, evaluability assessment, process evaluation (including formative evaluation), impact analysis (also termed summative evaluation), and efficiency (cost-benefit) analysis.

- Evaluation research raises complex ethical issues because it may involve withholding desired social benefits.

DISCUSSION QUESTIONS

1. Would you prefer that evaluation researchers use a stakeholder or a social science approach? Compare and contrast these perspectives and list at least four arguments for the one you favor.

2. Read and summarize an evaluation research report published in the journal *Evaluation and Program Planning*. Be sure to identify the type of evaluation research that is described. Discuss the strengths and weaknesses of the design.

3. Select one of the evaluation research studies described in this chapter, read the original report (book or article) about it, and review its adherence to the ethical guidelines for evaluation research. Which guidelines do you feel are most important? Which are most difficult to adhere to?

4. Is it ethical to assign people to receive some social benefit on a random basis? Form two teams and debate the ethics of the TARP randomized evaluation of welfare payments described in this chapter.

PRACTICE EXERCISES

1. Propose a randomized experimental evaluation of a social program with which you are familiar. Include in your proposal a description of the program and its intended outcomes. Discuss the strengths and weaknesses of your proposed design.

2. Identify the key stakeholders in a local social or educational program. Interview several stakeholders to determine what their goals are for the program and what tools they use to assess goal achievement. Compare and contrast the views of each stakeholder and try to account for any differences you find.

3. Review the evaluation lesson in the CD-ROM interactive exercises to learn more about the language and logic of evaluation research.

WEB EXERCISES

1. Inspect the Web site maintained by the Governmental Accounting Standards Board: http://www.seagov.org. Read and report on performance measurement in government as described in one of the case studies.

2. Describe the resources available for evaluation researchers at one of the following three Web sites: http://www.wmich.edu/evalctr/, http://www.stanford.edu/~davidf/empowermentevaluation.html, or http://www.worldbank.org/oed/.

3. You can check out the latest information regarding the D.A.R.E. program at www.dare.com. What is the current approach? Can you find information on the Web about current research on D.A.R.E.?

SPSS EXERCISES

1. Neighborhood and school integration has often been a focus of government social policy. Does the racial composition of a neighborhood have any association with attitudes related to racial issues?

Although we cannot examine the effects of social policies or programs directly in the GSS survey data, we can consider the association between neighborhood racial composition and attitudes related to race. The variable RACLIVE indicates whether the respondent lives in a racially integrated neighborhood. Request its frequency distribution as well as those for several attitudes related to race: RACMAR, RACPUSH, AFFRMACT, WRKWAYUP, BLKSIMP, and CLOSEBLK.

2. Do attitudes vary with the experience of living in a racially integrated neighborhood? Request the crosstabulation of RACMAR to CLOSEBLK by RACLIVE (request percentages on the column totals). Read the tables and explain what they tell us about attitudes and neighborhood. Does the apparent effect of racial integration vary with the different attitudes? How would you explain this variation in these "multiple outcomes"?

3. What other attitudes differ between whites who live in integrated and segregated neighborhoods? Review the GSS2000mini variable list to identify some possibilities and request crosstabulations for these variables Do you think that differences are more likely to be a consequence of a racially integrated neighborhood experience or a cause of the type of neighborhood that people choose to live in? Explain.

DEVELOPING A RESEARCH PROPOSAL

1. Develop a brief model for a program that might influence the type of attitude or behavior in which you are interested. List the key components of this model.

2. Design a program evaluation to test the efficacy of your program model, using an impact analysis approach.

3. Add to your plan a discussion of a program theory for your mode. In your methodological plan, indicate whether you will use qualitative or quantitative techniques and simple or complex outcomes.

4. Who are the potential stakeholders for your program? How will you relate to them before, during, and after your evaluation?

Chapter 11

HISTORICAL AND COMPARATIVE RESEARCH

Overview of Methods for Historical and Comparative Research

Historical Social Science Methods
Historical Events Research
  Event-Structure Analysis
  Oral History
Historical Process Research

Comparative Social Science Methods
Cross-Sectional Comparative Research
Comparative Historical Research

Secondary Data
Secondary Data Sources
  U.S. Bureau of the Census
  Integrated Public Use Microdata Series

  Bureau of Labor Statistics (BLS)
  Other U.S. Government Sources
  International Data Sources
  Survey Datasets
Challenges for Secondary Data Analyses

Demographic Analysis

Methodological Complications
Measuring Across Contexts
Sampling Across Time and Place
Identifying Causes

Ethical Issues in Historical and Comparative Research

Conclusions

Although the United States and several European nations have maintained democratic systems of governance for over 100 years, democratic rule has more often been brief and unstable, when it has occurred at all. What explains the presence of democratic practices in one country and their absence in another? Are democratic politics a realistic option for every nation? What about Bosnia? Congo? Iraq? Are there some prerequisites in historical experience, cultural values, or economic resources? Methodological tools that we can call "unobtrusive methods" allow us to investigate social processes at other times and in other places, when the actual participants in these processes are not available.

Unobtrusive methods for historical and comparative research can generate new insights into social processes due to their ability to focus on aspects of the social world beyond recent events in one country. They involve several different approaches and a diverse set of techniques, and they may have qualitative and/or quantitative components. These methods provide ways to investigate topics that usually cannot be studied with experiments, participant observation, or surveys. However, because this broader focus involves collecting data from records on the past or from other nations, unobtrusive methods used in historical and comparative investigations present unique challenges to social researchers.

In this chapter, I will review the major unobtrusive methods used by social scientists to understand historical processes and to compare different societies or regions. I will also highlight several sources of secondary data that can be useful in historical and comparative work, and I will point out the potential problems that can arise with secondary data. I will also introduce oral histories, a qualitative tool for historical investigations, as well as demographic methods, which can strengthen both historical and comparative studies. Throughout the chapter, I will draw many examples from research on democracy and the process of democratization.

OVERVIEW OF UNOBTRUSIVE METHODS FOR COMPARATIVE AND HISTORICAL RESEARCH

The central insight behind unobtrusive methods in historical and comparative investigations is that we can improve our understanding of social processes when we make comparisons to other times and places. Max Weber's comparative study of world religions (Bendix, 1962), Emile Durkheim's (1984) historical analysis of the division of labor, Karl Marx's (1967) investigation of political and economic change—each affirms the value of this insight. Beyond this similarity, however, historical and comparative methods are a diverse collection of approaches. Research may be historical, comparative, or both historical and comparative. Historical and comparative methods can be quantitative or qualitative, or a mixture of both. Both nomothetic and idiographic approaches to establishing causal effects can be used.

There are no hard-and-fast rules for determining how far in the past the focus of research must be in order to consider it historical, nor what types of comparisons are needed to warrant calling research comparative. In practice, research tends to be considered historical when it focuses on a period prior to the experience of most of those conducting research (Abbott, 1994:80). Research involving different nations is usually considered comparative, but so are studies of different regions within one nation if they emphasize interregional comparison. In recent years, the globalization of U.S. economic ties and the internationalization of scholarship have increased the use of unobtrusive methods for comparative research across many different countries (Kotkin, 2002).

Distinguishing research in terms of a historical and/or comparative focus results in four basic types of research: **historical events research, historical process research, cross-sectional comparative research,** and **comparative historical research.** Research that focuses

Exhibit 11.1 Types of Historical and Comparative Research

	Cross-Sectional	**Longitudinal**
Single Case	Historical Events Research	Historical Process Research
Multiple Cases	Cross-Sectional Comparative Research	Comparative Historical Research

on events in one short historical period is historical events research, whereas longitudinal research that traces a sequence of events over a number of years is historical process research (cf. Skocpol, 1984:359). There are also two types of comparative research, the first involving cross-sectional comparisons and the second comparing longitudinal data about historical processes between multiple cases. The resulting four types of research are displayed in Exhibit 11.1.

Historical events research   Research in which social events of one past time period are studied.

Historical process research   Research in which historical processes in a long time period are studied.

Cross-sectional comparative research   Research comparing data from one time period between two or more nations.

Comparative historical research   Research comparing data from more than one time period in more than one nation.

HISTORICAL SOCIAL SCIENCE METHODS

Both historical events research and historical process research investigate questions concerning past times. These methods are used increasingly by social scientists in sociology, anthropology, political science, and economics, as well as by many historians (Monkkonen, 1994). The late 20th and early 21st centuries have seen so much change in so many countries that many scholars have felt a need to investigate the background of these changes and to refine their methods of investigation (Hallinan, 1997; Robertson, 1993). The accumulation of large bodies of data about the past has stimulated more historically oriented research, but it has also led to the development of several different methodologies.

Much historical (and comparative) research is qualitative. This style of historical social science research tends to have several features that are similar to those used in other qualitative methodologies. Qualitative historical research is:

- *Case-oriented.* **Case-oriented research** focuses on the nation or other unit as a whole. This could be considered the most distinctive feature of qualitative research on historical processes.
- *Holistic.* It is concerned with the context in which events occurred and the interrelations among different events and processes: "how different conditions or parts fit together" (Ragin, 1987:25–26).
- *Conjunctural.* This is because, it is argued, "no cause ever acts except in complex conjunctions with others" (Abbott, 1994:101).
- *Temporal.* It becomes temporal by taking into account the related series of events that unfold over time.
- *Historically specific.* It is likely to be limited to the specific time(s) and place(s) studied, like traditional historical research.
- *Narrative.* It researches a story involving specific actors and other events occurring at the same time (Abbott, 1994:102), or one that takes account of the position of actors and events in time and in a unique historical context (Griffin, 1992). (You can think of this as a combination of the previous two features.) **Narrative explanations** involve idiographic causal reasoning (see Chapter 6).
- *Inductive.* The research develops an explanation for what happened from the details discovered about the past.

Case-oriented research   Research that focuses attention on the nation or other unit as a whole.

The focus on the past presents special methodological challenges:

- Documents and other evidence may have been lost or damaged.
- Available evidence may represent a sample biased toward more newsworthy figures.
- Written records will be biased toward those who were more prone to writing.
- Feelings of individuals involved in past events may be hard, if not impossible, to reconstruct.

Before you judge historical social science research as credible, you should look for convincing evidence that each of these challenges has been addressed.

Historical Events Research

Research on past events that does not follow processes for some long period of time—that is basically cross-sectional—is historical events research rather than historical process research. Investigations of past events may be motivated by the belief that they had a critical impact on subsequent developments or because they provide opportunities for testing the implications of a general theory (Kohn, 1987).

Event-Structure Analysis

One technique useful in historical events research, as well as in other types of historical and comparative research, is **event-structure analysis.** Event structure analysis is a qualitative approach that relies on a systematic coding of key events or national characteristics to identify the underlying structure of action in a chronology of events. The codes are then used to construct event sequences, to make comparisons between cases, and to develop an idiographic causal explanation for a key event.

An event structure analysis requires several steps:

1. Classifying historical information into discrete events

2. Ordering events into a temporal sequence

3. Identifying prior steps that are prerequisites for subsequent events

4. Representing connections between events in a diagram

5. Eliminating from the diagram connections that are not necessary to explain the focal event

Larry Griffin (1993) sought to explain a unique historical event, a lynching in 1930s Mississippi, with event-structure analysis. According to published accounts and legal records, the lynching occurred after David Harris, an African American who sold moonshine from his home, was accused of killing a white tenant farmer. After the killing was reported, the local deputy was called and a citizen search party was formed. The deputy did not intervene as the search party trailed Harris and then captured and killed him. Meanwhile, Harris's friends killed another African American who had revealed Harris's hiding place. This series of events is outlined in Exhibit 11.2.

Which among the numerous events occurring between the time that the tenant farmer confronted Harris and the time that the mob killed Harris had a causal influence on that outcome? To identify these idiographic causal links (see Chapter 6), Griffin identified plausible counterfactual possibilities—events that might have occurred but did not—and considered whether the outcome might have been changed if a counterfactual had occurred instead of a particular event. For example:

> If, contrary to what actually happened, the deputy had attempted to stop the mob, might the lynching have been averted? . . . Given what happened in comparable cases and the Bolivar County deputy's clear knowledge of the existence of the mob and of its early activities, his forceful intervention to prevent the lynching thus appears an objective possibility. (Griffin, 1993:1112)

So, Griffin concluded, nonintervention by the deputy had a causal influence on the lynching.

Exhibit 11.2   Event-Structure Analysis: Lynching Incident in the 1930s

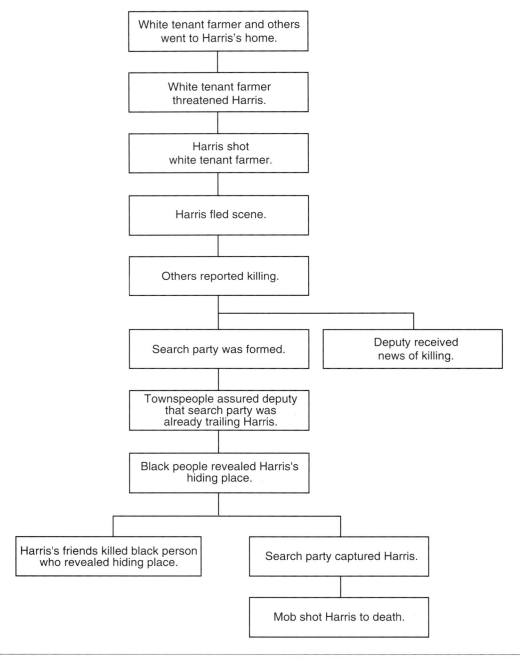

Source: Adapted from Griffin, 1993:1110. Reprinted with permission from the University of Chicago Press.

Oral History

History that is not written down is mostly lost to posterity (and social researchers). However, **oral histories** can be useful for understanding historical events that occurred within the lifetimes of living individuals. Although oral histories are not really "unobtrusive methods," they can sometimes result in a written record that can be analyzed by researchers at a later point in time, as the next example shows.

Thanks to a Depression-era writers project, Deanna Pagnini and S. Philip Morgan (1996) found that they could use oral histories to study attitudes toward births out of wedlock among African American and white women in the South during the 1930s.

Almost 70% of African American babies are born to unmarried mothers, compared to 22% of white babies (Pagnini & Morgan, 1996:1696). This difference often is attributed to contemporary welfare policies or problems in the inner city, but Pagnini and Morgan thought it might be due to more enduring racial differences in marriage and childbearing. To investigate these historical differences, they read 1,170 life histories recorded by almost 200 writers who worked for a New Deal program during the Depression of the 1930s, the Federal Writers' Project Life History Program for the Southeast. The interviewers had used a topic outline that included family issues, education, income, occupation, religion, medical needs, and diet.

In 1936, the divergence in rates of nonmarital births was substantial in North Carolina: 2.6% of white births were to unmarried women, compared to 28.3% of nonwhite births. The oral histories gave some qualitative insight into community norms that were associated with these patterns. A white seamstress who became pregnant at age 16 recalled that "I'm afraid he didn't want much to marry me, but my mother's threats brought him around" (Pagnini & Morgan, 1996:1705). There were some reports of suicides by unwed young white women who were pregnant. In comparison, African American women who became pregnant before they were married reported regrets, but rarely shame or disgrace. There were no instances of young black women committing suicide or getting abortions in these circumstances.

> We found that bearing a child outside a marital relationship was clearly not the stigmatizing event for African-Americans that it was for whites. . . . When we examine contemporary family patterns, it is important to remember that neither current marriage nor current childbearing patterns are "new" for either race. Our explanations for why African-Americans and whites organize their families in different manners must take into account past behaviors and values. (Pagnini & Morgan, 1996:1714–1715)

Whether oral histories are collected by the researcher or obtained from an earlier project, the stories they tell can be no more reliable than the memories that are recalled. Unfortunately, memories of past attitudes are "notoriously subject to modifications over time" (Banks, 1972:67), as are memories about past events, relationships, and actions. Use of corroborating data from documents or other sources should be used when possible to increase the credibility of descriptions based on oral histories.

Historical Process Research

Historical process research extends historical events research by focusing on a series of events that happened over a longer period of time. This longitudinal component allows for a

Exhibit 11.3   Variables for Historical Analysis of Environmental Protectionism

Dependent Variables	Definition	Data Source(s)	Period of Analysis
National parks and protected areas	Annual cumulative numbers of parks per nation-state	IUCN (1990)	1900–1990
Country chapters of international environmental nongovernmental associations	Annual numbers of chapters per nation-state	Fried (1905–1911); League of Nations (1921, 1938); UIA (1948–1990)	1900–1988
Nation-state memberships in intergovernmental environmental organizations	Annual numbers of memberships per nation-state	Fried (1905–1911); League of Nations (1921, 1938); UIA (1948–1990)	1900–1984
Environmental impact assessment laws	Year of founding	Wood (1995)	1966–1992
National environmental ministries	Year of founding	Europa Year Book (1970–1995)	1970–1995

Source: Frank et al., 2000:112.

much more complete understanding of historical developments than is often the case with historical events research, although it often uses techniques such as event history analysis and oral histories that are also used for research on historical events at one point in time.

Historical process research can also use quantitative techniques. The units of analysis in quantitative analyses of historical processes are nations or larger entities, and researchers use a longitudinal design in order to identify changes over time. For example, David John Frank, Ann Hironaka, and Evan Schofer (2000) treated the entire world as their "case" for their deductive test of alternative explanations for the growth of national activities to protect the natural environment during the 20th century. Were environmental protection activities a response to environmental degradation and economic affluence within nations, as many had theorized? Or, instead, were they the result of a "top-down" process in which a new view of national responsibilities was spread by international organizations? Their measures of environmental protectionism included the number of national parks among all countries in the world and memberships in international environmental organizations; one of their indicators of global changes was the cumulative number of international environmental agreements (see Exhibit 11.3 for a list of some of their data sources).

Exhibit 11.4a charts the growth of environmental activities identified around the world. Compare the pattern in this exhibit to the pattern of growth in the number of international environmental agreements and national environmental laws (Exhibit 11.4b), and you can see that environmental protectionism at the national level was rising at the same time that it was becoming more the norm in international relations. In more detailed analyses, Frank, Hironaka, and Schofer attempt to show that the growth in environmental protectionism was not explained by increasing environmental problems or economic affluence within nations.

Exhibit 11.4   International Environmental Activity

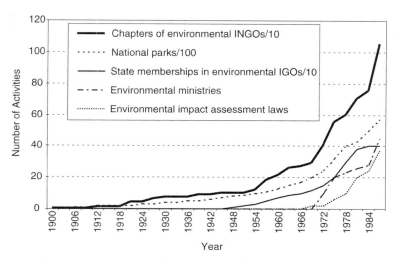

(a) Cumulative Numbers of Five National Environmental Activities, 1900 to 1988

Note: INGOs are international nongovernmental organizations; IGOs are intergovernmental organizations.

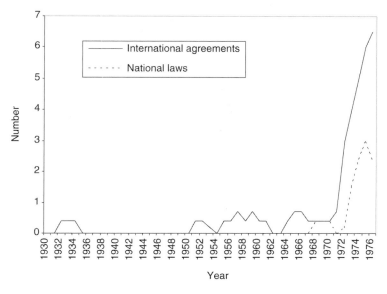

(b) Environmental Impact Assessment: International Agreements and National Laws, 1930 to 1977

Source: Frank et al., 2000:98, 102.

As in most research that relies on historical and/or comparative data, however, some variables that would indicate alternative influences (such as the strength of national environmental protest movements) could not be measured (Buttel, 2000). Further research is needed.

COMPARATIVE SOCIAL SCIENCE METHODS

The limitations of single-case historical research have encouraged many social scientists to turn to comparisons between nations. These studies allow for a broader vision about social relations than is possible with cross-sectional research limited to one country or other unit. From 1985 to 1990, more than 80 research articles in top sociology journals and 200 nonedited books were published in which the primary purpose was the comparison of two or more nations (Bollen, Entwisle, & Alderson, 1993). About half of this research used cross-sectional data rather than longitudinal data collected over a period of time.

Cross-Sectional Comparative Research

Comparisons between countries during one time period can help social scientists identify the limitations of explanations based on single-nation research. These comparative studies may focus on a period in either the past or the present.

Historical and comparative research that is quantitative may obtain data from national statistics or other sources of published data; if it is contemporary, such research may rely on cross-national surveys. Like other types of quantitative research, quantitative historical and comparative research can be termed **variable-oriented,** with a focus on variables representing particular aspects of the units studied (Demos, 1998).

Variable-oriented research   Research that focuses attention on variables representing particular aspects of the units studied and then examines the relations among these variables across sets of cases.

Causal reasoning in quantitative historical and comparative research is nomothetic and the approach is usually deductive, testing explicit hypotheses about relations among these variables (Kiser & Hechter, 1991). For example, Edgar Kiser and Michael Hechter (1991:20) deduced from rational choice theory a hypothesis about the probability of revolutions that is meant to apply across times and places: The relative power of rulers varies with the degree to which they are dependent on subjects for revenue and other resources.

Research on voter turnout also illustrates the value of cross-sectional comparative research. This research focuses on a critical issue in political science: Although free and competitive elections are a defining feature of democratic politics, elections themselves cannot orient governments to popular sentiment if citizens do not vote (LeDuc, Niemi, & Norris, 1996). As a result, the low levels of voter participation in U.S. elections have long been a source of practical concern and research interest.

International data give our first clue for explaining voter turnout: The rate of voter participation in the United States (54%, on average) is much lower than it is in many other countries

Exhibit 11.5   Percentage of Voters Who Participated in Elections, 1960–1995

Australia	95	Norway	81
Malta	94	Bulgaria	80
Austria	92	Israel	80
Belgium	91	Portugal	79
Italy	90	Finland	78
Luxembourg	90	Canada	76
Iceland	89	France	76
New Zealand	88	United Kingdom	75
Denmark	87	Ireland	74
Venezuela	85	Spain	73
Germany	86	Japan	71
Greece	86	Estonia	69
Latvia	86	Hungary	66
Lithuania	86	Russia	61
Sweden	86	India	58
Czech Republic	85	Switzerland	54
Brazil	83	United States	54
Netherlands	83	Poland	51
Costa Rica	81		

Source: Franklin, 1996:218.

that have free, competitive elections; in Australia, for example, 95% of voters usually turn out to vote (Exhibit 11.5).

Is this variation due to differences among voters in knowledge and wealth? Do media and political party get-out-the-vote efforts matter? Mark Franklin's (1996:219–222) analysis of these international data indicates that neither explanation accounts for much of the international variation in voter turnout. Instead, it is the structure of competition and the importance of issues that are important. Voter turnout is maximized where structural features maximize competition: compulsory voting, mail and Sunday voting, and multiday voting. Voter turnout also tends to be higher where the issues being voted on are important and where results are decided by proportional representation rather than on a winner-take-all basis—so individual votes are more important.

Franklin concludes that it is these characteristics that explain the low level of voter turnout in the United States, not the characteristics of individual voters. The United States lacks the structural features that make voting easier, the proportional representation that increases the impact of individuals' votes, and, often, the sharp differences between candidates that are found in countries with higher turnout. Because these structural factors generally do not vary within nations, we would never realize their importance if our analysis was limited to data from individuals in one nation.

Comparative Historical Research

Historical social scientists may use comparisons between cases "to highlight the particular features of each case" (Skocpol, 1984:370) or to identify general historical patterns across nations. Comparative historical research can also help to identify the causal processes at work within the nations or other entities (Lipset, 1968:34; Skocpol, 1984:374–386). Comparative historical research can result in historically conditional theory, in which the applicability of general theoretical propositions is limited to particular historical circumstances—for example, what explains the development of capitalism in Turkey may apply to some societies, but not to others (Paige, 1999).

The comparative historical approach focuses on sequences of events, rather than on some single past (or current) occurrence that might have influenced an outcome in the present. Comparisons of these sequences may be either quantitative or qualitative. Some studies collect quantitative longitudinal data about a number of nations and then use these data to test hypotheses about influences on national characteristics. (Theda Skocpol [1984:375] terms this "analytic historical sociology.") Others compare the histories or particular historical experiences of nations in a narrative form, noting similarities and differences and inferring explanations for key national events ("interpretive historical sociology" in Skocpol's terminology [1984:368]).

There are several stages for a systematic qualitative comparative historical study (Ragin 1987:44–52; Rueschemeyer, Stephens, & Stephens, 1992:36–39).

- Specify a theoretical framework and identify key concepts or events that should be examined to explain a phenomenon.
- Select cases (such as nations) that vary in terms of the key concepts or events.
- Identify similarities and differences between the cases in terms of these key concepts or events and the outcome to be explained.
- Propose a causal explanation for the historical outcome and check it against the features of each case. The criterion of success in this method is to explain the outcome for each case, without allowing deviations from the proposed causal pattern.

Dietrich Rueschemeyer, Evelyne Huber Stephens, and John Stephens (1992) used a method like this to explain why some nations in Latin America developed democratic politics, whereas others became authoritarian or bureaucratic-authoritarian states. First, Rueschemeyer, Stephens, and Stephens developed a theoretical framework that gave key attention to the power of social classes, state (government) power, and the interaction between social classes and the government. They then classified the political regimes in each nation over time (Exhibit 11.6). Next, they noted how each nation varied over time in terms of the variables they had identified as potentially important for successful democratization.

Their analysis identified several conditions for initial democratization: consolidation of state power (ending overt challenges to state authority); expansion of the export economy (reducing conflicts over resources); industrialization (increasing the size and interaction of middle and working classes); and some agent of political articulation of the subordinate classes (which could be the state, political parties, or mass movements). Historical variation in these conditions was then examined in detail.

SECONDARY DATA

Secondary data (most often the term is used in reference to quantitative data) are data that the researcher did not collect him- or herself to answer the research question of interest.

Exhibit 11.6 Classification of Regimes Over Time

	Constitutional Oligarchic	Authoritarian; Traditional, Populist, Military, or Corporatist	Restricted Democratic	Fully Democratic	Bureaucratic-Authoritarian
Argentina	before 1912	1930-46 1951-55 1955-58 1962-63	1958-62 1963-66	1912-30 1946-51 1973-76 1983-90	1966-73 1976-83
Brazil	before 1930	1930-45	1945-64 1985-90		1964-85
Bolivia	before 1930	1930-52 1964-82	1982-90	1952-64	
Chile	before 1920	1924-32	1920-24 1932-70 1990	1970-73	1973-89
Colombia	before 1936	1949-58	1936-49 1958-90		
Ecuador	1916-25	before 1916 1925-48 1961-78	1948-61 1978-90		
Mexico		up to 1990			
Paraguay		up to 1990			
Peru		before 1930 1930-39 1948-56 1962-63 1968-80	1939-48 1956-62 1963-68	1980-90	
Uruguay		before 1903 1933-42	1903-19	1919-33 1942-73 1984-90	1973-84
Venezuela		before 1935 1935-45	1958-68	1945-48 1968-90	

Source: Rueschemeyer, Stephens, & Stephens, 1992:160–161. Reprinted with permission from the University of Chicago Press.

Instead, secondary data are obtained from publicly available data archives, another researcher, or even from one's own previous projects that were designed to address some other research question. Historical and comparative research often relies on secondary data, although many other types of research can use secondary data. Many excellent secondary data sources are available.

Secondary Data Sources

After choosing one of the four research designs and deciding to use a quantitative or qualitative approach, a historical and comparative researcher must also select a data-collection technique. Quantitative researchers may use data available from the U.S. Bureau of the Census or other government agencies or from many other countries, as well as from world bodies like the World Bank, as reflected in Mark Franklin's (1996) study of international voting patterns and Edward Crenshaw's (1995) comparative study of democracy. Historical and comparative research may also rely on previously collected survey data.

Qualitative research often relies on information in published histories or other secondary sources, such as documents found in archival collections. Rueschemeyer, Stephens, and Stephens (1992) used a variety of sources to code key events in the histories of the nations they studied.

U.S. Bureau of the Census

The U.S. government has conducted a census of the population every 10 years since 1790; since 1940, this census also has included a census of housing (see also Chapter 5). This decennial Census of Population and Housing is a rich source of social science data (Lavin, 1994). The Census Bureau's monthly *Current Population Survey (CPS)* provides basic data on labor force activity that is then used in Bureau of Labor Statistics reports. The Census Bureau also collects data on agriculture, manufacturers, construction and other business, foreign countries, and foreign trade.

The U.S. Census of Population and Housing aims to survey an adult in every household in the United States. The basic "complete-count" census contains questions about household composition as well as ethnicity and income. More questions are asked in a longer form of the census that is administered to a sample of the households. A separate census of housing characteristics is conducted at the same time (Rives & Serow, 1988:15). Participation in the census is required by law, and confidentiality of the information obtained is mandated by law for 72 years after collection. Census data are reported for geographic units, including states, metropolitan areas, counties, census tracts (small, relatively permanent areas within counties), and even blocks (see Exhibit 11.7). These different units allow units of analysis to be tailored to research questions.

Census data are used to apportion seats in the U.S. House of Representatives and to determine federal and state legislative district boundaries, as well as to inform other decisions by government agencies. An interactive data retrieval system, *American FactFinder,* is the primary means for distributing results from the 2000 Census; those without direct Internet access can use 1,800 state data centers and 1,400 federal depository libraries, universities, and private organizations (U.S. Bureau of the Census, 1999:12). The U.S. Census Web site (http://www.census.gov) provides direct access to many statistics, and the catalog of the Inter-university Consortium for Political and Social Research (http://www.icpsr.umich.edu) lists many reports. Some detailed information is available only after paying a subscription fee of $40 per quarter for individuals (as of 1997). Summary tapes and CD-ROMs also can be

Exhibit 11.7   Census Small-Area Geography

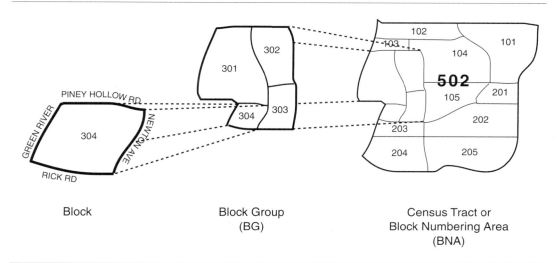

Block	Block Group (BG)	Census Tract or Block Numbering Area (BNA)

Source: U.S. Bureau of the Census, 1994:8.

purchased that contain census data in various geographic levels, including counties, cities, census tracts, and even blocks (for an example, check the following U.S. Census Web site: http://www.census.gov/apsd/www/TestDrive/usaprof.htm).

States also maintain census bureaus and may have additional resources. Some contain the original census data collected in the state 100 or more years ago. The ambitious historical researcher can use these returns to conduct detailed comparative studies at the county or state level (Lathrop, 1968:79).

Integrated Public Use Microdata Series

Individual-level samples from U.S. Census data for the years 1850 to 1990, as well as historical census files from several other countries, are available through the Integrated Public Use Microdata Series (IPUMS) at the University of Minnesota's Minnesota Population Center (MPC). These data are prepared in an easy-to-use format that provides consistent codes and names for all the different samples.

This exceptional resource offers 25 samples of the American population selected from 13 federal censuses, with at least 100,000 persons in each sample; in recent years the samples contained more than 1 million persons. Each sample is independently selected, so that individuals are not linked between samples. In addition to basic demographic measures, variables in the U.S. samples include educational, occupational, and work indicators; respondent income; disability status; immigration status; veteran status; and various household characteristics, including family composition and dwelling characteristics. The international samples include detailed characteristics from hundreds of thousands of individuals in countries ranging from France and Mexico to Kenya and Vietnam.

You can view these resources at www.ipums.umn.edu.

Bureau of Labor Statistics (BLS)

Another good source of data is the Bureau of Labor Statistics of the U.S. Department of Labor, which collects and analyzes data on employment, earnings, prices, living conditions, industrial relations, productivity and technology, and occupational safety and health (U.S. Bureau of Labor Statistics, 1991, 1997b). Some of these data are collected by the Bureau of the Census in the monthly *Current Population Survey (CPS);* other data are collected through surveys of establishments (U.S. Bureau of Labor Statistics, 1997a).

The *CPS* provides a monthly employment and unemployment record for the United States, classified by age, sex, race, and other characteristics. The *CPS* uses a stratified random sample of about 60,000 households (with separate forms for about 120,000 individuals). Detailed questions are included to determine the precise labor force status (whether they are currently working or not) of each household member over the age of 16. Statistical reports are published each month in the BLS's *Monthly Labor Review* and can also be inspected at its Web site (http://stats.bls.gov). Datasets are available on computer tapes and disks from the BLS and services like the Inter-university Consortium for Political and Social Research (ICPSR).

Other U.S. Government Sources

Many more datasets useful for historical and comparative research have been collected by federal agencies and other organizations. The National Technical Information Service (NTIS) of the U.S. Department of Commerce maintains a Federal Computer Products Center that collects and catalogs many of these datasets and related software.

By 1993, more than 1,850 datasets from 50 agencies were described in the NTIS *Directory.* The *Directory* is the essential source of information about the datasets and can be purchased from the U.S. Department of Commerce (National Technical Information Service, 1993). Dataset summaries can be searched in the *Directory* by either subject or agency. Government research reports cataloged by NTIS can be searched online at the NTIS Web site (http://www.fedworld.gov) and in a CD-ROM catalog available in some libraries.

International Data Sources

Comparative researchers can find datasets on population characteristics, economic and political features, and political events in many nations. Some of these are available from U.S. government agencies. For example, the Social Security Administration reports on the characteristics of social security throughout the world (Wheeler, 1995). This comprehensive report classifies nations in terms of their type of social security program and provides detailed summaries of the characteristics of each nation's programs. The 1999 volume is available on the Internet at http://www.ssa.gov/policy/docs/progdesc/ssptw/1999/index.html#toc. More recent data are organized by region. A broader range of data are available in the *World Handbook of Political and Social Indicators,* with political events and political, economic, and social data coded from 1948 to 1982 (http://www.icpsr.umich.edu:8080/ICPSR-STUDY/07761.xml) (Taylor & Jodice, 1986).

Many other sources of historical and comparative data are archived at the University of Michigan's Inter-university Consortium for Political and Social Research (ICPSR). The ICPSR was founded in 1962 by 21 universities collaborating with the University of Michigan's

Survey Research Center. It now includes more than 325 colleges and universities in North America and hundreds of institutions on other continents. The ICPSR archives include data from over 9,000 studies in more than 130 countries.

Do you have an interest in events and interactions between nations, such as threats of military force? A dataset collected by Charles McClelland includes characteristics of 91,240 such events (http://www.icpsr.umich.edu:8080/ICPSR-STUDY/05211.xml). The history of military interventions in nations around the world between 1946 and 1988 is coded in a dataset developed by Frederic Pearson and Robert Baumann. This dataset identifies the intervener and target countries, the starting and ending dates of military intervention, and a range of potential motives (such as foreign policies, related domestic disputes, and pursuit of rebels across borders).

Census data from other nations are also available through the ICPSR, as well as directly through the Internet. In the ICPSR archives, you can find a dataset from the Statistical Office of the United Nations on the 1966–1974 population of 220 nations throughout the world (http://www.icpsr.umich.edu:8080/ICPSR-STUDY/07623.xml). More current international population data are provided by the Center for International Research and the U.S. Census Bureau (http://www.icpsr.umich.edu:8080/ICPSR-STUDY/08490.xml).

Survey Datasets

Many survey datasets are also available on the Internet. These can be used by historical and comparative researchers to compare national attitudes and to examine trends over time. The Inter-university Consortium for Political and Social Research (1996) provides access to such surveys to researchers (including students) at many universities (http://www.icpsr. umich.edu).

Survey datasets obtained in the United States and in many other countries that are stored at the ICPSR provide data on topics ranging from elite attitudes to consumer expectations. For example, data collected in the British Social Attitudes Survey in 1998, designed by the University of Chicago's National Opinion Research Center, are available through the ICPSR (http://www.icpsr.umich.edu:8080/ICPSR-STUDY/03101.xml).

Data collected in a monthly survey of Spaniards' attitudes, by the Center for Research on Social Reality [Spain] Survey, are also available (http://www.icpsr.umich.edu:8080/ICPSR-SERIES/00017.xml). Survey data from Russia, Germany, and other countries can also be found in the ICPSR collection.

The ICPSR archives also include data from the U.S. census, election results, 19th-century French census materials, popular organizations, international events, and roll call votes in the U.S. House and Senate since 1790. More than 6 million variables are represented in the collection.

Appendix H includes some additional relevant Web sites.

Challenges for Secondary Data Analyses

Analysis of secondary data presents several challenges, ranging from uncertainty about the methods of data collection to the lack of maximal fit between the concepts that the primary study measured and each of the concepts that are the focus of the current investigation.

Responsible use of secondary data requires a good understanding of the primary data source. The researcher should be able to answer the following questions (most adapted from Riedel [2000:55–69] and Stewart [1984:23–30]):

1. What were the agency's goals in collecting the data? If the primary data were obtained in a research project, what were the project's purposes?

2. Who was responsible for data collection, and what were their qualifications? Are they available to answer questions about the data? Each step in the data-collection process should be charted and the personnel involved identified.

3. What data were collected, and what were they intended to measure?

4. When was the information collected?

5. What methods were used for data collection? Copies of the forms used for data collection should be obtained and the way in which these data are processed by the agency/agencies should be reviewed.

6. How is the information organized (by date, event, etc.)? Are there identifiers that are used to identify the different types of data available on the same case? In what form are the data available (computer tapes, disks, paper files)? Answers to these questions can have a major bearing on the work that will be needed to carry out the study.

7. How consistent are the data with data available from other sources?

8. What is known about the success of the data-collection effort? How are missing data indicated? What kind of documentation is available?

Answering these questions helps to ensure that the researcher is familiar with the data he or she will analyze and can help to identify any problems with it. For example, Pamela Paxton (2002) found that she could use only the number of international nongovernmental associations (INGOs) as a measure of secondary organizations in her study of the link between social capital and democracy in a sample of 101 countries, due to the unavailability of comparable figures on purely national associations. She cautioned that "INGOs represent only a specialized subset of all the associations present in a country" (Paxton, 2002:261).

Data quality is always a concern with secondary data, even when the data are collected by an official government agency. The need for concern is much greater in research across national boundaries, because different data-collection systems and definitions of key variables may have been used (Glover, 1996). Census counts can be distorted by incorrect answers to census questions as well as by inadequate coverage of the entire population (see Chapter 5; Rives & Serow, 1988:32–35). Social and political pressures may influence the success of a census in different ways in different countries. Some Mexicans were concerned that the results of Mexico's 2000 census would be "used against them" by the government, and nearly 200,000 communities were inaccessible for follow-up except by a day's mule travel (Burke, 2000). In rural China, many families who had flouted the government's official one-child policy sought to hide their "extra" children from census workers (Rosenthal, 2000).

Both historical and comparative analyses can be affected. For example, the percentage of the U.S. population not counted in the U.S. Census appears to have declined since 1880 from about 7% to 1%, but undercounting continues to be more common among poorer urban dwellers and recent immigrants (King & Magnuson, 1995; and see Chapter 5). The relatively successful 2000 U.S. Census reduced undercounting (Forero, 2000b), but still suffered from accusations of shoddy data-collection procedures in some areas (Forero, 2000a).

Researchers who rely on secondary data inevitably make trade-offs between their ability to use a particular dataset and the specific hypotheses they can test. If a concept that is critical to a hypothesis was not measured adequately in a secondary data source, the study might have to be abandoned until a more adequate source of data can be found. Alternatively, hypotheses or even the research question itself may be modified in order to match the analytic possibilities presented by the available data (Riedel, 2000:53).

DEMOGRAPHIC ANALYSIS

The social processes that are the focus of historical and comparative research are often reflected in and influenced by changes in the makeup of the population being studied. For example, the plummeting birth rates in European countries will influence the politics of immigration in those countries, their living standards, the character of neighborhoods, and national productivity (Bruni, 2002). **Demography** is the field that studies these dynamics. Demography is the statistical and mathematical study of the size, composition, and spatial distribution of human populations and how these features change over time. Demographers explain population change in terms of five processes: fertility, mortality, marriage, migration, and social mobility (Bogue, 1969:1).

Demographers obtain data from a census of the population (see Chapter 5) and from registries—records of events like births, deaths, migrations, marriages, divorces, diseases, and employment (Anderton, Barrett, & Bogue, 1997:54–79; Baum, 1993). They compute various statistics from these data to facilitate description and analysis (Wunsch & Termote, 1978). In order to use these data, you need to understand how they are calculated and the questions they are used to answer. Four concepts are key to understanding and using demographic methods: population change, standardization of population numbers, the demographic bookkeeping equation, and population composition.

Population change is a central concept in demography. The absolute population change is calculated simply as the difference between the population size in one census minus the population size in an earlier census. This measure of absolute change is of little value, however, because it does not take into account the total size of the population that was changing (Bogue, 1969:32–43). A better measure is the *intercensal percent change,* which is the absolute change in population between two censuses divided by the population size in the earlier census (and multiplied by 100 to obtain a percentage). With the percent change statistic, we can meaningfully compare the growth in two or more nations that differ markedly in size (as long as the intercensal interval does not vary between the nations) (White, 1993:1–2).

Standardization of population numbers, as with the calculation of intercensal percent change, is a key concern of demographic methods (Gill, Glazer, & Thernstrom, 1992:478–482; Rele, 1993). In order to make meaningful comparisons between nations and over time, numbers that describe most demographic events must be adjusted for the size of the population at risk for the event. For example, the fertility rate is calculated as the ratio of the number of births to women of childbearing age to the total number of women in this age range (multiplied by 1,000). Unless we make such adjustments, we will not know if a nation with a much higher number of births or deaths in relation to its total population size simply has more women in the appropriate age range or has more births per "eligible" woman.

The *demographic bookkeeping* (or *balancing*) *equation* is used to identify the four components of population growth during a time interval ($P_2 P_1$): births (B), deaths (D), and in- (M_i) and out-migration (M_o). The equation is written as follows: $P_2 = P_1 + (B - D) + (M_i - M_o)$. That is, population at a given point in time is equal to the population at an earlier time plus the excess of births over deaths during the interval and the excess of in-migration over out-migration (White, 1993:1–4). Whenever you see population size or change statistics used in a comparative analysis, you will want to ask yourself whether it is also important to know which component in the equation was responsible for the change over time or for the difference between countries (White, 1993:1–4).

Population composition refers to a description of a population in terms of such basic characteristics as age, race, sex, or marital status (White, 1993:1–7). Descriptions of population composition at different times or in different nations can be essential for understanding social dynamics identified in historical and comparative research. For example, Exhibit 11.8 compares the composition of the population in more developed and developing regions of the

Exhibit 11.8   Population Pyramids for More Developed and Developing Regions of the World: 1995

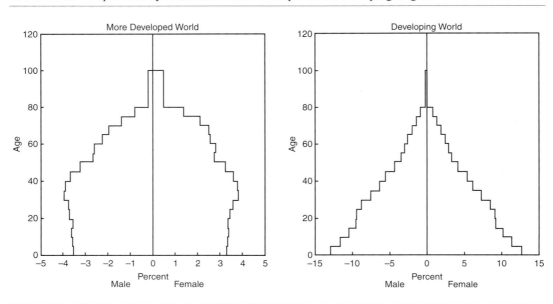

Source: Bogue, Arriaga, & Anderton, 1993:1–19.

world by age and sex in 1995, using United Nations data. By comparing these "population pyramids," we see that children comprise a much greater proportion of the population in less developed regions. The more developed regions' population pyramid also shows the greater proportion of women at older ages and the post-World War II "baby boom" bulge in the population.

Demographic analysis can be an important component of historical research (Bean, Mineau, & Anderton, 1990), but problems of data quality must be carefully evaluated (Vaessen, 1993). The hard work that can be required to develop demographic data from evidence that is hundreds of years old does not always result in worthwhile information. The numbers of people for which data are available in particular areas may be too small for statistical analysis; data that are easily available (such as a list of villages in an area) may not provide the information that is important (such as population size); and lack of information on the original data-collection procedures may prevent assessment of data quality (Hollingsworth, 1972:77).

METHODOLOGICAL COMPLICATIONS

Using unobtrusive methods for historical and comparative research can offer rich insights into other times and places, but the absence of the original sources—the people who collected the raw data or made the statements—creates some unique methodological complications. Small numbers of cases, spotty historical records, variable cross-national record-keeping practices, and different cultural and linguistic contexts limit the confidence that can be placed in measures, samples, and causal conclusions in many comparative historical studies. Consumers as well as designers of historical and comparative research must weigh carefully each of these potential complications.

Just to identify many of the potential problems for a comparative historical research project requires detailed knowledge of the times and of the nations or other units investigated (Kohn, 1987). This requirement itself often serves as a barrier to in-depth historical research and to comparisons between nations. An example of the problems posed by lack of intimate familiarity with another language, culture, and record-keeping system comes from the work of German sociologist Max Weber. Weber studied 18th-century Chinese law, which was contained in a volume from 1740 that had 436 statutes and 1,049 substatutes (Marsh, 2000:285). However, Weber "could not read Chinese, had no expert sinologist to help him," and had access to only a small portion of the documentary sources (Marsh, 2000:281–282). The result was a lack of appreciation for some features of the Chinese system and thus misclassification of the entire Chinese legal approach (Marsh, 2000).

Measuring Across Contexts

One common measurement problem in historical and comparative research projects is the lack of data from some historical periods or geographical units (Rueschemeyer, Stephens, & Stephens, 1992:4; Walters, James, & McCammon, 1997). The widely used U.S. Uniform Crime Reporting System did not begin until 1930 (Rosen, 1995). Missing data prevented Susan Olzak, Suzanne Shanahan, and Elizabeth McEneaney (1996:598) from including more than 55 out of a total of 212 standard metropolitan statistical areas (SMSAs) in their analysis of race riots. Sometimes alternative sources of documents or estimates for missing quantitative data can fill in gaps (Zaret, 1996), but even when measures can be created for key concepts, multiple measures of the same concepts are likely to be out of the question; as a result, tests of reliability and validity may not be feasible. Whatever the situation, researchers must assess the problem honestly and openly (Bollen, Entwisle, & Alderson, 1993; Paxton, 2002).

Those measures that are available are not always adequate. What is included in the historical archives may be an unrepresentative selection of materials that still remain from the past. At various times, some documents could have been discarded, lost, or transferred elsewhere for a variety of reasons. "Original" documents may be transcriptions of spoken words or handwritten pages and could have been modified slightly in the process; they could also be outright distortions (Erikson, 1966:172, 209–210; Zaret, 1996). When relevant data are obtained from previous publications, it is easy to overlook problems of data quality, but this simply makes it all the more important to evaluate the primary sources. Developing a systematic plan for identifying relevant documents and evaluating them is very important.

A somewhat more subtle measurement problem is that of establishing measurement equivalence. The meaning of concepts and the operational definitions of variables may change over time and between nations or regions (Erikson, 1966:xi). For example, the concept of being a "good son or daughter" refers to a much broader range of behaviors in China than in most Western countries (Ho, 1996). Rates of physical disability cannot be compared among nations due to a lack of standard definitions (Martin & Kinsella, 1995:364–365). Individuals in different cultures may respond differently to the same questions (Martin & Kinsella, 1995:385). Alternatively, different measures may have been used for the same concepts in different nations, and the equivalence of these measures may be unknown (van de Vijver & Leung, 1997:9). The value of statistics for particular geographic units like counties may vary over time simply due to changes in the boundaries of these units (Walters, James, & McCammon, 1997). Such possibilities should be considered, and any available opportunity should be taken to test for their effects.

A different measurement concern can arise as a consequence of the simplifications made to facilitate comparative analysis. In many qualitative comparative analyses, the values of continuous variables are dichotomized. For example, nations may be coded as "democratic" or "authoritarian." This introduces an imprecise and arbitrary element into the analysis (Lieberson, 1991). On the other hand, for some comparisons, qualitative distinctions such as "simple majority rule" or "unanimity required" may capture the important differences between cases better than quantitative distinctions. It is essential to inspect carefully the categorization rules for any such analysis and to consider what form of measurement is both feasible and appropriate for the research question being investigated (King, Keohane, & Verba, 1994:158–163).

Sampling Across Time and Place

The simplest type of sample is the selection of one case for a historical study. Although a great deal can be learned from the intensive focus on one nation or other unit, the lack of a comparative element shapes the type of explanations that are developed. Explanations for change within one nation are likely to focus on factors that have changed within it, such as the decisions of a political leader, rather than factors like political systems that vary between nations (Rueschemeyer, Stephens, & Stephens, 1992:31–36). However, comparisons between nations may reveal that differences in political systems are much more important than voluntary decisions by individual political leaders. It is only when the political system changes over time within one nation that its impact can be evaluated empirically (Rueschemeyer, Stephens, & Stephens, 1992:29).

Qualitative comparative historical studies are likely to rely on availability samples or purposive samples of cases. In an availability sample, researchers study a case or multiple cases simply because they are familiar with or have access to them. When using a purposive sampling strategy, researchers select cases because they reflect theoretically important distinctions. Quantitative historical comparative researchers often select entire populations of cases for which the appropriate measures can be obtained (see Chapter 5).

When geographic units like nations are sampled for comparative purposes, it is assumed that the nations are independent of each other in terms of the variables examined. Each nation can then be treated as a separate case for identifying possible chains of causes and effects. However, in a very interdependent world, this assumption may be misplaced—nations may develop as they do because of how other nations are developing (and the same can be said of cities and other units). As a result, comparing the particular histories of different nations may overlook the influence of global culture, international organizations, or economic dependency—just the type of influence identified in Frank, Hironaka, and Schofer's study of environmental protectionism (Skocpol, 1984:384; cf. Chase-Dunn & Hall, 1993). These common international influences may cause the same pattern of changes to emerge in different nations; looking within the history of these nations for the explanatory influences would lead to spurious conclusions. The possibility of such complex interrelations should always be considered when evaluating the plausibility of a causal argument based on a comparison between two apparently independent cases (Jervis, 1996).

Identifying Causes

The restriction of historical research to one setting in the past limits possibilities for testing causal connections, because explanations applied to these events can seem arbitrary (Skocpol, 1984:365). The researcher can reduce the problem by making some comparisons to other events in the past or present. However, the interdependence of sampled units (noted above) may mean that several cases available for comparison should be treated as just one larger case. There may also be too many possible combinations of causal factors to test and not enough cases to test them with.

The inductive approach taken by many qualitative comparative researchers can also make it seem that whatever the causal explanation developed, it has been tailored to fit the particulars of the historical record and so is unlikely to be confirmed by other cases (Rueschemeyer, Stephens, & Stephens, 1992:30).

Some comparative researchers use a systematic method for identifying causes that was developed by the English philosopher John Stuart Mill (1872). He called it the **method of agreement** (Exhibit 11.9). The core of this approach is the comparison of nations ("cases") in terms of similarities and differences on potential causal variables and the phenomenon to be explained. For example, suppose three nations that have all developed democratic political systems are compared in terms of four socioeconomic variables hypothesized by different

Exhibit 11.9   John Stuart Mill's Method of Agreement

Variable	The Method of Agreement*		
	Case 1	Case 2	Case 3
A	Different	Different	Different
B	Different	Same	Same
C	Different	Different	Different
D	Same	Same	Same
Outcome	Same	Same	Same

Source: Adapted from Skocpol, 1984:379.

*D is considered the cause of the outcome.

theories to influence democratization. If the nations differ in terms of three of the variables but are similar in terms of the fourth, this is evidence that the fourth variable influences democratization.

The features of the cases selected for comparison have a large impact on the ability to identify influences using the method of agreement. Cases should be chosen for their difference in terms of key factors hypothesized to influence the outcome of interest and their similarity on other, possibly confounding, factors (Skocpol, 1984:383). For example, in order to understand how industrialization influences democracy, you would need to select cases for comparison that differ in industrialization, so that you could then see if they differ in democratization (King, Keohane, & Verba, 1994:148–152).

This **deterministic causal approach** (Ragin, 1987:44–52) requires that there be no deviations from the combination of factors that are identified as determining the outcome for each nation. Yet there are likely to be exceptions to any explanatory rule that we establish (Lieberson, 1991). A careful analyst will evaluate the extent to which exceptions should be allowed in particular analyses.

With these cautions in mind, the combination of historical and comparative methods allows for rich descriptions of social and political processes in different nations or regions as well as for causal inferences that reflect a systematic, defensible weighing of the evidence. Data of increasingly good quality are available on a rapidly expanding number of nations, creating many opportunities for comparative research. We cannot expect one study comparing the histories of a few nations to control adequately for every plausible alternative causal influence, but repeated investigations can refine our understanding and lead to increasingly accurate causal conclusions (King, Keohane, & Verba, 1994:33).

ETHICAL ISSUES IN HISTORICAL AND COMPARATIVE RESEARCH

Analysis of historical documents or quantitative data collected by others does not create the potential for harm to human subjects that can be a concern when collecting primary data. It is still important to be honest and responsible in working out arrangements for data access when data must be obtained from designated officials or data archivists, but of course many data are available easily in libraries or on the Web. Researchers who conclude that they are being denied access to public records of the federal government may be able to obtain the data by filing a Freedom of Information Act (FOIA) request. The FOIA stipulates that all persons have a right to access all federal agency records unless the records are specifically exempted (Riedel, 2000:130–131). Researchers who review historical or government documents must also try to avoid embarrassing or otherwise harming named individuals or their descendants by disclosing sensitive information.

Ethical concerns are multiplied when surveys are conducted or other data are collected in other countries. If the outside researcher lacks much knowledge of local norms, values, and routine activities, the potential for inadvertently harming subjects is substantial. For this reason, cross-cultural researchers should spend time learning about each of the countries in which they plan to collect primary data and strike up collaborations with researchers in those countries (Hantrais & Mangen, 1996). Local advisory groups may also be formed in each country so that a broader range of opinion is solicited when key decisions must be made. Such collaboration can also be invaluable when designing instruments, collecting data, and interpreting results.

CONCLUSIONS

Historical and comparative social science investigations use a variety of techniques that range from narrative histories having much in common with qualitative methods to analyses of secondary data that are in many respects like traditional survey research. Each of these techniques can help the researcher gain new insights into processes like democratization. They encourage intimate familiarity with the course of development of the nations studied and thereby stimulate inductive reasoning about the interrelations among different historical events. Systematic historical and comparative techniques can be used to test deductive hypotheses concerning international differences as well as historical events.

Most historical and comparative methods encourage causal reasoning. They require the researcher to consider systematically the causal mechanism, or historical sequences of events, by which earlier events influence later outcomes. They also encourage attention to causal context, with a particular focus on the ways in which different cultures and social structures may result in different effects of other variables. There is much to be gained by learning and continuing to use and develop these methods.

KEY TERMS

Case-oriented research
Comparative historical research
Conjunctural
Cross-sectional comparative research
Demography
Deterministic causal approach
Event-structure analysis
Historical events research

Historical process research
Holistic
Method of agreement
Narrative explanation
Oral history
Secondary data
Temporal
Variable-oriented research

HIGHLIGHTS

- The central insight behind historical and comparative methods is that we can improve our understanding of social processes when we make comparisons to other times and places.

- There are four basic types of historical and comparative research methods: historical events research, historical process research, cross-sectional comparative research, and comparative historical research. Historical events research and historical process research are likely to be qualitative, whereas comparative studies are often quantitative; however, research of each type may be either quantitative or qualitative.

- Qualitative historical process research uses a narrative approach to causal explanation, in which historical events are treated as part of a developing story. Narrative explanations are temporal, holistic, and conjunctural.

- Methodological challenges for comparative and historical research include missing data, variation in the meaning of words and phrases and in the boundaries of geographic units across historical periods and between cultures, bias or inaccuracy of historical documents, lack of measurement equivalence, the need for detailed knowledge of the cases chosen, limited number of cases, case selection on an availability basis, reliance on dichotomous categorizations of cases, and interdependence of cases selected.

- Secondary data analysts should have a good understanding of the research methods used to collect the data they analyze. Data quality is always a concern, particularly with historical data.

- Central concepts for demographic research are population change, standardization of population numbers, the demographic bookkeeping equation, and population composition.

- Oral history provides a means of reconstructing past events. Data from other sources should be used whenever possible to evaluate the accuracy of memories.

- Secondary data for historical and comparative research are available from many sources. The Inter-university Consortium for Political and Social Research (ICPSR) provides the most comprehensive data archive.

DISCUSSION QUESTIONS

1. Review the differences between case-oriented, historically specific, inductive explanations and those that are more variable-oriented, theoretically general, and deductive. List several arguments for and against each approach. Which is more appealing to you and why?

2. Read the original article reporting one of the studies described in this chapter. Critique the article, using the article review questions presented in Appendix B as your guide. Focus particular attention on procedures for measurement, sampling, and establishing causal relations.

3. What historical events have had a major influence on social patterns in the nation? The possible answers are too numerous to list, ranging from any of the wars to major internal political conflicts, economic booms and busts, scientific discoveries, and legal changes. Pick one such event in your own nation for this exercise. Find one historical book on this event and list the sources of evidence used. What additional evidence would you suggest for a social science investigation of the event?

4. Consider the comparative historical research by Rueschemeyer, Stephens, and Stephens (1992) on democratic politics in Latin America. What does comparison among nations add to the researcher's ability to develop causal explanations?

5. Olzak, Shanahan, and McEneaney (1996) developed a nomothetic causal explanation of variation in racial rioting in the United States over time, whereas Griffin's (1993) explanation of a lynching can

be termed idiographic. Discuss the similarities and differences between these types of causal explanation. Use these two studies to illustrate the strengths and weaknesses of each.

6. Select one of the four types of historical and comparative methods for further study. Now search recent issues of journals like *American Journal of Sociology, American Sociological Review, American Political Science Review, Journal of Social History,* and *Social Science History* to find an article that uses this type of method. Read the abstracts of articles that appear to be historical and/or comparative. What difficulties do you have in classifying articles as historical or comparative? What rules would you suggest for making this classification? Now focus on the one article you have chosen. What strengths and limitations of the method you focused on does the article illustrate? (Refer to the "Methodological Issues" section of this chapter for a discussion of these issues.)

PRACTICE EXERCISES

1. The journals *Social Science History* and *Journal of Social History* report many studies of historical processes. Select one article from a recent journal issue about a historical process used to explain some event or other outcome. Summarize the author's explanation. Identify any features of the explanation that are temporal, holistic, and conjunctural. Prepare a chronology of the important historical events in that process. Do you agree with the author's causal conclusions? What additional evidence would strengthen the author's argument?

2. Exhibit 11.10 on page 364 identifies voting procedures and the level of turnout in 1 election for 10 countries. Do voting procedures appear to influence turnout in these countries? In order to answer this question using Mill's methods, you will first have to decide how to dichotomize the values of variables that have more than two values (postal voting, proxy voting, and turnout). You must also decide what to do about missing values. Apply Mill's method of agreement to the pattern in the table. Do any variables emerge as likely causes? What additional information would you like to have for your causal analysis?

3. Using your library's government documents collection or the U.S. Census site on the Web, select one report by the U.S. Bureau of the Census about the population of the United States or some segment of it. Outline the report and list all of the tables included in it. Summarize the report in two paragraphs. Suggest a historical or comparative study for which this report would be useful.

4. Review the survey datasets available through the Inter-university Consortium for Political and Social Research (ICPSR), using their Internet site (http://www.icpsr.umich.edu/index.html). Select two datasets that might be used to study a research question in which you are interested. Use the information ICPSR reports about them to answer Questions 1–5 from the "Challenges for Secondary Data Analyses" section of this chapter. Is the information adequate to answer these questions? What are the advantages and disadvantages of using one of these datasets to answer your research question compared to designing a new study?

5. Find a magazine or newspaper report on a demographic issue, such as population change or migration. Explain how one of the key demographic concepts could be used or was used to improve understanding of this issue.

6. Review the interactive exercises on the CD-ROM for a lesson that will help you to master the terms used in historical and comparative research.

WEB EXERCISES

1. The World Bank offers numerous resources that are useful for comparative research. Visit the World Bank Web site at http://www.worldbank.org. Click on "Countries & Regions" and then select "Africa—Sub-Saharan." Now choose "Angola" as your country and request the "Country Brief," and

Exhibit 11.10 Voting Procedures in 10 Countries

	Voting Age	Number of Days Polling Booth Open	Voting Day on Work Day or Rest Day	Postal Voting	Proxy Voting	Constituency Transfer	Advance Voting	Voter Turnout (in %)	Year (P=presidential, L = legislative election)
Switzerland	20	2	Rest day	Automatic for armed forces, otherwise by application 4 days before voting	Varies by canton	No	No	46	1991L
Taiwan	20	1	Rest day					72	1992L
Thailand	20	1	Rest day	No				62	1995L
Turkey	20	1	Rest day	No	No	Special polling stations at border posts for citizens residing abroad	No	80	1991L
Ukraine	18	1	Rest day	On application	On application	No	No	71.6	1994P
United Kingdom	18	1	Work day	On application	On application	No	No	77.8	1992L
United States	18	1	Work day	By application; rules vary across states	In some states for blind and disabled	No		51.5	1992P
Uruguay	18	1	Rest day	No	No	No	No	89.4	1994P
Venezuela	18	1	Rest day	No	"Assisted" voting for blind and disabled	No	No	60	1993P
Zambia		1	Work day		No			50	1991P

Source: LeDuc, Niemi, & Norris, 1996:19 (Figure 1.3).

examine the "Angola at a Glance" data. Now compare these data to those for another African country and summarize the differences and similarities you have identified between the countries.

2. The U.S. Bureau of Labor Statistics Web site provides extensive economic indicator data for regions, states, and cities. Go to the BLS Web page that offers statistics by location: http://stats.bls.gov/eag. Now click on a region and explore the types of data that are available. Write out a description of the steps you would have to take to conduct a comparative analysis using the data available from the BLS Web site.

3. The U.S. Census Bureau's home page can be found at http://www.census.gov. This site contains extensive reporting of census data including population data, economic indicators, and other information acquired through the U.S. Census. This Web site allows you to collect information on numerous subjects and topics. This information can then be used to make comparisons between different states or cities. Find the "State and County Quick Facts" option and choose your own state. Now pick the county in which you live and copy down several statistics of interest. Repeat this process for other counties in your state. Use the data you have collected to compare your county with other counties in the state. Write a one-page report summarizing your findings.

SPSS EXERCISES

1. In Chapter 2 you examined the relationship between support for capital punishment and region. In this exercise you will use Mill's method of agreement to examine regional differences again. For this cross-sectional comparative analysis, I have collapsed all the regions in the United States into East, Midwest, South, and West.
   a. First, examine the labels and response choices for each of the following variables:
      INCOME98, HHRACE, POLVIEW3, EDUCR3, ATTEND2, BIBLE2, BORN, SPKATH
      Which, if any, do you believe varies between regions? State at least five hypotheses.
   b. Now request the distributions for the above variables, within region. You can do this by requesting the crosstabulation of each variable by REGION4. Summarize what you have found in a table that indicates, for each region, whether it is "high" or "low" in terms of each variable, in comparison for each region. Repeat this procedure for the distribution of the variable CAPPUN. From the menu, click *Analyze|Descriptives|Crosstabs*
      In the Crosstabs window, set:
      Down: ATTEND2 (and the other variables)
      Across: REGION4
      Statistics: COLUMN %.
   c. Review your table of similarities and differences across the regions. See if on this basis you can develop a tentative explanation of regional variation in support for capital punishment using Mill's method of agreement.
   d. Discuss the possible weaknesses in the type of explanation you have constructed, following John Stuart Mill. Propose a different approach for a comparative historical analysis.

2. How do the attitudes of immigrants to the United States compare to those of people born in the United States? Request the crosstabulations (in percentage form) of the variables used in Question 1 by BORN (with BORN as the column variable). Inspect the output. Describe the similarities and differences you have found.

3. Because the GSS file is cross-sectional, we cannot use it to conduct historical research. However, we can develop some interesting historical questions by examining differences in the attitudes of Americans in different birth cohorts.
   a. Inspect the distributions of the same set of variables. Would you expect any of these attitudes and behaviors to have changed over the twentieth century? State your expectations in the form of hypotheses.

b. Request a crosstabulation of these variables by birth COHORTS. What appear to be the differences among the cohorts? Which differences do you think are due to historical change, and which do you think are due to the aging process? Which attitudes and behaviors would you expect to still differentiate the baby-boom generation and the post-Vietnam generation in 20 years?

DEVELOPING A RESEARCH PROPOSAL

Add a historical or comparative dimension to your proposed study.

1. Consider which of the four types of comparative/historical methods would be most suited to an investigation of your research question. Think of possibilities for qualitative and quantitative research on your topic with the method you prefer. Will you conduct a variable-oriented or case-oriented study? Write a brief statement justifying the approach you choose.

2. Review the possible sources of data for your comparative-historical project. Search the Web and relevant government, historical, and international organization sites or publications. Search the social science literature for similar studies and read about the data sources that they used.

3. Specify the hypotheses you will test or the causal sequences you will investigate. Describe what your cases will be (nations, regions, years, etc.). Explain how you will select cases. List the sources of your measures and describe the specific type of data you expect to obtain for each measure. Discuss how you will evaluate causal influences, and indicate whether you will take a nomothetic or idiographic approach to causality.

4. Review the list of potential problems in comparative/historical research and discuss those that you believe will be most troublesome in your proposed investigation. Explain your reasoning.

Chapter 12

DATA ANALYSIS

Introducing Statistics

Case Study: The Likelihood of Voting

Preparing Data for Analysis

Displaying Univariate Distributions

Graphs
Frequency Distributions
  Ungrouped Data
  Grouped Data
  Combined and Compressed
    Distributions

Summarizing Univariate Distributions

Measures of Central Tendency
  Mode
  Median
  Mean
  Median or Mean?
Measures of Variation
  Range

Interquartile Range
Variance
Standard Deviation

**Analyzing Data Ethically:
  How Not to Lie With Statistics**

Crosstabulating Variables

Graphing Association
Describing Association
Evaluating Association
Controlling for a Third Variable
  Intervening Variables
  Extraneous Variables
  Specification

Regressing Variables

**Analyzing Data Ethically: How Not to
  Lie About Relationships**

Conclusions

$\mathbf{T}$his chapter will introduce several common statistics used in social research and highlight the factors that must be considered when using and interpreting statistics. Think of it as a review of fundamental social statistics, if you have already studied them, or as an introductory overview, if you have not. Two preliminary sections lay the foundation for studying statistics. In the first, I will discuss the role of statistics in the research process, returning to themes and techniques with which you are already familiar. In the second preliminary section,

I will outline the process of preparing data for statistical analysis. In the rest of the chapter, I will explain how to describe the distribution of single variables and the relationship between variables. Along the way, I will address ethical issues related to data analysis. This chapter will have been successful if it encourages you to use statistics responsibly, to evaluate statistics critically, and to seek opportunities for extending your statistical knowledge.

Although many colleges and universities offer social statistics in a separate course, and for good reason (there's a *lot* to learn), I don't want you to think of this chapter as somehow on a different topic than the rest of this book. Data analysis is an integral component of research methods and it's important that any proposal for quantitative research include a plan for the data analysis that will follow data collection. (As you'll see in the next chapter, data analysis in qualitative projects often occurs in tandem with data collection.) You have to anticipate your data analysis needs if you expect your research design to secure the requisite data.

INTRODUCING STATISTICS

Statistics play a key role in achieving valid research results, in terms of measurement, causal validity, and generalizability. Some statistics are useful primarily to describe the results of measuring single variables and to construct and evaluate multi-item scales. These statistics include frequency distributions, graphs, measures of central tendency and variation, and reliability tests. Other statistics are useful primarily in achieving causal validity, by helping us to describe the association among variables and to control for or otherwise take account of other variables. Crosstabulation is the technique for measuring association and controlling other variables that is introduced in this chapter. All of these statistics are termed **descriptive statistics** because they are used to describe the distribution of and relationship among variables.

You already learned in Chapter 5 that it is possible to estimate the degree of confidence that can be placed in generalizations from a sample to the population from which the sample was selected. The statistics used in making these estimates are termed **inferential statistics.** In this chapter I will introduce the use of inferential statistics for testing hypotheses involving sample data.

Social theory and the results of prior research should guide our statistical choices, as they guide the choice of other research methods. There are so many particular statistics and so many ways for them to be used in data analysis that even the best statistician can become lost in a sea of numbers if she does not use prior research and theorizing to develop a coherent analysis plan. It is also important to choose for an analysis statistics that are appropriate to the level of measurement of the variables to be analyzed. As you learned in Chapter 4, numbers used to represent the values of variables may not actually signify different quantities, meaning that many statistical techniques will be inapplicable.

Case Study: The Likelihood of Voting

In this chapter I will use for examples data from the General Social Survey (GSS) on voting and the variables associated with it, and I will focus on a research question about political participation: What influences the likelihood of voting? Prior research on voting in both national and local settings provides a great deal of support for one hypothesis: The likelihood of voting increases with social status (Milbrath & Goel, 1977:92–95; Salisbury, 1975:326;

Exhibit 12.1   Voting and Social Status

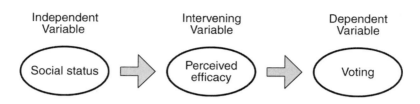

Verba & Nie, 1972:8–92). Research suggests that social status influences the likelihood of voting through the intervening variable of perceived political efficacy, or the feeling that one's vote matters (see Exhibit 12.1). But some research findings on political participation are inconsistent with the social status–voting hypothesis. For example, African Americans participate in politics at higher rates than do white Americans of similar social status (Verba & Nie, 1972; Verba, Nie, & Kim, 1978). This discrepant finding suggests that the impact of social status on voting and other forms of political participation varies with the social characteristics of potential participants.

If we are guided by prior research, a test of the hypothesis that likelihood of voting increases with social status should also take into account political efficacy and some social characteristics, such as race. We can find indicators for each of these variables except political efficacy in the 2000 General Social Survey (see Exhibit 12.2). We will substitute the variable "interpersonal trust " for political efficacy. I will use these variables to illustrate particular statistics throughout this chapter, drawing on complete 2000 GSS data. You can replicate my analysis with the subset of the 2000 GSS data that is included on your CD-ROM.

Exhibit 12.2   List of GSS2000 Variables for Analysis of Voting

Variable	SPSS Variable Name	Description
Social Status		
Family income	INCOM98R	Family income in 1998 (categories)
Education	EDUCR3	Years of education completed (categories)
Age	AGER	Years old (categories)
Gender	SEX	Sex
Marital status	MARITAL	Married, never married, widowed, divorced
Race	RACE	White, black, other
Politics Voting	VOTE96D	Voted in 1996 presidential election (yes/no)
Political views	POLVIEWS	Liberal to conservative rating
Interpersonal trust	TRUST	Believe other people can be trusted

Source: General Social Survey, National Opinion Research Center, 2000.

PREPARING DATA FOR ANALYSIS

My analysis of voting in this chapter is an example of what is called **secondary data analysis.** It is secondary because I received the data secondhand; I did not design the data-collection instrument. Using secondary data in this way has a major disadvantage: If you did not design the study yourself, it is unlikely that all the variables that you think should have been included actually were included *and* were measured in the way that you prefer. In addition, the sample may not represent just the population in which you are interested, and the study design may be only partially appropriate to your research question. For example, the 1991 GSS included one question that measured feelings of political efficacy, the 1996 version included several, but the 1998 and 2000 versions included none. Because it is a survey of individuals, the GSS lacks measures of political context (such as the dominant party in an area). Because the survey sample is selected only from the United States and because the questions concern just one presidential election, we will not be able to address directly the larger issues of political context that are represented in cross-national and longitudinal research (Verba, Nie, & Kim, 1978).

It is the availability of secondary data that makes their use preferable for many purposes. As you learned in Chapter 11, a great many high-quality datasets are available for reanalysis from the Inter-university Consortium for Political and Social Research (ICPSR) at the University of Michigan; many others can be obtained from the government, individual researchers, and other research organizations. Many of these datasets are stored online and can be downloaded directly for analysis; some can even be analyzed directly online. Others are available on CD-ROM. For a great many research problems, therefore, a researcher should first review the available datasets pertaining to that topic (and determine whether his or her university or other employer is a member of ICPSR). An enormous savings in time and resources may be the result.

If you have conducted your own survey or experiment, your quantitative data must be prepared in a format suitable for computer entry. Several options are available. Questionnaires or other data entry forms can be designed for scanning or direct computer entry (see Exhibit 12.3). Once the computer database software is programmed to recognize the response codes, the forms can be fed through a scanner and the data will then be entered directly into the database. If responses or other forms of data have been entered on nonscannable paper forms, a computer data entry program should be used that will allow the data to be entered into the database by clicking on boxes corresponding to the response codes. Alternatively, if a data entry program is not used, responses can be typed directly into a computer database. If data entry is to be done in this way, the questionnaires or other forms should be precoded. Precoding means that every response choice is represented by a number, and respondents are instructed to indicate their response to a question by checking a number. It will then be easier to type in the strings of numbers than to type in the responses themselves.

Whatever data entry method is used, the data must be checked carefully for errors—a process called **data cleaning.** The first step in data cleaning is to check responses before they are entered into the database to make sure that one and only one valid answer code has been clearly circled or checked for each question (unless multiple responses are allowed or a skip pattern was specified). Written answers can be assigned their own numerical codes. The next step in data cleaning is to make sure that no invalid codes have been entered. Invalid codes are codes that fall outside the range of allowable values for a given variable and those that

Exhibit 12.3 Data Entry Procedures

Bureau of Economic Analysis

Customer Satisfaction Survey

OMB Control No: 0691-0001
Expiration Date: 07/31/2003

On a scale of 1-5, please select the appropriate answer to each question.

1. Which data products do you use?	Frequently (every week)	Often (every month)	Infrequently	Rarely	Never	Don't know or not applicable
GENERAL DATA PRODUCTS						
Survey of Current Business	○ 5	○ 4	○ 3	○ 2	○ 1	● N/A
CD-ROMs	○ 5	○ 4	○ 3	○ 2	○ 1	● N/A
BEA Web site (www.bea.doc.gov)	○ 5	○ 4	○ 3	○ 2	○ 1	● N/A
STAT-USA Web site (www.stat-usa.gov)	○ 5	○ 4	○ 3	○ 2	○ 1	● N/A
Telephone access to staff	○ 5	○ 4	○ 3	○ 2	○ 1	● N/A
E-Mail access to staff	○ 5	○ 4	○ 3	○ 2	○ 1	● N/A
INDUSTRY DATA PRODUCTS						
Gross Product by Industry	○ 5	○ 4	○ 3	○ 2	○ 1	● N/A
Input-Output Tables	○ 5	○ 4	○ 3	○ 2	○ 1	● N/A
Satellite Accounts	○ 5	○ 4	○ 3	○ 2	○ 1	● N/A
INTERNATIONAL DATA PRODUCTS						
U.S. International Transactions (Balance of Payments)	○ 5	○ 4	○ 3	○ 2	○ 1	● N/A
U.S. Exports and Imports of Private Services	○ 5	○ 4	○ 3	○ 2	○ 1	● N/A
U.S. Direct Investment Abroad	○ 5	○ 4	○ 3	○ 2	○ 1	● N/A
Foreign Direct Investment in the United States	○ 5	○ 4	○ 3	○ 2	○ 1	● N/A
U.S. International Investment Position	○ 5	○ 4	○ 3	○ 2	○ 1	● N/A
NATIONAL DATA PRODUCTS						
National Income and Product Accounts (GDP)	○ 5	○ 4	○ 3	○ 2	○ 1	● N/A
NIPA Underlying Detail Data	○ 5	○ 4	○ 3	○ 2	○ 1	● N/A
Capital Stock (Wealth) and Investment by Industry	○ 5	○ 4	○ 3	○ 2	○ 1	● N/A
REGIONAL DATA PRODUCTS						
State Personal Income	○ 5	○ 4	○ 3	○ 2	○ 1	● N/A
Local Area Personal Income	○ 5	○ 4	○ 3	○ 2	○ 1	● N/A
Gross State Product by Industry	○ 5	○ 4	○ 3	○ 2	○ 1	● N/A
RIMS II Regional Multipliers	○ 5	○ 4	○ 3	○ 2	○ 1	● N/A

2. How satisfied are you with:	Very satisfied	Satisfied	Neither dissatisfied nor satisfied	Dissatisfied	Very dissatisfied	Don't know or not applicable
the overall quality of the BEA products/services?	○ 5	○ 4	○ 3	○ 2	○ 1	● N/A
the timeliness of BEA estimates?	○ 5	○ 4	○ 3	○ 2	○ 1	● N/A
the accuracy of BEA estimates?	○ 5	○ 4	○ 3	○ 2	○ 1	● N/A
the adaptation of BEA's methodologies to changes in the economy?	○ 5	○ 4	○ 3	○ 2	○ 1	● N/A
the format (ease of use) of BEA's data?	○ 5	○ 4	○ 3	○ 2	○ 1	● N/A
the documentation of BEA's data?	○ 5	○ 4	○ 3	○ 2	○ 1	● N/A
the courtesy of BEA staff?	○ 5	○ 4	○ 3	○ 2	○ 1	● N/A
the expertise of BEA staff?	○ 5	○ 4	○ 3	○ 2	○ 1	● N/A
BEA's responsiveness to your suggestions?	○ 5	○ 4	○ 3	○ 2	○ 1	● N/A
BEA's Web site (www.bea.doc.gov)?	○ 5	○ 4	○ 3	○ 2	○ 1	● N/A

Source: U.S. Bureau of Economic Analysis, 2002:11–12.

represent impossible combinations of responses to two or more questions. (For example, if a respondent says that he or she did not vote in an election, a response to a subsequent question indicating whom that person voted for would be invalid.) Most survey research organizations now use a database management program to control data entry. The program prompts the data entry clerk for each response code, checks the code to ensure that it represents a valid response for that variable, and saves the response code in the data file. This process reduces sharply the possibility of data entry errors.

If data are typed into a text file or entered directly through the data sheet of a statistics program, a computer program must be written to "define the data." A data definition program identifies the variables that are coded in each column or range of columns, attaches meaningful labels to the codes, and distinguishes values representing missing data. The procedures for doing so vary with the specific statistical package used. I used the Statistical Package for the Social Sciences (SPSS) for the analysis in this chapter; you will find examples of SPSS commands for defining and analyzing data in Appendix F. More detailed information on using SPSS is contained in SPSS manuals and in the Pine Forge Press volume, *Adventures in Social Research: Data Analysis Using SPSS 11.0/11.5 for Windows,* 5th edition by Earl Babbie, Fred Halley, and Jeanne Zaino (2003).

DISPLAYING UNIVARIATE DISTRIBUTIONS

The first step in data analysis is usually to display the variation in each variable of interest. For many descriptive purposes, the analysis may go no further. Graphs and frequency distributions are the two most popular approaches; both allow the analyst to display the distribution of cases across the categories of a variable. Graphs have the advantage of providing a picture that is easier to comprehend, although frequency distributions are preferable when exact numbers of cases having particular values must be reported and when many distributions must be displayed in a compact form.

Whichever type of display is used, the primary concern of the data analyst is to display accurately the distribution's shape, that is, to show how cases are distributed across the values of the variable. Three features of shape are important: **central tendency, variability,** and **skewness** (lack of symmetry). All three features can be represented in a graph or in a frequency distribution.

Central tendency The most common value (for variables measured at the nominal level) or the value around which cases tend to center (for a quantitative variable).

Variability The extent to which cases are spread out through the distribution or clustered in just one location.

Skewness The extent to which cases are clustered more at one or the other end of the distribution of a quantitative variable, rather than in a symmetric pattern around its center. Skew can be positive (a right skew), with the number of cases tapering off in the positive direction, or negative (a left skew), with the number of cases tapering off in the negative direction.

These features of a distribution's shape can be interpreted in several different ways, and they are not all appropriate for describing every variable. In fact, all three features of a distribution can be distorted if graphs, frequency distributions, or summary statistics are used inappropriately.

A variable's level of measurement is the most important determinant of the appropriateness of particular statistics. For example, we cannot talk about the skewness (lack of symmetry) of a qualitative variable (those measured at the nominal level). If the values of a variable cannot be ordered from lowest to highest—if the ordering of the values is arbitrary—we cannot say that the distribution is not symmetric because we could just reorder the values to make the distribution more (or less) symmetric. Some measures of central tendency and variability are also inappropriate for qualitative variables.

The distinction between variables measured at the ordinal level and those measured at the interval or ratio level should also be considered when selecting statistics to use, but social researchers differ in just how much importance they attach to this distinction. Many social researchers think of ordinal variables as imperfectly measured interval level variables and believe that in most circumstances statistics developed for interval level variables also provide useful summaries for ordinal variables. Other social researchers believe that variation in ordinal variables will often be distorted by statistics that assume an interval level of measurement. We will touch on some of the details in the following sections on particular statistical techniques.

We will now examine graphs and frequency distributions that illustrate these three features of shape. Summary statistics used to measure specific aspects of central tendency and variability will be presented in a separate section. There is a summary statistic for the measurement of skewness, but it is used only rarely in published research reports and will not be presented here.

Graphs

A picture often is worth some unmeasurable quantity of words. Even for the uninitiated, graphs can be easy to read, and they highlight a distribution's shape. They are useful particularly for exploring data because they show the full range of variation and identify data anomalies that might be in need of further study. And good, professional-looking graphs can now be produced relatively easily with software available for personal computers. There are many types of graphs, but the most common and most useful are bar charts, histograms, and frequency polygons. Each has two axes, the vertical axis (the *y*-axis) and the horizontal axis (the *x*-axis), and labels to identify the variables and the values, with tick marks showing where each indicated value falls along the axis.

A **bar chart** contains solid bars separated by spaces. It is a good tool for displaying the distribution of variables measured at the nominal level and other discrete categorical variables because there is, in effect, a gap between each of the categories. The bar chart of marital status in Exhibit 12.4 indicates that almost half of adult Americans were married at the time of the survey. Smaller percentages were divorced, separated, widowed, or never married. The most common value in the distribution is "married," so this would be the distribution's central tendency. There is a moderate amount of variability in the distribution, because the half who are not married are spread across the categories of widowed, divorced, separated, and never married. Because marital status is not a quantitative

Exhibit 12.4 Bar Chart of Marital Status

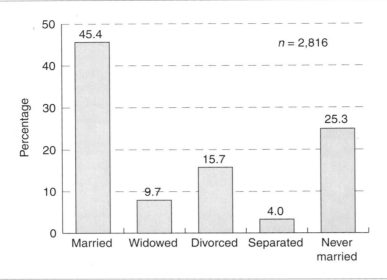

Source: General Social Survey, 2000.

Note: Percentages do not add up to 100 due to rounding error.

variable, the order in which the categories are presented is arbitrary, and so skewness is not relevant.

Histograms, in which the bars are adjacent, are used to display the distribution of quantitative variables that vary along a continuum that has no necessary gaps. Exhibit 12.5 shows a histogram of years of education from the 2000 GSS data. The distribution has a clump of cases centered at 12 years. The distribution is skewed, because there are more cases just above the central point than below it.

In a **frequency polygon,** a continuous line connects the points representing the number or percentage of cases with each value. The frequency polygon is an alternative to the histogram when the distribution of a quantitative, continuous variable must be displayed; this alternative is particularly useful when the variable has a wide range of values. It is easy to see in the frequency polygon of years of education in Exhibit 12.6 that the most common value is 12 years, high school completion, and that this value also seems to be the center of the distribution. There is moderate variability in the distribution, with many cases having more than 12 years of education and about one-quarter having completed at least 4 years of college (16 years). The distribution is highly skewed in the negative direction, with few respondents reporting less than 10 years of education.

If graphs are misused, they can distort, rather than display, the shape of a distribution. Compare, for example, the two graphs in Exhibit 12.7 (p. 376). The first graph shows that high school seniors reported relatively stable rates of lifetime use of cocaine between 1980 and 1985. The second graph, using exactly the same numbers, appeared in a 1986 *Newsweek* article on

Exhibit 12.5   Histogram of Years of Education

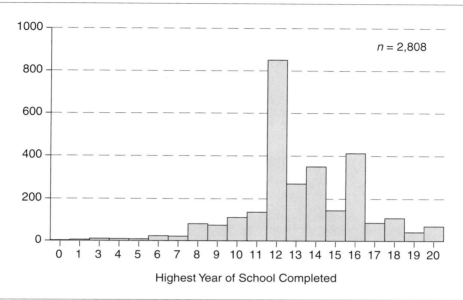

Source: General Social Survey, 2000.

Exhibit 12.6   Frequency Polygon of Years of Education

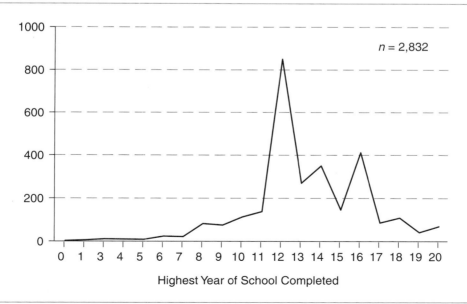

Source: General Social Survey, 2000.

Exhibit 12.7   Two Graphs of Cocaine Usage

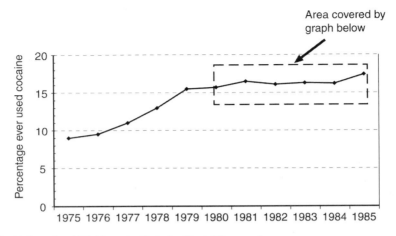

A. University of Michigan Institute for Social Research,
Time Series for Lifetime Prevalence of Cocaine Use

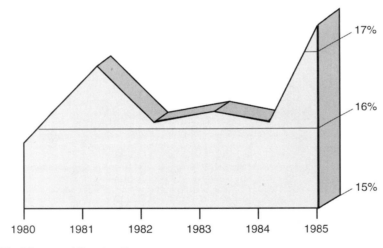

B. Final Stages of Construction

Source: Adapted from Orcutt & Turner, 1993. © 1993 by the Society for the Study of Social Problems.
Reprinted by permission.

the coke plague (Orcutt & Turner, 1993). To look at this graph, you would think that the rate
of cocaine usage among high school seniors had increased dramatically during this period.
But, in fact, the difference between the two graphs is due simply to changes in how the graphs
are drawn. In the plague graph, the percentage scale on the vertical axis begins at 15 rather

than at 0, making what was about a 1 percentage point increase look very big indeed. In addition, omission from the plague graph of the more rapid increase in reported usage between 1975 and 1980 makes it look as if the tiny increase in 1985 were a new, and thus more newsworthy, crisis.

Adherence to several guidelines (Tufte, 1983; Wallgren et al., 1996) will help you to spot these problems and to avoid them in your own work:

- The difference between bars can be exaggerated by cutting off the bottom of the vertical axis and displaying less than the full height of the bars. Instead, begin the graph of a quantitative variable at 0 on both axes. It may at times be reasonable to violate this guideline, as when an age distribution is presented for a sample of adults, but in this case be sure to mark the break clearly on the axis.
- Bars of unequal width, including pictures instead of bars, can make particular values look as if they carry more weight than their frequency warrants. Always use bars of equal width.
- Either shortening or lengthening the vertical axis will obscure or accentuate the differences in the number of cases between values. The two axes usually should be of approximately equal length.
- Avoid chart junk that can confuse the reader and obscure the distribution's shape (a lot of verbiage or umpteen marks, lines, lots of crosshatching, and the like).

Frequency Distributions

A **frequency distribution** displays the number, percentage (the relative frequencies), or both of cases corresponding to each of a variable's values or group of values. The components of the frequency distribution should be clearly labeled, with a title, a stub (labels for the values of the variable), a caption (identifying whether the distribution includes frequencies, percentages, or both), and perhaps the number of missing cases. If percentages are presented rather than frequencies (sometimes both are included), the total number of cases in the distribution (the **base number** *N*) should be indicated (see Exhibit 12.8).

Exhibit 12.8 Frequency Distribution of Voting in the 1996 Presidential Election

Value	Frequency	Valid Percentage
Voted	1,737	68.5%
Did not vote	799	31.5
Not eligible	201	–
Refused	9	–
Don't know	64	–
No answer	7	–
Total	2,817	100.0% (2,536)

Source: General Social Survey, 2000.

Exhibit 12.9   Frequency Distribution of Political Views

Value	Frequency	Valid Percentage
Extremely liberal	107	4.0%
Liberal	308	11.6
Slightly liberal	285	10.8
Moderate	1054	39.9
Slightly conservative	390	14.8
Conservative	411	15.5
Extremely conservative	89	3.4
Total	2,644	100.0%

Source: General Social Survey, 2000.

Ungrouped Data

Constructing and reading frequency distributions for variables with few values is not difficult. The frequency distribution of voting in Exhibit 12.8, for example, shows that 68.5% of the respondents eligible to vote said they voted and 31.5% reported they did not vote. The total number of respondents to this question was 2,536, although 2,817 actually were interviewed. The rest were ineligible to vote, just refused to answer the question, said they did not know whether they had voted or not, or gave no answer.

Political ideology was measured with a question having seven response choices, resulting in a longer but still relatively simple frequency distribution (see Exhibit 12.9). The most common response was moderate, with 39.9% of the sample choosing this label to represent their political ideology. The distribution has a symmetric shape, with somewhat more respondents identifying themselves as conservative than liberal. About 3% of the respondents identified themselves as extremely conservative and about 4% as extremely liberal.

If you compare Exhibits 12.9 and 12.6, you can see that a frequency distribution (Exhibit 12.9) can provide more precise information than a graph (Exhibit 12.6, p. 375) about the number and percentage of cases in a variable's categories. Often, however, it is easier to see the shape of a distribution when it is graphed. When the goal of a presentation is to convey a general sense of a variable's distribution, particularly when the presentation is to an audience that is not trained in statistics, the advantages of a graph outweigh those of a frequency distribution.

Grouped Data

Many frequency distributions (and graphs) require grouping of some values after the data are collected. There are two reasons for grouping:

- There are more than 15–20 values to begin with, a number too large to be displayed in an easily readable table.
- The distribution of the variable will be clearer or more meaningful if some of the values are combined.

Exhibit 12.10 Ungrouped and Grouped Age Distributions

Ungrouped		Grouped	
Age	Percentage	Age	Percentage
18	0.2%	18–19	1.8%
19	1.6	20–29	16.9
20	1.4	30–39	21.7
21	1.3	40–49	22.6
22	1.4	50–59	14.5
23	1.7	60–69	9.7
24	1.8	70–79	7.9
25	1.9	80–89	4.8
26	2.1		
27	1.7		100.0%
28	1.6		(2,809)
29	2.0		
30	2.2		
31	2.2		
32	2.7		
33	1.6		
34	2.0		
35	2.0		
36	2.2		
37	2.2		
38	2.7		
39	1.9		
40	2.6		
41	2.1		
42	2.6		
43	2.5		
44	2.5		
45	2.5		
46	2.0		
. . .	. . .		

Source: General Social Survey, 2000.

Inspection of Exhibit 12.10 should clarify these reasons. In the first distribution, which is only a portion of the entire ungrouped GSS age distribution, it is very difficult to discern any shape, much less the central tendency. In the second distribution, age is grouped in the familiar 10-year intervals (except for the first, abbreviated category), and the distribution's shape is immediately clear.

Once we decide to group values, or categories, we have to be sure that in doing so we do not distort the distribution. Adhering to the following guidelines for combining values in a frequency distribution will prevent many problems:

Exhibit 12.11   Years of Education Completed

Years of Education	Percentage
Less than 8	2.4%
8–11	15.1
12	29.3
13–15	28.2
16	14.0
17 or more	11.1
	100.0%
	(2,808)

Source: General Social Survey, 2000.

- Categories should be logically defensible and preserve the distribution's shape.
- Categories should be mutually exclusive and exhaustive, so that every case should be classifiable in one and only one category.

Violating these two guidelines is easier than you might think. If you were to group all the ages above 59 together, as 60 or higher, it would create the appearance of a bulge at the high end of the age distribution, with 22% of the cases. The same type of misleading impression could be created by combining other categories so that they include a wide range of values. In some cases, however, the most logically defensible categories will vary in size. A good example would be grouping years of education as less than 8 (did not finish grade school), 8–11 (finished grade school), 12 (graduated high school), 13–15 (some college), 16 (graduated college), and 17 or more (some postgraduate education). Such a grouping captures the most meaningful distinctions in the educational distribution and preserves the information that would be important for many analyses (see Exhibit 12.11).

It is also easy to imagine how the requirement that categories be mutually exclusive can be violated. You sometimes see frequency distributions or categories in questionnaires that use such overlapping age categories as 20–30, 30–40, and so on, instead of mutually exclusive categories like those in Exhibit 12.10. The problem is that we then can't tell which category to place someone in who is age 30, age 40, and so on.

Combined and Compressed Distributions

In a **combined frequency display,** the distributions for a set of conceptually similar variables having the same response categories are presented together. Exhibit 12.12 is a combined display reporting the frequency distributions in percentage form for 13 variables that indicate the level of confidence that GSS respondents placed in American institutions. The different variables are identified in the leftmost column and their values are labeled along the top. By looking at the table, you can see quickly that confidence is greatest in the scientific community and medicine; the military and the Supreme Court are also rated highly. A much smaller portion of the American public has much confidence in organized labor, the executive branch or Congress, the press, or TV. Note that the specific variables are ordered in decreasing order

Exhibit 12.12   Confidence in Institutions

Confidence in . . .	A Great Deal (%)	Only Some (%)	Hardly Any (%)	Total (%)	n
Scientific community	44.8	47.1	8.1	100.0	1739
Medicine	44.4	46.0	9.6	100.0	1860
Military	40.0	49.9	10.1	100.0	1818
U.S. Supreme Court	33.9	52.6	13.5	100.0	1772
Banks & financial institutions	29.9	55.6	14.4	100.0	1841
Major companies	29.1	59.4	11.4	100.0	1812
Organized religion	28.7	51.6	19.7	100.0	1809
Education	27.1	57.1	15.7	100.0	1869
Organized labor	14.1	56.6	29.4	100.0	1701
Executive branch of federal government	13.8	51.2	35.0	100.0	1805
Congress	12.6	57.9	29.5	100.0	1803
Press	10.4	47.8	41.8	100.0	1837
Television	10.0	47.5	42.5	100.0	1854

Source: General Social Survey, 2000.

Exhibit 12.13   Conditions When Abortion Should Be Allowed

Statement	% Agree	n
Woman's health seriously endangered	88.5	(1785)
Pregnant as result of rape	80.6	(1749)
Strong chance of serious defect	78.7	(1774)
Low income – can't afford more children	42.2	(1773)
Married & wants no more children	40.7	(1770)
Abortion if woman wants for any reason	39.9	(1768)
Not married	39.1	(1767)

Source: General Social Survey, 2000.

of confidence and that the source for the data is cited in the table's footnote. The number of cases on which the distributions are based is included for each variable.

Compressed frequency displays can also be used to present crosstabular data and summary statistics more efficiently, by eliminating unnecessary percentages (such as those corresponding to the second value of a dichotomous variable) and by reducing the need for repetitive labels. Exhibit 12.13 presents a compressed display of agreement that abortion should be allowed given particular conditions. Note that this display presents the number of cases on which the percentages are based in parentheses.

Combined and compressed statistical displays facilitate the presentation of a large amount of data in a relatively small space. They should be used with caution, however, because people who are not used to them may be baffled by them.

SUMMARIZING UNIVARIATE DISTRIBUTIONS

Summary statistics focus attention on particular aspects of a distribution and facilitate comparison among distributions. For example, if your purpose is to report variation in income by state in a form that is easy for most audiences to understand, you would usually be better off presenting average incomes; many people would find it difficult to make sense of a display containing 50 frequency distributions, although they could readily comprehend a long list of average incomes. A display of average incomes would also be preferable to multiple frequency distributions if your only purpose was to provide a general idea of income differences among states.

Of course, representing a distribution in one number loses information about other aspects of the distribution's shape, and so creates the possibility of obscuring important information. If you need to inform a discussion about differences in income inequality among states, for example, measures of central tendency and variability would miss the point entirely. You would either have to present the 50 frequency distributions or use some special statistics that represent the unevenness of a distribution. For this reason, analysts who report summary measures of central tendency usually also report a summary measure of variability, and sometimes several measures of central tendency, variability, or both.

Measures of Central Tendency

Central tendency is usually summarized with one of three statistics: the mode, the median, or the mean. For any particular application, one of these statistics may be preferable, but each has a role to play in data analysis. In order to choose an appropriate measure of central tendency, the analyst must consider a variable's level of measurement, the skewness of a quantitative variable's distribution, and the purpose for which the statistic is used. In addition, the analyst's personal experiences and preferences inevitably will play a role.

Mode

The **mode** is the most frequent value in a distribution. It is also termed the **probability average** because, being the most frequent value, it is the most probable. For example, if you were to pick a case at random from the distribution of political views (refer back to Exhibit 12.9, p. 378), the probability of the case being a moderate would be .40 out of 1, or 40%—the most probable value in the distribution.

The mode is used much less often than the other two measures of central tendency because it can so easily give a misleading impression of a distribution's central tendency. One problem with the mode occurs when a distribution is **bimodal**, in contrast to being **unimodal**. A bimodal (or trimodal, and so on) distribution has two or more categories with an equal number of cases and with more cases than any of the other categories. There is no single mode. Imagine that a particular distribution has two categories, each having just about the same number of cases (and these are the two most frequent categories). Strictly speaking, the mode would be the one with more cases, even though the other frequent category had only slightly fewer cases. Another potential problem with the mode is that it might happen to fall far from the main clustering of cases in a distribution. It would be misleading in most circumstances to say simply that the variable's central tendency was whatever the modal value was.

Nevertheless, there are occasions when the mode is very appropriate. Most important, the mode is the only measure of central tendency that can be used to characterize the central tendency of variables measured at the nominal level. We can't say much more about the central tendency of the distribution of marital status in Exhibit 12.4 (p. 374) than that the most common value is married. The mode also is often referred to in descriptions of the shape of a distribution. The terms *unimodal* and *bimodal* appear frequently, as do descriptive statements like "The typical [most probable] respondent was in her 30s." Of course, when the issue is what is the most probable value, the mode is the appropriate statistic. Which ethnic group is most common in a given school? The mode provides the answer.

Median

The **median** is the position average, or the point that divides the distribution in half (the 50th percentile). The median is inappropriate for variables measured at the nominal level because their values cannot be put in order, and so there is no meaningful middle position. In order to determine the median, we simply array a distribution's values in numerical order and find the value of the case that has an equal number of cases above and below it. If the median point falls between two cases (which happens if the distribution has an even number of cases), the median is defined as the average of the two middle values, and is computed by adding the values of the two middle cases and dividing by 2.

The median in a frequency distribution is determined by identifying the value corresponding to a cumulative percentage of 50. Starting at the top of the years of education distribution in Exhibit 12.11, for example, and adding up the percentages, we find that we have reached 46.8% in the 12 years category and then 75.0% in the 13–15 years category. The median is therefore 13–15.

With most variables, it is preferable to compute the median from ungrouped data because that method results in an exact value for the median, rather than an interval. In the grouped age distribution in Exhibit 12.10, for example, the median is in the 40s interval. But if we determine the median from the ungrouped data, we can state that the exact value of the median as 43.

Mean

The **mean,** or arithmetic average, takes into account the values of each case in a distribution—it is a weighted average. The mean is computed by adding up the value of all the cases and dividing by the total number of cases, thereby taking into account the value of each case in the distribution:

$$\text{Mean} = \text{Sum of value of cases/Number of cases}$$

In algebraic notation, the equation is: $\bar{Y} = \Sigma Y_i / N$. For example, to calculate the mean value of eight cases, we add the values of all the cases (ΣY_i) and divide by the number of cases (N):

$$(28 + 117 + 42 + 10 + 77 + 51 + 64 + 55) / 8 = 444/8 = 55.5$$

Because computing the mean requires adding up the values of the cases, it makes sense to compute a mean only if the values of the cases can be treated as actual quantities—that is, if they reflect an interval or ratio level of measurement, or if they are ordinal and we assume that ordinal measures can be treated as interval. It would make no sense to calculate the mean religion, for example. Imagine a group of four people in which there were two Protestants, one Catholic, and one Jew. To calculate the mean you would need to solve the equation (Protestant + Protestant + Catholic + Jew) ÷ 4 = ?. Even if you decide that Protestant = 1, Catholic = 2, and Jewish = 3 for data entry purposes, it still doesn't make sense to add these numbers because they don't represent quantities of religion.

Median or Mean?

Both the median and the mean are used to summarize the central tendency of quantitative variables, but their suitability for a particular application must be carefully assessed. The key issues to be considered in this assessment are the variable's level of measurement, the shape of its distribution, and the purpose of the statistical summary. Consideration of these issues will sometimes result in a decision to use both the median and the mean, and will sometimes result in neither measure being seen as preferable. But in many other situations, the choice between the mean and median will be clear-cut as soon as the researcher takes the time to consider these three issues.

Level of measurement is a key concern because to calculate the mean we must add up the values of all the cases—a procedure that assumes the variable is measured at the interval or ratio level. So even though we know that coding Agree as 2 and Disagree as 3 does not really mean that Disagree is 1 unit more of disagreement than Agree, the mean assumes this evaluation to be true. Because calculation of the median requires only that we order the values of cases, we do not have to make this assumption. Technically speaking, then, the mean is simply an inappropriate statistic for variables measured at the ordinal level (and you already know that it is completely meaningless for qualitative variables). In practice, however, many social researchers use the mean to describe the central tendency of variables measured at the ordinal level, for the reasons outlined earlier.

The shape of a variable's distribution should also be taken into account when deciding whether to use the median or mean. When a distribution is perfectly symmetric, so that the distribution of values below the median is a mirror image of the distribution of values above the median, the mean and median will be the same. But the values of the mean and median are affected differently by skewness, or the presence of cases with extreme values on one side of the distribution but not the other side. Because the median takes into account only the number of cases above and below the median point, not the value of these cases, it is not affected in any way by extreme values. Because the mean is based on adding the value of all the cases, it will be pulled in the direction of exceptionally high (or low) values. When the value of the mean is larger than the median, we know that the distribution is skewed in a positive direction, with proportionately more cases with higher than lower values. When the mean is smaller than the median, the distribution is skewed in a negative direction.

This differential impact of skewness on the median and mean is illustrated in Exhibit 12.14. On the first balance beam, the cases (bags) are spread out equally, and the median and mean are in the same location. On the second and third balance beams, the median corresponds to the value of the middle case, but the mean is pulled toward the value of the one case with an

Exhibit 12.14   The Mean as a Balance Point

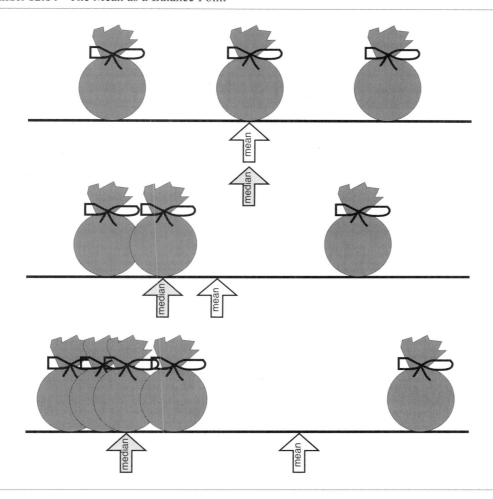

extremely high value. For this reason, the mean age (46.02) for the 2,809 cases represented partially in the detailed age distribution in Exhibit 12.10 is higher than the median age (43). Although in the distribution represented in Exhibit 12.10 the difference is small, in some distributions the two measures will have markedly different values, and in such instances the median may be preferred.

The single most important influence on the choice of the median or the mean for summarizing the central tendency of quantitative variables should be the purpose of the statistical summary. If the purpose is to report the middle position in one or more distributions, then the median is the appropriate statistic, whether or not the distribution is skewed. For example, with respect to the age distribution from the GSS, you could report that half the American population is younger than 42 years old and half the population is older than that. But if the

Exhibit 12.15   Insensitivity of Median to Variation at End of Distribution

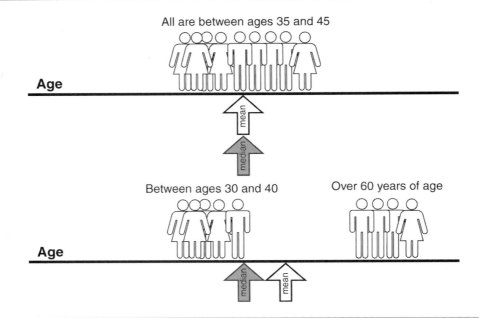

purpose is to show how likely different groups are to have age-related health problems, the measure of central tendency for these groups should take into account people's ages, not just the number who are older and younger than a particular age. For this purpose, the median would be inappropriate because it would not distinguish between two distributions like those represented in Exhibit 12.15. In the top distribution, everyone is between the ages of 35 and 45, with a median of 41. In the bottom distribution, the median is still 41 but half of the cases have ages above 60. The higher mean in the second distribution reflects the fact that it has more older people.

Keep in mind that it is not appropriate to use either the median or the mean as a measure of central tendency for variables measured at the nominal level, because at this level the different attributes of a variable cannot be ordered as higher or lower (as reflected in the following correspondence list). Technically speaking, the mode should be used to measure the central tendency of variables measured at the nominal level (and it can also be used with variables measured at the ordinal, interval, and ratio levels). The median is most suited to measure the central tendency of variables measured at the ordinal level (and it can also be used to measure the central tendency of variables measured at the interval and ratio levels). Finally, the mean is only suited to measure central tendency for variables measured at the interval and ratio levels.

It is not entirely legitimate to represent the central tendency of a variable measured at the ordinal level with the mean: Calculation of the mean requires summing the values of all cases, and at the ordinal level these values indicate only order, not actual numbers. Nonetheless, many social scientists use the mean with ordinal-level variables and find that this is potentially useful for comparisons among variables and as a first step in more complex statistical analyses. The median and mode can also be useful as measures of central tendency for variables measured at the interval and ratio levels, when the goal is to indicate middle position (the median) or the most frequent value (the mode):

Level of Measurement	Most Appropriate MCT	Potentially Useful MCT	Definitely Inappropriate MCT
Nominal	Mode	None	Median, Mean
Ordinal	Median	Mean	None
Interval, Ratio	Mean	Median, Mode	None

In general, the mean is the most commonly used measure of central tendency for quantitative variables, both because it takes into account the value of all cases in the distribution and because it is the foundation for many other more advanced statistics. However, the mean's very popularity results in its use in situations for which it is inappropriate. Keep an eye out for this problem.

Measures of Variation

You already have learned that central tendency is only one aspect of the shape of a distribution—the most important aspect for many purposes, but still just a piece of the total picture. A summary of distributions based only on their central tendency can be very incomplete, even misleading. For example, three towns might have the same median income but still be very different in their social character due to the shape of their income distributions. As illustrated in Exhibit 12.16, town A is a homogeneous middle-class community; town B is very heterogeneous; and town C has a polarized, bimodal income distribution, with mostly very poor and very rich people and few in between. However, all three towns have the same median income.

The way to capture these differences is with statistical measures of variation. Four popular measures of variation are the range, the interquartile range, the variance, and the standard deviation (which is the most popular measure of variability). In order to calculate each of these measures, the variable must be at the interval or ratio level (but many would argue that, like the mean, they can be used with ordinal-level measures, too). Statistical measures of variation are used infrequently with qualitative variables, so these measures will not be presented here.

It's important to realize that these measures of variation are summary statistics that capture only part of what we need to be concerned with about the distribution of a variable. In particular, they do not tell us about the extent to which a distribution is skewed, which we've seen is so important for interpreting measures of central tendency. Researchers usually evaluate the skewness of distributions just by eyeballing them.

Range

The **range** is a simple measure of variation, calculated as the highest value in a distribution minus the lowest value, plus 1:

$$\text{Range} = \text{Highest value} - \text{Lowest value} + 1$$

Exhibit 12.16 Distributions Differing in Variability but Not Central Tendency

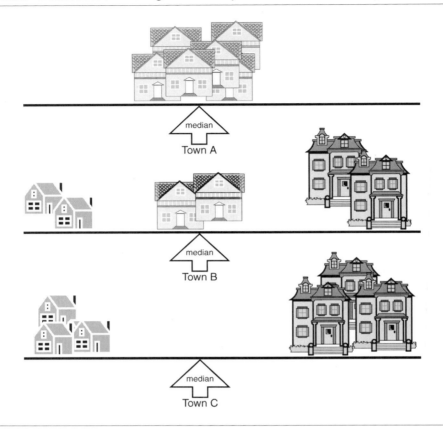

It often is important to report the range of a distribution, to identify the whole range of possible values that might be encountered. However, because the range can be drastically altered by just one exceptionally high or low value (termed an **outlier**), it does not do an adequate job of summarizing the extent of variability in a distribution.

Interquartile Range

A version of the range statistic, the **interquartile range** avoids the problem created by outliers. **Quartiles** are the points in a distribution corresponding to the first 25% of the cases, the first 50% of the cases, and the first 75% of the cases. You already know how to determine the second quartile, corresponding to the point in the distribution covering half of the cases—it is another name for the median. The first and third quartiles are determined in the same way, but by finding the points corresponding to 25% and 75% of the cases, respectively. The interquartile range is the difference between the first quartile and the third quartile (plus 1).

We can use the distribution of age for an example. If you add up the percentages corresponding to each value of age (ungrouped) in Exhibit 12.10 (p. 379), you'll find that you reach the first quartile (25% of the cases) at the age value of 32. If you were to continue, you would find that the age 57 corresponds to the third quartile—the point where you have covered 75% of the cases. So, the interquartile range for age, in the GSS2000 data, is 26:

$$\text{Third quartile} - \text{First quartile} + 1 = \text{Interquartile range.}$$
$$57 - 32 + 1 = 26$$

Variance

The **variance** is the average squared deviation of each case from the mean, so it takes into account the amount by which each case differs from the mean. An example of how to calculate the variance, using the following formula, appears in Exhibit 12.17:

$$\sigma^2 = \frac{\sum (Y_i - \bar{Y})^2}{N}$$

Symbol key: $\bar{Y}$ = mean; N = number of cases; Σ = sum over all cases; Y_i = value of case i on variable Y; σ^2 = variance.

You can see in Exhibit 12.17 two examples of summing over all cases, the operation represented by the Greek letter Σ in the formula.

The variance is used in many other statistics, although it is more conventional to measure variability with the closely related standard deviation than with the variance.

Exhibit 12.17   Calculation of the Variance

Case #	Score (X_i)	$X_i - \bar{X}$	$(X_i - \bar{X})^2$
1	21	−3.27	10.69
2	30	5.73	32.83
3	15	−9.27	85.93
4	18	−6.27	39.31
5	25	0.73	0.53
6	32	7.73	59.75
7	19	−5.27	27.77
8	21	−3.27	10.69
9	23	−1.27	1.61
10	37	12.73	162.05
11	26	1.73	2.99
	267		434.15

Mean: $\bar{X} = 267/11 = 24.27$
Sum of squared deviations = 434.15
Variance: $\sigma^2 = 434.15/11 = 39.47$

Standard Deviation

The **standard deviation** is simply the square root of the variance. It is the square root of the average squared deviation of each case from the mean:

$$\sigma^2 = \sqrt{\frac{\sum (Y_i - \overline{Y})^2}{N}}$$

Symbol key: $\overline{Y}$ = mean; N = number of cases; Σ = sum over all cases; Y_i = value of case i on variable Y; $\sqrt{}$ = square root; σ = standard deviation.

When the standard deviation is calculated from sample data, the denominator is supposed to be $N - 1$, rather than N, an adjustment that has no discernible effect when the number of cases is reasonably large. You also should note that the use of *squared* deviations in the formula accentuates the impact of relatively large deviations, because squaring a large number makes that number count much more.

The standard deviation has mathematical properties that increase its value for statisticians. You already learned about the **normal distribution** in Chapter 5. A normal distribution is a distribution that results from chance variation around a mean. It is symmetric and tapers off in a characteristic shape from its mean. If a variable is normally distributed (see Exhibit 12.18), 68% of the cases will lie between plus and minus 1 standard deviation from the distribution's mean, and 95% of the cases will lie between plus and minus 1.96 standard deviations from the mean.

This correspondence of the standard deviation to the normal distribution enables us to infer how confident we can be that the mean (or some other statistic) of a population sampled randomly is within a certain range of the sample mean. This is the logic behind calculating

Exhibit 12.18 The Normal Distribution

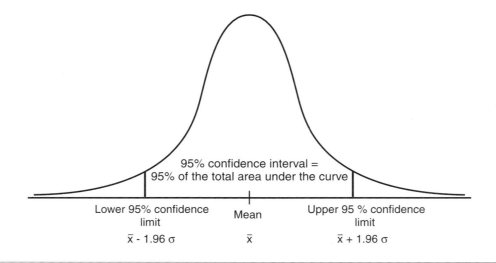

95% confidence interval = 95% of the total area under the curve

Lower 95% confidence limit

Mean

Upper 95 % confidence limit

$\bar{x} - 1.96\ \sigma$

$\bar{x}$

$\bar{x} + 1.96\ \sigma$

confidence limits around the mean, as we did in Chapter 5. Confidence limits indicate how confident we can be, given our particular random sample, that the value of some statistic in the population falls within a particular range.

ANALYZING DATA ETHICALLY: HOW NOT TO LIE WITH STATISTICS

Using statistics ethically means first and foremost being honest and open. Findings should be reported honestly, and the researcher should be open about the thinking that guided her decision to use particular statistics. Although this section has a humorous title (after Darrell Huff's [1954] little classic, *How to Lie with Statistics*), make no mistake about the intent: It is possible to distort social reality with statistics, and it is unethical to do so knowingly, even when the error is due more to carelessness than deceptive intent.

Summary statistics can easily be used unethically, knowingly or not. When we summarize a distribution in a single number, even in two numbers, we are losing much information. Neither central tendency nor variation describes a distribution's overall shape. And taken separately, neither measure tells us about the other characteristic of the distribution (central tendency or variation). So reports using measures of central tendency should normally also include measures of variation. And we also should inspect the shape of any distribution for which we report summary statistics in order to ensure that the summary statistic does not mislead us (or anyone else) because of an unusual degree of skewness.

It is possible to mislead those who read statistical reports by choosing summary statistics that accentuate a particular feature of a distribution. For example, imagine an unscrupulous realtor trying to convince a prospective home buyer in community B that it is a community with very high property values, when it actually has a positively skewed distribution of property values (see Exhibit 12.19). The realtor compares the mean price of homes in community B to that for community A (one with a homogeneous mid-priced set of homes) and therefore makes community B look much better. In truth, the higher mean in community B reflects a very skewed, lopsided distribution of property values— most residents own small, cheap homes. A median would provide a better basis for comparison.

You have already seen that it is possible to distort the shape of a distribution by ignoring some of the guidelines for constructing graphs and frequency distributions. Whenever you need to group data in a frequency distribution or graph, you can reduce the potential for problems by inspecting the ungrouped distributions and then using a grouping procedure that does not distort the distribution's basic shape. When you create graphs, be sure to consider how the axes you choose may change the distribution's apparent shape.

CROSSTABULATING VARIABLES

Most data analyses focus on relationships among variables in order to test hypotheses or just to describe or explore relationships. For each of these purposes, we must examine the

Exhibit 12.19 Using the Mean to Create a More Favorable Impression

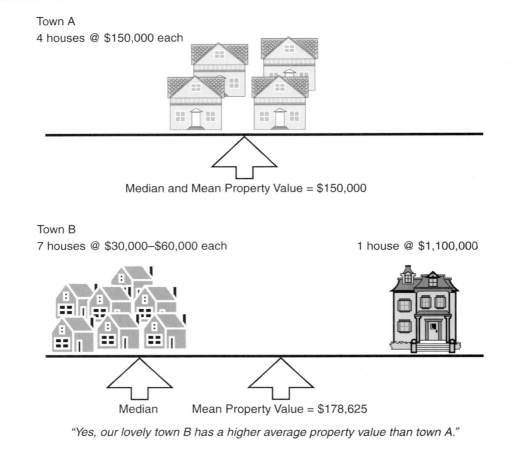

Town A
4 houses @ $150,000 each

Median and Mean Property Value = $150,000

Town B
7 houses @ $30,000–$60,000 each   1 house @ $1,100,000

Median   Mean Property Value = $178,625

"Yes, our lovely town B has a higher average property value than town A."

association among two or more variables. **Crosstabulation (crosstab)** is one of the simplest methods for doing so. A crosstabulation displays the distribution of one variable for each category of another variable; it can also be termed a *bivariate distribution*. You can also display the association between two variables in a graph; we will see an example in this section. Crosstabs provide a simple tool for statistically controlling one or more variables while examining the associations among others. In the next section you will learn how crosstabs used in this way can help to test for spurious relationships and evaluate causal models. We will examine several trivariate tables.

Exhibit 12.20 displays the crosstabulation of voting by income, so that we can test the hypothesis that likelihood of voting increases with this one social status indicator. The table is presented first with frequencies, and then again with percentages. In both tables, the *body* of the table is the part between the row and column labels and the row and column totals. The

Exhibit 12.20   Crosstabulation of Voting in 1996 by Family Income: Cell Counts and Percentages

		FAMILY INCOME: CELL COUNTS			
VOTING	<$20,000	$20,000–$34,999	$35,000–$59,999	$60,000 +	Total
Voted	331	306	375	464	1,476
Did not vote	361	229	235	155	980
Total (*n*)	(692)	(535)	(610)	(619)	(2,456)

		FAMILY INCOME: PERCENTAGES			
VOTING	<$20,000	$20,000–$34,999	$35,000–$59,999	$60,000+	Total
Voted	48%	57%	62%	75%	60%
Did not vote	52%	43%	38%	25%	40%
Total (*n*)	100%	100%	100%	100%	100%

Source: General Social Survey, 2000.

cells of the table are defined by combinations of row and column values. Each cell represents cases with a unique combination of values of the two variables, corresponding to that particular row and column. The **marginal distributions** of the table are on the right (the *row marginals*) and underneath (the *column marginals*). These are just the frequency distributions for the two variables (in number of cases, percentages, or both), considered separately. (The column marginals in Exhibit 12.20 are for family income; the row marginals are for the distribution of voting.) The independent variable is usually the column variable; the dependent variable then is the row variable. (Because voting is a socially desirable behavior, some people say that they voted when they didn't. Following Satoshi Kanazawa [2000], I lessen this response error by treating as voters only those who named the candidate for whom they voted.)

The first table in Exhibit 12.20 shows the number of cases with each combination of values of voting and family income. In it, you can see that 331 of those earning less than $20,000 per year voted, whereas 361 did not. On the other hand, 464 of those earning $60,000 or more voted, whereas 155 of these high-income respondents did not vote. It often is hard to look at a table in this form, with just the numbers of cases in each cell, and determine whether there is a relationship between the two variables. We need to convert the cell frequencies into **percentages**, as in the second table in Exhibit 12.20. This table presents the data as percentages within the categories of the independent variable (the column variable, in this case). In other words, the cell frequencies have been converted into percentages of the column totals (the *n* in each column). For example, in Exhibit 12.20, the number of people earning less than $20,000 who voted is 331 out of 692, or 48%. Because the cell frequencies have been converted to percentages of the column totals, the numbers add up to 100 in each column, but not across the rows.

To read the percentage table (the bottom panel of Exhibit 12.20), compare the percentage distribution of voting across the columns, starting with the lowest income category (in the left column) and moving from left to right. You see that as income increases, the percentage who voted also rises, from 48% of those with annual incomes under $20,000 (in the first cell in the first column), to 57% of those with incomes between $20,000 and $34,999, then 62% of those with incomes from $35,000 to $59,999, and then up to 75% of those with incomes of $60,000 or more (the last cell in the body of the table in the first row). This result is consistent with the hypothesis.

When a table is converted to percentages, usually just the percentages in each cell should be presented, not the number of cases in each cell. Include 100% at the bottom of each column (if the independent variable is the column variable) to indicate that the percentages add up to 100, as well as the *base number (n)* for each column (in parentheses). If the percentages add up to 99 or 101 due to rounding error, just indicate this in a footnote.

Follow these rules when you create and then read a percentage table:

1. Make the independent variable the column variable and the dependent variable the row variable.

2. Percentage the table column by column, on the column totals. The percents should add to 100 (or perhaps 99 or 101, if there has been rounding error) in each column.

3. Compare the distributions of the dependent variable (the row variable) across each column.

Skip ahead to the bottom panel of Exhibit 12.29 (page 402) and try your hand at the table reading process (as described by rule 3, above) with this larger table. This table describes the relationship between education and income. Examine the distribution of income for those with only a grade school education (first column). More than half (58%) reported an income under $20,000, whereas just 6% reported an income of $60,000 or more. Then examine the distribution of income for the respondents who had finished high school but gone no further. Here, the distribution of income has shifted upward, with just 29% reporting an income under $20,000 and 18% reporting incomes of $60,000 or more—that's three times the percentage in that category than we saw for those with a grade school education. You can see there are also more respondents in the $35,000–$59,999 category than there were for the grade schoolers. Now examine the column representing those who had completed at least some college. The percentage with incomes under $20,000 has dropped again, to 19%, whereas the percentage in the highest income category has risen to 35%. If you step back and compare the income distributions across the three categories of education, you see that incomes increased markedly and consistently. The relationship is positive (fortunately for all of us in the college crowd).

But the independent variable does not *have* to be the column variable; what is critical is to be consistent within a report or paper. You will find in published articles and research reports some percentage tables in which independent variable and dependent variable positions are reversed. If the independent variable is the row variable, we percentage the table on the row totals (the *n* in each row), and so the percentages add up to 100 across the rows (see Exhibit 12.21). When you read the table in Exhibit 12.21, you find that 35% of those in their 20s voted, compared to 54% of those in their 30s, 64% of those in their 40s, and 68–76% of those between 50 and 89 (the cell frequencies were omitted from this table).

Exhibit 12.21   Crosstabulation of Voting in 1996 by Age

	Voting			
Age	*Yes*	*No*	*Total*	*(n)*
18–19	0%	100%	100%	(51)
20–29	35%	65%	100%	(475)
30–39	54%	46%	100%	(610)
40–49	64%	36%	100%	(634)
50–59	71%	29%	100%	(408)
60–69	74%	26%	100%	(273)
70–79	76%	24%	100%	(222)
80–89	68%	32%	100%	(136)

Source: General Social Survey, 2000.

Exhibit 12.22   Race by Region of the United States

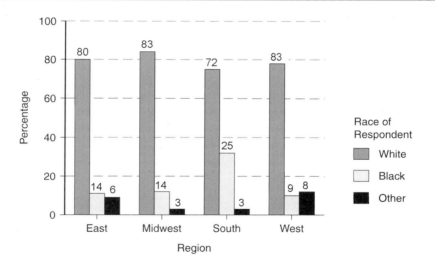

Source: Orcutt & Turner, 1993:196, 197.

Graphing Association

Graphs provide an efficient tool for summarizing relationships among variables. Exhibit 12.22 displays the relationship between race and region in graphic form. It shows that the percentage of the population that is black is highest in the South, whereas persons of "other" races are most common on the coasts.

Another good example of the use of graphs to show relationships is provided by a Bureau of Justice Statistics report on criminal victimization (Rand, Lynch, & Cantor, 1997:1).

Exhibit 12.23 Violent Crime Rates, 1973–1995*

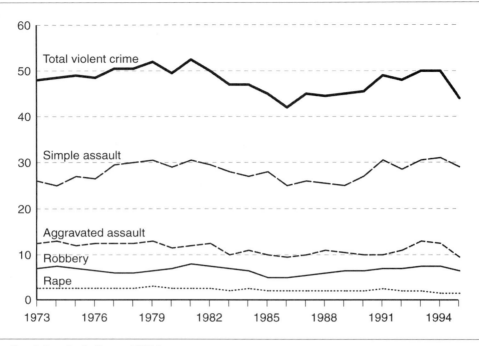

Source: Rand, Lynch, & Carter, 1997:1.

*Victimization rate per 1,000 persons age 12 or older.

Exhibit 12.23, taken from that report, shows how the rates of different violent crimes have varied over time, with most rates falling in the late 1980s, rising in the early 1990s, and then falling again by 1995.

Describing Association

A crosstabulation table reveals four aspects of the association between two variables:

- *Existence.* Do the percentage distributions vary at all between categories of the independent variable?
- *Strength.* How much do the percentage distributions vary between categories of the independent variable?
- *Direction.* For quantitative variables, do values on the dependent variable tend to increase or decrease with an increase in value on the independent variable?
- *Pattern.* For quantitative variables, are changes in the percentage distribution of the dependent variable fairly regular (simply increasing or decreasing), or do they vary (perhaps increasing, then decreasing, or perhaps gradually increasing, then rapidly increasing)?

Exhibit 12.24 Voting in 1996 by Interpersonal Trust

	People Can Be Trusted	
Voting	Agree	Disagree
Voted	70%	52%
Did not vote	30%	48%
Total	100%	100%
(*n*)	(662)	(1,093)

Source: General Social Survey, 2000.

In Exhibit 12.20 (page 393), an association exists; it is moderately strong (the difference in percentages between the first and last column is about 25 percentage points); and the direction of association between likelihood of voting and family income is positive. The pattern in this table is close to what is termed **monotonic**. In a monotonic relationship, the value of cases consistently increases (or decreases) on one variable as the value of cases increases on the other variable. The relationship in the table we examined in Exhibit 12.29, involving income and education, was also monotonic.

Monotonic is often defined a bit less strictly, with the idea being that as the value of cases on one variable increases (or decreases), the value of cases on the other variable tends to increase (or decrease), and at least does not change direction. This describes the relationship between voting and income: The likelihood of voting increases as family income increases, although the increase levels off in the middle two categories, with the result that the association is not strictly monotonic. There is also a moderately strong positive association between age and voting in Exhibit 12.21 (page 395), with likelihood of voting rising more than 40 percentage points between the ages of 20 and 79. However, the pattern of this relationship is **curvilinear** rather than monotonic: The increase in voting with age occurs largely between the ages of 20 and 50, before leveling off and then declining a bit for people in their 80s.

The relationship between the measure of trust and voting appears in Exhibit 12.24. There is an association, and in the direction I hypothesized: 70% of those who believe that people can be trusted voted, compared to 52% of those who believe that people cannot be trusted. Because both variables are dichotomies, there can be no pattern to the association beyond the difference between the two percentages. (Comparing the column percentages in either the first or the second row gives the same picture.)

Exhibit 12.25, by contrast, gives no evidence of an association between gender and voting. There is no difference between the percentage of men and women who voted (the one percentage point difference is too small to be considered meaningful). So that's all there is to say about the relationship.

Evaluating Association

You will find when you read research reports and journal articles that social scientists usually make decisions about the existence and strength of association on the basis of more statistics than just a crosstabulation table.

Exhibit 12.25 Voting in 1996 by Gender

Voting	Gender	
	Male	Female
Voted	59%	58%
Did not vote	41%	42%
Total	100%	100%
(*n*)	(1,229)	(1,588)

Source: General Social Survey, 2000.

A **measure of association** is a type of descriptive statistic used to summarize the strength of an association. There are many measures of association, some of which are appropriate for variables measured at particular levels. One popular measure of association in crosstabular analyses with variables measured at the ordinal level is **gamma.** As with many measures of association, the possible values of gamma vary from −1, meaning the variables are perfectly associated in an inverse direction; to 0, meaning there is no association of the type that gamma measures; to +1, meaning there is a perfect positive association of the type that gamma measures.

Inferential statistics are used in deciding whether it is likely that an association exists in the larger population from which the sample was drawn. Even when the association between two variables is consistent with the researcher's hypothesis, it is possible that the association was just due to the vagaries of sampling on a random basis (of course, the problem is even worse if the sample is not random). It is conventional in statistics to avoid concluding that an association exists in the population from which the sample was drawn unless the probability that the association was due to chance is less than 5%. In other words, a statistician normally will not conclude that an association exists between two variables unless he or she can be at least 95% confident that the association was not due to chance. This is the same type of logic that you learned about earlier in this chapter, which introduced the concept of 95% confidence limits for the mean. Estimation of the probability that an association is not due to chance will be based on one of several inferential statistics, **chi-square** being the one used in most crosstabular analyses. The probability is customarily reported in a summary form such as "$p < .05$," which can be translated as "The probability that the association was due to chance is less than 5 out of 100 (5%)."

When the analyst feels reasonably confident (at least 95% confident) that an association was not due to chance, it is said that the association is statistically significant. **Statistical significance** means that an association is not likely to be due to chance, according to some criterion set by the analyst. Convention (and the desire to avoid concluding that an association exists in the population when it doesn't) dictates that the criterion be a probability less than 5%.

But statistical significance is not everything. You may remember from Chapter 5 that sampling error decreases as sample size increases. For this same reason, an association is less likely to appear on the basis of chance in a larger sample than in a smaller sample. In a table with more than 1,000 cases, such as those involving the full 2000 GSS sample, the odds of a chance association are often very low indeed. For example, with our table based on 2,456 cases, the probability that the association between income and voting (Exhibit 12.20, p. 393) was due to chance was less than 1 in 1,000 ($p < .001$)! The association in that table was only moderate, as indicated by a gamma of .30. Even weak associations can be statistically significant with such a large random sample, which means that the analyst must be careful not to assume that just because a statistically significant association exists, it is therefore important. In a large sample, an association may be statistically significant but still be too weak to be substantively significant. All this boils down to another reason for evaluating carefully *both* the existence and the strength of an association.

Controlling for a Third Variable

Crosstabulation can also be used to study the relationship between two variables while controlling for other variables. We will focus our attention on controlling for a third variable in this section, but I will say a bit about controlling for more variables at the section's end. We will examine three different uses for three-variable crosstabulation: identifying an intervening variable, testing a relationship for spuriousness, and specifying the conditions for a relationship. Each type of three-variable crosstab helps to strengthen our understanding of the "focal relationship" involving our dependent and independent variable (Aneshenshel, 2002). Testing a relationship for possible spuriousness helps to meet the nonspuriousness criterion for causality; identifying an intervening variable can help to chart the causal mechanism by which variation in the independent variable influences variation in the dependent variable; and specifying the conditions when a relationship occurs can help to improve our understanding of the nature of that relationship.

All three uses for three-variable crosstabulation are aspects of **elaboration analysis:** the process of introducing control variables into a bivariate relationship in order to better understand the relationship (Davis, 1985; Rosenberg, 1968). We will examine the gamma and chi-square statistics for each table in this analysis.

Intervening Variables

We will first complete our test of one of the implications of the causal model of voting in Exhibit 12.1 (p. 369): that trust (or efficacy) intervenes in the relationship between social status and voting. You already have seen that both income (one of our social status indicators) and trust in people are associated with the likelihood of voting. Both relationships are predicted by the model: so far, so good. You can also see in Exhibit 12.26 that trust is related to income: Higher income is associated with the belief that people can be trusted (gamma = .27; $p < .001$). Another prediction of the model is confirmed. But in order to determine whether the trust variable is an **intervening variable** in this relationship, we must determine whether it explains (transmits) the influence of income on trust. We therefore examine the relationship between income and voting while controlling for the respondent's belief that people can be trusted.

According to the causal model, income (social status) influences voting (political participation) by influencing trust in people (our substitute for efficacy), which in turn influences voting. We can evaluate this possibility by reading the two subtables in Exhibit 12.27.

Exhibit 12.26   Crosstabulation of Interpersonal Trust by Income

| Trust in People | Family Income | | | |
	<$20,000	$20,000–$34,999	$35,000–$59,999	$60,000+
Agree	30%	41%	43%	56%
Disagree	70%	59%	57%	44%
Total	100%	100%	100%	100%
(n)	(439)	(350)	(408)	(428)

Source: General Social Survey, 2000.

Exhibit 12.27   Voting in 1996 by Family Income by Interpersonal Trust

"People can be trusted"

| Voting | Family Income | | | |
	<$20,000	$20,000–$34,999	$35,000 – $59,999	$60,000+
Voted	63%	62%	70%	81%
Did not vote	37%	38%	30%	19%
Total	100%	100%	100%	100%
(n)	(134)	(142)	(175)	(238)

"People can't be trusted"

| Voting | Family Income | | | |
	<$20,000	$20,000–$34,999	$35,000–$59,999	$60,000+
Voted	46%	53%	55%	66%
Did not vote	54%	47%	45%	34%
Total	100%	100%	100%	100%
(n)	(305)	(208)	(233)	(190)

Source: General Social Survey, 2000.

Subtables like those in Exhibit 12.27 describe the relationship between two variables within the discrete categories of one or more other control variables. The control variable in Exhibit 12.27 is trust in people, and the first subtable is the income-voting crosstab for only those respondents who believe that people *can* be trusted. The second subtable is for those respondents who believe that people *can't* be trusted. They are called subtables because together they make up the table in Exhibit 12.20 (p. 393). If trust in ordinary people intervened in the income–voting relationship, the effect of controlling for this third variable would be to eliminate, or at least substantially reduce, this relationship—the distribution of voting would be the same for every income category in both subtables in Exhibit 12.27.

A quick inspection of the subtables in Exhibit 12.27 reveals that trust in people does not intervene in the relationship between income and voting. There is only a modest difference in the strength of the income–voting association in the subtables (gamma is .35 in the first subtable and .18 in the second). In both subtables, the respondents with higher incomes—$20,000 or more, and in particular $35,000 or more—were more likely to vote than those with an income under $20,000. Of course, this finding does not necessarily mean that the causal model was wrong. This one measure is a measure of trust in people, which is not just the same as the widely studied concept of political efficacy; a better measure, from a different survey, might function as an intervening variable. But for now we should be less confident in the model.

Extraneous Variables

Another reason for introducing a third variable into a bivariate relationship is to see whether that relationship is spurious due to the influence of an **extraneous variable**—a variable that influences both the independent and dependent variables, creating an association between them that disappears when the extraneous variable is controlled. Ruling out possible extraneous variables will help to strengthen considerably the conclusion that the relationship between the independent and dependent variables is causal, particularly if all the variables that seem to have the potential for creating a spurious relationship can be controlled.

One variable that might create a spurious relationship between income and voting is education. You have already seen that the likelihood of voting increases with income. Is it not possible, though, that this association is spurious due to the effect of education? Education, after all, is associated with both income and voting, and we might surmise that it is what students learn in school about civic responsibility that increases voting, not income itself. Exhibit 12.28 diagrams this possibility, and Exhibit 12.29 shows the bivariate associations among education and voting, and education and income. As the model in Exhibit 12.28

Exhibit 12.28   A Causal Model of a Spurious Effect

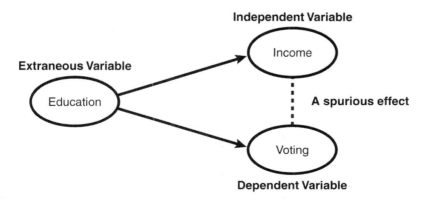

Exhibit 12.29   Voting in 1996 by Education and Income by Education

Voting by Education

| | Education | | |
| | Grade School | High School | Some College |
Voting			
Voted	38%	56%	67%
Did not vote	62%	44%	33%
Total	100%	100%	100%
(*n*)	(490)	(823)	(1,495)

Income by Education

| | Education | | |
| | Grade School | High School | Some College |
Income			
<$20,000	58%	29%	19%
$20,000–$34,999	23%	27%	19%
$35,000–$59,999	14%	26%	27%
$60,000+	6%	18%	35%
Total	101%*	100%	100%
(*n*)	(403)	(718)	(1,331)

Source: General Social Survey, 2000.

*Percentages do not add to 100 due to rounding error.

predicts, education is associated with both income and voting. So far, so good. If education actually does create a spurious relationship between income and voting, there should be no association between income and voting after controlling for education. Because we are using crosstabs, this means there should be no association in any of the income–voting subtables for any value of education.

The trivariate crosstabulation in Exhibit 12.30 shows that the relationship between voting and income is not spurious due to the effect of education; if it was, each of the subtables would have a pattern like that in the "grade school" subtable, where the association between voting and income really doesn't appear—there is only a two percentage point increase in voting between the lowest and the highest income categories (see also the "Grade School" bars in Exhibit 12.31, p. 404). Gamma is .00 for this first subtable.

But there is an association between income and voting in the other two subtables in Exhibit 12.30, for respondents with a high school or some college education. The strength of that association is not much weaker in these two subtables than it was in the original bivariate table: gamma is −.23 and −.25 in the second and third subtables; it was .30 in the original bivariate table (Exhibit 12.20, p. 393). So our hypothesis, that income as a social status indicator has a causal effect on voting, is specified by education, but it does not appear that it was spurious. The next section elaborates on this more complex pattern.

Exhibit 12.30   Voting in 1996 by Income by Education

Education = Grade School

Voting	Family Income			
	<$20,000	$20,000–$34,999	$35,000–$59,999	$60,000+
Voted	37%	36%	38%	39%
Did not vote	63%	64%	62%	61%
Total	100%	100%	100%	100%
(*n*)	(233)	(91)	(56)	(23)

Education = High School

Voting	Family Income			
	<$20,000	$20,000–$34,999	$35,000–$59,999	$60,000+
Voted	49%	54%	61%	71%
Did not vote	51%	46%	39%	29%
Total	100%	100%	100%	100%
(*n*)	(210)	(193)	(188)	(127)

Education = Some College

Voting	Family Income			
	<$20,000	$20,000–$34,999	$35,000–$59,999	$60,000+
Voted	56%	67%	66%	78%
Did not vote	44%	33%	34%	22%
Total	100%	100%	100%	100%
(*n*)	(248)	(251)	(365)	(467)

Source: General Social Survey, 2000.

Specification

By adding a third variable to an evaluation of a bivariate relationship, the data analyst can also specify the conditions under which the bivariate relationship occurs. A **specification** occurs when the association between the independent and dependent variables varies across the categories of one or more other control variables. This is what we just found in Exhibit 12.30. The pattern is displayed graphically in Exhibit 12.31.

The subtables in Exhibit 12.32 allow an evaluation of whether race specifies the effect of income on voting, as suggested by previous research. The percentages who voted in each of the income categories vary more among whites (gamma = −.31) than for minorities (gamma = −.19). Race therefore does appear to specify somewhat the association between income and voting: The likelihood of white respondents having voted varies more with their

Exhibit 12.31   Chart of Voting in 1996 by Family Income by Education

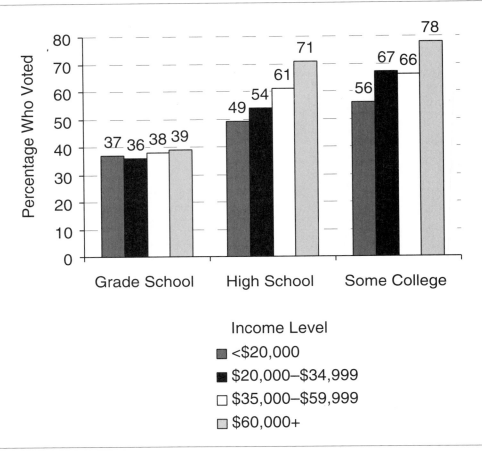

Source: General Social Survey, 2000.

income than it does among minority respondents. It is the very high rate of voting among the highest income whites (for example, 77% of whites who earned $60,000 per year or more voted) that accounts for this specification; investigation of the reason for this would make for an interesting contribution to the literature. Is it because whites in the high income category actually earn more on average than minorities in that income category? Or do high income whites feel more connected to the political system than do high income minorities? Can you think of other possibilities?

I should add one important caution about constructing tables involving three or more variables. Because the total number of cells in the subtables becomes large as the number of categories of the control (third) variable increases, the number of cases that each cell percentage is based on will become correspondingly small. This effect has two important consequences. First, the number of comparisons that must be made in order to identify the

Exhibit 12.32   Voting in 1996 by Income by Race

RACE = WHITE

	FAMILY INCOME			
VOTING	*<$20,000*	*$20,000–$34,999*	*$35,000–$59,999*	*$60,000 +*
Voted	50%	60%	63%	77%
Did not vote	50%	40%	37%	23%
Total	100%	100%	100%	100%
(n)	(483)	(426)	(511)	(538)

RACE = AFRICAN AMERICAN AND OTHER MINORITY

	FAMILY INCOME			
VOTING	*<$20,000*	*$20,000–$34,999*	*$35,000–$59,999*	*$60,000 +*
Voted	44%	47%	52%	63%
Did not vote	56%	53%	48%	37%
Total	100%	100%	100%	100%
(n)	(209)	(109)	(99)	(81)

Source: General Social Survey, 2000.

patterns in the table as a whole becomes very substantial—and the patterns may become too complex to make much sense of them. Second, as the number of cases per category decreases, the odds that the distributions within these categories could be due to chance become greater. This problem of having too many cells and too few cases can be lessened by making sure that the control variable has only a few categories and by drawing a large sample, but often neither of these steps will be sufficient to resolve the problem completely.

REGRESSING VARIABLES

My goal in introducing you to crosstabulation has been to help you think about the association among variables and to give you a relatively easy tool for describing association. In order to read most statistical reports and to conduct more sophisticated analyses of social data, you will have to extend your statistical knowledge. Many statistical reports and articles published in social science journals use a statistical technique called **regression analysis** or **correlational analysis** to describe the association between two or more quantitative variables. The terms actually refer to different aspects of the same technique. Statistics based on regression and correlation are used very often in social science and have many advantages over crosstabulation—as well as some disadvantages.

Exhibit 12.33   Occupational Prestige by Years of Education

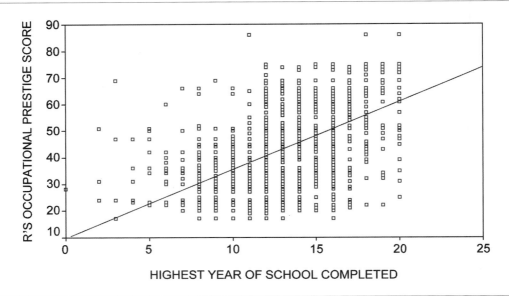

Source: General Social Survey, 2000.

I'll only give you an overview here of this approach. Take a look at Exhibit 12.33. It's a plot, termed a *scatterplot,* of the relationship in the GSS 2000 sample between years of education and occupational prestige (a score that ranges from 0 to 100, reflecting the prestige accorded to the respondent's occupation by people in America). You can see that I didn't collapse the values of either of these variables into categories, as I had to do in order to use them in the preceding crosstabular analysis. Instead, the scatterplot shows the location of each case in the data in terms of years of education (the horizontal axis) and occupational prestige level (the vertical axis).

You can see that the data points in the scatterplot tend to run from the lower left to the upper right of the chart, indicating a positive relationship: The more the years of education, the higher the occupational prestige. The line drawn through the points is the *regression line.* The regression line summarizes this positive relationship between years of education, the independent variable (often simply termed *X* in regression analysis) and occupational prestige, the dependent variable (often simply termed *Y* in regression analysis). This regression line is the "best fitting" straight line for this relationship—it is the line that lies closest to all the points in the chart, according to certain criteria.

How well does the regression line fit the points? In other words, how close does the regression line come to the points? (Actually, it's the square of the vertical distance, on the *y*-axis, between the points and the regression line that is used as the criterion.) The **correlation coefficient,** also called "Pearson's *r*," or just "*r*," gives an answer to that question. The value of *r* for this relationship is .52, which indicates a moderately strong positive linear relationship (if it were a negative relationship, *r* would have a negative sign). The value of *r* is 0 when there is absolutely no linear relationship between the two variables, and 1 when all the points representing all the cases lie exactly on the regression line (which would mean that the regression line describes the relationship perfectly).

So the correlation coefficient does for a scatterplot like this what gamma does for a crosstabulation table: It is a summary statistic that tells us about the strength of the association between the two variables. Values of r close to 0 indicate that the relationship is weak; values of r close to 1 indicate the relationship is strong—in between there is a lot of room for judgment.

You can also use correlation coefficients and regression analysis to study simultaneously the association between three or more variables. For example, you could test to see whether several other variables in addition to education are associated with occupational prestige scores.

You will need to learn more about when correlation coefficients and regression analysis are appropriate (such as, both variables have to be quantitative and the relationship has to be linear [not curvilinear]). But that's for another time and place. In order to learn more about correlation coefficients and regression analysis, you'll have to take a statistics course. For now, this short introduction will enable you to make sense of more of the statistical analyses you find in research articles.

ANALYZING DATA ETHICALLY: HOW NOT TO LIE ABOUT RELATIONSHIPS

When the data analyst begins to examine relationships among variables in some real data, social science research becomes most exciting. The moment of truth, it would seem, has arrived. Either the hypotheses are supported or not. But, in fact, this is also a time to proceed with caution, and to evaluate the analyses of others with even more caution. Once large datasets are entered into a computer, it becomes very easy to check out a great many relationships; when relationships are examined among three or more variables at a time, the possibilities become almost endless. In fact, regression analysis (extended to what is termed *multiple regression analysis*), allows a researcher to test easily for many relationships at the same time.

This range of possibilities presents a great hazard for data analysis. It becomes very tempting to search around in the data until something interesting emerges. Rejected hypotheses are forgotten in favor of highlighting what's going on in the data. It's not wrong to examine data for unanticipated relationships; the problem is that inevitably some relationships among variables will appear just on the basis of chance association alone. If you search hard and long enough, it will be possible to come up with something that really means nothing.

A reasonable balance must be struck between deductive data analysis to test hypotheses and inductive analysis to explore patterns in a dataset. Hypotheses formulated in advance of data collection must be tested as they were originally stated; any further analyses of these hypotheses that involve a more exploratory strategy must be labeled in research reports as such. Serendipitous findings do not need to be ignored, but they must be reported as such. Subsequent researchers can try to test deductively the ideas generated by our explorations.

We also have to be honest about the limitations of using survey data to test causal hypotheses. The usual practice for those who seek to test a causal hypothesis with non-experimental survey data is to test for the relationship between the independent and dependent variables, controlling for other variables that might possibly create a spurious relationship. This is what we did by examining the relationship between income and voting while controlling for education (Exhibit 12.30, p. 403). (These subtables actually show that education specifies the relationship between family income and voting—there is no relationship for those with only a grade school education, but the relationship exists for those who finished high school and those who attended college. Education does not actually explain the income–voting relationship)

But finding that a hypothesized relationship is not altered by controlling for just one variable does not establish that the relationship is causal. Nor does controlling for two, three, or many more variables. There always is a possibility that some other variable that we did not think to control, or that was not even measured in the survey, has produced a spurious relationship between the independent and dependent variables in our hypothesis (Lieberson, 1985). We have to think about the possibilities and be cautious in our causal conclusions.

It is also important to understand the statistical techniques we are using and to use them appropriately. In particular, the analyst who uses regression analysis has to make a number of assumptions about the variables in the analysis; when these assumptions are violated, regression results can be very misleading. (You just might want to rush right out to buy the Pine Forge Press statistics text at this point, *Statistics for a Diverse Society* by Chava Frankfort-Nachmias and Anna Leon-Guerrero.)

CONCLUSIONS

This chapter has demonstrated how a researcher can describe social phenomena, identify relationships among them, explore the reasons for these relationships, and test hypotheses about them. Statistics provide a remarkably useful tool for developing our understanding of the social world, a tool that we can use both to test our ideas and to generate new ones.

Unfortunately, to the uninitiated, the use of statistics can seem to end debate right there—you can't argue with the numbers. But you now know better than that. The numbers will be worthless if the methods used to generate the data are not valid; and the numbers will be misleading if they are not used appropriately, taking into account the type of data to which they are applied. And even assuming valid methods and proper use of statistics, there's one more critical step, because the numbers do not speak for themselves. Ultimately, it is how we interpret and report the statistics that determines their usefulness.

KEY TERMS

Bar chart	Compressed frequency display
Base number (*N*)	Correlation coefficient
Bimodal	Correlational analysis
Central tendency	Crosstabulation (crosstab)
Chi-square	Curvilinear
Combined frequency display	Data cleaning

Descriptive statistics
Elaboration analysis
Extraneous variable
Frequency distribution
Frequency polygon
Gamma
Histogram
Inferential statistics
Interquartile range
Intervening variable
Marginal distribution
Mean
Measure of association
Median
Mode
Monotonic

Normal distribution
Outlier
Percentage
Probability average
Quartile
Range
Regression analysis
Secondary data analysis
Skewness
Specification
Standard deviation
Statistical significance
Subtable
Unimodal
Variability
Variance

HIGHLIGHTS

- Data entry options include direct collection of data through a computer, use of scannable data entry forms, and use of data entry software. All data should be cleaned during the data entry process.

- Use of secondary data can save considerable time and resources, but may limit data analysis possibilities.

- Bar charts, histograms, and frequency polygons are useful for describing the shape of distributions. Care must be taken with graphic displays to avoid distorting a distribution's apparent shape.

- Frequency distributions display variation in a form that can be easily inspected and described. Values should be grouped in frequency distributions in a way that does not alter the shape of the distribution. Following several guidelines can reduce the risk of problems.

- Summary statistics are often used to describe the central tendency and variability of distributions. The appropriateness of the mode, mean, and median vary with a variable's level of measurement, the distribution's shape, and the purpose of the summary.

- The variance and standard deviation summarize variability around the mean. The interquartile range is usually preferable to the range to indicate the interval spanned by cases, due to the effect of outliers on the range. The degree of skewness of a distribution is usually described in words rather than with a summary statistic.

- Some of the data in many reports can be displayed more efficiently by using combined and compressed statistical displays.

- Honesty and openness are the key ethical principles that should guide data summaries.

- Crosstabulations should normally be percentaged within the categories of the independent variable. A crosstabulation can be used to determine the existence, strength, direction, and pattern of an association.

- Elaboration analysis can be used in crosstabular analysis to test for spurious and mediating relationships and to specify the conditions under which relationships occur.

- Inferential statistics are used with sample-based data to estimate the confidence that can be placed in a statistical estimate of a population parameter. Estimates of the probability that an association between variables may have occurred on the basis of chance are also based on inferential statistics.

- Regression analysis is a statistical technique for characterizing the relationship between two quantitative variables with a linear equation and for summarizing the extent to which the linear equation represents that relationship. Correlation coefficients summarize the fit of the relationship to the regression line.

DISCUSSION QUESTIONS

1. Create frequency distributions from lists in U.S. Bureau of the Census reports on the characteristics of cities or counties, or any similar listing of data for at least 100 cases. You will have to decide on a grouping scheme for the distribution of variables like average age and population size, how to deal with outliers in the frequency distribution, and how to categorize qualitative variables like the predominant occupation. Decide what summary statistics to use for each variable. How well were the features of each distribution represented by the summary statistics? Describe the shape of each distribution. Propose a hypothesis involving two of these variables, and develop a crosstab to evaluate the support for this hypothesis. Describe each relationship in terms of the four aspects of an association, after percentaging each table within the categories of the independent variable. Does the hypothesis appear to have been supported? To begin, go to www.census.gov.

2. Become a media critic. For the next week, scan a newspaper or some magazines for statistics. How many can you find using frequency distributions, graphs, and the summary statistics introduced in this chapter? Are these statistics used appropriately and interpreted correctly? Would any other statistics have been preferable or useful in addition to those presented?

PRACTICE EXERCISES

1. Exhibit 12.34 shows a frequency distribution of "trust in people" as produced by the Statistical Package for the Social Sciences (SPSS) with the GSS 2000 data. As you can see, the table includes abbreviated labels for the variable and its response choices, as well as the raw frequencies and three percentage columns. The first percentage column (Percent) shows the percentage in each category; the next percentage column (Valid Percent) is based on the total number of respondents who gave valid answers (2,817 in this instance). It is the Valid Percent column that normally should be used to construct a frequency distribution for presentation. The last percentage column is Cumulative Percent, adding up the valid percents from top to bottom.

Redo the table for presentation, using the format of the frequency distributions presented in the text.

2. Try your hand at recoding. Start with the distribution of the political ideology variable from Exhibit 12.9. It is named POLVIEWS in the GSS. Recode it to just three categories. What decision did you make about grouping? What was the consequence of this decision for the shape of the distribution? For the size of the middle category?

3. Crosstabulations produced by most statistical packages are not in the proper format for inclusion in a report, and so they have to be reformatted. Referring to Exhibit 12.35, rewrite the table in presentational format, using one of the other tables as your guide. Describe the association in the table in terms of each of the four aspects of association. A chi-square test of statistical significance resulted in a *p* value of .000, meaning that the actual value was less than .001. State the level of confidence that you can have that the association in the table is not due to chance.

Exhibit 12.34 Distribution of "Can People Be Trusted?"

		Frequency	Percent	Valid Percent	Cumulative Percent
Valid	CAN TRUST	662	23.5	35.2	35.2
	CANNOT TRUST	1093	38.8	58.2	93.4
	DEPENDS	124	4.4	6.6	100.0
	Total	1879	66.7	100.0	
Missing	NAP	921	32.7		
	DK	9	.3		
	NA	8	.3		
	Total	938	33.3		
Total		2817	100.0		

Source: General Social Survey, 2000.

Exhibit 12.35 Vote in 1996 Election by Education (Trichotomized)

			Education Trichotomized			
			Grade School	High School	Some College	Total
Vote in 1996 Election Indicated	Voted	Count	184	457	1008	1649
		% within Education Trichotomized	37.6%	55.5%	67.4%	58.7%
	Did Not Vote	Count	306	366	487	1159
		% within Education Trichotomized	62.4%	44.5%	32.6%	41.3%
Total		Count	490	823	1495	2808
		% within Education Trichotomized	100.0%	100.0%	100.0%	100.0%

Source: General Social Survey, 2000.

4. What if you had to answer this question: What was the income distribution of voters in the 1996 presidential election, and how did it compare to the income distribution for those who didn't vote? Can you answer this question exactly with Exhibit 12.20, page 393? If not, change the column percentages in the table to row percentages. In order to do this, you will first have to convert the column percentages back to cell frequencies (although the frequencies are included in the table, so you can check your work). You can do this by multiplying the column percentage by the number of cases in the column, and then dividing by 100 (you will probably have fractional values because of rounding error). Then compute the row percentages from these frequencies and the row totals.

5. Exhibit 12.35 contains a crosstabulation of voting by education (recoded) directly as output by SPSS from the 2000 GSS dataset. Describe the row and column marginal distributions. Try to calculate a cell percentage using the frequency (count) in that cell and the appropriate base number of cases.

WEB EXERCISES

1. Search the Web for a social science example of statistics. Using the Key Terms from this chapter, describe the set of statistics you have identified. What social phenomena does this set of statistics describe? What relationships, if any, do the statistics identify?

2. Go to the Roper Center for Public Opinion Research Web site at http://www.ropercenter.uconn.edu. Choose any two U.S. presidents from Franklin. D. Roosevelt to the present. By using the Web site links, locate the presidential job performance poll data for the two presidents you have chosen.

Based on poll data on presidential job performance, create a brief report that includes the following for each president you chose: the presidents you chose and their years in office; the questions asked in the polls; and bar charts showing years when polls were taken, average of total percentage approving of job performance, average of total percentage disapproving of job performance, and average of total percentage with no opinion on job performance. Write a brief summary comparing and contrasting your two bar charts.

3. Do a Web search for information on a social science subject you are interested in. How much of the information you find relies on statistics as a tool for understanding the subject? How do statistics allow researchers to test their ideas about the subject and generate new ideas? Write your findings in a brief report, referring to the Web sites that you relied on.

SPSS EXERCISES

1. Develop a description of the basic social and demographic characteristics of the U.S. population in 1998. Examine each characteristic with three statistical techniques: a graph, a frequency distribution, and a measure of central tendency (and a measure of variation, if appropriate).
   a. From the menu, select *Graphs\Bar.* From the Bar Graph window, select *Simple Define* [Marital—Category Axis]. *Bars represent % of cases.* Select *Options* (do not display groups defined by missing values). Finally, select *Histogram* [EDUC,EARNRS,TVHOURS, ATTEND].
   b. Describe the distribution of each variable.
   c. Generate frequency distributions and descriptive statistics for these variables. From the menu, select *Analyze\Descriptive statistics\Frequencies.* From the Frequencies window, set MARITAL,EDUC,EARNRS,TVHOURS,ATTEND. For the Statistics, choose the mean, median, range, and standard deviation.
   d. Collapse the categories for each distribution. Be sure to adhere to the guidelines on pages 379-380. Does the general shape of any of the distributions change as a result of changing the categories?
   e. Which statistics are appropriate to summarize the central tendency and variation of each variable? Do the values of any of these statistics surprise you?

2. Try describing relationships with support for capital punishment by using graphs. Select two relationships you identified in previous exercises and represent them in graphic form. Try drawing the graphs on lined paper (graph paper is preferable).

3. If you have the CD-ROM that came with this book, which contains a copy of a subset of the 2000 General Social Survey, it will be easy for you to replicate the tables in this chapter. It would be a good exercise for you to do so, but remember that if you are using the GSS2000mini file, your tables will contain only a sample of cases from the complete GSS2000 file that I used. The computer output you

get will probably not look like the tables shown here, because I reformatted the tables for presentation, as you should do before preparing a final report. At this point, I'll let you figure out the menu commands required to generate these graphs, frequency distributions, and crosstabulations.

4. Propose a variable that might have created a spurious relationship between income and voting. Explain your thinking. Propose a variable that might result in a conditional effect of income on voting, so that the relationship between income and voting would vary across the categories of the other variable. Test these propositions with three-variable crosstabulations. Were any supported? How would you explain your findings?

DEVELOPING A RESEARCH PROPOSAL

Use the GSS data to add a pilot study to your proposal. A pilot study is a preliminary effort to test out the procedures and concepts that you have proposed to research.

1. In SPSS, review the GSS2000mini variable list and identify some variables that have at least some connection to your research problem. If possible, identify one variable that might be treated as independent in your proposed research and one that might be treated as dependent.

2. Request frequencies for these variables.

3. Request a crosstabulation of the dependent variable by the independent variable (if you were able to identify any). If necessary, recode the independent variable to five or fewer categories.

4. Write a brief description of your findings and comment on their implications for your proposed research. Did you learn any lessons from this exercise for your proposal?

Chapter 13

QUALITATIVE DATA ANALYSIS AND CONTENT ANALYSIS

Features of Qualitative Data Analysis

Qualitative Data Analysis as an Art
Research Questions for Qualitative Data
    Analysis
The Case Study

Techniques of Qualitative Data Analysis

Documentation
Conceptualization, Coding, and
    Categorizing
Examining Relationships and Displaying
    Data
Authenticating Conclusions
Reflexivity

Alternatives in Qualitative Data Analysis

Traditional Ethnography
Qualitative Comparative Analysis
Narrative Analysis
Grounded Theory

**Computer-Assisted Qualitative Data
    Analysis**

Content Analysis

Ethics in Qualitative Data Analysis

Conclusions

*I was at lunch standing in line and he [another male student] came up to my face
and started saying stuff and then he pushed me. I said . . . I'm cool with you, I'm
your friend and then he push me again and calling me names. I told him to stop
pushing me and then he push me hard and said something about my mom. And
then he hit me, and I hit him back. After he fell I started kicking him.*

—Morrill et al., 2000:521

Unfortunately, this statement was not made by a soap opera actor, but by a real student
writing an in-class essay about conflicts in which he had participated. But then you already
knew that such conflicts are common in many high schools, so perhaps it will be reassuring

to know that this statement was elicited by a team of social scientists who were studying conflicts in high schools in order to better understand their origins and to inform prevention policies.

Does it surprise you that the text excerpt above is data used in a qualitative research project? That is the first difference between qualitative and quantitative data analysis—the data to be analyzed is text, rather than numbers, at least when the analysis first begins. Does it trouble you to learn that there are no variables and hypotheses in this qualitative analysis by Calvin Morrill, Christine Yalda, Madeleine Adelman, Michael Musheno, and Cindy Bejarano (2000)? This, too, is another difference between the typical qualitative and quantitative approaches to analysis, although there are some exceptions.

I will present in this chapter the features that most qualitative data analyses share and I will illustrate these features with research on youth conflict and on being homeless. You will quickly learn that there is no one way to analyze textual data. To quote Michael Quinn Patton (2002:432),

> Qualitative analysis transforms data into findings. No formula exists for that transformation. Guidance, yes. But no recipe. Direction can and will be offered, but the final destination remains unique for each inquirer, known only when—and if—arrived at.

So I will discuss some of the different types of qualitative data analysis before focusing on content analysis, an approach to analyzing text that relies on quantitative techniques. You will also learn about computer programs for qualitative data analysis, and you will see that these programs are blurring the distinctions between quantitative and qualitative approaches to textual analysis.

FEATURES OF QUALITATIVE DATA ANALYSIS

The distinctive features of qualitative data collection methods that you studied in Chapter 9 are also reflected in the methods used to analyze that data. The focus on text—on qualitative data rather than on numbers—is the most important feature of qualitative analysis. In addition, qualitative and quantitative data analysis differ in the priority given to the views of the researcher and to the subjects of the research. Qualitative data analysts seek to describe their textual data in ways that capture the setting or people who produced this text on their own terms, rather than in terms of predefined measures and hypotheses. What this means is that qualitative data analysis tends to be inductive—the analyst identifies important categories in the data, as well as patterns and relationships, through a process of discovery. There are often no predefined measures or hypotheses. Anthropologists term this an **emic focus,** which means representing the setting in terms of the participants, rather than an **etic focus,** in which the setting and its participants are represented in terms that the researcher brings to the study.

Emic focus   Representing a setting with the participants' terms.

Etic focus   Representing a setting with the researchers' terms.

Qualitative data analysis is an iterative and reflexive process that begins as data are being collected, rather than after data collection has ceased (Stake, 1995). Next to her field notes or interview transcripts, the qualitative analyst jots down ideas about the meaning of the text and how it might relate to other issues. This process of reading through the data and interpreting it continues throughout the project. The analyst adjusts the data collection process itself when it begins to appear that additional concepts need to be investigated or new relationships explored. This process is termed **progressive focusing** (Parlett & Hamilton, 1976).

We emphasize placing an interpreter in the field to observe the workings of the case, one who records objectively what is happening but simultaneously examines its meaning and redirects observation to refine or substantiate those meanings. Initial research questions may be modified or even replaced in mid-study by the case researcher. The aim is to thoroughly understand [the case]. If early questions are not working, if new issues become apparent, the design is changed. (Stake, 1995:9)

Progressive focusing   The process by which a qualitative analyst interacts with the data and gradually refines her focus.

Elijah Anderson (2003:38) describes the progressive focusing process in his memoir about his study of Jelly's Bar:

I also wrote conceptual memos to myself to help me sort out my findings. Usually not more than a page long, they represented theoretical insights that emerged from my engagement with the data in my field notes. As I gained tenable hypotheses and propositions, I began to listen and observe selectively, focusing in on those events that I thought might bring me alive to my research interests and concerns. This method of dealing with the information I was receiving amounted to a kind of dialogue with the data, sifting out ideas, weighing new notions against the reality with which I [was] faced there on the streets and back at my desk.

Carrying out this process successfully is more likely if the analyst reviews a few basic guidelines when he or she starts the process of analyzing qualitative data (Miller & Crabtree, 1999b:142–143)

- Know yourself, your biases and preconceptions.
- Know your question.
- Seek creative abundance. Consult others and keep looking for alternative interpretations.
- Be flexible.
- Exhaust the data. Try to account for all the data in the texts, then publicly acknowledge the unexplained and remember the next principle.
- Celebrate anomalies. They are the windows to insight.
- Get critical feedback. The solo analyst is a great danger to self and others.
- Be explicit. Share the details with yourself, your team members, and your audiences.

You'll also want to keep in mind features of qualitative data analysis that are shared with those of quantitative data analysis. Both quantitative and qualitative data analysis can involve making distinctions about textual data. You also know that textual data can be transposed to quantitative data through a process of categorization and counting.

Qualitative Data Analysis as an Art

If you find yourself longing for the certainty of predefined measures and deductively derived hypotheses, you are beginning to understand the difference between setting out to analyze data quantitatively and planning to do so with a qualitative approach in mind. Perhaps you are also now understanding better the difference between the positivist and interpretivist research philosophies that I summarized in Chapter 3. When it comes right down to it, the process of qualitative data analysis is even described by some as involving as much "art" as science—as a "dance," in the words of William Miller and Benjamin Crabtree (1999b:138–139).

> Interpretation is a complex and dynamic craft, with as much creative artistry as technical exactitude, and it requires an abundance of patient plodding, fortitude, and discipline. There are many changing rhythms; multiple steps; moments of jubilation, revelation, and exasperation. . . . The dance of interpretation is a dance for two, but those two are often multiple and frequently changing, and there is always an audience, even if it is not always visible. Two dancers are the interpreters and the texts.

The "dance" of qualitative data analysis is represented in Exhibit 13.1, which captures the alternation between immersion in the text to identify meanings and editing the text to create categories and codes. The process involves three different modes of reading the text:

1. When the researcher reads the text *literally* (L, in Exhibit 13.1), she is focused on its literal content and form, so the text "leads" the dance.

2. When the researcher reads the text *reflexively* (R), she focuses on how her own orientation shapes her interpretations and focus. Now, the researcher leads the dance.

3. When the researcher reads the text *interpretively* (I), she tries to construct her own interpretation of what the text means.

So there is no one way to read a text during the process of analysis; instead, you should use a mixture of approaches, just as you do during the process of collecting qualitative data.

Qualitative data analyses also tend to be guided by more exploratory types of research questions than are quantitative analyses, and they often focus attention on the interrelated aspects of the setting or group under investigation—the case—rather than breaking the whole up into separate parts. Each of these components—an emic focus, progressive focusing, a reflexive and iterative analysis, exploratory research questions, and a focus on the whole case—is represented in a traditional ethnography, in which the qualitative analyst represents the cultural life of the group. If you are ready to examine this diverse collection of approaches, then we can proceed.

Exhibit 13.1   Dance of Qualitative Analysis

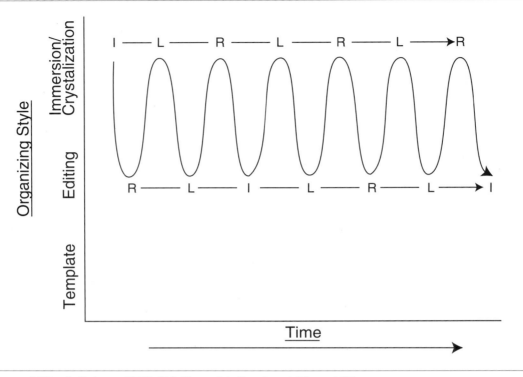

Source: Miller & Crabtree, 1999b:139, Figure 7.1. Based on Addison, 1999.

Research Questions for Qualitative Data Analysis

You already know that research designs should be selected and refined to reflect the research questions that they are intended to answer. This principle applies even more to qualitative data analysis plans. A typical research question for a qualitative project appears in a proposal that my colleagues and I submitted to the National Institute of Mental Health to compare the value of independent and group homes for homeless mentally ill persons. Although the literature on mental health services contains a substantial amount of information on typical group homes, our plan was "to develop client-managed Evolving Consumer Households (ECH) which offer significant advantages over both Independent Living and existing models of group living." We therefore posed several research questions about the process by which this evolution might occur (Goldfinger et al., 1990:43):

> What is the process by which group homes can evolve into independent consumer operated households? Can a model which fosters increasing consumer independence and management be replicated in multiple residences? What is the natural history of the unfolding of the transition of control and decision making from paid staff to resident consumers?

The open-ended nature of these questions suggested an exploratory analysis that would describe a wide range of activities and events in the group homes.

Daniel M. Cress and David A. Snow (2000) found more specific deficits in their review of prior research on social movements, as they formulated analysis plans for their study of the outcomes achieved by homeless mobilization organizations.

> [O]ur understanding of the consequences of social movements is conspicuously under-developed. . . . hampered by conceptual and causal confusion. . . . what counts as an outcome clearly is open to debate. . . . On a causal level, the precise influence of social movement activity in relation to specifiable outcomes is difficult to ascertain. . . . [T]here is debate about which factors associated with social movements are most important. . . . [T]he potential influence of cultural and ideational factors in the determination of movement outcomes has been glaringly absent in most theoretical discussions and research explorations of the problems. (Cress & Snow, 2000:1064)

This evaluation of the deficits of prior research led to the specific research question that Cress and Snow (2000:1072) sought to answer:

> [T]he ways in which organizational, tactical, political mediation, and framing factors interact and combine to account for variation in the outcomes achieved by the 15 homeless SMOs [social movement organizations] we studied.

Cress and Snow turned to qualitative techniques in order to answer this question for five reasons: (1) the relative inaccessibility of the homeless SMOs; (2) the lack of much prior research about homeless SMOs; (3) the need to explore different possible outcome measures; (4) the intensive data needed to assess the range of potentially important influences; and (5) the multiple possible ways in which these influences might interact to affect outcomes.

Calvin Morrill and his colleagues (2000:524) turned to qualitative methods for their study of youth violence when they concluded that traditional quantitatively oriented gang and delinquency researchers "narrowly construct youth experience with peer conflict." What is needed, they proposed, is a "youth-centered study of conflict" that "puts youths' voices and orientations toward conflict at the center of concern." With this goal in mind, they (Morrill et al., 2000:528) sought a methodology that would do the following:

- Treat "young people's experiences and pronouncements contextually."
- Recognize "that youths actively construct meaningful cultural representations."
- "Facilitate self-representation by youth."
- Consider schools as "strategic sites where youths struggle to make sense of the worlds they create and re-create with peers and adults."

Morrill et al. (2000:531) concluded from this review of prior research on youth violence that a new approach was necessary. They decided to conduct a "narrative survey," in which students in ninth-grade English classes at one high school were asked to write a story about a time they experienced a conflict with another student. Five specific exploratory research questions guided their analysis:

1. How do youths represent everyday conflict in their stories?

2. What decision-making and reasoning processes do youths produce in their stories about conflict?

3. How do young people represent various means for handling peer conflict?

4. How is violence portrayed in their narratives?

5. How are adults situated in youth conflict narratives?

We will see in a later section how segments of the youths' conflict narratives provided some answers to these questions.

Each of these examples illustrates how the research questions that serve as starting points for qualitative data analyses do not simply emerge from the setting studied, but are shaped by the investigator. As Harry Wolcott (1995:156) explains, the research question

> is not embedded within the lives of those whom we study, demurely waiting to be discovered. Quite the opposite: *We instigate the problems we investigate.* There is no point in simply sitting by, passively waiting to see what a setting is going to "tell" us or hoping a problem will "emerge."

My focus on the importance of the research question as a tool for guiding qualitative data analyses should not obscure the iterative nature of the analytic process. The research question can change, narrow, expand, or multiply throughout the processes of data collection and analysis.

The Case Study

To many qualitative data analysts, the focus on variables and hypotheses in quantitative research is needless "slicing and dicing" of a social world that really functions as an integrated whole. Instead, their focus is on understanding "the case." The case may be an organization, community, social group, family, or even an individual and, as far as the qualitative analyst is concerned, it must be understood in its entirety. **Case study** is not so much a single method as a way of thinking about what qualitative data analysis can, or perhaps should, focus on. Educational researcher Robert Stake (1995:xi, xii) presents the logic of the case study approach:

> Case study is the study of the particularity and complexity of a single case, coming to understand its activity within important circumstances. . . . The qualitative researcher emphasizes episodes of nuance, the sequentiality of happenings in context, the wholeness of the individual.

Central to much qualitative case study research is the goal of creating a **thick description** of the setting studied—a description that provides a sense of what it is like to experience that setting from the standpoint of the natural actors in that setting (Geertz, 1973). Robert Stake's (1995:150) description of "a case within a case," a student in a school he studied, illustrates how a thick description gives a feel of the place and persons within it.

At 8:30 A.M. on Thursday morning, Adam shows up at the cafeteria door. Breakfast is being served but Adam doesn't go in. The woman giving out meal chits has her hands on him, seems to be sparring with him, verbally. And then he disappears. Adam is one of five siblings, all arrive at school in the morning with less than usual parent attention. Short, with a beautifully sculpted head . . . Adam is a person of notice.

At 8:55 he climbs the stairs to the third floor with other upper graders, turning to block the girls behind them and thus a string of others. Adam manages to keep the girls off-balance until Ms. Crain . . . spots him and gets traffic moving again. Mr. Garson . . . notices Adam, has a few quiet words with him before a paternal shove toward the room.

Case study   A setting or group that the analyst treats as an integrated social unit that must be studied holistically and in its particularity.

Thick description   A rich description that conveys a sense of what it is like from the standpoint of the natural actors in that setting.

You will learn in the next sections how qualitative data analysts can become structured in their approach, classifying cases or instances in conceptual categories and then identifying patterns and relationships. You will also see how these techniques differ when applied to textual data and how alternative qualitative data analytic approaches can seem sharply divergent from or somewhat similar to the logic of quantitative data analysis.

TECHNIQUES OF QUALITATIVE DATA ANALYSIS

Exhibit 13.2 outlines the phases of qualitative data analysis:

1.   Documentation of the data and the process of data collection

2.   Organization/categorization of the data into concepts

3.   Connection of the data to show how one concept may influence another

4.   Corroboration/legitimization, by evaluating alternative explanations and disconfirming evidence and searching for negative cases

5.   Representing the account (reporting the findings)

The analysis of qualitative research notes begins in the field, at the time of observation and/or interviewing, as the researcher identifies problems and concepts that appear likely to help in understanding the situation. Simply reading the notes or transcripts is an important step in the analytic process. Researchers should make frequent notes in the margins to identify important statements and to propose ways of coding the data: "husband/wife conflict," perhaps, or "tension reduction strategy."

An interim stage may consist of listing the concepts reflected in the notes and diagramming the relationships among concepts (Maxwell, 1996:78–81). In large projects, weekly team meetings are an important part of this process. Susan Miller described this process in

Exhibit 13.2   Flow Model of Qualitative Data Analysis Components

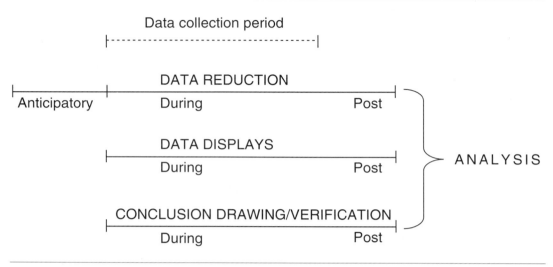

Source: Miles & Huberman, 1994:10, Figure 1.3. Used with permission.

her study of neighborhood police officers. Her research team met both to go over their field notes and to resolve points of confusion, as well as to dialogue with other skilled researchers who helped to identify emerging concepts (Bachman & Schutt, 2001:309):

> The fieldwork team met weekly to talk about situations that were unclear and to troubleshoot any problems. We also made use of peer-debriefing techniques. Here, multiple colleagues, who were familiar with qualitative data analysis but not involved in our research, participated in preliminary analysis of our findings. (Miller, 1999:233)

This process continues throughout the project and should assist in refining concepts during the report-writing phase, long after data collection has ceased. Let's examine each of the stages of qualitative research in more detail.

Documentation

The data for a qualitative study most often are notes jotted down in the field or during an interview—from which the original comments, observations, and feelings are reconstructed—or text transcribed from audiotapes. "The basic data are these observations and conversations, the actual words of people reproduced to the best of my ability from the field notes" (Diamond, 1992:7). What to do with all this material? Many field research projects have slowed to a halt because a novice researcher becomes overwhelmed by the quantity of information that has been collected. A one-hour interview can generate 20 to 25 pages of single-spaced text (Kvale, 1996:169). Analysis is less daunting, however, if the researcher maintains a disciplined transcription schedule.

Usually, I wrote these notes immediately after spending time in the setting or the next day. Through the exercise of writing up my field notes, with attention to "who" the speakers and actors were, I became aware of the nature of certain social relationships and their positional arrangements within the peer group. (Anderson, 2003:38)

You can see the analysis already emerging from this simple process of taking notes.

The first formal analytical step is documentation. The various contacts, interviews, written documents, and whatever it was that preserves a record of what happened all need to be saved and listed. Documentation is critical to qualitative research for several reasons: It is essential for keeping track of what will be a rapidly growing volume of notes, tapes, and documents; it provides a way of developing an outline for the analytic process; and it encourages ongoing conceptualizing and strategizing about the text.

Miles and Huberman (1994:53) provide a good example of a contact summary form that was used to keep track of observational sessions in a qualitative study of a new school curriculum (Exhibit 13.3).

Conceptualization, Coding, and Categorizing

Identifying and refining important concepts is a key part of the iterative process of qualitative research. Sometimes conceptualization begins with a simple observation that is interpreted directly, "pulled apart" and then put back together more meaningfully. Robert Stake provides an example (1995:75).

When Adam ran a pushbroom into the feet of the children nearby, I jumped to conclusions about his interactions with other children: aggressive, teasing, arresting. Of course, just a few minutes earlier I had seen him block the children climbing the steps in a similar moment of smiling bombast. So I was aggregating, and testing my unrealized hypotheses about what kind of kid he was, not postponing my interpreting. . . . My disposition was to keep my eyes on him. (Stake, 1995:74)

The focus in this conceptualization "on the fly" is to provide a detailed description of what was observed and a sense of why that was important.

More often, analytic insights are tested against new observations, the initial statement of problems and concepts is refined, the researcher then collects more data, interacts with it again, and the process continues. Elijah Anderson (2003) recounts how his conceptualization of social stratification at Jelly's Bar developed over a long period of time:

I could see the social pyramid, how certain guys would group themselves and say in effect, "I'm here and you're there." I made sense of these crowds [initially] as the "respectables," the "non-respectables," and the "near-respectables." . . . Inside, such non-respectables might sit on the crates, but if a respectable came along and wanted to sit there, the lower status person would have to move. (Anderson, 2003:18, 19)

But this initial conceptualization changed with experience, as Anderson realized that the participants themselves used other terms to differentiate social status: "winehead," "hoodlum," and "regular" (Anderson, 2003:28). What did they mean by these terms? "The 'regulars'

Exhibit 13.3   Example of a Contact Summary Form

Contact type:			Site:	Tindale
Visit	X		Contact date:	11/28-29/79
Phone			Today's date:	12/28/79
	(with whom)		Written by:	BLT

1. What were the main issues or themes that struck you in this contact?

    Interplay between highly prescriptive, "teacher-proof" curriculum that is top-down imposed and the actual writing of the curriculum by the teachers themselves.

    Split between the "watchdogs" (administrators) and the "house masters" (dept. chairs & teachers) vis a vis job foci.

    District curric, coord'r as decision maker re school's acceptance of research relationship.

2. Summarize the information you got (or failed to get) on each of the target questions you had for this contact.

Question	Information
History of dev. of innov'n	Conceptualized by Curric., Coord'r, English Chairman & Assoc. Chairman; written by teachers in summer; revised by teachers following summer with field testing data
School's org'l structure	Principal & admin'rs responsible for discipline; dept chairs are educ'l leaders
Demographics	Racial conflicts in late 60's; 60% black stud. pop.; heavy emphasis on discipline & on keeping out non-district students slipping in from Chicago
Teachers' response to innov'n	Rigid, structured, etc. at first; now, they say they like it/NEEDS EXPLORATION
Research access	Very good; only restriction: teachers not required to cooperate

3. Anything else that struck you as salient, interesting, illuminating or important in this contact?
    Thoroughness of the innov'n's development and training.

    Its embeddedness in the district's curriculum, as planned and executed by the district curriculum coordinator.

    The initial resistance to its high prescriptiveness (as reported by users) as contrasted with their current acceptance and approval of it (again, as reported by users).

4. What new (or remaining) target questions do you have in considering the next contact with this site?

    How do users really perceive the innov'n? If they do indeed embrace it, what accounts for the change from early resistance?

    Nature and amount of networking among users of innov'n.

    Information on "stubborn" math teachers whose ideas weren't heard initially – who are they? Situation particulars? Resolution?

    Follow-up on English teacher Reilly's "fall from the chairmanship."

    Follow a team through a day of rotation, planning, etc.

    CONCERN: The consequences of eating school cafeteria food two days per week for the next four or five months . . .

    Stop

Source: Miles & Huberman, 1994:53, Figure 4.1.

basically valued 'decency.' They associated decency with conventionality but also with 'working for a living,' or having a 'visible means of support'" (Anderson, 2003:29). In this way, Anderson progressively refined his concept as he gained experience in the setting.

Howard S. Becker (1958:658) provides another excellent illustration of this iterative process of conceptualization in his study of medical students:

> When we first heard medical students apply the term "crock" to patients, we made an effort to learn precisely what they meant by it. We found, through interviewing students about cases both they and the observer had seen, that the term referred in a derogatory way to patients with many subjective symptoms but no discernible physical pathology. Subsequent observations indicated that this usage was a regular feature of student behavior and thus that we should attempt to incorporate this fact into our model of student-patient behavior. The derogatory character of the term suggested in particular that we investigate the reasons students disliked these patients. We found that this dislike was related to what we discovered to be the students' perspective on medical school: the view that they were in school to get experience in recognizing and treating those common diseases most likely to be encountered in general practice. "Crocks," presumably having no disease, could furnish no such experience. We were thus led to specify connections between the student-patient relationship and the student's view of the purpose of his professional education. Questions concerning the genesis of this perspective led to discoveries about the organization of the student body and communication among students, phenomena which we had been assigning to another [segment of the larger theoretical model being developed]. Since "crocks" were also disliked because they gave the student no opportunity to assume medical responsibility, we were able to connect this aspect of the student-patient relationship with still another tentative model of the value system and hierarchical organization of the school, in which medical responsibility plays an important role. (Becker, 1958:658)

This excerpt shows how the researcher first was alerted to a concept by observations in the field, then refined his understanding of this concept by investigating its meaning. By observing the concept's frequency of use, he came to realize its importance. Then he incorporated the concept into an explanatory model of student–patient relationships.

A well-designed chart, or **matrix,** can facilitate the coding and categorization process. Exhibit 13.4 shows an example of a coding form designed by Miles and Huberman (1994:93–95) to represent the extent to which teachers and teachers' aides ("users") and administrators at a school gave evidence of various supporting conditions that indicated preparedness for a new reading program. The matrix condenses data into simple categories, reflects further analysis of the data to identify "degree" of support, and provides a multidimensional summary that will facilitate subsequent, more intensive analysis. Direct quotes still impart some of the flavor of the original text.

Examining Relationships and Displaying Data

Examining relationships is the centerpiece of the analytic process, because it allows the researcher to move from simple description of the people and settings to explanations of

Exhibit 13.4   Example of Checklist Matrix

Presence of Supporting Conditions

Condition	For Users	For Administrators
Commitment	*Strong*—"wanted to make it work."	*Weak* at building level. Prime movers in central office committed; others not.
Understanding	"*Basic*" ("felt I could do it, but I just wasn't sure how.") for teacher. *Absent* for aide ("didn't understand how we were going to get all this.")	*Absent* at building level and among staff. *Basic* for 2 prime movers ("got all the help we needed from developer.") *Absent* for other central office staff.
Materials	*Inadequate*: ordered late, puzzling ("different from anything I ever used"), discarded.	N.A.
Front-end training	"*Sketchy*" for teacher ("it all happened so quickly"); no demo class. *None* for aide: ("totally unprepared. I had to learn along with the children.")	Prime movers in central office had training at developer site; none for others.
Skills	*Weak-adequate* for teacher. "*None*" for aide.	One prime mover (Robeson) skilled in substance; others unskilled.
Ongoing inservice	*None*, except for monthly committee meeting; no substitute funds.	*None*
Planning, coordination time	*None*: both users on other tasks during day; lab tightly scheduled, no free time.	*None*
Provisions for debugging	*None* systematized; spontaneous work done by users during summer.	*None*
School admin. support	*Adequate*	N.A.
Central admin. support	*Very Strong* on part of prime movers.	Building admin. only acting on basis of central office commitment.
Relevant prior experience	*Strong* and useful in both cases: had done individualized instruction, worked with low achievers. But aide no diagnostic experience.	*Present* and useful in central office, esp. Robeson (specialist).

Source: Miles & Huberman, 1994:95, Table 5.2. Used with permission.

why things happened as they did with those people in that setting. The process of examining relationships can be captured in a matrix that shows how different concepts are connected, or perhaps what causes are linked with what effects.

Exhibit 13.5 Coding Form for Relationships: Stakeholders' Stakes

How high are the stakes for various primary stakeholders?	*Estimate of Various Stakeholders' Inclination Toward the Program*		
	Favorable	Neutral or Unknown	Antagonistic
High			
Moderate			
Low			

Source: Patton, 2002:472.

Note: Construct illustrative case studies for each cell based on fieldwork.

Exhibit 13.5 displays a matrix used to capture the relationship between the extent to which stakeholders in a new program had something important at stake in the program and the researcher's estimate of their favorability toward the program. Each cell of the matrix was to be filled in with a summary of an illustrative case study. In other matrix analyses, quotes might be included in the cells to represent the opinions of these different stakeholders, or the number of cases of each type might appear in the cells. The possibilities are almost endless. Keeping this approach in mind will generate many fruitful ideas for structuring a qualitative data analysis.

The simple relationships that are identified with a matrix like that shown in Exhibit 13.5 can be examined and then extended to create a more complex causal model. Such a model represents the multiple relationships among the constructs identified in a qualitative analysis as important for explaining some outcome. A great deal of analysis must precede the construction of such a model, with careful attention to identification of important variables and the evidence that suggests connections between them. Exhibit 13.6 provides an example of these connections from a study of the implementation of a school program.

Authenticating Conclusions

No set standards exist for evaluating the validity or "authenticity" of conclusions in a qualitative study, but the need to consider carefully the evidence and methods on which conclusions are based is just as great as with other types of research. Individual items of information can be assessed in terms of at least three criteria (Becker, 1958):

- *How credible was the informant?* Were statements made by someone with whom the researcher had a relationship of trust, or by someone the researcher had just met? Did the informant have reason to lie? If the statements do not seem to be trustworthy as indicators of actual events, can they at least be used to help understand the informant's perspective?
- *Were statements made in response to the researcher's questions, or were they spontaneous?* Spontaneous statements are more likely to indicate what would have been said had the researcher not been present.

Exhibit 13.6 Example of a Causal Network Model

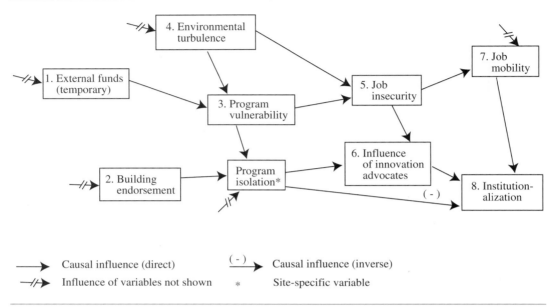

Source: Miles & Huberman, 1994:159, Figure 6.5.

- *How does the presence or absence of the researcher or the researcher's informant influence the actions and statements of other group members?* Reactivity to being observed can never be ruled out as a possible explanation for some directly observed social phenomenon. However, if the researcher carefully compares what the informant says goes on when the researcher is not present, what the researcher observes directly, and what other group members say about their normal practices, the extent of reactivity can be assessed to some extent.

A qualitative researcher's conclusions should also be assessed by their ability to provide a credible explanation for some aspect of social life. That explanation should capture group members' **tacit knowledge** of the social processes that were observed, not just their verbal statements about these processes. Tacit knowledge—"the largely unarticulated, contextual understanding that is often manifested in nods, silences, humor, and naughty nuances"—is reflected in participants' actions as well as their words and in what they fail to state but nonetheless feel deeply and even take for granted (Altheide & Johnson, 1994:492–493). These features are evident in Whyte's analysis of Cornerville social patterns:

> The corner-gang structure arises out of the habitual association of the members over a long period of time. The nuclei of most gangs can be traced back to early boyhood. . . . Home plays a very small role in the group activities of the corner boy. . . .
> . . . The life of the corner boy proceeds along regular and narrowly circumscribed channels.
> . . . Out of [social interaction within the group] arises a system of mutual obligations which

is fundamental to group cohesion. . . . The code of the corner boy requires him to help his friends when he can and to refrain from doing anything to harm them. When life in the group runs smoothly, the obligations binding members to one another are not explicitly recognized. (Whyte, 1955:255–257)

Comparing conclusions from a qualitative research project to those obtained by other researchers conducting similar projects can also increase confidence in their authenticity. Miller's (1999) study of neighborhood police officers (NPOs) found striking parallels in the ways they defined their masculinity to processes reported in research about males in nursing and other traditionally female jobs (Bachman & Schutt, 2001:315):

In part, male NPOs construct an exaggerated masculinity so that they are not seen as feminine as they carry out the social-work functions of policing. Related to this is the almost defiant expression of heterosexuality, so that the men's sexual orientation can never truly be doubted even if their gender roles are contested. Male patrol officers' language—such as their use of terms like "pansy police" to connote neighborhood police officers—served to affirm their own heterosexuality. . . . In addition, the male officers, but not the women, deliberately wove their heterosexual status into conversations, explicitly mentioning their female domestic partner or spouse and their children. This finding is consistent with research conducted in the occupational field. The studies reveal that men in female-dominated occupations, such as teachers, librarians, and pediatricians, over-reference their heterosexual status to ensure that others will not think they are gay. (Miller, 1999:222)

Reflexivity

Confidence in the conclusions from a field research study is also strengthened by an honest and informative account about how the researcher interacted with subjects in the field, what problems he or she encountered, and how these problems were or were not resolved. Such a "natural history" of the development of the evidence enables others to evaluate the findings. Such an account is important first and foremost because of the evolving and variable nature of field research: To an important extent, the researcher "makes up" the method in the context of a particular investigation rather than applying standard procedures that are specified before the investigation begins.

Barrie Thorne provides a good example of this final element of the analysis:

Many of my observations concern the workings of gender categories in social life. For example, I trace the evocation of gender in the organization of everyday interactions, and the shift from boys and girls as loose aggregations to "the boys" and "the girls" as self-aware, gender-based groups. In writing about these processes, I discovered that different angles of vision lurk within seemingly simple choices of language. How, for example, should one describe a group of children? A phrase like "six girls and three boys were chasing by the tires" already assumes the relevance of gender. An alternative description of the same event—"nine fourth-graders were chasing by the tires"—emphasizes age and downplays gender. Although I found no tidy solutions, I have tried to be thoughtful about such choices. . . . After several months of observing at Oceanside, I realized that my fieldnotes were peppered with the words "child" and "children," but that the children themselves rarely used the term. "What do they call themselves?" I badgered in an entry in my fieldnotes. The answer it turned out, is that children use the same practices as adults. They refer to one another by using given names ("Sally," "Jack") or language specific to a given context ("that guy on first base"). They rarely have occasion to use age-generic terms. But when pressed to locate themselves in an age-based way, my informants used "kids" rather than "children." (Thorne, 1993:8–9)

Qualitative data analysts, more often than quantitative researchers, display real sensitivity to how a social situation or process is interpreted from a particular background and set of values and not simply based on the situation itself (Altheide & Johnson, 1994). Researchers are only human, after all, and must rely on their own senses and process all information through their own minds. By reporting how and why they think they did what they did, they can help others determine whether, or how, the researchers' perspectives influenced their conclusions. "There should be clear 'tracks' indicating the attempt [to show the hand of the ethnographer] has been made" (Altheide & Johnson, 1994:493).

Elijah Anderson's (2003) memoir about the Jelly's Bar research illustrates the type of "tracks" that an ethnographer makes as well as how he can describe those tracks. He acknowledges that his tracks began as a child (Anderson, 2003:1–2):

While growing up in the segregated black community of South Bend, from an early age, I was curious about the goings on in the neighborhood, but particularly streets, and more particularly, the corner taverns that my uncles and my dad would go to hang out and drink in. . . . Hence, my selection of Jelly's as a field setting was a matter of my background, intuition, reason, and with a little bit of luck.

After starting to observe at Jelly's, Anderson's (2003:4) "tracks" led to Herman:

After spending a couple of weeks at Jelly's, I met Herman and I felt that our meeting marked a big achievement. We would come to know each other well. . . . something of an informal leader at Jelly's. . . . We were becoming friends. . . . he seemed to genuinely like me, and he was one person I could feel comfortable with.

So we learn that Elijah Anderson's observations were to be shaped in part by Herman's perspective, but we also find out that Anderson maintained some engagement with fellow students. This contact outside the bar helped to shape his analysis: "By relating my experiences to my fellow students, I began to develop a coherent perspective or a 'story' of the place which complemented the accounts that I had detailed in my accumulating field notes" (Anderson, 2003:6).

In this way, the outcome of Anderson's analysis of qualitative data resulted in part from the way in which he "played his role" as a researcher and participant, not just from the setting itself.

ALTERNATIVES IN QUALITATIVE DATA ANALYSIS

The qualitative data analyst can choose from many interesting alternative approaches. Of course, the research question under investigation should shape the selection of an analytic approach, but the researcher's preferences and experiences inevitably also will have an important influence on the method chosen. The four alternative approaches I present here (traditional ethnography, qualitative comparative analysis, narrative analysis, and grounded theory) give you a good sense of the different possibilities—but be forewarned that I selected these four from a long and growing list (Patton, 2002).

Traditional Ethnography

Ethnography is the study of a culture or cultures that some group of people share (Van Maanen, 1995:4). As a method, it usually is meant to refer to the process of participant observation by a single investigator who immerses himself or herself in the group for a long period of time (often one or more years). As you learned in Chapter 9, anthropological field research has traditionally been ethnographic, and much sociological field work shares these same characteristics. But there are no particular methodological techniques associated with ethnography, other than just "being there." The analytic process relies on the thoroughness and insight of the researcher to "tell us like it is" in the setting, as he or she experienced it.

Code of the Street, Elijah Anderson's (1999:10–11) award-winning study of Philadelphia's inner city, captures the flavor of this approach:

> My primary aim in this work is to render ethnographically the social and cultural dynamics of the interpersonal violence that is currently undermining the quality of life of too many urban neighborhoods. . . . How do the people of the setting perceive their situation? What assumptions do they bring to their decision making?

The methods of investigation are described in the book's preface: participant observation, including direct observation and in-depth interviews, impressionistic materials drawn from various social settings around the city, and interviews with a wide variety of people. Like most traditional ethnographers, Anderson (1999:11) describes his concern with being "as objective as possible" and using his training as other ethnographers do, "to look for and to recognize underlying assumptions, their own and those of their subjects, and to try to override the former and uncover the latter."

From analysis of the data obtained in these ways, a rich description emerges of life in the inner city. Although we often do not "hear" the residents speak, we feel the community's pain in Anderson's (1999:138) description of "the aftermath of death":

> When a young life is cut down, almost everyone goes into mourning. The first thing that happens is that a crowd gathers about the site of the shooting or the incident. The police then arrive, drawing more of a crowd. Since such a death often occurs close to the victim's house, his mother or his close relatives and friends may be on the scene of the killing. When they arrive, the women and girls often wail and moan, crying out their grief for all to hear, while the young men simply look on, in studied silence. . . . Soon the ambulance arrives.

Elijah Anderson uses these descriptions as a foundation on which he develops the key concepts in his analysis, such as "code of the street":

The "code of the street" is not the goal or product of any individual's actions but is the fabric of everyday life, a vivid and pressing milieu within which all local residents must shape their personal routines, income strategies, and orientations to schooling, as well as their mating, parenting, and neighbor relations. (Anderson, 1999:326)

Anderson's report on his Jelly's Bar study illustrates how an ethnographic analysis deepened as he became more socially integrated into the Jelly's Bar group. He thus became more successful at "blending the local knowledge one has learned with what we already know sociologically about such settings" (Anderson, 2003:39):

I engaged the denizens of the corner and wrote detailed field notes about my experiences, and from time to time looked for patterns and relationships in my notes. In this way, an understanding of the setting came to me in time, especially as I participated more fully in the life of the corner and wrote my field notes about my experiences; as my notes accumulated, and as I reviewed them occasionally and supplemented them with conceptual memos to myself, their meanings became more clear, while even more questions emerged. (Anderson, 2003:15)

This rich ethnographic tradition is being abandoned by some qualitative data analysts, however. Many have become skeptical of the ability of social scientists to perceive the social world in a way that is not distorted by their own subjective biases or to receive impressions from the actors in that social world that are not altered by the fact of being studied (Van Maanen, 2002). As a result, both specific techniques and alternative approaches to qualitative data analysis have proliferated. The next sections introduce several of these alternative approaches.

Qualitative Comparative Analysis

Recall from earlier in the chapter how Daniel Cress and David Snow (2000) asked a series of very specific questions about social movement outcomes in their study of homeless social movement organizations (SMOs). They collected qualitative data about 15 SMOs in 8 cities. A content analysis of newspaper articles indicated that these cities represented a range of outcomes, and the SMOs within them were also relatively accessible to Cress and Snow due to prior contacts. In each of these cities, Cress and Snow used a snowball sampling strategy to identify the homeless SMOs and the various supporters, antagonists, and significant organizational bystanders with whom they interacted. They then gathered information from representatives of these organizations, including churches, other activist organizations, police departments, mayors' offices, service providers, federal agencies, and of course the SMOs themselves.

In order to answer their research questions, Cress and Snow needed to operationalize each of the various conditions that they believed might affect movement outcomes, using coding procedures that were much more systematic than those often employed in qualitative research. For example, Cress and Snow (2000:1078) defined "sympathetic allies" operationally as

the presence of one or more city council members who were supportive of local homeless mobilization. This was demonstrated by attending homeless SMO meetings and rallies and by taking initiatives to city agencies on behalf of the SMO. (Seven of the 15 SMOs had such allies.)

Cress and Snow also chose a structured method of analysis, **qualitative comparative analysis (QCA)**, to assess how the various conditions influenced SMO outcomes. This procedure identifies the combination of factors that had to be present across multiple cases to produce a particular outcome (Ragin, 1987). Cress and Snow (2000:1079) explain why QCA was appropriate for their analysis:

> QCA . . . is conjunctural in its logic, examining the various ways in which specified factors interact and combine with one another to yield particular outcomes. This increases the prospect of discerning diversity and identifying different pathways that lead to an outcome of interest and thus makes this mode of analysis especially applicable to situations with complex patterns of interaction among the specified conditions.

Exhibit 13.7 summarizes the results of much of Cress and Snow's (2000:1097) analysis. It shows that homeless SMOs that were coded as organizationally viable, used disruptive tactics, had sympathetic political allies, and presented a coherent diagnosis and program in response to the problem they were protesting were very likely to achieve all four valued outcomes: representation, resources, protection of basic rights, and some form of tangible relief. Some other combinations of the conditions were associated with increased likelihood of achieving some valued outcomes, but most of these alternatives less frequently had positive effects.

Exhibit 13.7 Multiple Pathways to Outcomes and Level of Impact

Pathways	Outcomes	Impact
1. VIABLE * DISRUPT * ALLIES * DIAG * PROG ……….............	Representation, Resources, Rights, and Relief	Very strong
2. VIABLE * disrupt * CITY * DIAG * PROG …………..............	Representation and Rights	Strong
3. VIABLE * ALLIES * CITY * DIAG * PROG …………..............	Resources and Relief	Moderate
4. viable * DISRUPT * allies * diag * PROG ………...............	Relief	Weak
5. viable * allies * city * diag * PROG …………....................	Relief	Weak
6. viable * disrupt * ALLIES * CITY * diag * prog ……..............	Resources	Weak

Source: Cress & Snow, 2000:1097, Table 6. Reprinted with permission from the University of Chicago Press.

Note:—Uppercase letters indicate presence of condition and lowercase letters indicate the absence of a condition. Conditions not in the equation are considered irrelevant. Multiplication signs (∗) are read as "and."

The qualitative textual data on which the codes were based indicate how particular combinations of conditions exerted their influence. For example, one set of conditions that increased the likelihood of achieving increased protection of basic rights for homeless persons included avoiding disruptive tactics in cities that were more responsive to the SMOs. Cress and Snow (2000:1089) use a quote from a local SMO leader to explain this process:

> We were going to set up a picket, but then we got calls from two people who were the co-chairs of the Board of Directors. They have like 200 restaurants. And they said, "Hey, we're not bad guys, can we sit down and talk?" We had been set on picketing . . . Then we got to thinking, wouldn't it be better . . . if they co-drafted those things [rights guidelines] with us? so that's what we asked them to do. We had a work meeting, and we hammered out the guidelines.

Narrative Analysis

Narrative "displays the goals and intentions of human actors; it makes individuals, cultures, societies, and historical epochs comprehensible as wholes" (Richardson, 1995:200). **Narrative analysis** focuses on "the story itself" and seeks to preserve the integrity of personal biographies or a series of events that cannot adequately be understood in terms of their discrete elements (Riessman, 2002:218). The coding for a narrative analysis is typically of the narratives as a whole, rather than of the different elements within them. The coding strategy revolves around reading the stories and classifying them into general patterns.

For example, Calvin Morrill and his colleagues (2000:534) read through 254 conflict narratives written by the ninth graders they studied and found four different types of stories:

1. *Action tales,* in which the author represents him- or herself and others as acting within the parameters of taken-for-granted assumptions about what is expected for particular roles among peers.

2. *Expressive tales,* in which the author focuses on strong, negative emotional responses to someone who has wronged him or her.

3. *Moral tales,* in which the author recounts explicit norms that shaped his or her behavior in the story and influenced the behavior of others.

4. *Rational tales,* in which the author represents him- or herself as a rational decision maker navigating through the events of the story.

In addition to these dominant distinctions, Morrill et al. (2000:534–535) also distinguished the stories in terms of four stylistic dimensions: plot structure (such as whether the story unfolds sequentially), dramatic tension (how the central conflict is represented), dramatic resolution (how the central conflict is resolved), and predominant outcomes (how the story ends). Coding reliability was checked through a discussion by the two primary coders, who found that their classifications agreed for a large percentage of the stories.

The excerpt that begins this chapter exemplifies what Morrill et al. (2000:536) termed an "action tale." Such tales unfold in matter-of-fact tones kindled by dramatic tensions that begin with a disruption of the quotidian order of everyday routines. A shove, a bump, a look . . . triggers a response. . . . Authors of action tales typically organize their plots as linear streams of events as they move briskly through the story's scenes. . . . this story's dramatic tension finally resolves through physical fighting, but . . . only after an attempted conciliation.

You can contrast that "action tale" with the following narrative, which Morrill et al. (2000:545–546) classify as a "moral tale," in which the student authors "explicitly tell about their moral reasoning, often referring to how normative commitments shape their decisionmaking":

I . . . got into a fight because I wasn't allowed into the basketball game. I was being harassed by the captains that wouldn't pick me and also many of the players. The same type of things had happened almost every day where they called me bad words so I decided to teach the ring leader a lesson. I've never been in a fight before but I realized that sometimes you have to make a stand against the people that constantly hurt you, especially emotionally. I hit him in the face a couple of times and I got respect I finally deserved.

Morrill et al. (2000:553) summarize their classification of the youth narratives in a simple table that highlights the frequency of each type of narrative and the characteristics associated with each of them (Exhibit 13.8). How does such an analysis contribute to our understanding of youth violence? Morrill et al. (2000:551) first emphasize that their narratives "suggest that consciousness of conflict among youths—like that among adults—is not a singular entity, but comprises a rich and diverse range of perspectives."

Exhibit 13.8   Summary Comparison of Youth Narratives*

Representation of	*Action Tales (N = 144)*	*Moral Tales (N = 51)*	*Expressive Tales (N = 35)*	*Rational Tales (N = 24)*
Bases of everyday conflict	disruption of everyday routines & expectations	normative violation	emotional provocation	goal obstruction
Decisionmaking	intuitive	principled stand	sensual	calculative choice
Conflict handling	confrontational	ritualistic	cathartic	deliberative
Physical violence†	in 44% (N = 67)	in 27% (N = 16)	in 49% (N = 20)	in 29% (N = 7)
Adults in youth conflict control	invisible or background	sources of rules	agents of repression	institutions of social control

Source: Morrill et al., 2000:551, Table 1. Copyright 2000. Reprinted with permission of Blackwell Publishing, Ltd.

* Total *N* = 254.

† Percentages based on the number of stories in each category.

Theorizing inductively, Morrill et al. (2000:553–554) then attempt to explain why action tales were much more common than the more adult-oriented normative, rational, or emotionally expressive tales. One possibility is Gilligan's theory of moral development, which suggests that younger students are likely to limit themselves to the simpler action tales that "concentrate on taken-for-granted assumptions of their peer and wider cultures, rather than on more self-consciously reflective interpretation and evaluation." More generally, Morrill et al. (2000:556) argue, "we can begin to think of the building blocks of cultures as different narrative styles in which various aspects of reality are accentuated, constituted, or challenged, just as others are deemphasized or silenced."

In this way, Morrill et al.'s narrative analysis allowed an understanding of youth conflict to emerge from the youths' own stories while also informing our understanding of broader social theories and processes.

Grounded Theory

Theory development occurs continually in qualitative data analysis (Coffey & Atkinson, 1996:23). The goal of many qualitative researchers is to create **grounded theory**—that is, to build up inductively a systematic theory that is "grounded" in, or based on, the observations. The observations are summarized into conceptual categories, which are tested directly in the research setting with more observations. Over time, as the conceptual categories are refined and linked, a theory evolves (Glaser & Strauss, 1967; Huberman & Miles, 1994:436). Exhibit 13.9 diagrams this process. Notice that it corresponds to the inductive portion of the research circle, which was introduced in Chapter 2 (see Exhibit 2.6, p. 45).

As observation, interviewing, and reflection continue, researchers refine their definitions of problems and concepts and select indicators. They can then check the frequency and

Exhibit 13.9   The Development of Grounded Theory

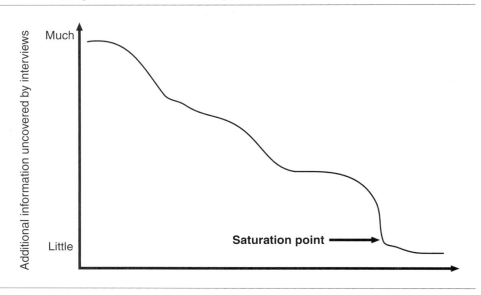

distribution of phenomena: How many people made a particular type of comment? How often did social interaction lead to arguments? Social system models may then be developed, which specify the relationships among different phenomena. These models are modified as researchers gain experience in the setting. For the final analysis, the researchers check their models carefully against their notes and make a concerted attempt to discover negative evidence that might suggest the model is incorrect.

COMPUTER-ASSISTED QUALITATIVE DATA ANALYSIS

The analysis process can be enhanced in various ways by using a computer. Programs designed for qualitative data can speed up the analysis process, make it easier for researchers to experiment with different codes, test different hypotheses about relationships, and facilitate diagrams of emerging theories and preparation of research reports (Coffey & Atkinson, 1996; Richards & Richards, 1994). The steps involved in **computer-assisted qualitative data analysis** parallel those used traditionally to analyze such text as notes, documents, or interview transcripts: preparation, coding, analysis, and reporting. We use two of the most popular programs to illustrate these steps: HyperRESEARCH and QSR NVivo. (See Appendix G for an extended introduction to HyperRESEARCH. Check out the software itself and the HyperRESEARCH tutorials on the CD-ROM that accompanies this text.)

Text preparation begins with typing or scanning text in a word processor or, with NVivo, directly into the program's rich text editor. NVivo will create or import a rich text file. HyperRESEARCH requires that your text be saved as a text file (as "ASCII" in most word processors) before you transfer it into the analysis program. HyperRESEARCH expects your text data to be stored in separate files corresponding to each unique case, such as an interview with one subject.

Coding the text involves categorizing particular text segments. This is the foundation of much qualitative analysis. Either program allows you to assign a code to any segment of text (in NVivo, you drag through the characters to select them; in HyperRESEARCH, you click on the first and last words to select text). You can both make up codes as you go through a document and assign codes that you have already developed to text segments. Exhibit 13.10 shows the screens that appear in the two programs at the coding stage, when a particular text segment is being labeled. You can also have the programs "autocode" text by identifying a word or phrase that should always receive the same code, or, in NVivo, by coding each section identified by the style of the rich text document—for example, each question or speaker (of course, you should check carefully the results of autocoding). Both programs also let you examine the coded text "in context"—embedded in its place in the original document.

In qualitative data analysis, coding is not a one-time-only or one-code-only procedure. Both HyperRESEARCH and NVivo allow you to be inductive and holistic in your coding: You can revise codes as you go along, assign multiple codes to text segments, and link your own comments ("memos") to text segments. In NVivo you can work "live" with the coded text to alter coding or create new, more subtle categories. You can also place hyperlinks to other documents in the project or any multimedia files outside it.

Analysis focuses on reviewing cases or text segments with similar codes and examining relationships among different codes. You may decide to combine codes into larger concepts.

Exhibit 13.10a   HyperRESEARCH Coding Stage

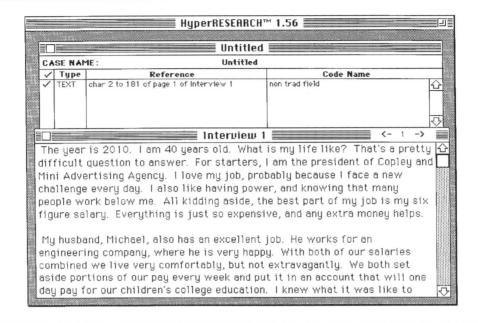

Exhibit 13.10b   NVivo Coding Stage

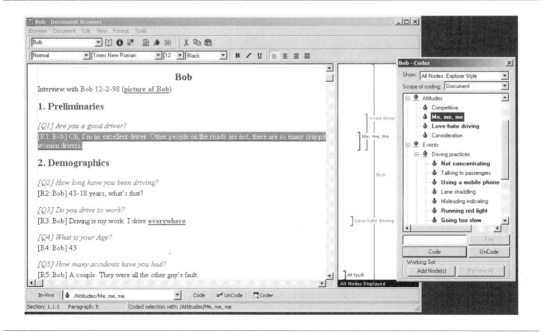

Exhibit 13.11 A Free-Form Model in NVivo

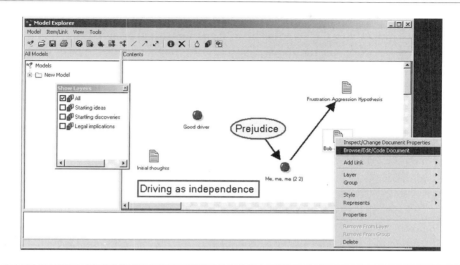

You may specify additional codes to capture more fully the variation among cases. You can test hypotheses about relationships among codes. NVivo allows development of an indexing system to facilitate thinking about the relationships among concepts and the overarching structure of these relationships. It will also allow you to draw more free-form models (see Exhibit 13.11). In HyperRESEARCH, you can specify combinations of codes that identify cases that you want to examine.

Reports from both programs can include text to illustrate the cases, codes, and relationships that you specify. You can also generate counts of code frequencies and then import these counts into a statistical program for quantitative analysis. However, the many types of analyses and reports that can be developed with qualitative analysis software do not lessen the need for a careful evaluation of the quality of the data on which conclusions are based.

In reality, using a qualitative data analysis computer program is not always as straightforward as it appears (Bachman & Schutt, 2001:314). Scott Decker and Barrik Van Winkle (1996:53–54) describe the difficulty they faced in using a computer program to identify instances of the concept of "drug sales":

The software we used is essentially a text retrieval package. . . . One of the dilemmas faced in the use of such software is whether to employ a coding scheme within the interviews or simply to leave them as unmarked text. We chose the first alternative, embedding conceptual tags at the appropriate points in the text. An example illustrates this process. One of the activities we were concerned with was drug sales. Our first chore (after a thorough reading of all the transcripts) was to use the software to "isolate" all of the transcript sections dealing with drug sales. One way to do this would be to search the transcripts for every instance in which the word "drugs" was used. However, such a strategy would have the disadvantages of providing information of too general a character while often missing important statements about drugs. Searching on the word "drugs" would have produced a file including every time the word was used, whether it was in reference to drug sales, drug use, or drug availability, clearly more information than we were interested. However, such a search would have failed to find all of the slang used to refer to drugs ("boy" for heroin, "Casper" for crack cocaine) as well as the more common descriptions of drugs, especially rock or crack cocaine.

Decker and Van Winkle solved this problem by parenthetically inserting conceptual tags in the text whenever talk of drug sales was found. This process allowed them to examine all of the statements made by gang members about a single concept (drug sales). As you can imagine, however, this still left the researchers with many pages of transcript material to analyze.

CONTENT ANALYSIS

Content analysis is "the systematic, objective, quantitative analysis of message characteristics" (Neuendorf, 2002:1) that facilitates making inferences from text (Weber, 1985:9). You can think of a content analysis as a "survey" of some documents or other records of prior communication. In fact, a content analysis is a survey designed with fixed-choice responses so that it produces quantitative data that can be analyzed statistically. This method was first applied to the study of newspaper content and then to the analysis of Nazi propaganda broadcasts in World War II, but it can also be used to study historical documents, records of speeches, and other "voices from the past."

As a form of textual analysis, content analysis is like qualitative data analysis. Like the methods we have just been studying, it involves coding and categorizing text and identifying relationships among constructs identified in the text. However, as a quantitative procedure, content analysis overlaps with qualitative data analysis only at the margins—the points where qualitative analysis takes on quantitative features or where content analysis focuses on qualitative features of the text.

Kimberly Neuendorf's (2002:3) analysis of medical prime-time network television programming highlights both aspects of content analysis: As Exhibit 13.12 shows, medical programming has been dominated by noncomedy shows, but there have been two significant periods of comedy medical shows—during the 1970s and early 1980s and then again in the early 1990s. But it took a qualitative analysis of medical show content to reveal that the 1960s shows represented a very distinct "physician-as-God" era, which shifted to a more human view of the medical profession in the 1970s and 1980s. This era has been followed in turn by a mixed period that has had no dominant theme.

The units that are "surveyed" in a content analysis can range from newspapers, books, or TV shows to persons referred to in other communications, themes expressed in documents, or propositions made in different statements. Words or other features of these units are then coded in order to measure the variables involved in the research question. The content analysis proceeds through several stages (Weber, 1985):

Identify a population of documents or other textual sources for study. This population should be selected so that it is appropriate to the research question of interest. Perhaps the population will be all newspapers published in the United States, college student newspapers,

Exhibit 13.12 Medical Primetime Network Television Programming, 1951 to 1998

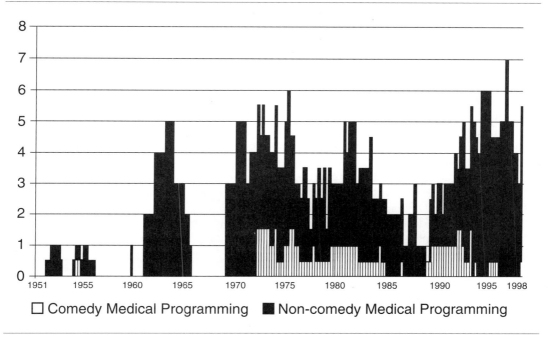

□ Comedy Medical Programming   ■ Non-comedy Medical Programming

Source: Neuendorf, 2002:3, Figure 1.1. Copyright 2002. Reprinted with permission from Sage Publications, Inc.

nomination speeches at political party conventions, or "state of the nation" speeches by national leaders.

Determine the units of analysis. These could be items such as newspaper articles, whole newspapers, speeches, or political conventions.

Select a sample of units from the population. The simplest strategy might be a simple random sample of documents. However, a stratified sample might be needed to ensure adequate representation of community newspapers in large and small cities, or of weekday and Sunday papers, or of political speeches during election years and in off years (see Chapter 4).

Design coding procedures for the variables to be measured. This requires deciding what unit of text to code, such as words, sentences, themes, or paragraphs. Then the categories into which the text units are to be coded must be defined. These categories may be broad, such as "supports democracy," or narrow, such as "supports universal suffrage."

Test and refine the coding procedures. Clear instructions and careful training of coders are essential.

Base statistical analyses on counting occurrences of particular words, themes, or phrases, and test relations between different variables. These analyses would use some of the statistics introduced in Chapter 12, including frequency distributions, measures of central tendency and variation, cross-tabulations, and correlation analysis.

Developing reliable and valid coding procedures is not an easy task. The meaning of words and phrases is often ambiguous. Homographs create special problems (words such as *mine* that have different meanings in different contexts), as do many phrases that have special meanings (such as "point of no return") (Weber, 1985:30). As a result, coding procedures cannot simply categorize and count words; text segments in which the words are embedded must also be inspected before codes are finalized. Because different coders may perceive different meanings in the same text segments, explicit coding rules are required to ensure coding consistency. Special dictionaries can be developed to keep track of how the categories of interest are defined in the study (Weber, 1984:24–34).

After coding procedures are developed, their reliability should be assessed by comparing different coders' codes for the same variables. Computer programs for content analysis can be used to enhance reliability (Weber, 1984). Whatever the rules are that the computer is programmed to use to code text, these rules will be applied consistently. Validity can be assessed with a construct validation approach by determining the extent to which theoretically predicted relationships occur (see Chapter 4).

These various steps are represented in the flowchart in Exhibit 13.13 (pp. 444-445). Note that each of these steps is comparable to the procedures in quantitative survey research; they overlap with qualitative data analysis techniques primarily at the point of developing coding schemes. Use this flowchart as a checklist when you design or critique a content analysis project.

Exhibit 13.14 (pp. 446-447) is a segment of the coding form I developed for a content analysis of union literature that I collected during a study of union political processes (Schutt, 1986). My sample was of 362 documents: all union newspapers and a stratified sample of union leaflets given to members during the years of my investigation. My coding scheme included measures of the source and target for the communication, as well as of concepts that my theoretical framework indicated were important in organizational development: types of goals, tactics for achieving goals, organizational structure, and forms of participation. The analysis documented a decline in concern with client issues and an increase in focus on organizational structure, which were both trends that also emerged in interviews with union members.

ETHICS IN QUALITATIVE DATA ANALYSIS

The qualitative data analyst is never far from ethical issues and dilemmas. Throughout the analytic process, the analyst must consider how the findings will be used and how participants in the setting will react. Miles and Huberman (1994:204–205) suggest several specific questions that should be kept in mind:

> *Research integrity and quality.* Is my study being conducted carefully, thoughtfully, and correctly in terms of some reasonable set of standards? Real analyses have real consequences, so you owe it to yourself and those you study to adhere strictly to the analysis methods that you believe will produce authentic, valid conclusions.

Ownership of data and conclusions. Who owns my field notes and analyses: I, my organization, my funders? And once my reports are written, who controls their diffusion? Of course these concerns arise in any social research project, but the intimate involvement of the qualitative researcher with participants in the setting studied makes conflicts of interest between different stakeholders much more difficult to resolve. Working through the issues as they arise is essential.

Use and misuse of results. Do I have an obligation to help my findings be used appropriately? What if they are used harmfully or wrongly? It is prudent to develop understandings early in the project with all major stakeholders that specify what actions will be taken in order to encourage appropriate use of project results and to respond to what is considered misuse of these results.

CONCLUSIONS

The variety of approaches to qualitative data analysis makes it difficult to provide a consistent set of criteria for interpreting their quality. Norman Denzin's (2002:362–363) "interpretive criteria" are a good place to start. Denzin suggests that at the conclusion of their analyses, qualitative data analysts ask the following questions about the materials they have produced. Reviewing several of them will serve as a fitting summary for your understanding of the qualitative analysis process.

- *Do they illuminate the phenomenon as lived experience?* In other words, do the materials bring the setting alive in terms of the people in that setting?
- *Are they based on thickly contextualized materials?* We should expect thick descriptions that encompass the social setting studied.
- *Are they historically and relationally grounded?* There must be a sense of the passage of time between events and the presence of relationships between social actors.
- *Are they processual and interactional?* The researcher must have described the research process and his or her interactions within the setting.
- *Do they engulf what is known about the phenomenon?* This includes situating the analysis in the context of prior research and also acknowledging the researcher's own orientation upon first starting the investigation.

When an analysis of qualitative data is judged as successful in terms of these criteria, we can conclude that the goal of "authenticity" has been achieved.

In contrast, the criteria for judging quantitative content analyses of text are the same standards of validity applied to data collected with other quantitative methods. We must review the sampling approach, the reliability and validity of the measures, and the controls used to strengthen any causal conclusions. But you have seen in this chapter that there is no sharp demarcation between what is considered a qualitative or a quantitative analysis. As a research methodologist, you must be ready to use both types of techniques, evaluate research findings in terms of both sets of criteria, and mix and match the methods as required by the research problem to be investigated and the setting in which it is to be studied.

Exhibit 13.13 Flowchart for the Typical Process of Content Analysis Research

1. *Theory and rationale*: *What* content will be examined, and *why*? Are there certain *theories* or perspectives that indicate that this particular message content is important to study? Library work is needed here to conduct a good literature review. Will you be using an integrative model, linking content analysis with other data to show relationships with source or receiver characteristics? Do you have *research questions*? *Hypotheses?*

2. *Conceptualizations:* What *variables* will be used in the study, and how do you define them *conceptually* (i.e., with dictionary-type definitions)? Remember, you are the boss! There are many ways to define a given construct, and there is no one right way. You may want to screen some examples of the content you're going to analyze, to make sure you've covered everything you want.

3. *Operationalizations (measures):* Your measures should match your conceptualizations . . . What *unit of data collection* will you use? You may have more than one unit (e.g., a by-utterance coding scheme and a by-speaker coding scheme). Are the variables measured well (i.e., at a high *level of measurement,* with categories that are *exhaustive and mutually exclusive)?* An *a priori* coding scheme describing all measures must be created. Both face validity and content validity may also be assessed at this point.

Human Coding   Computer Coding

4a. *Coding schemes:* You need to create the following materials:

   a. *Codebook* (with all variable measures *fully* explained)

   b. *Coding form*

4b. *Coding schemes:* With computer text content analysis, you still need a code book of sorts—a full explanation of your *dictionaries* and method of applying them. You may use standard dictionaries (e.g., those in Hart's program, *Diction*) or originally created dictionaries. When creating custom dictionaries, be sure to first generate a frequencies list from your text sample and examine for key words and phrases.

Human Coding   Computer Coding

Exhibit 13.13 Continued

5. *Sampling:* Is a census of the content possible? (If yes, go to #6.) How will you *randomly sample* a subset of the content? This could be by time period, by issue, by page, by channel, and so forth.

6. *Training and pilot reliability:* During a training session in which coders work together, find out whether they can agree on the coding of variables. Then, in an independent coding test, note the *reliability* on each variable. At each stage, *revise* the codebook or coding form as needed.

7a. *Coding:* Use at least two coders, to establish intercoder reliability. Coding should be done independently, with at least 10% overlap for the reliability test.

7b. *Coding:* Apply dictionaries to the sample text to generate per-unit (e.g., per-news-story) frequencies for each dictionary. Do some spot checking for validation.

Human Coding

Computer Coding

8. *Final reliability:* Calculate a reliability figure (percent agreement, Scott's *pi*, Spearman's *rho*, or Pearson's *r*, for example) for each variable.

9. *Tabulation and reporting:* See various examples of content analysis results to see the ways in which results can be reported. Figures and statistics may be reported one variable at a time (univariate), or variables may be cross-tabulated in different ways (bivariate and multivariate techniques). Over-time trends are also a common reporting method. In the long run, relationships between content analysis variables and other measures may establish criterion and construct validity.

Source: Neuendorf, 2002:50–51. Copyright 2002. Reprinted with permission from Sage Publications, Inc.

Exhibit 13.14 Union Literature Coding Form*

I. *Preliminary Codes*

    1. Document # _____

    2. Date _____
              mo   yr

    3. Length of text _____ pp. (round up to next 1/4 page; count legal size as 1.25)

    4. Literature Type
        1. General leaflet for members/employees
        2. Newspaper/Newsletter article
        3. Rep Council motions
        4. Other material for Reps, Stewards, Delegates (e.g., budget, agenda)
        5. Activity reports of officers, President's Report
        6. Technical information-filing grievances, processing forms
        7. Buying plans/Travel packages
        8. Survey Forms, Limited Circulation material (correspondence)
        9. Non-Union
        10. Other _____ (specify)

    4A. If newspaper article   4B. If Rep Council motion
         Position   Sponsor
          1. Headline story   1. Union leadership
          2. Other front page   2. Office
          3. Editorial   3. Leadership faction
          4. Other   4. Opposition faction
                                       5. Other

    5. Literature content-Special issues
        1. First strike (1966)
        2. Second strike (1967)
        3. Collective bargaining (1977)
        4. Collective bargaining (1979)
        5. Election/campaign literature
        6. Affiliation with AFSCME/SEIU/other national union
        7. Other

II. *Source and Target*

    6. Primary source (code in terms of those who prepared this literature for distribution).
        1. Union-newspaper (Common Sense; IUPAE News)
        2. Union-newsletter (Info and IUPAE Bulletin)
        3. Union-unsigned
        4. Union officers
        5. Union committee
        6. Union faction (the Caucus; Rank-and-Filers; Contract Action, other election slate; PLP News; Black Facts)
        7. Union members in a specific work location/office
        8. Union members-other
        9. Dept. of Public Aid/Personnel
        10. DVR/DORS

*Coding instruction available from author.

Exhibit 13.14 Union Literature Coding Form* (Continued)

11. Credit Union
12. Am. Buyers' Assoc.
13. Other non-union

7. Secondary source (use for lit. at least in part reprinted from another source, for distribution to members)
   1. Newspaper-general circulation
   2. Literature of other unions, organizations
   3. Correspondence of union leaders
   4. Correspondence from DPA/DVR-DORS/Personnel
   5. Correspondence from national union
   6. Press release
   7. Credit Union, Am. Buyers'
   8. Other—————————————-(specify)
   9. None

8. Primary target (the audience for which the literature is distributed)
   1. Employees-general (if mass-produced and unless otherwise stated)
   2. Employees-DVR/DORS
   3. Union members (if refers only to members or if about union elections)
   4. Union stewards, reps, delegates committee
   5. Non-unionized employees (recruitment lit, etc.)
   6. Other—————————————(specify)
   7. Unclear

III. *Issues*

   A. Goal

   B. Employee conditions/benefits (Circle up to 5)
      1. Criteria for hiring
      2. Promotion
      3. Work out of Classification, Upgrading
      4. Step increases
      5. Cost-of-living, pay raise, overtime pay, "money"
      6. Layoffs (non-disciplinary); position cuts
      7. Workloads, Redeterminations, "30 for 40", GA Review
      8. Office physical conditions, safety
      9. Performance evaluations
      10. Length of workday
      11. Sick Benefits/Leave—holidays, insurance, illness, vacation, voting time
      12. Educational leave
      13. Grievances—change in procedures
      14. Discrimination (race, sex, age, religion, national origin)
      15. Discipline-political (union-related)
      16. Discipline—performance, other
      17. Procedures with clients, at work
      18. Quality of work, "worthwhile jobs"—other than relations with clients

Source: Schutt, 1986:208-209. Copyright 1986, State University of New York; reprinted with permission from the State University of New York Press. All rights reserved.

KEY TERMS

Case study
Computer-assisted qualitative data analysis
Content analysis
Emic focus
Ethnography
Etic focus
Grounded theory

Matrix
Narrative analysis
Progressive focusing
Qualitative comparative analysis (QCA)
Tacit knowledge
Thick description

HIGHLIGHTS

• Qualitative data analysts are guided by an emic focus of representing persons in the setting on their own terms, rather than by an etic focus on the researcher's terms.

• Case studies use thick description and other qualitative techniques to provide a wholistic picture of a setting or group.

• Ethnographers attempt to understand the culture of a group.

• Narrative analysis attempts to understand a life or a series of events as they unfolded, in a meaningful progression.

• Grounded theory connotes a general explanation that develops in interaction with the data and is continually tested and refined as data collection continues.

• Special computer software can be used for the analysis of qualitative, textual, and pictorial data. Users can record their notes, categorize observations, specify links between categories, and count occurrences.

• Content analysis is a tool for systematic quantitative analysis of documents and other textual data. It requires careful testing and control of coding procedures to achieve reliable measures.

DISCUSSION QUESTIONS

1. List the primary components of qualitative data analysis strategies. Compare and contrast each of these components with those relevant to quantitative data analysis. What are the similarities and differences? What difference do these make?

2. Does qualitative data analysis result in trustworthy results? Why would anyone question its use? What would you reply to the doubters?

3. Which analytic alternative do you prefer? Why?

4. Read the complete text of one of the qualitative studies presented in this chapter and evaluate its conclusions for authenticity, using the criteria in this chapter.

PRACTICE EXERCISES

1. Attend a sports game as an ethnographer. Write up your analysis and circulate it for criticism.

2. Write a narrative in class about your first date, car, college course, or something else that you and your classmates agree on. Then collect all the narratives and analyze them in a "committee of the whole." Follow the general procedures discussed in the example of narrative analysis in this chapter.

3. Select a current social or political topic that has been the focus of news articles. Propose a content analysis strategy for this topic, using newspaper articles or editorials as your units of analysis. Your strategy should include a definition of the population, selection of the units of analysis, a sampling plan, and coding procedures for key variables. Now find an article on this topic and use it to develop your coding procedures. Test and refine your coding procedures with another article on the same topic.

WEB EXERCISES

1. The Qualitative Report is an online journal about qualitative research. Inspect the table of contents for a recent issue at http://www.nova.edu/ssss/QR/index.html. Read one of the articles and write a brief article review.

2. Be a qualitative explorer! Go to the list of qualitative research Web sites and see what you can find that enriches your understanding of qualitative research (http://www.ualberta.ca/~jrnorris/qual.html). Be careful to avoid textual data overload.

HYPERRESEARCH EXERCISES

1. Eight essays written by college-aged women in Hesse-Biber's (1989) "Cinderella Study" are saved on the CD-ROM. The essays touch on how young women feel about combining work and family roles. Using HYPERRESEARCH, the qualitative software program on the CD-ROM, open the Cinderella Study. Look over the preliminary code categories that have already been applied to each essay. Do you agree with the code categories/themes already selected? Do they capture the meaning for each of these cases (essays)? What new code categories would you add and why? Which would you delete? Why? What are some of the common themes/codes you see that cut across all 8 cases concerning how young women think about what their life will be like 20 years from now?

2. Work through the tutorials on the CD-ROM. How does it seem that qualitative analysis software facilitates the analysis process? Does it seem to you that it might hinder the analysis process in some ways? Explain your answers.

DEVELOPING A RESEARCH PROPOSAL

1. Which qualitative data analysis alternative is most appropriate for the qualitative data you proposed to collect for your project? Using this approach, develop a strategy for using the techniques of QDA to analyze your textual data.

2. Now identify a potential source of textual data that would be appropriate for a content analysis related to your research question. Develop a complete content analysis plan by answering each of the questions posed in Exhibit 13.13 on pages 444-445.

Chapter 14

REPORTING RESEARCH

Social Research Proposals, Part II
Case Study: Treating Substance Abuse

Comparing Research Designs
Performing Meta-Analyses
  Case Study: Broken Homes and
    Delinquency

Writing Research

Reporting Research
Journal Articles
Applied Research Reports

Ethics, Politics, and Research
  Reports

Conclusions

You learned in Chapter 2 that research is a circular process, so it is appropriate that we end this book where we began. The stage of reporting research results is also the point at which the need for new research is identified. It is the time when, so to speak, "the rubber hits the road"—when we have to make our research make sense to others. To whom will our research be addressed? How should we present our results to them? Will we seek to influence how our research report is used?

The primary goals of this chapter are to guide you in developing research proposals, comparing completed research studies, and writing worthwhile reports of your own. I will introduce one new research technique—meta-analysis, which is a quantitative method for statistically evaluating the results of a large body of prior research on a specific topic. This chapter also gives particular attention to the writing process itself and points out how that process can differ when writing up qualitative rather than quantitative research. We will conclude by considering some of the ethical issues unique to the reporting process.

SOCIAL RESEARCH PROPOSALS, PART II

It is time to return to the basic outline of a research proposal that I introduced in Chapter 2 and fill in more of the details.

Most research proposals will have at least six sections (Locke, Spirduso, & Silverman, 2000):

- *An introductory statement of the research problem,* in which you clarify what it is that you are interested in studying.
- *A literature review,* in which you explain how your problem and plans build on what has already been reported in the literature on this topic.
- *A methodological plan,* detailing just how you will respond to the particular mix of opportunities and constraints you face.
- *A budget,* presenting a careful listing of the anticipated costs.
- *An ethics statement,* identifying human subjects issues in the research and how you will respond to them in an ethical fashion.
- *A statement of limitations,* reviewing weaknesses of the proposed research and presenting plans for minimizing their consequences.

When you develop a research proposal, it will help to ask yourself a series of questions like those in Exhibit 14.1 (also see Herek, 1995). It is too easy to omit important details and to avoid being self-critical while rushing to put a proposal together. However, it is even more painful to have a proposal rejected (or to receive a low grade). Better to make sure the proposal covers what it should and confronts the tough issues that reviewers (or your professor) will be sure to spot.

The series of questions in Exhibit 14.1 can serve as a map to the preceding chapters in this book and as a checklist of decisions that must be made throughout any research project. The questions are organized in five sections, each concluding with a *checkpoint* at which you should consider whether to proceed with the research as planned, modify the plans, or stop the project altogether. The sequential ordering of these questions obscures a bit the way in which they should be answered: not as single questions, one at a time, but as a unit—first as five separate stages, and then as a whole. Feel free to change your answers to earlier questions on the basis of your answers to later questions.

We will learn how to apply the decision checklist with an example from a proposal focused on treatment for substance abuse.

Case Study: Treating Substance Abuse

Particular academic departments, grant committees, and funding agencies will have more specific proposal requirements. As an example, Exhibit 14.2 lists the primary required sections of the "Research Plan" for proposals to the National Institutes of Health (NIH), together with excerpts from a proposal I submitted in this format to the National Institute of Mental Health (NIMH) with colleagues from the University of Massachusetts Medical School. The Research Plan is limited by NIH guidelines to 25 pages. It must be preceded by an abstract (which I have excerpted), a proposed budget, biographical sketches of project personnel, and a discussion of the available resources for the project. Appendixes may include research instruments, prior publications by the authors, and findings from related work.

As you can see from the excerpts, our proposal (Schutt et al., 1992) was to study the efficacy of a particular treatment approach for homeless mentally ill persons who abuse

Exhibit 14.1 Decisions in Research

PROBLEM FORMULATION (Chapters 1–3)

1. Developing a research question
2. Assessing researchability of the problem
3. Consulting prior research
4. Relating to social theory
5. Choosing an approach:
   Deductive? Inductive? Descriptive?
6. Reviewing research guidelines

> CHECKPOINT 1
> Alternatives: • Continue as planned.
> • Modify the plan.
> • STOP. Abandon the plan.

RESEARCH VALIDITY (Chapters 4–6)

7. Establishing measurement validity:
   • How are concepts defined?
   • Choose a measurement strategy.
   • Assess available measures or develop new measures.
   • What evidence of reliability and validity is available or can be collected?
8. Establishing generalizability:
   • Was a representative sample used?
   • Are the findings applicable to particular subgroups?
   • Does the population sampled correspond to the population of interest?
9. Establishing causality:
   • What is the possibility of experimental or statistical controls?
   • How to assess the causal mechanism?
   • Consider the causal context.
10. Data required: Longitudinal or cross-sectional?
11. Units of analysis: Individuals or groups?
12. What are major possible sources of causal invalidity?

> CHECKPOINT 2
> Alternatives: • Continue as planned.
> • Modify the plan.
> • STOP. Abandon the plan.

RESEARCH DESIGN (Chapters 7–11)

13. Choosing a research design and procedures:
    Experimental? Survey? Participant observation?
    Historical, comparative? Multiple methods?
14. Specifying the research plan: Type of surveys, observations, etc.
15. Secondary analysis? Availability of suitable data sets?

(Continued)

Exhibit 14.1 Continued

16 Causal approach: Idiographic or nomothetic?
17. Assessing ethical concerns

> CHECKPOINT 3
> Alternatives: • Continue as planned.
>   • Modify the plan.
>   • STOP. Abandon the plan.

DATA ANALYSIS (Chapters 12–13)

18. Choosing a statistical approach:
    • Statistics and graphs for describing data
    • Identifying relationships between variables
    • Deciding about statistical controls
    • Testing for interaction effects
    • Evaluating inferences from sample data to the population

> CHECKPOINT 4
> Alternatives: • Continue as planned.
>   • Modify the plan.
>   • STOP. Abandon the plan.

REVIEWING, PROPOSING, REPORTING RESEARCH (Chapters 2,14)

19. Clarifying research goals
20. Identifying the intended audience
21. Searching the literature and the Web
22. Organizing the text
23. Reviewing ethical and practical constraints

> CHECKPOINT 5
> Alternatives: • Continue as planned.
>   • Modify the plan.
>   • STOP. Abandon the plan.

substances. The proposal included a procedure for recruiting subjects in two cities, randomly assigning half of the subjects to a recently developed treatment program, and measuring a range of outcomes. The NIMH review committee (composed of social scientists expert in these issues) approved the project for funding but did not rate it highly enough so that it actually was awarded funds (it often takes several resubmissions before even a worthwhile proposal is funded). The committee members recognized the proposal's strengths, but also identified several problems that they believed had to be overcome before the proposal could be funded. The problems were primarily methodological, stemming from the difficulties associated with providing services to, and conducting research on, this particular segment of the homeless population.

Exhibit 14.2 A Grant Proposal to the National Institute of Mental Health

Relapse Prevention for Homeless Dually Diagnosed

Abstract

This project will test the efficacy of shelter-based treatment that integrates Psychosocial Rehabilitation with Relapse Prevention techniques adapted for homeless mentally ill persons who abuse substances. Two hundred and fifty homeless persons, meeting . . . criteria for substance abuse and severe and persistent mental disorder, will be recruited from two shelters and then randomly assigned to either an experimental treatment condition . . . or to a control condition.

For one year, at the rate of three two-hour sessions per week, the treatment group ($n = 125$) will participate for the first six months in "enhanced" Psychosocial Rehabilitation . . . , followed by six months of Relapse Prevention training. . . . The control group will participate in a Standard Treatment condition (currently comprised of a twelve-step peer-help program along with counseling offered at all shelters). . . .

Outcome measures include substance abuse, housing placement and residential stability, social support, service utilization, level of distress. . . . The integrity of the experimental design will be monitored through a process analysis. Tests for the hypothesized treatment effects . . . will be supplemented with analyses to evaluate the direct and indirect effects of subject characteristics and to identify interactions between subject characteristics and treatment condition. . . .

Research Plan

1. Specific Aims

The research demonstration project will determine whether an integrated clinical shelter-based treatment intervention can improve health and well-being among homeless persons who abuse alcohol and/or drugs and who are seriously and persistently ill—the so-called "dually diagnosed." . . . We aim to identify the specific attitudes and behaviors that are most affected by the integrated psychosocial rehabilitation/relapse prevention treatment, and thus to help guide future service interventions.

2. Background and Significance

Relapse is the most common outcome in treating the chronically mentally ill, including the homeless. . . . Reviews of the clinical and empirical literature published to date indicate that treatment interventions based on social learning experiences are associated with more favorable outcomes than treatment interventions based on more traditional forms of psychotherapy and/or chemotherapy. . . . However, few tests of the efficacy of such interventions have been reported for homeless samples.

3. Progress Report/Preliminary Studies

Four areas of Dr. Schutt's research help to lay the foundation for the research demonstration project here proposed. . . . The 1990 survey in Boston shelters measured substance abuse with selected ASI [Addiction Severity Index] questions. . . . About half of the respondents evidenced a substance abuse problem.

Just over one-quarter of respondents had ever been treated for a mental health problem. . . . At least three-quarters were interested in help with each of the problems mentioned other than substance abuse. Since help with benefits, housing, and AIDS prevention will each be provided to all study participants in the proposed research demonstration project, we project that this should increase the rate of participation and retention in the study. . . . Results [from co-investigator Dr. Walter Penk's research] . . . indicate that trainers were more successful in engaging the dually diagnosed in Relapse Prevention techniques. . . .

4. Research Design and Methods

Study Sample.
Recruitment. The study will recruit 350 clients beginning in month 4 of the study and running through month 28 for study entry. The span of treatment is 12 months and is followed by 12 months of follow-up. . . .

Study Criteria.
Those volunteering to participate will be screened and declared eligible for the study based upon the following characteristics:
1. Determination that subject is homeless using criteria operationally defined by one of the accepted definitions summarized by . . .

Attrition.
Subject enrollment, treatment engagement, and subject retention each represent potentially significant challenges to study integrity and have been given special attention in all phases of the project. Techniques have been developed to address engagement and retention and are described in detail below. . . .

Research Procedures.
All clients referred to the participating shelters will be screened for basic study criteria. . . . Once assessment is completed, subjects who volunteer are then randomly assigned to one of two treatment conditions–RPST or Standard Treatment. . . .

Research Variables and Measures.
Measures for this study . . . are of three kinds: subject selection measures, process measures, and outcome measures. . . .

5. Human Subjects

Potential risks to subjects are minor. . . . Acute problems identified . . . can be quickly referred to appropriate interventions. Participation in the project is voluntary, and all subjects retain the option to withdraw . . . at any time, without any impact on their access to shelter care or services regularly offered by the shelters. Confidentiality of subjects is guaranteed. . . . [They have] . . . an opportunity to learn new ways of dealing with symptoms of substance abuse and mental illness.

Source: Schutt, Penk, et al., 1992.

The proposal has many strengths, including the specially tailored intervention derived from psychiatric rehabilitation technology developed by Liberman and his associates and relapse prevention methods adapted from Marlatt. [T]his fully documented treatment . . . greatly facilitates the generalizability and transportability of study findings. . . . The investigative team is excellent . . . also attuned to the difficulties entailed in studying this target group. . . . While these strengths recommend the proposal . . . eligibility criteria for inclusion of subjects in the study are somewhat ambiguous. . . . This volunteer procedure could substantially underrepresent important components of the shelter population. . . . The projected time frame for recruiting subjects . . . also seems unrealistic for a three-year effort. . . . Several factors in the research design seem to mitigate against maximum participation and retention.

If you get the impression that researchers cannot afford to leave any stone unturned in working through procedures in an NIMH proposal, you are right. It is very difficult to convince a government agency that a research project is worth spending a lot of money on (we requested about $2 million). And that is as it should be: Your tax dollars should be used only for research that has a high likelihood of yielding findings that are valid and useful. But even when you are proposing a smaller project to a more generous funding source—or just presenting a proposal to your professor—you should scrutinize the proposal carefully before submission and ask others to comment on it. Other people will often think of issues you neglected to consider, and you should allow yourself time to think about these issues and to reread and redraft the proposal. Besides, you will get no credit for having thrown together a proposal as best you could in the face of an impossible submission deadline.

Let's review the issues identified in Exhibit 14.1 as they relate to the NIMH relapse prevention proposal submitted by me, Dr. Walter E. Penk, and our collaborators. The research question concerned the effectiveness of a particular type of substance abuse treatment in a shelter for homeless persons—an evaluation research question [Question 1]. This problem certainly was suitable for social research, and it was one that could have been handled for the money we requested [Question 2]. Prior research demonstrated clearly that our proposed treatment had potential and also that it had not previously been tried with homeless persons [3]. The treatment approach was connected to psychosocial rehabilitation theory [4] and, given prior work in this area, a deductive, hypothesis-testing stance was called for [5]. Our review of research guidelines continued up to the point of submission and we felt that our proposal took each into account [6]. So it seemed reasonable to continue to develop the proposal (Checkpoint 1).

Measures were to include direct questions, observations by field researchers, and laboratory tests (of substance abuse) [7]. The proposal's primary weakness was in the area of generalizability [8]. We proposed to sample persons in only two homeless shelters in two cities, and we could offer only weak incentives to encourage potential participants to start and stay in the study. The review committee believed that these procedures might result in an unrepresentative group of initial volunteers beginning the treatment and perhaps an even less representative group continuing through the entire program. The problem was well suited to a randomized, experimental design [9] and was best addressed with longitudinal data [10], involving individuals [11]. Our randomized design controlled for selection bias and endogenous change, but external events, treatment contamination, and treatment misidentification were potential sources of causal invalidity [12]. Clearly we should have modified the proposal with some additional recruitment and retention strategies—although it may be that the research could not actually be carried out without some major modification of the research question (Checkpoint 2).

A randomized experimental design was preferable because this was to be a treatment-outcome study, but we did include a field research component so that we could evaluate treatment implementation [13, 14]. Because the effectiveness of our proposed treatment strategy had not been studied before among homeless persons, we could not propose doing a secondary data analysis or meta-analysis [15]. We sought only to investigate causation from a nomothetic perspective, without attempting to show how the particular experiences of each participant may have led to their outcome [16]. Because participation in the study was to be voluntary and everyone received *something* for participation, the research design seemed ethical (and it was approved by the University of Massachusetts Medical School's Institutional Review Board and by the state mental health agency's human subjects committee) [17]. We planned several statistical tests, but here the review committee remarked that we should have been more specific [18]. Our goal was to use our research as the basis for several academic articles, and we expected that the funding agency would also require us to prepare a report for general distribution [19, 20]. We had reviewed the research literature carefully [21], but as is typical in most research proposals, we did not develop our research reporting plans any further [22, 23].

COMPARING RESEARCH DESIGNS

The central features of experiments, surveys, qualitative methods, and comparative historical methods provide distinct perspectives even when used to study the same social processes. Comparing subjects randomly assigned to a treatment and to a comparison group, asking standard questions of the members of a random sample, observing while participating in a natural social setting, recording published statistics on national characteristics, and reading historical documents involve markedly different decisions about measurement, causality, and generalizability. As you can see in Exhibit 14.3, not one of these methods can reasonably be graded as superior to the others in all respects, and each varies in its suitability to different research questions and goals. Choosing among them for a particular investigation requires consideration of the research problem, opportunities and resources, prior research, philosophical commitments, and research goals.

Experimental designs are strongest for testing nomothetic causal hypotheses and are most appropriate for studies of treatment effects (see Chapter 6). Research questions that are believed to involve basic social psychological processes are most appealing for laboratory studies, because the problem of generalizability is reduced. Random assignment reduces the possibility of preexisting differences between treatment and comparison groups to small,

Exhibit 14.3   Comparison of Research Methods

Design	Measurement Validity	Generalizability	Type of Causal Assertions	Causal Validity
Experiments	+	−	Nomothetic	+
Surveys	+	+	Nomothetic	−/+[a]
Qualitative Methods	−/+[b]	−	Idiographic	−
Comparative [c]	−	−/+	Idiographic or Nomothetic	−

[a] Surveys are a weaker design for identifying causal effects than true experiments, but use of statistical controls can strengthen causal arguments.

[b] Reliability is low compared to surveys, and systematic evaluation of measurement validity is often not possible. However, direct observations may lead to great confidence in the validity of measures.

[c] All conclusions about this type of design vary with the specific approach used. See Chapter 11.

specifiable, chance levels, so many of the variables that might create a spurious association are controlled. But in spite of this clear advantage, an experimental design requires a degree of control that cannot always be achieved outside of the laboratory (see Chapter 7). It can be difficult to ensure in real-world settings that a treatment was delivered as intended and that other influences did not intrude. As a result, what appears to be a treatment effect or noneffect may be something else altogether. Field experiments thus require careful monitoring of the treatment process. Unfortunately, most field experiments also require more access arrangements and financial resources than can often be obtained.

Laboratory experiments permit much more control over conditions, but at the cost of less generalizable findings. People must volunteer for most laboratory experiments, and so there is a good possibility that experimental subjects differ from those who do not volunteer. Ethical and practical constraints limit the types of treatments that can be studied experimentally (you can't assign social class or race experimentally). The problem of generalizability in an experiment using volunteers lessens when the object of investigation is an orientation, behavior, or social process that is relatively invariant among people, but it is difficult to know which orientations, behaviors, or processes are so invariant. If a search of the research literature on the topic identifies many prior experimental studies, the results of these experiments will suggest the extent of variability in experimental effects and point to the unanswered questions about these effects.

Both surveys and experiments typically use standardized, quantitative measures of attitudes, behaviors, or social processes. Closed-ended questions are most common and are well suited for the reliable measurement of variables that have been studied in the past and whose meanings are well understood (see Chapter 4). Of course, surveys often include measures of many more variables than are included in an experiment (Chapter 8), but this feature is not inherent in either design. Phone surveys may be quite short, whereas some experiments can involve very lengthy sets of measures (see Chapter 7). The set of interview questions we used at baseline in the Boston housing study (Chapter 10), for example, required more than 10 hours to complete. The level of funding for a survey will often determine which type of survey is conducted and thus how long the questionnaire is.

Most social science surveys rely on random sampling for their selection of cases from some larger population, and it is this feature that makes them preferable for descriptive research that seeks to develop generalizable findings (see Chapter 5). However, survey questionnaires can only measure what respondents are willing to report verbally; they may not be adequate for studying behaviors or attitudes that are regarded as socially unacceptable. Surveys are also often used to test hypothesized causal relationships. When variables that might create spurious relationships are included in the survey, they can be controlled statistically in the analysis and thus eliminated as rival causal influences.

Qualitative methods presume an intensive measurement approach in which indicators of concepts are drawn from direct observation or in-depth commentary (see Chapter 9). This approach is most appropriate when it is not clear what meaning people attach to a concept or what sense they might make of particular questions about it. Qualitative methods are also admirably suited to the exploration of new or poorly understood social settings, when it is not even clear what concepts would help to understand the situation. They may also be used instead of survey methods when the population of interest is not easily identifiable or seeks to remain hidden. For these reasons, qualitative methods tend to be preferred when exploratory research questions are posed or when new groups are investigated. But, of course, intensive measurement necessarily makes the study of large numbers of cases or situations difficult, resulting in the limitation of many field research efforts to small numbers of people or unique social settings. The individual field researcher may not require many financial resources, but the amount of time required for many field research projects serves as a barrier to many would-be field researchers.

When qualitative methods can be used to study several individuals or settings that provide marked contrasts in terms of a presumed independent variable, it becomes possible to evaluate nomothetic causal hypotheses with these methods. However, the impossibility of taking into account many possible extraneous influences in such limited comparisons makes qualitative methods a weak approach to hypothesis testing. Qualitative methods are more suited to the elucidation of causal mechanisms. In addition, qualitative methods can be used to identify the multiple successive events that might have led to some outcome, thus identifying idiographic causal processes.

Historical and comparative methods range from cross-national quantitative surveys to qualitative comparisons of social features and political events (see Chapter 11). Their suitability for exploration, description, explanation, and evaluation varies in relation to the particular method used, but they are essential for research on historical processes and national differences. If the same methods are used to study multiple eras or nations rather than just one nation at one time, the results are likely to be enhanced generalizability and causal validity.

Performing Meta-Analyses

A **meta-analysis** is a quantitative method for identifying patterns in findings across multiple studies of the same research question (Cooper & Hedges, 1994). Unlike a traditional literature review, which describes previous research studies verbally, meta-analyses treat previous studies as cases whose features are measured as variables and are then analyzed statistically. It is like conducting a survey in which the "respondents" are previous studies. Meta-analysis shows how evidence about social processes varies across research studies. If the methods used in these studies varied, then meta-analysis can describe how this variation affected study findings. If social contexts varied across the studies, then meta-analysis will indicate how social context affected study findings.

Meta-analysis can be used when a number of studies have attempted to answer the same research question with similar quantitative methods, most often experiments. It is not appropriate for evaluating results from qualitative studies, nor from multiple studies that used different methods or measured different dependent variables. It is also not very sensible to use meta-analysis to combine study results when the original case data from these studies are available and can actually be combined and analyzed together (Lipsey & Wilson, 2001). Meta-analysis is a technique for combination and statistical analysis of published research reports.

After a research problem is formulated about the findings of such research, then the literature must be searched systematically to identify the entire population of relevant studies. Typically, multiple bibliographic databases are used; some researchers also search for relevant dissertations and conference papers. Once the studies are identified, their findings, methods, and other features are coded (for example, sample size, location of sample, strength of the association between the independent and dependent variables). Eligibility criteria must be specified carefully in order to determine which studies to include and which to omit as too different. Mark Lipsey and David Wilson (2001:16–21) suggest that eligibility criteria include:

- *Distinguishing features.* This includes the specific intervention tested and perhaps the groups compared.
- *Research respondents.* These specify the population to which generalization is sought.
- *Key variables.* These must be sufficient to allow tests of the hypotheses of concern and controls for likely additional influences.
- *Research methods.* Apples and oranges cannot be directly compared, but some tradeoff must be made between including the range of studies about a research question and excluding those that are so different in their methods as not to yield comparable data.
- *Cultural and linguistic range.* If the study population is going to be limited to English language publications, or limited in some other way, this must be acknowledged and the size of the population of relevant studies in other languages should be estimated.
- *Time frame.* Social processes relevant to the research question may have changed for such reasons as historical events or new technologies, so temporal boundaries around the study population must be considered.
- *Publication type.* Will the analysis focus only on published reports in professional journals, or will it include dissertations and/or unpublished reports?

Statistics are then calculated to identify the average effect of the independent variable on the dependent variable, as well as the effect of methodological and other features of the studies (Cooper & Hedges, 1994). The **effect size** statistic is the key to capturing the association between the independent and dependent variables across multiple studies. The effect size statistic is a standardized measure of association—often the difference between the mean of the experimental group and the mean of the control group on the dependent variable, adjusted for the average variability in the two groups (Lipsey & Wilson, 2001).

The meta-analytic approach to synthesizing research results can result in much more generalizable findings than those obtained with just one study. Methodological weaknesses in the studies included in the meta-analysis are still a problem, however; it is only when other studies without particular methodological weaknesses are included that we can estimate effects with some confidence. In addition, before we can place any confidence in the results of a meta-analysis, we must be confident that all (or almost all) relevant studies were included and that the information we need to analyze was included in all (or most) of the studies (Matt & Cook, 1994).

Case Study: Broken Homes and Delinquency

Many studies have tested the hypothesis that juveniles from broken homes have higher rates of delinquency than those from homes with intact families, but findings have been inconclusive. L. Edward Wells and Joseph Rankin (1991) were able to find 50 studies that tested this hypothesis, with estimates of the increase in delinquency among juveniles from broken homes ranging from 1% to 50%. In order to explain this variation, Wells and Rankin coded key characteristics of the research studies, such as the population sampled—the general population? a specific age range?—and the measures used: Did researchers take account of stepparents? Did they measure juveniles' relations with the absent parent? Was

Exhibit 14.4   Delinquency by Broken Homes

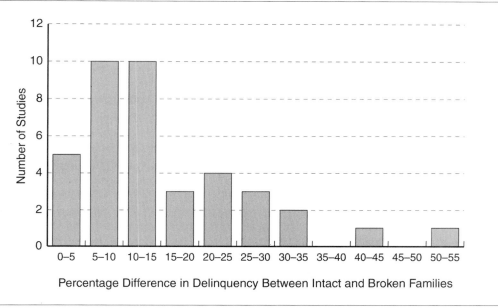

Source: Adapted from Wells & Rankin, 1991:80.

delinquency measured with official records or by self-report? What types of delinquency were measured?

The average effect of broken homes across the studies was to increase the likelihood of delinquency by about 10% to 15% (see Exhibit 14.4). Effects varied with the studies' substantive features and their methods, however. Juveniles from broken homes were more likely to be involved in status offenses (such as truancy and running away) and drug offenses but were no more likely to commit crimes involving theft or violence than were juveniles from intact homes. Juveniles' race, sex, and age and whether a stepparent was present did not have consistent effects. On the other hand, differences in methods accounted for much of the variation among the studies in the estimated effect of broken homes. The effect of broken homes on delinquency tended to be greater in studies using official records rather than surveys and in studies of smaller special populations rather than of the general population. In general, the differences in estimates of the association between broken homes and delinquency were due primarily to differences in study methods and only secondarily to differences in the social characteristics of the people studied.

Meta-analyses like the Wells and Rankin study make us aware of how hazardous it is to base understanding of social processes on single studies that are limited in time, location, and measurement. Although one study may not support the hypothesis that we deduced from what seemed to be a compelling theory, this is not a sufficient basis for discarding the theory itself, nor even for assuming that the hypothesis is no longer worthy of consideration in future research. You can see that a meta-analysis combining the results of many studies may identify conditions for which the hypothesis is supported and others for which it is not.

Of course we need to have our wits about us when we read reports of meta-analytic studies. It is not a good idea to assume that a meta-analysis is the definitive word on a research question just because it cumulates the results of multiple studies. Fink (1998:215–237) suggests evaluating meta-analytic studies in terms of the following seven criteria:

- *Clear statement of the analytic objectives.* The study's methods cannot be evaluated without knowledge of the objectives they were intended to achieve. Meta-analyses are most appropriate for summarizing research conducted to identify the effect of some type of treatment or some other readily identifiable individual characteristic.
- *Explicit inclusion and exclusion criteria.* On what basis were research reports included in the analysis? Were high-quality studies distinguished from low-quality studies? If low-quality studies were included, were they analyzed separately, so that effects could be identified separately for only the population of high-quality studies?
- *Satisfactory search strategies.* Both electronic and written reference sources should be searched. Was some method used to find studies that were conducted but not published? It may be necessary to write directly to researchers in the field and to consult lists of papers presented at conferences.
- *A standardized protocol for screening the literature.* Screening involves rating the quality of the study and its relevance to the research question. This screening should be carried out with a simple rating form.
- *A standardized protocol for collecting data.* It is best to have two reviewers use a standard form for coding the characteristics of the reported research. The level of agreement between these reviewers should be assessed.
- *Complete explanation of the method of combining results.* Some checks should be conducted to determine where variable study features influenced the size of the treatment effect.
- *Report of results, conclusions, and limitations.* This seems obvious, but it's easy for a researcher to skirt over study limitations or some aspects of the findings.

WRITING RESEARCH

The goal of research is not just to discover something, but to communicate that discovery to a larger audience: other social scientists, government officials, your teachers, the general public—perhaps several of these audiences. Whatever the study's particular outcome, if the intended audience for the research comprehends the results and learns from them, the research can be judged a success. If the intended audience does not learn about the study's results, the research should be judged a failure—no matter how expensive the research, how sophisticated its design, or how much you (or others) invested in it.

Successful research reporting requires both good writing and a proper publication outlet. We will first review guidelines for successful writing before we look at particular types of research publications.

Consider the following principles formulated by experienced writers (Booth, Colomb, & Williams, 1995:150–151):

- Respect the complexity of the task and don't expect to write a polished draft in a linear fashion. Your thinking will develop as you write, causing you to reorganize and rewrite.
- Leave enough time for dead ends, restarts, revisions, and so on, and accept the fact that you will discard much of what you write.
- Write as fast as you comfortably can. Don't worry about spelling, grammar, and so on until you are polishing things up.
- Ask anyone whom you trust for their reactions to what you have written.
- Write as you go along, so you have notes and report segments drafted even before you focus on writing the report.

It is important to outline a report before writing it, but neither the report's organization nor the first written draft should be considered fixed. As you write, you will get new ideas about how to organize the report. Try them out. As you review the first draft, you will see many ways to improve your writing. Focus particularly on how to shorten and clarify your statements. Make sure each paragraph concerns only one topic. Remember the golden rule of good writing: Writing is revising!

You can ease the burden of report writing in several ways:

- Draw on the research proposal and on project notes.
- Use a word processing program on a computer to facilitate reorganizing and editing.
- Seek criticism from friends, teachers, and other research consumers before turning in the final product.

I often find it helpful to use what I call **reverse outlining:** After you have written a first complete draft, outline it on a paragraph-by-paragraph basis, ignoring the actual section headings you used. See if the paper you wrote actually fits the outline you planned. How could the organization be improved?

Most important, leave yourself enough time so that you *can* revise, several times if possible, before turning in the final draft. Here are one student's reflections on writing and revising:

I found the process of writing and revising my paper longer than I expected. I think it was something I was doing for the first time—working within a committee—that made the process not easy. The overall experience was very good, since I found that I have learned so much. My personal computer also did help greatly.

Revision is essential until complete clarity is achieved. This took most of my time. Because I was so close to the subject matter, it became essential for me to ask for assistance in achieving clarity. My committee members, English editor, and fellow students were extremely helpful. Putting it on disk was also, without question, a timesaver. Time was the major problem.

The process was long, hard and time-consuming, but it was a great learning experience. I work full time so I learned how to budget my time. I still use my time productively and am very careful of not wasting it. (Graduate Program in Applied Sociology, 1990)

For more suggestions about writing, see Becker (1986), Booth et al. (1995), Cuba (2002), Strunk and White (2000), and Turabian (1996).

REPORTING RESEARCH

You began writing your research report when you worked on the research proposal, and you will find that the final report is much easier to write, and more adequate, if you write more material for it as you work out issues during the project. It is very disappointing to discover that something important was left out when it is too late to do anything about it. And I don't need to point out that students (and professional researchers) often leave final papers (and reports) until the last possible minute (often for understandable reasons, including other coursework and job or family responsibilities). But be forewarned: *The last-minute approach does not work for research reports.*

Journal Articles

Writing for academic journals is perhaps the toughest form of writing, because articles are submitted to several experts in your field for careful review—anonymously, with most journals—prior to acceptance for publication. Perhaps it wouldn't be such an arduous process if so many academic journals did not have rejection rates in excess of 90% and turnaround times for reviews that are usually several months. Even the best articles, in the judgment of the reviewers, are given a "revise and resubmit" after the first review and then are evaluated all over again after the revisions are concluded.

But there are some important benefits of journal article procedures. First and foremost is the identification of areas in need of improvement, as the author(s) eyes are replaced by those of previously uninvolved subject matter experts and methodologists. A good journal editor makes sure that he or she has a list of many different types of experts available for reviewing whatever types of articles the journal is likely to receive. There is a parallel benefit for the author(s): It is always beneficial to review criticisms of your own work by people who know the field well. It can be a painful and time-consuming process, but the entire field moves forward as researchers continually critique and suggest improvements in each others' research reports.

Exhibit 14.5 presents an outline of the sections in an academic journal article, with some illustrative quotes. The article's introduction highlights the importance of the problem selected—the relationship between marital disruption (divorce) and depression. The introduction also states clearly the gap in the research literature that the article is meant to fill—the untested possibility that depression might cause marital disruption, rather than, or in addition to, marital disruption causing depression. The findings section (labeled "Results") begins by presenting the basic association between marital disruption and depression. Then it elaborates on this association by examining sex differences, the impact of prior marital quality, and various mediating and modifying effects. As indicated in the combined discussion and conclusions section, the analysis shows that marital disruption does indeed increase depression and specifies the time frame (3 years) during which this effect occurs.

These basic article sections present research results well, but many research articles include subsections tailored to the issues and stages in the specific study being reported. Most journals require a short abstract at the beginning that summarizes the research question and findings.

Exhibit 14.5 Sections in a Journal Article

Aseltine, Robert H., Jr. and Ronald C. Kessler. 1993. "Marital Disruption and Depression in a Community Sample." Journal of Health and Social Behavior, *34 (September): 237–251.*

INTRODUCTION
    Despite 20 years of empirical research, the extent to which marital disruption causes poor mental health remains uncertain. The reason for this uncertainty is that previous research has consistently overlooked the potentially important problems of selection into and out of marriage on the basis of prior mental health. (p. 237)

SAMPLE AND MEASURES
Sample
Measures

RESULTS
The Basic Association Between Marital Disruption and Depression
Sex Differences
The Impact of Prior Marital Quality
The Mediating Effects of Secondary Changes
The Modifying Effects of Transitions to Secondary Roles

DISCUSSION [includes conclusions]

. . . According to the results, marital disruption does in fact cause a significant increase in depression compared to pre-divorce levels within a period of three years after the divorce. (p. 245)

Source: Aseltine & Kessler, 1993:237–251.

Applied Research Reports

Applied research reports are written for a different audience than the professional social scientists and students who read academic journals. Typically, an applied report is written with a wide audience of potential users in mind and to serve multiple purposes. Often, both the audience and the purpose are established by the agency or other organization that funded the research project on which the report is based. Sometimes, the researcher may use the report to provide a broad descriptive overview of study findings that will be presented more succinctly in a subsequent journal article. In either case, an applied report typically provides much more information about a research project than does a journal article and relies primarily on descriptive statistics rather than only those statistics useful for the specific hypothesis tests that are likely to be the primary focus of a journal article.

Exhibit 14.6 outlines the sections in an applied research report. This particular report was mandated by the California state legislature in order to review a state-funded

Exhibit 14.6 Sections in an Applied Report

Vernez, Georges, M. Audrey Burnam, Elizabeth A. McGlynn, Sally Trude, and Brian S. Mittman. 1988. Review of California's Program for the Homeless Mentally Disabled. *Santa Monica: The RAND Corporation.*

SUMMARY
    In 1986, the California State Legislature mandated an independent review of the HMD programs that the counties had established with the state funds. The review was to determine the accountability of funds; describe the demographic and mental disorder characteristics of persons served; and assess the effectiveness of the program. This report describes the results of that review. (p. v)

INTRODUCTION
    Background
    California's Mental Health Services Act of 1985 ... allocated $20 million annually to the state's 58 counties to support a wide range of services, from basic needs to rehabilitation. (pp. 1–2)
        Study Objectives
        Organization of the Report

HMD PROGRAM DESCRIPTION AND STUDY METHODOLOGY
        The HMD Program
        Study Design and Methods
        Study Limitations

COUNTING AND CHARACTERIZING THE HOMELESS
        Estimating the Number of Homeless People
        Characteristics of the Homeless Population

THE HMD PROGRAM IN 17 COUNTIES
        Service Priorities
        Delivery of Services
        Implementation Progress
        Selected Outcomes
        Effects on the Community and on County Service Agencies
        Service Gaps

DISCUSSION
        Underserved Groups of HMD
        Gaps in Continuity of Care
    A particularly large gap in the continuum of care is the lack of specialized housing alternatives for the mentally disabled. The nature of chronic mental illness limits the ability of these individuals to live completely independently. But their housing needs may change, and board-and-care facilities that are acceptable during some periods of their lives may become unacceptable at other times. (p. 57)

        Improved Service Delivery
        Issues for Further Research

Exhibit 14.6 Continued

Appendix
A. SELECTION OF 17 SAMPLED COUNTIES
B. QUESTIONNAIRE FOR SURVEY OF THE HOMELESS
C. GUIDELINES FOR CASE STUDIES
D. INTERVIEW INSTRUMENTS FOR TELEPHONE SURVEY
E. HOMELESS STUDY SAMPLING DESIGN, ENUMERATION, AND SURVEY
   WEIGHTS
F. HOMELESS SURVEY FIELD PROCEDURES
G. SHORT SCREENER FOR MENTAL AND SUBSTANCE USE DISORDERS
H. CHARACTERISTICS OF THE COUNTIES AND THEIR HMD-FUNDED
   PROGRAMS
I. CASE STUDIES FOR FOUR COUNTIES' HMD PROGRAMS

Source: Vernez, Burnam, McGlynn, Trude, & Mittman, 1988. Reprinted with permission.

program for the homeless mentally disabled. The goals of the report are described as both description and evaluation. The body of the report presents findings on the number and characteristics of homeless persons and on the operations of the state-funded program in each of 17 counties. The discussion section highlights service needs that are not being met. Nine appendixes then provide details on the study methodology and the counties studied.

One of the major differences between an applied research report and a journal article is that an article must focus on answering a particular research question, whereas an applied report is likely to have the broader purpose of describing a wide range of study findings and attempting to meet the needs of diverse audiences that have divergent purposes in mind for the research. But a research report that simply describes "findings" without some larger purpose in mind is unlikely to be effective in reaching any audience. Anticipating the needs of the audience (or audiences) for the report and identifying the ways in which the report can be useful to them will result in a product that is less likely to be ignored.

A Congressional briefing by social scientists Ronald J. Angel, P. Lindsay Chase-Lansdale, Andrew Cherlin, and Robert Moffitt (2002) on the impact of new welfare-to-work policies is an example of a report informed by a keen understanding of current concerns and the key questions of their audience. Prepared under the auspices of the Consortium of Social Science Associations, with funding from the W.K. Kellogg Foundation, the report was titled *Welfare, Children, and Families: Results From a Three City Study.*

The starting point for the briefing was recognition that welfare reform has been a success, as commonly measured in terms of the number of recipients who have left public welfare and the high rates of employment these "leavers" have obtained (50–70%). But economist Robert Moffitt knew that the picture was more complex than that, and that policy makers needed a broader picture of what has been happening. Based on research done in the impoverished areas of Boston, Chicago, and San Antonio, he focused attention on the differences between families that had remained on welfare and those who had left, and the problems that seemed to make leaving difficult:

- Incomes for welfare "leavers" are only modestly higher, by 20% after 2 years.
- Women who remain on welfare have far fewer people to help them than those who leave.
- Many leavers no longer participated in the food stamp or Medicaid programs, even though they were still eligible.
- Stayers were much more disadvantaged than leavers, with 39% not having a high school degree, 25% having a serious health problem, and more reporting problems like depression and experiences with domestic violence
- Women who work and remain on welfare earn higher income than those who leave.
- More disadvantaged welfare recipients are more likely to be forced off welfare for technical noncompliance with rules.

With these findings in mind, Moffitt (and his coauthors, at other points in the briefing), pointed out some of the policy implications (Moffitt, 2002:8–11): "it is not clear that sanctions are a good substitute for financial incentives"; "You can stay on [welfare] and do quite well and can work"; "significant health problems, the domestic violence problems, the mental health problems, and the low skills problems . . . prevent them from working more." Finally, "there is room for improvement in the structure of supports both on and off welfare, and I think that some of the tradeoffs are well illustrated by our data."

What can be termed the **front matter** and the **back matter** of an applied report also are important. Applied reports usually begin with an executive summary: a summary list of the study's main findings, often in bullet fashion. Appendixes, the back matter, may present tables containing supporting data that were not discussed in the body of the report. Applied research reports also often append a copy of the research instrument(s).

An important principle for the researcher writing for a nonacademic audience is to make the findings and conclusions engaging and clear. You can see how I did this in a report from a class research project I designed with my graduate methods students (and in collaboration with several faculty knowledgeable about substance abuse) (Exhibit 14.7). These report excerpts indicate how I summarized key findings in an executive summary (Schutt et al., 1996:iv), emphasized the importance of the research in the introduction (Schutt et al., 1996:1), used formatting and graphing to draw attention to particular findings in the body of the text (Schutt et al., 1996:5), and tailored recommendations to our own university context (Schutt et al., 1996:26).

ETHICS, POLITICS, AND RESEARCH REPORTS

It is at the time of reporting research results that the researcher's ethical duty to be honest becomes paramount. Here are some guidelines:

- *Provide an honest accounting of how the research was carried out and where the initial research design had to be changed.* Readers do not have to know about every change you made in your plans and each new idea you had, but they should be informed about major changes in hypotheses or research design.
- *Maintain a full record of the research project so that questions can be answered if they arise.* Many details will have to be omitted from all but the most comprehensive

Exhibit 14.7   Student Substance Abuse, Report Excerpts

Executive Summary

- Rates of substance abuse were somewhat lower at UMass–Boston than among nationally selected samples of college students.
- Two-thirds of the respondents reported at least one close family member whose drinking or drug use had ever been of concern to them—one-third reported a high level of concern.
- Most students perceived substantial risk of harm due to illicit drug use, but just one-quarter thought alcohol use posed a great risk of harm.

Introduction

Binge drinking, other forms of alcohol abuse, and illicit drug use create numerous problems on college campuses. Deaths from binge drinking are too common and substance abuse is a factor in as many as two-thirds of on-campus sexual assaults (Finn, 1997; National Institute of Alcohol Abuse and Alcoholism, 1995). College presidents now rate alcohol abuse as the number one campus problem (Wechsler, Davenport, Dowdall, Moeykens, & Castillo, 1994) and many schools have been devising new substance abuse prevention policies and programs. However, in spite of increasing recognition of and knowledge about substance abuse problems at colleges as a whole, little attention has been focused on substance abuse at commuter schools.

Findings

The composite index identifies 27% of respondents as at risk of substance abuse (an index score of 2 or higher).[1] One-quarter reported having smoked or used smokeless tobacco in the past two weeks.

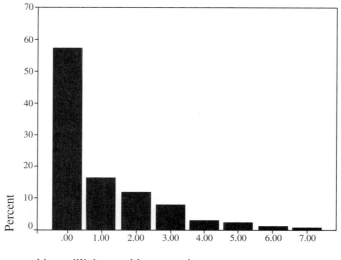

27% of respondents were identified as at risk of substance abuse.

binge+illicty+problem experience

(Continued)

Exhibit 14.7 Continued

Recommendations

1. Enforce campus rules and regulations about substance use. When possible and where appropriate, communications from campus officials to students should heighten awareness of the UMass Boston commitment to an alcohol- and drug-free environment.
2. Encourage those students involved in campus alcohol or drug-related problems or crises to connect with the PRIDE program.
3. Take advantage of widespread student interest in prevention by forming a university-wide council to monitor and stimulate interest in prevention activities.

Source: Schutt et al., 1996.

reports, but these omissions should not make it impossible to track down answers to specific questions about research procedures that may arise in the course of data analysis or presentation.

- *Avoid "lying with statistics" or using graphs to mislead.* See Chapter 12 for more on this topic.
- *Acknowledge the sponsors of the research.* This is important, in part, so that others can consider whether this sponsorship may have tempted you to bias your results in some way
- *Thank staff who made major contributions.* This is an ethical as well as a political necessity. Let's maintain our social relations!
- *Be sure that the order of authorship for coauthored reports is discussed in advance and reflects agreed-upon principles.* Be sensitive to coauthors' needs and concerns.

Ethical research reporting should not mean ineffective reporting. You need to tell a coherent story in the report and avoid losing track of the story in a thicket of minuscule details. You do not need to report every twist and turn in the conceptualization of the research problem or the conduct of the research. But be suspicious of reports that don't seem to admit to the possibility of any room for improvement. Social science is an ongoing enterprise in which one research report makes its most valuable contribution by laying the groundwork for another, more sophisticated research project. Highlight important findings in the research report, but also use the research report to point out what are likely to be the most productive directions for future researchers.

Even following appropriate guidelines like these, however, will not prevent controversy and conflict over research on sensitive issues. Sociologist Peter Rossi (1999) recounts the controversy that arose when he released a summary of findings conducted in his 1986 study of homeless persons in Chicago (see Chapter 5). In spite of important findings about the causes and effects of homelessness, media attention focused on Rossi's markedly smaller estimate of the numbers of homeless persons in Chicago compared to the "guesstimates" that had been publicized by local advocacy groups. "Moral of the story: Controversy is news, to which careful empirical findings cannot be compared" (Rossi, 1999:2).

Does this mean that ethical researchers should avoid political controversy by sidestepping media outlets for their work? Many social scientists argue that the media offers one of the best ways to communicate the practical application of sociological knowledge, and that when we avoid these opportunities, "some of the best sociological insights never reach policy makers because sociologists seldom take advantage of useful mechanisms to get their ideas out" (Wilson, 1998:435).

Sociologist William Julius Wilson (1998:438) urges the following principles for engaging the public through the media:

1. focus on issues of national concern, issues that are high on the public agenda;

2. develop creative and thoughtful arguments that are clearly presented and devoid of technical language; and

3. present the big picture whereby the arguments are organized and presented so that the readers can see how the various parts are interrelated.

Ultimately, each researcher must make a decision about the most appropriate and important outlets for their work.

CONCLUSIONS

A well-written research article or report requires (to be just a bit melodramatic) blood, sweat, and tears—and more time than you will at first anticipate. But the process of writing one will help you to write the next. And the issues you consider, if you approach your writing critically, will be sure to improve your subsequent research projects and sharpen your evaluations of other investigators' research projects.

Good critical skills are essential when evaluating research reports, whether your own or those produced by others. There are *always* weak points in any research, even published research. It is an indication of strength, not weakness, to recognize areas where one's own research needs to be, or could have been, improved. And it is really not just a question of sharpening your knives and going for the jugular. You need to be able to weigh the strengths and weaknesses of particular research results, and to evaluate a study in terms of its contribution to understanding the social world—not in terms of whether it gives a definitive answer for all time.

But this is not to say that anything goes. Much research lacks one or more of the three legs of validity—measurement validity, causal validity, or generalizability—and contributes more confusion than understanding about the social world. Top journals generally maintain very high standards, partly because they have good critics in the review process and distinguished editors who make the final acceptance decisions. But some daily newspapers do a poor job of screening, and research reporting standards in many popular magazines, TV shows, and books are often abysmally poor. Keep your standards high and your view critical when reading research reports, but not so high or so critical that you turn away from studies that make tangible contributions to understanding the social world—even if they don't provide definitive answers. And don't be so intimidated by the need to maintain high standards that you shrink from taking advantage of opportunities to conduct research yourself.

The growth of social science methods from its infancy to adolescence, perhaps to young adulthood, ranks as a key intellectual accomplishment of the 20th century. Opinions about the causes and consequences of homelessness no longer need depend on the scattered impressions of individuals; criminal justice policies can be shaped by systematic evidence of their effectiveness; and changes in the distribution of poverty and wealth in populations can be identified and charted. Employee productivity, neighborhood cohesion, and societal conflict may each be linked to individual psychological processes and to international economic strains.

Of course, social research methods are no more useful than the commitment of researchers to their proper application. Research methods, like all knowledge, can be used poorly or well, for good purposes or bad, when appropriate or not. A claim that a belief is based on social science research in itself provides no extra credibility. As you have learned throughout this book, we must first learn which methods were used, how they were applied, and whether interpretations square with the evidence. To investigate the social world, we must keep in mind the lessons of research methods.

KEY TERMS

Back matter

Effect size

Front matter

Meta-analysis

Reverse outlining

HIGHLIGHTS

- Research reports should be evaluated systematically, using the review guide in Appendix B and also taking account of the interrelations among the design elements.

- Proposal writing should be a time for clarifying the research problem, reviewing the literature, and thinking ahead about the report that will be required. Trade-offs between different design elements should be considered and the potential for mixing methods evaluated.

- Different types of reports typically pose different problems. Authors of student papers must be guided in part by the expectations of their professor. Thesis writers have to meet the requirements of different committee members, but can benefit greatly from the areas of expertise represented on a typical thesis committee. Applied researchers are constrained by the expectations of the research sponsor; an advisory committee from the applied setting can help to avoid problems. Journal articles must pass a peer review by other social scientists and often are much improved in the process.

- Research reports should include an introductory statement of the research problem, a literature review, a methodology section, a findings section with pertinent data displays, and a conclusions section that identifies any weaknesses in the research design and points out implications for future research and theorizing. This basic report format should be modified according to the needs of a particular audience.

- All reports should be revised several times and critiqued by others before being presented in final form.

- The central ethical concern in research reporting is to be honest. This honesty should include providing a truthful accounting of how the research was carried out, maintaining a full record about the project, using appropriate statistics and graphs, acknowledging the research sponsors, and being sensitive to the perspectives of coauthors.

DISCUSSION QUESTIONS

1. A good place to start developing your critical skills would be with one of the articles reviewed in this chapter. Try reading one, and fill in the answers to the article review questions that I did not cover

(Appendix B). Do you agree with my answers to the other questions? Could you add some points to my critique, or to the lessons on research designs that I drew from these critiques?

2. Read the journal article "Marital Disruption and Depression in a Community Sample," by Aseltine and Kessler, in the September 1993 issue of *Journal of Health and Social Behavior.* How effective is the article in conveying the design and findings of the research? Could the article's organization be improved at all? Are there bases for disagreement about the interpretation of the findings?

3. Rate four journal articles for the overall quality of the research and for the effectiveness of the writing and data displays. Discuss how each could have been improved.

PRACTICE EXERCISES

1. Call a local social or health service administrator or a criminal justice official and arrange for an interview. Ask the official about his or her experience with applied research reports and conclusions about the value of social research and the best techniques for reporting to practitioners.

2. Interview a student who has written an independent paper or thesis based on collecting original data. Ask her to describe her experiences while writing the thesis. Review the decisions she made in designing her research, and ask about the stages of research design, data collection and analysis, and report writing that proved to be difficult.

WEB EXERCISES

1. Go to the National Science Foundation's Sociology Program Web site at http://www.nsf.gov/sbe/ses/sociol/start.htm. What are the components that the National Science Foundation's Sociology Program looks for in a proposed piece of research? Outline a research proposal to study a subject of your choice to be submitted to the National Science Foundation for funding.

2. The National Academy of Sciences wrote a lengthy report on ethics issues in scientific research. Visit the site and read the report: http://www.nap.edu/readingroom/books/obas. Summarize the information and guidelines in the report.

3. Using the Web, find five different examples of social science research projects that have been completed. Briefly describe each. How does each differ in its approach to reporting the research results? Who do you think the author(s) of each is "reporting" to (i.e., who is the "audience")? How do you think the predicted audience has helped to shape the author's approach to reporting the results? Be sure to note the Web sites at which you located each of your five examples.

SPSS EXERCISES

1. Review the output you have generated in previous SPSS exercises. Select the distributions, statistics, and crosstabs that you believe provide a coherent and interesting picture of support for capital punishment in America.

2. Prepare these data displays in presentation format and number them (Table 1, Table 2, etc.).

3. Write a short report. Include in your report a brief introduction and literature review (you might use the articles I referred to in Chapters 1 and 2). In a short methods section, review the basics of the GSS2000 and list the variables you have used for the analysis.

4. In your conclusions section include some suggestions for additional research on support for capital punishment.

DEVELOPING A RESEARCH PROPOSAL

Now it's time to bring all the elements of your proposal together.

1. Organize the proposal material you wrote for previous chapters in a logical order (see page 451). Select what you feel is the strongest research method (Chapters 7–11) as your primary method.

2. Add a multiple method component to your research design with one of the other methods sections you prepared in Chapters 7–11.

3. Rewrite the entire proposal, adding an introduction. Also add sections that outline a budget and state the limitations of your study.

4. Review the proposal with the "decision checklist" (Exhibit 14.1, pp. 452-453). Answer each question and justify your decision at each checkpoint.

Appendix A

SUMMARIES OF FREQUENTLY CITED RESEARCH ARTICLES

Actual research studies are used throughout the text to illustrate particular research approaches and issues. You can use the following summaries at any point to review the design of each study. The chapter number in brackets indicates the text chapter in which the study is introduced.

Anderson, Elijah. 1999. *Code of the Street: Decency, Violence, and the Moral Life of the Inner City.* New York: W. W. Norton. [Chapter 13]. Ethnographic study of social life in an impoverished urban community based on participant observation. Develops contextually based understanding of what the "code of the street" means and how it is maintained.

Anderson, Elijah. 2003. "Jelly's Place: An Ethnographic Memoir." *Symbolic Interaction,* forthcoming. [Chapter 13]. Review of field methods used in study of Jelly's Bar. Recounts process of gaining entry to the bar and gaining the trust of its customers.

Anspach, Renee R. 1991. "Everyday Methods for Assessing Organizational Effectiveness." *Social Problems,* 38(February):1–19. [Chapter 8]. Study of effectiveness of mental health systems with a snowball sample of administrators, case managers, clients, and family members in four community mental health systems. Responses to open-ended interviews indicated that the programs were failing in many ways, but that the respondents wanted the interviewer to believe in the program's effectiveness.

Aronson, Elliot and Judson Mills. 1959. "The Effect of Severity of Initiation on Liking for a Group." *Journal of Abnormal and Social Psychology,* 59:177–181. [Chapter 7]. Classic experimental study of students at an all-women's college in the 1950s. Students were assigned randomly to either read embarrassing words or listen to a boring, taped discussion prior to being allowed to join a group. Subjects who participated in the more severe initiation procedure reported greater liking for the group.

Bennett, Lauren, Lisa Goodman, and Mary Ann Dutton. 1999. "Systemic Obstacles to the Criminal Prosecution of a Battering Partner: A Victim Perspective." *Journal of Interpersonal Violence,* 14:761–772. [Chapter 2]. Inductive exploration of why victims of domestic battering often decide not to press charges. Forty-nine victims were interviewed in one court, in which one researcher also worked as a victim advocate. There were four reasons that victims failed to press charges: confusion about court procedures, frustration due to delays, paralysis by fear of retribution, and a desire to keep the batterer out of jail.

Bushman, Brad J., Roy F. Baumeister, and Angela D. Stack. 1999. "Catharsis, Aggression, and Persuasive Influence: Self-Fulfilling or Self-Defeating Prophecies?" *Journal of Personality and Social Psychology,* 76:367–376. [Chapter 6]. Experimental study of the effect of catharsis on aggression, in which 707 introductory psychology students participated. Students read either a positive statement about catharsis, a negative statement about catharsis, or no statement. After several other steps, students were engaged in a competitive reaction-time task, and their aggressiveness toward their competitor was measured. Students who had read the procatharsis message exhibited more aggressive responses than did those who read the anticatharsis message or no message.

Cohen, Susan G. and Gerald E. Ledford, Jr. 1994. "The Effectiveness of Self-Managing Teams: A Quasi-Experiment." *Human Relations*, 47:13–43. [Chapter 7]. A study of the effectiveness of self-managing teams using an ex post facto design. Work teams were studied in a telecommunications company in which some work teams were self-managing and some were traditionally managed by a supervisor. Each work group identified as self-managing was matched with a traditionally managed work group that produced the same product or service. Self-reported quality of work life was higher in the self-managing groups than in the traditionally managed groups. Job performance also seemed higher in the self-managing groups in clerical and craft functions but not in small business offices. A special review of operations in small business offices revealed that their work did not lend itself to a team approach. This finding helped to specify the context in which the hypothesized cause would have its effect.

Cole, Jeffrey I. 2001. *The UCLA Internet Report 2001: Surveying the Digital Future, Year Two.* Los Angeles: Center for Communications Policy. [Chapter 1]. National survey of a representative sample of Americans to identify frequency and types of Internet use and to explore possible causes of Internet use. More than two-thirds of the population went online in 2001, a higher proportion than in the previous year, and most were satisfied with the experience. The most popular activities were e-mail and Web browsing, and most reported that it does not detract from their work or in-person social activities.

Coleman, James S. and Thomas Hoffer. 1987. *Public and Private High Schools: The Impact of Communities.* New York: Basic Books. [Chapter 6]. Study of student achievement in private and public high schools using an event-based (cohort) panel design. Verbal and math achievement test scores of Catholic school students increased more over 2 years than did those of public school students; change in performance of students in non-Catholic private schools was more mixed.

Cress, Daniel M. and David A. Snow. 2000. "The Outcomes of Homeless Mobilization: The Influence of Organization, Disruption, Political Mediation, and Framing." *American Journal of Sociology,* 4:1063–1104. [Chapter 13]. Qualitative analysis of differences between homeless mobilization efforts and the influence of different factors on successful mobilization. Uses qualitative comparative analysis techniques to assess how various conditions influenced SMO outcomes.

Diamond, Timothy. 1992. *Making Gray Gold: Narratives of Nursing Home Care.* Chicago: University of Chicago Press. [Chapter 9]. A participant observation study of the inside of three Chicago nursing homes and the attitudes and actions of their staffs. The central research questions were, in Diamond's words, "What was life like inside, day in and day out? Who lived in nursing homes, and what did they do there?" He began the study by going to school for 6 months to obtain a required state certificate for nursing home employees; he then worked for several months at each of the three nursing homes. The nursing homes were selected to differ in location and in the proportion of their residents on Medicaid. Diamond's in-depth descriptions and idiographic connections of sequences of events enabled him to explore human experiences in depth and to carefully analyze the social contexts in which these experiences occurred.

Drake, Robert E., Gregory J. McHugo, Deborah R. Becker, William A. Anthony, and Robin E. Clark. 1996. "The New Hampshire Study of Supported Employment for People with Severe Mental Illness." *Journal of Consulting and Clinical Psychology*, 64:391–399. [Chapter 10]. A test of the value of two different approaches to providing employment services for people diagnosed with severe mental disorders that used a variant of the classic randomized comparative change design. One approach, Group Skills Training (GST), emphasized pre-employment skills training and used separate agencies to provide vocational and mental health services. The other approach, Individual Placement and Support (IPS), provided vocational and mental health services in a single program and placed people directly into jobs without pre-employment skills training. Both groups received posttests, at 6, 12, and 18 months. The researchers hypothesized that GST participants would be more likely to obtain jobs than would IPS participants, but the IPS participants proved to be twice as likely to obtain a competitive job as the GST participants.

Fischer, Constance T. and Frederick J. Wertz. 2002. "Empirical Phenomenological Analyses of Being Criminally Victimized." Pp. 275–304 in *The Qualitative Researcher's Companion,* edited by A. Michael Huberman and Matthew B. Miles. Thousand Oaks, CA: Sage. [Chapter 9]. A phenomenological analysis of being criminally victimized, based on recounting crime victims' stories and then identifying common themes in these stories.

Frank, David John, Ann Hironaka, and Evan Schofer. 2000. "The Nation-State and the Natural Environment over the Twentieth Century." *American Sociological Review,* 65:96–116. [Chapter 11]. Investigation of why national activities to protect the natural environment grew during the 20th century. Measures of national and international environmental protectionist activities were recorded from various documents. The growth in environmental protectionism was not explained by increasing environmental problems or economic affluence within nations, but by a growing norm of environmental protection in international organizations.

Franklin, Mark N. 1996. "Electoral Participation." Pp. 216–235 in *Comparing Democracies: Elections and Voting in Global Perspective*, edited by Lawrence LeDuc, Richard G. Niemi, and Pippa Norris. Thousand Oaks, CA: Sage. [Chapter 11]. An analysis of international data to explain variation in voter turnout. Voter turnout is maximized where such structural features as compulsory voting and mail and Sunday voting maximize competition. Voter turnout also tends to be higher where the issues being voted on are important and where results are decided by proportional representation rather than on a winner-take-all basis (so individual votes are more important). Franklin concluded that it is the lack of these characteristics that explains the low level of voter turnout in the United States, not the characteristics of individual voters.

Goldfinger, Stephen M., Russell K. Schutt, Larry J. Seidman, Winston M. Turner, Walter E. Penk, and George S. Tolomiczenko. 1996. "Self-Report and Observer Measures of Substance Abuse Among Homeless Mentally Ill Persons in the Cross-Section and Over Time." *The Journal of Nervous and Mental Disease*, 184(11):667–672. [Chapter 4]. In this study of housing for homeless mentally ill persons, we assessed substance abuse with several different sets of direct questions as well as with reports from subjects' case managers and others. We found that the observational reports were often inconsistent with self-reports and that different self-report measures were not always in agreement—hence they were unreliable. A more reliable measure was initial reports of lifetime substance abuse problems, which identified all those who subsequently abused substances during the project. We concluded that the lifetime measure was a valid way to identify persons at risk for substance abuse problems. No single measure was adequate to identify substance abusers at a particular point in time during the project. Instead, we constructed a composite of observer and self-report measures that seemed to be a valid indicator of substance abuse over 6-month periods.

Goldfinger, Stephen M., Russell K. Schutt, George S. Tolomiczenko, Winston M. Turner, Norma Ware, Walter E. Penk, et al. 1997. "Housing Persons Who Are Homeless and Mentally Ill: Independent Living or Evolving Consumer Households?" Pp. 29–49 in *Mentally Ill and Homeless: Special Programs for Special Needs*, edited by William R. Breakey and James W. Thompson. Amsterdam, The Netherlands: Harwood Academic Publishers. [Chapter 10]. Field experiment to evaluate the impact of two types of housing on residential stability, health, and other outcomes for formerly homeless mentally ill persons. Individuals living in shelters were assigned randomly to permanent housing either in an "independent living" site (an efficiency apartment) or in an "evolving consumer household" site (a group home from which support staff were withdrawn as residents took over management responsibilities). Participants were evaluated with lengthy interview instruments, neuropsychological tests, and personality inventories for an 18-month period after housing placement. Anthropologists observed interaction in the group homes, and case managers reported on the services delivered to subjects. We found that residents assigned to group homes had a higher rate of housing retention than those assigned to independent apartments; that housing loss was higher among substance abusers and those whom clinicians recommended for group homes; and that individuals assigned to independent apartments were more satisfied with their residences. However, the type of housing did not affect residents' symptoms of mental illness or their feelings about the quality of their lives.

Gottfredson, Michael R. and Don M. Gottfredson. 1988. *Decision Making in Criminal Justice: Toward the Rational Exercise of Discretion*, 2nd ed. New York: Plenum. [Chapter 3]. Analysis of crime data collected in the National Crime Survey, 1973–1977, U.S. Department of Justice. Supports the rational choice prediction that cost-benefit calculations influence crime and crime reporting.

Griffin, Larry J. 1993. "Narrative, Event-Structure Analysis, and Causal Interpretation in Historical Sociology." *American Journal of Sociology,* 98:1094–1133. [Chapter 11]. Analysis of the events leading up to a lynching in Mississippi in the 1930s. Event-structure analysis is used to develop an idiographic explanation that highlights the structure of action underlying the series of events.

Hampton, Keith N. and Barry Wellman. 1999. "Netville On-line and Off-line: Observing and Surveying a Wired Suburb." *American Behavioral Scientist,* 43:475–492. [Chapter 1]. Study of the impact of universal access to electronic communication on social relations. Surveys, participant observation (for 2 years), and analysis of online messages and discussions resulted in a comprehensive investigation. With Internet access, connected residents had larger and less geographically concentrated circles of friends than did unconnected residents.

Hampton, Keith N. and Barry Wellman. 2001. "Long Distance Community in the Network Society: Contact and Support Beyond Netville." *American Behavioral Scientist,* 45:4 76-495. [Chapter 1]. Examination of effect of computer network connections on social relations outside of the immediate community. Survey results indicate that computer-medicated communication increases social ties primarily to immediately adjacent neighborhoods, not to physically distant locations.

Haney, C., C. Banks, and Philip G. Zimbardo. 1973. "Interpersonal Dynamics in a Simulated Prison." *International Journal of Criminology and Penology,* 1:69–97. [Chapter 2]. Classic study of the impact of social position—being a prisoner or a prison guard—on behavior. Male volunteers signed a contract to participate for 2 weeks in a simulated prison. Prisoners became passive and disorganized, whereas guards became verbally and physically aggressive. The experiment was terminated after 6 days and has been a focus for discussion about experimental ethics ever since.

Harris, David R. and Jeremiah Joseph Sim. 2002. "Who Is Multiracial? Assessing the Complexity of Lived Race." *American Sociological Review,* 67:614–627. [Chapter 4]. Analysis of racial self-classification based on a national survey of youths. Researchers found that racial self-classification can vary with social context, and that youths were less likely to self-identify as multiracial, rather than monoracial, in the presence of a parent.

Hirsch, Eric L. 1990. "Sacrifice for the Cause: Group Processes, Recruitment, and Commitment in a Student Social Movement." *American Sociological Review,* 55(April):243–254. [Chapter 9]. Study of 1985 anti-apartheid student movement at Columbia University. Used mixed methods—participant observation, intensive interviewing, and standardized survey. Consciousness raising seemed to play a key role in increasing support for the campaign to make the university divest its stock in companies that did business in South Africa.

Horney, Julie, D. Wayne Osgood, and Ineke Haen Marshall. 1995. "Criminal Careers in the Short-Term: Intra-Individual Variability in Crime and Its Relation to Local Life Circumstances." *American Sociological Review*, 60:655–673. [Chapter 6]. An example of the use of retrospective data. The researchers interviewed 658 newly convicted male offenders sentenced to a Nebraska state prison. In a 45- to 90-minute interview, they recorded each inmate's report of his life circumstances and of his criminal activities for the previous 2 to 3 years. They then found that criminal involvement was related strongly to adverse changes in life circumstances, such as marital separation or drug use.

Loader, Brian, Steve Muncer, Roger Burrows, Nicolas Pleace, and Sarah Nettleton. 2002. "Medicine on the Line? Computer-Mediated Social Support and Advice for People with Diabetes." *International Journal of Social Welfare*, 11:53–65. [Chapter 1]. Qualitative analysis of all interactions (postings) on a British diabetes newsgroup in 1 week in 1998. Each of 149 different "threads" (chains of interrelated messages on a topic) was categorized for the type of social support it provided. The newsgroup seemed to be "a reasonably active network of people with diabetes, who find value in sharing their experiences and lay knowledge of living with their condition in an informal virtual self-help forum."

Milgram, Stanley. 1965. "Some Conditions of Obedience and Disobedience to Authority." *Human Relations,* 18:57–75. [Chapter 7]. Attempt to identify through laboratory experiments the conditions under which ordinary citizens would resist instructions from authority figures to inflict pain on others. Men were recruited through local newspaper ads. Each participant was told he was to participate in a study of the learning process. The recruit was then designated to play the role of the teacher while another "volunteer" (actually the researcher's confederate) went into another room for the rest of the experiment (in most versions of the experiment). The experimenter then instructed the teacher/subject to help the "student" memorize words by administering an electric shock (with a phony machine) every time the student failed to remember the correct word, the voltage level increased for each successive shock. The researcher patiently encouraged the subject to continue administering the shocks even when the dial on the machine moved to "Extreme Intensity Shock" and "Danger: Severe Shock." Many subjects continued to administer shocks beyond the level they believed would hurt or even kill the subject.

Morrill, Calvin, Christine Yalda, Madeleine Adelman, Michael Musheno, and Cindy Bejarano. 2000. "Telling Tales in School: Youth Culture and Conflict Narratives." *Law & Society Review,* 34:521–565. [Chapter 13]. Narrative analysis of study of youth violence. Uses a "narrative survey," in which students in ninth-grade English classes at one high school were asked to write a story about a time they experienced a conflict with another student.

Morris, Michael W. and Paul C. Moore. 2000. "The Lessons We (Don't) Learn: Counterfactual Thinking and Organizational Accountability After a Close Call." *Administrative Science Quarterly*, 45:737–765. [Chapter 7]. Classic experiment to test the impact of organizational accountability on learning from experience. Forty-two Stanford University students were paid to use a flight simulator, and then told they were either private or commercial "pilots" and asked to land their "plane" under very difficult conditions. Student pilots who had been told they were working for a company were less likely to engage in upward comparisons than were students who had been told they were private pilots.

National Geographic. 2000. *Survey 2000.* http://www.survey2000.nationalgeographic.com. [Chapter 1]. International survey about Internet usage that was conducted on the Internet, in which 80,012 individuals from 178 countries and territories responded. The interactive questionnaire included measures of feelings about communities and personal behavior and preferences. Survey responses suggested that the Internet supplemented but did not displace community ties.

Needleman, Carolyn. 1981. "Discrepant Assumptions in Empirical Research: The Case of Juvenile Court Screening." *Social Problems,* 28:247–262. [Chapter 8]. Participant observation study of how probation officers screened cases in two New York juvenile court intake units. The study revealed that the concepts most researchers believe they are measuring with official records differ markedly from the meaning attached to those records by probation officers. Probation officers often decided how to handle cases first and then created an official record that appeared to justify their decisions.

Nie, Norman H. and Lutz Erbring. 2000. *Internet and Society: A Preliminary Report.* Palo Alto, CA: Stanford Institute for the Quantitative Study of Society. [Chapter 1]. An innovative survey conducted to investigate the effect of the Internet on social relations. Each member of the sample of 4,113 adults in the United States was given a free Web TV connected to the Internet. Survey questions were asked and answered through the Web TVs. More Internet use was associated with less time on other social activities.

Pagnini, Deanna L. and S. Philip Morgan. 1996. "Racial Differences in Marriage and Childbearing: Oral History Evidence from the South in the Early Twentieth Century." *American Journal of Sociology*, 101:1694–1715. [Chapter 11]. Oral histories were studied to reveal attitudes toward births out of wedlock among African American and white women in the South during the 1930s. Pagnini and Morgan read 1,170 life histories recorded by almost 200 writers who worked for a New Deal program during the Depression of the 1930s. The interviewers had used a topic outline that included family issues, education, income, occupation, religion, medical needs, and diet. The analysis gave some insight into community norms that were associated with higher rates of unwed births among African American women. Bearing a child outside a marital relationship did not seem to be the stigmatizing event for African Americans that it was for whites.

Pate, Antony M. and Edwin E. Hamilton. 1992. "Formal and Informal Deterrents to Domestic Violence: The Dade County Spouse Assault Experiment." *American Sociological Review,* 57 (October):691–697. [Chapter 2]. A replication of the Minneapolis Domestic Violence

Experiment on the police response to domestic violence, funded by the U.S. Department of Justice. This study extended the deterrence framework used by Sherman and Berk to include informal sanctions, and found that the informal sanctioning experienced by persons who were employed and married increased the deterrent effect of arrest.

Paternoster, Raymond, Robert Brame, Ronet Bachman, and Lawrence W. Sherman. 1997. "Do Fair Procedures Matter? The Effect of Procedural Justice on Spouse Assault." *Law & Society Review*, 31(1):163–204. [Chapter 2]. A secondary analysis of data collected in the Milwaukee Domestic Violence Experiment, one of the replications of Sherman and Berk's study of the police response to domestic violence. Paternoster and his colleagues tested a prediction of procedural justice theory that people will comply with the law out of a sense of duty and obligation if they are treated fairly by legal authorities. The procedural justice hypothesis was supported: Persons who were arrested in the Milwaukee experiment became more likely to reoffend only if they had been treated unfairly by the police. Otherwise, their rate of rearrest was similar to that for the persons who were not arrested.

Pew Internet & American Life Project. 2000. *Tracking Online Life: How Women Use the Internet to Cultivate Relationships with Family and Friends.* Washington, DC: The Pew Internet & American Life Project. www.pewinternet.org. [Chapter 1]. Survey of 3,533 adults residing in the continental United States to investigate Internet use and its impact on social relations. Most respondents reported that the Internet had improved their connections to members of their family; women were somewhat more positive than men about the Internet's impact.

Phillips, David P. 1982. "The Impact of Fictional Television Stories on U.S. Adult Fatalities: New Evidence on the Effect of the Mass Media on Violence." *American Journal of Sociology,* 87:1340–1359. [Chapter 7]. Quasi-experimental study of the effect of TV soap opera suicides on the number of actual suicides in the United States, using a multiple group before-and-after design. Soap-opera suicides in 1977 were identified, and then the suicide rates in the week prior to and during the week of each suicide story were compared. Deaths due to suicide increased from the control period to the experimental period in 12 of the 13 comparisons.

Presley, Cheryl A., Philip W. Meilman, and Rob Lyerla. 1994. "Development of the Core Alcohol and Drug Survey: Initial Findings and Future Directions." *Journal of American College Health*, 42:248–255. [Chapter 4]. The Core Alcohol and Drug Survey was developed by a committee of grantees of the U.S. Department of Education's Fund for the Improvement of Postsecondary Education (FIPSE) to assist universities in obtaining reliable information about the effectiveness of their efforts to prevent substance abuse. The instrument measures the nature, scope, and consequences of the use of alcohol and other drugs among college students. It is administered annually on 800 campuses and has resulted in a database with over half a million respondents. Almost half of students report binge drinking within the preceding 2 weeks, and the average number of drinks declines as GPA increases. However, 87% of students report that they prefer not to have drugs around, and 33% prefer not to have alcohol present on campus.

Price, Richard H., Michelle Van Ryn, and Amiram D. Vinokur. 1992. "Impact of a Preventive Job Search Intervention on the Likelihood of Depression Among the Unemployed." *Journal of Health and Social Behavior,* 33:158–167. [Chapter 7]. Field experiment to test the hypothesis that a job search program to help newly unemployed persons could also reduce their risk of depression. Unemployed persons who volunteered for job search help at Michigan Employment Security Commission offices were randomly assigned either to participate in eight 3-hour group training seminars over a 2-week period (the treatment) or to receive self-help information on job search in the mail (the comparison condition). The authors found fewer depressive symptoms among the subjects who had participated in the group training seminars.

Ringwalt, Christopher L., Jody M. Greene, Susan T. Ennett, Ronaldo Iachan, Richard R. Clayton, and Carl G. Leukefeld. 1994. *Past and Future Directions of the D.A.R.E. Program: An Evaluation Review.* Research Triangle, NC: Research Triangle Institute. [Chapter 10]. Evaluation of D.A.R.E. with site visits, informal interviews, discussions, and surveys of D.A.R.E. program coordinators and advisors. These data indicated that D.A.R.E. was operating as designed and was running relatively smoothly, and that drug prevention coordinators in D.A.R.E. school districts rated the program components as much more satisfactory than did coordinators in school districts with other types of alcohol and drug prevention programs. However, D.A.R.E. did not decrease subsequent rates of drug use.

Ross, Catherine E. 1990. "Work, Family and the Sense of Control: Implications for the Psychological Well-Being of Women and Men" Proposal submitted to the National Science Foundation. Columbus: The Ohio State University. [Chapter 8]. Investigation of relationship between family and work roles, sense of control, and mental health. A national probability sample of 2,031 adult Americans was contacted by telephone and selected with random digit dialing. Publications from this research focused on the relationship between health lifestyle and perceived health, physical impairment and income, gender, parenthood, and anger.

Ross, Catherine E. and Chia-ling Wu. 1995. "The Links Between Education and Health." *American Sociological Review,* 60:719–745. [Chapter 8]. A 1990 telephone survey of a random sample of 2,031 adult Americans to identify the psychological effects of changes in household structure. Ross proposed a theory to link women's and men's objective positions at home and in the labor force to their subjective sense of control over life, and in turn to emotional and physical well-being. The questionnaire measured conditions of work and home; sociodemographic characteristics such as employment and marital status, socioeconomic status, and age; the sense of control; and depression, anxiety, anger, and other psychological outcomes. Ross and her collaborators found that high educational attainment improves health directly, and it improves health indirectly through work and economic conditions, social-psychological resources, and health lifestyle.

Rossi, Peter H. 1989. *Down and Out in America: The Origins of Homelessness.* Chicago: University of Chicago Press. [Chapter 5]. Survey of homeless and other extremely poor persons in Chicago to determine, in part, why people become homeless. Cluster sampling techniques were used to select shelter users as well as homeless persons found late at night on blocks selected for the likelihood that they would have homeless persons. Homeless persons were extremely poor but had more health problems, particularly substance abuse and mental illness, than extremely poor persons who were housed.

Rueschemeyer, Dietrich, Evelyne Huber Stephens, and John D. Stephens. 1992. *Capitalist Development and Democracy.* Chicago: University of Chicago Press. [Chapter 11]. A comparative historical analysis to explain why some nations in Latin America developed democratic politics while others became authoritarian states. The researchers developed a theoretical framework that gave key attention to the power of social classes, state (government) power, and the interaction between social classes and the government. They then classified the political regimes in each nation over time, noting how each nation varied in terms of the variables they had identified as potentially important for successful democratization. Their analysis identified several conditions for initial democratization: consolidation of state power, expansion of the export economy, industrialization, and some agent of political articulation for the subordinate classes.

Sampson, Robert J. 1987. "Urban Black Violence: The Effect of Male Joblessness and Family Disruption." *American Journal of Sociology,* 93:348–382. [Chapter 6]. Study of the causes of urban violence (rates of homicide and robbery) using city-level data from the 1980 U.S. Census. The specific hypothesis was that higher rates of black family disruption (the percentage of black households with children headed by females) result in more violence was supported.

Sampson, Robert J. and John H. Laub. 1990. "Crime and Deviance Over the Life Course: The Salience of Adult Social Bonds." *American Sociological Review,* 55:609–627. [Chapter 6]. Longitudinal study of the effect of childhood deviance on adult crime. A sample of white males in Boston was first studied when they were between 10 and 17 years old and then again in their adult years. Data were collected from multiple sources, including interviews with the subjects themselves and criminal justice records. Children who had been committed to a correctional school for persistent delinquency were much more likely to have committed crimes as adults.

Sampson, Robert J. and John H. Laub. 1993. "Structural Variations in Juvenile Court Processing: Inequality, the Underclass, and Social Control." *Law and Society Review,* 27(2):285–311. [Chapter 3]. Analysis of official records to test the hypothesis that juvenile justice is harsher in areas characterized by racial poverty and a large underclass. A random sample of 538,000 cases from 322 counties was drawn and combined with census data on county social characteristics. In counties having a relatively large underclass and poverty concentrated among minorities, juvenile cases were more likely to be treated harshly. These relationships occurred for both black and white juveniles, but were particularly strong for blacks, and they were not related to counties' average income levels or to criminal justice system resources.

Sampson, Robert J. and Stephen W. Raudenbush. 1999. "Systematic Social Observation of Public Spaces: A New Look at Disorder in Urban Neighborhoods." *American Journal of Sociology,* 105:603–651. [Chapter 6]. Cross-sectional study of the effect of visible public social and physical disorder on the crime rate in Chicago neighborhoods. The researchers hypothesized that variation in crime rates would be explained by the strength of informal social control rather than by the "broken windows" theory that visible signs of disorder caused crime. Visible disorder was measured by observers riding in vans; these observational data were complemented by a survey of residents and an examination of police records. Informal social control was a much more important factor in the neighborhood crime rate than visible social and physical disorder.

Sampson, Robert J., Jeffrey D. Morenoff, and Felton Earls. 1999. "Beyond Social Capital: Spatial Dynamics of Collective Efficacy for Children." *American Sociological Review,* 64:633–660. [Chapter 3]. Investigation of the social mechanisms by which neighborhood structural characteristics influence "collective efficacy" for children. Data are combined from the 1990 Census and a 1995 survey of 8,782 Chicago residents. Residential stability and concentrated affluence were associated with more interaction between children and adults and more interchanges about childrearing among adults. Concentrated disadvantage and proximity to neighborhoods with a high level of disadvantage were associated with lower levels of perceived collective efficacy for children.

Sampson, Robert J., Stephen W. Raudenbush, and Felton Earls. 1997. "Neighborhoods and Violent Crime: A Multilevel Study of Collective Efficacy." *Science,* 277:918–924. [Chapter 6]. A survey-based study of influences on violent crime in Chicago neighborhoods. Collective efficacy was one variable hypothesized to influence the neighborhood crime rate. The variable is a characteristic of the neighborhood but was measured with responses of individual residents to questions about their neighbors' helpfulness and trustworthiness. Neighborhood variation in collective efficacy explained variation in the rate of violent crime between neighborhoods.

Schutt, Russell K. 1986. *Organization in a Changing Environment: Unionization of Welfare Employees.* Albany: State University of New York Press. [Chapter 13]. My study of the development of a public employee union and how it changed over time from a participatory democratic structure to a more bureaucratic form of organization. I surveyed union members and other welfare employees with two mailed questionnaires, observed the delegate meetings of a public-employee union for about 4 years, and content-analyzed union literature. My explanation of union development combined a historical account of the union's development (an idiographic explanation) with survey findings that union members in expanding occupations were less likely than union members in stagnant or shrinking occupations to support a participatory democratic structure (a nomothetic explanation).

Schutt, Russell K., Suzanne Gunston, and John O'Brien. 1992. "The Impact of AIDS Prevention Efforts on AIDS Knowledge and Behavior Among Sheltered Homeless Adults." *Sociological Practice Review,* 3(1):1–7. [Chapter 4]. Interview survey of homeless persons living in shelters to determine what they knew about HIV transmission and AIDS, whether they had been exposed to any prevention activities, and what effect the exposure might have had on their knowledge and on their risk-related behaviors. Respondents were selected from three large shelters using systematic random sampling procedures; one of these shelters had hosted an active AIDS prevention program. There was no association between the average

AIDS knowledge score and exposure to prevention activities. However, exposure to specific prevention activities was associated with more knowledge about the specific risks the activities were designed to reduce.

Sherman, Lawrence W. and Richard A. Berk. 1984. "The Specific Deterrent Effects of Arrest for Domestic Assault." *American Sociological Review,* 49:261–272. [Chapter 2]. A field experiment to determine whether arresting accused abusers on the spot would deter repeat incidents, as predicted by deterrence theory. Police in Minneapolis were randomly assigned domestic assault cases to result either in an arrest, in an order that the offending spouse leave the house for 8 hours, or in some type of verbal advice by the police officers. Accused batterers who were arrested had lower recidivism rates than those who were ordered to leave the house or were just warned. Several replications of this experiment produced different results.

Skoll, Geoffrey R. 1992. *Walk the Walk and Talk the Talk: An Ethnography of a Drug Abuse Treatment Facility.* Philadelphia: Temple University Press. [Chapter 3]. Ethnographic study of a drug abuse treatment facility. Symbolic interaction conceptual framework highlights how the continual threat of punishment engenders distrust and deviance.

Thorne, Barrie. 1993. *Gender Play: Girls and Boys in School.* New Brunswick, NJ: Rutgers University Press. [Chapter 9]. A participant observation study of children's social interaction at two similar public elementary schools in California and Michigan. Thorne took the role of complete observer, after receiving permission from school authorities to observe in classrooms and on playgrounds. The research focused on children's social relations, how they organized and gave meaning to social situations, and how children and adults create and re-create gender in their daily interactions.

Udry, J. Richard. 1988. "Biological Predispositions and Social Control in Adolescent Sexual Behavior." *American Sociological Review,* 53:709–722. [Chapter 3]. Study of 8th-, 9th, and 10th-grade public school students in a southern U.S. city. Students completed questionnaires about their sexual behavior and attitudes and gave blood samples. Both testosterone levels and social variables such as church attendance were related to sexual behavior, but these influences interacted with gender and participation in sports.

U.S. Department of Commerce. 2002. *A Nation Online: How Americans Are Expanding Their Use of the Internet.* Washington, DC: National Telecommunications and Information Administration, Economics and Statistics Administration, U.S. Department of Commerce. [Chapter 1]. Analysis of Internet use based on the U.S. Census Bureau's Current Population Survey of 57,000 households. The analysis documents the rapid growth of Internet use, with half of the nation online in September 2001, and increasing rates across all income ranges. Children and teenagers use computers and the Internet more than any other age group.

Verba, Sidney, Norman Nie, and Jae-On Kim. 1978. *Participation and Political Equality: A Seven-Nation Comparison.* New York: Cambridge University Press. [Chapter 11]. International survey of voting and other forms of political participation. Social status has the strongest, most consistent effect on voting, but ethnicity and other social characteristics can modify this influence.

Wageman, Ruth. 1995. "Interdependence and Group Effectiveness." *Administrative Science Quarterly,* 40:145–180. [Chapter 7]. Quasi-experimental study of effect of task design and reward allocation on work team functioning. More than 800 Xerox service technicians in 152 teams participated. Survey data were collected 1 month prior to the intervention and 4 months after it began. Team performance was influenced positively by management that stressed either interdependence or autonomy, but hybrid management models were associated with poorer team performance.

Wechsler, Henry, Jae Eun Lee, Meichun Kuo, and Hang Lee. 2000. "College Binge Drinking in the 1990s: A Continuing Problem. Results of the Harvard School of Public Health 1999 College Alcohol Study." http://www.hsph.harvard.edu/cas/rpt2000/CAS2000rpt2.html. [Chapter 4]. Survey of students attending colleges throughout the United States about drinking behavior and its consequences. Binge drinking was operationalized in terms of both the quantity of alcohol consumed in one episode and the recency of that episode, with different quantities of alcohol specified for rating men and women as binge drinkers. Of the students, 44% were binge drinkers. The rates of binge drinking varied significantly by college. Students at schools with moderate or high levels of binging were more likely than students at schools with low levels of binging to experience problems that result from the drinking behavior of other students.

Wellman, Barry, Anabel Quan Haase, James Witte, and Keith Hampton. 2001. "Does the Internet Increase, Decrease, or Supplement Social Capital? Social Networks, Participation, and Community Commitment." *American Behavioral Scientist*, 45:436-455. [Chapter 1]. Study of social connections and the Internet using data from the 1998 National Geographic Society Web-based survey. The focus is on 39,211 persons in North America. Findings indicate that people's interaction online supplements their face-to-face and telephone communication without increasing or decreasing it. The authors conclude that the Internet is becoming normalized as it is incorporated into everyday life.

Wells, L. Edward and Joseph H. Rankin. 1991. "Families and Delinquency: A Meta-Analysis of the Impact of Broken Homes." *Social Problems,* 38:71–93. [Chapter 14]. Meta-analysis to test the hypothesis that juveniles from broken homes have higher rates of delinquency than those from homes with intact families. Features and findings of 50 previous studies of this hypothesis were coded. The average effect of broken homes was to increase the likelihood of delinquency by about 10%–15%, but effects varied with the studies' features—primarily with their methods and secondarily with the social characteristics of the people studied.

Whyte, William Foote. 1955. *Street Corner Society.* Chicago: University of Chicago Press. [Chapter 9]. Classic exploratory field research study using participant observation of individuals in a poor Boston community. Whyte lived and socialized in the community, talking with many individuals and participating in a range of activities. He found a corner-gang structure that was relatively independent of the influence of older adults in the community and was based on long-term interaction and a system of mutual obligations.

Appendix B

QUESTIONS TO ASK
ABOUT A RESEARCH ARTICLE

1. What is the basic research question, or problem? Try to state it in just one sentence. (Chapter 2)

2. Is the purpose of the study explanatory, evaluative, exploratory, or descriptive? Did the study have more than one purpose? (Chapter 1)

3. What prior literature was reviewed? Was it relevant to the research problem? To the theoretical framework? Does the literature review appear to be adequate? Are you aware of (or can you locate) any important omitted studies? (Chapter 2)

4. Was a theoretical framework presented? What was it? Did it seem appropriate for the research question addressed? Can you think of a different theoretical perspective that might have been used? (Chapters 2, 3)

5. How well did the study live up to the guidelines for science? Do you need additional information in any areas to evaluate the study? To replicate it? (Chapter 3)

6. Did the study seem consistent with current ethical standards? Were any trade-offs made between different ethical guidelines? Was an appropriate balance struck between adherence to ethical standards and use of the most rigorous scientific practices? (Chapter 2)

7. Were any hypotheses stated? Were these hypotheses justified adequately in terms of the theoretical framework? In terms of prior research? (Chapter 2)

8. What were the independent and dependent variables in the hypothesis or hypotheses? Did these variables reflect the theoretical concepts as intended? What direction of association was hypothesized? Were any other variables identified as potentially important? (Chapter 2)

9. What were the major concepts in the research? How, and how clearly, were they defined? Were some concepts treated as unidimensional that you think might best be thought of as multidimensional? (Chapter 4)

10. Did the instruments used, the measures of the variables, seem valid and reliable? How did the authors attempt to establish this? Could any more have been done in the study to establish measurement validity? (Chapter 4)

11. Was a sample or the entire population of elements used in the study? What type of sample was selected? Was a probability sampling method used? Did the authors think the sample was generally representative of the population from which it was drawn? Do you? How would you evaluate the likely generalizability of the findings to other populations? (Chapter 5)

12. Was the response rate or participation rate reported? Does it appear likely that those who did not respond or participate were markedly different from those who did participate? Why or why not? Did the author(s) adequately discuss this issue? (Chapters 5, 8)

13. What were the units of analysis? Were they appropriate for the research question? If some groups were the units of analysis, were any statements made at any point that are open to the ecological fallacy? If individuals were the units of analysis, were any statements made at any point that suggest reductionist reasoning? (Chapter 6)

14. Was the study design cross-sectional or longitudinal, or did it use both types of data? If the design was longitudinal, what type of longitudinal design was it? Could the longitudinal design have been improved in any way, as by collecting panel data rather than trend data, or by decreasing the dropout rate in a panel design? If cross-sectional data were used, could the research question have been addressed more effectively with longitudinal data? (Chapter 6)

15. Were any causal assertions made or implied in the hypotheses or in subsequent discussion? What approach was used to demonstrate the existence of causal effects? Were all five issues in establishing causal relationships addressed? What, if any, variables were controlled in the analysis to reduce the risk of spurious relationships? Should any other variables have been measured and controlled? How satisfied are you with the internal validity of the conclusions? (Chapter 6)

16. Was an experimental, survey, participant observation, historical comparative or some other research design used? How well was this design suited to the research question posed and the specific hypotheses tested, if any? Why do you suppose the author(s) chose this particular design? How was the design modified in response to research constraints? How was it modified in order to take advantage of research opportunities? (Chapters 7–11)

17. Was this an evaluation research project? If so, which type of evaluation was it? Which design alternatives did it use? (Chapter 10)

18. Was a historical comparative design used? Which type was it? Were problems due to using historical and/or cross-national data addressed? (Chapter 11)

19. Was any attention given to social context? To biological processes? If so, what did this add? If not, would it have improved the study? Explain. (Chapter 3)

20. Summarize the findings. How clearly were statistical and/or qualitative data presented and discussed? Were the results substantively important? (Chapters 12, 13)

21. Did the author(s) adequately represent the findings in the discussion and/or conclusions sections? Were conclusions well grounded in the findings? Are any other interpretations possible? (Chapter 14)

22. Compare the study to others addressing the same research question. Did the study yield additional insights? In what ways was the study design more or less adequate than the design of previous research? (Chapter 14)

23. What additional research questions and hypotheses are suggested by the study's results? What light did the study shed on the theoretical framework used? On social policy questions? (Chapters 2, 3, 14)

Appendix C

HOW TO READ
A RESEARCH ARTICLE

The discussions of research articles throughout the text may provide all the guidance you need to read and critique research on your own. But reading about an article in bits and pieces in order to learn about particular methodologies is not quite the same as reading an article in its entirety in order to learn what the researcher found out. The goal of this appendix is to walk you through an entire research article, answering the review questions introduced in Appendix B. Of course, this is only one article and our "walk" will take different turns than would a review of other articles, but after this review you should feel more confident when reading other research articles on your own.

We will use for this example an article by South and Spitze (1994) on housework in marital and nonmarital households, reprinted on pages C8-C28 of this appendix. It focuses on a topic related to everyone's life experiences as well as to important questions in social theory. Moreover, it is a solid piece of research published in a top journal, the American Sociological Association's *American Sociological Review*.

I have reproduced below each of the article review questions from Appendix C, followed by my answers to them. After each question, I indicate the chapter where the question was discussed and after each answer I cite the article page or pages that I am referring to. You can also follow my review by reading through the article itself and noting my comments.

1. *What is the basic research question, or problem? Try to state it in just one sentence.* (Chapter 2)

The clearest statement of the research question—actually three questions—is that "we seek to determine how men and women in these [six] different situations [defined by marital status and living arrangement] compare in the amounts of time they spend doing housework, whether these differences can be attributed to differences in other social and economic characteristics, and which household tasks account for these differences" (p. 328). Prior to this point, the authors focus in on this research question, distinguishing it from the more general issue of how housework is distributed within marriages and explaining why it is an important research question.

2. *Is the purpose of the study explanatory, evaluative, exploratory, or descriptive? Did the study have more than one purpose?* (Chapter 1)

The problem statement indicates that the study will have both descriptive and explanatory purposes: it will "determine how men and women . . . compare" and then try to explain the differences in housework between them. The literature review that begins on p. 328 also makes it clear that the primary purpose of the research was explanatory, since the authors review previous explanations for gender differences in housework and propose a new perspective (pp. 328–333).

3. *What prior literature was reviewed? Was it relevant to the research problem? To the theoretical framework? Does the literature review appear to be adequate? Are you aware of (or can you locate) any important studies that have been omitted?* (Chapter 2, 3)

Literature is reviewed from the article's first page until the "data and methods" section (pp. 327–333). It all seems relevant to the particular problem as well as to the general theoretical framework. In the first few paragraphs, several general studies are mentioned to help clarify the importance of the research problem (pp. 327–328). In the "models of household labor" section, alternative theoretical perspectives used in other studies are reviewed and the strength of the support for them is noted (pp. 328–330). After identifying the theoretical perspective they will use, the authors then introduce findings from particular studies that are most relevant to their focus on how housework varies with marital status (pp. 330–333). I leave it to you to find out whether any important studies were omitted.

4. *Was a theoretical framework presented? What was it? Did it seem appropriate for the research question addressed? Can you think of a different theoretical perspective that might have been used?* (Chapters 2, 3)

The "gender perspective" is used as a framework for the research (p. 329). This perspective seems very appropriate to the research question addressed because it highlights the importance of examining differences between married and other households. The authors themselves discuss three other theoretical perspectives on the division of household labor that might have been used as a theoretical framework, but identify weaknesses in each of them (pp. 328–329).

5. *How well did the study live up to the guidelines for science? Do you need additional information in any areas to evaluate the study? To replicate it?* (Chapter 3)

It would be best to return to this question after reading the whole article. The study clearly involves a test of ideas against empirical reality as much as that reality could be measured; it was carried out systematically and disclosed, as far as we can tell, fully. Since the authors used an available dataset, others can easily obtain the complete documentation for the study and try to replicate the authors' findings. The authors explicitly note and challenge assumptions made in other theories of the division of housework (p. 329), although they do not clarify their own assumptions as such. Two of their assumptions are that the appropriation of another's work is likely to occur "perhaps only" in heterosexual couple households (p. 329) and that "a woman cannot display love for or subordination to a man through housework when no man is present" (p. 330). The authors also assume that respondents' reports of the hours they have spent on various tasks are reasonably valid (p. 334). These seem to me to be reasonable assumptions, but a moment's reflection should convince you that they are, after all, unproved assumptions that could be challenged. This is not in itself a criticism of the research, since some assumptions must be made in any study. The authors specified the meaning of key terms, as required in scientific research. They also searched for regularities in their data, thus living up to another guideline. A skeptical stance toward current knowledge is apparent in the literature review and in the authors' claim that they have found only "suggestive evidence" for their theoretical perspective (p. 344). They aim clearly to build social theory and encourage others to build on their findings, "to further specify the conditions" (p. 344). The study thus seems to exemplify adherence to basic scientific guidelines and to be very replicable.

6. *Did the study seem consistent with current ethical standards? Were any trade-offs made between different ethical guidelines? Was an appropriate balance struck between adherence to ethical standards and use of the most rigorous scientific practices?* (Chapter 2)

The authors use survey data collected by others and so encounter no ethical problems in their treatment of human subjects. The reporting seems honest and open. Although the research should help inform social policy, the authors' explicit focus is on how their research can inform social theory. This is quite appropriate for research reported in a scientific journal, so there are no particular ethical problems raised about the uses to which the research is put. The original survey used by the authors does not appear at all likely to have violated any ethical guidelines concerning the treatment of human subjects, although it would be necessary to inspect the original research report to evaluate this.

7. *Were any hypotheses stated? Were these hypotheses justified adequately in terms of the theoretical framework? In terms of prior research?* (Chapter 2)

Five primary hypotheses are stated, although they are labeled as "several important contrasts" that are suggested by the "doing gender" approach, rather than as hypotheses. For example, the first hypothesis is that "women in married-couple households [are expected] to spend more time doing housework than women in any other living situation" (p. 330). A more general point is made about variation in housework across household types before these specific hypotheses are introduced. Several more specific hypotheses are then introduced about variations among specific types of households (pp. 330–331). Some questions about patterns of housework in households that have not previously been studied are presented more as speculations than as definite hypotheses (pp. 332–333). Three additional hypotheses are presented concerning the expected effects of the control variables (p. 333).

8. *What were the independent and dependent variables in the hypothesis(es)? Did these variables reflect the theoretical concepts as intended? What direction of association was hypothesized? Were any other variables identified as potentially important?* (Chapter 2)

The independent variable in the first hypothesis is marital status (married versus other); the dependent variable is time spent doing housework. The hypothesis states that more time will be spent by married women than by other women, and it is stated that this expectation is "net of other differences among the household types" (p. 330). Can you identify the variables in the other hypotheses [the second and fourth hypotheses about men just restate the preceding hypotheses for women]? Another variable, gender differences in time spent on housework, is discussed throughout the article, but it is not in itself measured; rather, it is estimated by comparing the aggregate distribution of hours for men and women.

> 9. *What were the major concepts in the research? How, and how clearly, were they defined? Were some concepts treated as unidimensional that you think might best be thought of as multidimensional?* (Chapter 4)

The key concept in the research is that of "doing gender"; it is discussed at length and defined in a way that becomes reasonably clear when it is said that "housework 'produces' gender through the everyday enactment of dominance, submission, and other behaviors symbolically linked to gender" (p. 329). The central concept of housework is introduced explicitly as "a major component of most people's lives" (p. 330), but it is not defined conceptually—presumably because it refers to a widely understood phenomenon. A conceptual definition would have helped to justify the particular operationalization used, and the decision to exclude child care from what is termed housework (p. 334). (A good, practical reason for this exclusion is given in footnote 2.) The concept of housework is treated as multidimensional by distinguishing what are termed "male-typed," "female-typed," and "gender-neutral" tasks (p. 342). Another key concept is that of marital status, which the authors define primarily by identifying its different categories (pp. 330–333).

> 10. *Did the instruments used, the measures of the variables, seem valid and reliable? How did the authors attempt to establish this? Could any more have been done in the study to establish measurement validity?* (Chapter 4)

The measurement of the dependent variable was straightforward, but required respondents to estimate the number of hours per week they spent on various tasks. The authors report that some other researchers have used a presumably more accurate method—time diaries—to estimate time spent on household tasks, and that the results they obtain are very similar to those of the recall method used in their study This increases confidence in the measurement approach used, although it does not in itself establish the validity or reliability of the self-report data. Measures of marital status and other variables involved relatively straightforward questions and do not raise particular concerns about validity The researchers carefully explain in footnotes how they handled missing data.

> 11. *Was a sample or the entire population of elements used in the study? What type of sample was selected? Was a probability sampling method used? Did the authors think the sample was generally representative of the population from which it was drawn? Do you? How would you evaluate the likely generalizability of the findings to other populations?* (Chapter 5)

The sample was a random (probability) sample of families and households. A disproportionate stratified sampling technique was used to ensure the representation of adequate numbers of single-parent families, cohabitors, and other smaller groups that are of theoretical interest (pp. 333–334). The sample is weighted in the analysis to compensate for the disproportionate sampling method and is said to be representative of the U.S. population. The large size of the sample ($N = 11,016$ after cases with missing values were excluded) indicates that the confidence limits around sample statistics will be very small. Do you think the findings could be generalized to other countries with different cultural values about gender roles and housework?

12. *Was the response rate or participation rate reported? Does it appear likely that those who did not respond or participate were markedly different from those who did participate? Why or why not? Did the author(s) adequately discuss this issue?* (Chapters 5, 8)

The response rate was not mentioned—a major omission, although it could be found in the original research report. The authors omitted 2,001 respondents from the obtained sample due to missing data and adjusted values of variables having missing data for some other cases. In order to check the consequences of these adjustments, the authors conducted detailed analyses of the consequences of various adjustment procedures. They report that the procedures they used did not affect their conclusions (pp. 333–334). This seems reasonable.

13. *What were the units of analysis? Were they appropriate for the research question? If some groups were the units of analysis, were any statements made at any point that are open to the ecological fallacy? If individuals were the units of analysis, were any statements made at any point that suggest reductionist reasoning?* (Chapter 6)

The survey sampled adults, although it was termed a survey of families and households; and it is data on individuals (and the households in which they live) that are analyzed. You can imagine this same study being conducted with households forming the units of analysis, and the dependent variable being the percentage of total time in the family spent on housework, rather than the hours spent by individuals on housework. The conclusions generally are appropriate to the use of individuals as the units of analysis, but there is some danger in reductionist misinterpretation of some of the interpretations, such as that "men and women must be 'doing gender' when they live together" (p. 344). Conclusions like this would be on firmer ground if they were based on household-level data that revealed whether one person's approach to housework did, in fact, vary in relation to that of his or her partner.

14. *Was the study design cross-sectional or longitudinal, or did it use both types of data? If the design was longitudinal, what type of longitudinal design was it? Could the longitudinal design have been improved in any way, as by collecting panel data rather than trend data, or by decreasing the dropout rate in a panel design? If cross-sectional data were used, could the research question have been addressed more effectively with longitudinal data?* (Chapter 6)

The survey was cross-sectional. The research question certainly could have been addressed more effectively with longitudinal data that followed people over their adult lives, since many of the authors' interpretations reflect their interest in how individuals' past experiences with housework shape their approach when they enter a new marital status (pp. 344–345).

15. *Were any causal assertions made or implied in the hypotheses or in subsequent discussion? What approach was used to demonstrate the existence of causal effects? Were all five issues in establishing causal relationships addressed? What, if any, variables were controlled in the analysis to reduce the risk of spurious relationships? Should any other variables have been measured and controlled? How satisfied are you with the internal validity of the conclusions?* (Chapter 6)

The explanatory hypotheses indicate that the authors were concerned with causality. Mention is made of a possible causal mechanism when it is pointed out that "doing gender"—the presumed causal influence—may operate at both unconscious and conscious levels (p. 329). In order to reduce the risk of spuriousness in the presumed causal relationship (between marital status and housework time), variables such as age, education, earnings, and the presence of children are controlled (p. 335). There are, of course, other variables that might have created a spurious relationship, but at least several of the most likely contenders have been controlled. For example, the use of cross-sectional data leaves us wondering whether some of the differences attributed to marital status might really be due to generational differences—the never-married group is likely to be younger and the widowed group older; controlling for age gives us more confidence that this is not the case. On the other hand, the lack of longitudinal data means that we do not know whether the differences in housework might have preceded marital status: perhaps women who got married also did more housework even before they were married than women who remained single.

16. *Was an experimental, survey, participant observation, or some other research design used? How well was this design suited to the research question posed and the specific hypotheses tested, if any? Why do you suppose the author(s) chose this particular design? How was the design modified in response to research constraints? How was it modified in order to take advantage of research opportunities?* (Chapters 7–11)

Survey research was the method of choice, and probably was used for this article because the dataset was already available for analysis. Survey research seems appropriate for the research questions posed, but the limitation of the survey to one point in time was a major constraint (p. 333).

17. *Was this an evaluation research project? If so, which type of evaluation was it? Which design alternatives did it use?* (Chapter 10)

This study did not use an evaluation research design. The issues on which it focuses might profitably be studied in some program evaluations.

18. *Was a historical comparative design used? Which type was it? Were problems due to using historical and/or cross-national data addressed?* (Chapter 11)

This study did not use any type of historical or comparative design. It is interesting to consider how the findings might have differed if comparisons to other cultures or to earlier times had been made.

19. *Was any attention given to social context? To biological processes? If so, what did this add? If not, would it have improved the study? Explain.* (Chapter 3)

In a sense, the independent variable in this study *is* social context: the combinations of marital status and living arrangements distinguish different social contexts in which gender roles are defined. However, no attention is given to the potential importance of larger social contexts, such as neighborhood, region, or nation. It is also possible to imagine future research that tests the influence of biological factors on the household division of labor, as in Udry's (1988) study of adolescents.

20. *Summarize the findings. How clearly were statistical and/or qualitative data presented and discussed? Were the results substantively important?* (Chapters 12, 13)

Statistical data are presented clearly using descriptive statistics (multiple regression analysis (a multivariate statistical technique), and graphs that highlight the most central findings. In fact, the data displays are exemplary, because they effectively convey findings to a wide audience and also subject the hypotheses to rigorous statistical tests. No qualitative data are presented. The findings seem substantively important, since they identify large differences in the household roles of men and women and in how these roles vary in different types of household (pp. 336–343).

21. *Did the author(s) adequately represent the findings in the discussion and/or conclusions sections? Were conclusions well grounded in the findings? Are any other interpretations possible?* (Chapter 14)

The findings are well represented in the discussion and conclusions section (pp. 343–345). The authors point out in their literature review that a constant pattern of gender differences in housework across household types would "cast doubt on the validity of the gender perspective" (p. 330), and the findings clearly rule this out. However, the conclusions give little consideration to the ways in which the specific findings might be interpreted as consistent or inconsistent with reasonable predictions from each of the three other theoretical perspectives reviewed. You might want to consider yourself what other interpretations of the findings might be possible. Remember that other interpretations always are possible for particular findings—it is a question of the weight of the evidence, the persuasiveness of the theory used, and the consistency of the findings with other research.

22. *Compare the study to others addressing the same research question. Did the study yield additional insights? In what ways was the study design more or less adequate than the design of previous research?* (Chapter 14)

The study investigated an aspect of the question of gender differences in housework that had not previously received much attention (variation in gender differences across different types of household). This helped the authors to gain additional insights into gender and housework, although the use of cross-sectional data and a retrospective self-report measure of housework made their research in some ways less adequate than others.

23. *What additional research questions and hypotheses are suggested by the study's results? What light did the study shed on the theoretical framework used? On social policy questions?* (Chapter 2, 3, 14)

The article suggests additional questions for study about "the conditions under which [the dynamics of doing gender] operate" and how equity theory might be used to explain the division of labor in households (p. 344). The authors make a reasonable case for the value of their "gender perspective." Social policy questions are not addressed directly, but the article would be of great value to others concerned with social policy.

HOUSEWORK IN MARITAL AND NONMARITAL HOUSEHOLDS*

SCOTT J. SOUTH   GLENNA SPITZE
State University of New York at Albany   *State University of New York at Albany*

Although much recent research has explored the division of household labor between husbands and wives, few studies have examined housework patterns across marital statuses. This paper uses data from the National Survey of Families and Households to analyze differences in time spent on housework by men and women in six different living situations: never married and living with parents, never married and living independently, cohabiting, married, divorced, and widowed. In all situations, women spend more time than men doing housework, but the gender gap is widest among married persons. The time women spend doing housework is higher among cohabitants than among the never-married, is highest in marriage, and is lower among divorcees and widows. Men's housework time is very similar across both never-married living situations, in cohabitation, and in marriage. However, divorced and widowed men do substantially more housework than does any other group of men, and they are especially more likely than their married counterparts to spend more time cooking and cleaning. In addition to gender and marital status, housework time is affected significantly by several indicators of workload (e.g., number of children, home ownership) and time devoted to nonhousehold activities (e.g., paid employment, school enrollment)—most of these variables have greater effects on women's housework time than on men's. An adult son living at home increases women's housework, whereas an adult daughter at home reduces housework for women and men. These housework patterns are generally consistent with an emerging perspective that views housework as a symbolic enactment of gender relations. We discuss the implications of these findings for perceptions of marital equity.

Until 20 years ago, social science research on housework was largely nonexistent (Glazer-Malbin 1976; Huber and Spitze 1983), but since then, research on the topic has exploded. Patterns of housework and how housework is experienced by participants have been documented in both qualitative (e.g., Hochschild with Machung 1989; Oakley 1974) and quantitative studies (e.g., Berk 1985; Blair and Lichter 1991; Coverman and Sheley 1986; Goldscheider and Waite 1991; Rexroat and Shehan 1987; Ross 1987; Shelton 1990; Spitze 1986; Walker and Woods 1976). The vast majority of these studies have focused on married couples, but a few have examined cohabiting couples as well (e.g., Blumstein and Schwartz 1983; Shelton and John 1993; Stafford, Backman, and Dibona 1977). The rationale for focusing on couples is typically a research interest in equity (Benin and Agostinelli 1988; Blair and Johnson 1992; Ferree 1990; Peterson and Maynard 1981; Thompson 1991) and in how changes in women's employment and gender roles have changed, or failed to change, household production functions.

Very few studies have examined housework as performed in noncouple households composed of never-married, separated or divorced, or widowed persons (e.g., Grief 1985; Sanik and Mauldin 1986). Such studies are important for two reasons. First, people are spending increasing amounts of time in such households at various points in their lives due to postponed marriages, higher divorce rates, and a preference among adults in all age categories (including the later years) for independent living. For example, the proportion of households that includes married couples decreased from 76.3 percent to 60.9 percent between 1940 and 1980 (Sweet and Bumpass 1987), and the number of years adult women spend married has decreased by about seven years during the past several decades (Watkins, Menken, and Bon-

*Direct all correspondence to Scott J. South or Glenna Spitze, Department of Sociology, State University of New York at Albany, Albany, NY 12222. The authors contributed equally to this research and are listed alphabetically. We acknowledge with gratitude the helpful comments of several anonymous *ASR* reviewers.

gaarts 1987). It is important to learn how housework is experienced by this substantial segment of the population to understand the household production function in general and because performance of housework is related to decisions about paid work and leisure time for people in these categories.

Second, the housework experiences of single, divorced, and widowed persons go with them if they move into marriage or cohabitation—these experiences are part of the context in which they negotiate how to accomplish tasks jointly with a partner. People may use those prior experiences or assumptions about what they *would* do if the marriage or cohabiting relationship dissolved to set an alternative standard when assessing an equitable division of household labor, rather than simply comparing their own investment in housework to their partner's. Thus, by understanding factors affecting housework contributions by men and women not living in couple relationships, we can better understand what happens when they do form those relationships.

Our broadest objective in this paper is to analyze how time spent doing housework by men and women varies by marital status and to interpret this analysis in relation to the "gender perspective" on household labor. Focusing on six situations defined by marital status and living arrangement, we seek to determine how men and women in these different situations compare in the amounts of time they spend doing housework, whether these differences can be attributed to differences in other social and economic characteristics, and which household tasks account for these differences. We are particularly interested in those persons who are living independently and who are not married or cohabiting, since previous research has focused heavily on married persons and, to a lesser extent, on cohabiting couples (Shelton and John 1993; Stafford et al. 1977) and children still living at home (Benin and Edwards 1990; Berk 1985; Blair 1991; Goldscheider and Waite 1991; Hilton and Haldeman 1991).

MODELS OF HOUSEHOLD LABOR

Beginning with Blood and Wolfe's (1960) classic study, sociologists have attempted to explain the division of household labor between husbands and wives and to determine whether the division is changing over time. The *re-source-power perspective* originating in that work focuses on the economic and social contexts in which husbands and wives bring their individual resources (such as unequal earnings) to bear in bargaining over who will do which household chores. This resource-power theory has since been modified and elaborated upon in several ways, focusing on determining which resources are important and the conditions under which they are useful for bargaining. Rodman's (1967) theory of resources in cultural context and Blumberg and Coleman's (1989) theory of gender stratification (as applied to housework) suggest that there are limits on how effectively resources can be used, especially by women. Several observers suggest that wives' resources may be "discounted" by male dominance at the societal level (Aytac and Teachman 1992; Blumberg and Coleman 1989; Ferree 1991b; Gillespie 1971).

Two other perspectives are used frequently in the study of household labor. One focuses on *socialization and gender role attitudes*, suggesting that husbands and wives perform household labor in differing amounts depending upon what they have learned and have come to believe about appropriate behavior for men and women (see Goldscheider and Waite 1991). An alternative perspective, the *time availability hypothesis*, suggests that husbands and wives perform housework in amounts relative to the time left over after paid work time is substracted. A variation on this, the demand response capability hypothesis (Coverman 1985), is somewhat broader and includes factors that increase the total amount of work to be done and spouses' availability to do it. The focus on time allocation as a rational process is akin to the economic perspective, most closely associated with Becker (1981; see also critique in Berk 1985). However, sociologists and economists differ in their views on this perspective: Economists assume that time allocation to housework and paid work is jointly determined and based on the relative efficiency of husbands and wives in both arenas; sociologists assume that decisions about paid work are causally prior (Godwin 1991; Spitze 1986).

The above three perspectives (power-resources, socialization-gender roles, and time availability) have guided much of the sociological research on household labor over the past 20 years (see reviews of these theories and their variations in Ferree 1991a; Godwin 1991; Shelton 1992; Spitze 1988). However, they have produced mixed results, and, as several reviewers have pointed out, much more variance is explained by gender per se than by any of the other factors in these models (Ferree 1991a; Thompson and Walker 1991). Moreover, studies show that women who earn more than their husbands often do a disproportionate share of the housework, perhaps in an attempt to prevent those earnings from threatening the husband's self-esteem (Thompson and Walker 1991). While both husbands' and wives' time in paid employment does affect the time they spend doing housework (Goldscheider and Waite 1991), it is argued that the basic distribution of household labor calls for an explanation of its gendered, asymmetrical nature (Thompson and Walker 1991).

A new direction in the explanation of household labor originates in West and Zimmerman's (1987) concept of "doing gender." They argue that gender can be understood as "a routine accomplishment embedded in everyday interaction" (1987:125). Berk (1985) applied their perspective to the division of household labor, observing that the current situation among husbands and wives is neither inherently rational (as the New Home Economics had argued; see Becker 1981) nor fair. Thus, Berk concludes that more than goods and services are "produced" through household labor. She describes the marital household as a "gender factory" where, in addition to accomplishing tasks, housework "produces" gender through the everyday enactment of dominance, submission, and other behaviors symbolically linked to gender (Berk 1985; see also Hartmann 1981; Shelton and John 1993).

Ferree (1991a) elaborates on the "gender perspective" and its application to household labor and argues that it challenges three assumptions of resource theory. First, as Berk pointed out in her critique of economic analyses of housework, housework is not allocated in the most efficient manner. Second, gender is more influential than individual resources in determining the division of household labor. And third, housework is not necessarily defined as "bad" and to be avoided. On the contrary, in addition to expressing subordination, housework can also express love and care, particularly for women (Ferree 1991a). Relatedly, DeVault (1989) describes in detail how the activities surrounding the planning and prepara-

tion of meals are viewed not only as labor but also as an expression of love. In support of the general argument that housework has important symbolic meanings, Ferree (1991a) points out that "housework-like chores are imposed in other institutions to instill discipline" (p. 113), such as KP in the army.

The process of "doing gender" is not assumed to operate at a conscious level; on the contrary, Berk (1985) points out that it goes on "without much notice being taken" (p. 207). Ferree (1991a) finds it "striking how little explicit conflict there is over housework in many families" (p. 113). Hochschild's (with Machung 1989) pathbreaking study shows how gender ideologies are enacted through the performance of housework and may operate in a contradictory manner at conscious and unconscious levels. She discovers through in-depth case studies that people's ideas about gender are often "fractured and incoherent" (p. 190) and that contradictions abound between what people say they believe, what they seem to feel, and how these beliefs and feelings are reflected in their household behavior.

This developing "doing gender" approach suggests several important contrasts between couple households (especially those of married couples) and other household types. Indeed, one could argue that *only* by examining a range of household types, including those *not* formed by couples, can one determine the usefulness of this explanation for the behavior of married or cohabiting persons. If gender is being "produced," one would expect this process to be more important in heterosexual couple households than in other household types—there would be less need or opportunity for either men or women to display dominance and subordination or other gender-linked behaviors when they are not involved in conjugal relations. Berk (1985) argues that "in households where the appropriation of *another's* work is possible, in practice the expression of work and the expression of gender become inseparable" (p. 204). Of course, we recognize that gender role socialization is likely to produce gender differentials, even among unmarried persons. However, this *appropriation* seems likely to occur mainly, or perhaps only, in heterosexual couple households, particularly when the couples are married. Berk observes a sharp contrast in the housework patterns of married couples versus same-sex roommate arrangements, the latter seeming "so uncomplicated" to respondents (1985:204).

If heterosexual couples indeed produce gender through performing housework, we would expect women in married-couple households to spend more time doing housework than women in any other living situation; we would expect men's time spent doing housework to be lower in married-couple households than in other household types. These expectations are net of other differences between the household types, such as the presence of children, that affect housework. We would expect women to display submission to and/or love for their husbands or male partners by performing a disproportionate share of the housework, whereas men would display their gender/dominance by avoiding housework that they might perform in other household settings—in particular female-typed housework that constitutes the vast majority of weekly housework time in households. Because a woman cannot display love for or subordination to a man through housework when no man is present, this avenue for displaying gender does not exist in one-adult households. Thus, we would predict smaller gender differences in noncouple than couple household settings once other relevant factors are controlled.

An alternative empirical outcome—one that would cast doubt on the validity of the gender perspective—would be a pattern across household type involving a more or less constant gender difference. We know that there is a gender gap in time spent doing housework between married men and women and between teenage boys and girls. We do not know, however, whether that gap is constant across other situations. If, for example, gender differences in childhood training produce standards or skill levels that vary with gender, one might argue that men and women would carry these attitudes or behaviors with them as they move among different household situations.

HOUSEWORK AND MARITAL STATUS

Housework is a major component of most people's lives, just as is paid work. It is first experienced in childhood as "chores" and continues into retirement. Yet, while housework is performed prior to marriage and after its dissolution, most studies of household labor focus exclusively on husbands and wives. This tends to create the false impression that housework occurs only within marital households.

Our analysis of housework is based on a categorization by marital status. We focus on men and women who have *never married*, or are currently *married, divorced,* or *widowed*. However, because a key aspect of our theoretical argument focuses on gender relations in heterosexual households, we add a "cohabiting" category, which includes persons who are currently cohabiting whether or not they have ever been married, divorced, or widowed. Further, the situation of never-married persons (who are not cohabiting) varies greatly depending upon whether they are *living independently* or *living in a parental household*; thus we divide never-married persons into two groups based on living situation. In the sections below, we review studies of housework performed by persons in each of these six categories.

Never-Married Persons Living in Their Parents' Homes

The performance of household chores is one of many gender-differentiated socialization experiences gained in families of origin. A number of studies have examined housework performed by boys and girls up to the age of 18 who are living with their parents. These studies have focused on three kinds of questions: how parents define the meaning of housework (White and Brinkerhoff 1981a), how children's contributions relate to or substitute for mothers' or fathers' work (Berk 1985; Goldscheider and Waite 1991), and how housework varies by the gender of the child, mother's employment, and number of parents in the household (e.g., Benin and Edwards 1990; Blair 1991; Hilton and Haldeman 1991).

Housework done by boys and by girls mirrors that of adults, with girls doing stereotypical "female" chores and spending more time doing housework than boys (Benin and Edwards 1990; Berk 1985; Blair 1991; Goldscheider and Waite 1991; Hilton and Haldeman 1991; Timmer, Eccles, and O'Brien 1985; White and Brinkerhoff 1981b). Patterns by gender and age suggest that, under certain conditions, children (particularly older girls) actually assist their parents. Gender differences increase with age, so that in the teenage years girls are spending about twice as much time per week as boys doing housework (Timmer et al.

1985), and the gender-stereotyping of tasks is at a peak. This pattern holds even in single-father families, where one might expect less traditional gender-typed behavior (Grief 1985). Adolescent girls' housework time has been shown to substitute for that of their mothers, while boys' housework time does not (Bergen 1991; Goldscheider and Waite 1991). Differences between single-parent and two-parent families also suggest more actual reliance on girls' work: Boys in single-parent households do less housework than do boys in two-parent households, while girls in single-parent households do more (Hilton and Haldeman 1991). Similar differences have been found between single- and dual-earner two-parent families. Again, girls do more when parents' time is constrained (dual earners) while boys do less, suggesting that parents actually rely on girls to substitute for their mothers' time doing housework (Benin and Edwards 1990).

One would expect parallel differences in the behavior of young adult men and women who still live with their parents. To our knowledge, only three studies have examined housework performed by adult children living in parental households. Ward, Logan, and Spitze (1992) find that adult children living with parents perform only a small proportion of total household tasks when compared to their parents, and parents whose adult children do not live at home actually perform fewer household tasks per month than do parents whose adult children live with them. There are also major differences between adult sons and adult daughters in the amount of housework they do, with daughters performing more tasks than sons when they live in a parent's home. This holds for all parent age groups, particularly those under 65. These gender differences are consistent with results on adult children's share of household tasks reported by Goldscheider and Waite (1991). Hartung and Moore (1992) report qualitative findings that are consistent with the conclusion that adult children, especially sons, contribute little to household chores and typically add to their mothers' burdens.

Never-Married Persons Living Independently

We know of no empirical research that focuses specifically on never-married persons living independently, so we will speculate briefly about factors affecting them. One likely consequence of experiences with housework in the parental home is that girls acquire the skills required for independent living, including shopping, cooking, cleaning, and laundry. To the extent that they have already been doing significant amounts of housework at home, girls' transitions to independent living may not create a major change in the amount or types of housework they perform. The skills boys are more likely to learn in the parental home (e.g., yard work) may be less useful, particularly if their first independent living experience is in an apartment. They may reach adulthood enjoying housework less than women, feeling less competent at household tasks, holding lower standards of performance, embracing gender-stereotyped attitudes about appropriateness of tasks, and preferring to pay for substitutes (e.g., laundry, meals eaten out). On the other hand, single men living independently (and not cohabiting) are forced, to a certain extent, to do their own housework (Goldscheider and Waite 1991), because their living situations are unlikely to provide household services. Thus, the time spent by single men doing housework should increase when they move out of parental households.

Cohabiters

Cohabiting couples share some characteristics of both married and single persons (Shelton and John 1993; Stafford et al. 1977). As Rindfuss and VandenHeuvel (1992) point out, most discussions have used married persons as the comparison group, viewing cohabitation as an alternative kind of marriage or engagement. The division of household labor between cohabiters may be closer to that of married persons, but in other areas such as fertility plans, employment, school enrollment, and home ownership, cohabiters more closely resemble single persons (Rindfuss and VandenHeuvel 1992). Thus, we would expect cohabiters to fall at an intermediate position, between never-married living independently and married persons, in the allocation of time to housework.

A few empirical studies have examined housework by heterosexual cohabiting couples. One early study (Stafford et al. 1977) uses a relative contribution measure of housework and finds cohabiting couples to be fairly "traditional" in their division of household labor. A more recent study using an absolute measure of time expenditure in housework (Shelton and John 1993) sheds more light on the comparison between cohabiting and married couples. Adjusted means of time spent doing housework for cohabiting men are not significantly different from those for married men, but cohabiting women do less housework than do married women. These results are consistent with Blumstein and Schwartz's (1983) comparisons of married and cohabiting men and women. Blair and Lichter (1991) find no significant differences between married and cohabiting men's housework time, but find less task segregation by gender among cohabitants. As is true of comparisons on other dimensions (Rindfuss and VandenHeuvel 1992), studies of housework among cohabiting couples have used married persons as the comparison group, and there have been few comparisons of housework patterns in cohabiting relationships to patterns in other marital statuses.

Married Persons

Marriage often entails a number of changes that increase housework, including parenthood and home ownership, but it also might increase housework for less tangible reasons. Marriage and parenthood entail responsibility for the well-being of others, which is likely to be reflected in higher standards of cleanliness and nutrition, and thus require that more time be devoted to housework. However, the net result of this increase in total work is different for men and for women, and this gender division of household labor has been the subject of much research and theorizing in recent years. Averages tend to range widely depending on the definitions of housework used, but women generally report performing over 70 percent of total housework, even if they are employed (Bergen 1991; Ferree 1991a). One recent study reported married women (including nonemployed) doing 40 hours of housework per week and men 19 hours (Shelton and John 1993), and countless studies have documented that wives' employment has little effect on married men's housework load (see reviews in Spitze 1988; Thompson and Walker 1991). Clearly, wives are responsible for the vast bulk of household chores and for maintaining standards of cleanliness and health in the family. Married men have been described as doing less

housework than they create (Hartmann 1981). Further, when they do contribute to household chores, men are more likely to take on those jobs which are more pleasant, leaving women with those than can be described as "unrelenting, repetitive, and routine" (Thompson and Walker 1991:86). Thus, past empirical results for married persons are consistent with the gender perspective, but comparative analyses that include persons in other marital statuses are needed.

Divorced Persons

To our knowledge there have been no studies of the time divorced persons spend doing housework except those studies focusing on children's housework. Divorced persons (who are not cohabiting) have had the prior experience of living with a heterosexual partner. Women may experience a decrease in housework hours if in fact their partner was creating more housework than he was doing. Men's experience, on the other hand, may be similar to that of moving out of the parental household, that is, of having to do some household tasks for themselves that were previously performed by others. Those who never lived independently before may have to do some of these chores for the first time. Gove and Shin (1989) point out that both divorced and widowed men have more difficulty carrying out their daily household routines than do their female counterparts, who are more likely to experience economic strains.

Widowed Persons

In empirical studies, housework has been identified as an important source of strain for widowed men. Widowed men reduce the time they spend doing housework as the years since widowhood pass, and they are more likely than widows to have help doing it as time goes on (Umberson, Wortman, and Kessler 1992). Of course, today's widows and widowers came of age when the gendered division of labor in households was much more segregated than it is today and when living independently before or between marriages was much less common. While we expect widowed men today to have entered widowhood with relatively little experience in certain kinds of household chores, this may not be true in the future.

Widowed women may share some characteristics with divorced women; they may actually feel some relief from the strain of doing the bulk of household tasks for two (Umberson et al. 1992). Like widowed men, however, current cohorts of widowed women may have little experience in certain kinds of chores, in this case traditionally male chores such as yard work, car care, or financial management.

Other Factors Influencing Time Doing Housework

Men and women in different marital statuses are likely to differ on a variety of factors that can influence the performance of housework, such as their health, employment status, presence of children and other adults, and home ownership. We would expect the performance of housework to vary by marital status both because of these factors and because of the ways in which the marital status itself (or experience in a previous status) influences housework behavior. Here, we describe a model of time spent in housework that can be applied to persons in all marital situations. This model will then guide us in choosing control variables for the analysis of housework.

A person is expected to spend more time in housework as the *total amount to be done* increases. (Berk [1985] calls this the total "pie" in her study of married couple households.) We would expect the amount of housework to increase as the number of children increases, particularly when children are young, but to some extent for older children as well (Bergen 1991; Berk 1985; Ishii-Kuntz and Coltrane 1992; Rexroat and Shehan 1987). The amount of work will also increase with the addition of adults to the household, although of course they may perform housework as well. Work may also increase with the size of house and the responsibilities that go with home ownership, car ownership, and presence of a yard (Bergen 1991; Berk 1985).[1]

Note that the total housework to be done is to some extent a subjective concept. Two households with the same composition and type of home may accomplish different amounts of housework for several reasons. The standards held by the adults in the household will vary (Berk 1985) and may even vary systematically along dimensions such as education and age. Also, some households purchase more services than others, due to available income (Bergen 1991) and time constraints.

A second factor influencing the amount of housework a person does is the number of *other people* there are in the household with whom to share the work. Other people are most helpful if they are adults, and women are likely to contribute more than men. Teenagers and even grade-school-age children may be helpful, and their contribution may also vary by gender. The way that household labor is divided, and thus the amount performed by a particular man or woman, may also relate to gender-role attitudes that may vary with education, age, race, and other factors.

Third, persons with more *time and energy* will do more housework. Available time would be limited by hours spent in paid work, school enrollment status, health and disability status, and age (Coltrane and Ishii-Kuntz 1992; Ishii-Kuntz and Coltrane 1992; Rexroat and Shehan 1987). Concurrent roles, in addition to that of homemaker, detract from the time available to be devoted to housework.

DATA AND METHODS

Data for this study are drawn from the National Survey of Families and Households (NSFH), a national probability sample of 13,017 adults interviewed between March of 1987 and May of 1988 (Sweet, Bumpass, and Call 1988). The NSFH includes a wide variety of questions on sociodemographic background, household composition, labor force behavior, and marital and cohabitation experiences, as well as items describing respondents' allocation of time to household tasks. The NSFH oversamples single-parent families and cohabiters (as well as minorities and recently married persons), thus facilitating comparisons of household labor among persons in different—and relatively rare—household situations. Sample weights are used throughout the

---

[1] While owning appliances would be expected to decrease time spent doing housework, it has had much less clear-cut effects than expected, both over time and in cross-sectional studies (Gershuny and Robinson 1988).

analysis to achieve the proper representation of respondents in the U.S. population.

The dependent variable, hours devoted to housework in the typical week, is derived from a series of questions asking respondents how many hours household members spend on various tasks. Respondents were provided with a chart and instructed: "Write in the approximate number of hours per week that you, your spouse/partner, or others in the household normally spend doing the following things." Nine household tasks include "preparing meals," "washing dishes and cleaning up after meals," "cleaning house," "outdoor and other household maintenance tasks (lawn and yard work, household repair, painting, etc.)," "shopping for groceries and other household goods," "washing, ironing, mending," "paying bills and keeping financial records," "automobile maintenance and repair," and "driving other household members to work, school, or other activities." This analysis uses only the number of hours that the respondents report *themselves* as spending on these tasks. To construct the dependent variable, we sum the number of hours spent on each of the nine tasks.[2]

We make two adjustments to this dependent variable. First, because a few respondents reported spending inordinate numbers of hours on specific tasks, we recode values above the 95th percentile for each task to the value at that percentile. This adjustment reduces skewness in the individual items and therefore in the summed variable as well. Second, so we can include respondents who omit one or two of the nine questionnaire items, we impute values for the household tasks for these respondents.[3] In-

dividuals who failed to respond to more than two of the questions are excluded from the analysis. Omitting these respondents and excluding cases with missing values on the independent variables leaves 11,016 respondents available for analysis.

Given our focus on differences in housework between unmarried and married persons, it is essential that the dependent variable records the absolute number of hours devoted to housework rather than the proportional distribution of hours (or tasks) performed by various household members (e.g., Waite and Goldscheider 1992; Spitze 1986). Of course, estimates of time spent on household tasks made by respondents (as recorded in the NSFH) are likely to be less accurate than estimates from time diaries (for a review of validity studies dealing with time use, see Gershuny and Robinson 1988). Yet, estimates of the relative contribution of wives and husbands to household labor are generally comparable across different reporting methods (Warner 1986). Moreover, the effects of respondent characteristics on the time spent on housework shown here are quite similar to the effects observed in time diary studies. The size of the NSFH (approximately five times larger than the typical time-use survey), its oversampling of atypical marital statuses, and its breadth of coverage of respondent characteristics adequately compensate for the lack of time-diary data.

The key explanatory variable combines respondents' marital status' with aspects of their

---

[2] The research literature on housework is inconsistent regarding the inclusion of time spent in childcare. Many data sets commonly used to analyze household labor do not include childcare in their measure (e.g., Bergen 1991; Rexroat and Shehan 1987) or, as is the case here, childcare time is not included as a separate task (Coltrane and Ishii-Kuntz 1992), in part because respondents have difficulty separating time spent in childcare from leisure and from time spent in other tasks. Thus, we are not able to include childcare in our measure. This probably creates a downward bias in estimates of household labor time.

[3] The NSFH assigns four different codes to the household task items for respondents who did not give a numerical reply: some unspecified amount of time spent; inapplicable; don't know; and no answer. Our imputation procedure substitutes a value of 0 for

those who did not answer this question (but answered at least seven of the nine items) or who said the task was inapplicable. In the former case, skipping the item most likely indicates that the respondent spent no time on that task; in the latter case, the respondent most likely could not logically spend time on that task (e.g., persons without cars could not spend any time maintaining them). For respondents who indicated spending some unspecified amount of time on a task and for those who indicated they didn't know, our imputation procedure substitutes the mean value for that task. In both of these instances, respondents presumably spent at least some time on that task. Our explorations of alternative ways of handling missing data, including omitting respondents who failed to answer one or more of the questions, treating all nonnumerical responses as 0, and substituting all nonnumerical responses with the mean, showed quite clearly that our substantive conclusions are unaffected by the method used to handle missing data.

living arrangements. (For stylistic convenience, we refer to this variable simply as marital status.) We distinguish six mutually exclusive statuses: never married and living in the parental household, never married (not cohabiting) and living independently, cohabiting, currently married, divorced or separated (not cohabiting), and widowed (not cohabiting). Because we are interested in the impact of a spouse or partner on respondents' time doing housework, cohabiters include divorced, separated, and widowed cohabiters as well as never-married cohabiters.

The other explanatory variables measure respondents' demographic background, socioeconomic standing, household composition, concurrent roles, and disability status. As suggested above, several of these factors may help explain any differences that we observe in housework time by marital status and gender. *Age* is measured in years. Because housework demands are likely to peak during the middle adult years and to moderate at older ages, we also include *age squared* as an independent variable. *Education* is measured by years of school completed. *Household earnings* refers to the wage, salary, and self-employment income of all members of the household.[4] *Home ownership* is a dummy variable scored 1 for respondents who own their own home and 0 for those who do not.

Several variables reflect the presence in the household of persons who may create or perform housework. *Children* in the household are

divided into the number of children younger than 5 years old, the number age 5 through 11, and the number age 12 through 18. Among the latter group, girls might be expected to create less (or perform more) housework than boys (Goldscheider and Waite 1991), and thus we include separate counts of male and female teenagers. We use several dummy variables to indicate the presence in the household of an *adult male* or *adult female* other than the respondent's spouse or cohabiting partner. Adult females are expected to reduce respondent's time devoted to housework, while adult males are expected to increase it. We further distinguish between adult household members who are the children of the respondent and those who are not.

Respondents who invest their time in activities outside the home are anticipated to devote less time to domestic labor. Employment status is measured by the usual number of *hours worked per week* in the labor force. And, whether the respondent is currently *attending school* is indicated by a dummy variable scored 1 for currently enrolled respondents and 0 for those not attending school.

Finally, *disability status* is measured by the response to the question, do you "have a physical or mental condition that limits your ability to do day-to-day household tasks?" Individuals reporting such a condition are scored 1 on this dummy variable; unimpaired respondents are scored 0.[5]

Our primary analytic strategy is to estimate OLS regression equations that examine the impact of gender, marital status, and the other explanatory variables on the time spent doing housework. Of particular importance for our theoretical model is whether marital status differences in housework time vary by gender—that is, do gender and marital status interact in affecting time spent doing housework? The "gender perspective" implies that marital status differences in housework will be more pronounced for women than for men and that the gender differences in housework will be greatest for married persons. The regression models are also used to determine the extent to which marital status differences in time doing

---

[4] So as not to lose an inordinate number of cases to missing data, we substituted the mean for missing values on household earnings, and we included a dummy variable for these respondents in the regression models (coefficients not shown). One potential difficulty with this procedure is that all respondents who were not the householder or the spouse of the householder receive the mean value, because respondents were not asked the earnings of other household members. Equations estimated only with respondents who are householders revealed effects almost identical to those reported in the text, although never-married respondents living in the parental household are necessarily excluded from these equations. Given that households with adult children include more adults than other households, the household earnings of these latter respondents are likely to be higher than average, but any bias in the effect of earnings is apt to be slight. With one exception (see footnote 5), the amount of missing data on the other explanatory variables is small.

[5] To retain the 5 percent of respondents who did not reply to the question on disability status, the regression equations also include a dummy variable for these respondents (coefficients not shown).

Table 1. Descriptive Statistics for Hours Spent in Housework per Week and for Explanatory Variables, by Gender: U.S. Men and Women, 1987 to 1988

Variable	Women		Men	
	Mean	Standard Deviation	Mean	Standard Deviation
Housework hours per week	32.62	18.18	18.14	12.88
Marital Status[a]				
Never married/living in parental home	.06	.23	.11	.32
Never married/living independently	.10	.30	.11	.32
Cohabiting	.04	.19	.04	.20
Married	.57	.50	.63	.48
Divorced/separated	.12	.33	.08	.26
Widowed	.12	.33	.03	.17
Number of children ages 0 to 4	.26	.59	.22	.55
Number of children ages 5 to 11	.33	.70	.29	.66
Number of girls ages 12 to 18	.16	.44	.15	.43
Number of boys ages 12 to 18	.17	.45	.15	.43
Adult male child present (0 = no; 1 = yes)	.10	.29	.07	.25
Adult male nonchild present (0 = no; 1 = yes)	.09	.29	.18	.38
Adult female child present (0 = no; 1 = yes)	.08	.27	.05	.22
Adult female nonchild present (0 = no; 1 = yes)	.14	.35	.17	.38
Home ownership (0 = no; 1 = yes)	.59	.49	.58	.49
Household earnings (in $1,000s)	28.72	37.69	31.64	36.51
Education 12.45	2.93	12.94	3.32	
Age	44.30	17.99	42.24	17.07
Age squared (/100)	22.86	17.81	20.75	16.38
Hours employed per week	18.43	20.01	31.81	22.55
School enrollment (0 = no; 1 = yes)	.06	.24	.07	.26
Disabled (0 = no; 1 = yes)	.06	.24	.05	.22
Number of cases	6,764		4,252	

[a]May not add to 1.00 because of rounding.

housework can be explained by other respondent characteristics and to assess whether the gender-specific impact of the explanatory variables holds for the general population (including unmarried people) in ways previously shown for married persons.

RESULTS

Table 1 presents descriptive statistics for all variables in the analysis. Immediately apparent is the sharp but unsurprising difference between men and women in the amount of time spent doing housework. In this sample, women report spending almost 33 hours per week on household tasks, while men report spending slightly more than 18 hours. Both figures are roughly comparable to the findings of prior studies, although of course those studies did not include unmarried persons.

Gender differences in current marital status are relatively slight. Men are somewhat more likely than women to have never married, reflecting longstanding differences in age at marriage. And, among the never married, men are more likely than women to reside in the parental household. Women are more likely than men to be currently divorced or widowed, a probable consequence of their lower remarriage rates following divorce and men's higher mortality. Four percent of both sexes are co-habiters.

Differences between women and men on the other explanatory variables are also generally small. The sole exception is the number of hours worked outside the home, with women averaging approximately 18 hours per week and men 32 hours.

The regression analysis of time spent on housework is shown in Table 2. In our initial equations (not shown here), we pooled the male and female respondents and regressed housework hours on the explanatory variables, including dummy variables for gender and marital status. We then added to this equation product terms representing the interaction of gender and marital status. As predicted by the theoretical model, allowing marital status and gender to interact in their effects on housework significantly increases the variance explained ($F = 67.06$; $p < .001$). And specifically, the difference in housework hours between married women and married men is significantly larger than the housework hours differences between women and men in each of the other marital statuses. Product terms representing the interaction of gender with the other explanatory variables also revealed that several of the effects varied significantly by gender; thus, we estimate and present the equations separately for women and for men.[6]

The first equation in Table 2 is based only on the women respondents and regresses weekly housework hours on dummy variables representing five of the six marital statuses, with married respondents serving as the reference category. Persons in all five marital statuses work significantly fewer hours around the house than do the married respondents; at the extreme, married women spend over 17 hours more per week on housework than do never-married women who reside in the parental household. As anticipated, the amount of time spent on housework by women who are never-

---

[6] The distribution of some of the factors that explain variation in housework hours differs by age group. For example, enrollment in school and the presence of children in the household are most prevalent for younger respondents, while disability and widowhood are more common among the aged. Yet, the correlation matrices showed little evidence of multicollinearity, and disaggregating the equations by age revealed patterns and determinants quite similar to those for the sample as a whole.

married and living independently, cohabiting, divorced (including separated), or widowed falls between that of women who have not married (and remain in the parental home) and those who have married.

The third column of Table 2 presents the parallel equation for men. As reflected in the constant term, married men report spending almost 18 hours per week in housework, compared to almost 37 hours for their female counterparts (the constant term in column 1). More importantly, marital status differences in housework hours among men are relatively small compared to the analogous differences among women. Married men do significantly more housework than never-married men who still live with their parents and significantly less than divorced and widowed men, but most of these differences are modest. Moreover, the pattern of time spent doing housework across marital statuses differs substantially between men and women; it is greatest for men during widowhood and greatest for women during marriage.

Equation 2 in Table 2 re-estimates marital status differences in housework hours for men and women, controlling for the other explanatory variables. As shown in column 2, differences among women in these additional variables account for some, though by no means all, of the marital status differences in housework. Controlling for these variables reduces the differences between married women and other women by between 17 percent (for widows) and 66 percent (for cohabiters). Further, the difference between married women and cohabiting women is no longer statistically significant once these variables are controlled. Thus, among women a moderate proportion of the marital status differences in time spent doing housework is attributable to compositional differences. Particularly important in accounting for these marital status differences in housework hours are the number of hours the respondent works outside the home and the presence of children in the household; both variables vary significantly by marital status and are at least moderately related to time spent doing housework. We discuss these and the other effects of the explanatory variables in detail below.

For men, in contrast, controlling for the other explanatory variables does somewhat less to explain marital status differences in house-

Table 2. OLS Coefficients for Regression of Hours Spent in Housework per Week on Marital Status and Other Explanatory Variables, by Gender: U.S. Men and Women, 1987 to 1988

Independent Variable	Women		Men	
	(1)	(2)	(1)	(2)
Marital Status				
Never married/living in parental home	−17.41***†	−9.73***	−2.90***†	−.52†
	(.93)	(1.34)	(.63)	(1.18)
Never married/living independently	−11.62***†	−6.45***	1.09†	1.43†
	(.74)	(.84)	(.63)	(.80)
Cohabitating	−5.54***†	−1.86†	1.34†	1.73†
	(1.14)	(1.14)	(.98)	(1.03)
Married	Reference		Reference	
Divorced/separated	−5.30***†	−3.68***	3.73***†	4.58***†
	(.66)	(.68)	(.75)	(.80)
Widowed	−9.08***	−7.51***	5.66***†	6.97***†
	(.67)	(.77)	(1.16)	(1.21)
Number of children ages 0 to 4	—	3.63***	—	.67†
		(.38)		(.39)
Number of children ages 5 to 11	—	3.77***	—	.85***
		(.31)		(.32)
Number of girls ages 12 to 18	—	1.62***†	—	−.64†
		(.46)		(.46)
Number of boys ages 12 to 18	—	1.88**	—	.74
		(.47)		(.47)
Adult male child parent (0 = no; 1 = yes)	—	1.79*	—	.91
		(.74)		(.82)
Adult male nonchild present (0 = no; 1 = yes)	—	−.10	—	−.37
		(.97)		(.72)
Adult female child present (0 = no; 1 = yes)	—	−2.46**	—	−2.93**
		(.80)		(.92)
Adult female nonchild present (0 = no; 1 = yes)	—	−1.18	—	−1.40
		(.85)		(.84)
Home ownership (0 = no; 1 = yes)	—	2.24**	—	−1.22*
		(.52)		(.52)
Household earnings (in $1,000s)	—	−.03***†	—	−.02***†
		(.01)		(.01)
Education	—	−.44***†	—	.14**†
		(.08)		(.06)
Age	—	.40***†	—	.05†
		(.08)		(.08)
Age squared (/100)	—	−.44***†	—	−.15†
		(.08)		(.08)
Hours employed per week	—	−.17***	—	−.08***
		(.01)		(.01)
School enrollment (0 = no; 1 = yes)	—	−4.07**	—	−2.48**
		(.91)		(.82)
Disabled (0 = no; 1 = yes)	—	−5.34**	—	−2.96**
		(.86)		(.94)
Constant	36.67**	34.26**	17.83**	19.87**
	(.28)	(2.07)	(.25)	(2.08)
Root mean squared error	17.39	16.37	12.76	12.57
R^2	.08	.19	.02	.05
Number of cases	6,764	6,764	4,252	4,252

*$p < .05$ **$p < .01$ (two-tailed tests)

Note: Numbers in parentheses are standard errors. Equations in columns 2 and 4 include dummy variables for missing values on household earnings and disabled.

†Difference in coefficients for women and men is statistically significant at $p < .05$.

work. Although the difference between never-married men living in the parental home and married men becomes statistically nonsignificant when these variables are controlled, the absolute size of the decline (about 2.5 hours per week) is small. More important, with these controls the initially larger differences between married men and both divorced and widowed men actually increase.

Most of the explanatory variables have significant effects on time spent doing housework for either the men *or* the women, and many have significant effects for both sexes. Several variables have stronger effects among one sex than the other. The presence of children in the household creates more housework, especially for women, with pre-teenagers creating slightly more work than older children. The impact of children on housework hours tends to be significantly stronger for women than for men, a finding also found in studies limited to married couples (Bergen 1991; Rexroat and Shehan 1987). The presence in the household of the respondent's adult children also significantly affects housework hours, but the direction of the effect depends on both the sex of the adult children and the respondent. For female respondents, the presence of an adult male child increases housework hours, while for both female and male respondents the presence of an adult female child significantly reduces time allocated to housework. These findings are consistent with the view that men create housework, while women perform work men would otherwise do themselves (Hartmann 1981). Adults who are *not* children of the respondent do not add or subtract significantly, on average, from the respondent's housework time. This may be because the household is a heterogeneous group, including some roommates, siblings and other relatives, and elderly parents. Some household members may be helpful and others may be a burden, and their effects may cancel out.[7]

As expected, home ownership significantly increases housework time, and it appears to do so about equally for men and women. This may be due to larger amounts of living space to be cleaned and to the increase in yard work and maintenance and repair chores among homeowners. Total household earnings reduce housework significantly more for women than for men, suggesting that purchased household services substitute more for women's than for men's domestic labor.[8] Among women, education is inversely associated with housework, while for men the association is positive and significant. Educated women and men tend to hold egalitarian attitudes, which may lead to greater symmetry in their housework patterns (Huber and Spitze 1983). The hypothesized curvilinear (bell-shaped) association between age and housework emerges for women, but not for men.

As indicated by the significant effects of employment and school enrollment on time spent doing housework, investing time in nonhousehold activities significantly reduces household labor. The impact of hours employed is significantly greater for women than for men, a finding consistent with prior research (Gershuny and Robinson 1988; Rexroat and Shehan 1987). This suggests that women have less discretionary time than men, so that increased expenditures of time outside the home must necessarily divert time away from housework.[9]

---

[7] While it is possible to separate persons in heterogeneous households into a number of categories and attempt to sort out those who tend to help and those who create more work, the small number of respondents with *any* other adult present suggests that this would not be a useful refinement to the analysis.

[8] The gender difference in the effect of household earnings on housework is complicated by the fact that, for couple households, wife's (or female cohabiting partner's) hours employed per week is controlled for in the women's equation, but not in the men's equation. If hours employed are deleted from both equations, the gender difference in the effect of household earnings becomes statistically nonsignificant. Hence, this difference, which is barely significant to begin with, should be interpreted cautiously.

[9] From the perspective of the New Home Economics, the amount of time allocated to housework and to paid labor are frequently considered to be jointly determined, and thus the inclusion of employment hours as a predictor of housework has been questioned (Godwin 1991). We believe that for most persons, and particularly persons in nonmarital households, decisions regarding the allocation of time to the paid labor force are made prior to decisions about housework time (especially given that our measure of housework excludes childcare), and thus that the treatment of paid employment as an explanatory variable is justified. In any event, omitting respondent's hours employed per week from the equations does not

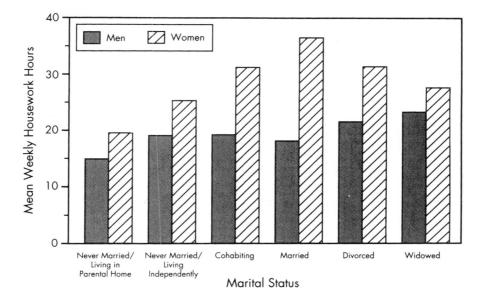

Figure 1. Mean Hours Spent Doing Housework Each Week, by Gender and Marital Status

Because the combined effects of gender and marital status are moderately complex, we present Figure 1 to help clarify the nature of their interaction. This figure graphs the (unadjusted) mean housework hours for men and women along the most common temporal sequence of marital statuses. In all marital statuses, women spend more hours than men on housework. The gender gap among never-married men and women living in the parental home is about 4 hours. Both never-married women and men who live independently do more housework than their counterparts who remain at home, but because the increase is slightly greater for women than for men (almost a 6-hour increase for women versus 4 hours for men), the gender difference in housework in this group grows to a little over 6 hours. Presumably, both men and women who live independently perform household tasks that previously had been done for them by their parents when the respondents resided in the parental homes.

The gender difference in housework hours widens dramatically as one moves to the couple households—cohabiters and married persons. Cohabiting women do more housework than never-married women (regardless of the latter's living arrangements), while cohabiting men work about the same hours around the house as never-married men living independently. The result of these discrepant trajectories is that the gender difference among cohabiters increases to approximately 12 hours per week. The gender gap in housework hours reaches its zenith among married women and men, at approximately 19 hours per week. This disparity is primarily a consequence of married women doing substantially more housework than never-married and cohabiting women, although these differences diminish with controls, as shown in Table 2. Rather than simply maintaining a behavioral pattern established prior to forming a conjugal union, married and, to a lesser extent, cohabiting women appear to increase substantially the time they devote to housework. In contrast, the amount of housework done by married men is fairly similar to that done by never-married and cohabiting men. Hence, as the "gender perspective" would suggest, it is in marital and cohabiting

---

appreciably alter the effects of marital status and gender that are the crux of our analysis, nor does the omission modify the impact of the other explanatory variables.

Table 3. Mean Hours Spent per Week in Various Household Tasks, by Marital Status and Gender: U.S. Men and Women, 1987 to 1988

Household Task[b]	Marital Status[a]					
	Never Married/ Living in Parental Home	Never Married/ Living Independently	Cohabiting	Married	Divorced	Widowed
Women						
Preparing meals	3.64	6.74	7.99	10.14	8.15	7.96
Washing dishes	3.92	4.38	5.51	6.11	5.14	4.73
Cleaning house	3.95	5.16	7.10	8.31	6.68	5.68
Washing/ironing	2.45	2.63	3.44	4.16	3.37	2.50
Outdoor maintenance	1.39	1.24	1.34	2.06	1.94	2.26
Shopping	1.72	2.28	2.69	2.86	2.67	2.40[ns]
Paying bills	.81[ns]	1.53	1.66	1.52	1.70	1.48[ns]
Car maintenance	.48	.42	.28	.16	.40	.20
Driving	.90[ns]	.65	1.10[ns]	1.34	1.30	.38[ns]
Total housework hours	19.26	25.04	31.12	36.67	31.37	27.59
Number of cases	383	649	248	3,838	829	817
Men						
Preparing meals	2.23	5.06	3.71	2.69	5.50	6.48
Washing dishes	1.92	2.77	2.63	2.15	3.24	3.87
Cleaning house	2.20	2.97	2.60	2.03	3.54	3.38
Washing/ironing	1.30	1.92	1.16	.70	1.75	1.67
Outdoor maintenance	3.56	1.56	3.18	4.94	2.60	3.38
Shopping	.83	1.92	1.73	1.58	1.93	2.14[ns]
Paying bills	.90[ns]	1.38	1.35	1.32	1.45	1.65[ns]
Car maintenance	1.23	.92	1.51	1.37	.99	.52
Driving	.75[ns]	.42	1.28[ns]	1.04	.57	.41[ns]
Total housework hours	14.93	18.92	19.16	17.83	21.56	23.49
Number of cases	477	476	181	2,668	323	127

[a] All associations between marital status and time spent on household tasks are significant at the $p < .05$ level.

[b] Within marital status and task type, all gender differences are significant at the $p < .05$ level with the following exceptions (marked ns): for never married in parental home—paying bills and driving; for cohabitors—driving; for widows—shopping, paying bills, and driving.

unions that gender differences in housework are most evident.

Among the formerly married, hours spent on housework by men and women begin to converge. Relative to their married counterparts, women who are divorced or widowed do less housework, while divorced or widowed men do more, with or without controlling for other variables. For women, this difference is perhaps best explained by a reduction in the total amount of housework required brought about by the absence of a husband in the household. For men, divorce and widowhood means doing household tasks previously done by a wife.

In general, then, patterns of time spent in housework across different marital statuses appear at least broadly consistent with the emerging "gender perspective." While there is a gender gap in housework in all marital statuses, this disparity varies dramatically and, as predicted, is widest for men and women in couple households (i.e., married or cohabiting relationships). However, to determine the extent to which these totals reflect behavior that becomes more gender-differentiated in couple households, we examine marital status differences in the completion of particular household tasks.

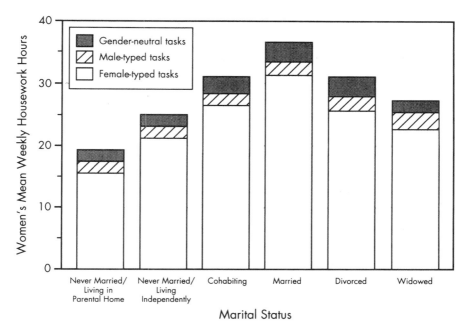

Figure 2. Mean Hours Spent by Women Doing Housework each Week, by Sex Type of Task and Marital Status

Accordingly, Table 3 presents the mean hours spent per week in each of the individual nine household tasks, disaggregated by gender and marital status. Figures 2 and 3 summarize the information in Table 3, graphing for women and men the (unadjusted) amounts of time spent in "female-typed" tasks (preparing meals, washing dishes, cleaning house, washing and ironing, and shopping), "male-typed" tasks (outdoor chores and automobile maintenance), and "gender-neutral" tasks (paying bills and driving other household members).[10] Among women, the marital status differences in *total* housework hours shown in Figure 1 are replicated for the female-typed tasks, which constitute in each marital status category the vast bulk of housework hours (see Figure 2). Of the female-typed tasks, the largest differences are in the number of hours spent prepar-

ing meals and cleaning house, although all five tasks consume more time for married women than for any of the other groups (Table 3). Because in each marital status the amount of time allocated to male-typed tasks is small, *differences* by marital status in these tasks are also slight. Married women do less car maintenance than do other women, but, with the exception of widows, spend slightly more time on outdoor maintenance. For women, then, marital status differences in total housework hours are largely a consequence of differences in hours spent on female-typed tasks.

Among men, however, marital status differences in gender-specific tasks do not always reflect those for housework as a whole. For example, as shown in Figure 3, although the difference in *total* housework hours between never-married men living independently and married men is small (about 1 hour), the difference is composed of several counterbalancing components. Never-married men living independently spend over 5 hours more per week than married men on female-typed tasks, but offset most of this difference by spending less time on male-typed tasks. Similarly, never-married men living independently spend al-

[10] This categorization is consistent with other analyses, including those by Ferree (1991b) and Aytac and Teachman (1992). Shelton (1992) shows shopping to be somewhat intermediate between female- and neutral-typed tasks, and others (e.g., Presser 1993) have treated it as a gender-neutral task.

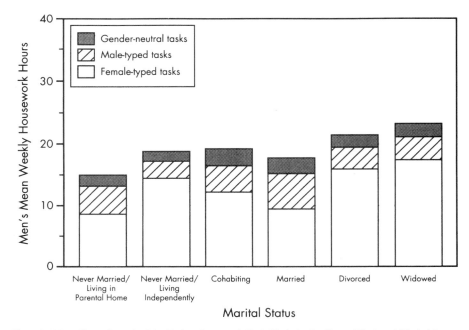

Figure 3. Mean Hours Spent by Men Doing Housework Each Week, by Sex Type of Task and Marital Status

most 3 hours per week more than cohabiting men in female-typed chores, but cohabiting men more than compensate for this difference by spending more time doing male-typed and gender-neutral tasks. Hence, to the extent that cohabiting men differ from never-married men living independently, they do so not by greater participation in female-typed chores, but by increasing their time doing stereotypically male tasks (e.g., automobile maintenance and outdoor chores) and gender-neutral tasks (e.g., driving other household members). On a smaller scale, the difference between cohabiting men and married men in total housework (about 1.3 hours per week) masks an important difference: Cohabiting men spend over 2.5 more hours per week than do married men on traditionally female chores, but married men make up over half of this difference by spending more time on outdoor maintenance. Like never-married men living independently, cohabiting men do more female-typed tasks than do married men, although they do not work on outdoor maintenance tasks to the same degree as their married counterparts.

The difference in total housework hours between married men and divorced men and between married men and widowed men is also composed of counterbalancing chores. Divorced and widowed men spend 6 to 8 hours more per week than married men on female-typed tasks, but the greater time expenditures by married men on outdoor and automobile maintenance partially offset this difference. In general, the distribution of housework hours by the sex-type of task appears consistent with the gender perspective: Married and cohabiting men spend less time on female-typed tasks and more time on male-typed tasks than do men in most other marital statuses.

DISCUSSION AND CONCLUSION

Doing housework is a significant part of many people's lives, yet few studies have explored housework patterns and determinants across household types. Indeed, because much prior research has been motivated by concerns about marital equity, the erroneous impression may exist that housework is performed only by members of married-couple families. Clearly, this is not the case.

Our results suggest that even never-married men, who might be expected to eschew housework, spend almost half as much time working around the home as they do in the paid labor force. Given prior studies suggesting little contribution by adult sons who live at home (Hartung and Moore 1992; Ward et al. 1992), the amount of housework reported being done by never-married men living in parental homes may seem surprisingly high — approximately 2 hours per day. However, the largest single component of this time (approximately one-quarter of it) is spent on outdoor maintenance, and outdoor and automobile maintenance together constitute one-third of the total time spent. Further, it is likely that much of the time spent in other chores, such as cooking, cleaning, or laundry, is directed more toward self-maintenance than to the well-being of the entire household (Hartung and Moore 1992). Thus, given this context, the amount of housework reported by never-married men living in the parental home appears reasonable.

The performance of housework by men is substantially similar across marital statuses. Differences in total housework hours among never-married, cohabiting, and married men are rather small and are partly attributable to differences in other social and economic characteristics. The most noteworthy differences among men in housework hours involve the appreciable differences between divorced and widowed men and the men in other marital statuses. The number of hours married women spend doing housework approaches a typical full-time work week and is termed the "second shift" by Hochschild (1989). But women in other living situations that do not include a male partner also spend 20 to 30 hours a week doing household chores. The gender gap in housework hours is highest in marriage, but is evident in other marital statuses as well. Although social and economic differences among women in various marital situations (especially the presence of children and hours spent in paid work) account for approximately half of these differences in housework hours, marital status differences in housework among women are generally greater than the corresponding differences among men.

From these patterns and from our detailed analysis of individual household tasks, we have concluded that there is suggestive evidence for the "gender perspective." Housework that women perform for and in the presence of men displays gender more so than the same work performed with no man present. We find that the gender gap in housework time is greatest in married couple households relative to other households, and that much of this difference *cannot* be explained by the fact that marriage often brings children and reduced hours of paid work for women. Thus, we conclude that men and women must be "doing gender" when they live together. Moreover, relative to their unmarried counterparts, married men spend very little time in the traditionally female tasks of cooking and cleaning.

Of course, there are also significant gender gaps among persons in nonmarital households, implying that the dynamics of doing gender are not entirely absent in other household situations. However, we view our analysis and the patterns displayed in couple and noncouple households to be suggestive evidence that these dynamics operate differentially across household types. Perhaps our analysis and tentative interpretation will encourage those theorists working in the new gender perspective to further specify the conditions under which these processes operate so that future empirical tests can be more precise.

Analysis across household type and marital status may also have implications for the application of equity theory to the allocation of household labor. While most analyses of equity in household labor have used a comparison between husbands and wives as the implicit or explicit base for judging fairness, several recent discussions have raised the possibility that other standards may be used as well. Thompson (1991) discusses the issue of comparison referents and points out that husbands may compare themselves with *other husbands* and wives with *other wives*, while both Ferree (1990) and Kollock, Blumstein, and Schwartz (1988) present empirical comparisons between the predictive value of intracouple and intragender standards. To our knowledge, however, the idea that spouses may compare themselves to *their own past or projected experiences in another marital status*, or even to others who are not currently married, has not been discussed in the empirical literature on housework equity, although fear of divorce was certainly a potent factor in the ideological and behavioral choices of Hochschild's (1989) female respondents. Although this is necessarily speculative, we suggest that married men might use their experience prior to marriage as a reference point for both negotiating and evaluating their own contribution to household labor within marriage. People are spending increasing amounts of time in nonmarital statuses, particularly never-married, cohabiting, and divorced. During their lives, they often go through transitions which include a sequence from being never married to cohabiting to married to divorced or widowed. By examining the time men and women spend doing housework in each of these living situations we may be better able to understand what occurs when people negotiate how housework will be divided within marriage.

SCOTT J. SOUTH is Associate Professor of Sociology at the State University of New York at Albany. His recent research focuses on the social demography of American families, with particular emphasis given to contextual influences on patterns of family formation and dissolution. He is Co-Editor (with Stewart E. Tolnay) of The Changing American Family: Sociological and Demographic Perspectives *(Westview Press, 1992).*

GLENNA SPITZE is Professor of Sociology and Women's Studies at the State University of New York at Albany. In addition to her research on household labor, she is working on a book with John R. Logan based on their research on family structure and intergenerational relations.

REFERENCES

Aytac, Isik A. and Jay D. Teachman. 1992. "Occupational Sex Segregation, Marital Power, and Household Division of Labor." Paper presented at the meetings of the American Sociological Association, 20–24 Aug., Pittsburgh, PA.

Becker, Gary. 1981. *A Treatise on the Family*. Chicago, IL: University of Chicago.

Benin, Mary H. and Joan Agostinelli. 1988. "Husbands' and Wives' Satisfaction with the Division of Labor." *Journal of Marriage and the Family* 50:349–61.

Benin, Mary Holland and Debra A. Edwards. 1990. "Adolescents' Chores: The Difference Between Dual and Single-Earner Families." *Journal of Marriage and the Family* 52:361–73.

Bergen, Elizabeth. 1991. "The Economic Context of Labor Allocation." *Journal of Family Issues* 12:140–57.

Berk, Sarah Fenstermaker. 1985. *The Gender Factory*. New York: Plenum.

Blair, Sampson Lee. 1991. "The Sex-Typing of Children's Household Labor: Parental Influence on Daughters' and Sons' Housework." Paper presented at the meeting of the American Sociological Association, 23–27 Aug., Cincinnati, OH.

Blair, Sampson Lee and Michael P. Johnson. 1992. "Wives' Perceptions of the Fairness of the Division of Household Labor: The Intersection of Housework and Ideology." *Journal of Marriage and the Family* 54:570–81.

Blair, Sampson Lee and Daniel T. Lichter. 1991. "Measuring the Division of Household Labor: Gender Segregation Among American Couples." *Journal of Family Issues* 12:91–113.

Blood, Robert O. and Donald M. Wolfe. 1960. *Husbands and Wives*. New York: Free Press.

Blumberg, Rae Lesser and Marion Tolbert Coleman. 1989. "A Theoretical Look at the Gender Balance of Power in the American Couple." *Journal of Family Issues* 10:255–50.

Blumstein, Philip and Pepper Schwartz. 1983. *American Couples*. New York: William Morrow.

Coltrane, Scott and Masako Ishii-Kuntz. 1992. "Men's Housework: A Life-Course Perspective." *Journal of Marriage and the Family* 54:43–57.

Coverman, Shelley. 1985. "Explaining Husbands' Participation in Domestic Labor." *Sociological Quarterly* 26:81–97.

Coverman, Shelley and Joseph F. Sheley. 1986. "Changes in Men's Housework and Child-Care Time, 1965–1975." *Journal of Marriage and the Family* 48:413–22.

DeVault, Marjorie L. 1991. *Feeding the Family: The Social Organization of Caring as Gendered Work*. Chicago, IL: University of Chicago.

Ferree, Myra Marx. 1990. "Gender and Grievances in the Division of Household Labor: How Husbands and Wives Perceive Fairness." Paper presented at the meeting of the American Sociological Association, 11–15 Aug., Washington, DC.

———. 1991a. "Feminism and Family Research." Pp. 103–21 in *Contemporary Families*, edited by A. Booth. Minneapolis, MN: National Council on Family Relations.

———. 1991b. "The Gender Division of Labor in Two-Earner Marriages: Dimensions of Variability and Change." *Journal of Family Issues* 12:158–80.

Gershuny, Jonathan and John P. Robinson. 1988. "Historical Changes in the Household Division of Labor." *Demography* 25:537–52.

Gillespie, Dair L. 1971. "Who Has the Power: The Marital Struggle." *Journal of Marriage and the Family* 33:445–58.

Glazer-Malbin, Nona. 1976. "Housework." *Signs* 1:905–22.

Godwin, Deborah D. 1991. "Spouses' Time Allocation to Household Work: A Review and Critique." *Lifestyles: Family and Economic Issues* 12:253–94.

Goldscheider, Frances K. and Linda J. Waite. 1991. *New Families, No Families? The Transformation of the American Home*. Berkeley, CA: University of California.

Gove, Walter R. and Hee-Choon Shin. 1989. "The Psychological Well-Being of Divorced and Widowed Men and Women: An Empirical Analysis." *Journal of Family Issues* 10:122–44.

Grief, Geoffrey L. 1985. "Children and Housework in the Single Father Family." *Family Relations* 34:353–57.

Hartmann, Heidi I. 1981. "The Family as the Locus of Gender, Class, and Political Struggle: The Example of Housework." *Signs* 6:366–94.

Hartung, Beth and Helen A. Moore, 1992. "The Return of the 'Second Shift': Adult Children Who Return Home." Paper presented at the meeting of the American Sociological Association, 20–24 Aug., Pittsburgh, PA.

Hilton, Jeanne M. and Virginia A. Haldeman. 1991. "Gender Differences in the Performance of Household Tasks by Adults and Children in Single-Parent and Two-Parent, Two-Earner Families." *Journal of Family Issues* 12:114–30.

Hochschild, Arlie with Anne Machung. 1989. *The Second Shift: Working Parents and the Revolution at Home.* New York: Viking.

Huber, Joan and Glenna Spitze. 1983. *Sex Stratification: Children, Housework, and Jobs.* New York: Academic Press.

Ishii-Kuntz, Masako and Scott Coltrane. 1992. "Remarriage, Stepparenting, and Household Labor." *Journal of Family Issues* 13:215–33.

Kollock, Peter, Philip Blumstein, and Pepper Schwartz. 1988. "The Judgment of Equity in Intimate Relationships." Paper presented at the meeting of the American Sociological Association, 24–28 Aug., Atlanta, GA.

Oakley, Ann. 1974. *The Sociology of Housework.* New York: Pantheon.

Peterson, Larry R. and Judy L. Maynard. 1981. "Income, Equity, and Wives' Housekeeping Role Expectations." *Pacific Sociological Review* 24: 87–105.

Presser, Harriet B. 1993. "Gender, Work Schedules, and the Division of Family Labor." Paper presented at the meeting of the Population Association of American, 1–3 April, Cincinnati, OH.

Rexroat, Cynthia and Constance Shehan. 1987. "The Family Life Cycle and Spouses' Time in Housework." *Journal of Marriage and the Family* 49:737–50.

Rindfuss, Ronald R. and Audrey VandenHeuvel. 1992. "Cohabitation: A Precursor to Marriage or an Alternative to Being Single?" Pp. 118–42 in *The Changing American Family: Sociological and Demographic Perspectives*, edited by S. J. South and S. E. Tolnay. Boulder, CO: Westview Press.

Rodman, Hyman, 1967. "Marital Power in France, Greece, Yugoslavia, and the United States: A Cross-National Discussion." *Journal of Marriage and the Family* 29:320–24.

Ross, Catherine E. 1987. "The Division of Labor at Home." *Social Forces* 65:816–33.

Sanik, Margaret Mietus and Teresa Mauldin. 1986.

"Single Versus Two-Parent Families: A Comparison of Mothers' Time." *Family Relations* 35:53–56.

Shelton, Beth Anne. 1990. "The Distribution of Household Tasks: Does Wife's Employment Status Make a Difference?" *Journal of Family Issues* 11:115–35.

———. 1992. *Women, Men and Time.* New York: Greenwood Press.

Shelton, Beth Anne and Daphne John. 1993. "Does Marital Status Make a Difference? Housework Among Married and Cohabiting Men and Women." *Journal of Family Issues* 14:401–20.

Spitze, Glenna. 1986. "The Division of Task Responsibility in U.S. Households: Longitudinal Adjustments to Change." *Social Forces* 64:689–701.

———. 1988. "Women's Employment and Family Relations: A Review." *Journal of Marriage and the Family* 50:595–618.

Stafford, Rebecca, Elaine Backman, and Pamela Dibona. 1977. "The Division of Labor Among Cohabiting and Married Couples." *Journal of Marriage and the Family* 39:43–57.

Sweet, James, Larry Bumpass, and Vaughn Call. 1988. "The Design and Content of the National Survey of Families and Households." (Working Paper NSFH-1). Center for Demography and Ecology, University of Wisconsin, Madison, WI.

Sweet, James A. and Larry L. Bumpass. 1987. *American Families and Households.* New York: Russell Sage Foundation.

Thompson, Linda and Alexis J. Walker. 1991. "Gender in Families." Pp. 76–102 in *Contemporary Families*, edited by A. Booth. Minneapolis, MN: National Council on Family Relations.

Thompson, Linda. 1991. "Family Work: Women's Sense of Fairness." *Journal of Family Issues* 12: 181–96.

Timmer, Susan G., Jacquelynne Eccles, and Keith O'Brien. 1985. "How Children Use Time." Pp. 353–82 in *Time, Goods, and Well-Being*, edited by T. F. Juster and F. P. Stafford. Ann Arbor, MI: Institute for Social Research, University of Michigan.

Umberson, Debra, Camille B. Wortman, and Ronald C. Kessler. 1992. "Widowhood and Depression: Explaining Long-Term Gender Differences in Vulnerability." *Journal of Health and Social Behavior* 33:10–24.

Waite, Linda and Frances K. Goldscheider. 1992. "Work in the Home: The Productive Context of Family Relationships." Pp. 267–99 in *The Changing American Family: Sociological and Demographic Perspectives*, edited by S. J. South and S. E. Tolnay. Boulder, CO: Westview Press.

Walker, Kathryn E. and Margaret E. Woods. 1976. *Time Use: A Measure of Household Production of Goods and Services.* Washington, DC: American Home Economics Association.

Ward, Russell, John Logan, and Glenna Spitze. 1992. "The Influence of Parent and Child Needs on

Coresidence in Middle and Later Life." *Journal of Marriage and the Family* 54:209–21.

Warner, Rebecca A. 1986. "Alternative Strategies for Measuring Household Division of Labor: A Comparison." *Journal of Family Issues* 7:179–95.

Watkins, Susan Cotts, Jane A. Menken, and John Bongaarts. 1987. "Demographic Foundations of Family Change." *American Sociological Review* 52:346–58.

West, Candace and Don H. Zimmerman. 1981. "Doing Gender." *Gender and Society* 1:125–51.

White, Lynn K. and David B. Brinkerhoff. 1981a. "Children's Work in the Family: Its Significance and Meaning." *Journal of Marriage and the Family* 43:789–98.

———. 1981b. "The Sexual Division of Labor: Evidence from Childhood." *Social Forces* 60:170–81.

Appendix D

FINDING INFORMATION

ELIZABETH SCHNEIDER, MLS

This appendix complements Chapter 2, which presented general principles and methods for finding information related to your research questions. The purpose of this appendix is to provide you with specific, practical pointers for finding high quality information in a timely and efficient manner.

SEARCHING THE LITERATURE

In Chapter 2, you learned about the most frequently used indexes in the social sciences: *Sociological Abstracts* and *Psychological Abstracts.* You might also find relevant literature in *EconLit,* which indexes the economic literature, and in *ContempWomenIss,* which indexes literature on contemporary women's issues. It is most likely that your college library will have subscriptions to the online version of *Sociological Abstracts (Sociofile)* and *Psychological Abstracts (Psychinfo).* It will save you a lot of time in the long run if you ask a librarian to teach you the best techniques for retrieving the most relevant articles to answer your questions. Keep in mind, however, that many online databases only go back to the early 1990s, so you will have to use print indexes to identify articles published before then.

The *Social Science Citation Index (SSCI)* is another very useful source of bibliographic information for articles and books published across the social sciences. *SSCI* has a unique "citation searching" feature that allows you to look up articles or books and see who else has cited them in their work. This is an excellent and efficient way to assemble a number of references that are highly relevant to your research and to find out which articles and books have had the biggest impact in a field. Unfortunately, some college libraries do not subscribe to *SSCI,* either in its print, CD-ROM, or online version, due to its expense, but if you have access to *SSCI,* you should consider using it whenever you want to make sure that you develop the strongest possible literature review for your topic. You'll find that as you use *SSCI,* you will learn the extent to which there is agreement about a common "paradigm" about a topic (see Chapter 3).

Whatever database you use, the next step after finding your references is to obtain the articles themselves. You will probably find the full text of many articles available online, but this will be determined by what journals your library subscribes to. Older articles published before 1990 probably will not be online. Keep in mind that your library will not have anywhere near all the journals (and books) that you run across in your literature search, so you will have to add another step to your search: checking the "holdings" information.

If an article that appears to be important for your topic isn't available from your own library, either online or in print, don't give up yet. Here are some additional strategies for tracking it down:

- Find out if your college has reciprocal arrangements with other colleges that would allow you to use their materials.
- Find out if colleges in your area allow students from other colleges to use their collections and databases.
- Do not overlook your public library—you may be pleasantly surprised.
- Check to see if your library can get the desired resource for you from another library (through interlibrary loan).
- Check with a commercial vendor such as PubList (http://www.publist.com) to see if you can purchase the article.

SEARCHING THE WEB

In order to find useful information on the Web, you have to be even more vigilant than when you search the literature directly. With billions of Web pages on the Internet, there is no limit to the amount of time you can squander and the volume of useless junk you can find as you conduct your research on the Web. However, I can share with you some good ways to avoid the biggest pitfalls.

Direct Addressing

Knowing the exact address (uniform resource locator, or URL) of a useful Web site is the most efficient way to find a resource on the Web. Appendix H contains many URLs relevant to social science research, but the following sections highlight a few categories and examples that may prove helpful to you.

Professional Organizations

- American Sociological Association (http://www.asanet.org)
- American Psychological Association (http://www.apa.org)
- National Association of Social Workers (http://www.naswdc.org)
- American Association of Criminology (http://www.asc41.com)

Government Sites

- U.S. Office of Justice Programs (http://www.ojp.usdoj.gov)
- U.S. Bureau of the Census (http://www.census.gov)

Journals and Newspapers

- Annual Review of Sociology (http://www.annualreviews.org)
- The New York Times (http://www.nytimes.com)

Bibliographic Formats for Citing Electronic Information

- Electronic reference formats suggested by the American Psychological Association (http://www.apastyle.org/elecref.html)
- A compendium from Dartmouth College on how to cite sources from a variety of media, with examples (http://www.dartmouth.edu/~sources/)

When you find Web sites that you expect you will return to often, you can save their addresses as "bookmarks" or "favorites" in your Web browser. However, since these can very quickly multiply, you should try to be selective.

Browsing Subject Directories

Subject directories (also called guides, indexes, or clearinghouses) contain links to other Web resources that are organized by subject. They vary in quality and authoritativeness, but a good one can be invaluable to your research and save you much time. The main advantage to using subject directories is that they contain links to resources that have been selected, evaluated, and organized by human beings, and thus present a much more manageable number of resources. If the person managing the guide is an expert in the field of concern, or just a careful and methodological evaluator of Web resources, their guide can help you to identify good sites that contain useful and trustworthy information, without feeling like you should try to wade through thousands of "hits" and evaluate all the sites yourself.

The following are some examples of subject directories:

- Argus Clearinghouse (http://www.clearinghouse.net/searchbrowse.html) is a guide to subject directories on the Internet, and classifies them under subject headings.
- Virtual Library (http://vlib.org) is the original subject guide, and actually consists of a number of directories produced by different individuals and organizations residing on Web sites scattered around the world. There is a Virtual Library for the Social Sciences (http://vlib.org/SocialSciences.html) that includes listings for anthropology, demographics, psychology, social policy and evaluation, sociology, women's studies, and other areas.
- Another virtual library for the social sciences (http://www.clas.ufl.edu/users/gthursby/socsci/) includes a large number of links to a diverse array of resources, including professional societies and online journals.
- Infomine:Scholarly Internet Resource Collections (http://lib-www.ucr.edu) is produced by librarians across several campuses of the University of California system, and it includes a subject directory for the social sciences.
- SOSIG—Social Science Information Gateway (http://www.sosig.ac.uk) is a British site that aims to be comprehensive. It is classified according to the Dewey Decimal System—the classification system used by most public libraries.

- Yahoo! (http://www.yahoo.com) is often mistaken for a search engine, but it is actually a subject directory—and a monster one at that. Unlike search engines, when you search Yahoo!, you are not searching across the Web, but rather just within the Web pages that Yahoo! has cataloged. Yahoo! has a subject directory for the social sciences with more specific listings, including one for social work (http://dir.yahoo.com/social_ science/ social_work/).

Many other Internet subject directories are maintained by academic departments, professional organizations, and individuals. It's often hard to determine whether a particular subject directory like this is up-to-date and reasonably comprehensive, but you can have some confidence in subject directories published by universities or government agencies. *The Internet Research Handbook* is an excellent source for more information on subject directories (O'Dochartaigh, 2002).

Search Engines

Chapter 2 outlined the major points to consider when using search engines to find information for your research. Search engines are powerful Internet tools—it is already impossible to imagine life without them. The biggest problem is the huge number of results that come back to you. Chapter 2 suggested phrase searching as a way to reduce that number. If the number of results is still unmanageable, you can try a title search. Exhibit D.1 shows the results of typing the following into the Google search box: *ti: "informal social control."* This search will retrieve those pages that have that phrase in their title as opposed to anywhere on the page. This practice usually results in a dramatically smaller yield of results. If you are looking for graphical information such as a graph or a chart, you can limit your search to those pages that contain an image. On Google, this just requires clicking on the "Images" link located above the search box.

There are many search engines, and none of them will give you identical results when you use them to search the Web. Different search engines use different strategies to find Web sites and offer somewhat different search options for users. Due to the enormous size of the Web and its constantly changing content, it simply isn't possible to identify one search engine that will give you completely up-to-date and comprehensive results. You can find the latest information about search engines at http://searchenginewatch.com. Although there are many search engines, you may find the following to be particularly useful for general searching:

- Google (http://www.google.com) has become the leading search engine for many users in recent years. Its coverage is relatively comprehensive and it does a good job of ranking search results by their relevancy (based on the terms in your search request). Google also allows you to focus your search just on images, discussions, or directories.
- All The Web is a more recent comprehensive search engine that also does a good job of relevancy ranking and allows searches restricted to images and so on. You can find it at http://www.alltheweb.com.
- Microsoft's search engine (http://search.msn.com) adds a unique feature: Editors review and pick the most popular sites. As a result, your search request may result in a "popular topics" list that can help you to focus your search.

Exhibit D.1   The Results of a Google Search

In conclusion, use the appropriate tool for your searches. Do not use a search engine in place of searching literature that is indexed in tools such as *Sociological Abstracts*. Bookmark the key sites that you find in your area of interest. Become familiar with subject directories that cover your areas of interest, and look there before going to a search engine. And when you do use a search engine, take a moment to learn about how it works and what steps you should take to get the best results in the least amount of time.

Appendix E

TABLE OF RANDOM NUMBERS

Line/Col.	(1)	(2)	(3)	(4)	(5)	(6)	(7)	(8)	(9)	(10)	(11)	(12)	(13)	(14)
1	10480	15011	01536	02011	81647	91646	69179	14194	62590	36207	20969	99570	91291	90700
2	22368	46573	25595	85393	30995	89198	27982	53402	93965	34095	52666	19174	39615	99505
3	24130	48360	22527	97265	76393	64809	15179	24830	49340	32081	30680	19655	63348	58629
4	42167	93093	06243	61680	07856	16376	39440	53537	71341	57004	00849	74917	97758	16379
5	37570	39975	81837	16656	06121	91782	60468	81305	49684	60672	14110	06927	01263	54613
6	77921	06907	11008	42751	27756	53498	18602	70659	90655	15053	21916	81825	44394	42880
7	99562	72905	56420	69994	98872	31016	71194	18738	44013	48840	63213	21069	10634	12952
8	96301	91977	05463	07972	18876	20922	94595	56869	69014	60045	18425	84903	42508	32307
9	89579	14342	63661	10281	17453	18103	57740	84378	25331	12566	58678	44947	05585	56941
10	85475	36857	43342	53988	53060	59533	38867	62300	08158	17983	16439	11458	18593	64952
11	28918	69578	88231	33276	70997	79936	56865	05859	90106	31595	01547	85590	91610	78188
12	63553	40961	48235	03427	49626	69445	18663	72695	52180	20847	12234	90511	33703	90322
13	09429	93969	52636	92737	88974	33488	36320	17617	30015	08272	84115	27156	30613	74952
14	10365	61129	87529	85689	48237	52267	67689	93394	01511	26358	85104	20285	29975	89868
15	07119	97336	71048	08178	77233	13916	47564	81056	97735	85977	29372	74461	28551	90707
16	51085	12765	51821	51259	77452	16308	60756	92144	49442	53900	70960	63990	75601	40719
17	02368	21382	52404	60268	89368	19885	55322	44819	01188	65255	64835	44919	05944	55157
18	01011	54092	33362	94904	31273	04146	18594	29852	71585	85030	51132	01915	92747	64951
19	52162	53916	46369	58586	23216	14513	83149	98736	23495	64350	94738	17752	35156	35749
20	07056	97628	33787	09998	42698	06691	76988	13602	51851	46104	88916	19509	25625	58104
21	48663	91245	85828	14346	09172	30168	90229	04734	59193	22178	30421	61666	99904	32812
22	54164	58492	22421	74103	47070	25306	76468	26384	58151	06646	21524	15227	96909	44592
23	32639	32363	05597	24200	13363	38005	94342	28728	35806	06912	17012	64161	18296	22851
24	29334	27001	87637	87308	58731	00256	45834	15398	46557	41135	10367	07684	36188	18510
25	02488	33062	28834	07351	19731	92420	60952	61280	50001	67658	32586	86679	50720	94953
26	81525	72295	04839	96423	24878	82651	66566	14778	76797	14780	13300	87074	79666	95725
27	29676	20591	68086	26432	46901	20849	89768	81536	86645	12659	92259	57102	80428	25280
28	00742	57392	39064	66432	84673	40027	32832	61362	98947	96067	64760	64584	96096	98253
29	05366	04213	25669	26422	44407	44048	37937	63904	45766	66134	75470	66520	34693	90449
30	91921	26418	64117	94305	26766	25940	39972	22209	71500	64568	91402	42416	07844	69618
31	00582	04711	87917	77341	42206	35126	74087	99547	81817	42607	43808	76655	62028	76630
32	00725	69884	62797	56170	86324	88072	76222	36086	84637	93161	76038	65855	77919	88006
33	69011	65797	95876	55293	18988	27354	26575	08625	40801	59920	29841	80150	12777	48501

(Continued)

Appendix E (Continued)

Line/Col.	(1)	(2)	(3)	(4)	(5)	(6)	(7)	(8)	(9)	(10)	(11)	(12)	(13)	(14)
34	25976	57948	29888	88604	67917	48708	18912	82271	65424	69774	33611	54262	85963	03547
35	09763	83473	73577	12908	30883	18317	28290	35797	05998	41688	34952	37888	38917	88050
36	91567	42595	27958	30134	04024	86385	29880	99730	55536	84855	29080	09250	79656	73211
37	17955	56349	90999	49127	20044	59931	06115	20542	18059	02008	73708	83317	36103	42791
38	46503	18584	18845	49618	02304	51038	20655	58727	28168	15475	56942	53389	20562	87338
39	92157	89634	94824	78171	84610	82834	09922	25417	44137	48413	25555	21246	35509	20468
40	14577	62765	35605	81263	39667	47358	56873	56307	61607	49518	89656	20103	77490	18062
41	98427	07523	33362	64270	01638	92477	66969	98420	04880	45585	46565	04102	46880	45709
42	34914	63976	88720	82765	34476	17032	87589	40836	32427	70002	70663	88863	77775	69348
43	70060	28277	39475	46473	23219	53416	94970	25832	69975	94884	19661	72828	00102	66794
44	53976	54914	06990	67245	68350	82948	11398	42878	80287	88267	47363	46634	06541	97809
45	76072	29515	40980	07391	58745	25774	22987	80059	39911	96189	41151	14222	60697	59583
46	90725	52210	83974	29992	65831	38857	50490	83765	55657	14361	31720	57375	56228	41546
47	64364	67412	33339	31926	14883	24413	59744	92351	97473	89286	35931	04110	23726	51900
48	08962	00358	31662	25388	61642	34072	81249	35648	56891	69352	48373	45578	78547	81788
49	95012	68379	93526	70765	10593	04542	76463	54328	02349	17247	28865	14777	62730	92277
50	15664	10493	20492	38391	91132	21999	59516	81652	27195	48223	46751	22923	32261	85653
51	16408	81899	04153	53381	79401	21438	83035	92350	36693	31238	59649	91754	72772	02338
52	18629	81953	05520	91962	04739	13092	97662	24822	94730	06496	35090	04822	86772	98289
53	73115	35101	47498	87637	99016	71060	88824	71013	18735	20286	23153	72924	35165	43040
54	57491	16703	23167	49323	45021	33132	12544	41035	80780	45393	44812	12515	98931	91202
55	30405	83946	23792	14422	15059	45799	22716	19792	09983	74353	68668	30429	70735	25499
56	16631	35006	85900	98275	32388	52390	16815	69298	82732	38480	73817	32523	41961	44437
57	96773	20206	42559	78985	05300	22164	24369	54224	35083	19687	11052	91491	60383	19746
58	38935	64202	14349	82674	66523	44133	00697	35552	35970	19124	63318	29686	03387	59846
59	31624	76384	17403	53363	44167	64486	64758	75366	76554	31601	12614	33072	60332	92325
60	78919	19474	23632	27889	47914	02584	37680	20801	72152	39339	34806	08930	85001	87820
61	03931	33309	57047	74211	63445	17361	62825	39908	05607	91284	68833	25570	38818	46920
62	74426	33278	43972	10119	89917	15665	52872	73823	73144	88662	88970	74492	51805	99378
63	09066	00903	20795	95452	92648	45454	09552	88815	16553	51125	79375	97596	16296	66092
64	42238	12426	87025	14267	20979	04508	64535	31355	86064	29472	47689	05974	52468	16834
65	16153	08002	26504	41744	81959	65642	74240	56302	00033	67107	77510	70625	28725	34191
66	21457	40742	29820	96783	29400	21840	15035	34537	33310	06116	95240	15957	16572	06004

Line/Col.	(1)	(2)	(3)	(4)	(5)	(6)	(7)	(8)	(9)	(10)	(11)	(12)	(13)	(14)
67	21581	57802	02050	89728	17937	37621	47075	42080	97403	48626	68995	43805	33386	21597
68	55612	78095	83197	33732	05810	24813	86902	60397	16489	03264	88525	42786	05269	92532
69	44657	66999	99324	51281	84463	60563	79312	93454	68876	25471	93911	25650	12682	73572
70	91340	84979	46949	81973	37949	61023	43997	15263	80644	43942	89203	71795	99533	50501
71	91227	21199	31935	27022	84067	05462	35216	14486	29891	68607	41867	14951	91696	85065
72	50001	38140	66321	19924	72163	09538	12151	06878	91903	18749	34405	56087	82790	70925
73	65390	05224	72958	28609	81406	39147	25549	48542	42627	45233	57202	94617	23772	07896
74	27504	96131	83944	41575	10573	08619	64482	73923	36152	05184	94142	25299	84387	34925
75	37169	94851	39117	89632	00959	16487	65536	49071	39782	17095	02330	74301	00275	48280
76	11508	70225	51111	38351	19444	66499	71945	05422	13442	78675	84081	66938	93654	59894
77	37449	30362	06694	54690	04052	53115	62757	95348	78662	11163	81651	50245	34971	52924
78	46515	70331	85922	38329	57015	15765	97161	17869	45349	61796	66345	81073	49106	79860
79	30986	81223	42416	58353	21532	30502	32305	86482	05174	07901	54339	58861	74818	46942
80	63798	64995	46583	09765	44160	78128	83991	42865	92520	83531	80377	35909	81250	54238
81	82486	84846	99254	67632	43218	50076	21361	64816	51202	88124	41870	52689	51275	83556
82	21885	32906	92431	09060	64297	51674	64126	62570	26123	05155	59194	52799	28225	85762
83	60336	98782	07408	53458	13564	59089	26445	29789	85205	41001	12535	12133	14645	23541
84	43937	46891	24010	25560	86355	33941	25786	54990	71899	15475	95434	98227	21824	19585
85	97656	63175	89303	16275	07100	92063	21942	18611	47348	20203	18534	03862	78095	50136
86	03299	01221	05418	38982	55758	92237	26759	86367	21216	98442	08303	56613	91511	75928
87	79626	06486	03574	17668	07785	76020	79924	25651	83325	88428	85076	72811	22717	50585
88	85636	68335	47539	03129	65651	11977	02510	26113	99447	68645	34327	15152	55230	93448
89	18039	14367	61337	06177	12143	46609	32989	74014	64708	00533	35398	58408	13261	47908
90	08362	15656	60627	36478	65648	16764	53412	09013	07832	41574	17639	82163	60859	75567
91	79556	29068	04142	16268	15387	12856	66227	38358	22478	73373	88732	09443	82558	05250
92	92608	82674	27072	32534	17075	27698	98204	63863	11951	34648	88022	56148	34925	57031
93	23982	25835	40055	67006	12293	02753	14827	22235	35071	99704	37543	11601	35503	85171
94	09915	96306	05908	97901	28395	14186	00821	80703	70426	75647	76310	88717	37890	40129
95	50937	33300	26695	62247	69927	76123	50842	43834	86654	70959	79725	93872	28117	19233
96	42488	78077	69882	61657	34136	79180	97526	43092	04098	73571	80799	76536	71255	64239
97	46764	86273	63003	93017	31204	36692	40202	35275	57306	55543	53203	18098	47625	88684
98	03237	45430	55417	63282	90816	17349	88298	90183	36600	78406	06216	95787	42579	90730
99	86591	81482	52667	61583	14972	90053	89534	76036	49199	43716	97548	04379	46370	28672
100	38534	01715	94964	87288	65680	43772	39560	12918	86537	62738	19636	51132	25739	56947

Source: Beyer, 1968.

Appendix F

HOW TO USE
A STATISTICAL PACKAGE

WITH THE ASSISTANCE OF LISA M. GILMAN
AND WITH CONTRIBUTIONS BY JOAN SAXTON WEBER

Computers and statistical software such as the Statistical Package for the Social Sciences (SPSS) make complex statistical computations simple and fast. SPSS is one of the most popular comprehensive statistical software packages used in the social sciences. You can use it to calculate a great many statistics and to create charts and tables for presentations with just a few clicks of the mouse.

This appendix provides a basic introduction to SPSS. Even if you are unfamiliar with computers or apprehensive about statistics, you will find that SPSS for Windows is very user friendly. Please bear in mind that all of the examples use version 11.5 of SPSS, with data from the 2000 version of the General Social Survey (GSS); if you are using a different SPSS version or another year of the GSS, you may find some slight differences in procedures or answers.

BASIC PROCEDURES

To start SPSS for Windows, click or double-click on the SPSS icon using the left mouse button. If you are unable to locate the SPSS icon, click the Start button, then click on Programs, and then click on SPSS.

A new screen will open with a "What would you like to do?" box superimposed on the screen. For now, click on the Cancel button in the "What would you like to do?" box, to get it out of the way. You are now looking at the SPSS Data Editor window. This screen is where data to be analyzed are entered or data files that have already been created (datasets) are loaded.

To access the data for this appendix, click:

File ∅ Open ∅ Data (or just click on the open folder icon).

Select (highlight) the GSS2000mini file. If the GSS2000mini file hasn't been transferred to your hard disk, you can find it on the CDROM that came with this text.

Exhibit F.1   SPSS Data Editor

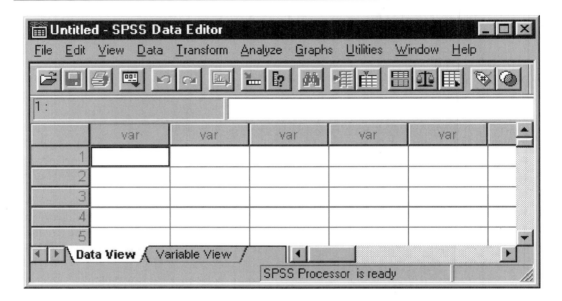

The Data View in the Data Editor consists of columns and rows, with each column representing a different variable—their names are at the top—and each row representing one case or "observation" (Exhibit F.1). If you are using the student version of SPSS, you are limited to no more than 50 variables and 1,500 observations. (The GSS2000mini dataset has 1,404 cases, or observations, and 48 variables. You can confirm this by moving the scroll bars on the bottom and right of the Data View). There are no variable/observation limits in the commercial version.

Another screen you should be familiar with is the Variable View screen. To access the variable view screen, click on the Variable View tab at the bottom left of the Data Editor (not available in early versions of SPSS for Windows). The Variable View screen contains a list of all the variables included in the data set and their characteristics. Each row corresponds to a single variable. Variable characteristics are indicated at the top of each column. When you are in the Variable View mode, you can create, edit, or view variable information. Now click on the Data View tab to return to the data view mode.

Looking at the Data

There are several ways to learn more about the variables and numbers that you see in the Data View screen. The names of the variables are listed across the top of the screen. You can also see the list of variables in the GSS2000mini file by clicking on the variable list icon at the top of the data editor screen. When you click on any variable in the resulting window, you can see the details that show how it was coded. But the easiest way to learn about the variables in the dataset is to switch from the Data View to the Variable View screen by clicking on the tab in the lower left.

You can tell what some variables are just by their SPSS variable names, like SEX. However, many variables are responses to specific questions and we can't tell just what they are on the basis of the shorthand variable name. Instead, we can inspect the variable label in the "Label" column corresponding to that variable in the Variable View screen (you may need to widen the Label column by dragging the separator line at the top of the column with your mouse).

SPSS understands numbers much better than text, so all the answers to each GSS question have been coded. This means that, for every variable, each response category has been assigned a numerical value. For some variables, such as AGE and EDUC, the number you see is simply the number of years. For other variables, such as SEX and RACE, each number corresponds to a particular response category. For example, go to the Variable View screen and click on the "Values" cell in the row corresponding to the variable SEX. Now click on the gray box in that cell and you can see the labels for specific codes, which show that men are coded "1" and women are coded "2."

Values that stand in for missing data are indicated in the "Missing" column. Special labels identifying the reason for missing data, such as DK for Don't Know or NA for No Answer, also appear in the Value Labels column. For ABRAPE, the variables dialog box showed that 8 corresponds with DK (don't know) and 9 corresponds with NA (not available). Therefore, for the variable ABRAPE, both 8 and 9 are missing values.

For most statistical calculations, SPSS ignores missing values and calculates the statistic based on the responses of the respondents who answered the question. In general, however, you should make sure missing values are not inadvertently included in your analysis. Common values used to identify missing data are –1, 0, 8, and 9. If the variable is two digits wide, such as AGE, the missing values are usually 97, 98, and/or 99.

What if you have data for new cases to enter, or new variables that you need to define? You can simply enter the data in the Data View and enter the labels and missing value codes in the Variable View. Click on File—Save after you are sure that everything is correct.

Before you proceed to the next step, make one minor adjustment in the display options. Click:

Edit ∅ Options

The Options dialog box will open. You will see a series of "tabs" along the top of the window. You should be looking at the General options (if not, click on the General tab). On the upper left side of the General options screen you will see the Variable Lists options.

Under Variable Lists, click the radio button next to Display Names (to mark it with a small dot). This will display the convenient short variable names rather than the descriptive variable label in some of the selection boxes.

UNIVARIATE STATISTICS

Now that you have an open data file and are somewhat familiar with the data itself, you can begin exploring the data statistically (statistics are discussed in Chapter 12).

Frequencies

A *frequency distribution* is a table that displays how many and what percentage of observations fall into given categories for a variable of interest. In other words, a frequency distribution tells you how many people said yes, how many people said no, and so on. The purpose of obtaining a frequency distribution is to summarize the data so that they are easy to understand. The variable ABRAPE (pregnant as a result of rape) will serve as a good example for a frequency distribution. Click:

Analyze ∅ Descriptive Statistics ∅ Frequencies

The frequencies dialog box will open, as shown in Exhibit F.2. Choose ABRAPE by clicking on it from the list on the left. Click the arrow in the center of the dialog box to move the ABRAPE to the "variable(s)" box on the right. Then click OK.

Exhibit F.2   The Frequencies Dialogue Box

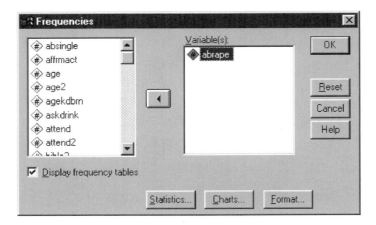

After SPSS has processed the command, the results appear in a new window titled "Output1–SPSS Viewer." The Output window has two panes. The left pane is referred to as the "output navigator." The output navigator contains an outline of everything you ask SPSS to do from the beginning of the session. It allows you to easily refer back to any given table or graph. To go to a specific table, you find it in the output navigator, click on the table you want, and it will be displayed in the right pane. As indicated, the right pane contains the actual output for the commands you gave SPSS. It is often referred to as the "output" or the "results."

In the example above, SPSS created a frequency distribution for the variable ABRAPE. SPSS produces two boxes (Exhibit F.3). The first box just displays the valid number of cases (*N*) and the total number of missing cases for the variable of interest. The second box contains the actual frequency distribution. If the entire table is not visible, use the scroll bar on the right to move down the output window. The distribution shows that about 80% of respondents believe abortion is permissible when a pregnancy is the result of rape, whereas 20% of respondents do not believe that abortion is permissible in this circumstance.

Exhibit F.3   SPSS Frequencies Output

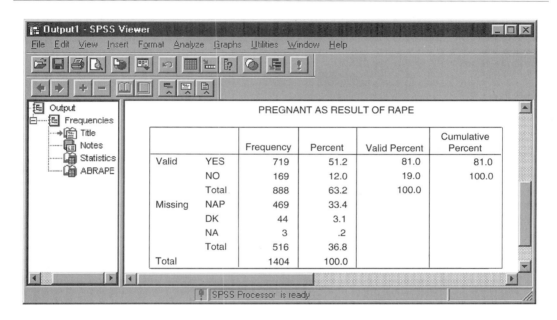

Descriptive Statistics

If you need to calculate the mean, median, or standard deviation of an interval or ratio level variable, you can do so simply with the Descriptive Statistics procedure. Click:

Analyze ∅ Descriptive Statistics ∅ Descriptives

and click the EDUC variable over into the Variables window before clicking OK.

Graphing

Another method of describing the distribution of a single variable is through the use of a histogram. A histogram is useful for graphically displaying the distribution of a given variable. Histograms are useful when the variable(s) you are interested in are continuous in nature (interval/ratio) and have a large number of categories. For example, if you want to look at the number of respondents within certain age groups, it is much simpler to visually display the data than to look at counts. Let's look at how age is distributed in the GSS200mini data included with this book. Click:

Graphs ∅ Histogram

Click on the AGE variable in the variable list and move it to the Variable box and click OK (Exhibit F.4).

Exhibit F.4   Selecting a Variable for a Histogram

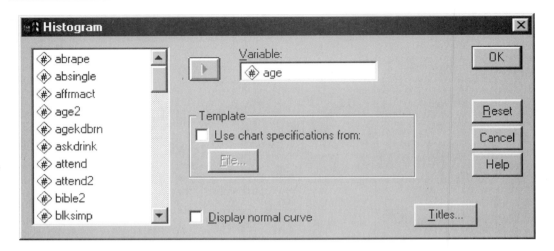

When you look at the histogram (Exhibit F.5), you can see that the age distribution has a slight positive skew. The majority of respondents are under the age of 60. The statistics to the right of the histogram indicate that the mean age of the respondents for this sample is approximately 46 years old with a standard deviation of about 17 years.

Exhibit F.5   Histogram of Age

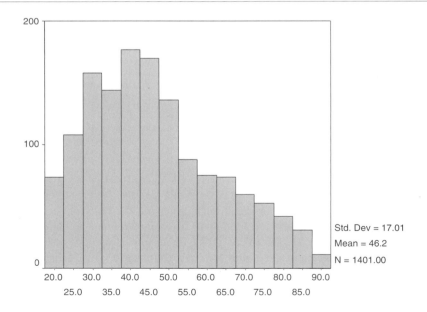

AGE OF RESPONDENT

A similar graphic device for nominal or ordinal variables is the bar chart. You can create a bar chart for Race by clicking:

Graphs * Bar

and then highlighting the options Simple, and "Summaries for groups of cases" before clicking Define. Now scroll through the variable list to find race, click this into the Category Axis box, and select the Bars Represent . . . % of cases option. Under Options, unclick the box for "Display Groups Defined by Missing Values." Now, back in the "Define Simple Bar" window, click OK. And there you have it.

RECODING VARIABLES

In some instances, variables with many categories may be confusing to use and/or interpret. At other times, your research question may make it necessary to limit your analysis to certain categories. The variable EDUC (highest year of education completed) is a good example. You seldom want to know if people with 11 years of education are different from people who have 10 years of education. It might be better to examine differences of opinion among high school graduates versus college graduates.

To create these groups it will be necessary to recode the EDUC variable. When recoding a variable, be sure to check the missing values and to look at the minimum and maximum values for valid responses with a frequency distribution.

Let's recode EDUC into the following four categories:

Those who have 0 to 11 years of education are put into category 1

Those who have exactly 12 years of education are put into category 2

Those who have 13 to 15 years of education are put into category 3

Those who have 16 or more years of education are put into category 4

In this example, you will collapse the original 21 categories (years of education from 0 to 20) into the 4 categories indicated above. To do this, you will create a new variable called ED4CAT. (You should always recode variables into "different variables" to retain the original variable.) Click:

Transform ∅ Recode ∅ Into Different Variables

This takes you to the first recode dialog box, in which you tell SPSS the name of the old variable you are recoding from (EDUC) and the name of your new recoded variable (ED4CAT) (see Exhibit F.6). Using the scroll bar, find EDUC in the variable list on the left and move it to the "Numeric Variable ∅ Output Variable" box. Under the "Output Variable" section, type the name of the new variable (ED4CAT) and a variable label, then click Change. Be sure to recode any missing values (these could be collapsed into a single category).

Exhibit F.6   Selecting Variable for Recoding

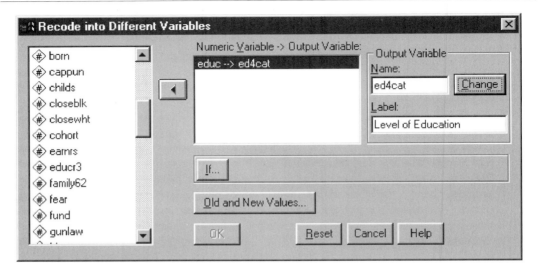

After doing this, click the "Old and New Values . . ." button. A new dialog box will open (Exhibit F.7). This second box is where you tell SPSS what categories you want to recode the original data into. To do this, you identify the original ("old") values of the variable on the left side of the box, and you put the values for your new variable on the right side of the box. Click the Add button to proceed with the conversion.

Exhibit F.7   Recoding Instructions

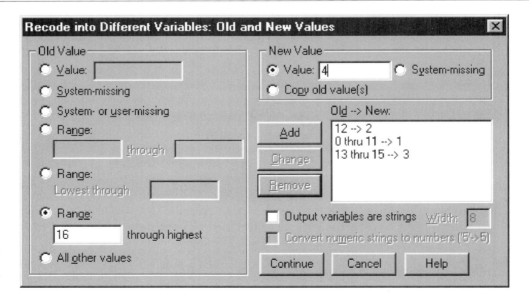

After you have created the desired categories click OK. You will be returned to the first recode box and will need to click OK again. The newly created variable (ED4CAT) will be located at the end of the data matrix. Obtain a frequency distribution for ED4CAT. You will notice that there are no value labels. Therefore, to make this output easier to read it will be necessary to attach value labels to the numeric codes. Go back to the Data View window. Scroll to the far right of the data matrix. Double-click the name of the new variable ED4CAT. This will put you in Variable View mode, which will allow you to edit the characteristics of the variable.

Using the right arrow key on the keyboard, go to the "Values" cell. Click on the button located next to the word "None." A box entitled "Value Labels" will appear. Enter each category value and the corresponding value label where indicated (Exhibit F.8). After all value labels are entered, click OK.

Exhibit F.8   Defining Value Labels

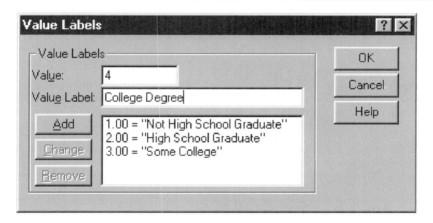

Remember, you must also tell SPSS what the missing values are for your recoded variable. To do this, using the right arrow key on the keyboard, move to the "Missing" cell (this is located next to the "Values" cell). Click the button located in that cell. Identify each missing value as a "Discrete Missing Value" and then click OK.

Computing a New Variable

Recoding is very useful when you want to alter the format of a given variable. However, sometimes it may be necessary to combine multiple variables. For example, you may have a survey measuring aggressive behavior. To best measure levels of aggressiveness it would make sense to build an additive index from the data so that each respondent has an aggressiveness score (see Chapter 4). To do this, it is necessary to modify the data through the use of the Compute command. This command works well for combining two or more variables and for performing other types of mathematical transformations of the data.

Using the Compute command, let's calculate the age of each respondent's eldest child. Click:

Transform ∅ Compute

The Compute command will create a new variable based on the mathematical functions you select—the target variable. Name the target variable CHLDAGE. To compute this, we need to calculate the difference between the respondents' age and the age of the respondent when his/her first child was born. Therefore, move the AGE variable to the "Numeric Expression" box. Using your mouse or keypad, click on the subtraction symbol. Now, move the AGEKDBRN variable into the "Numeric Expression" box, and click OK. The new variable will be created to the far right of the existing variables.

If you scroll to the right, you will notice a number of cells with a "." in them. This is SPSS's default for "missing" data. The age of the eldest child could not be calculated for those individuals who did not have any children. Therefore, SPSS uses the "." to indicate that there were no data (or the data were missing) for those cases.

BIVARIATE AND MULTIVARIATE STATISTICS

Frequency distributions are good for describing the distribution of the variables in the dataset. However, to examine the relationship between two or more variables, a different set of statistical techniques are necessary. These are referred to as bivariate (two variable) and multivariate (multiple variable) statistics.

Crosstabulation

One way of exploring the relationship between two variables is through the use of a contingency table, more commonly referred to as a crosstab. Crosstabs are useful for exploring relationships between categorical variables. For example, we can use a crosstab to explore the relationship between level of education as measured by DEGREE and attitudes toward abortion for any reason (ABANY). Click:

Analyze ∅ Descriptive Statistics ∅ Crosstabs

For this analysis, DEGREE is the independent variable and ABANY is the dependent variable. Therefore, you will want DEGREE in the columns and ABANY in the rows. Locate these variables in the variable list (Exhibit F.9). Using the arrow buttons, place DEGREE and ABANY in their respective boxes.

Exhibit F.9   Requesting Crosstabs

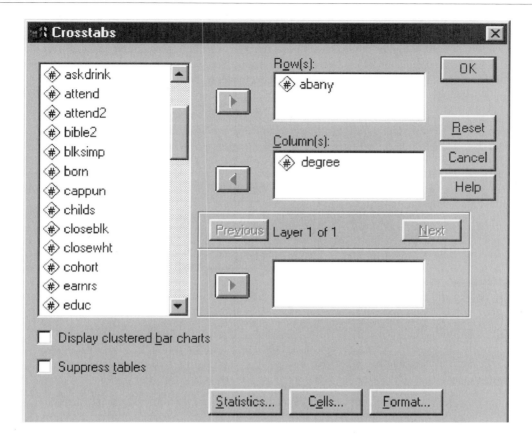

SPSS automatically computes cell counts (the number of respondents that fall within each category). However, you should also have SPSS calculate percentages for the independent variable to interpret differences. Therefore, click the Cells. . . button, choose the column percentages, and then click Continue to return to the first dialog box. If you have previous knowledge of statistics, you may want SPSS to also calculate a specific statistical test, such as chi-square. To do this, click the Statistics . . . button, make the appropriate choices, then click Continue. Click OK to run the crosstab command.

Now repeat this procedure, substituting INCOMR2 for DEGREE. This will generate a crosstabulation of support for abortion by respondent's income.

The results indicate that support for abortion due to being single increases with education (rising from about 33% to over 50% across the five education categories), but only to a limited extent with income (an increase of about 6% between the two income categories).

Three-Variable Crosstabs

In the last example it was determined that there was only a weak relationship between income and support for abortion. Could this relationship be due to an extraneous factor? A three-variable crosstab can be created to assess whether controlling for another variable eliminates the apparent influence of income on support for abortion.

You have already seen that support for abortion increases with degree. Because income also increases with degree, and we know that maximum educational attainment most often precedes employment as an adult, it is possible that support for abortion varies with income because both of these variables are in turn influenced directly by level of education. If this is the case, the relationship between income and support for abortion would be spurious—that is, it would be due to the extraneous factor of education.

We can control for degree in order to assess the effects of education on the relationship between income and support for abortion. To do this, click:

Analyze ∅ Descriptive Statistics ∅ Crosstabs

You should click ABANY into the rows box and INCOMR2 into the columns box in the Crosstabs dialog box (unless they are still there after your last procedure). Select the variable DEGREE from the variables list and move it to the empty box on the bottom titled "Layer 1 of 1." Select the column percentages and the chi-square statistic, if desired, then click OK.

The results indicate that when controlling for the influence of degree, the relationship between income and support for abortion is eliminated for HIGH SCHOOL, but somewhat stronger for JUNIOR COLLEGE and GRADUATE. (Compare the "yes" percentages in the columns corresponding to the two income categories.) In other words, in this sample degree seems to be the critical influence on support for abortion, with income possibly making a difference for those with a junior college and graduate degree. You might take a minute to speculate about what might account for this pattern (although if you have had a course in statistics, and check the chi-square statistic for these tables, you may realize that we cannot reject the possibility that the relationship between support for abortion and income is simply due to chance).

Comparing Means

How would you compare mean years of education of whites and minorities? This type of question requires a comparison of means. A comparison of means is useful when you want to look at differences between two or more groups, such as by race or gender.

Click:

Analyze ∅ Compare Means ∅ Means

You must choose two variables: a dependent variable, which must be an interval/ratio level variable (or an ordinal variable that you are treating as interval), and an independent variable, which should be nominal or ordinal. For this example, EDUC is the dependent variable and RACE is the independent variable (Exhibit F.10).

Exhibit F.10   Requesting a Comparison of Means

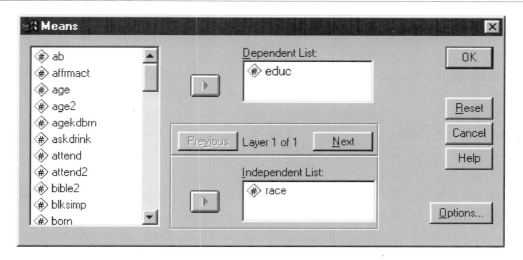

After you identify your dependent and independent variables, click OK. SPSS will produce a table that shows the mean years of education for each category within the RACE variable.

The results indicate that the mean years of education for whites is about one year higher than the mean number of years of education for blacks, but less than half a year higher than for individuals in the "other" category.

SAVING AND RETRIEVING FILES IN SPSS

A number of the exercises in this book require you to recode variables. To eliminate the need to recreate variables you created via the Recode command, it is a good idea to save the dataset as a new file—with a new name—on either your hard drive or a floppy disk. In the Student Version of SPSS, the maximum number of variables allowed in any given dataset is 50. If you exceed the 50-variable limit, SPSS will save only the first 50 variables. You can delete variables you do not need by highlighting the corresponding column in Data View and pressing Delete on your keyboard. In any case, do *not* save the dataset with the same name. You might unintentionally make a permanent change in the values of variables in the dataset and later come to regret it.

Saving SPSS Data Files

To save the dataset as a new file, click:
File ∅ Save As
The Save As dialog box will open. It should be similar to the File_Open dialog box shown at the beginning of this appendix.

If you are saving the file to your hard drive, you should save it in the SPSS folder or My Documents folder to find it easily later. After you type in the new name, click the Save As button.

Be forewarned: Output files can quickly take up a *lot* of space on your hard disk, or on a floppy. In most cases, you should just print the output instead of saving it in a file.

Opening Output Files

To open the output file(s) you saved, simply click:
File ∅ Open ∅ Output
The Open File dialog box will open. From the "Look in" drop-down text box, locate the folder where you saved the output file. Click on "ABANYFreq.spo" (or any other Viewer output file you want to open) to highlight it, and then click Open. The file will open in the Output window.

PRINTING YOUR OUTPUT

There are two ways to print from SPSS: from the menu bar and from the tool bar. First let's look at how to print from the menu bar. Click:
File ∅ Print
From the print dialog box you can choose to print all of your output or only selected items, the type of printer, and then number of copies to print. After you have made your selections, click OK. If you want to print only part of the output, you can select multiple portions by depressing the Ctrl key while clicking on each portion you would like to print (this must be done prior to selecting the print option). Then, from the print dialog box click on the radio button for Selection in the "Print Range" section (to mark it with a small dot), and then click OK. Exhibit F.11 shows an illustration of some of these features in the print dialog box.

Exhibit F.11   Print Dialog Box

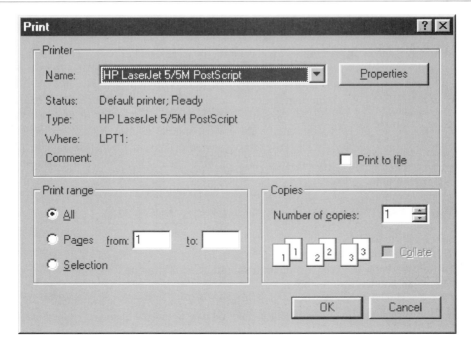

In addition to printing from the menu bar, you can also print by clicking the "Print" button on the tool bar (the printer icon). This brings up the same print dialog box.

Now that you have been introduced to a variety of different ways to communicate with SPSS, you may be feeling a bit overwhelmed. While you are still familiarizing yourself with SPSS, you may want to stick to the menu bar options as they guide you on how to proceed. When you become more comfortable using SPSS, you may like the convenience of the tool bar shortcuts. Keep in mind, you don't have to learn everything all at once.

CONCLUSION

At this point you should be familiar with SPSS and able to complete all the exercises included in this book. Remember, the more you practice, the more comfortable you will be with using SPSS and statistics. If you have trouble, don't be afraid to refer to the SPSS help file or Statistical Tutor, which are available from the Help drop-down menu, or ask your instructor or the computer lab consultant. Everyone runs into problems, but you can solve problems more quickly if you do the following:

- Write down the error message you are getting.
- Try to determine whether your problem is an SPSS problem. If so, look for help from the many sources of assistance out there: the Help drop-down menu in SPSS, the SPSS manual, some campus computer lab consultants, your instructor, and quite possibly your classmates.
- Try to determine whether your problem is a Windows problem or a computer hardware problem. If so, your college probably offers computer lab technical support. Introductory books for Windows are an excellent resource because they typically describe problems common to Windows and to many software programs.

Box F.1   Summary of SPSS Drop-Down Menus

The **File** menu enables you to open and save data files, import data created by other software, and print the contents of the data editor.
Use the **Edit** menu to cut, copy, and paste data; find data within the open data set; and change options settings.
The **View** menu allows you to change how the data editor looks by changing fonts, turning toolbars on and off, turning grid lines on and off, and turning value labels on and off.
Use the **Data** menu to sort, select, or weight cases.
The **Transform** menu lets you make changes to selected variables, compute new variables, recode the values of existing ones, and replace missing values.
Use the **Analyze** menu to select the statistical procedure you want to use.
The **Graphs** menu allows you to produce a variety of two- and three-dimensional graphical displays of your data for purposes of data analysis and presentation.
Use the **Utilities** menu to obtain information about the variables in the open data set and select a list of variables to appear in dialog boxes.
The **Window** menu lets you switch between SPSS windows or minimize all open SPSS windows.
Use the **Help** menu to access SPSS help topics and run the tutorial.

Appendix G

How to Use a Qualitative™
Analysis Package

Ann Dupuis

You may have noticed the "HyperRESEARCH" option on the computer CD bundled with this book, and wondered what it's about. The short answer is: This is the demo version of the HyperRESEARCH software (for both Macintosh and Windows), including an electronic manual and a full set of tutorials with all necessary support and sample files.

For the long answer, please read on.

WHAT IS HyperRESEARCH?

HyperRESEARCH is a software tool for qualitative data analysis, developed by ResearchWare, Inc. (www.researchware.com). It is one of several CAQDAS packages available. (CAQDAS is an acronym for computer-assisted qualitative data analysis software.) Like many CAQDAS programs, HyperRESEARCH's essential capabilities are for qualitative analysis—code-and-retrieve data analysis features, report-generating capabilities, multimedia support (for data including graphics, video, and audio as well as text), and theory-building tools. These features are packaged within an easy-to-use package that helps you, the user, take control.

NOTE: Ann Dupuis is a Technical Support and Documentation Specialist at ResearchWare, Inc. (support@research-ware.com). This appendix is copyright ©2002 by ResearchWare, Inc. HyperRESEARCH™ is a trademark of Research Ware, Inc.

A demo version of HyperRESEARCH is available on the accompanying CD. (You also can download HyperRESEARCH from www.researchware.com.) This version of the software is fully functional; however, you are limited to using "demo mode," which places limits on the size of your study (your Master Code List is limited to 75 code names, you may have only seven cases, and you may apply only 50 code instances to each case). You can purchase a "license key" from ResearchWare, Inc. or any of its reseller partners to unlock the software (lift the restrictions imposed in demo mode).

If you are a student, you may find that the free demo version of the software is adequate to your needs while you learn how to conduct qualitative research. If you are an instructor, you should note that the demo version of HyperRESEARCH is free for you and your students to use. ResearchWare, Inc. also has a promotional program in which qualifying educators will receive a free license key to unlock the unrestricted version of HyperRESEARCH for their own use. Visit its Web site at www.researchware.com for more information.

Exhibit G.1   HyperRESEARCH Basic Interface: Study Window, Code List Editor, Source Window, and Annotation Window; Not Shown: Hypothesis Tester, Report Generator, Code Map, and Other Specialized Functions

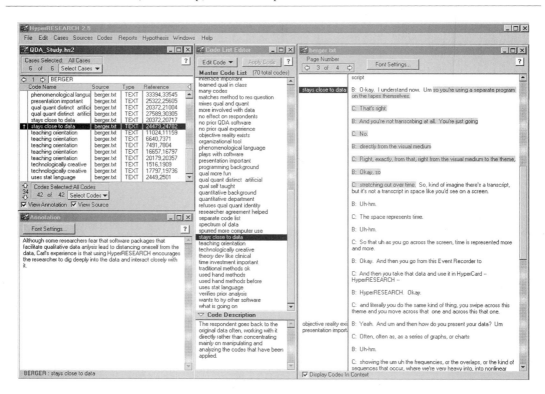

A QUICK TOUR OF HʏᴘᴇʀRESEARCH

This introduction to HyperRESEARCH briefly shows the major features of the software. For a more in-depth, step-by-step look at how HyperRESEARCH facilitates qualitative data analysis, it is recommended that you use the tutorials on the CD. You can install HyperRESEARCH on your computer and follow the step-by-step tutorials to learn first hand how to use the software. The CD includes sample research materials and HyperRESEARCH studies you can use in conjunction with the tutorials, or to explore the software's capabilities on your own.

HyperRESEARCH's Flexible Structure and Point-and-Click Interface

HyperRESEARCH allows you to organize your data in many ways. A study consists of one or more cases (a case is the unit of analysis in a HyperRESEARCH study) (Exhibit G.2). You decide what a case will represent, such as an individual, a time period, or a focus group. HyperRESEARCH allows you to choose your codes and code relationships, the depth of your analysis, and the source of your data (i.e., text, graphic, audio, and video sources). HyperRESEARCH allows you to apply codes for multiple sourcefiles to a single case (or a single source file to multiple cases). You also can assign multiple codes to any chunk of source material.

Exhibit G.2 Graphic Representation of the Structure of a HyperRESEARCH Study

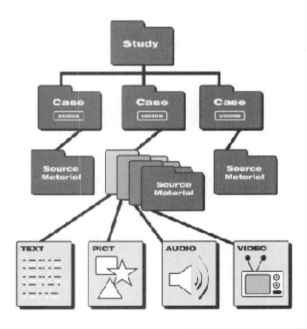

HyperRESEARCH's point-and-click interface features pull-down menus, click-and-drag selection, and keyboard shortcuts for those who prefer keyboard commands to mouse clicks.

The Study Window

The Study window is the main HyperRESEARCH window, where your cases and code references are displayed. The Study window also shows you how many cases are currently in your study, and how many code instances have been applied to the current case (Exhibit G.3).

You can view the code references of one case at a time. Each code reference consists of a code name (from your Master Code List, entered into the Code List Editor), the source file name, the source type (text, audio, video, graphic), and a code reference (HyperRESEARCH's reference points for recalling the source material).

With the View Source option selected, clicking on any code reference will recall the underlying source material. HyperRESEARCH will open the file in a Source window, with the underlying source material highlighted.

Exhibit G.3   Study and Source Windows Showing Highlighted Code and Source Material

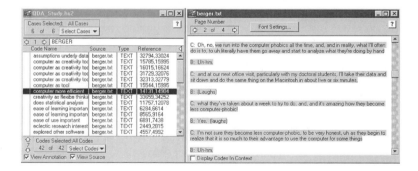

While working in your Study window, you also can manipulate your code instances. The Codes menu offers a variety of commands you can use with your codes, including duplicating code instances (applying additional codes to the same source material referenced by the original code), recoding (changing the code name applied to the referenced source material), and deleting (removing one or more specific code instances from the case) (Exhibit G.4).

Exhibit G.4   Codes Menu Showing Options Available While Working With Code Instances in the Study Window

You can also sort the code instances in your study by name, by reference, by type, by source file, or by any combination of these criteria.

The Select Cases and Select Codes commands allow you to concentrate on subsets of your cases and codes. These powerful commands facilitate quick review of themes and patterns in your data and coding. Used in conjunction with the report generator and the hypothesis tester, code and case selections allow you to temporarily ignore extraneous data when generating reports or testing hypotheses.

You may select codes by name, by type (text, audio, etc.), by criteria (including Code Proximity functions), or via the Code Map. The codes you select will appear in the Study window. Codes not included in the selection will be hidden from view. You can recall them at any time by altering your code selection parameters (Exhibit G.5).

The Code List Editor

The Code List Editor allows you to create, view, and manipulate your Master Code List. You can add codes, edit codes (with changes being reflected in the individual code references throughout your study), and enter detailed definitions or descriptions for your master codes (Exhibit G.6).

You can use the Code List Editor to enter a Code Description for any of your master codes. It's great for quick reference when deciding exactly which code to apply to a source chunk (a block of text), especially when several researchers are working on the same study.

Exhibit G.5   Study Window Showing Codes Selected By Name (All Other Codes Are Hidden)

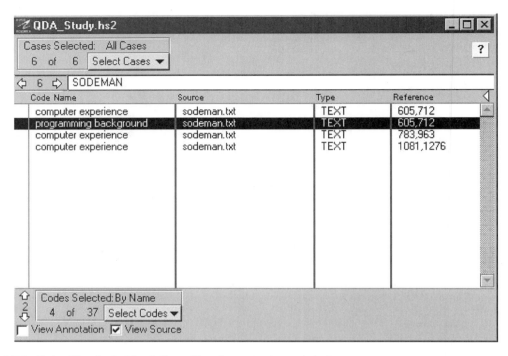

Exhibit G.6   The Code List Editor, Showing a Code Description

Any changes you make to the Master Code List will be reflected in the individual code instances applied to the cases in your study. Thus, if you wish to rename all instances of a master code throughout your study, you would use the global Rename command available from the Edit Code menu in the Code List Editor.

To affect specific code instances, rather than all codes throughout your study, use the main Codes menu commands in conjunction with individual code instances in the Study window.

The Source Windows

HyperRESEARCH has four Source window types, one for each of the four types of source material (text, graphics, audio, and video). Displayed reports include hyperlinks to underlying source material. HyperRESEARCH's ability to work with multiple data types, such as text, graphic, audio, and video sources, provides the flexibility to integrate all of the data necessary to conduct your research.

The Text Source Window

The text Source window displays text files. You can customize the Font Settings (typeface and size) and also choose whether to Display Codes in Context (code names appear in the left margin). This window is fully resizable and movable.

HyperRESEARCH 2.5 allows you to select any chunk of text (from one character to an entire file) and apply any number of codes to it. Text source files also can be split into multiple pages, if you wish (Exhibit G.7).

Exhibit G.7   Source Window (Text)

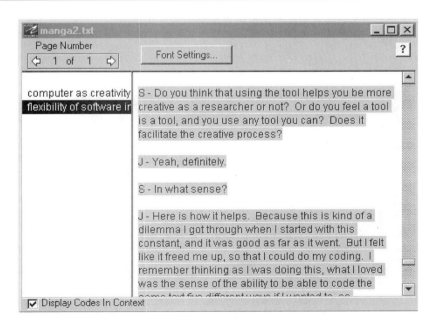

View your codes adjacent to the source material by using Display Codes In Context. The material can be sent to a printer with the codes appearing in the left margin. The Codes In Context feature also can be turned off, maximizing the space available for text (with no margin for viewing code names).

To select text for coding, simply click and drag over the desired chunk. Then use the Code List Editor to apply one or more codes to the source selection.

The Graphic Source Window

The graphic Source window allows you to display still images (.gif, .jpg, or similar graphic files) and assign codes to selected portions of the image (Exhibit G.8).

Exhibit G.8   Source Window (Graphic)

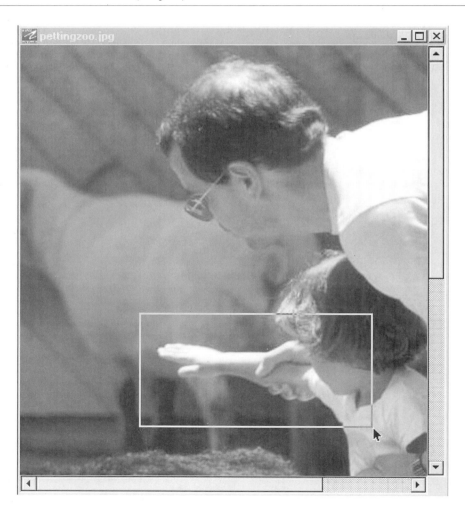

To select a portion of a graphic for coding, click and drag from one corner of a rectangular chunk to the opposite corner. Then use the Code List Editor to apply one or more codes to the graphic selection.

The Movie Source Window

The movie Source window displays movie files (with their audio tracks, if any) using Apple's QuickTime software. You can select and code any number of frames, which can be replayed when recalling the source material from the Study window or in a hyperlinked report (Exhibit G.9).

Exhibit G.9   Source Window (Video)

To select a video segment for coding, simply click and drag along the slide track while holding down the Shift key. Alternatively, position the slide bar at the beginning of the desired segment, then hold the Shift key down and click on the Play button. Release the Shift key when you reach the end of the desired segment.

After you have selected a video segment, you can fine-tune your selection. The video window controls offer frame-by-frame precision.

As with text selections, you can apply more than one code to a given chunk.

The Audio Source Window

The audio Source window uses Apple's QuickTime software to allow you to play back an audio file and select portions for coding. Viewing the coded source material of an audio file (either by selecting the code reference on the Study window with the View Source feature active, or clicking on a hyperlinked code reference in a report) recalls and replays the selected portion of the audio track (Exhibit G.10).

Exhibit G.10 Source Window (Audio)

The audio Source window controls are identical to the video Source window controls.

The Annotation Window

The Annotation window allows you to add a memo or annotation to any code reference in your study. Unlike a Code Definition, which applies to a master code, an Annotation is specific to an individual code reference and its underlying source material (Exhibit G.11).

Exhibit G.11 Annotation Window

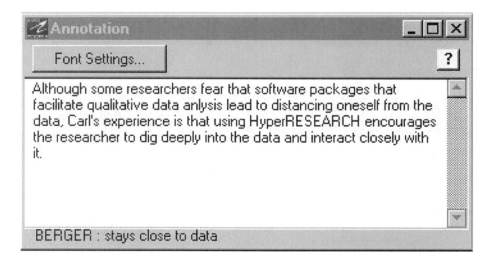

To annotate a code, select a code reference on a case card, choose the Annotate command, and add up to 32,000 characters of information per reference. Annotations can be used as a built-in memo system. All annotations are fully editable and can be included in reports.

The Report Window

The Report window presents the report generation options. Use this window to customize the data you wish retrieved for a given report.

Generate custom reports and display them on your screen or save them as text to output to a word processor, spreadsheet, or statistical package. Hyperlinked reports allow you to click on any code reference to view the source material (Exhibit G.12).

Exhibit G.12 Report Window Showing Report Element Options

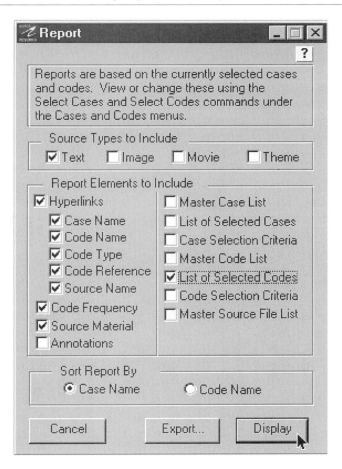

In addition to specifying which elements you wish included in a report, you can use the Select Cases and Select Codes commands to specify precisely which cases and codes you wish included in the report. Generate a report that includes all codes across your entire study, or report on any subset of cases and codes.

If you choose any report elements from the right column (Master Case List through Master Source File List), the report generator will also display a header page with the specified information (Exhibit G.13).

Exhibit G.13 Report Display Window with Header Information

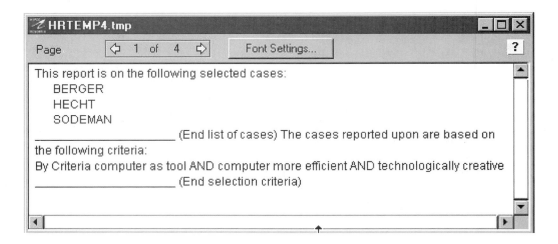

The body of the report will present results based on the current selection of cases and code instances in your Study window. You may choose to include the source material and any annotations for reported codes as well as the code names themselves.

If the Hyperlinks elements are all included, the code reference lines will actually be hyperlinks. Clicking on a code reference (e.g., "MACKEY used hand methods before 1 TEXT 13109,13334 mackey.txt") will open the underlying source material in a Source window. This allows you to view the source material in the context of the rest of the file if you wish (Exhibit G.14).

Exhibit G.14   Report Display Window Showing Hyperlinked Code References
and Source Material

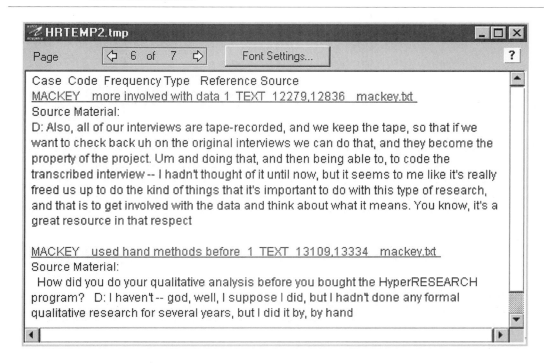

You can save report settings (including the current selection of cases and codes in your study) to run the same report again. You also can export the generated report to a text file, which you can work further with in a word processor or other program.

LEARNING MORE ABOUT THE BASICS

We've covered the basics of HyperRESEARCH: coding and retrieving, code manipulation, and generating reports. You may want to stop reading now, and start experimenting with the software itself. Tutorials One through Four on the CD offer step-by-step "walkthroughs" for the procedures for starting a study (or opening an existing one), coding source material, manipulating code instances, and generating reports. Tutorial Five covers coding and retrieving graphic, video, and audio source material. After you've mastered these procedures, you'll be ready for the more advanced and specialized capabilities HyperRESEARCH offers.

For an introduction to HyperRESEARCH's advanced features (covered in depth in Tutorials Six and Seven), read on.

ADVANCED FEATURES

In addition to the basic code-and-retrieve features HyperRESEARCH offers, there are several more advanced features available.

Autocoding

With Autocode, you can automatically assign a code to multiple sources and multiple cases, looking for several phrases or words in a single pass. Specify a number of characters, words, or lines before and/or after the found phrases to be included in the chunk selected for autocoding.

First you assign source files to the proper cases. Then you specify the phrase (or phrases) to search for and how much surrounding source material to include (Exhibit G.15).

Exhibit G.15 Autocode (Phrases) Window Set to Select Entire Paragraphs Around Each Occurrence of the Specified Phrases, in Selected Sources

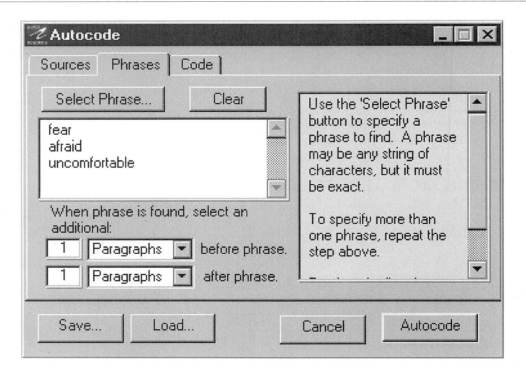

Finally, you select the codes to apply to the matching source materials (Exhibit G.16).

Exhibit G.16 Autocode (Code) Window With Code Names to Assign

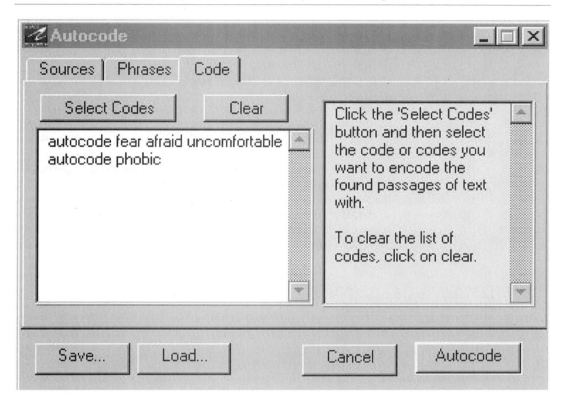

The Autocode button becomes active when all necessary parameters are supplied. HyperRESEARCH will apply the selected code or codes to all instances of the selected phrase it finds, and place the code references in the Study window for the specified cases.

Autocoding is best used as a first-pass tool, to earmark certain sections of your textual data for more precise coding. You may wish to use separate code names for autocoded passages (such as the "autocode phobic" code name in the example pictured in Exhibit G.15). These code names would then be replaced with final code names (such as "evidence of computer phobia") when you examine the actual source material and select a more precise segment of text to code.

Code Proximity Searches

HyperRESEARCH lets you conveniently reference overlapping code instances with Code Proximity searches. One of several code- and case-selection tools available, the Code

Proximity functions will seek out specific relationships between two code names (Exhibit G.17).

Available functions are:

- *Equals*—The code references for "code 1" and "code 2" match exactly. With text files, the starting and ending character placement for the source material selection will be exactly the same for the code references being compared.
- *Excludes*—The source material for "code 1" completely excludes any source material coded with "code 2." There are no overlapping characters, pixels, or video or audio segments.
- *Includes*—The source material for "code 1" completely includes the source material for "code 2." For example, a textual selection of two paragraphs coded with "code 1" will include the source material for "code 2" if "code 2" has been applied to one of those paragraphs (and no other source material outside the selection for "code 1").
- *Overlaps*—The source material for "code 1" overlaps one or more characters coded with "code 2." Code references that qualify for the equals or includes functions will also qualify for the overlaps function. However, the matches for overlaps don't need to be as specific as those for includes or equals. Coded text segments that share even one character can qualify as overlapping. With graphics, video, and audio files, the overlapping of even one pixel or time segment is enough to qualify for the overlaps function.

Exhibit G.17 Selection of Codes Based on Code Proximity Functions

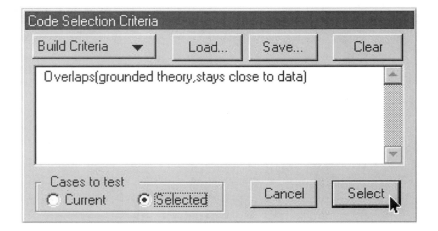

You can use the Code Proximity functions to select subsets of your codes or subsets of your cases, based on the relative placement of the codes segments within your source files.

The Code Map Window

The Code Map window allows you to explore graphic representations of the relationships between your master codes. You can group codes in any way you wish, and visually link master code names to one another. Arrange your codes visually to indicate code families, trees, or networks (Exhibit G.18).

Exhibit G.18 The Code Map Window

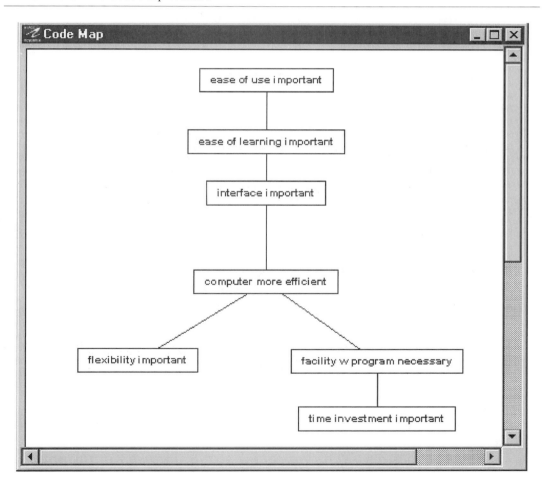

You can select codes using your Code Map and apply that selection to the Study window, which will then display only those code references corresponding to the selected master codes. Selections of mapped codes can be made by selecting each code individually, or by selecting one code and then expanding the selection based on code links. In Exhibit G.18, commanding HyperRESEARCH to select all codes within two links of the "computer more efficient" code would select everything but "ease of use important."

Thus, the Code Map can be used as a visually oriented code selection tool as well as a visualization tool.

The Hypothesis Window

The Hypothesis Tester is an "expert system" that helps you build theories and test them against the codes you've applied to your data. Like the Report Generator, the Hypothesis Tester consists of two windows: the Hypothesis Test window and a Report Display window.

The Hypothesis Test window includes a section that displays the current Hypothesis Test Rules, and a section that allows you to edit those rules (Exhibit G.19).

Exhibit G.19 The Hypothesis Window Showing Part of a Hypothesis Rule List

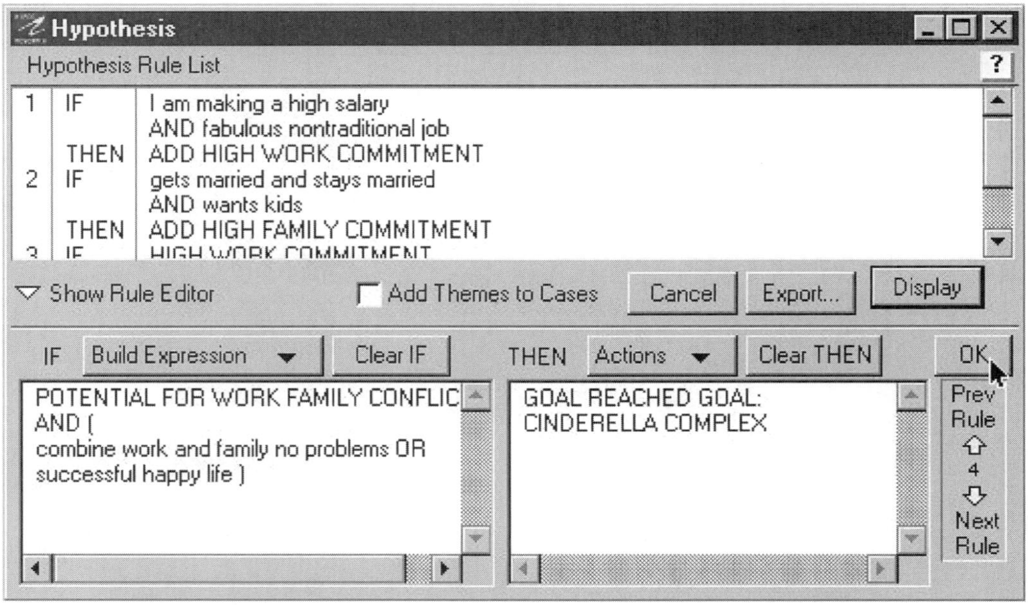

When the Hypothesis Rule List is complete, you can Export the hypothesis test report to a text file, or Display it to the Report Display window. You can also save the hypothesis for later use, or open an already-constructed hypothesis (Exhibit G.20).

Exhibit G.20 The Hypothesis Menu

Although the Hypothesis Tester may seem complicated at first, at its heart it's another way to examine your cases, looking for combinations of the presence and/or absence of code names. It utilizes Boolean expressions (delineating the code combinations to search for with the use of logical AND, OR, and NOT) and can also utilize the Code Proximity functions to look specifically for coded segments that overlap one another.

You can also use the Hypothesis Tester to add Theme codes to your case. Say you'd like to find every case that has been coded with both "gets married and stays married" and "wants kids." You'd like to apply the code "high family commitment" to each relevant case.

You could do this by selecting cases by criteria ("gets married and stays married" AND "wants kids"). You could then go to each selected case and either duplicate one or more "gets married and stays married" and "wants kids" with the "high family commitment" code, or you could open the relevant source file, select a passage (possibly one related to those already coded), and apply the "high family commitment" code directly.

Alternatively, you can do this by creating a hypothesis test that does essentially the same thing. Such a test would have one rule:

IF ("gets married and stays married" AND "wants kids") THEN ADD CODE "HIGH FAMILY COMMITMENT".

(Using all capital letters for the code name helps distinguish it as a Theme code.)

With the Add Themes to Cases option checked, running this hypothesis test would tell HyperRESEARCH to find any case that had one or more instances of "gets married and stays married" and also one or more instances of "wants kids" already coded to it. HyperRESEARCH would then add the "HIGH FAMILY COMMITMENT" code name as a Theme code. This code would not point to any specific source file or source material. It would, however, be considered in any Select Cases or Select Codes command, and would show up on your Reports (provided you chose to include Theme types as a Report Element) (Exhibit G.21).

Exhibit G.21 Study Window With Theme Code "HIGH FAMILY COMMITMENT" Applied

Code Name	Source	Type	Reference
successful happy life	Interview 6.txt	TEXT	221,276
gets married and stays married	Interview 6.txt	TEXT	736,836
wants kids	Interview 6.txt	TEXT	891,948
combine work and family no problems	Interview 6.txt	TEXT	1086,1205
works in traditional field	Interview 6.txt	TEXT	1633,1776
takes major responsibility for family work	Interview 6.txt	TEXT	1483,1872
successful happy life	Interview 6.txt	TEXT	1779,1872
concern about getting old	Interview 6.txt	TEXT	2,218
HIGH FAMILY COMMITMENT	Cinderella Complex.hhp	THEME	2

Cinderella Study.hs2

Cases Selected: All Cases
8 of 8 Select Cases ▼

6 Case 06

Codes Selected: All Codes
9 of 9 Select Codes ▼
View Annotation   View Source

LEARNING MORE ABOUT HᴜᴘᴇʀRESEARCH

The best way to learn more about HyperRESEARCH is to dive right into the materials on the CD. Install the software (both Macintosh and Windows versions are included), print out the tutorials (at least Tutorials One through Four, which cover the basics), and play around with the sample studies (the Cinderella Study and the Qualitative Data Analysis Study).

You also can visit ResearchWare's Web site at www.researchware.com. You'll find instructions there on how to join the HyperRESEARCH email discussion list. The Web site also lists events (workshops, conferences, and trade shows), links for online resources for qualitative data analysis, and more.

Welcome to the world of CAQDAS!

Appendix H

ANNOTATED LIST OF WEB SITES

http://www.abanet.org/domviol/mrdv/identify.html

The American Bar Association's Commission on Domestic Violence. Includes a definition of domestic violence, procedures for identifying a person as a victim of domestic violence, and a list of "basic warning signs."

http://www.apa.org

American Psychological Association. Includes much useful information about the APA, the psychology profession, and the results of selected research studies.

http://www.asc41.com

American Society of Criminology. Includes much useful information for students, academicians, and practitioners in the many disciplines related to criminal justice.

http://www.asanet.org

American Sociological Association. Includes lists of publications, Ethics Code, Employment Bulletin, and summaries of research funding opportunities.

http://soc.annurev.org

Annual Reviews of Sociology online. Abstracts from volumes can be searched by subject or by keywords. Offers downloads of complete text of articles for a fee.

http://www.apastyle.org/elecref.html

APA style. Electronic reference formats suggested by the American Psychological Association.

http://www.clearinghouse.net/searchbrowse.html

Argus Clearinghouse. Provides subject guides on the Internet and classifies them under subject headings.

http://www.rci.rutgers.edu/~cas2/

Center of Alcohol Studies. Offers links to numerous sites related to alcohol, alcoholism, and so on. A comprehensive index of a wealth of information on the subject.

http://www.socstats.soton.ac.uk/cass/

Centre for Applied Social Surveys (CASS). Offers access to the Question Bank (a reference source for information on how questions are formatted and worded in major social surveys) and general knowledge about survey data collection methods, design, and measurement. Access to CASS newsletters and CASS courses as well as links to other research sites of interest such as articles on social survey methodology.

http://www.c-s-i.org

Crime Stoppers International, an organization devoted to fighting crime and violence around the world. Offers links to interesting sites related to the subjects of crime and violence.

http://www.dartmouth.edu/~sources/

Dartmouth College Sources. A compendium on how to cite sources from a variety of media, with examples.

http://www.sociology.org

Electronic Journal of Sociology. Full text of articles published only online.

http://plsc.uark.edu/book/books/ethics/index.htm

Ethics site maintained by the University of Arkansas. Cases are described that involve various ethical and moral dilemmas confronted in social science research, public administration, policy making, and so on. Each case offers a different example of an ethical issue. Lists of questions allow the reader to explore the complexity of the ethics issues involved and reflect on his or her own opinions regarding the cases.

http://www.library.cornell.edu/okuref/research/webeval/html

Evaluating Web Sites: Criteria and Tools. Developed by the Olin Kroch Uris Libraries at Cornell University. Guidelines for evaluating Web sites and links to many sites with more detailed information.

http://sobek.colorado.edu/SOC/RES/family.html

Family Sociology Resources. University of Colorado site with links to family sociology resources. (Note: SOC/RES/ in the URL must be all caps.)

http://www.fbi.gov

Federal Bureau of Investigation. Much interesting information on crime.

http://www.gallup.com

Gallup poll. This site contains election poll results dating back to 1936 and information from polls on current events.

http://www.icpsr.umich.edu/gss/

General Social Survey. Search all years of the GSS for variables of interest. Check wording of questions and response choices, see frequency distributions for variables in different sets of years, obtain lists of GSS publications, and download GSS datasets.

http://www.lib.umich.edu/govdocs/

Government Resources on the Web. A subject directory of government information compiled by the University of Michigan Documents Center.

http://www.hsph.harvard.edu/cas/

Harvard School of Public Health. The latest findings about student substance abuse.

http://lib-www.ucr.edu

INFOMINE (Scholarly Internet Resource Collections). This is one example of a site that scholars can use to link to other sites containing a wide range of scholarly materials.

http://www.infopeople.org

InfoPeople Search Engines Quick Guide. Comprehensive and comparative data on most of the major search engines.

http://www.criminaljusticestudies.com/weblinks/ICJS_Links.htm

Institute for Criminal Justice Studies Web Links. "One of the most comprehensive web links pages for Criminal Justice Information on the Internet."

http://www.uakron.edu/hefe/lib1.html

Library resources and links. Library of Congress, presidential libraries, database of academic research journals, academic libraries with Web servers.

http://www.nap.edu/readingroom/books/obas/

The National Academy of Science report "On Being a Scientist: Responsible Conduct in Research." Discusses ethical issues in scientific research.

http://www.naswdc.org

National Association of Social Workers. Contains a wealth of information for social work practitioners and students.

http://www.nationalhomeless.org

The National Coalition for the Homeless. Current statistics, publications, legislative developments, and links to other resources.

http://www.umich.edu/~nes/

National Election Studies. Includes responses to questions asked since 1952, a test of the 1996 NES questionnaire, and data for online analysis. Searchable by keyword.

http://survey2000.nationalgeographic.com

The National Geographic Society's site for their Survey 2000 project. Detailed compilation of findings and many interesting displays.

http://www.niaaa.nih.gov

National Institute on Alcoholism and Alcohol Abuse. Provides many of the most popular measures of substance abuse.

http://www.nih.gov

National Institutes of Health. Information about NIH programs and grants.

http://www.nsf.gov/sbe/ses/

National Science Foundation's Social and Economic Sciences. Information regarding the Sociology Program, research funding, current and past supported projects, and so forth.

http://www.fedworld.gov

National Technical Information Service for ordering government publications.

http://www.nytimes.com

The *New York Times* Web edition. Regular news stories and other regular newspaper sections. Some pictures and audio files. Also, special news sections for Web users; online forums, allowing you to read comments on some issue—and to send a comment yourself; and search options.

http://www.bedfordstmartins.com/online/citex.html

Online! A guide to proper citation of different types of online sources, with examples conforming to MLA style, APA style, Chicago style, and more.

http://www.socialpsychology.org/expts.htm

Online Social Psychology Studies. A site at which you can participate in a social psychology experiment on the Web.

http://www.ukans.edu/cwis/units/coms2/po/index.html

Online Survey Research/Public Opinion Centers: A Worldwide Listing. University of Kansas site with a listing of and links to a great many different survey research organizations.

http://www.umich.edu/~psid/

The Panel Study of Income Dynamics. Provides data and publications based on these data.

http://www.pewinternet.org

The Pew Internet Project site. Detailed results and project description.

http://www.policefoundation.org

The Police Foundation site. Lists current and past research projects and summarizes their impact.

http://www.lib.umich.edu/govdocs/polisci.html

Political Science Resources on the Web. A subject directory compiled by the University of Michigan Documents Center.

http://popindex.princeton.edu

Population Index on the Web. Population index for 1986–1996.

http://www.publist.com

PubList. Quick and easy access to information on thousands of publications. Many of the publications listed can be purchased for a fee.

http://qb.soc.surrey.ac.uk/docs/home.htm

Question Bank from the Centre for Applied Social Surveys. Contains questions used in different surveys.

http://www.erols.com/bainbri/qf.htm

The Question Factory. A laboratory for exploring survey instruments. Allows Web users to participate in interactive survey creation and gives access to survey results.

http://www.randomizer.org

Research Randomizer. A site at which you can explore the process of randomization.

http://www.ropercenter.uconn.edu

The Roper Center. General information on the center and poll results on presidential performance.

http://www.searchenginewatch.com

Search Engine Watch. A helpful site to visit to learn about search engines.

http://www.sosig.ac.uk

Social Science Information Gateway. An omnibus source offering a comprehensive index of links to multiple resources in sociology, including research methods sites, professional associations, and research centers. A good reference source for social science browsing on the Web.

http://www.sociolog.com

Sociolog. Links to lists of professional associations, sociology departments, university catalogs, data archives.

http://www.socresonline.org.uk/socresonline/

Sociological Research Online. Full text articles published only online.

http://www.trinity.edu/~mkearl/index.html

A Sociological Tour Through Cyberspace. Trinity University site with links to many resources, including government statistics, data sources, and theory groups.

http://www.digeratiweb.com/sociorealm

Sociorealm. Contains summaries of social theories and links to many sites with information about contemporary and classical social theory.

http://www.pscw.uva.nl/sociosite/

SocioSite. Social science information system based at the University of Amsterdam. Offers links and access to a vast number of helpful sites on the Internet related to sociology. Can be used as a reference source for sociology on the Web.

http://www.stanford.edu/group/siqss/

Stanford Institute for the Quantitative Study of Society's Internet survey. Description of the study and descriptive data.

http://www.lib.umich.edu/govdocs/stats.html

Statistical Resources on the Web. A subject directory compiled by the Documents Center at the University of Michigan.

http://www.samhsa.gov

Substance Abuse and Mental Health Services Administration. Offers summaries of publications, reports, and statistical information on SAMHSA research.

http://thomas.loc.gov

Thomas, Legislative Information on the Internet. Federal legislation, including pending and past legislation, and committee composition.

http://www.census.gov

U.S. Bureau of the Census home page. Contains tables and graphs reporting detailed census data. Population data and economic indicators.

http://www.ojp.usdoj.gov

U.S. Bureau of Justice. Information about programs, with extensive data on legal issues.

http://stats.bls.gov

U.S. Bureau of Labor Statistics, Department of Labor. A significant source of data on employment and earnings.

http://www.worldbank.org

World Bank. Resources that are useful for comparative research. Includes detailed maps and statistical data on many countries.

http://libraries.mit.edu/humanities/WomensStudies/wscd.html

WSSLINKS (Women's Studies Section Links). A subject guide compiled by the Women's Studies Section Collection Development Committee of the American Association of College and Research Libraries.

http://vlib.org

The WWW Virtual Library. The original Internet subject guide that covers many disciplines including the Social Sciences.

http://yahoo.com

Yahoo! A large and comprehensive Internet subject directory.

REFERENCES

Abbott, Andrew. 1992. "From Causes to Events: Notes on Narrative Positivism." *Sociological Methods and Research,* 20 (May): 428–455.

Abbott, Andrew. 1994. "History and Sociology: The Lost Synthesis." Pp. 77–112 in *Engaging the Past: The Uses of History Across the Social Sciences,* edited by Eric H. Monkkonen. Durham, NC: Duke University Press.

Abel, David. 2000. "Census May Fall Short at Colleges." *The Boston Sunday Globe,* March 26, pp. B1, B4.

Abel, David. 2002. "A Way Out." *The Boston Globe,* July 18, pp. B1, B8.

Abrams, Philip. 1982. *Historical Sociology.* Ithaca, NY: Cornell University Press.

Adair, G., T. W. Dushenko, and R. C. L. Lindsay. 1985. "Ethical Regulations and Their Impact on Research Practice." *American Psychologist,* 40: 59–72.

Addison, Richard B. 1999. "A Grounded Hermeneutic Editing Approach." Pp. 145–161 in *Doing Qualitative Research,* edited by Benjamin F. Crabtree and William L. Miller. Thousand Oaks, CA: Sage.

Aguirre, Adalberto, Jr. and David V. Baker. 1993. "Racial Prejudice and the Death Penalty: A Research Note." *Social Justice,* 20: 150–155.

Alfred, Randall. 1976. "The Church of Satan." Pp. 180–202 in *The New Religious Consciousness,* edited by Charles Glock and Robert Bellah. Berkeley: University of California Press.

Allport, Gordon. 1954. *The Nature of Prejudice.* Cambridge: Addison-Wesley.

Altheide, David L. and John M. Johnson. 1994. "Criteria for Assessing Interpretive Validity in Qualitative Research." Pp. 485–499 in *Handbook of Qualitative Research,* edited by Norman K. Denzin and Yvonna S. Lincoln. Thousand Oaks, CA: Sage.

Altman, Drew, Ellen L. Bassuk, William R. Breakey, A. Alan Fischer, Charles R. Halpern, Gloria Smith, Louisa Stark, Nathan Stark, Bruce C. Vladeck, and Phyllis Wolfe. 1989. "Health Care for the Homeless." *Society,* 26 (May/June): 4–5.

Altman, Lawrence. 1998. "Getting It Right on the Facts of Death." *The New York Times,* December 22, p. D7.

Alvarez, Lizette. 1996. "Who Needs Emergency Family Shelter? Try Asking Mothers Who Are There." *The New York Times,* September 2, pp. 23, 25.

American Psychiatric Association. 1994. *Diagnostic Criteria from DSM IV.* Washington, DC: American Psychiatric Association.

American Sociological Association. 1997. *Code of Ethics.* Washington, DC: American Sociological Association.

Aminzade, Ronald. 1992. "Historical Sociology and Time." *Sociological Methods & Research,* 20: 456–480.

Anderson, Elijah. 1990. *Streetwise: Race, Class, and Change in an Urban Community.* Chicago: University of Chicago Press.

Anderson, Elijah. 1999. *Code of the Street: Decency, Violence, and the Moral Life of the Inner City.* New York: W. W. Norton.

Anderson, Elijah. 2003. "Jelly's Place: An Ethnographic Memoir." *Symbolic Interaction*, forthcoming.

Anderson, Margo J. and Stephen E. Fienberg. 1999. *Who Counts? The Politics of Census-Taking in Contemporary America.* New York: Russell Sage Foundation.

Anderton, Douglas L., Richard E. Barrett, and Donald J. Bogue. 1997. *The Population of the United States.* New York: Free Press.

Aneshensel, Carol S. 2002. *Theory-Based Data Analysis for the Social Sciences.* Thousand Oaks, CA: Pine Forge Press.

Angel, Ronald J., P. Lindsay Chase-Lansdale, Andrew Cherlin and Robert Moffitt. 2002. *Welfare, Children, and Families: Results from a Three City Study. A Congressional Briefing,* May 17. Washington, DC: Consortium of Social Science Associations.

Anspach, Renee R. 1991. "Everyday Methods for Assessing Organizational Effectiveness." *Social Problems,* 38 (February): 1–19.

Aponte, Robert. 1990. "Definitions of the Underclass: A Critical Analysis." Pp. 117–137 in *Sociology in America,* edited by Herbert J. Gans. Newbury Park, CA: Sage.

Applebome, Peter. 1993. "Racial Divisions Persist 25 Years After King Killing." *The New York Times,* April 4, p. 16.

Applebome, Peter. 1999. "The On-Line Revolution Is Not the End of Civilization as We Know It. But Almost. Education.com." *Education Life, The New York Times,* April 4, pp. 26–37.

Armas, Genaro C. 2002. "Government Won't File Appeal in Census Case." *The Boston Globe,* November 23, p. A1.

Arnold, David. 1994. "Manners Found, Good and Bad . . ." *Boston Globe,* July 7, pp. 1, 31.

Aronson, Elliot and Judson Mills. 1959. "The Effect of Severity of Initiation on Liking for a Group." *Journal of Abnormal and Social Psychology,* 59 (September): 177–181.

Artemov, Viktor. 1998. "Work and Free Time of the Employed Rural Population in Siberia: Time-Budget Trends (1970s to 1990s)." *Society and Leisure,* 21: 379–398.

Aseltine, Robert H., Jr., and Ronald C. Kessler. 1993. "Marital Disruption and Depression in a Community Sample." *Journal of Health and Social Behavior,* 34 (September): 237–251.

Ashenfelter, Orley. 1973. "Discrimination and Trade Unions." Pp. 88–112 in *Discrimination in Labor Markets,* edited by Orley Ashenfelter and Albert Rees. Princeton, NJ: Princeton University Press.

Babbie, Earl, Fred Halley, and Jeanne Zaino. 2003. *Adventures in Social Research: Data Analysis Using SPSS 11.0/11.5 for Windows,* 5th ed. Thousand Oaks, CA: Pine Forge Press.

Babor, Thomas F., Robert S. Stephens, and G. Alan Marlatt. 1987. "Verbal Report Methods in Clinical Research on Alcoholism: Response Bias and Its Minimization." *Journal of Studies on Alcohol,* 48(5): 410–424.

Bachman, Ronet and Russell K. Schutt. 2002. *The Practice of Research in Criminology and Criminal Justice,* 2nd edn. Thousand Oaks, CA: Pine Forge Press.

Bahr, Howard M. and Theodore Caplow. 1973. *Old Men Drunk and Sober.* New York: New York University Press.

Bailey, William C. 1990. "Murder, Capital Punishment, and Television: Execution Publicity and Homicide Rates." *American Sociological Review,* 55 (October): 628–633.

Bainbridge, William Sims. 1989. *Survey Research: A Computer-Assisted Introduction.* Belmont, CA: Wadsworth.

Bandura, Albert, Dorothea Ross, and Sheila A. Ross. 1963. "Imitation of Film-Mediated Aggressive Models." *Journal of Abnormal and Social Psychology,* 66: 3–11.

Banks, J. A. 1972. "Historical Sociology and the Study of Population." Pp. 55–70 in *Population and Social Change,* edited by D. V. Glass and Roger Revelle. London: Edward Arnold.

Barclay, George W. 1958. *Techniques of Population Analysis.* New York: Wiley.

Bargh, John A., Katelyn Y. A. McKenna, and Grainne M. Fitzsimons. 2002. "Can You See Me? Activation and Expression of the 'True Self' on the Internet." *Journal of Social Issues,* 58: 33–48.

Barkan, Steven B. and Steven F. Cohn. 1994. "Racial Prejudice and Support for the Death Penalty by Whites." *Journal of Research in Crime and Delinquency,* 31: 202–209.

Barringer, Felicity. 1993. "Majority in Poll Back Ban on Handguns." *The New York Times,* June 4, p. A14.

Barsade, Sigal G., Andrew G. Ward, Jean D. F. Turner, and Jeffrey A. Sonnenfeld. 2000. "To Your Heart's Content: A Model of Affective Diversity in Top Managament Teams." *Administrative Science Quarterly,* 45: 802–836.

Baum, Samuel. 1993. "Sources of Demographic Data." Pp. 3-1–3-50 in *Readings in Population Research Methodology. Vol. 1, Basic Tools,* edited by Donald J. Bogue, Eduardo E. Arriaga, and Douglas L. Anderton. Chicago: Social Development Center, for the United National Population Fund.

Baxter, Ellen and Kim Hopper. 1984. "Shelter and Housing for the Homeless Mentally Ill." Pp. 109–139 in *The Homeless Mentally Ill,* edited by H. Richard Lamb. Washington, DC: American Psychiatric Association.

Bean, Lee L., Geraldine P. Mineau, and Douglas L. Anderton. 1990. *Fertility Change on the American Frontier: Adaptation and Innovation.* Berkeley: University of California Press.

Becker, Gary S. 1971. *The Economics of Discrimination,* 2nd ed. Chicago: University of Chicago Press.

Becker, Howard S. 1958. "Problems of Inference and Proof in Participant Observation." *American Sociological Review,* 23: 652–660.

Becker, Howard S. 1963. *The Outsiders: Studies in the Sociology of Deviance.* New York: Free Press.

Becker, Howard S. 1986. *Writing for Social Scientists.* Chicago: University of Chicago Press. (This can be ordered directly from the American Sociological Association, 1722 N Street, NW, Washington, DC 20036, 202-833-3410.)

Bellah, Robert N., Richard Madsen, William M. Sullivan, Ann Swidler, and Steven M. Tipton. 1985. *Habits of the Heart: Individualism and Commitment in American Life.* New York: Harper & Row.

Bendix, Reinhard. 1962. *Max Weber: An Intellectual Portrait.* Garden City, NY: Doubleday/Anchor.

Bennett, Lauren, Lisa Goodman, and Mary Ann Dutton. 1999. "Systemic Obstacles to the Criminal Prosecution of a Battering Partner: A Victim Perspective." *Journal of Interpersonal Violence,* 14: 761–772.

Berger, Peter L. and Thomas Luckmann. 1966. *The Social Construction of Reality: A Treatise in the Sociology of Knowledge.* New York: Doubleday.

Berk, Richard A., Alec Campbell, Ruth Klap, and Bruce Western. 1992. "The Deterrent Effect of Arrest: A Bayesian Analysis of Four Field Experiments." *American Sociological Review,* 57 (October): 698–708.

Beyer, William H. (Ed.). 1968. *CRC Handbook of Tables for Probability and Statistics,* 2nd ed. Boca Raton, FL: CRC Press.

Binder, Arnold and James W. Meeker. 1993. "Implications of the Failure to Replicate the Minneapolis Experimental Findings." *American Sociological Review,* 58 (December): 886–888.

Black, Donald J. 1976. *The Behavior of Law.* New York: Academic Press.

Black, Donald J. (Ed.). 1984. *Toward a General Theory of Social Control.* Orlando, FL: Academic Press.

Blakely, Edward J., and Mary Gail Snyder. 1997. *Fortress America: Gated Communities in the United States.* Washington, DC, and Cambridge, MA: Brookings Institution Press and Lincoln Institute of Land Policy.

Blalock, Hubert M., Jr. 1967. *Toward a Theory of Minority-Group Relations.* New York: Wiley.

Blalock, Hubert M., Jr. 1969. *Theory Construction: From Verbal to Mathematical Formulations.* Englewood Cliffs, NJ: Prentice-Hall.

Blau, Peter M. 1964. *Exchange and Power in Social Life.* New York: Wiley.

Blauner, Robert. 1964. *Alienation and Freedom: The Factory Worker and His Industry.* Chicago: University of Chicago Press.

Bogdewic, Stephan P. 1999. "Participant Observation." Pp. 33–45 in *Doing Qualitative Research,* 2nd ed., edited by Benjamin F. Crabtree and William L. Miller. Thousand Oaks, CA: Sage.

Bogue, Donald J. 1969. *Principles of Demography.* New York: Wiley.

Bogue, Donald J., Eduardo E. Arriaga, and Douglas L. Anderton. 1993. *Readings in Population Research Methodology. Vol. 1, Basic Tools.* Chicago: Social Development Center, for the United Nations Population Fund.

Bollen, Kenneth A., Barbara Entwisle, and Arthur S. Alderson. 1993. "Macrocomparative Research Methods." *Annual Review of Sociology,* 19: 321–351.

Booth, Wayne C., Gregory G. Colomb, and Joseph M. Williams. 1995. *The Craft of Research.* Chicago: University of Chicago Press.

Borg, Marian J. 1997. "The Southern Subculture of Punitiveness? Regional Variation in Support for Capital Punishment." *Journal of Research in Crime and Delinquency,* 34: 25–45.

Borg, Marian J. 1998. "Vicarious Homicide Victimization and Support for Capital Punishment: A Test of Black's Theory of Law." *Criminology,* 36: 537–567.

Boruch, Robert F. 1997. *Randomized Experiments for Planning and Evaluation: A Practical Guide.* Thousand Oaks, CA: Sage.

Bourgois, Philippe, Mark Lettiere, and James Quesada. 1997. "Social Misery and the Sanctions of Substance Abuse: Confronting HIV Risk Among Homeless Heroin Addicts in San Francisco." *Social Problems,* 44: 155–173.

Bradshaw, York W. and Michael Wallace. 1996. *Global Inequalities.* Thousand Oaks, CA: Sage.

Bray, Hiawatha. 1999. "Plugging in to the Electronic Campus." *The Boston Globe Magazine,* April 11, pp. 20–30.

Brent, Edward and Alan Thompson. 1996. *Methodologist's Toolchest™ for Windows: User's Guide and Reference Manual.* Columbia, MO: Idea Works.

Brewer, John and Albert Hunter, 1989. *Multimethod Research: A Synthesis of Styles.* Newbury Park, CA: Sage.

Bridges, George S. and Joseph G. Weis. 1989. "Measuring Violent Behavior: Effects of Study Design on Reported Correlates of Violence." Pp. 14–34 in *Violent Crime, Violent Criminals,* edited by Neil Alan Weiner and Marvin E. Wolfgang. Newbury Park, CA: Sage.

Brown, Judith Belle. 1999. "The Use of Focus Groups in Clinical Research." Pp. 109–124 in *Doing Qualitative Research,* 2nd ed., edited by Benjamin F. Crabtree and William L. Miller. Thousand Oaks, CA: Sage.

Brown, S. A., M. S. Goldman, A. Inn, and L. R. Anderson. 1980. "Expectations of Reinforcement from Alcohol: Their Domain and Relation to Drinking Patterns." *Journal of Consulting and Clinical Psychology,* 48: 419–426.

Bruni, Frank. 2002. "Persistent Drop in Fertility Reshapes Europe's Future." *The New York Times,* December 26, pp. A1, A10.

Burke, Garance. 2000. "Mexico's Census Battles Perception of Corruption." *The Boston Globe,* March 2, p. A2.

Burt, Martha R. 1996. "Homelessness: Definitions and Counts." Pp. 15–23 in *Homelessness in America,* edited by Jim Baumohl. Phoenix, AZ: Oryx.

Bushman, Brad J. 1995. "Moderating Role of Trait Aggressiveness in the Effects of Violent Media on Aggression." *Journal of Personality and Social Psychology,* 69(5): 950–960.

Bushman, Brad J., and Roy F. Baumeister, 1998. "Threatened Egotism, Narcissism, Self-Esteem, and Direct and Displaced Aggression: Does Self-Love or Self-Hate Lead to Violence?" *Journal of Personality and Social Psychology,* 75: 219–229.

Bushman, Brad J., Roy F. Baumeister, and Angela D. Stack. 1999. "Catharsis, Aggression, and Persuasive Influence: Self-Fulfilling or Self-Defeating Prophecies?" *Journal of Personality and Social Psychology,* 76: 367–376.

Butler, Dore· and Florence Geis. 1990. "Nonverbal Affect Responses to Male and Female Leaders: Implications for Leadership Evaluations." *Journal of Personality and Social Psychology,* 58 (January): 48–59.

Buttel, Frederick H. 2000. "World Society, the Nation-State, and Environmental Protection: Comment on Frank, Hironaka, and Schofer." *American Sociological Review,* 65: 117–121.

Butterfield, Fox. 1996a. "After 10 Years, Juvenile Crime Begins to Drop." *The New York Times,* August 9, pp. A1, A25.

Butterfield, Fox. 1996b. "Gun Violence May Be Subsiding, Studies Find." *The New York Times,* October 14, p. A10.

Butterfield, Fox. 1997. "Serious Crime Decreased for Fifth Year in a Row." *The New York Times,* January 5, p. 10.

Butterfield, Fox. 2000. "As Murder Rates Edge Up, Concern, But Few Answers." *The New York Times,* June 18, p. A12.

Buzawa, Eve S. and Carl G. Buzawa (Eds.). 1996. *Do Arrests and Restraining Orders Work?* Thousand Oaks, CA: Sage.

Cain, Leonard D., Jr. 1967. "The AMA and the Gerontologists: Uses and Abuses of 'A Profile of the Aging: USA.'" Pp. 78–114 in *Ethics, Politics, and Social Research,* edited by Gideon Sjoberg. Cambridge, MA: Schenkman.

Cambanis, Thanassis. 2002. "Juror Scrutiny Reaches New Level." *The Boston Globe,* July 12, pp. B1, B3.

Campbell, Donald T. and M. Jean Russo. 1999. *Social Experimentation.* Thousand Oaks, CA: Sage.

Campbell, Donald T. and Julian C. Stanley. 1966. *Experimental and Quasi-Experimental Designs for Research.* Chicago: Rand McNally.

Campbell, Richard T. 1992. "Longitudinal Research." Pp. 1146–1158 in *Encyclopedia of Sociology,* edited by Edgar F. Borgatta and Marie L. Borgatta. New York: Macmillan.

Campbell, Wilson. 2002. "A Statement from The Governmental Accounting Standards Board and Performance Measurement Staff." American Society for Public Administration, http://www.aspanet. org/cap/forum_statement.html#top, July 20, 2002.

Carmines, Edward G. and Richard A. Zeller. 1979. *Reliability and Validity Assessment.* Quantitative Applications in the Social Sciences, #17. Beverly Hills, CA: Sage.

Center for Survey Research, University of Massachusetts at Boston. 1987. "Methodology: Designing Good Survey Questions." *Newsletter,* April, p. 3.

Chase-Dunn, Christopher and Thomas D. Hall. 1993. "Comparing World-Systems: Concepts and Working Hypotheses." *Social Forces,* 71: 851–886.

Chen, Huey-Tsyh. 1990. *Theory-Driven Evaluations.* Newbury Park, CA: Sage.

Chen, Huey-Tsyh and Peter H. Rossi. 1987. "The Theory-Driven Approach to Validity." *Evaluation and Program Planning,* 10: 95–103.

Chen, Xiangming. 1994. "The Changing Roles of Free Economic Zones in Development: A Comparative Analysis of Capitalist and Socialist Cases in East Asia." *Studies in Comparative International Development,* 29: 3–25.

Clements, Mark. 1994. "What Americans Say About the Homeless." *Parade Magazine,* January 9, pp. 4–6.

Clymer, Adam. 2001. "The Unbearable Lightness of Public Opinion Polls." *The New York Times,* July 22, p. WK3.

Clymer, Adam. 2002. "World Survey Says Negative Views of U.S. Are Rising." *The New York Times,* December 5, p. A11.

Coffey, Amanda and Paul Atkinson. 1996. *Making Sense of Qualitative Data: Complementary Research Strategies.* Thousand Oaks, CA: Sage.

Cohen, Gary E. and Barbara A. Kerr. 1998. "Computer-Mediated Counseling: An Empirical Study of a New Mental Health Treatment." *Computers in Human Services,* 15: 13–26.

Cohen S., R. Mermelstein, T. Kamarck, and H. M. Hoberman. 1985. "Measuring the Functional Components of Social Support." Pp. 73–94 in *Social Support: Theory, Research and Applications,* edited by I. G. Sarason and B. R. Sarason. The Hague, The Netherlands: Martinus Nijhoff.

Cohen, Sheldon. 1992. "Stress, Social Support, and Disorder." Pp. 109–124 in *The Meaning and Measurement of Social Support,* edited by Hans O. F. Veiel and Urs Baumann. New York: Hemisphere.

Cohen, Susan G. and Gerald E. Ledford, Jr. 1994. "The Effectiveness of Self-Managing Teams: A Quasi-Experiment." *Human Relations, 47*: 13–43.

Coleman, James S. 1990. *Foundations of Social Theory.* Cambridge, MA: Harvard University Press.

Coleman, James S. and Thomas Hoffer. 1987. *Public and Private High Schools: The Impact of Communities.* New York: Basic Books.

Coleman, James S., Thomas Hoffer, and Sally Kilgore. 1982. *High School Achievement: Public, Catholic, and Private Schools Compared.* New York: Basic Books.

Collins, Randall. 1994. *Four Sociological Traditions.* New York: Oxford University Press.

Connolly, Francis J. and Charley Manning. 2001. "What 'Push Polling' Is and What It Isn't." *The Boston Globe,* August 16, p. A21.

Converse, Jean M. 1984. "Attitude Measurement in Psychology and Sociology: The Early Years." Pp. 3–40 in *Surveying Subjective Phenomena,* vol. 2, edited by Charles F. Turner and Elizabeth Martin. New York: Russell Sage Foundation.

Cook, Thomas D. and Donald T. Campbell. 1979. *Quasi-Experimentation: Design and Analysis Issues for Field Settings.* Chicago: Rand McNally.

Cooley, Charles Horton. 1902. *Human Nature and the Social Order.* New York: Scribner's.

Cooper, Harris and Larry V. Hedges. 1994. "Research Synthesis as a Scientific Enterprise." Pp. 3–14 in *The Handbook of Research Synthesis,* edited by Harris Cooper and Larry V. Hedges. New York: Russell Sage Foundation.

Cooper, Kathleen B. and Nancy J. Victory. 2002. "Foreword." P. iv in *A Nation Online: How Americans Are Expanding Their Use of the Internet.* Washington, D.C.: National Telecommunications and Information Administration, Economics and Statistics Administration, U.S. Department of Commerce.

Core Institute. 1994. "Core Alcohol and Drug Survey: Long Form." Carbondale, IL: FIPSE Core Analysis Grantee Group, Core Institute, Student Health Programs, Southern Illinois University.

Correll, Joshua, Bernadette Park, Charles M. Judd, and Bernd Wittenbrink. 2002. "The Police Officer's Dilemma: Using Ethnicity to Disambiguate Potentially Threatening Individuals." *Journal of Personality and Social Psychology,* 83: 1314–1329.

Corse, Sara J., Nancy B. Hirschinger, and David Zanis. 1995. "The Use of the Addiction Severity Index with People with Severe Mental Illness." *Psychiatric Rehabilitation Journal,* 19(1): 9–18.

Costner, Herbert L. 1989. "The Validity of Conclusions in Evaluation Research: A Further Development of Chen and Rossi's Theory-Driven Approach." *Evaluation and Program Planning,* 12: 345–353.

Couper, Mick P., Reginald P. Baker, Jelke Bethlehem, Cynthia Z. F. Clark, Jean Martin, William L. Nicholls II, and James M. O'Reilly (Eds.). 1998. *Computer Assisted Survey Information Collection.* New York: Wiley.

Crenshaw, Edward M. 1995. "Democracy and Demographic Inheritance: The Influence of Modernity and Proto-Modernity on Political and Civil Rights, 1965 to 1980." *American Sociological Review,* 60: 702–718.

Cress, Daniel M. and David A. Snow. 2000. "The Outcomes of Homeless Mobilization: The Influence of Organization, Disruption, Political Mediation, and Framing." *American Journal of Sociology,* 4: 1063–1104.

Crossen, Cynthia. 1994. "How 'Tactical Research' Muddied Diaper Debate." *The Wall Street Journal,* May 17, pp. B1, B9.

Cuba, Lee J. 2002. *A Short Guide to Writing About Social Science,* 4th ed. New York: Addison-Wesley.

CyberAtlas staff. 2003. The World's Online Population. Retrieved February 2, 2003 from http://cyberatlas. internet.com/big_picture/geographics/article/0,1323,5911_151151,00.html

Czaja, Ronald and Bob Blair. 1995. *Survey Research.* Newbury Park, CA: Pine Forge Press.

Damasio, Antonio R. 1994. *Descartes' Error: Emotion, Reason, and the Human Brain.* New York: Grosset/Putnam.

Daniels, Arlene Kaplan. 1967. "The Low-Caste Stranger in Social Research." Pp. 267–296 in *Ethics, Politics, and Social Research,* edited by Gideon Sjoberg. Cambridge, MA: Schenkman.

Dannefer, W. Dale and Russell K. Schutt. 1982. "Race and Juvenile Justice Processing in Court and Police Agencies." *American Journal of Sociology,* 87 (March): 1113–1132.

Davies, Paul. 1993. "The Holy Grail of Physics." *The New York Times Book Review,* March 7, pp. 11–12.

Davies, Philip, Anthony Petrosino, and Iain Chalmers. 1999. *Report and Papers from the Exploratory Meeting for The Campbell Collaboration.* London: School of Public Policy, University College.

Davis, James A. 1985. *The Logic of Causal Order.* Sage University Paper Series on Quantitative Applications in the Social Sciences, series no. 07–055. Beverly Hills, CA: Sage.

Davis, James A. and Tom W. Smith. 1992. *The NORC General Social Survey: A User's Guide.* Newbury Park, CA: Sage.

Davis, Ryan. 1999. "Study: Search Engines Can't Keep Up With Expanding Net." *The Boston Globe,* July 8, pp. C1, C3.

Dawes, Robyn. 1995. "How Do You Formulate a Testable Exciting Hypothesis?" Pp. 93–96 in *How to Write a Successful Research Grant Application: A Guide for Social and Behavioral Scientists,* edited by Willo Pequegnat and Ellen Stover. New York: Plenum Press.

Decker, Scott H. and Barrik Van Winkle. 1996. *Life in the Gang: Family, Friends, and Violence.* Cambridge, England: Cambridge University Press.

Demos, John. 1998. "History Beyond Data Bits." *The New York Times,* December 30, p. A23.

Dennis, Michael. 1998. "Return Rate on Quex." Posted message to the Topical Evaluation Network Outcome Research List (outcmten@maelstrom.stjohns.edu). October 25.

Dentler, Robert A. 2002. *Practicing Sociology: Selected Fields.* Westport, CT: Praeger.

Denzin, Norman K. 2002. "The Interpretive Process." Pp. 349–368 in *The Qualitative Researcher's Companion,* edited by A. Michael Huberman and Matthew B. Miles. Thousand Oaks, CA: Sage.

Denzin, Norman K. and Yvonna S. Lincoln. 1994. "Introduction: Entering the Field of Qualitative Research." Pp. 1–17 in *Handbook of Qualitative Research,* edited by Norman K. Denzin and Yvonna S. Lincoln. Thousand Oaks, CA: Sage.

DeParle, Jason. 1999. "Project to Rescue Needy Stumbles Against the Persistence of Poverty." *The New York Times,* May 15, pp. A1, A10.

De Ritis, Anthony. 2001. Quoted in "The E-Learning Road," by Cate Coulacos Prato. *Boston Globe,* July 15, pp. B1, B10.

Devine, Joel A. and James D. Wright. 1993. *The Greatest of Evils: Urban Poverty and the American Underclass.* New York: Aldine de Gruyter.

Diamond, Jared. 1987. "Soft Sciences Are Often Harder Than Hard Sciences." *Discover* (August), pp. 34–39.

Diamond, Larry, Juan Linz, and Seymour Martin Lipset. 1990. *Politics in Developing Countries: Comparing Experiences with Democracy.* Boulder, CO: Lynne Rienner.

Diamond, Timothy. 1992. *Making Gray Gold: Narratives of Nursing Home Care.* Chicago: University of Chicago Press.

DiClemente, C. C., J. P. Carbonari, R. P. G. Montgomery, and S. O. Hughes. 1994. "The Alcohol Abstinence Self-Efficacy Scale." *Journal of Studies on Alcohol,* 55: 141–148.

Dillman, Don A. 1978. *Mail and Telephone Surveys: The Total Design Method.* New York: Wiley.

Dillman, Don A. 1982. "Mail and Other Self-Administered Questionnaires." Chapter 12 in *Handbook of Survey Research,* edited by Peter Rossi, James Wright, and Andy Anderson. New York: Academic Press. As reprinted on pp. 637–638 in Delbert C. Miller, 1991. *Handbook of Research Design and Social Measurement,* 5th ed. Newbury Park, CA: Sage.

Dillman, Don A. 2000. *Mail and Internet Surveys: The Tailored Design Method,* 2nd ed. New York: Wiley.

Dillman, Don A., James A. Christenson, Edwin H. Carpenter, and Ralph M. Brooks. 1974. "Increasing Mail Questionnaire Response: A Four-State Comparison." *American Sociological Review*, 39 (October): 744–756.

Dolnick, Edward. 1984. "Why Have the Pollsters Been Missing the Mark?" *The Boston Globe*, July 16, pp. 27–28.

Donath, Judith S. 1999. "Identity and Deception in the Virtual Community." Pp. 29–59 in *Communities in Cyberspace*, edited by Peter Kollock and Marc A. Smith. New York: Routledge.

Drago, Robert, Robert Caplan, David Costanza, Tanya Brubaker, Darnell Cloud, Susan Donohue, Naomi Harris, and Tammy Riggs. 1998. "Time for Surveys: Do Busy People Complete Time Diaries?" *Society and Leisure*, 21: 555–562.

Drake, Robert E., Gregory J. McHugo, Deborah R. Becker, William A. Anthony, and Robin E. Clark. 1996. "The New Hampshire Study of Supported Employment for People with Severe Mental Illness." *Journal of Consulting and Clinical Psychology*, 64: 391–399.

Drake, Robert E., Gregory J. McHugo, and Jeremy C. Biesanz. 1995. "The Test-Retest Reliability of Standardized Instruments Among Homeless Persons with Substance Use Disorders." *Journal of Studies on Alcohol*, 56(2): 161–167.

Duncan, Otis Dudley and Stanley Lieberson. 1959. "Ethnic Segregation and Assimilation." *American Journal of Sociology*, 64: 364–374.

Durkheim, Emile. 1951. *Suicide*. New York: Free Press.

Durkheim, Emile. 1956 [1906]. "The Evolution and the Role of Secondary Education in France." Pp. 135–154 in *Education and Sociology*, translated by Sherwood D. Fox. New York: Free Press.

Durkheim, Emile. 1966. *Suicide: A Study in Sociology*. Translated by John A. Spaulding and George Simpson. New York: Free Press.

Durkheim, Emile. 1984. *The Division of Labor in Society*. Translated by W. D. Halls. New York: Free Press.

Dykema, Jennifer and Nora Cate Schaeffer. 2000. "Events, Instruments, and Reporting Errors." *American Sociological Review*, 65: 619–629.

Earley, P. Christopher. 1994. "Self or Group: Cultural Effects of Training on Self-Efficacy and Performance." *Administrative Science Quarterly*, 39: 89–117.

Egan, Timothy. 1995. "Many Seek Security in Private Communities." *The New York Times*, September 3, pp. 1, 22.

Emerson, Michael O., George Yancey, and Karen J. Chai. 2001. "Does Race Matter in Residential Segregation? Exploring the Preferences of White Americans." *American Sociological Review*, 66: 922–935.

Emerson, Robert M. (Ed.). 1983. *Contemporary Field Research*. Prospect Heights, IL: Waveland.

Emerson, Robert M., Rachel I. Fretz, and Linda L. Shaw. 1995. *Writing Ethnographic Fieldnotes*. Chicago: University of Chicago Press.

Emirbayer, Mustafa. 1996. "Durkheim's Contribution to the Sociological Analysis of History." *Sociological Forum*, 11: 263–284.

Erikson, Kai T. 1966. *Wayward Puritans: A Study in the Sociology of Deviance*. New York: Wiley.

Erikson, Kai T. 1967. "A Comment on Disguised Observation in Sociology." *Social Problems*, 12: 366–373.

Fallows, Deborah. 2002. *Email at Work*. Washington, D.C.: Pew Internet and American Life Project. http://www.pewinternet.org.

Farley, Reynolds. 1977. "Trends in Racial Inequalities: Have the Gains of the 1960s Disappeared in the 1970s?" *American Sociological Review*, 42: 189–208.

Fears, Darryl. 2002. "For Latinos in U.S., Race Not Just Black or White." *The Boston Globe*, December 30, p. A3.

Fenno, Richard F., Jr. 1978. *Home Style: House Members in Their Districts*. Boston: Little, Brown.

Fine, Gary Alan. 1980. "Cracking Diamonds: Observer Role in Little League Baseball Settings and the Acquisition of Social Competence." Pp. 117–131 in *Fieldwork Experience: Qualitative Approaches to Social Research,* edited by William B. Shaffir, Robert A. Stebbins, and Allan Turowetz. New York: St. Martin's Press.

Fink, Arlene. 1998. *Conducting Research Literature Reviews: From Paper to the Internet.* Thousand Oaks, CA: Sage.

Fischer, Constance T. and Frederick J. Wertz. 2002. "Empirical Phenomenological Analyses of Being Criminally Victimized." Pp. 275–304 in *The Qualitative Researcher's Companion,* edited by A. Michael Huberman and Matthew B. Miles. Thousand Oaks, CA: Sage.

Forero, Juan. 2000a. "Census Takers Say Supervisors Fostered Filing of False Data." *The New York Times,* July 28, p. A21.

Forero, Juan. 2000b. "Census Takers Top '90 Efforts in New York City, with More to Go." *The New York Times,* June 12, p. A29.

Fowler, Floyd J. 1988. *Survey Research Methods,* revised ed. Newbury Park, CA: Sage.

Fowler, Floyd J. 1995. *Improving Survey Questions: Design and Evaluation.* Thousand Oaks, CA: Sage.

Fowler, Floyd J. 1998. Personal communication, January 7. Center for Survey Research, University of Massachusetts, Boston.

Fox, Nick and Chris Roberts. 1999. "GPs in Cyberspace: The Sociology of a 'Virtual Community.'" *The Sociological Review,* 47: 643–669.

Fraker, Thomas and Rebecca Maynard. 1987. "Evaluating Comparison Group Designs with Employment-Related Programs." *Journal of Human Resources,* 22(2): 194–227.

Frank, David John, Ann Hironaka, and Evan Schofer. 2000. "The Nation-State and the Natural Environment Over the Twentieth Century." *American Sociological Review,* 65: 96–116.

Frankfort-Nachmias, Chava and Anna Leon-Guerrero. 2002. *Social Statistics for a Diverse Society,* 3rd ed. Thousand Oaks, CA: Pine Forge.

Franklin, Mark N. 1996. "Electoral Participation." Pp. 216–235 in *Comparing Democracies: Elections and Voting in Global Perspective,* edited by Lawrence LeDuc, Richard G. Niemi, and Pippa Norris. Thousand Oaks, CA: Sage.

Freedman, David A. 1991. "Statistical Models and Shoe Leather." Pp. 291–313 in *Sociological Methodology,* vol. 21, edited by Peter V. Marsden. Oxford: Basil Blackwell.

Freeman, Richard B. 1974. "Alternative Theories of Labor-Market Discrimination: Individual and Collective Behavior." Pp. 33–49 in *Patterns of Racial Discrimination,* vol. 2, edited by George von Furstenburg, Ann Horowitz, and Bennett Harrison. Lexington, MA: Heath.

Fremont, Allen M. and Chloe E. Bird. 1999. "Integrating Sociological and Biological Models: An Editorial." *Journal of Health and Social Behavior,* 40:126–129.

Friedlander, Daniel, James Riccio, and Stephen Freedman. 1993. *GAIN: Two-Year Impacts in Six Counties.* New York: Manpower Demonstration Research Corporation.

Garrett, Gerald R. and Russell K. Schutt. 1990. "Homelessness in Massachusetts: Description and Analysis." Pp. 73–90 in *Homeless in the United States: State Surveys,* edited by Jamshid Momeni. New York: Greenwood.

Geertz, Clifford. 1973. "Thick Description: Toward an Interpretive Theory of Culture." Pp. 3–30 in *The Interpretation of Cultures,* edited by Clifford Geertz. New York: Basic Books.

Gilchrist, Valerie J. and Robert L. Williams. 1999. "Key Informant Interviews." Pp. 71–88 in *Doing Qualitative Research,* 2nd ed., edited by Benjamin F. Crabtree and William L. Miller. Thousand Oaks: Sage.

Gill, Richard T., Nathan Glazer, and Stephan A. Thernstrom. 1992. *Our Changing Population.* Englewood Cliffs, NJ: Prentice Hall.

Glaser, Barney G. and Anselm L. Strauss. 1967. *The Discovery of Grounded Theory: Strategies for Qualitative Research.* London: Weidenfeld and Nicholson.

Glasgow, Douglas G. 1980. *The Black Underclass: Poverty, Unemployment, and Entrapment of Ghetto Youth.* San Francisco: Jossey-Bass.

Glashow, Sheldon. 1989. "We Believe That the World Is Knowable." *The New York Times,* October 22, p. E24.

Gleick, James. 1990. "The Census: Why We Can't Count." *The New York Times Magazine,* July 15, pp. 22–26, 54.

Glover, Judith. 1996. "Epistemological and Methodological Considerations in Secondary Analysis." Pp. 28–38 in *Cross-National Research Methods in the Social Sciences,* edited by Linda Hantrais and Steen Mangen. New York: Pinter.

Glover, Robert W. and Ray Marshall. 1977. "The Response of Unions in the Construction Industry to Antidiscrimination Efforts." Pp. 121–140 in *Equal Rights and Industrial Relations,* edited by Leonard J. Hausman, Orley Ashenfelter, Bayard Rustin, R. F. Schubert, and D. Slaiman. Madison, WI: Industrial Relations Research Association.

Glueck, Sheldon and Elenor Glueck. 1950. *Unraveling Juvenile Delinquency.* New York: Commonwealth Fund.

Goffman, Erving. 1961. *Asylums: Essays on the Social Situation of Mental Patients and Other Inmates.* Garden City, NY: Doubleday.

Goldenberg, Sheldon. 1992. *Thinking Methodologically.* New York: HarperCollins.

Goldfinger, Stephen M., Barbara Dickey, Sondra Hellman, Martha O'Bryan, Walter Penk, Russell Schutt, and Larry J. Seidman. 1990. *Apartments v. Evolving Consumer Households for the HMI.* Boston: Harvard Medical School. Grant proposal to the National Institute of Mental Health.

Goldfinger, Stephen M. and R. K. Schutt. 1996. "Comparison of Clinicians' Housing Recommendations and Preferences of Homeless Mentally Ill Persons." *Psychiatric Services,* 47: 413–415.

Goldfinger, Stephen M., Russell K. Schutt, Larry J. Seidman, Winston M. Turner, Walter E. Penk, and George S. Tolomiczenko. 1996. "Self-Report and Observer Measures of Substance Abuse Among Homeless Mentally Ill Persons in the Cross-Section and Over Time." *The Journal of Nervous and Mental Disease,* 184(11): 667–672.

Goldfinger, Stephen M., Russell K. Schutt, G. S. Tolomiczenko, L. Seidman, W. Penk, W. Turner, and B. Caplan. 1999. "Housing Placement and Subsequent Days Homeless Among Formerly Homeless Adults with Mental Illness." *Psychiatric Services,* 50: 674–679.

Goldfinger, Stephen M., Russell K. Schutt, G. S. Tolomiczenko, W. Turner, N. Ware, W. E. Penk et al. 1997. "Housing Persons Who Are Homeless and Mentally Ill: Independent Living or Evolving Consumer Households?" Pp. 29–49 in *Mentally Ill and Homeless: Special Programs for Special Needs,* edited by William R. Breakey and James W. Thompson. Amsterdam: Harwood.

Goleman, Daniel. 1993a. "Placebo Effect Is Shown to Be Twice as Powerful as Expected." *The New York Times,* August 17, p. C3.

Goleman, Daniel. 1993b. "Pollsters Enlist Psychologists in Quest for Unbiased Results." *The New York Times,* September 7, pp. C1, C11.

Goleman, Daniel. 1995. *Emotional Intelligence.* New York: Bantam.

Gordon, Raymond. 1992. *Basic Interviewing Skills.* Itasca, IL: Peacock.

Gottfredson, Michael R. and Don M. Gottfredson. 1988. *Decision Making in Criminal Justice: Toward the Rational Exercise of Discretion,* 2nd ed. New York: Plenum.

Graduate Program in Applied Sociology. 1990. *Handbook for Thesis Writers.* Boston: University of Massachusetts–Boston.

Grady, John. 1996. "The Scope of Visual Sociology." *Visual Sociology,* 11: 10–24.

Greenberg, David H. & Mark Shroder. 1997. *The Digest of Social Experiments*, 2nd ed. Washington, D.C.: Urban Institute Press.

Griffin, Larry J. 1992. "Temporality, Events, and Explanation in Historical Sociology: An Introduction." *Sociological Methods & Research,* 20: 403–427.

Griffin, Larry J. 1993. "Narrative, Event-Structure Analysis, and Causal Interpretation in Historical Sociology." *American Journal of Sociology,* 98 (March): 1094–1133.

Grimes, William. 1995. "Does Life Imitate Violence on Film?" *The New York Times,* November 30, p. B1.

Grinnell, Frederick. 1992. *The Scientific Attitude,* 2nd ed. New York: Guilford.

Gross, Jane. 1992. "Divorced, Middle-Aged and Happy: Women, Especially, Adjust to the 90s." *The New York Times,* December 7, p. A14.

Groves, Robert M. 1989. *Survey Errors and Survey Costs.* New York: Wiley.

Groves, Robert M. and Mick P. Couper. 1998. *Nonresponse in Household Interview Surveys.* New York: Wiley.

Groves, Robert M. and Robert L. Kahn. 1979. *Surveys by Telephone: A National Comparison with Personal Interviews.* New York: Academic Press. As adapted in Delbert C. Miller, 1991. *Handbook of Research Design and Social Measurement,* 5th ed. Newbury Park, CA: Sage.

Gruenewald, Paul J., Andrew J. Treno, Gail Taff, and Michael Klitzner. 1997. *Measuring Community Indicators: A Systems Approach to Drug and Alcohol Problems.* Thousand Oaks, CA: Sage.

Grunwald, Michael. 1997. "Gateway to a New America: Illinois Community Defends Its Barricade to 'Unwelcome' Outsiders." *The Boston Globe,* August 25, pp. A1, A8.

Guba, Egon G. and Yvonna S. Lincoln. 1989. *Fourth Generation Evaluation.* Newbury Park, CA: Sage.

Guba, Egon G. and Yvonna S. Lincoln. 1994. "Competing Paradigms in Qualitative Research." Pp. 105–117 in *Handbook of Qualitative Research,* edited by Norman K. Denzin and Yvonna S. Lincoln. Thousand Oaks, CA: Sage.

Gubrium, Jaber F. and James A. Holstein. 1997. *The New Language of Qualitative Method.* New York: Oxford University Press.

Gurstein, Penny. 1995. *Planning for Telework and Home-Based Employment: A Canadian Survey on Integrating Work into Residential Environments.* Vancouver, British Columbia: Canada Mortgage and Housing Corporation. As cited in Michelson, 1998:458.

Hadaway, C. Kirk, Penny Long Marler, and Mark Chaves. 1993. "What the Polls Don't Show: A Closer Look at U.S. Church Attendance." *American Sociological Review,* 58 (December): 741–752.

Hafner, Katie. 2002. "Lessons Learned the Hard Way at Dot-Com University." *The New York Times,* May 2, pp. E1, E8.

Hagan, John. 1994. *Crime and Disrepute.* Thousand Oaks, CA: Pine Forge.

Hage, Jerald and Barbara Foley Meeker. 1988. *Social Causality.* Boston: Unwin Hyman.

Haight, Catherine. 1994. "A Preview of This Year's Fortune 500." *Fortune Magazine,* 129: 6.

Haines, Herb. 1992. "Flawed Executions, the Anti-Death Penalty Movement, and the Politics of Capital Punishment." *Social Problems,* 39: 125–138.

Hallinan, Maureen T. 1997. "The Sociological Study of Social Change." *American Sociological Review,* 62: 1–11.

Hamilton, V. Lee and Joseph Sanders. 1983. "Universals in Judging Wrongdoing: Japanese and Americans Compared." *American Sociological Review,* 48 (April): 199–211.

Hampton, Keith N. and Barry Wellman. 1999. "Netville On-line and Off-line: Observing and Surveying a Wired Suburb." *American Behavioral Scientist,* 43: 475–492.

Hampton, Keith N. and Barry Wellman. 2000. "Examining Community in the Digital Neighborhood: Early Results from Canada's Wired Suburb." Pp. 475–492 in *Digital Cities: Technologies, Experiences, and Future Perspectives,* edited by Toru Ishida and Katherine Isbister. Berlin: Springer-Verlag.

Hampton, Keith and Barry Wellman. 2001. "Long Distance Community in the Network Society." *American Behavioral Scientist,* 45: 476–495.

Haney, C., C. Banks, and Philip G. Zimbardo. 1973. "Interpersonal Dynamics in a Simulated Prison." *International Journal of Criminology and Penology,* 1: 69–97.

Hantrais, Linda and Steen Mangen. 1996. "Method and Management of Cross-National Social Research." Pp. 1–12 in *Cross-National Research Methods in the Social Sciences,* edited by Linda Hantrais and Steen Mangen. New York: Pinter.

Harding, Sandra. 1989. "Value-Free Research Is a Delusion." *The New York Times,* October 22, p. E24.

Harris, Anthony R., Stephen H. Thomas, Gene A. Fisher, and David J. Hirsch. 2002. "Murder and Medicine: The Lethality of Criminal Assault 1960–1999." *Homicide Studies,* 6: 128–166.

Harris, David R. and Jeremiah Joseph Sim. 2002. "Who Is Multiracial? Assessing the Complexity of Lived Race." *American Sociological Review,* 67: 614–627.

Hart, Chris. 1998. *Doing a Literature Review: Releasing the Social Research Imagination.* Thousand Oaks, CA: Sage.

Heckathorn, Douglas D. 1997. "Respondent-Driven Sampling: A New Approach to the Study of Hidden Populations." *Social Problems,* 44: 174–199.

Heckathorn, Douglas D. 2002. "Respondent-Driven Sampling II: Deriving Valid Population Estimates from Chain-Referral Samples of Hidden Populations." *Social Problems,* 49: 11–34.

Heilbroner, Robert L. 1970. *The Making of Economic Society,* 3rd ed. Englewood Cliffs, NJ: Prentice Hall.

Herek, Gregory. 1995. "Developing a Theoretical Framework and Rationale for a Research Proposal." Pp. 85–91 in *How to Write a Successful Research Grant Application: A Guide for Social and Behavioral Scientists,* edited by Willo Pequegnat and Ellen Stover. New York: Plenum Press.

Hesse-Biber, Sharon. 1989. "Eating Problems and Disorders in a College Population: Are College Women's Eating Problems a New Phenomenon?" *Sex Roles,* 20: 71–89.

Hirsch, Eric L. 1990. "Sacrifice for the Cause: Group Processes, Recruitment, and Commitment in a Student Social Movement." *American Sociological Review,* 55 (April): 243–254.

Hirsch, Kathleen. 1989. *Songs from the Alley.* New York: Doubleday.

Hite, Shere. 1987. *Women and Love: A Cultural Revolution in Progress.* New York: Alfred A. Knopf.

Ho, D. Y. F. 1996. "Filial Piety and Its Psychological Consequences." Pp. 155–165 in *Handbook of Chinese Psychology,* edited by M. H. Bond. Hong Kong: Oxford University Press.

Hochschild, Arlie Russell. 1997. *The Time Bind: When Work Becomes Home and Home Becomes Work.* New York: Metropolitan Books.

Holden, Constance. 1986. "Homelessness: Experts Differ on Root Causes." *Science,* 232: 562–570.

Hollingsworth, T. H. 1972. "The Importance of the Quality of Data in Historical Demography." Pp. 71–86 in *Population and Social Change,* edited by D. V. Glass and Roger Revelle. London: Edward Arnold.

Holmes, Steven A. 1994. "Census Officials Plan Big Changes in Gathering Data." *The New York Times,* May 16, pp. A1, A13.

Holmes, Steven A. 1996. "In a First, 2000 Census Is to Use Sampling." *The New York Times,* February 29, p. A18.

Holmes, Steven A. 2000. "Stronger Response by Minorities Helps Improve Census Reply Rate." *The New York Times,* May 4, pp. A1, A22.

Holmes, Steven A. 2001a. "Census Officials Ponder Adjustments Crucial to Redistricting." *The New York Times,* February 12, p. A17.

Holmes, Steven A. 2001b. "The Confusion Over Who We Are." *The New York Times,* June 3, p. WK 1.

Hoover, Kenneth R. 1980. *The Elements of Social Scientific Thinking,* 2nd ed. New York: St. Martin's.

Horney, Julie, D. Wayne Osgood, and Ineke Haen Marshall. 1995. "Criminal Careers in the Short-Term: Intra-Individual Variability in Crime and Its Relation to Local Life Circumstances." *American Sociological Review,* 60: 655–673.

Hrobjartsson, Asbjorn and Peter C. Gotzsche. 2001. "Is the Placebo Powerless? An Analysis of Clinical Trials Comparing Placebo With No Treatment." *New England Journal of Medicine,* 344: 1594–1602.

Huberman, A. Michael and Matthew B. Miles. 1994. "Data Management and Analysis Methods." Pp. 428–444 in *Handbook of Qualitative Research,* edited by Norman K. Denzin and Yvonna S. Lincoln. Thousand Oaks, CA: Sage.

Huff, Darrell. 1954. *How to Lie with Statistics.* New York: W. W. Norton.

Humphrey, Nicholas. 1992. *A History of the Mind: Evolution and the Birth of Consciousness.* New York: Simon & Schuster.

Humphreys, Laud. 1970. *Tearoom Trade: Impersonal Sex in Public Places.* Chicago: Aldine.

Hunt, Morton. 1985. *Profiles of Social Research: The Scientific Study of Human Interactions.* New York: Russell Sage Foundation.

Hurwitz, Arthur C. 2000. "Letter to the Editor." *The New York Times,* February 16, p. A22.

Inter-university Consortium for Political and Social Research. 1996. *Guide to Resources and Services 1995–1996.* Ann Arbor, MI: ICPSR.

Irvine, Leslie. 1998. "Organizational Ethics and Fieldwork Realities: Negotiating Ethical Boundaries in Codependents Anonymous." Pp. 167–183 in *Doing Ethnographic Research: Fieldwork Settings.* Thousand Oaks, CA: Sage.

Janesick, Valerie J. 1994. "The Dance of Qualitative Research Design: Metaphor, Methodolatry, and Meaning." Pp. 209–219 in *Handbook of Qualitative Research,* edited by Norman K. Denzin and Yvonna S. Lincoln. Thousand Oaks, CA: Sage.

Jencks, Christopher. 1992. *Rethinking Social Policy: Race, Poverty, and the Underclass.* New York: HarperPerennial.

Jencks, Christopher. 1994. *The Homeless.* Cambridge, MA: Harvard University Press.

Jervis, Robert. 1996. "Counterfactuals, Causation, and Complexity." Pp. 309–316 in *Counterfactual Thought Experiments in World Politics: Logical, Methodological, and Psychological Perspectives,* edited by Philip E. Tetlock and Aaron Belkin. Princeton, NJ: Princeton University Press.

Jesnadum, Anick. 2000. "Researchers Fear Privacy Breaches with Online Research." www.digitalmass.com/news/daily/09/15/researchers.html.

Johnson, Dirk. 1997. "Party Animals in Fraternities Face the Threat of Extinction." *The New York Times,* May 15, pp. A1, A29.

Kagay, Michael R. with Janet Elder. 1992. "Numbers Are No Problem for Pollsters. Words Are." *The New York Times,* October 9, p. E5.

Kahn, Ric. 1997. "A Last Drink on New Year's." *The Boston Globe,* January 3, pp. B1–B2.

Kaku, Michio. 1997. *Visions: How Science Will Revolutionize the 21st Century.* New York: Anchor.

Kamin, Leon. 1974. *The Science and Politics of IQ.* Potomac, MD: Erlbaum.

Kanazawa, Satoshi. 2000. "A New Solution to the Collective Action Problem: The Paradox of Voter Turnout." *American Sociological Review,* 65: 433–442.

Kandel, Denise and Kazuo Yamaguchi. 1993. "From Beer to Crack: Developmental Patterns of Drug Involvement." *American Journal of Public Health,* 83: 851–855.

Kane, Emily W. and Howard Schuman. 1991. "Open Survey Questions as Measures of Personal Concern with Issues: A Reanalysis of Stouffer's *Communism, Conformity, and Civil Liberties.*" Pp. 81–96 in *Sociological Methodology,* vol. 21, edited by Peter V. Marsden. Oxford: Basil Blackwell.

Kaplan, Fred. 2002. "NY Continues to See Plunge in Number of Felonies." *The Boston Globe,* April 15, p. A3.

Kass, Seymour. 2000. "Letter to the Editor." *The New York Times,* February 16, p. A22.

Kaufman, Sharon R. 1986. *The Ageless Self: Sources of Meaning in Late Life.* Madison: University of Wisconsin Press.

Kay, Tess. 1998. "Having It All or Doing It All? The Construction of Women's Lifestyles in Time-Crunched Households." *Society and Leisure,* 21: 435–454.

Kenney, Charles. 1987. "They've Got Your Number." *The Boston Globe Magazine,* August 30, pp. 12, 46–56, 60.

Kershaw, David and Jerilyn Fair. 1976. *The New Jersey Income-Maintenance Experiment.* Vol. 1. New York: Academic Press.

Kershaw, Sarah. 2000. "In a Black Community, Mistrust of Government Hinders Census." *The New York Times,* May 16, p. A20.

Kershaw, Sarah. 2002. "Report Shows Serious Crime Rose in 2001." *The New York Times,* June 24, p. A10.

Kifner, John. 1994. "Pollster Finds Error on Holocaust Doubts." *The New York Times,* May 20, p. A12.

Kincaid, Harold. 1996. *Philosophical Foundations of the Social Sciences: Analyzing Controversies in Social Research.* Cambridge: Cambridge University Press.

King, Gary, Robert O. Keohane, and Sidney Verba. 1994. *Scientific Inference in Qualitative Research.* Princeton, NJ: Princeton University Press.

King, Miriam L. and Diana L. Magnuson. 1995. "Perspectives on Historical U.S. Census Undercounts." *Social Science History,* 19: 455–466.

Kiser, Edgar and Michael Hechter. 1991. "The Role of General Theory in Comparative-Historical Sociology." *American Journal of Sociology,* 97: 1–30.

Knight, JR, Henry Wechsler, Meichun Kuo, Mark Seibring, E. R. Weitzman, & M. A. Schuckit. 2002. "Alcohol Abuse and Dependence Among US College Students." *Journal of Studies on Alcohol,* 63: 263–270.

Knox, Richard A. 1997. "Time Running Out for Key Women's Study: Push Is on for Volunteers." *The Boston Globe,* September 8, pp. C1, C3.

Knulst, Wim and Andires van den Broek. 1998. "Do Time-Use Surveys Succeed in Measuring 'Busyness'? Some Observations of the Dutch Case." *Society and Leisure,* 21: 563–572.

Koegel, Paul. 1987. *Ethnographic Perspectives on Homeless and Homeless Mentally Ill Women.* Washington, DC: Alcohol, Drug Abuse, and Mental Health Administration, Public Health Service, U.S. Department of Health and Human Services.

Koegel, Paul and M. Audrey Burnam. 1992. "Problems in the Assessment of Mental Illness Among the Homeless: An Empirical Approach." Pp. 77–99 in *Homelessness: A National Perspective,* edited by Marjorie J. Robertson and Milton Greenblatt. New York: Plenum.

Kohn, Melvin L. 1987. "Cross-National Research as an Analytic Strategy." *American Sociological Review,* 52: 713–731.

Kohut, Andrew. 1988. "Polling: Does More Information Lead to Better Understanding?" *The Boston Globe,* November 7, p. 25.

Kolata, Gina. 1993. "Family Aid to Elderly Is Very Strong, Study Shows." *The New York Times,* May 3, p. A16.

Kolbert, Elizabeth. 1992. "Test-Marketing a President." *The New York Times Magazine,* August 30, pp. 18–21, 60, 68, 72.

Kollock, Peter and Marc A. Smith. 1999. "Communities in Cyberspace." Pp. 3–25 in *Communities in Cyberspace,* edited by Peter Kollock and Marc A. Smith. New York: Routledge.

Kolodinsky, Jane and JoAnne LaBrecque. 1996. "The Allocation of Time to Grocery Shopping: A Comparison of Canadian and U.S. Households." *Journal of Family and Economic Issues,* 17:393–408.

Kotkin, Stephen. 2002. "A World War Among Professors." *The New York Times,* September 7: Arts pp. 1, 17.

Kotre, John. 1995. *White Gloves: How We Create Ourselves Through Memory.* New York: Free Press.

Kraemer, Helena Chmura and Sue Thiemann. 1987. *How Many Subjects? Statistical Power Analysis in Research.* Newbury Park, CA: Sage.

Krauss, Clifford. 1996. "New York Crime Rate Plummets to Levels Not Seen in 30 Years." *The New York Times,* December 20, pp. A1, B4.

Kraut, Robert, Sara Kiesler, Bonka Boneva, Jonathon Cummings, Vicki Helgeson, and Anne Crawford. 2002. "Internet Paradox Revisited." *Journal of Social Issues,* 58: 49–74.

Krippendorff, Klaus. 1980. *Content Analysis: An Introduction to Its Methodology.* Thousand Oaks, CA: Sage.

Krueger, Richard A. 1988. *Focus Groups: A Practical Guide for Applied Research.* Newbury Park, CA: Sage.

Kubey, Robert. 1990. "Television and the Quality of Family Life." *Communication Quarterly,* 38 (Fall): 312–324.

Kuhn, Thomas S. 1970. *The Structure of Scientific Revolutions,* 2nd ed. Chicago: University of Chicago Press.

Kuzel, Anton J. 1999. "Sampling in Qualitative Inquiry." Pp. 33–45 in *Doing Qualitative Research,* 2nd ed., edited by Benjamin F. Crabtree and William L. Miller. Thousand Oaks, CA: Sage.

Kvale, Steinar. 1996. *Interviews: An Introduction to Qualitative Research Interviewing.* Thousand Oaks, CA: Sage.

Kvale, Steinar. 2002. "The Social Construction of Validity." Pp. 299–325 in *The Qualitative Inquiry Reader,* edited by Norman K. Denzin and Yvonna S. Lincoln. Thousand Oaks, CA: Sage.

Labaw, Patricia J. 1980. *Advanced Questionnaire Design.* Cambridge, MA: ABT Books.

La Gory, Mark, Ferris J. Ritchey, and Jeff Mullis. 1990. "Depression Among the Homeless." *Journal of Health and Social Behavior,* 31 (March): 87–101.

Laireiter, Anton and Urs Baumann. 1992. "Network Structures and Support Functions—Theoretical and Empirical Analyses." Pp. 33–55 in *The Meaning and Measurement of Social Support,* edited by Hans O. F. Veiel and Urs Baumann. New York: Hemisphere.

Lakshmanan, Indira A. R. 1993. "Do You Think Jurassic Park Is Too Scary for Children?" *The Boston Globe,* June 16, p. 28.

LaLonde, Robert J. 1986. "Evaluating the Econometric Evaluations of Training Programs with Experimental Data." *The American Economic Review,* 76: 604–620.

Langford, Terri. 2000. "Census Workers in Dallas Find the Well-Off Hard to Count." *The Boston Globe,* June 1:A24.

Larson, Calvin J. 1993. *Pure and Applied Sociological Theory: Problems and Issues.* New York: Harcourt Brace Jovanovich.

Larson, Calvin J. and Gerald R. Garrett. 1996. *Crime, Justice and Society,* 2nd ed. Dix Hills, NY: General Hall.

Laslett, Peter. 1973. *The World We Have Lost,* 2nd ed. New York: Scribner.

Lathrop, Barnes F. 1968. "History from the Census Returns." Pp. 79–101 in *Sociology and History: Methods,* edited by Seymour Martin Lipset and Richard Hofstadter. New York: Basic Books.

Latour, Francie. 2002. "Marching Orders: After 10 Years, State Closes Prison Boot Camp." *Boston Sunday Globe,* June 16, pp. B1, B7.

Lavin, Danielle and Douglas W. Maynard. 2001. "Standardization vs. Rapport: Respondent Laughter and Interviewer Reaction During Telephone Surveys." *American Sociological Review,* 66: 453–479.

Lavin, Michael R. 1994. *Understanding the 1990 Census: A Guide for Marketers, Planners, Grant Writers and Other Data Users.* Kenmore, NY: Epoch Books.

Lavrakas, Paul J. 1987. *Telephone Survey Methods: Sampling, Selection, and Supervision.* Newbury Park, CA: Sage.

Lazarsfeld, Paul F. and Anthony R. Oberschall. 1965. "Max Weber and Empirical Research." *American Sociological Review* (April): 185–199.

LeDuc, Lawrence, Richard G. Niemi, and Pippa Norris (Eds.). 1996. *Comparing Democracies: Elections and Voting in Global Perspective.* Thousand Oaks, CA: Sage.

Lee, Barrett A., Sue Hinze Jones, and David W. Lewis. 1990. "Public Beliefs About the Causes of Homelessness." *Social Forces,* 69: 253–265.

Lehto, Anna-Maija. 1998. "Time Pressure as a Stress Factor." *Society and Leisure,* 21: 491–511.

Lempert, Richard. 1989. "Humility Is a Virtue: On the Publicization of Policy-Relevant Research." *Law and Society Review,* 23: 146–161.

Lempert, Richard and Joseph Sanders. 1986. *An Invitation to Law and Social Science: Desert, Disputes, and Distribution.* New York: Longman.

Levi, Margaret. 1996. "The Institution of Conscription." *Social Science History,* 20: 133–167.

Levine, James P. 1976. "The Potential for Crime Overreporting in Criminal Victimization Surveys." *Criminology,* 14: 307–330.

Levine, Robert V., Todd Simon Martinez, Gary Brase et al. "Helping in 36 U.S. Cities." *Journal of Personality and Social Psychology,* 67 (July): 69–82.

Levy, Paul S. and Stanley Lemeshow. 1999. *Sampling of Populations: Methods and Applications,* 3rd ed. New York: Wiley.

Lewin, Tamar. 2001a. "Surprising Result in Welfare-to-Work Studies." *The New York Times,* July 31, p. A16.

Lewin, Tamar. 2001b. "Income Education Is Found to Lower Risk of New Arrest." *The New York Times,* November 16, p. A18.

Liang, Diane Wei, Richard Moreland, and Linda Argote. 1995. "Group Versus Individual Training and Group Performance: The Mediating Role of Transactive Memory." *Personality and Social Psychology Bulletin,* 21: 384–393.

Lichtblau, Eric. 2000. "Crime Dip Levels Off; Assault, Rape Up." *The New York Times,* December 19, p. A2.

Lieberson, Stanley. 1985. *Making It Count: The Improvement of Social Research and Theory.* Berkeley: University of California Press.

Lieberson, Stanley. 1991. "Small N's and Big Conclusions: An Examination of the Reasoning in Comparative Studies Based on a Small Number of Cases." *Social Forces,* 70: 307–320.

Lieberson, Stanley. 1992. "Einstein, Renoir, and Greeley: Some Thoughts About Evidence in Sociology." *American Sociological Review,* 57 (February): 1–15.

Liebow, Elliot. 1967. *Tally's Corner: A Study of Negro Streetcorner Men.* Boston: Little, Brown.

Link, Bruce G., Jo C. Phelan, Ann Stueve, Robert E. Moore, Michaeline Brenahan, and Elmer L. Struening. 1996. "Public Attitudes and Beliefs About Homeless People." Pp. 143–148 in *Homelessness in America,* edited by Jim Baumohl. Phoenix, AZ: Oryx.

Lipset, Seymour Martin. 1968. *Revolution and Counterrevolution.* New York: Basic Books.

Lipset, Seymour Martin. 1990. *Continental Divide: The Values and Institutions of the United States and Canada.* New York: Routledge.

Lipset, Seymour Martin, Martin Trow, and James Coleman. 1956. *Union Democracy.* New York: Free Press.

Lipsey, Mark W. and David B. Wilson. 2001. *Practical Meta-Analysis.* Thousand Oaks, CA: Sage.

Lipsky, Michael. 1980. *Street-Level Bureaucracy.* New York: Russell Sage Foundation.

Litwin, Mark S. 1995. *How to Measure Survey Reliability and Validity.* Thousand Oaks, CA: Sage.

Loader, Brian D., Steve Muncer, Roger Burrows, Nicolas Pleace, and Sarah Nettleton. 2002. "Medicine on the Line? Computer-Mediated Social Support and Advice for People with Diabetes." *International Journal of Social Welfare,* 11: 53–65.

Locke, Lawrence F., Stephen J. Silverman, and Waneen Wyrick Spirduso. 1998. *Reading and Under-standing Research.* Thousand Oaks, CA: Sage.

Locke, Lawrence F., Waneen Wyrick Spirduso, and Stephen J. Silverman. 2000. *Proposals That Work: A Guide for Planning Dissertations and Grant Proposals,* 4th ed. Thousand Oaks, CA: Sage.

Lodge, Milton. 1981. *Magnitude Scaling: Quantitative Measurement of Opinions.* Quantitative Applications in the Social Sciences, #25. Beverly Hills, CA: Sage.

Lofland, John and Lyn H. Lofland. 1984. *Analyzing Social Settings: A Guide to Qualitative Observation and Analysis,* 2nd ed. Belmont, CA: Wadsworth.

Loth, Renee. 1992. "Bush May Be Too Far Back, History of Polls Suggests." *The Boston Globe,* October 25, p. 19.

Lynch, Michael and David Bogen. 1997. "Sociology's Asociological 'Core': An Examination of Textbook Sociology in Light of the Sociology of Scientific Knowledge." *American Sociological Review,* 62: 481–493.

Mangione, Thomas W. 1995. *Mail Surveys: Improving the Quality.* Thousand Oaks, CA: Sage.

Marini, Margaret Mooney and Burton Singer. 1988. "Causality in the Social Sciences." Pp. 347–409 in *Sociological Methodology,* vol. 18, edited by Clifford C. Clogg. Washington, DC: American Sociological Association.

Markoff, John. 2000. "A Newer, Lonelier Crowd Emerges in Internet Study." *The New York Times.* February 16, pp. A1, A15.

Marsh, Robert M. 2000. "Weber's Misunderstanding of Traditional Chinese Law." *American Journal of Sociology,* 106: 281–302.

Marshall, Catherine and Gretchen B. Rossman. 1999. *Designing Qualitative Research,* 3rd ed. Thousand Oaks, CA: Sage.

Marshall, Ray and Vernon V. Briggs, Jr. 1967. "Negro Participation in Apprenticeship Programs." *Journal of Human Resources,* 2: 51–59.

Martin, Lawrence L. and Peter M. Kettner. 1996. *Measuring the Performance of Human Service Programs.* Thousand Oaks, CA: Sage.

Martin, Linda G. and Kevin Kinsella. 1995. "Research on the Demography of Aging in Developing Countries." Pp. 356–403 in *Demography of Aging,* edited by Linda G. Martin and Samuel H. Preston. Washington, DC: National Academy Press.

Marx, Karl. 1967. *Capital: A Critique of Political Economy.* New York: International Publishers.

Marx, Karl and Friedrich Engels. 1961. "The Communist Manifesto." Pp. 13–44 in *Essential Works of Marxism,* edited by Arthur P. Mendel. New York: Bantam.

Maticka-Tyndale, Eleanor. 1992. "Social Construction of HIV Transmission and Prevention Among Heterosexual Young Adults." *Social Problems,* 39 (August): 238–252.

Matt, Georg E. and Thomas D. Cook. 1994. "Threats to the Validity of Research Syntheses." Pp. 503–520 in *The Handbook of Research Synthesis,* edited by Harris Cooper and Larry V. Hedges. New York: Russell Sage Foundation.

Maxwell, Joseph A. 1996. *Qualitative Research Design: An Interactive Approach.* Thousand Oaks, CA: Sage.

Mayr, Ernst. 1982. *The Growth of Biological Thought: Diversity, Evolution, and Inheritance.* Cambridge, MA: Harvard University Press.

McCarty, John A. and L. J. Shrum. 2000. "The Measurement of Personal Values in Survey Research: A Test of Alternative Rating Procedures." *Public Opinion Quarterly,* 64: 271–298.

McLellan, A. Thomas, Lester Luborsky, John Cacciola, Jeffrey Griffith, Frederick Evans, Harriet L. Barr, and Charles P. O'Brien. 1985. "New Data from the Addiction Severity Index: Reliability and Validity in Three Centers." *The Journal of Nervous and Mental Disease,* 173(7): 412–423.

Mead, George Herbert. 1934. *Mind, Self, and Society.* Chicago: University of Chicago Press.

Merton, Robert K. 1957. *Social Theory and Social Structure,* revised and enlarged edition. Glencoe, IL: Free Press.

Merton, Robert K., Marjorie Fiske, and Patricia L. Kendall. 1956. *The Focused Interview.* Glencoe, IL: Free Press.

Metro Social Services. 1987. *PATH Community Survey.* Nashville, TN: Metro Social Services, Nashville-Davidson County.

Meyer, John W., John Boli, George M. Thomas, and Francisco O. Ramirez. 1997. "World Society and the Nation-State." *American Journal of Sociology,* 103: 144–181.

Michelson, William. 1998. "Time Pressure and Human Agency in Home-Based Employment." *Society and Leisure,* 21: 455–472.

Miczek, Klaus A., Joseph F. DeBold, Margaret Haney, Jennifer Tidey, Jeffrey Vivian, and Elise M. Weerts. 1994. "Alcohol, Drugs of Abuse, Aggression, and Violence." Pp. 377–570 in *Understanding and Preventing Violence. Vol. 3, Social Influences,* edited by Albert J. Reiss, Jr., and Jeffrey A. Roth. Washington, DC: National Academy Press.

Mieczkowski, Tom. 1997. "Hair Assays and Urinalysis Results for Juvenile Drug Offenders." in *National Institute of Justice Research Preview.* Washington, DC: U.S. Department of Justice.

Milbrath, Lester and M. L. Goel. 1977. *Political Participation,* 2nd ed. Chicago: Rand McNally.

Miles, Matthew B. and A. Michael Huberman. 1994. *Qualitative Data Analysis,* 2nd ed. Thousand Oaks, CA: Sage.

Milgram, Stanley. 1965. "Some Conditions of Obedience and Disobedience to Authority." *Human Relations,* 18: 57–75.

Mill, John Stuart. 1872. *A System of Logic: Ratiocinative and Inductive,* 8th ed., vol. 2. London: Longmans, Green, Reader, & Dyer.

Miller, Delbert C. 1991. *Handbook of Research Design and Social Measurement,* 5th ed. Newbury Park, CA: Sage.

Miller, Susan. 1999. *Gender and Community Policing: Walking the Talk.* Boston: Northeastern University Press.

Miller, Warren E. and Santa Traugott. 1989. *American National Election Data Sourcebook, 1952–1986.* Cambridge, MA: Harvard University Press.

Miller, William L. and Benjamin F. Crabtree. 1999a. "Clinical Research: A Multimethod Typology and Qualitative Roadmap." Pp. 3–30 in *Doing Qualitative Research,* 2nd ed., edited by Benjamin F. Crabtree and William L. Miller. Thousand Oaks, CA: Sage.

Miller, William L. and Benjamin F. Crabtree. 1999b. "The Dance of Interpretation." Pp. 127–143 in *Doing Qualitative Research,* edited by Benjamin F. Crabtree and William L. Miller. Thousand Oaks, CA: Sage.

Miller, William L. and Benjamin F. Crabtree. 1999c. Pp. 89-107 in *Doing Qualitative Research,* edited by Benjamin F. Crabtree and William L. Miller. Thousand Oaks, CA: Sage.

Mills, C. Wright. 1959. *The Sociological Imagination.* New York: Oxford University Press.

Mirowsky, John. 1995. "Age and the Sense of Control." *Social Psychology Quarterly,* 58: 31–43.

Mirowsky, John and Paul Nongzhuang Hu. 1996. "Physical Impairment and the Diminishing Effects of Income." *Social Forces,* 74: 1073–1096.

Mirowsky, John and Catherine E. Ross. 1991. "Eliminating Defense and Agreement Bias from Measures of the Sense of Control: A 2 x 2 Index." *Social Psychology Quarterly,* 54: 127–145.

Mirowsky, John and Catherine E. Ross. 1992. "Age and Depression." *Journal of Health and Social Behavior,* 33: 187–205.

Mirowsky, John and Catherine E. Ross. 1999. "Economic Hardship Across the Life Course." *American Sociological Review,* 64: 548–569.

Mitchell, Richard G., Jr. 1993. *Secrecy and Fieldwork.* Newbury Park, CA: Sage.

Moffitt, Robert Moffitt. 2002. "The Impact of Welfare Reform on Employment and Income." Pp. 8–11 in *Welfare, Children, and Families: Results from a Three City Study. A Congressional Briefing,* by Ronald J. Angel, P. Lindsay Chase-Lansdale, Andrew Cherlin and Robert Moffitt, May 17. Washington, DC: Consortium of Social Science Associations.

Mohr, Lawrence B. 1992. *Impact Analysis for Program Evaluation.* Newbury Park, CA: Sage.

Monkkonen, Eric H. 1994. "Introduction." Pp. 1–8 in *Engaging the Past: The Uses of History Across the Social Sciences.* Durham, NC: Duke University Press.

Mooney, Christopher Z. and Mei Hsien Lee. 1995. "Legislating Morality in the American States: The Case of Abortion Regulation Reform." *American Journal of Political Science,* 39: 599–627.

Moore, David W. 1992. "The Sure Thing That Got Away." *The New York Times,* October 25, p. E15.

Morrill, Calvin, Christine Yalda, Madeleine Adelman, Michael Musheno, and Cindy Bejarano. 2000. "Telling Tales in School: Youth Culture and Conflict Narratives." *Law & Society Review,* 34: 521–565.

Morris, Michael W. and Paul C. Moore. 2000. "The Lessons We (Don't) Learn: Counterfactual Thinking and Organizational Accountability After a Close Call." *Administrative Science Quarterly*, 45: 737–765.

Mosher, Clayton J., Terance D. Miethe, and Dretha M. Phillips. 2002. *The Mismeasure of Crime.* Thousand Oaks, CA: Sage.

Mueser, Kim T., Paul R. Yarnold, Douglas F. Levinson, Hardeep Singhy, Alan S. Bellack, Kimmy Kee, Randall L. Morrison, and Kashinath G. Yadalam. 1990. "Prevalence of Substance Abuse in Schizophrenia: Demographic and Clinical Correlates." *Schizophrenia Bulletin,* 16(1): 31–56.

Munger, Frank. 1993. "From the Editor." *Law and Society Review,* 27 (2): 251–254.

Myers, Steven Lee. 2002. "Russia Takes Stock of a Nation's Transformation." *The New York Times,* September 29, p. 3.

Nagourney,, Adam. 2002. "Cellphones and Caller ID Are Making It Harder for Pollsters to Pick a Winner." *The New York Times,* November 5, p. A20.

National Geographic Society. 2000. *Survey 2000.* survey2000.nationalgeographic.com.

National Institute of Alcohol Abuse and Alcoholism. 1994. "Alcohol-Related Impairment." *Alcohol Alert,* 25 (July): 1–5.

National Institute of Alcohol Abuse and Alcoholism. 1995. "College Students and Drinking." *Alcohol Alert,* 29 (July): 1–6.

National Institute of Alcohol Abuse and Alcoholism. 1997. "Alcohol Metabolism." *Alcohol Alert,* 35 (January): 1–4.

National Opinion Research Center (NORC). 1992. National Data Program for the Social Sciences. *The NORC General Social Survey: Questions and Answers.* Chicago: Mimeographed.

National Opinion Research Center (NORC). 1996. *General Social Survey.* Chicago: National Opinion Research Center, University of Chicago.

National Technical Information Service, U.S. Department of Commerce. 1993. *Directory of U.S. Government Datafiles for Mainframes and Microcomputers.* Washington, DC: Federal Computer Products Center, National Technical Information Service, U.S. Department of Commerce.

Navarro, Mireya. 1990. "Census Questionnaire: Link to Democracy and Source of Data." *The New York Times,* March 25, p. 36.

Needleman, Carolyn. 1981. "Discrepant Assumptions in Empirical Research: The Case of Juvenile Court Screening." *Social Problems,* 28 (February): 247–262.

Netcraft. 2002. Survey Highlights December, Retrieved February 2, 2003 from http://serverwatch.com/stats/netcraft/article.php/1559261

Neuendorf, Kimberly A. 2002. *The Content Analysis Guidebook.* Thousand Oaks, CA: Sage.

Newport, Frank. 1992. "Look at Polls as a Fever Chart of the Electorate." Letter to the Editor, *The New York Times,* November 6, p. A28.

Newport, Frank. 2000. "Popular Vote in Presidential Race Too Close to Call." http://www.gallup.com/poll/releases/pr001107.asp. 12/13/00. Princeton, NJ: The Gallup Organization.

Nie, Norman H. and Lutz Erbring. 2000. *Internet and Society: A Preliminary Report.* Palo Alto, CA: Stanford Institute for the Quantitative Study of Society.

Norusis, Marija J. and SPSS Inc. 1993. *SPSS for Windows Base System User's Guide, Release 6.0.* Chicago: SPSS Inc.

Novak, David. 2003. "The Evolution of Internet Research: Shifting Allegiances." *Online,* 27: 21.

Nunberg, Geoffrey. 2002. "The Shifting Lexicon of Race." *The New York Times,* December 22, p. WK 3.

Ó Dochartaigh, Niall. 2002. *The Internet Research Handbook: A Practical Guide for Students and Researchers in the Social Sciences.* Thousand Oaks, CA: Sage.

Oberschall, Anthony. 1972. "The Institutionalization of American Sociology." Pp. 187–251 in *The Establishment of Empirical Sociology: Studies in Continuity, Discontinuity, and Institutionalization,* edited by Anthony Oberschall. New York: Harper & Row.

Olzak, Susan, Suzanne Shanahan, and Elizabeth H. McEneaney. 1996. "Poverty, Segregation, and Race Riots: 1960 to 1993." *American Sociological Review,* 61: 590–613.

Onishi, Norimitsu. 1997. "Life and Death Under the Highways." *The New York Times,* February 17, p. 29.

Orcutt, James D. and J. Blake Turner. 1993. "Shocking Numbers and Graphic Accounts: Quantified Images of Drug Problems in the Print Media." *Social Problems,* 49 (May): 190–206.

Oreskes, Michel and Robin Toner. 1989. "The Homeless at the Heart of Poverty and Policy." *The New York Times,* January 29, p. E5.

Orr, Larry L. 1999. *Social Experiments: Evaluating Public Programs With Experimental Methods.* Thousand Oaks, CA: Sage.

Orshansky, Mollie. 1977. "Memorandum for Daniel P. Moynihan. Subject: History of the Poverty Line." Pp. 232–237 in *The Measure of Poverty. Technical Paper I: Documentation of Background*

Information and Rationale for Current Poverty Matrix, edited by Mollie Orshansky. Washington, DC: U.S. Department of Health, Education, and Welfare.

Pagnini, Deanna L. and S. Philip Morgan. 1996. "Racial Differences in Marriage and Childbearing: Oral History Evidence from the South in the Early Twentieth Century." *American Journal of Sociology,* 101: 1694–1715.

Paige, Jeffery M. 1999. "Conjuncture, Comparison, and Conditional Theory in Macrosocial Inquiry." *American Journal of Sociology,* 105: 781–800.

Papineau, David. 1978. *For Science in the Social Sciences.* London: Macmillan.

Parks, Malcolm and Kory Floyd. 1996. "Making Friends in Cyberspace." *Journal of Computer-Mediated Communication,* 1: 1–16. www.ascusc.org/jcmc/vol1/issue4/parks.html.

Parlett, Malcolm and David Hamilton. 1976. "Evaluation as Illumination: A New Approach to the Study of Innovative Programmes." Pp. 140–157 in *Evaluation Studies Review Annual,* vol. 1, edited by G. Glass. Beverly Hills, CA: Sage.

Passell, Peter. 1993. "Like a New Drug, Social Programs Are Put to the Test." *The New York Times,* March 9, pp. C1, C10.

Pate, Antony M. and Edwin E. Hamilton. 1992. "Formal and Informal Deterrents to Domestic Violence: The Dade County Spouse Assault Experiment." *American Sociological Review,* 57 (October): 691–697.

Paternoster, Raymond, Robert Brame, Ronet Bachman, and Lawrence W. Sherman. 1997. "Do Fair Procedures Matter? The Effect of Procedural Justice on Spouse Assault." *Law & Society Review,* 31(1): 163–204.

Patterson, Orlando. 1997. "The Race Trap." *The New York Times,* July 11, p. A25.

Patton, Michael Quinn. 2002. *Qualitative Research & Evaluation Methods,* 3rd ed. Thousand Oaks, CA: Sage.

Paxton, Pamela. 2002. "Social Capital and Democracy: An Interdependent Relationship." *American Sociological Review,* 67: 254–277.

Pepinsky, Harold E. 1980. "A Sociologist on Police Patrol." Pp. 223–234 in *Fieldwork Experience: Qualitative Approaches to Social Research,* edited by William B. Shaffir, Robert A. Stebbins, and Allan Turowetz. New York: St. Martin's.

Peterson, Robert A. 2000. *Constructing Effective Questionnaires.* Thousand Oaks, CA: Sage.

Pew Internet & American Life Project. 2000. *Tracking Online Life: How Women Use the Internet to Cultivate Relationships with Family and Friends.* Washington, DC: The Pew Internet & American Life Project. www.pewinternet.org.

Phillips, David P. 1982. "The Impact of Fictional Television Stories on U.S. Adult Fatalities: New Evidence on the Effect of the Mass Media on Violence." *American Journal of Sociology,* 87 (May): 1340–1359.

Phillips, Derek L. 1971. *Knowledge from What? Theories and Methods in Social Research.* Chicago: Rand McNally.

Plessy v. Ferguson, 163 U.S. 537 (1896).

Pollner, Melvin and Richard E. Adams. 1994. "The Interpersonal Context of Mental Health Interviews." *Journal of Health and Social Behavior,* 35: 283–290.

Posavac, Emil J. and Raymond G. Carey. 1997. *Program Evaluation: Methods and Case Studies,* 5th ed. Upper Saddle River, NJ: Prentice Hall.

Presley, Cheryl A., Philip W. Meilman, and Rob Lyerla. 1994. "Development of the Core Alcohol and Drug Survey: Initial Findings and Future Directions." *Journal of American College Health,* 42: 248–255.

Presser, Stanley. 1985. "The Use of Survey Data in Basic Research in the Social Sciences." Pp. 93–114 in *Surveying Subjective Phenomena,* vol. 2, edited by Charles F. Turner and Elizabeth Martin. New York: Russell Sage Foundation.

Presser, Stanley and Johnny Blair. 1994. "Survey Pretesting: Do Different Methods Produce Different Results?" Pp. 73–104 in *Sociological Methodology.* San Francisco: Jossey-Bass.

Prewitt, Kenneth. 2000. Letter to The Honorable Dan Miller. Washington, DC: U.S. Department of Commerce, Bureau of the Census. September 27. www.census.gov/Press-Release/www/2000/cb00cn58.html, 1/19/2003.

Price, Richard H., Michelle Van Ryn, and Amiram D. Vinokur. 1992. "Impact of a Preventive Job Search Intervention on the Likelihood of Depression Among the Unemployed." *Journal of Health and Social Behavior,* 33 (June): 158–167.

Punch, Maurice. 1994. "Politics and Ethics in Qualitative Research." Pp. 83–97 in *Handbook of Qualitative Research,* edited by Norman K. Denzin and Yvonna S. Lincoln. Thousand Oaks, CA: Sage.

Purdy, Matthew. 1994. "Bronx Mystery: 3rd-Rate Service for 1st-Class Mail." *The New York Times,* March 12, pp. 1, 3.

Putnam, Israel. 1977. "Poverty Thresholds: Their History and Future Development." Pp. 272–283 in *The Measure of Poverty. Technical Paper I: Documentation of Background Information and Rationale for Current Poverty Matrix,* edited by Mollie Orshansky. Washington, DC: U.S. Department of Health, Education, and Welfare.

Radin, Charles A. 1997. "Partnerships, Awareness Behind Boston's Success." *The Boston Globe,* February 19, pp. A2, B7.

Radloff, Lenore. 1977. "The CES-D Scale: A Self-Report Depression Scale for Research in the General Population." *Applied Psychological Measurement,* 1: 385–401.

Ragin, Charles C. 1987. *The Comparative Method: Moving Beyond Qualitative and Quantitative Strategies.* Berkeley: University of California Press.

Ragin, Charles C. 1994. *Constructing Social Research.* Thousand Oaks, CA: Pine Forge Press.

Rand, Michael R., James P. Lynch, and David Cantor. 1997. *Criminal Victimization, 1973–95.* Washington, DC: Office of Justice Programs, U.S. Department of Justice.

Rashbaum, William K. 2002. "Reasons for Crime Drop in New York Elude Many." *The New York Times,* November 29, p. A28.

Reed, Wornie L., Jodi Nudelman, Robert W. Adams, Jane Dockery, Nicol Nealeigh, and Rodney W. Thomas. 1997. *Infant Immunization Coverage Cluster Survey.* Cleveland, OH: Urban Child Research Center, Cleveland State University.

Reisman, David. 1969 [1950]. *The Lonely Crowd: A Study of the Changing American Character.* New Haven, CT: Yale University Press.

Reiss, Albert J., Jr. 1971a. *The Police and the Public.* New Haven, CT: Yale University Press.

Reiss, Albert J., Jr. 1971b. "Systematic Observations of Natural Social Phenomena." Pp. 3–33 in *Sociological Methodology,* vol. 3, edited by Herbert Costner. San Francisco: Jossey-Bass.

Rele, J. R. 1993. "Demographic Rates: Birth, Death, Marital, and Migration." Pp. 2-1–2-26 in *Readings in Population Research Methodology. Vol. 1, Basic Tools,* edited by Donald J. Bogue, Eduardo E. Arriaga, and Douglas L. Anderton. Chicago: Social Development Center, for the United National Population Fund.

Reynolds, Paul Davidson. 1979. *Ethical Dilemmas and Social Science Research.* San Francisco: Jossey-Bass.

Richards, Thomas J. and Lyn Richards. 1994. "Using Computers in Qualitative Research." Pp. 445–462 in *Handbook of Qualitative Research,* edited by Norman K. Denzin and Yvonna S. Lincoln. Thousand Oaks, CA: Sage.

Richardson, Laurel. 1995. "Narrative and Sociology." Pp. 198–221 in *Representation in Ethnography,* edited by John Van Maanen. Thousand Oaks, CA: Sage.

Ricketts, Erol R. and Isabel Sawhill. 1988. "Defining and Measuring the Underclass." *Journal of Policy Analysis and Management,* 7(2): 316–325.

Riedel, Marc. 2000. *Research Strategies for Secondary Data: A Perspective for Criminology and Criminal Justice.* Thousand Oaks, CA: Sage.

Riessman, Catherine Kohler. 2002. "Narrative Analysis." Pp. 217–270 in *The Qualitative Researcher's Companion,* edited by A. Michael Huberman and Matthew B. Miles. Thousand Oaks, CA: Sage.

Ringwalt, Christopher L., Jody M. Greene, Susan T. Ennett, Ronaldo Iachan, Richard R. Clayton, and Carl G. Leukefeld. 1994. *Past and Future Directions of the D.A.R.E. Program: An Evaluation Review.* Research Triangle, NC: Research Triangle Institute.

Rives, Norfleet W., Jr., and William J. Serow. 1988. *Introduction to Applied Demography: Data Sources and Estimation Techniques.* Sage University Paper Series on Quantitative Applications in the Social Sciences, series no. 07–039. Thousand Oaks, CA: Sage.

Robertson, David Brian. 1993. "The Return to History and the New Institutionalism in American Political Science." *Social Science History,* 17: 1–36.

Robinson, John P. 1973. "Toward a More Appropriate Use of Guttman Scaling." *Public Opinion Quarterly,* 37: 260–267.

Robinson, John P. 1998. "Activity Patterns of Time-Diary Dropouts." *Society and Leisure,* 21: 551–554.

Robinson, John P. and Ann Bostrom. 1994. "The Overestimated Workweek? What Time Diary Measures Suggest." *Monthly Labor Review,* August, pp. 11–23.

Robinson, John P. and Geoffrey Godbey. 1997a. *Time for Life: The Surprising Ways Americans Use Their Time.* University Park, PA: Pennsylvania State University Press.

Robinson, John P. and Geoffrey Godbey. 1997b. "Trend, Gender, and Status Differences in Americans' Perceived Stress." *Society and Leisure,* 21: 473–489.

Rohsenow, D. J. 1983. "Drinking Habits and Expectancies About Alcohol's Effects for Self Versus Others." *Journal of Consulting and Clinical Psychology,* 51: 752–756.

Rohsenow, D. J. and J. A. Bachorowski. 1984. "Effects of Alcohol and Expectancies on Verbal Aggression in Men and Women." *Journal of Abnormal Psychology,* 93: 418–432.

Rohsenow, D. J., P. M. Monti, D. B. Abrams, A. V. Rubonis, R. S. Niaura, A. D. Sirota, and S. M. Colby. 1992. "Cue Elicited Urge to Drink and Salivation in Alcoholics: Relationship to Individual Differences." *Advances in Behavioral Research and Therapy,* 14: 195–210.

Rosen, Lawrence. 1995. "The Creation of the Uniform Crime Report: The Role of Social Science." *Social Science History,* 19: 215–238.

Rosenbaum, David E. 2000. "Seeking Answers, Census Is Raising Privacy Questions." *The New York Times,* April 1, pp. A1, A9.

Rosenberg, Morris. 1965. *Society and the Adolescent Self-Image.* Princeton, NJ: Princeton University Press.

Rosenberg, Morris. 1968. *The Logic of Survey Analysis.* New York: Basic Books.

Rosenthal, Elisabeth. 2000. "Rural Flouting of One-Child Policy Undercuts China's Census." *The New York Times,* April 14, p. A10.

Rosenthal, Rob. 1994. *Homeless in Paradise: A Map of the Terrain.* Philadelphia: Temple University Press.

Ross, Catherine E. 1989. "Work, Family, and the Sense of Control. SES-8916154." Final summary report submitted to the National Science Foundation. Columbus: The Ohio State University.

Ross, Catherine E. 1990. "Work, Family, and the Sense of Control: Implications for the Psychological Well-Being of Women and Men." Proposal submitted to the National Science Foundation. Urbana: University of Illinois.

Ross, Catherine E. and Chloe E. Bird. 1994. "Sex Stratification and Health Lifestyle: Consequences for Men's and Women's Perceived Health." *Journal of Health and Social Behavior,* 35: 161–178.

Ross, Catherine E. and Marieke Van Willigen. 1996. "Gender, Parenthood, and Anger." *Journal of Marriage and the Family,* 58: 572–584.

Ross, Catherine E., John R. Reynolds, and Karlyn J. Geis. 2000. "The Contingent Meaning of Neighborhood Stability for Residents' Psychological Well-Being." *American Sociological Review,* 65: 581–597.

Ross, Catherine E. and Chia-ling Wu. 1995. "The Links Between Education and Health." *American Sociological Review,* 60: 719–745.

Ross, Catherine E. and Chia-ling Wu. 1996. "Education, Age, and the Cumulative Advantage in Health." *Journal of Health and Social Behavior,* 37: 104–120.

Rossi, Peter H. 1989. *Down and Out in America: The Origins of Homelessness.* Chicago: University of Chicago Press.

Rossi, Peter H. 1999. "Half Truths with Real Consequences: Journalism, Research, and Public Policy. Three Encounters." *Contemporary Sociology,* 28: 1–5.

Rossi, Peter H. and Howard E. Freeman. 1989. *Evaluation: A Systematic Approach,* 4th ed. Newbury Park, CA: Sage.

Rossman, Gretchen B. and Sharon F. Rallis. 1998. *Learning in the Field: An Introduction to Qualitative Research.* Thousand Oaks, CA: Sage.

Roth, Dee. 1990. "Homelessness in Ohio: A Statewide Epidemiologial Study." Pp. 145–163 in *Homeless in the United States, Vol. 1: State Surveys,* edited by Jamshid Momeni. New York: Greeenwood.

Roth, Dee, J. Bean, N. Lust, and T. Saveanu. 1985. *Homelessness in Ohio: A Study of People in Need.* Columbus, OH: Department of Mental Health.

Rubin, Herbert J. and Irene S. Rubin. 1995. *Qualitative Interviewing: The Art of Hearing Data.* Thousand Oaks, CA: Sage.

Rueschemeyer, Dietrich, Evelyne Huber Stephens, and John D. Stephens. 1992. *Capitalist Development and Democracy.* Chicago: University of Chicago Press.

Ruggles, Patricia. 1990. *Drawing the Line: Alternative Poverty Measures and Their Implications for Public Policy.* Washington, DC: The Urban Institute Press.

Ruster, Bernd, Bruno Simma, and Michael Bock (Eds.). 1983. *International Protection of the Environment: Treaties and Related Documents.* Dobbs Ferry, NY: Oceana.

Sacks, Stanley, Karen McKendrick, George DeLeon, Michael T. French, and Kathryn E. McCollister. 2002. "Benefit-Cost Analysis of a Modified Therapeutic Community for Mentally Ill Chemical Abusers." *Evaluation & Program Planning,* 25: 137–148.

Salisbury, Robert H. 1975. "Research on Political Participation." *American Journal of Political Science,* 19 (May): 323–341.

Sampson, Robert J. 1987. "Urban Black Violence: The Effect of Male Joblessness and Family Disruption." *American Journal of Sociology,* 93 (September): 348–382.

Sampson, Robert J. and John H. Laub. 1990. "Crime and Deviance Over the Life Course: The Salience of Adult Social Bonds." *American Sociological Review,* 55 (October): 609–627.

Sampson, Robert J. and John H. Laub. 1993. "Structural Variations in Juvenile Court Processing: Inequality, the Underclass, and Social Control." *Law and Society Review,* 27(2): 285–311.

Sampson, Robert J. and John H. Laub. 1994. "Urban Poverty and the Family Context of Delinquency: A New Look at Structure and Process in a Classic Study." *Child Development,* 65: 523–540.

Sampson, Robert J. and Janet L. Lauritsen. 1994. "Violent Victimization and Offending: Individual-, Situational-, and Community-Level Risk Factors." Pp. 1–114 in *Understanding and Preventing Violence. Vol. 3, Social Influences,* edited by Albert J. Reiss, Jr., and Jeffrey A. Roth. Washington, DC: National Academy Press.

Sampson, Robert J., Jeffrey D. Morenoff, and Felton Earls. 1999. "Beyond Social Capital: Spatial Dynamics of Collective Efficacy for Children." *American Sociological Review,* 64: 633–660.

Sampson, Robert J. and Stephen W. Raudenbush. 1999. "Systematic Social Observation of Public Spaces: A New Look at Disorder in Urban Neighborhoods." *American Journal of Sociology,* 105: 603–651.

Sampson, Robert J. and Stephen W. Raudenbush. 2001. "Disorder in Urban Neighborhoods—Does It Lead to Crime?" *Research in Brief.* Washington, DC: National Institute of Justice, U.S. Department of Justice.

Sampson, Robert J., Stephen W. Raudenbush, and Felton Earls. 1997. "Neighborhoods and Violent Crime: A Multilevel Study of Collective Efficacy." *Science,* 277: 918–924.

Savelsberg, Joachim L., Ryan King, and Lara Cleveland. 2002. "Politicized Scholarship? Science on Crime and the State." *Social Problems*, 49:3 27–348.

Schalock, Robert and John Butterworth. 2000. *A Benefit-Cost Analysis Model for Social Service Agencies.* Boston: Institute for Community Inclusion.

Schlenger, W.E., J. M. Caddell, L. Ebert et al. 2002. "Psychological Reactions to Terrorist Attacks: Findings From the National Study of Americans' Reactions to September 11." *Journal of the American Medical Association,* 288: 581–588.

Schober, Michael F. 1999. "Making Sense of Survey Questions." Pp. 77–94 in *Cognition and Survey Research,* edited by Monroe G. Sirken, Douglas J. Herrmann, Susan Schechter, Norbert Schwartz, Judith M. Tanur, and Roger Tourangeau. New York: Wiley.

Schofield, Janet Ward. 2002. "Increasing the Generalizability of Qualitative Research." Pp. 171–203 in *The Qualitative Researcher's Companion,* edited by A. Michael Huberman and Matthew B. Miles. Thousand Oaks, CA: Sage.

Schorr, Lisbeth B. and Daniel Yankelovich. 2000. "In Search of a Gold Standard for Social Programs." *The Boston Globe,* February 18, p. A19.

Schuman, Howard and Otis Dudley Duncan. 1974. "Questions About Attitude Survey Questions." Pp. 232–251 in *Sociological Methodology 1973–1974,* edited by Herbert L. Costner. San Francisco: Jossey-Bass.

Schuman, Howard and Stanley Presser. 1981. *Questions and Answers in Attitude Surveys: Experiments on Question Form, Wording, and Context.* New York: Academic Press.

Schuster, M.A., B. D. Stein, L. H. Jaycox, R. L. Collins, G. N. Marshall, M. N. Elliott, et al. 2001. "A National Survey of Stress Reactions After the September 1, 2001, Terrorist Attacks." *New England Journal of Medicine,* 345: 1507–1512.

Schutt, Russell K. 1986. *Organization in a Changing Environment.* Albany, NY: State University of New York Press.

Schutt, Russell K. 1987a. "Craft Unions and Minorities: Determinants of Change in Admission Practices." *Social Problems,* 34 (October): 388–402.

Schutt, Russell K. 1987b. "Recent Research Methods Texts: Means for Achieving Course Goals?" *Teaching Sociology,* 15 (April): 203–213.

Schutt, Russell K. 1988. *Shelter Staff Questionnaire.* Unpublished questionnaire. Boston: Department of Sociology, University of Massachusetts.

Schutt, Russell K. 1989. "Objectivity Versus Outrage." *Society,* 26 (May/June): 14–16.

Schutt, Russell K. 1990. "The Quantity and Quality of Homelessness: Research Results and Policy Implications." *Sociological Practice Review,* 1(2): 77–87.

Schutt, Russell K. 1992. "The Perspectives of DMH Shelter Staff: Their Clients, Their Jobs, Their Shelters and the Service System." A report to the Metro Boston Region of the Massachusetts Department of Mental Health. University of Massachusetts, Boston. Unpublished report.

Schutt, Russell K., Hubert M. Blalock, and Theodore C. Wagenaar. 1984. "Goals and Means for Research Methods Courses." *Teaching Sociology,* 11 (April): 235–258.

Schutt, Russell K., Robert Burke, Marsha Hogan, Patricia Ingraham, Richard Lyons, Tatjana Meschede, Richard Ryan, Joan Sinkiewicz, Helene Stern, and Andrew Walker. 1991. *The Shattuck Shelter Staff: Work Experience, Orientations to Work and AIDS Awareness.* Unpublished report to Shattuck Shelter. Boston: University of Massachusetts.

Schutt, Russell K. and Herbert L. Costner. 1993. "Another Edsel: The Collective Misperception of the Demand for the Certification of MA Sociologists." *The American Sociologist,* 23(3): 57–71.

Schutt, Russell K. and W. Dale Dannefer. 1988. "Detention Decisions in Juvenile Cases: JINS, JDs and Gender." *Law and Society Review,* 22(3): 509–520.

Schutt, Russell K., Xiaogang Deng, Gerald R. Garrett, Stephanie Hartwell, Sylvia Mignon, Joseph Bebo, Matthew O'Neill, Mary Aruda, Pat Duynstee, Pam DiNapoli, and Helen Reiskin. 1996. *Substance Use and Abuse Among UMass Boston Students.* Boston: Department of Sociology, University of Massachusetts–Boston.

Schutt, Russell K. and M. L. Fennell. 1992. "Shelter Staff Satisfaction with Services, the Service Network and Their Jobs." *Current Research on Occupations and Professions,* 7: 177–200.

Schutt, Russell K. and Gerald R. Garrett. 1992. *Responding to the Homeless: Policy and Practice.* New York: Plenum.

Schutt, Russell K. and Stephen M. Goldfinger. 1996 "Housing Preferences and Perceptions of Health and Functioning Among Homeless Mentally Ill Persons.*" Psychiatric Services,* 47: 381–386.

Schutt, Russell K., Stephen M. Goldfinger, and Walter E. Penk, 1992. "The Structure and Sources of Residential Preferences Among Seriously Mentally Ill Homeless Adults." *Sociological Review,* 3(3): 148–156.

Schutt, Russell K., Stephen M. Goldfinger, and Walter E. Penk. 1997. "Satisfaction with Residence and with Life: When Homeless Mentally Ill Persons Are Housed." *Evaluation and Program Planning,* 20(2): 185–194.

Schutt, Russell K., Suzanne Gunston, and John O'Brien. 1992. "The Impact of AIDS Prevention Efforts on AIDS Knowledge and Behavior Among Sheltered Homeless Adults." *Sociological Practice Review,* 3(1): 1–7.

Schutt, Russell K., Tatjana Meschede, and Jill Rierdan. 1994. "Distress, Suicidality, and Social Support Among Homeless Adults." *Journal of Health and Social Behavior,* 35 (June): 134–142.

Schutt, Russell K., Alan Orenstein, and Theodore C. Wagenaar (Eds.). 1982. *Research Methods Courses: Syllabi, Assignments, and Projects.* Washington, DC: Teaching Resources Center, American Sociological Association.

Schutt, Russell K., Walter E. Penk, Paul J. Barreira, Robert Lew, William H. Fisher, Angela Browne, and Elizabeth Irvine, 1999. Relapse Prevention for Dually Diagnosed Homeless. Proposal to National Institute of Mental Health, for Mental Health Research on Homeless Persons, PA-91-60. Worcester, MA: University of Massachusetts Medical School.

Schutt, Russell K., Theodore C. Wagenaar, and Kevin P. Mulvey (Eds.). 1987. *Research Methods Courses: Syllabi, Assignments, and Projects,* 2nd ed. Washington, DC: American Sociological Association.

Schutt, Russell K. (with the assistance of Tatjana Meschede). 1992. *The Perspectives of DMH Shelter Staff: Their Clients, Their Jobs, Their Shelters and the Service System.* Unpublished report to the Metro Boston Region of the Massachusetts Department of Mental Health. Boston: Department of Sociology, University of Massachusetts.

Schwandt, Thomas A. 1994. "Constructivist, Interpretivist Approaches to Human Inquiry." Pp. 118–137 in *Handbook of Qualitative Research,* edited by Norman K. Denzin and Yvonna S. Lincoln. Thousand Oaks, CA: Sage.

Schwartz, Mildred A. 1974. *Politics and Territory: The Sociology of Regional Persistence in Canada.* Montreal: McGill-Queen's University Press.

Scott, Janny. 2001. "A Nation by the Numbers, Smudged." *The New York Times,* July 1, p. 21, 22.

Scriven, Michael. 1972a. "The Methodology of Evaluation." Pp. 123–136 in *Evaluating Action Programs: Readings in Social Action and Education,* edited by Carol H. Weiss. Boston: Allyn & Bacon.

Scriven, Michael. 1972b. "Prose and Cons About Goal-Free Evaluation." *Evaluation Comment,* 3: 1–7.

Scull, Andrew T. 1988. "Deviance and Social Control." Pp. 667–693 in *Handbook of Sociology,* edited by Neil J. Smelser. Newbury Park, CA: Sage.

Sechrest, Lee and Souraya Sidani. 1995. "Quantitative and Qualitative Methods: Is There an Alternative?" *Evaluation and Program Planning,* 18: 77–87.

Seidman, Larry J. 1997. "Neuropsychological Testing." Pp. 498–508 in *Psychiatry,* vol. 1, edited by Allan Tasman, Jerald Kay, and Jeffrey Lieberman. Philadelphia: W. B. Saunders.

Seligman, Martin E. P. 1975. *Helplessness.* San Francisco: W. H. Freeman.

Sexton, Joe. 1994. "A Fatal Spiral to the Street: For Winter's First Exposure Victim, a Swift, Brutal Decline." *The New York Times,* January 2, pp. 19, 21.

Shadish, William R. 1995. "Philosophy of Science and the Quantitative-Qualitative Debates: Thirteen Common Errors." *Evaluation and Program Planning,* 18: 63–75.

Shadish, William R., Thomas D. Cook, and Laura C. Leviton, eds. 1991. *Foundations of Program Evaluation: Theories of Practice.* Thousand Oaks, CA: Sage.

Shepherd, Jane, David Hill, Joel Bristor, and Pat Montalvan. 1996. "Converting an Ongoing Health Study to CAPI: Findings from the National Health and Nutrition Study." Pp. 159–164 in *Health Survey Research Methods Conference Proceedings,* edited by Richard B. Warnecke. Hyattsville, MD: U.S. Department of Health and Human Services.

Sherman, Lawrence W. 1992. *Policing Domestic Violence: Experiments and Dilemmas.* New York: Free Press.

Sherman, Lawrence W. 1993. "Implications of a Failure to Read the Literature." *American Sociological Review,* 58: 888–889.

Sherman, Lawrence W. and Richard A. Berk. 1984. "The Specific Deterrent Effects of Arrest for Domestic Assault." *American Sociological Review,* 49: 261–272.

Sherman, Lawrence W. and Ellen G. Cohn. 1989. "The Impact of Research on Legal Policy: The Minneapolis Domestic Violence Experiment." *Law and Society Review,* 23: 117–144.

Sherman, Lawrence W. and Douglas A. Smith, with Janell D. Schmidt and Dennis P. Rogan. 1992. "Crime, Punishment, and Stake in Conformity." *American Sociological Review,* 57: 680–690.

Sieber, Joan E. 1992. *Planning Ethically Responsible Research: A Guide for Students and Internal Review Boards.* Thousand Oaks, CA: Sage.

Silver, Roxane Cohen, E. Alison Holman, Daniel N. McIntosh, Michael Poulin, and Virginia Gil-Rivas. 2002. "Nationwide Longitudinal Study of Psychological Responses to September 11." *JAMA: The Journal of the American Medical Association,* 288: 1235–1244.

Simon, Rita J. and Sandra Baxter. 1989. "Gender and Violent Crime." Pp. 171–197 in *Violent Crime, Violent Criminals,* edited by Neil Alan Weiner and Marvin E. Wolfgang. Newbury Park, CA: Sage.

Sirken, Monroe G., Douglas J. Herrmann, Susan Schechter, Norbert Schwartz, Judith M. Tanur, and Roger Tourangeau (Eds.). 1999. *Cognition and Survey Research.* New York: Wiley.

Sjoberg, Gideon (Ed.). 1967. *Ethics, Politics, and Social Research.* Cambridge, MA: Schenkman.

Sjoberg, Gideon and Roger Nett. 1968. *A Methodology for Social Research.* New York: Harper & Row.

Skinner, Harvey A. and Wen-Jenn Sheu. 1982. "Reliability of Alcohol Use Indices: The Lifetime Drinking History and the MAST." *Journal of Studies on Alcohol,* 43(11): 1157–1170.

Skocpol, Theda. 1984. "Emerging Agendas and Recurrent Strategies in Historical Sociology." Pp. 356–391 in *Vision and Method in Historical Sociology,* edited by Theda Skocpol. New York: Cambridge University Press.

Skocpol, Theda. 2002. "Will 9/11 and the War on Terror Revitalize American Civic Democracy?" *PS: Political Science & Politics,* 35: 537–540.

Skoll, Geoffrey R. 1992. *Walk the Walk and Talk the Talk: An Ethnography of a Drug Abuse Treatment Facility.* Philadelphia: Temple University Press.

Smith, Adam. 1937 [1776]. *An Inquiry into the Nature and Causes of the Wealth of Nations.* Edited by Edwin Cannan, with an introduction by Max Lerner. New York: Random House.

Smith, Joel. 1991. "A Methodology for Twenty-First Century Sociology." *Social Forces,* 70: 1–17.

Smith, Marc A. 1999. "Invisible Crowds in Cyberspace: Mapping the Social Structure of the Usenet." Pp. 195–219 in *Communities in Cyberspace,* edited by Peter Kollock and Marc A. Smith. New York: Routledge.

Smith, Tom W. 1984. "Nonattitudes: A Review and Evaluation." Pp. 215–255 in *Surveying Subjective Phenomena,* vol. 2, edited by Charles F. Turner and Elizabeth Martin. New York: Russell Sage Foundation.

Snow, David A. and Leon Anderson. 1987. "Identity Work Among the Homeless: The Verbal Construction and Avowal of Personal Identities." *American Journal of Sociology,* 92 (May): 1336–1371.

Sobell, Linda C., Mark B. Sobell, Diane M. Riley, Reinhard Schuller, D. Sigfrido Pavan, Anthony Cancilla, Felix Klajner, and Gloria I. Leo. 1988. "The Reliability of Alcohol Abusers' Self-Reports of Drinking and Life Events That Occurred in the Distant Past." *Journal of Studies on Alcohol,* 49(2): 225–232.

Sociological Abstracts, Inc. 1987. *Sociological Abstracts.* San Diego, CA: Sociological Abstracts, Inc.

Sosin, Michael R., Paul Colson, and Susan Grossman. 1988. *Homelessness in Chicago: Poverty and Pathology, Social Institutions and Social Change.* Chicago: Chicago Community Trust.

South, Scott J. and Glenna Spitze. 1994. "Housework in Marital and Nonmarital Households." *American Sociological Review,* 59: 327–347.

Specter, Michael. 1994. "Census-Takers Come Calling and Get a Scolding." *The New York Times,* March 3, p. A4.

Stake, Robert E. 1995. *The Art of Case Study Research.* Thousand Oaks, CA: Sage.

Stewart, David W. 1984. *Secondary Research: Information Sources and Methods.* Thousand Oaks, CA: Sage.

Stille, Alexander. 2000. "A Happiness Index with a Long Reach: Beyond G.N.P. to Subtler Measures." *The New York Times,* May 20, pp. A17, A19.

Stone, P. J., D. C. Dunphy, M. S. Smith, and D. M. Ogilvie. 1966. *The General Inquirer: A Computer Approach to Content Analysis.* Cambridge, MA: MIT Press.

Stout, David. 1997a. "Officials Are Starting Early in Their Defense of the 2000 Census." *The New York Times,* March 23, p. 37.

Stout, David. 1997b. "Senate Panel Opposes Use of Sampling in Next Census." *The New York Times,* May 4, p. 31.

Strunk, William, Jr., and Elwyn Brooks White. 2000. *The Elements of Style,* 4th ed. New York: Allyn & Bacon.

Sudman, Seymour. 1976. *Applied Sampling.* New York: Academic Press.

"Survey on Adultery: 'I Do' Means 'I Don't.'" 1993. *The New York Times,* October 19, p. A20.

Survey Research Laboratory. 1990a. *SRL Study 688: Work, Family, and the Sense of Control. Interviewer Instructions.* Unpublished. Urbana: University of Illinois.

Survey Research Laboratory. 1990b, August. *Work, Family, and the Sense of Control.* Unpublished questionnaire. Urbana: University of Illinois. August.

Swarns, Rachel L. 1996. "Moscow Sends Homeless to Faraway Hometowns." *The New York Times,* October 15, pp. A1, A12.

Tarnas, Richard. 1991. *The Passion of the Western Mind: Understanding the Ideas That Have Shaped Our World View.* New York: Ballantine.

Tavernise, Sabrina. 2002. "How Many Russians? Let Us Weigh the Count, Cooperation or No." *The New York Times,* October 10, p. A13.

Taylor, Jerry. 1999. "DARE gets updated in some area schools, others drop program." *The Boston Sunday Globe,* May 16, p. 1, 11.

Tenner, Edward. 1999. "Let's Not Get Too Wired" (editorial). *The New York Times on the Web,* July 22.

Tetlock, Philip E. and Aaron Belkin. 1996. "Counterfactual Thought Experiments in World Politics: Logical, Methodological, and Psychological Perspectives." Pp. 3–38 in *Counterfactual Thought Experiments in World Politics: Logical, Methodological, and Psychological Perspectives,* edited by Philip E. Tetlock and Aaron Belkin. Princeton, NJ: Princeton University Press.

Thorne, Barrie. 1993. *Gender Play: Girls and Boys in School.* New Brunswick, NJ: Rutgers University Press.

Timmer, Doug A., D. Stanley Eitzen, and Kathryn D. Talley. 1993. *Paths to Homelessness: Extreme Poverty and the Urban Housing Crisis.* Boulder, CO: Westview Press.

Tobler, Nancy S. 1986. "Meta-Analysis of 143 Adolescent Drug Prevention Programs: Quantitative Outcome Results of Program Participants Compared to a Control or Comparison Group." *The Journal of Drug Issues,* 16(4): 537–567.

Toby, Jackson. 1957. "Social Disorganization and Stake in Conformity: Complementary Factors in the Predatory Behavior of Hoodlums." *Journal of Criminal Law, Criminology and Police Science,* 48: 12–17.

Toppo, Greg. 2002. "Antidrug Program Backed by Study." *The Boston Globe,* October 29, p. A10.

Tourangeau, Roger. 1999. "Context Effects." Pp. 111–132 in *Cognition and Survey Research,* edited by Monroe G. Sirken, Douglas J. Herrmann, Susan Schechter, Norbert Schwartz, Judith M. Tanur, and Roger Tourangeau. New York: Wiley.

Tufte, Edward R. 1983. *The Visual Display of Quantitative Information.* Cheshire, CT: Graphics Press.

Turabian, Kate L. 1996. *A Manual for Writers of Term Papers, Theses, and Dissertations,* 6th ed. Chicago: University of Chicago Press.

Turner, Charles F. and Elizabeth Martin (Eds.). 1984. *Surveying Subjective Phenomena,* vols. I and II. New York: Russell Sage Foundation.

Tyler, Tom R. 1990. "The Social Psychology of Authority: Why Do People Obey an Order to Harm Others?" *Law and Society Review,* 24: 1089-1102.

Uchitelle, Louis. 1997. "Measuring Inflation: Can't Do It, Can't Stop Trying." *The New York Times,* March 16, p. 4.

Uchitelle, Louis. 1999. "Devising New Math to Define Poverty." *The New York Times,* October 16, pp. A1, A14.

UCLA Center for Communication Policy. 2001. *The UCLA Internet Report 2001—"Surveying the Digital Future."* Los Angeles: UCLA Center for Communication Policy.

Udry, J. Richard. 1988. "Biological Predispositions and Social Control in Adolescent Sexual Behavior." *American Sociological Review,* 53: 709–722.

U.S. Bureau of the Census. 1994. *Census Catalog and Guide, 1994.* Washington, DC: Department of Commerce, U.S. Bureau of the Census.

U.S. Bureau of the Census. 1996. *Census Catalog and Guide, 1996.* Washington, DC: Department of Commerce, U.S. Bureau of the Census.

U.S. Bureau of the Census. 1999. *United States Census 2000, Updated Summary: Census 2000 Operational Plan.* Washington, DC: U.S. Department of Commerce, Bureau of the Census, February.

U.S. Bureau of the Census. 2000a. "Census 2000 Efficiencies Result in $305 Million Savings." Washington, DC: U.S. Department of Commerce, Bureau of the Census, September 27. www.census.gov/Press-Release/www/2000/cn58.html (1/19/2003).

U.S. Bureau of the Census. 2000b. "Census Bureau Director Says 92 Percent of U.S. Households Accounted For; Thanks President and Vice President for Message to Census Workers." *United States Department of Commerce News,* May 31. www.census.gov/Press-Release/www/2000/ cb00cn41.html.

U.S. Bureau of the Census. 2000c. "Response Rate for Census 2000 Matches 1990 Rate." *United States Department of Commerce News,* April 19. www.census.gov/Press-Release/www/2000/ cb00cn35.html.

U.S. Bureau of the Census. 2000d. "U.S. Commerce Secretary William M. Daley Delegates Decision to Census Bureau on Adjusting Census 2000." *United States Department of Commerce News,* June 14. www.census.gov/Press-Release/www/2000.html.

U.S. Bureau of the Census. 2000e. "Well Done, America!" Washington, DC: U.S. Department of Commerce, Bureau of the Census, September 19. www.census.gov/Press-Release/www/2000/ cn57.html (1/19/2003).

U.S. Bureau of the Census. 2001. "Statement by William G. Barron Jr. on the Current Status of Results of Census 2000 Accuracy and Coverage Evaluation Survey." Washington, DC: U.S. Department of Commerce, Bureau of the Census, July 13. www.census.gov/Press-Release/www/2001/cb01cs06.html (1/19/2003).

U.S. Bureau of the Census. 2003. "Census Bureau to Test Changes in Questionnaire, New Response Technology." Washington, DC: U.S. Department of Commerce, Bureau of the Census, January 16. www.census.gov/Press-Release/www/2003/cb03cn02.html (1/19/2003).

U.S. Bureau of Labor Statistics, Department of Labor. 1991. *Major Programs of the Bureau of Labor Statistics.* Washington, DC: U.S. Bureau of Labor Statistics, Department of Labor.

U.S. Bureau of Labor Statistics, Department of Labor. 1997a. *Employment and Earnings.* Washington, DC: U.S. Bureau of Labor Statistics, Department of Labor.

U.S. Bureau of Labor Statistics, Department of Labor. 1997b. *Handbook of Methods.* Washington, DC: U.S. Bureau of Labor Statistics, Department of Labor.

U.S. Department of Commerce. 2002. *A Nation Online: How Americans Are Expanding Their Use of the Internet.* Washington, DC: National Telecommunications and Information Administration, Economics and Statistics Administration, U.S. Department of Commerce.

U.S. Department of Health, Education, and Welfare. 1976. *The Measure of Poverty.* Washington, DC: U.S. Department of Health, Education, and Welfare.

U.S. Department of Health and Human Services, Substance Abuse and Mental Health Services Administration, Center for Mental Health Services. 1995. *Client-Level Evaluation Procedure Manual.* Washington, DC: U.S. Department of Health and Human Services.

U.S. Department of Justice, Bureau of Justice Statistics. *National Crime Surveys: National Sample, 1973–1977* [Computer file]. 1977. Conducted by U.S. Department of Commerce, Bureau of the Census. Ann Arbor, MI: Inter-university Consortium for Political and Social Research [producer and distributor].

U.S. Government Accounting Office. (June 2001). *Health and Human Services: Status of Achieving Key Outcomes and Addressing Major Management Challenges.* Retrieved April 8, 2003, from www.gao.gov/new.items/d01748.pdf.

U.S. Office of Management and Budget. 2002. Government and Performance Results Act of 1993. Washington, DC: U.S. Office of Management and Budget, Executive Office of the President.

Vaessen, Martin. 1993. "Evaluation of Population Data: Errors and Deficiencies." Pp. 4-1–4-69 in *Readings in Population Research Methodology. Vol. 1, Basic Tools,* edited by Donald J. Bogue, Eduardo E. Arriaga, and Douglas L. Anderton. Chicago: Social Development Center, for the United Nations Population Fund.

Vaillant, George E. 1995. *The Natural History of Alcoholism Revisited.* Cambridge, MA: Harvard University Press.

Valenzuela, Arturo. 1990. "Chile: Origins, Consolidation, and Breakdown of a Democratic Regime." Pp. 38–86 in *Politics in Developing Countries: Comparing Experiences with Democracy,* edited by Larry Diamond, Juan J. Linz, and Seymour Martin Lipset. Boulder, CO: Lynne Rienner.

van de Vijver, Fons and Kwok Leung. 1997. *Methods and Data Analysis for Cross-Cultural Research.* Thousand Oaks, CA: Sage.

Van Maanen, John. 1982. "Fieldwork on the Beat." Pp. 103–151 in *Varieties of Qualitative Research,* edited by John Van Maanen, James M. Dabbs, Jr., and Robert R. Faulkner. Beverly Hills: Sage.

Van Maanen, John. 1995. "An End to Innocence: The Ethnography of Ethnography." Pp. 1–35 in *Representation in Ethnography,* edited by John Van Maanen. Thousand Oaks, CA: Sage.

Van Maanen, John. 2002. "The Fact of Fiction in Organizational Ethnography." Pp. 101–117 in *The Qualitative Researcher's Companion,* edited by A. Michael Huberman and Matthew B. Miles. Thousand Oaks, CA: Sage.

Verba, Sidney and Norman Nie. 1972. *Political Participation: Political Democracy and Social Equality.* New York: Harper & Row.

Verba, Sidney, Norman Nie, and Jae-On Kim. 1978. *Participation and Political Equality: A Seven-Nation Comparison.* New York: Cambridge University Press.

Vernez, Georges, M. Audrey Burnam, Elizabeth A. McGlynn, Sally Trude, and Brian S. Mittman. 1988. *Review of California's Program for the Homeless Mentally Disabled.* Santa Monica, CA: RAND.

Vidich, Arthur J. and Stanford M. Lyman. 1994. "Qualitative Methods: Their History in Sociology and Anthropology." Pp. 23–59 in *Handbook of Qualitative Research,* edited by Norman K. Denzin and Yvonna S. Lincoln. Thousand Oaks, CA: Sage.

Wageman, Ruth. 1995. "Interdependence and Group Effectiveness." *Administrative Science Quarterly,* 40: 145–180.

Wallace, Walter L. 1971. *The Logic of Science in Sociology.* Chicago: Aldine.

Wallace, Walter L. 1983. *Principles of Scientific Sociology.* New York: Aldine.

Wallgren, Anders, Britt Wallgren, Rolf Persson, Ulf Jorner, and Jan-Aage Haaland. 1996. *Graphing Statistics and Data: Creating Better Charts.* Thousand Oaks, CA: Sage.

Walters, Pamela Barnhouse, David R. James, and Holly J. McCammon. 1997. "Citizenship and Public Schools: Accounting for Racial Inequality in Education for the Pre- and Post-Disfranchisement South." *American Sociological Review,* 62: 34–52.

Warr, Mark. 1995. "The Polls-Poll Trends: Public Opinion on Crime and Punishment." *Public Opinion Quarterly,* 59: 296–310.

Watson, Charles G., Curt Tilleskjor, E. A. Hoodecheck-Schow, John Pucel, and Lyle Jacobs. 1984. "Do Alcoholics Give Valid Self-Reports?" *Journal of Studies on Alcohol,* 45(4): 344–348.

Watson, Roy E. L. 1986. "The Effectiveness of Increased Police Enforcement as a General Deterrent." *Law and Society Review,* 20(2): 293–299.

Weatherby, Norman L., Richard Needle, Helen Cesari, Robert Booth, Clyde B. McCoy, John K. Waters, Mark Williams, and Dale D. Chitwood. 1994. "Validity of Self-Reported Drug Use Among Injection Drug Users and Crack Cocaine Users Recruited Through Street Outreach." *Evaluation and Program Planning,* 17(4): 347–355.

Webb, Eugene J., Donald T. Campbell, Richard D. Schwartz, and Lee Sechrest. 2000. *Unobtrusive Measures,* rev. ed. Thousand Oaks, CA: Sage.

Webb, Eugene, Donald T. Campbell, Richard D. Schwartz, and Lee Sechrest. 1966. *Unobtrusive Measures: Nonreactive Research in the Social Sciences.* Chicago: Rand McNally.

Weber, Max. 1947. *The Theory of Social and Economic Organization.* Translated by A. M. Henderson and Talcott Parsons. New York: Free Press.

Weber, Max. 1949. *The Methodology of the Social Sciences.* Translated and edited by Edward A. Shils and Henry A. Finch. New York: Free Press.

Weber, Max. 1958. *The Protestant Ethic and the Spirit of Capitalism.* New York: Scribner's.

Weber, Robert Philip. 1985. *Basic Content Analysis.* Thousand Oaks, CA: Sage.

Wechsler, Henry, Andrea Davenport, George Dowdall, Barbara Moeykens, and Sonia Castillo. 1994. "Health and Behavioral Consequences of Binge Drinking in College: A National Survey of Students at 140 Campuses." *JAMA: The Journal of the American Medical Association,* 272(21): 1672–1677.

Wechsler, Henry, Jae Eun Lee, Meichun Kuo, and Hang Lee. 2000. "College Binge Drinking in the 1990s: A Continuing Problem. Results of the Harvard School of Public Health 1999 College Alcohol Study." www.hsph.harvard.edu/cas/rpt2000/CAS2000rpt2.html.

Wechsler, Henry, Jae Eun Lee, Meichun Kuo, Mark Seibring, Toben F. Nelson, and Hang Lee. 2002. "Trends in College Binge Drinking During a Period of Increased Prevention Efforts." *Journal of American College Health,* 50: 203–217.

Wechsler, Henry, Toben Nelson, and Elissa Weitzman. 2000. "From Knowledge to Action: How Harvard's College Alcohol Study Can Help Your Campus Design a Campaign Against Student Alcohol Abuse." *Change,* 32: 38–43.

Weinberg, Darin. 2000. "'Out There': The Ecology of Addiction in Drug Abuse Treatment Discourse." *Social Problems,* 47: 606–621.

Wellman, Barry and Milena Gulia. 1999. "Virtual Communities as Communities: Net Surfers Don't Ride Alone." Pp. 167–194 in *Communities in Cyberspace,* edited by Peter Kollock and Marc A. Smith. New York: Routledge.

Wellman, Barry, Anabel Quan Haase, James Witte, and Keith Hampton. 2001. "Does the Internet Increase, Decrease, or Supplement Social Capital? Social Networks, Participation, and Community Commitment." *American Behavioral Scientist,* 45: 436–455.

Wellman, Barry and Keith Hampton. 1999. "Living Networked in a Wired World." *Comparative Sociology,* 28: 1–12.

Wells, L. Edward and Joseph H. Rankin. 1991. "Families and Delinquency: A Meta-Analysis of the Impact of Broken Homes." *Social Problems,* 38 (February): 71–93.

Wheeler, Peter M. 1995. *Social Security Programs Throughout the World—1995.* Research Report #64, SSA Publication No. 13–11805. Washington, DC: Office of Research and Statistics, Social Security Administration.

Wheeler, Peter M. 1996. *Income of the Aged Chartbook, 1994.* Washington, DC: Office of Research, Evaluation, and Statistics, Social Security Administration.

White, Michael J. 1993. "Measurement of Population Size, Composition, and Distribution." Pp. 1-1–1-29 in *Readings in Population Research Methodology. Vol. 1, Basic Tools,* edited by Donald J. Bogue, Eduardo E. Arriaga, and Douglas L. Anderton. Chicago: Social Development Center, for the United Nations Population Fund.

Wholey, J. S. 1979. *Evaluation: Promise and Performance.* Washington, DC: Urban Institute.

Whyte, William Foote. 1955. *Street Corner Society.* Chicago: University of Chicago Press.

Whyte, William Foote. 1991. *Social Theory for Social Action: How Individuals and Organizations Learn to Change.* Newbury Park, CA: Sage.

Wickham-Crowley, Timothy P. 1992. *Guerrillas and Revolution in Latin America: A Comparative Study of Insurgents and Regimes Since 1956.* Princeton, NJ: Princeton University Press.

Williams, Kirk R. and Richard Hawkins. 1986. "Perceptual Research on General Deterrence: A Critical Review." *Law and Society Review,* 20: 545–572.

Wilson, William Julius. 1987. *The Truly Disadvantaged: The Inner City, the Underclass, and Public Policy.* Chicago: University of Chicago Press.

Wilson, William Julius. 1998. "Engaging Publics in Sociological Dialogue Through the Media." *Contemporary Sociology,* 27: 435–438.

Witkin, Belle Ruth and James W. Altschuld. 1995. *Planning and Conducting Needs Assessments: A Practical Guide.* Thousand Oaks, CA: Sage.

Wolcott, Harry F. 1995. *The Art of Fieldwork.* Walnut Creek, CA: AltaMira Press.

Women In World History. 2001. "The Plight of Women's Work in the Early Industrial Revolution in England and Wales." Women In World History Curriculum. http://www.womeninworldhistory. com/lesson7.html, retrieved February 2, 2003.

Wood, Christopher. 1995. *Environmental Impact Assessment: A Comparative Review.* New York: Wiley.

World Bank. 1994. *World Development Report 1994.* New York: Oxford University Press.

Wright, James D. and Eleanor Weber. 1987. *Homelessness and Health.* New York: McGraw-Hill.

Wunsch, Guillaume J. and Marc G. Termote. 1978. *Introduction to Demographic Analysis: Principles and Methods.* New York: Plenum Press.

Young, Robert L. 1992. "Religious Orientation, Race and Support for the Death Penalty." *Journal for the Scientific Study of Religion,* 31: 76–87.

Zaret, David. 1996. "Petitions and the 'Invention' of Public Opinion in the English Revolution." *American Journal of Sociology,* 101: 1497–1555.

Zarozny, Sharon (Ed.). 1987. *The Federal Database Finder: A Directory of Free and Fee-Based Databases and Files Available from the Federal Government,* 2nd ed. Chevy Chase, MD: Information US.

Zetterberg, Hans L. 1965. *On Theory and Verification in Sociology,* 3rd ed. Totowa, NJ: Bedminster Press.

Zielbauer, Paul. 2000. "2 Cities Lag Far Behind the U.S. in Heeding the Call of the Census." *The New York Times,* April 21, p. A21.

Zitner, Aaron. 1996. "A Cloudy Gaze into a Crystal Ball." The New York Times, September 26, pp. D1, D14.

Zullow, Harold M. 1991. "Pessimistic Rumination in Popular Songs and Newsmagazines Predict Economic Recession Via Decreased Consumer Optimism and Spending." *Journal of Economic Psychology,* 12: 501–526.

GLOSSARY/INDEX

Abbott, Andrew, 179, 180, 338, 340
Abel, David, 127, 135
Abortion
    laws, 101
    surveys on attitudes, 244-245
Abt Associates, 311
Action research, 327
Adair, G., 55
Adams, Richard E., 259
Addiction Severity Index (ASI),
        114, 115
Adelman, Madeleine, 415
Adolescents
    conflicts among, 414-415, 419-420,
        434-436, 435e
    effects of welfare-to-work
        programs, 325
    sexuality, 81
    substance abuse, 102
    See also Delinquency
African Americans
    attitudes toward births out of
        wedlock, 343
    children and neighborhoods, 65
    lynchings, 341, 342e
    neighborhood racial composition, 219
    political participation, 369
    poverty and juvenile delinquency, 81
    racial classifications, 107-108
    See also Race
Aggression, effects of catharsis, 181-182, 182e,
    183-184, 183e, 186-187, 188

Agreement bias, 235-236
AIDS
    discovery of virus, 52
    prevention education, 100
Alcohol. *See* Substance abuse
Alcohol Abstinence Self-Efficacy Scale,
        100, 101e
Alderson, Arthur S., 346, 358
Alfred, Randall, 286
Allport, Gordon, 87
Alternate-forms reliability   A procedure for
        testing the reliability of responses to survey
        questions in which subjects' answers are
        compared after the subjects have been asked
        slightly different versions of the questions or
        when randomly selected halves of the sample
        have been administered slightly different
        versions of the questions, 117
Altheide, David L., 428, 430
Altman, Lawrence, 94
Altschuld, James W., 317
American Evaluation Association, 312-313
American FactFinder, 350
American Jewish Committee, 233
American Medical Association, 52
American Psychiatric Association, 88
American Sociological Association (ASA) ethics
        code, 53-54, 220
American Sociological Review, 30, 38, 105
Anderson, Elijah, 180, 416, 423-425, 430, 431-432
Anderson, Margo J., 135
Anderton, Douglas L., 355-357

Note: Page numbers followed by *e* refer to exhibits.

Aneshensel, Carol S., 399

Angel, Ronald J., 467-468

Anomalous findings Unexpected findings in data analysis that are inconsistent with most other findings with that data, 49

Anonymity Provided by research in which no identifying information is recorded that could be used to link respondents to their responses, 269, 304

Anspach, Renee R., 268

Anthony, William A., 321

Anthropology, field research, 280, 282, 431

Applebome, Peter, 7-8

Applied research reports, 465
  audience, 468
  differences from journal articles, 467
  example, 469-470*e*
  front and back matter, 468
  sections, 465-467, 466-467*e*, 468

Appreciative inquiry, 327

Archives, 93

Armas, Genaro C., 135

Aronson, Elliot, 220-221

Arriaga, Eduardo, 356

Articles. *See* Journal articles

ASA. *See* American Sociological Association

ASI. *See* Addiction Severity Index

Association A criterion for establishing a nomothetic causal relationship between two variables: variation in one variable is related to variation in another variable, 181, 183
  crosstabulation, 391-394, 396
  curvilinear, 397
  direction of, 46-47, 396
  evaluating, 397-399
  graphing, 395-396, 395*e*
  in nonexperiments, 211
  in quasi-experiments, 208
  in true experiments, 203
  measures of, 398
  monotonic, 397
  specification, 403-405

Atkinson, Paul, 436, 437

Attributes, 107

Authenticity When the understanding of a social process or social setting is one that reflects fairly the various perspectives of participants in that setting, 16, 17, 20, 427-429

Authority
  obedience to, 132-133, 218

uncritical agreement with, 7-8

Availability sampling Sampling in which elements are selected on the basis of convenience, 147-148, 359

Averages. *See* **Mean**; **Mode**

Babbie, Earl, 372

Babor, Thomas F., 117

Bachman, Ronet, 41, 43, 422, 429, 439

Back matter The section of an applied research report that may include appendixes, tables, and the research instrument(s), 468

Bainbridge, William Sims, 138

Banks, C., 54

Bar chart A graphic for qualitative variables in which the variable's distribution is displayed with solid bars separated by spaces, 373-374, 374*e*

Bargh, John A., 11, 20

Barrett, Richard E., 355

Barringer, Felicity, 169

Barsade, Sigal G., 210

Base number *N* The total number of cases in a distribution, 377

Baumann, Robert, 353

Baumeister, Roy F., 181-182, 183-184, 188

Bean, Lee L., 357

Becker, Deborah R., 321

Becker, Howard S., 43, 425, 427, 463

Before-and-after design A quasi-experimental design consisting of several before-after comparisons involving the same variables but different groups, 204, 205*e*, 206
  fixed-sample panel designs, 171-173, 206
  multiple group, 206-207
  repeated measures panel designs, 207
  time series designs, 207-208

Behavior coding Observation in which the research categorizes according to strict rules the number of times certain behaviors occur, 241, 242

Bejerano, Cindy, 415

Bell Core Research, Inc., 253

Bellah, Robert N., 78, 298, 300-301

Bendix, Reinhard, 67, 338

Bennett, Lauren, 50-51

Bennett, William J., 87

Berger, Peter L., 79

Berk, Richard A., 30, 38, 42, 47, 48, 50, 52, 55, 71, 73, 74, 187, 189, 195, 203, 212, 215, 216, 221-222, 317-318, 329-330

Biesanz, Jeremy C., 120

Bimodal A distribution, in which two nonadjacent categories have about the same number of cases, and these categories have more cases than any others, 382, 383

Binder, Arnold, 52

Bird, Chloe E., 81, 269

Bivariate distributions, 392

Black box evaluation This type of evaluation occurs when an evaluation of program outcomes ignores, and does not identify, the process by which the program produced the effect, 325

Black, Donald J., 31-32, 90

Blair, Bob, 229

Blair, Johnny E., 241, 242, 253, 257, 258, 266

Blalock, Hubert M., Jr., 65

Blau, Peter M., 231

BLS. *See* Bureau of Labor Statistics

Boas, Franz, 280

Bogdewic, Stephan P., 284, 287, 289, 293, 295

Bogen, David, 75

Bogue, Donald J., 355, 356

Bollen, Kenneth A., 346, 358

Boot camps, 329, 330

Booth, Wayne C., 462-463

Boruch, Robert F., 220, 221, 312, 321, 331, 332, 333

Boston
    Cornerville study, 285, 287-288, 289, 295, 304, 428-429
    juvenile delinquents, 171
    Ten Point Coalition, 329

Boston Globe, 127

Boston McKinney Project, 315-316

Bourgeois, Philippe, 147

Bradshaw, York W., 67

Brain, emotional responses, 79, 80*e*

Brame, Robert, 41, 43

Bray, Hiawatha, 7

Brazil, racial classifications, 107

Brewer, John, 16, 49, 105, 112, 113

Bridges, George S., 175

Bristor, Joel, 259

British Social Attitudes Survey, 353

Broken windows theory, 166, 167*e*, 185

Brooks, Ralph M., 251

Brown, Judith Belle, 302, 303

Brown, S. A., 88

Bruni, Frank, 355

Bureau of Justice Statistics, 395-396

Bureau of Labor Statistics (BLS), 350, 352

Bureau of the Census. *See* U.S. Census Bureau

Burke, Garance, 354

Burrows, Roger, 12-13

Burt, Martha R., 129

Bush, George H. W., 237, 256

Bush, George W., 138

Bushman, Brad J., 181-182, 183-184, 186-187, 188, 195, 202-203

Butler, Dore, 102

Buttel, Frederick H., 346

Buzawa, Carl G., 51

Buzawa, Eve S., 51

Cain, Leonard D., Jr., 52

California State Legislature, 465-467, 466-467*e*

Campbell, Alec, 48

Campbell Collaboration, 313

Campbell, Donald T., 15, 73, 103, 186, 204, 214, 215, 216, 334

Campbell, Richard T., 167, 168, 172

Campbell, Wilson, 312, 323

Cantor, David, 395-396

CAPI. *See* **Computer-assisted personal interview**

Capitalism, 67

Carey, Raymond G., 314, 315, 320, 333

Carmines, Edward G., 91

Carpenter, Edwin H., 251

Case reports, 76-77

Case study A setting or group that the analyst treats as an integrated social unit that must be studied holistically and in its particularity, 420-421
    one-shot, 210

Case-oriented research Research that focuses attention on the nation or other unit as a whole, 340

Case-oriented understanding An understanding of social processes in a group, formal organization, community, or other collectivity that reflects accurately the standpoint of participants, 180-181

CATI. *See* **Computer-assisted telephone interview**

Causal effect
    criteria for relationship, 181, 183-189, 203
    in historical and comparative research, 359-360
    in nonexperiments, 211
    in quasi-experiments, 208
    in true experiments, 202-203

Causal effect (idiographic perspective) When a series of concrete events, thoughts, or actions result in a particular event or individual outcome, 177, 179-180, 278

Causal effect (nomothetic perspective)   When variation in one phenomenon, an independent variable, leads to or results in variation in another phenomenon, the dependent variable, all other things being equal, 177-179

Causal validity   Exists when a conclusion that A leads to or results in B is correct; also called internal validity, 16, 17, 20
in experiments, 211-212, 216
sources of invalidity, 212-215

Census   Research in which information is obtained through the responses that all available members of an entire population give to questions, 134-135
Chinese, 354
data available, 350-351, 353
data quality, 354-355
Mexican, 354
Russian, 135
state, 351

Census Bureau. *See* U.S. Census Bureau

Center for Epidemiologic Studies Depression Index (CES-D), 98, 99*e*, 240

Center for International Research, 353

Center for Mental Health Services, ACCESS Program, 102

Center for Research on Social Reality [Spain] Survey, 353

Center for Survey Research, University of Massachusetts at Boston, 96

Central tendency   The most common value (for variables measured at the nominal level), or the value around which cases tend to center (for a quantitative variable), 372
mean, 383-387
median, 383, 384-387
mode, 382-383

CES-D. *See* Center for Epidemiologic Studies Depression Index

Ceteris paribus   Latin phrase meaning "other things being equal," 177

Chai, Karen J., 219

Chalmers, Iain, 313

Chance sampling error. *See* **Random sampling error**

Charlotte (North Carolina), domestic violence experiment, 48

Chase-Dunn, Christopher, 359

Chase-Lansdale, P. Lindsay, 467-468

Chaves, Mark, 94

Chen, Huey-Tsyh, 319, 325, 326, 327, 328

Cherlin, Andrew, 467-468

Chicago
homeless, 130, 145-146, 146*e*, 470
influences on crime rates, 166-167, 174-175, 185

Children
as research subjects, 54, 284
gender and behavior, 277, 278
influence of neighborhoods on development, 65, 66*e*

China, census, 354

Chi-square   An inferential statistic used to test hypotheses about relationships between two or more variables in a crosstabulation, 398

Cholera, 7

Christenson, James A., 251

Church attendance, 104, 105*e*

Clark, Robin E., 321

Cleveland, Lara, 79

Clinton, Bill, 237

Closed-ended (fixed-choice) question   A survey question that provides preformatted response choices for the respondent to circle or check, 95-96
"don't know" responses, 236-238
mutually exclusive and exhaustive choices, 95-96, 235, 238-239
number of response categories, 239

Cluster   A naturally occurring, mixed aggregate of elements of the population, 144

Cluster sampling   Sampling in which elements are selected in two or more stages, with the first stage being the random selection of naturally occurring clusters and the last stage being the random selection of elements within clusters, 144-146, 145*e*

Clymer, Adam, 238

Codependents Anonymous, 304

Coffey, Amanda, 436, 437

Cognitive functioning, 79

Cognitive interview   A technique for evaluating questions in which researchers ask people test questions, then probe with follow-up questions to learn how they understood the question and what their answers mean, 120, 239, 241

Cohen, S., 90-91

Cohen, Susan G., 209-210

Cohn, Ellen G., 74

Cohort   Individuals or groups with a common starting point. Examples include college class of 1997, people who graduated from high school in the 1980s, General Motors employees who started work between 1990 and the year 2000, and people who were born in the late 1940s or the 1950s (the "baby boom generation"), 173

Cohort studies. *See* **Event-based design**

Coleman, James S., 67, 173, 174

Collective efficacy, 167, 168*e*, 175

Collins, Randall, 64

Colomb, Gregory G., 462-463

Colorado Springs (Colorado), domestic violence experiment, 48

Colson, Paul, 130-131

Columbia University, 301-302

Combined frequency display   A table that presents together the distributions for a set of conceptually similar variables having the same response categories; common headings are used for the responses, 380-381, 381*e*

Communist Manifesto, 66

Community, as basis of social organization, 63

Community Mental Health Act Amendments of 1975, 312

Community mental health systems, 268

Comparative historical research   Research comparing data from more than one time period in more than one nation, 338, 339, 347-348

Comparative research
   causality, 359-360
   compared to other research designs, 459
   cross-sectional, 338, 339, 346-347
   ethical issues, 360-361
   methodological complications, 357-360
   overview, 338-339
   sampling, 358-359
   types, 338-339, 339*e*
   See also **Secondary data**

Comparison group   In an experiment, a group that has been exposed to a different treatment (or value of the independent variable) than the experimental group, 195-197
   See also **Control group**

Compensatory rivalry (John Henry effect)   A type of contamination in experimental and quasi-experimental designs that occurs when control group members are aware that they are being denied some advantage and increase their efforts by way of compensation, 214

Complete observation   A role in participant observation in which the researcher does not participate in group activities and is publicly defined as a researcher, 282, 284

Complete participation   A role in field research in which the researcher does not reveal his or her identity as a researcher to those who are observed, 282, 285-287, 304

Compressed frequency display   A table that presents cross-classification data efficiently by eliminating unnecessary percentages, such as the percentage corresponding to the second value of a dichotomous variable, 381, 381*e*

Compstat, 165

Computer-assisted personal interview (CAPI)   A personal interview in which the laptop computer is used to display interview questions and to process responses that the interviewer types in, as well as to check that these responses fall within allowed ranges, 259

Computer-assisted qualitative data analysis   Uses special computer software to assist qualitative analyses through creation, application, and refinement of categories; tracing linkages between concepts; and making comparisons between cases and events, 437-440
   challenges, 439-440
   coding, 437-439, 438*e*
   reports, 439
   text preparation, 437

Computer-assisted telephone interview (CATI)   A telephone interview in which a questionnaire is programmed into a computer, along with relevant skip patters, and only legal entries are allowed; incorporates the tasks of interviewing, data entry, and some data cleaning, 257-258

Computers
   bibliographic databases, 32, 33*e*, 37
   processing power, 62
   See also Internet; Software

Concept   A mental image that summarizes a set of similar observations, feelings, or ideas, 86-87
   overlapping dimensions, 97-98, 98*e*

Conceptualization   The process of specifying what we mean by a term. In deductive research, conceptualization helps to translate portions of an abstract theory into specific variables that can be used in testable hypotheses. In inductive research, conceptualization is an important part of the process used to make sense of related observations, 87-89

Concurrent validity The type of validity that exists when scores on a measure are closely related to scores on a criterion measured at the same time, 114

Confidence intervals, 157-159, 390-391, 398

Confidentiality Provided by research in which identifying information that could be used to link respondents to their responses is available only to designated research personnel for specific research needs, 55, 268-269, 304-305, 332-333

Conflict theory Identifies conflict between social groups as the primary force in society; understanding the bases and consequences of conflict is the key to understanding social processes, 64, 66-67, 70

Congress. *See* U.S. House of Representatives; U.S. Senate

Conjunctural A feature of narrative explanation; no cause is ever understood to have an effect except in complex conjunctions with other causes, 340

Connolly, Francis J., 235

Consortium of Social Science Organizations, 467

Constant A number that has a fixed value in a given situation; a characteristic or value that does not change, 91

Construct validity The type of validity that is established by showing that a measure is related to other measures as specified in a theory, 114-115

Constructivist paradigm Methodology based on rejection of belief in an external reality; it emphasizes the importance of exploring the way in which different stakeholders in a social setting construct their beliefs, 76

Contamination A source of causal invalidity that occurs when either the experimental and/or the comparison group is aware of the other group and is influenced in the posttest as a result, 212, 214

Content analysis A research method for systematically analyzing and making inferences from text, 104, 440-442
  coding, 441, 442, 446-447*e*
  document population, 440-441
  flowchart, 442, 444-445*e*
  reliability and validity, 442, 443
  statistical analyses, 441-442

Content validity The type of validity that exists when the full range of a concept's meaning is covered by the measure, 113

Context A focus of idiographic causal explanation; a particular outcome is understood as part of a larger set of interrelated circumstances, 181, 188-189
  in nonexperiments, 211
  in quasi-experiments, 208
  in true experiments, 203

Context effects Occur in a survey when one or more questions influence how subsequent questions are interpreted, 244-245

Contextual effects Relationships among variables that vary among geographic units or other contexts, 80-81

Contingent question A question that is asked of only a subset of survey respondents, 234

Control group A comparison group that receives no treatment, 183, 196
  contamination of, 214
  matching, 198, 200*e*
  nonequivalent control group designs, 204-205, 212-213
  random assignment to, 184, 198
  selection bias, 212-213
  See also **Comparison group**

Control theory, 49

Convergent validity The type of validity achieved when one measure of a concept is associated with different types of measures of the same concept, 115

Converse, Jean M., 228

Cook, Thomas D., 186, 204, 214, 215, 216, 327, 460

Cooley, Charles Horton, 69

Cooper, Harris, 459, 460

Cooper, Kathleen B., 9

Copernicus, 71

Core Alcohol and Drug Survey, 95, 108, 108*e*, 110, 110*e*, 112

Core Institute, Southern Illinois University, 95, 98, 110, 112

Cornerville study, 285, 287-288, 289, 295, 304, 428-429

Correlation coefficient A summary statistic that varies from 0 to 1 or −1, with 0 indicating the absence of a linear relationship between two quantitative variables and 1 or −1 indicating that the relationship is completely described by the line representing the regression of the dependent variable on the independent variable, 406-407

Correlational analysis A statistical technique that summarizes the strength of a relationship between two quantitative variables in terms of its adherence to a linear pattern, 405-407

Correll, Joshua, 120

Corse, Sara J., 117

Cost-benefit analysis A type of evaluation research that compares program costs to the economic value of program benefits, 323, 324e, 331

Cost-effectiveness analysis A type of evaluation research that compares program costs to actual program outcomes, 323

Costner, Herbert L., 187

Counterfactual The outcome that would have occurred if the subjects who were exposed to the treatment actually were not exposed, but otherwise had had identical experiences to those they underwent during the experiment, 178, 178e

Couper, Mick P., 231, 259, 261

Cover letter The letter sent with a mailed questionnaire. It explains the survey's purpose and auspices and encourages the respondent to participate, 249, 250e

Covert participation. *See* **Complete participation**

Crabtree, Benjamin F., 279, 298, 416, 417

Crawford, Aileen, 281

Crenshaw, Edward M., 350

Cress, Daniel M., 419, 432-434

Crime
    causes of crime rate changes, 165-166
    collective efficacy and, 167, 168e, 175
    disorder and, 166, 167e, 185, 297
    effects on victims, 180-181
    informal social control and, 31-32, 166-167, 167e, 181, 185
    life circumstances and, 168
    media violence and, 178, 178e
    rates, 174-175, 395-396, 396e
    relationship to family disruption, 186
    statistics, 94, 105, 357
    thefts reported, 68, 69e
    See also Delinquency; Domestic violence

Crime Control and Safe Streets Act, 332-333

Criterion validity The type of validity that is established by comparing the scores obtained on the measure being validated to those obtained with a more direct or already validated measure of the same phenomenon (the criterion), 113-114, 115

Cronbach's alpha A statistic commonly used to measure interitem reliability, 117

Cross-population generalizability Exists when findings about one group, population, or setting hold true for other groups, populations, or settings; also called external validity, 18-19, 19e
    evaluating, 131, 132
    in experiments, 216

Cross-sectional comparative research Research comparing data from one time period between two or more nations, 338, 339, 346-347

Cross-sectional research design A study in which data are collected at only one point in time, 166-167
    causality, 210
    repeated, 169-171
    time order in, 167-169

Crosstabulation (crosstab) In the simplest case, a bivariate (two-variable) distribution, showing the distribution of one variable for each category of another variable; can also be elaborated using three or more variables, 391-394
    aspects of association, 396
    controlling for third variables, 399

Cuba, Lee J., 463

Current Population Survey, 3, 350, 352

Curvilinear Any pattern of association between two quantitative variables that does not involve a regular increase or decrease, 397

Czaja, Ronald, 229

Dannefer, W. Dale, 81, 267

D.A.R.E. (Drug Abuse Resistance Education), 310-311, 318-319, 318e, 320-321

Data analysis
    ethical issues, 391, 407-408
    preparing data, 370-372
    See also Qualitative data analysis; **Secondary data analysis**; Statistics

Data cleaning The process of checking data for errors after the data have been entered in a computer file, 370-372

Data collection
    observations, 102-103
    qualitative data, 416
    self-reports, 104, 105, 105e, 113-114, 117-119
    unobtrusive measures, 103-104

See also **Participant observation**; **Qualitative methods**; **Survey research**

Data, secondary. *See* **Secondary data**

Davies, Philip, 313

Davis, James A., 188, 230, 399

Davis, Ryan, 34

Dawes, Robyn, 57

De Ritis, Anthony, 7

Debriefing   A researcher's informing subjects after an experiment about the experiment's purposes and methods, and evaluating subjects' personal reactions to the experiment, 55, 221

Deception, 220-221

Decker, Scott H., 439-440

Deductive research   The type of research in which a specific expectation is deduced from a general premise and is then tested; compare to inductive research, 44

theory and data in, 41, 42*e*, 44

Delinquency

broken homes and, 460-461, 461*e*

factors in, 187, 188*e*, 189*e*

juvenile court records, 267-268, 267*e*

relationship to adult crime, 171-172, 172*e*, 184

relationship to poverty, 81

See also Crime

Democracy

in Latin America, 348, 349*e*

international comparisons, 337-338, 346-347, 347*e*

social capital and, 354

See also Elections; Voter participation

Demography   The statistical and mathematical study of the size, composition, and spatial distribution of human populations and how these features change over time, 355-357

Demos, John, 346

Dennis, Michael, 231

Dentler, Robert A., 311, 331

Denzin, Norman K., 154, 278, 443

Dependent variable   A variable that is hypothesized to vary depending on or under the influence of another variable, 44, 45

Depression

index, 98, 99*e*, 240

of unemployed, 196-197, 197*e*, 203, 213-214, 216, 221

sense of control and, 228

Descriptive research   Research in which social phenomena are defined and described, 10

examples, 11-12

inductive approach, 51

Descriptive statistics   Statistics used to describe the distribution of and relationship among variables, 368

Deterministic causal approach   An approach in which there is a relationship between an independent and a dependent variable; the independent variable has an effect on the dependent variable in every case under consideration, 360

Deterrence theory, 30, 38, 43, 44*e*, 48, 71, 73

Detroit Area Study, 235

Deviance, primary and secondary, 43

Dewey, Thomas E., 138

Diabetes, 12-13, 19, 21

Diagnostic and Statistical Manual, IV (DSM-IV), 88

Diamond, Timothy, 276-277, 278, 280-282, 285, 286, 287, 290, 293, 296, 422

Dichotomy   Variables having only two values, 111

DiClemente, C. C., 100

Differential attrition (mortality)   A problem that occurs in experiments when comparison groups become different because subjects are more likely to drop out of one of the groups for various reasons, 212

Dillman, Don A., 229, 231, 233, 234, 235, 236, 238, 239, 241, 244, 245, 248, 249, 251, 252, 261, 264, 266

Direct observations, 102-103

Direction of association   A pattern in a relationship between two variables—the values of variables tend to change consistently in relation to change on the other variable. The direction of association can be either positive or negative, 46-47, 396

Discriminant validity   An approach to construct validation; the scores on the measure to be validated are compared to scores on another measure of the same variable and to scores on variables that measure different but related concepts. Discriminant validity is achieved if the measure to be validated is related most strongly to its comparison measure and less so to the measures of other concepts, 115

Disproportionate stratified sampling   Sampling in which elements are selected from strata in different proportions from those that appear in the population, 142, 143*e*, 145-146

Dissertations, 40

Distribution of benefits   An ethical issue about how much researchers can influence the benefits subjects receive as part of the treatment being studied in a field experiment, 221-222, 331-332

Distributions
 base number *N*, 377
 bimodal, 382, 383
 bivariate, 392
 central tendency, 372, 382-387
 mean, 157-158
 normal, 155-156, 157-158, 157*e*, 390, 390*e*
 sampling, 154-155
 skewness, 372
 summarizing, 382
 unimodal, 382, 383
 univariate, 372-373
 variability, 372
 See also **Frequency distribution**
Division of labor, 64-65, 65*e*, 194-195, 338
Domestic violence
 decision to press charges, 50-51
 deterrent effects of arrest and employment status, 39, 39*e*, 49-50, 216
 extent of problem, 27, 51
 fair arrest procedures, 41
 informal sanctions, 38, 49
 See also Minneapolis Domestic Violence Experiment
Donath, Judith S., 17
Double negative   A question or statement that contains two negatives, which can muddy the meaning of the question, 233
Double-barreled question   A single survey question that actually asks two questions but allows only one answer, 233
Double-blind procedure   An experimental method in which neither the subjects nor the staff delivering experimental treatments know which subjects are getting the treatment and which are receiving a placebo, 214
Drake, Robert E., 120, 321
Drugs. *See* Substance abuse
DSM-IV. See Diagnostic and Statistical Manual, IV
Dukakis, Michael, 256
Durkheim, Emile, 9, 64-65, 194, 338
Dushenko, T. W., 55
Dutton, Mary Ann, 50-51
Dykema, Jennifer, 239

Earls, Felton, 65, 175
Ecological fallacy   An error in reasoning in which incorrect conclusions about individual-level

processes are drawn from group-level data, 175, 176*e*
Education
 achievement test scores in public and private schools, 173-174
 in women's prisons, 322
 Internet use by level, 3, 3*e*, 4
 occupational prestige and, 406, 406*e*
 relationship to income, 394, 401-402, 402*e*
 relationship to voting, 401-402, 401*e*, 402*e*
Effect size   A standardized measure of association—often the difference between the mean of the experimental group and the mean of the control group on the dependent variable, adjusted for the average variability in the two groups, 460
Efficiency analysis   A type of evaluation research that compares program costs to program effects. It can be either a cost-benefit analysis or a cost-effectiveness analysis, 323-324
Ego-based commitments, 7
Eitzen, D. Stanley, 149
Elaboration analysis   The process of introducing a third variable into an analysis in order to better understand—to elaborate–the bivariate (two-variable) relationship under consideration. Additional control variables also can be introduced, 399
Elder, Janet, 233
Elections
 focus groups, 303
 presidential, 137-139, 138*e*, 169, 237-238, 256
 push polling, 235
 See also Voter participation
Electronic survey   A survey that is sent and answered by computer, either through e-mail or on the Web, 261
 compared to other survey designs, 247-248, 247*e*, 264-266, 265*e*
 confidentiality, 269
 costs, 248
 drawbacks, 264
 formats, 264
 interactive voice response, 264
Elements   The individual members of the population whose characteristics are to be measured, 128, 129
E-mail. *See* Internet
E-mail survey   A survey that is sent and answered through e-mail, 261
 See also **Electronic survey**

Emerson, Michael O., 219
Emerson, Robert M., 103, 293
Emic focus   Representing a setting with the participants' terms, 415
Empirical generalization   A statement that describes patterns found in data, 47, 51
Employees
job satisfaction, 78
participation, 78
team organization, 204-205, 206*e*
See also Work
Endogenous change   A source of causal invalidity that occurs when natural developments or changes in the subjects (independent of the experimental treatment itself) account for some or all of the observed change from the pretest to the posttest, 212, 213
Engels, Friedrich, 66
England
British Social Attitudes Survey, 353
Industrial Revolution, 63
Entwisle, Barbara, 346, 358
Enumeration units   Units that contain one or more elements and that are listed in a sampling frame, 129
Environmental protection, historical research, 344-346, 344*e*, 345*e*
Erbring, Lutz, 4, 10, 11, 13, 14, 17, 18, 21, 22, 128, 131
Erikson, Kai T., 286-287, 358
Errors in reasoning, 4, 5-8
Errors of nonobservation   Errors caused by the omission from a survey or other research of some cases that should be included, 230
Errors of observation   Errors caused by poor measurement of observed cases, 230
ESM. *See* **Experience sampling method**
Ethical issues
American Sociological Association ethics code, 53-54, 220
anonymity, 269, 304
comparative research, 360-361
confidentiality, 55, 268-269, 304-305, 332-333
data analysis, 391, 407-408
deception, 220-221
distribution of benefits, 221-222, 331-332
evaluating, 55-56
evaluation research, 331-333
experimental research, 220-222
historical research, 360-361

honesty and openness, 52
informed consent, 54-55, 220, 304
participant observation, 285, 286-287, 304
qualitative data analysis, 442-443
qualitative research, 285, 286-287, 303-305
research reporting, 468-471
survey research, 55, 268-269
uses of science, 52-53
Ethnography   The study of a culture or cultures that some group of people share, using participant observation over an extended period of time, 417, 431-432
Etic focus   Representing a setting with the researchers' terms, 415
European Association for Telematic Applications, 9, 10*e*
Evaluability assessment   A type of evaluation research conducted to determine whether it is feasible to evaluate a program's effects within the available time and resources, 317
Evaluation research   Research that describes or identifies the impact of social policies and programs, 11, 311
black box approach, 325
challenges, 333
compared to traditional social science research, 314-315
design alternatives, 324-331
efficiency analysis, 323-324
ethical issues, 331-333
evaluability assessment, 317
examples, 14, 310-312
experimental research, 321
federal government requirements, 312, 323
growth of, 312, 312*e*
history, 311-313
impact analysis, 320-322
needs assessment, 315-317
process evaluation, 317-320
process of, 313-314
professional organizations, 312-313
program theory approach, 325-326, 326*e*
qualitative methods, 320, 328-329
quality assurance reviews, 312
quantitative methods, 328, 329
quasi-experiments, 321-322
research firms, 311, 312
researcher or stakeholder orientation, 326-328
simple or complex outcomes, 329-331
systems model, 313-314, 313*e*

Event-based design   A type of longitudinal study in which data are collected at two or more points in time from individuals in a cohort. Also known as cohort study, 173-174

Event-structure analysis   A systematic method of developing a causal diagram showing the structure of action underlying some chronology of events; the end result is an idiographic causal explanation, 341, 342*e*

Ex post facto control group design
A nonexperimental design in which comparison groups are selected after the treatment, program, or other variation in the independent variable has occurred, 208-210, 209*e*

Exhaustive attribute   Every case can be classified as having at least one attribute (or value) for the variable, 107

Expectations of experimental staff   A source of treatment misidentification in experiments and quasi-experiments that occurs when change among experimental subjects is due to the positive expectations of the staff who are delivering the treatment, rather than to the treatment itself; also called a self-fulfilling prophecy, 214

Experience sampling method (ESM)
A technique for drawing a representative sample of everyday activities, thoughts, and experiences; participants carry a pager and are beeped at random times over several days or weeks; upon hearing the beep, participants complete a report designed by the researcher, 292

Experimental designs
    compared to other research designs, 457-458
    criteria for causal relationships, 181,
        183-189, 203
    ethical issues, 220-222
    generalizability, 215-217
    in evaluation research, 321
    laboratory, 202-203, 458
    process analysis, 217-218
    randomized comparative change
        designs, 198
    randomized comparative posttest designs,
        199-201
    use of, 195
    validity, 211-215, 216
    See also **Control group**; **Field experiment**;
        Quasi-experimental design; **True**
        experiment

Experimental group   In an experiment, the group of subjects that receives the treatment or experimental manipulation, 183, 195-197
    matching, 198, 200*e*
    random assignment to, 184, 198
    selection bias, 212-213

Explanatory research   Seeks to identify causes and effects of social phenomena and to predict how one phenomenon will change or vary in response to variation in some other phenomenon, 11, 13

Exploratory research   Seeks to find out how people get along in the setting under question, what meanings they give to their actions, and what issues concern them, 10-11
    examples, 12-13
    inductive approach, 50-51, 278
    qualitative methods, 278

External events   A source of causal invalidity that occurs when events external to the study influence posttest scores; also called an effect of history, 213-214

External validity. *See* **Cross-population generalizability**

Extraneous variable   A variable that influences both the independent and dependent variables so as to create a spurious association between them that disappears when the extraneous variable is controlled, 188, 189*e*, 401-402

Face validity   The type of validity that exists when an inspection of items used to measure a concept suggests that they are appropriate "on their face," 113

Factorial survey   A survey in which randomly selected subsets of respondents are asked different questions, or are asked to respond to different vignettes, in order to determine the causal effect of the variables represented by these differences, 218-220

Fallows, Deborah, 13, 14

Families
    disruption and crime, 186, 460-461, 461*e*
    incomes, 155, 156*e*
    television viewing habits, 292
    work and, 227-228, 234-235, 240

Fears, Darryl, 107

Federal Bureau of Investigation (FBI), Uniform Crime Reports (UCR), 94, 357

Federal Writers' Project Life History Program for the Southeast, 343

Feedback Information about service delivery system outputs, outcomes, or operations that is available to any program inputs, 314

Fence-sitters Survey respondents who see themselves as being neutral on an issue and choose a middle (neutral) response that is offered, 236, 238

Fenno, Richard F., Jr., 284, 288, 290-291, 295, 301

Field experiment A study conducted in a real-world setting, 202
generalizability, 215-216
lack of control over conditions, 202
resources needed, 458
selection bias, 212
See also Experimental designs

Field notes Notes that describe what has been observed, heard, or otherwise experienced in a participant observation study. These notes usually are written after the observational session, 293-295
analysis of, 421, 422-423
contact summary forms, 423, 424*e*

Field research Research in which natural social processes are studied as they happen and left relatively undisturbed, 280, 282
See also **Participant observation**

Fienberg, Stephen E., 135

Filter question A survey question used to identify a subset of respondents who then are asked other questions, 234, 234*e*, 239, 244

Fink, Arlene, 462

FIPSE Core Analysis Grantee Group, 95

Fischer, Constance T., 180-181

Fiske, Marjorie, 302

Fitzsimons, Grainne M., 11, 20

Fixed-choice questions. *See* **Closed-ended (fixed-choice) question**

Fixed-sample panel design A type of longitudinal study in which data are collected from the same individuals—the panel—at two or more points in time. In another type of panel design, panel members who leave are replaced with new members. Also known as panel study, 171-173, 206

Floaters Survey respondents who provide an opinion on a topic in response to a closed-ended question that does not include a "don't know" option, but who will choose "don't know" if it is available, 236-238, 237*e*

Floyd, Kory, 6

Focus groups A qualitative method that involves unstructured group interviews in which the focus group leader actively encourages discussion among participants on the topics of interest, 241, 277, 302-303

FOIA. *See* Freedom of Information Act

Food and Drug Administration, 53

Forced-choice questions Closed-ended survey questions that do not include "don't know" as an explicit response choice, 237-238

Forero, Juan, 134, 355

Formative evaluation Process evaluation that is used to shape and refine program operations, 319-320

Fowler, Floyd J., 95, 120, 229, 241, 250, 261, 266

Fox, James Alan, 165

Fox, Nick, 10

Frank, David John, 344, 359

Frankfort-Nachmias, Chava, 408

Franklin, Mark N., 347, 350

Freedman, David A., 7

Freedom of Information Act (FOIA), 361

Freeman, Howard E., 198, 204, 208, 209, 222, 311, 315, 319, 320

Fremont, Allen M., 81

Frequency distribution Numerical display showing the number of cases, and usually the percentage of cases (the relative frequencies), corresponding to each value or group of values of a variable, 372-373, 377, 377*e*
combined frequency displays, 380-381, 381*e*
compressed frequency displays, 381, 381*e*
grouped data, 378-380, 379*e*, 380*e*, 391
ungrouped data, 377*e*, 378, 378*e*

Frequency polygon A graphic for quantitative variables in which a continuous line connects data points representing the variable's distribution, 374, 375*e*

Fretz, Rachel I., 293

Front matter The section of an applied research report that includes an executive summary, abstract, and table of contents, 468

Functionalism A social theory that explains social patterns in terms of their consequences for society as a whole and emphasizes the interdependence of social institutions and their common interest in maintaining the social order, 64-65, 70

GAFS. *See* Global Assessment of Functioning Scale

Gallup, George, 138

Gallup polls, 138, 233, 237-238, 256

Gamma   A measure of association that is sometimes used in crosstabular analysis, 398

GASB. *See* Governmental Accounting Standards Board

Gatekeeper   A person in a field setting who can grant researchers access to the setting, 288

Geertz, Clifford, 420

Geis, Florence, 102

Gemeinschaft societies   Societies based on community; they are homogeneous, with social relations based on kinship and, often, a common religion, 63

Gender
  children's behavior, 277, 278
  masculinity of police officers, 429
  voter participation and, 397, 398*e*

General Social Survey (GSS)
  administration of, 94, 230
  family incomes, 155, 156*e*
  length, 229
  nonrespondents, 260, 260*e*
  questions, 94, 229, 259
  voter participation data, 368, 369, 369*e*, 370, 398-399

Generalizability   Exists when a conclusion holds true for the population, group, setting, or event that we say it does, given the conditions that we specify, 16, 17
  importance, 19-20
  in qualitative research, 154
  in survey research, 229
  of experimental designs, 215-217
  problems with, 17-18
  See also **Cross-population generalizability**; **Sample generalizability**

Gesellschaft societies   Societies based on association; they are individualistic and competitive, with a developed division of labor, 63

Gilchrist, Valerie J., 289

Gill, Richard T., 355

Gilligan, Carol, 436

Glaser, Barney G., 290, 436

Glazer, Nathan, 355

Global Assessment of Functioning Scale (GAFS), 103, 117, 118*e*

Glover, Judith, 354

Glueck, Eleanor, 187

Glueck, Sheldon, 187

Goal-free evaluation, 327-328

Goel, M. L., 368

Goffman, Erving, 286

Goldfinger, Stephen M., 120, 173, 293, 315, 316, 418, 451

Goleman, Daniel, 79, 215, 239

Goodman, Lisa, 50-51

Google, 35, 36*e*

Gordon, Raymond, 234

Gore, Al, 138

Gottfredson, Don M., 68, 71

Gottfredson, Michael R., 68, 71

Gotzsche, Peter C., 215

Government Performance and Results Act of 1993, 312

Governmental Accounting Standards Board (GASB), 312, 323

Graduate Program in Applied Sociology, 463

Grady, John, 295

Grand tour question   A broad question at the start of an interview that seeks to engage the respondent in the topic of interest, 298

Graphs, 373
  advantages, 372
  bar charts, 373-374, 374*e*
  frequency polygons, 374, 375*e*
  guidelines, 377, 391
  histograms, 374, 375*e*
  misuse of, 374-377, 376*e*
  relationships shown in, 395-396, 395*e*
  scatterplots, 406, 406*e*

Griffin, Larry J., 340, 341

Grinnell, Frederick, 74

Grossman, Susan, 130-131

Grounded theory   Systematic theory developed inductively, based on observations that are summarized into conceptual categories, reevaluated in the research setting, and gradually refined and linked to other conceptual categories, 436-437, 436*e*

Group-administered survey   A survey that is completed by individual respondents who are assembled in a group, 252
  compared to other survey designs, 247-248, 247*e*, 264-266, 265*e*
  ethical issues, 268
  See also **Survey research**

Groves, Robert M., 229, 231, 258, 259, 261

Gruenewald, Paul J., 86, 93, 94

GSS. *See* General Social Survey

Guba, Egon G., 73, 76-77, 327

Gubrium, Jaber F., 20

Gunston, Suzanne, 100
Guttman scaling, 102

Haase, Anabel Quan, 11, 12, 20
Hadaway, C. Kirk, 94, 104
Hafner, Katie, 7
Hagan, John, 43
Hage, Jerald, 179, 188
Hall, Thomas D., 359
Halley, Fred, 372
Hallinan, Maureen T., 340
Hamburg, Germany, cholera epidemic, 7
Hamilton, David, 416
Hamilton, Edwin E., 38-40, 48, 49
Hampton, Keith, 11, 12, 14, 20, 128
Hampton, Keith N., 1, 9, 15
Haney, C., 54
Hantrais, Linda, 361
Harris, Anthony R., 166
Harris, David, 107-108, 341
Harris, Louis, 169
Hawkins, Richard, 38
Hawthorne effect   A type of contamination in experimental and quasi-experimental designs that occurs when members of the treatment group change in terms of the dependent variable because their participation in the study makes them feel special, 215
HCFA. *See* Health Care Finance Administration
Health Care Finance Administration (HCFA), 320
Health Research Extension Act of 1985, 332
Hechter, Michael, 346
Heckathorn, Douglas D., 152
Hedges, Larry V., 459, 460
Heilbroner, Robert L., 63
Herek, Gregory, 451
Hermeneutic circle   Represents the dialectical process in which the researcher obtains information from multiple stakeholders in a setting, refines his or her understanding of the setting, and then tests that understanding with successive respondents, 76, 77*e*
High schools, conflicts in, 414-415, 419-420, 434-436
Hill, David, 259
Hironaka, Ann, 344, 359
Hirsch, Eric L., 301-302
Hirsch, Kathleen, 179
Hirschinger, Nancy B., 117
Histogram   A graphic for quantitative variables in which the variable's distribution is displayed with adjacent bars, 374, 375*e*

Historical events research   Research in which social events are studied at one past time period, 338-339, 340-341
event-structure analysis, 341, 342*e*
oral histories, 343
Historical process research   Research in which historical processes are studied over a long period of time, 338, 339, 343-346
Historical research
causality, 359-360
challenges, 340
comparative, 338, 339, 347-348
compared to other research designs, 459
content analysis, 440-442
demographic analysis, 357
ethical issues, 360-361
methodological complications, 357-360
methods, 339-340
overview, 338-339
qualitative methods, 340, 344, 346
sampling, 358-359
types, 338-339, 339*e*
See also **Secondary data**
History effect   A source of causal invalidity that occurs when something other than the treatment influences outcome scores; also called an effect of external events, 212, 213-214
Ho, D. Y. F., 358
Hoffer, Thomas, 173, 174
Holistic   A feature of idiographic causal explanations, involving concern with context or understanding a particular outcome as part of a larger set of interrelated circumstances, 340
Hollingsworth, T. H., 357
Holmes, Steven A., 108, 135, 251
Holstein, James A., 20
Homeless
AIDS prevention education for, 100
estimated numbers, 470
housing alternatives, 173
sampling, 128, 129-131, 145-146, 146*e*, 151
social movement organizations, 432-434
substance use measurement, 120
substance use programs, 127
Homeless mentally ill
housing for, 120, 293-295, 315-316, 316*e*, 418
observations by interviewers, 102
shelter staff views of, 96
substance abuse treatment, 451-457
Honesty, 52

Horney, Julie, 168

House of Representatives. *See* U.S. House of Representatives

Housing segregation, 219

Hrobjartsson, Asbjorn, 215

Hu, Paul Nongzhuang, 269

Huberman, A. Michael, 423, 425, 436, 442-443

Huff, Darrell, 391

Human subjects, research on
    anonymity, 269, 304
    children, 54, 284
    confidentiality, 332-333
    ethical standards, 53-56
    informed consent, 54-55, 220, 304
    institutional review boards, 53, 332
    potential harm, 54, 55, 304
    withholding beneficial treatment, 55, 221-222

Humphrey, Nicholas, 6

Humphreys, Laud, 286

Hunt, Morton, 214, 217, 221

Hunter, Albert, 16, 49, 105, 112, 113

HyperRESEARCH, 437, 438*e*, 439, 523-543

Hypothesis A tentative statement about empirical reality involving a relationship between two or more variables, 44, 45
    direction of association, 46-47
    examples, 46*e*
    wording, 46

ICPSR. *See* Inter-university Consortium for Political and Social Research

Idiographic causal explanation An explanation that identifies the concrete, individual sequence of events, thoughts, or actions that resulted in a particular outcome for a particular individual or that led to a particular event; may be termed an individualist or historicist explanation, 177, 179-180, 278

Idiosyncratic variation Variation in responses to questions that is caused by individuals' reactions to particular words or ideas in the question instead of by variation in the concept that the question is intended to measure, 97

Illogical reasoning When we prematurely jump to conclusions or argue on the basis of invalid assumptions, 6, 8, 22

IMF. *See* International Monetary Fund

Impact evaluation (or analysis) The extent to which a treatment or other service has an effect, 320-322

Inaccurate observation Observations based on faulty perceptions of empirical reality, 5-6, 8, 21

Independent variable A variable that is hypothesized to cause, or lead to, variation in another variable, 44, 45

Index A composite measure based on summing, averaging, or otherwise combining the responses to multiple questions that are intended to measure the same concept, 97-98
    cautions, 98-100
    examples, 98, 99*e*
    multidimensional, 100
    preexisting, 98, 240
    score calculations, 100
    subscales, 100
    weighted, 100-102

Indicator The question or other operation used to indicate the value of cases on a variable, 91, 92, 92*e*

Inductive research The type of research in which general conclusions are drawn from specific data; compare to deductive research, 49
    examples, 49-50
    historical, 340
    qualitative, 50-51, 278
    theory and data in, 41, 42*e*, 49

Industrial Revolution, 63, 67

Inferential statistics A mathematical tool for estimating how likely it is that a statistical result based on data from a random sample is representative of the population from which the sample is assumed to have been selected, 155, 368, 398

Informal social control
    delinquency and, 187, 188*e*
    effects on crime rates, 31-32, 166-167, 167*e*, 181, 185
    spouse abuse and, 38, 49

Informants, key, 289

Informed consent, 54-55, 220, 304

Initiation, severity of, 220-221

In-person interview A survey in which an interviewer questions respondents face-to-face and records their answers, 258
    advantages, 258
    compared to other survey designs, 247-248, 247*e*, 264-266, 265*e*
    computer-assisted, 259
    costs, 229, 248

interacting with respondents, 258-259

interviewer training, 258

maximizing response, 260-261

third-party presence, 259-260

See also **Survey research**

Inputs   The resources, raw materials, clients, and staff that go into a program, 313, 314

Institute for Survey Research, 55

Institutional review board (IRB)   A group of organizational and community representatives required by federal law to review the ethical issues in all proposed research that is federally funded, involves human subjects, or has any potential for harm to subjects, 53, 332

Integrated Public Use Microdata Series (IPUMS), 351

Integrative approach   An orientation to evaluation research that expects researchers to respond to the concerns of people involved with the program—stakeholders—as well as to the standards and goals of the social scientific community, 328

Intensive (depth) interviewing   A qualitative method that involves open-ended, relatively unstructured questioning in which the interviewer seeks in-depth information on the interviewee's feelings, experiences, and perceptions, 277, 297-298

combined with participant observation, 301-302

preparations, 298

questions, 298-299, 300-301

recording, 301

relations with respondents, 299-300

researcher roles, 298

saturation point, 151, 299, 299*e*

selection of respondents, 299

Interactive voice response (IVR)   A survey in which respondents receive automated calls and answer questions by pressing numbers on their touch-tone phones or speaking numbers that are interpreted by computerized voice recognition software, 264

Intercensal percent change, 355

Interitem reliability   An approach that calculates reliability based on the correlation among multiple items used to measure a single concept; also known as internal consistency, 116-117

Internal consistency. *See* **Interitem reliability**

Internal validity. *See* **Causal validity**

International Monetary Fund (IMF), 311

Internet

ages of users, 4

annotated Web site list, 544-550

citing sources on, 37

education levels and use of, 3, 3*e*, 4

fictitious identities, 17

impact on social relations, 1-4, 8-9, 10-11, 13-14, 15*e*, 22

literature searches, 32, 34-37, 500-503

medical self-help groups, 12-13, 19, 21

number of users, 62

percentage of U.S. households with access, 3, 261

research on discussion groups, 305

search engines, 34-36, 36*e*, 502-503

self-presentation on, 20, 21*e*

social uses, 12, 12*e*, 14

subject directories, 34, 501-502

worldwide survey, 11-12, 14, 17-18, 20, 21

See also **Electronic survey**

Interobserver reliability   When similar measurements are obtained by different observers rating the same persons, events, or places, 117

Interpretive questions   Questions included in a questionnaire or interview schedule to help explain answers to other important questions, 242-243

Interpretivism   Methodology based on the belief that reality is socially constructed and that the goal of social scientists is to understand what meanings people give to that reality, 75-76, 154

case reports, 76-77

goals, 78

hermeneutic circle, 76, 77*e*

research guidelines, 77

Interquartile range   The range in a distribution between the end of the first quartile and the beginning of the third quartile, 388-389

Intersubjective agreement   Agreement between scientists about the nature of reality; often upheld as a more reasonable goal for science than certainty about an objective reality, 73

Inter-university Consortium for Political and Social Research (ICPSR), 94, 230, 350, 352-353, 370

Interval level of measurement   A measurement of a variable in which the numbers indicating a variable's values represent fixed measurement units, but have no absolute, or fixed, zero point, 106e, 109-110, 373

Intervening variables   Variables that are influenced by an independent variable and in turn influence variation in a dependent variable, thus helping to explain the relationship between the independent and dependent variables, 187, 188e, 399-401

Interview schedule   The survey instrument containing the questions asked by the interviewer in an in-person or phone survey, 240

for phone surveys, 253, 254-256e

length, 229

See also **Questionnaire**

Interviews

observational questions, 103

See also **Cognitive interview**; **In-person interview**

Intrarater (or intraobserver) reliability   Consistency of ratings by an observer of an unchanging phenomenon at two or more points in time, 116

IPUMS. *See* Integrated Public Use Microdata Series

IRB. *See* **Institutional review board**

Irvine, Leslie, 304

IVR. *See* **Interactive voice response**

James, David R., 357, 358

Janesick, Valerie J., 81

Jervis, Robert, 359

Jesnadum, Anick, 305

John Henry effect. *See* **Compensatory rivalry**

Johnson, John M., 428, 430

Jottings   Brief notes written in the field about highlights of an observation period, 293

Journal articles

bibliographic databases, 32, 33e, 37

differences from applied research reports, 467

evaluating, 37-38, 488-490, 491-498

rejection rates, 464

review process, 31, 37, 40, 464

searching for, 31-34

sections, 464, 465e

Judd, Charles M., 120

Kagay, Michael R., 233

Kahn, Robert L., 229

Kaku, Michio, 62

Kanazawa, Satoshi, 393

Kandel, Denise, 102

Kaplan, Fred, 165

Kaufman, Sharon R., 278, 298

Kendall, Patricia L., 302

Kenney, Charles, 138

Keohane, Robert O., 29, 178, 290, 358, 360

Kershaw, Sarah, 135, 165

Kettner, Peter M., 314

Key informant   An insider who is willing and able to provide a field researcher with superior access and information, including answers to questions that arise in the course of the research, 289

Kifner, John, 233

Kilgore, Sally, 173

Kim, Jae-On, 369, 370

Kincaid, Harold, 73, 74

King, Gary, 29, 178, 290, 358, 360

King, Miriam, 355

King, Ryan, 79

Kinsella, Kevin, 358

Kiser, Edgar, 346

Klap, Ruth, 48

Klitzner, Michael, 86

Knight, J. R., 85

Kohn, Melvin L., 341, 357

Kohut, Andrew, 256

Kolbert, Elizabeth, 303

Kollock, Peter, 10

Kotkin, Stephen, 338

Kraemer, Helena Chmura, 159

Kraut, Robert, 22

Krueger, Richard A., 302, 303

Kubey, Robert, 292

Kuhn, Thomas S., 71-72

Kuo, Meichun, 85

Kuzel, Anton J., 290

Kvale, Steinar, 20, 299, 300, 422

Labaw, Patricia J., 229, 242, 243, 245

Labeling theory, 30-31, 43, 44e

Laboratory experiments, 202-203, 458

Landers, Ann, 4

Landon, Alfred M., 138

Langford, Terri, 135

Larson, Calvin J., 55

Laslett, Peter, 63

Lathrop, Barnes F., 351

Latin America, regime types, 348, 349e

Latour, Francie, 330

Laub, John H., 171, 172, 184, 187

Lavin, Danielle, 79

Lavin, Michael R., 350
Lavrakas, Paul J., 253
Learning, effects of organizational accountability, 199-201, 201*e*, 202-203, 202*e*
Ledford, Gerald E., Jr., 209-210
LeDuc, Lawrence, 346
Lee, Hang, 85
Lee, Jae Eun, 85
Lee, Mei Hsien, 101
Lemeshow, Stanley, 129, 145, 159, 229, 252, 253
Lempert, Richard, 43, 52
Leon-Guerrero, Anna, 408
Lettiere, Mark, 147
Leung, Kwok, 358
Level of measurement The mathematical precision with which the values of a variable can be expressed. The nominal level of measurement, which is qualitative, has no mathematical interpretation; the quantitative levels of measurement—ordinal, interval, and ratio—are progressively more precise mathematically, 106
   comparison of, 111-112, 111*e*
   interval, 106*e*, 109-110, 373
   nominal, 106*e*, 107-108, 373
   ordinal, 106*e*, 108-109, 373
   ratio, 106*e*, 110-111, 373
   selecting, 112
   statistics used, 373, 387
Levine, James P., 105
Levitan, Laura C., 327
Levy, Paul S., 129, 145, 159, 229, 252, 253
Lewin, Tamar, 322, 325
Lichtblau, Eric, 165
Lieberson, Stanley, 358, 360, 408
Lincoln, Yvonna S., 73, 76-77, 278, 327
Lindsay, R. C. L., 55
Link, Bruce G., 139-140
Lipset, Seymour Martin, 348
Lipsey, Mark W., 459, 460
Lipsky, Michael, 268
Literary Digest, 138
Literature reviews
   integrated, 40-41
   single-article, 38-40
   writing, 33-34, 37-38
Literature searches
   on Internet, 32, 34-37, 500-503
   procedures, 31-34, 499-500
Litwin, Mark S., 117
Loader, Brian D., 11, 12-13, 14, 18, 49, 104

Locke, Lawrence F., 40, 56, 451
Lofland, John, 277
Lofland, Lyn H., 277
Longitudinal research design A study in which data are collected that can be ordered in time; also defined as research in which data are collected at two or more points in time, 166, 169
   event-based designs, 173-174
   fixed-sample panel designs, 171-173
   repeated cross-sectional designs, 169-171
   types, 170*e*
Lotteries, 136
Luckman, Thomas, 79
Lyerla, Rob, 95
Lyman, Stanford M., 280
Lynch, James P., 395-396
Lynch, Michael, 75
Lynchings, 341, 342*e*

Madsen, Richard, 298, 300-301
Magnuson, Diana L., 355
Mailed survey A survey involving a mailed questionnaire to be completed by the respondent, 248
   compared to other survey designs, 247-248, 247*e*, 264-266, 265*e*
   costs, 229, 248
   cover letters, 249, 250*e*
   follow-up mailings, 248, 249
   incentives, 251
   incomplete responses, 252
   nonrespondents, 136, 251
   procedure, 248-249
   questionnaires, 229
   response rates, 248, 250-252, 265-266
   See also **Survey research**
Malinowski, Bronislaw, 280
Mangen, Steen, 361
Mangione, Thomas W., 250, 269
Manning, Charley, 235
Manpower Demonstration Research Corporation, 325
Marginal distribution The summary distributions in the margins of a crosstabulation that correspond to the frequency distribution of the row variable and of the column variable, 393
Marini, Margaret Mooney, 186
Marlatt, G. Alan, 117
Marler, Penny Long, 94
Marsh, Robert M., 357

Marshall, Ineke Haen, 168

Martin, Elizabeth, 97, 230, 235, 239, 245

Martin, Lawrence L., 314

Martin, Linda G., 358

Marx, Karl, 64, 66-67, 194-195, 338

MAST. *See* Michigan Alcoholism Screening Test

Matching   A procedure for equating the characteristics of individuals in different comparison groups in an experiment. Matching can be done on either an individual or an aggregate basis. For individual matching, individuals who are similar in terms of key characteristics are paired prior to assignment, and then the two members of each pair are assigned to the two groups. For aggregate matching, groups are chosen for comparison that are similar in terms of the distribution of key characteristics, 198, 200*e*

Matrix questions, 245, 246*e*

Matrix   A form on which can be recorded systematically particular features of multiple cases or instances that a qualitative data analyst needs to examine, 425, 426, 426*e*, 427*e*

Matt, Georg E., 460

Maxwell, Joseph A., 278-279, 288, 421

Maynard, Douglas W., 79

McCammon, Holly J., 357, 358

McCarty, John A., 109

McClelland, Charles, 353

McEneaney, Elizabeth H., 357-358

McHugo, Gregory J., 120, 321

McKenna, Katelyn Y. A., 11, 20

McLellan, A. Thomas, 114, 115

Mead, George Herbert, 69

Mean   The arithmetic, or weighted, average, computed by adding up the value of all the cases and dividing by the total number of cases, 383-387

of normal distributions, 157-158

of random samples, 155

Measure of association   A type of descriptive statistic that summarizes the strength of an association, 398

See also **Association**

Measurement   The process of linking abstract concepts to empirical indicants, 91

choice of method, 104

combining operations, 104-105

developing new measures, 120

errors, 104-105

in historical and comparative research, 357-358

in qualitative research, 121

questions, 94-97

See also Data collection; **Level of measurement**

Measurement validity   Exists when a measure measures what we think it measures, 16, 17, 112-113

construct validity, 114-115

content validity, 113

criterion validity, 113-114, 115

face validity, 113

problems with, 17

Mechanism   A discernible process that creates a causal connection between two variables, 181, 186-188

in nonexperiments, 211

in quasi-experiments, 208

in true experiments, 203

Media

content analysis, 104

interviews, 127

research reported in, 470-471

violence in, 178, 178*e*

See also Television

Median   The position average, or the point that divides a distribution in half (the 50th percentile), 383, 384-387

Medical self-help groups, 12-13, 19, 21

Medical students, 425

Meeker, Barbara Foley, 179, 188

Meeker, James W., 52

Meilman, Philip W., 95

Mental health

community mental health systems, 268

employment services for mentally ill, 321, 322*e*

Global Assessment of Functioning Scale, 103, 117, 118*e*

See also Depression; Homeless mentally ill

Merton, Robert K., 71, 302

Meta-analysis   The quantitative analysis of findings from multiple studies, 459

case study, 460-461

evaluating, 462

process, 459-460

studies included, 459-460

Method of agreement   A method proposed by John Stuart Mill for establishing a causal relation, in which the values of cases that agree on an outcome variable also agree on the value of the variable hypothesized to have a causal effect, while they differ in terms of other variables, 359-360, 360*e*

Mexico, census, 354
Miami-Dade Spouse Assault Experiment, 38-40, 48
Michigan Alcoholism Screening Test (MAST), 113
Michigan Employment Security Commission, 196
Michigan Survey Research Center, 235
Mieczkowski, Tom, 114
Miethe, Terance D., 94
Milbrath, Lester, 368
Miles, Matthew B., 423, 425, 436, 442-443
Milgram, Stanley, 132-133, 218
Mill, John Stuart, 359-360
Miller, Delbert C., 172, 240, 250, 257
Miller, Susan, 421-422, 429
Miller, William L., 279, 298, 416, 417
Mills, C. Wright, 28
Mills, Judson, 220-221
Milwaukee (Wisconsin)
    domestic violence experiment, 41, 48
    Project New Hope, 330-331, 330*e*
Mineau, Geraldine P., 357
Minneapolis Domestic Violence Experiment
    articles on, 30, 52-53
    background, 51
    causal mechanisms studied, 187
    critiques of, 74
    definition of domestic assault, 74
    deterrence theory, 30, 43, 44*e*, 48, 71
    ethical issues, 55, 221-222
    generalizability, 215
    hypothesis, 47
    influence, 27-28, 52-53
    labeling theory, 30-31, 43, 44*e*
    outcomes, 329-330
    publicity, 52-53
    random assignment of arrests, 55, 73, 74,
        212, 317-318
    replication studies, 28, 29, 38-40, 41, 47-48,
        53, 73, 74, 187, 189
    research circle and, 47-48, 48*e*
    research design, 47, 317-318
    resources needed, 30
    theoretical background, 30-31, 42-43, 44*e*, 71
    unemployment rates, 189
    See also Domestic violence
Minnesota Population Center (MPC), 351
Miringoff, Marc, 87
Mirowsky, John, 240, 269
Mitchell, Richard G., Jr., 286
Mixed-mode surveys Surveys that are
    conducted by more than one method,
    allowing the strengths of one survey design to
    compensate for the weaknesses of another and
    maximizing the likelihood of securing data
    from different types of respondents; for
    example, nonrespondents in a mailed survey
    may be interviewed in person or over the
    phone, 264, 265
Mode The most frequent value in a distribution;
    also termed the probability average, 382-383
Moffitt, Robert, 467-468
Mohr, Lawrence B., 198, 201, 204, 213, 329, 330
Monkkonen, Eric H., 339
Monotonic A pattern of association in which the
    value of cases on one variable increases or
    decreases fairly regularly across the categories
    of another variable, 397
Montalvan, Pat, 259
Mooney, Christopher Z., 101
Moore, David W., 237
Moore, Paul C., 199-201, 202-203
Morenoff, Jeffrey D., 65
Morgan, S. Philip, 343
Morrill, Calvin, 414, 415, 419-420, 434-436
Morris, Michael W., 199-201, 202-203
Mosher, Clayton J., 94
MPC. *See* Minnesota Population Center
Mueser, Kim T., 88
Multidimensional index An index containing
    subsets of questions that measure different
    aspects of the same concept, 100
Multinational corporations, power of, 67, 68*e*
Multiple group before-and-after design A type
    of quasi-experimental design in which several
    before-and-after comparisons are made
    involving the same independent and dependent
    variables but different groups, 206-207
Multiple regression analysis, 407
Muncer, Steve, 12-13
Musheno, Michael, 415
Mutually exclusive A variable's attributes
    (or values) are mutually exclusive when every
    case can be classified as having only one
    attribute (or value), 107

Nader, Ralph, 138
Nagourney, Adam, 231
Narrative analysis A form of qualitative
    analysis in which the analyst focuses on how
    respondents impose order on the flow of
    experience in their lives and so make sense
    of events and actions in which they have
    participated, 434-436, 435*e*

Narrative explanation   An idiographic causal explanation that involves developing a narrative of events and processes that indicate a chain of causes and effects, 340

National Geographic Society, survey of worldwide Internet use, 11-12, 14, 17-18, 20, 21, 22, 128, 131

National Incident-Based Reporting System (NIBRS), 94

National Institute of Alcohol Abuse and Alcoholism (NIAAA), 86, 113

National Institute of Justice, 47

National Institute of Mental Health (NIMH), 120, 418
    grant proposals, 451, 454-455e
    review committee, 453-457

National Institutes of Health (NIH)
    Office for Protection from Research Risks, 53
    Research Plan, 451

National Opinion Research Center, 230, 353

National Science Foundation, 228

National Technical Information Service (NTIS), 352

Natural environment, 81

Needleman, Carolyn, 267

Needs assessment   A type of evaluation research that attempts to determine the needs of some population that might be met with a social program, 315-317

Neighborhoods, influence on children's development, 65, 66e

Nelson, Toben F., 85

Netcraft, 62

Nett, Roger, 78

Nettleton, Sarah, 12-13

Netville, 1-2, 14, 15e, 18, 19, 22, 128, 131

Neuendorf, Kimberly A., 440

New Deal, 343

New Jersey Income Maintenance Experiment, 311-312, 317

New York City
    cholera epidemic, 7
    violent crime rate, 165

Newport, Frank, 138, 237-238

Newsweek, 374-377

NIAAA. *See* National Institute of Alcohol Abuse and Alcoholism

NIBRS. *See* National Incident-Based Reporting System

Nie, Norman, 369, 370

Nie, Norman H., 4, 10, 11, 13, 14, 17, 18, 21, 22, 128, 131

Niemi, Richard G., 346

NIH. *See* National Institutes of Health

NIMH. *See* National Institute of Mental Health

Nixon, Richard M., 233

Nominal level of measurement   Variables whose values have no mathematical interpretation; they vary in kind or quality, but not in amount, 106e, 107-108, 373

Nomothetic causal explanation   An explanation that identifies common influences on a number of cases or events, 177-179, 181
    See also Experimental designs

Nonequivalent control group design   A quasi-experimental design in which there are experimental and comparison groups that are designated before the treatment occurs but are not created by random assignment, 204-205, 205e, 212-213

Nonexperimental designs, 208
    causality, 211
    criteria for relationship, 181, 183, 184, 185
    ex post facto control group designs, 208-210, 209e
    intervening variables, 187
    one-shot case studies, 210

Nonprobability sampling methods   Sampling methods in which the probability of selection of population elements is unknown, 135, 146-147
    availability sampling, 147-148, 359
    purposive sampling, 150-151, 290, 359
    quota sampling, 148-150, 149e, 150e, 290
    snowball sampling, 151-152, 268, 290, 432

Nonrespondents   People or other entities who do not participate in a study although they are selected for the sample, 136
    to General Social Survey, 260, 260e
    to mailed surveys, 136, 251
    to phone surveys, 231
    to surveys, 230, 231

Nonspuriousness   A criterion for establishing a causal relation between two variables; a relationship between two variables is nonspurious when it is not due to variation in a third variable, 181, 184-186, 399
    in nonexperiments, 211
    in quasi-experiments, 208
    in true experiments, 203
    See also **Spurious relationship**

Normal distribution A symmetric, bell-shaped distribution that results from chance variation around a mean, 155-156, 157-158, 157*e*, 390, 390*e*

Normal science Research that accepts the dominant scientific paradigm and attempts to test or refine predictions made within that paradigm, 71

Norris, Pippa, 346

Notes. *See* **Field notes**

Novak, David, 34

NTIS. *See* National Technical Information Service

Nunberg, Geoffrey, 87

Nursing homes, 276-277, 278, 280-282, 290

NVivo, 437, 438*e*, 439, 439*e*

O'Brien, John, 100

Observations
    direct, 102-103
    errors of, 230
    systematic, 296-297
    See also **Participant observation**

O'Dochartaigh, Niall, 34

Office of Management and the Budget, 312

Olzak, Susan, 357-358

Omaha (Nebraska), domestic violence experiment, 48, 53

Omnibus survey A survey that covers a range of topics of interest to different social scientists, 229-230

One-shot case studies, 210

Open-ended question A survey question to which the respondent replies in his or her own words, either by writing or by talking, 96

Openness, 52

Operation A procedure for identifying or indicating the value of cases on a variable, 91

Operationalization The process of specifying the operations that will indicate the value of cases on a variable, 89-92, 90*e*

Optical illusions, 6, 6*e*

Oral history Data collected through intensive interviews with participants in past events, 343

Orcutt, James D., 376

Ordinal level of measurement A measurement of a variable in which the numbers indicating a variable's values specify only the order of the cases, permitting "greater than" and "less than" distinctions, 106*e*, 108-109, 373

Orr, Larry L., 311, 323

Orshansky, Mollie, 89

Osgood, D. Wayne, 168

Outcomes The impact of the program process on the cases processed, 313-314, 329-331

Outlier An exceptionally high or low value in a distribution, 388

Outputs The services delivered or new products produced by the program process, 313, 314

Overgeneralization Occurs when we unjustifiably conclude that what is true for some cases is true for all cases, 5*e*, 6, 8, 21

Pagnini, Deanna, 343

Paige, Jeffery M., 348

Panel studies. *See* **Fixed-sample panel design**

Papineau, David, 188

Paradigm shift A major shift in scientific beliefs, including a change in presuppositions, theories, and accepted research findings, 71-72

Park, Bernadette, 120

Parks, Malcolm, 6

Parlett, Malcolm, 416

Participant observation A qualitative method for gathering data that involves developing a sustained relationship with people while they go about their normal activities, 277, 282
    combined with intensive interviews, 301-302
    complete observation, 282, 284
    complete participation, 282, 285-287, 304
    developing relationships, 288-290
    entering field, 287-288
    ethical issues, 285, 286-287, 304
    illegal activities, 285
    notes, 293-295
    participation and observation, 282, 284-285
    personal dimensions, 295-296
    reactive effects, 284, 428
    researcher roles, 282-287, 283*e*
    sampling, 290-292, 291*e*

Participatory action research A type of research in which the researcher involves some organizational members as active participants throughout the process of studying an organization; the goal is making changes in the organization, 78

Participatory research, 327

Part-whole question effects These occur when responses to a general or summary question about a topic are influenced by responses to an earlier, more specific question about that topic, 245

Pate, Antony M., 38-40, 48, 49

Paternoster, Raymond, 41, 43
Patterson, Orlando, 108
Patton, Michael Quinn, 312, 317, 320, 322, 326,
    327, 328-329, 415, 431
Paxton, Pamela, 354, 358
Pearson, Frederic, 353
Penk, Walter E., 173, 456
Pepinsky, Harold E., 285
Percentages   Relative frequencies, computed by
    dividing the frequency of cases in a particular
    category by the total number of cases, and
    multiplying by 100, 393-394, 395*e*
Periodicity   A sequence of elements (in a list to be
    sampled) that varies in some regular, periodic
    pattern, 141, 141*e*
Personal interviews. *See* **In-person interview**;
    Interviews
Peterson, Robert A., 95, 233, 239, 241, 244, 245,
    258, 264
Petrosino, Anthony, 313
Pew Internet & American Life Project, 17, 22
Phillips, David P., 206-207
Phillips, Dretha M., 94
Phone survey   A survey in which interviewers
    question respondents over the phone and then
    record their answers, 252-253
    compared to other survey designs, 247-248,
        247*e*, 264-266, 265*e*
    computer-assisted, 257-258
    costs, 229, 248
    interview schedules, 253, 254-256*e*
    interviewer instructions, 256, 257*e*
    interviewer training, 257
    maximizing response, 256-258, 266
    nonresponse, 231
    political polls, 229
    random digit dialing, 139-140, 253
    rapport with respondents, 79
    reaching sample units, 253, 256
    response rates, 258
    See also **Survey research**
Pilot studies, 57
Placebo effect   A source of treatment
    misidentification that can occur when subjects
    receive a treatment that they consider likely to
    be beneficial, and improve because of that
    expectation rather than because of the
    treatment itself, 215
Planetary Society, 232
Pleace, Nicolas, 12-13
Plessy, Homer, 107

Plessy v. Ferguson, 107
Police
    D.A.R.E. program, 310-311, 318-319,
        318*e*, 320-321
    masculinity of neighborhood officers, 429
    New York City, 165
    observation of, 102, 288-289
    See also Minneapolis Domestic Violence
        Experiment
Police Foundation, 27, 38
Pollner, Melvin, 259
Polls. *See* **Survey research**
Population   The entire set of individuals or other
    entities to which study findings are to be
    generalized, 128, 129
    defining, 129-131
    diversity, 132-134, 137
    target, 132
Population change, 355
Population composition, 356-357, 356*e*
Population parameter   The value of a statistic,
    such as a mean, computed using the data for
    the entire population; a sample statistic is an
    estimate of a population parameter, 157
Posavac, Emil J., 314, 315, 320, 333
Positivism   The philosophical view that an
    external, objective reality exists apart from
    human perceptions of it, 72, 73-75, 78
Postpositivism   A philosophical view that
    modifies the positivist premise of an external,
    objective reality by recognizing its complexity,
    the limitations of human observers, and
    therefore the impossibility of developing
    more than a partial understanding of reality,
    73, 74, 78
Posttest   In experimental research, the
    measurement of an outcome (dependent)
    variable after an experimental intervention or
    after a presumed independent variable has
    changed for some other reason, 197, 213
Poverty
    definitions, 88-89
    measurement of, 92
    relationship to delinquency, 81
Predictive validity   The type of validity that exists
    when a measure predicts scores on a criterion
    measured in the future, 114
Prejudice, 87
Presley, Cheryl A., 95
Presser, Stanley, 218, 234, 235, 236, 238,
    241, 243, 245

Pretest   In experimental research, the measurement of an outcome (dependent) variable prior to an experimental intervention or change in a presumed independent variable for some other reason. The pretest is exactly the same "test" as the posttest, but it is administered at a different time, 197-198
  influence on posttest scores, 213
  interaction with treatment, 216-217
Pretest-posttest control group design. *See* **Randomized comparative change design**
Prewitt, Kenneth, 134
Price, Richard H., 196-197, 202, 203, 213-214, 216, 221
Prisons
  boot camps, 329, 330
  education in women's, 322
  simulation study, 54, 55
  studies of released prisoners, 319, 319*e*
Probability average. *See* **Mode**
Probability of selection   The likelihood that an element will be selected from the population for inclusion in the sample. In a census of all the elements of a population, the probability that any particular element will be selected is 1.0. If half the elements in the population are sampled on the basis of chance (say, by tossing a coin), the probability of selection for each element is one-half, or .5. As the size of the sample as a proportion of the population decreases, so does the probability of selection, 135-136
Probability sampling method   A sampling method that relies on a random, or chance, selection method so that the probability of selection of population elements is known, 135-137
  cluster sampling, 144-146
  simple random sampling, 139-140
  stratified random sampling, 141-143, 145-146, 149, 150*e*
  systematic random sampling, 140-141
Probation officers, 267
Procedural justice, 41, 43
Process analysis   A research design in which periodic measures are taken to determine whether a treatment is being delivered as planned, usually in a field experiment, 217-218, 328-329

Process evaluation   Evaluation research that investigates the process of service delivery, 317-320
Program process   The complete treatment or service delivered by the program, 313, 314
Program theory   A descriptive or prescriptive model of how a program operates and produces effects, 325-326, 326*e*
Progressive focusing   The process by which a qualitative analyst interacts with the data and gradually refines her focus, 416
Project New Hope, 330-331, 330*e*
Proportionate stratified sampling   Sampling method in which elements are selected from strata in exact proportion to their representation in the population, 142, 143*e*
Proposals. *See* Research proposals
Protestant Reformation, 67
Punch, Maurice, 287
Purdy, Matthew, 229
Purposive sampling   A nonprobability sampling method in which elements are selected for a purpose, usually because of their unique position, 150-151, 290, 359
Push polling, 235
Putnam, Israel, 89

QCA. *See* **Qualitative comparative analysis**
QSR NVivo. *See* NVivo
Qualitative comparative analysis (QCA)   A systematic type of qualitative analysis that identifies the combination of factors that had to be present across multiple cases to produce a particular outcome, 432-434, 433*e*
Qualitative data analysis
  alternative approaches, 430-437
  as art, 417
  authenticity of conclusions, 427-429
  coding, 425, 426*e*, 427*e*
  computer-assisted, 437-440
  conceptualization, 423-425
  "dance" of, 417, 418*e*
  difference from quantitative, 415
  documentation, 422-423
  emic focus, 415
  ethical issues, 442-443
  ethnography, 417, 431-432
  examining relationships, 425-427, 428*e*
  features, 415-417
  grounded theory, 436-437, 436*e*
  narrative analysis, 434-436, 435*e*

phases, 421-422, 422e
qualitative comparative analysis,
    432-434, 433e
quality criteria, 443
reflexivity, 429-430
research questions, 418-420
software, 437-440, 523-543
See also **Content analysis**
Qualitative methods   Methods such as participant
    observation, intensive interviewing, and focus
    groups that are designed to capture social life
    as participants experience it, rather than in
    categories predetermined by the researcher.
    These methods typically involve exploratory
    research questions, inductive reasoning,
    an orientation to social context, human
    objectivity, and the meanings attached by
    participants to events and to their lives, 14-15
authenticity as goal, 17, 20, 427-429
case study, 280-282
characteristics, 278-279
combining with other methods, 267-268
compared to other research designs, 458-459
distinction from experimental and survey
    research, 278
distinction from quantitative methods, 15, 16
ethical issues, 285, 286-287, 303-305
generalizability, 154
in evaluation research, 320, 328-329
in historical and comparative research, 340,
    344, 346
interpretivism, 75-78, 154
measurement, 121
origins, 280
process, 279-280, 279e
reflexive process, 278-279, 279e, 429-430
researcher roles, 279
sampling, 290-292
sampling methods, 146-147
use of, 15
See also **Focus groups**; **Intensive interviewing**;
    Participant observation
Quality assurance reviews, 312
Quantitative methods   Methods such as surveys
    and experiments that record variation in social
    life in terms of categories that vary in amount.
    Data that are treated as quantitative are either
    numbers or attributes that can be ordered in
    terms of magnitude, 14
distinction from qualitative methods, 15, 16
use of, 15

Quartiles   The points in a distribution
    corresponding to the first 25% of the cases, the
    first 50% of the cases, and the last 25% of the
    cases, 388
Quasi-experimental design   A research design in
    which there is a comparison group that is
    comparable to the experimental group in
    critical ways, but in which subjects are not
    randomly assigned to the comparison and
    experimental groups, 198, 203-204
before-and-after designs, 204, 205e,
    206-208
causality, 208
in evaluation research, 321-322
in historical research, 340
nonequivalent control group designs, 204-205,
    205e, 212-213
validity, 211
Quesada, James, 147
Questionnaire   The survey instrument
    containing the questions in a self-administered
    survey, 240
context effects, 244-245
data entry from, 370, 371e
designing, 240, 244
existing instruments, 240
instructions, 246-247
layout, 245-247
length, 229
pilot studies, 241-242
precoding, 370
pretesting, 239, 241-242
question order, 244-245
skip patterns, 234, 234e, 246
See also **Interview schedule**
Questions
agreement bias and, 235-236
bias in, 234-235
constructing, 94-95, 231-232
contingent, 234
disadvantages, 104
filter, 234, 234e, 239, 244
forced-choice, 237-238
"grand tour," 298
in intensive interviews, 298-299, 300-301
interpretive, 242-243
matrix, 245, 246e
open-ended, 96
pretesting, 239, 241-242
refining, 241-242
sequence of, 244-245

sets, 97
single, 95-96
wording, 218, 232-235
See also **Closed-ended question**
Quota sampling A nonprobability sampling method in which elements are selected to ensure that the sample represents certain characteristics in proportion to their prevalence in the population, 148-150, 149*e*, 150*e*, 290

Race
by region of United States, 395, 395*e*
classifications, 107-108
housing preferences and, 219
voting, income, and, 403-404, 405*e*
See also African Americans; White Americans
Ragin, Charles C., 290, 340, 348, 360
Rallis, Sharon F., 287, 288, 289, 298
RAND Corporation, 311
Rand, Michael R., 395-396
Random assignment A procedure by which each experimental subject is placed in a group randomly, 184, 185*e*, 198
distinction from random sampling, 198, 199*e*
Random digit dialing The random dialing by a machine of numbers within designated phone prefixes, which creates a random sample for phone surveys, 139-140, 253
Random number table A table containing lists of numbers that are ordered solely on the basis of chance; it is used for drawing a random sample, 139, 505-507
Random sampling A method of sampling that relies on a random, or chance, selection method so that every element of the sampling frame has a known probability of being selected, 136
distinction from random assignment, 198, 199*e*
probability of selection, 135-136
simple, 139-140
stratified, 141-143, 145-146, 149, 150*e*
systematic, 140-141
weighted, 142-143, 144*e*
Random sampling error Differences between the population and the sample that are due only to chance factors (random error), not to systematic sampling error. Random sampling error may or may not result in an unrepresentative sample. The magnitude of sampling error due to chance factors can be

estimated statistically. Also known as chance sampling error, 156
Randomization The random assignment of cases, as by the toss of a coin, 184, 198, 212
Randomized comparative change design The classic true experimental design in which subjects are assigned randomly to two groups; both these groups receive a pretest, one group then receives the experimental intervention, and then both groups receive a posttest. Also called the posttest-only control group design, 198, 321, 322*e*
Randomized comparative posttest design A true experimental design in which subjects are assigned randomly to two groups—one group then receives the experimental intervention and both groups receive a posttest; there is no pretest, 199-201
Range The true upper limit in a distribution minus the true lower limit (or the highest rounded value minus the lowest rounded value, plus one), 387-388
interquartile, 388-389
Rankin, Joseph H., 460-461
Rashbaum, William K., 165
Ratio level of measurement A measurement of a variable in which the numbers indicating a variable's values represent fixed measuring units and an absolute zero point, 106*e*, 110-111, 373
Rational choice theory Explains social processes in terms of rational cost/benefit calculations that shape individual behavior, 43, 44*e*, 64, 67-68, 70
See also Deterrence theory
Raudenbush, Stephen W., 166-167, 175, 177, 181, 182, 183, 184, 185, 297
Reactive effects The changes in an individual or group behavior that are due to being observed or otherwise studied, 284, 428
Reasoning, errors in, 4, 5-8
Reductionist fallacy (reductionism) An error in reasoning that occurs when incorrect conclusions about group-level processes are based on individual-level data. Also known as individualist fallacy, 176, 176*e*
Reflexive research design, 278-279, 279*e*
Regression analysis A statistical technique for characterizing the pattern of a relationship between two quantitative variables in terms of a linear equation and for summarizing

the strength of this relationship in terms of its deviation from that linear pattern, 405-407

Regression effect A source of causal invalidity that occurs when subjects who are chosen for a study because of their extreme scores on the dependent variable become less extreme on the posttest due to natural cyclical or episodic change in the variable, 213

Reisman, David, 9

Reiss, Albert J., Jr., 102, 297

Rele, J. R., 355

Reliability A measurement procedure yields consistent scores when the phenomenon being measure is not changing, 115-116
  alternate-forms, 117
  comparison to validity, 119*e*
  improving, 117-121
  interitem, 116-117
  interobserver, 117
  intraobserver, 116
  split-halves, 117
  test-retest, 116, 120

Reliability measures Statistics that summarize the consistency among a set of measures. Cronbach's alpha is the most common measure of the reliability of a set of items included in an index, 98

Repeated cross-sectional design A longitudinal study in which data are collected at two or more points in time from different samples of the same population; also called trend study, 169-171

Repeated measures panel design A quasi-experimental design consisting of several pretest and posttest observations of the same group, 207

Replacement sampling A method of sampling in which sample elements are returned to the sampling frame after being selected, so they may be sampled again. Random samples may be selected with or without replacement, 139

Replications Repetitions of a study using the same research methods to answer the same research question, 47-48, 74

Reports, research
  applied reports, 465-468
  coauthored, 470
  controversial, 470
  critiquing, 37-38
  ethical issues, 468-471
  evaluating, 471
  media outlets, 470-471
  organization, 463
  writing, 462-463
  See also Journal articles

Representative sample A sample that "looks like" the population from which it was selected in all respects that are potentially relevant to the study. The distribution of characteristics among the elements of a representative sample is the same as the distribution of those characteristics among the total population. In an unrepresentative sample, some characteristics are overrepresented or underrepresented, 133-134, 133*e*, 137

Requests for proposals (RFPs), 29

Research circle A diagram of the elements of the research process, including theories, hypotheses, data collection, and data analysis, 44, 45*e*
  application of, 47-48, 48*e*, 49-50, 50*e*

Research designs
  combined methods, 267-268
  comparison, 457-459, 457*e*
  cross-sectional, 166-171, 210
  longitudinal, 166, 169-174
  reflexive, 278-279, 279*e*
  triangulation, 15-16
  See also Comparative research; Experimental designs; Historical research; Non-experimental designs; **Qualitative methods**; **Survey research**

Research organizations, 40, 311, 312

Research proposals
  case study, 451-457
  developing, 451, 452-453*e*
  reviews, 453-457
  sections, 56, 451
  writing, 56

Research questions. *See* **Social research question**

Research reports. *See* Reports, research

Research Triangle Institute, 318

Resistance to change The reluctance to change our ideas in light of new information, 7-8, 22

Respondent-driven sampling, 151-152, 152*e*, 153*e*
  See also **Snowball sampling**

Respondents
  anonymity, 269, 304
  confidentiality, 55, 268-269, 304-305, 332-333
  fence-sitters, 236, 238

floaters, 236-238, 237*e*
See also Human subjects, research on;
   Nonrespondents
Reverse outlining   Outlining the sections in an
   already written draft of a paper or report in
   order to improve its organization in the next
   draft, 463
Revolutions, 346
Reynolds, Paul Davidson, 54, 55
RFPs. *See* Requests for proposals
Richards, Lyn, 437
Richards, Thomas J., 437
Richardson, Laurel, 179, 434
Riedel, Marc, 354, 355, 361
Riessman, Catherine Kohler, 434
Ringwalt, Christopher L., 311, 318, 319
Rives, Norfleet W., Jr., 350, 354
Roberts, Chris, 10
Robertson, David Brian, 340
Robinson, John P., 102
Rohsenow, D. J., 88
Roosevelt, Franklin Delano, 138
Roper polls, 233
Rosenbaum, David E., 134
Rosenberg, Morris, 240, 399
Rosenthal, Elizabeth, 354
Rosenthal, Rob, 151
Ross, Catherine E., 228, 229, 230, 234-235, 238,
   239, 240, 242, 243, 244, 247, 253, 256, 269
Rossi, Peter H., 94, 145, 198, 204, 208, 209, 222,
   311, 315, 319, 320, 328, 470
Rossman, Gretchen B., 287, 288, 289, 298
Roth, Dee, 151
Rubin, Herbert J., 75, 150-151, 298, 299, 300
Rubin, Irene S., 75, 150-151, 298, 299, 300
Rueschemeyer, Dietrich, 348, 350, 357, 359
Ruggles, Patricia, 89
Russia, census, 135
Russo, M. Jean, 15, 73, 216, 334

Sacks, Stanley, 324
Salisbury, Robert H., 368
Sample   A subset of a population that is used to
   study the population as a whole, 128
   components, 128-131
   fraction of population, 137
   in historical and comparative research,
      358-359
   in qualitative research, 290-292
   planning, 128-135
   quality, 152-154

representative, 133-134, 133*e*, 137
   sizes, 137, 159-160
Sample generalizability   Exists when a conclusion
   based on a sample, or subset, of a larger
   population holds true for that population,
   18, 19*e*
   evaluating, 131-132
   in experiments, 215-216
Sample statistic   The value of a statistic,
   such as a mean, computed from sample
   data, 155, 157
Sampling distributions, 154-155, 157
   See also Distributions
Sampling error   Any difference between the
   characteristics of a sample and the
   characteristics of a population. The larger the
   sampling error, the less representative the
   sample, 131, 137
   estimating, 155
   in survey research, 230
   random, 156
   systematic, 136-137, 138-139
Sampling frame   A list of all elements or other
   units containing the elements in a population,
   128, 129
   adequacy, 136
   for surveys, 230
Sampling interval   The number of cases from one
   sampled case to another in a systematic
   random sample, 140, 141*e*
Sampling methods. *See* **Nonprobability sampling
   methods**; **Probability sampling method**;
   Theoretical sampling
Sampling units   Units listed at each stage of a
   multistage sampling design, 129
   primary, 129, 130*e*, 145
   secondary, 129, 130*e*
Sampson, Robert J., 31, 65, 71, 166-167, 171, 172,
   175, 176-177, 181, 182, 183, 184, 185, 186,
   187, 297
Sanders, Joseph, 43
Saturation point   The point at which
   subject selection is ended in intensive
   interviewing, when new interviews seem
   to yield little additional information, 151,
   299, 299*e*
Savelsberg, Joachim L., 79
Scale   A composite measure based on combining
   the responses to multiple questions pertaining
   to a common concept after these questions are
   differentially weighted, so that questions

judged on some basis to be more important for the underlying concept contribute more to the composite score, 100-102

Scatterplots, 406, 406*e*

Schaeffer, Nora Cate, 239

Schober, Michael F., 244

Schofer, Evan, 344, 359

Schofield, Janet Ward, 154

Schorr, Lisbeth B., 329

Schuckit, M. A., 85

Schuman, Howard, 218, 234, 235, 236, 238, 243, 245

Schutt, Russell K., 81, 96, 100, 173, 267, 315, 422, 429, 439, 456, 468

Schwandt, Thomas A., 75

Schwartz, Richard D., 103

Science A set of logical, systematic, documented methods for investigating nature and natural processes; the knowledge produced by these investigations, 8
normal, 71
positivism, 72, 73-75, 78
uses of, 52-53

Scientific paradigm The accepted theories, research findings, and unquestioned presuppositions that guide scientific work in an area, 71

Scientific revolution A sudden, radical change that overturns a paradigm (the prevailing wisdom in a scientific field), 71

Scott, Janny, 111

Scriven, Michael, 201, 328

Scull, Andrew T., 43

Search engines, 34-36, 502-503

Seattle-Denver Income Maintenance Experiment, 312

Sechrest, Lee, 16, 103

Secondary data Data analyzed to answer a research question by a researcher who did not participate in the study in which the data were collected, 348-350
demographic, 355-357
disadvantages, 370
quality, 93-94, 354, 358
sources, 93, 94, 350-353, 370
survey datasets, 94, 230, 353, 370

Secondary data analysis Analysis of data collected by someone other than the researcher or the researcher's assistants, 353-355, 370

Segregation, housing, 219

Seibring, Mark, 85

Seidman, Larry J., 79

Selection bias A source of internal (causal) invalidity that occurs when characteristics of experimental and comparison group subjects differ in any way that influences the outcome, 212-213

Selective observation Choosing to look only at things that are in line with our preferences or beliefs, 5-6, 5*e*, 8, 21

Self-fulfilling prophecy. *See* **Expectancies of experimental staff**

Seligman, Martin E. P., 240

Senate. *See* U.S. Senate

Serendipitous findings Unexpected patterns in data, which stimulate new ideas or theoretical approaches; also known as anomalous findings, 49, 407

Serow, William J., 350, 354

Sexuality
marital infidelity, 259
of adolescents, 81

Shadish, William R., 327

Shanahan, Suzanne, 357-358

Shaw, Linda L., 293

Shepherd, Jane, 259

Sherman, Lawrence W., 27, 28, 29, 30, 38, 41, 42, 43, 47, 48, 52, 53, 55, 71, 73, 74-75, 187, 189, 195, 203, 212, 215, 216, 221-222, 317-318, 329-330

Sheu, Wen-Jenn, 113

Shrum, L. J., 109

Sidani, Souraya, 16

Sieber, Joan A., 53, 54, 55, 56

Silverman, Stephen J., 40, 56, 451

Sim, Jeremiah Joseph, 107-108

Simple random sampling A method of sampling in which every sample element is selected only on the basis of chance, through a random process, 139-140

Singer, Burton, 186

Sjoberg, Gideon, 55, 78

Skewness The extent to which cases are clustered more at one or the other end of the distribution of a quantitative variable, rather than in a symmetric pattern around its center. Skew can be positive (a right skew), with the number of cases tapering off in the positive direction, or negative (a left skew), with the number of cases tapering off in the negative direction, 372, 384-385, 385*e*

Skinner, Harvey A., 113

Skip pattern   The unique combination of questions created in a survey by filter questions and contingent questions, 234, 234*e*, 246

Skocpol, Theda, 339, 347, 348, 359, 360

Skoll, Geoffrey R., 69, 71

Smith, Adam, 64, 67

Smith, Douglas A., 29

Smith, Joel, 78

Smith, Marc A., 10

Smith, Tom W., 230, 238

Smutylo, Terry, 322

Snow, David A., 419, 432-434

Snow, John, 7

Snowball sampling   A method of sampling in which sample elements are selected as they are identified by successive informants or interviewees, 151-152, 268, 290, 432

Soap opera suicides, 206-207, 207*e*

Sobell, Linda C., 116

Social class, 66, 92
   See also Social status

Social control, 90
   See also Informal social control

Social exchange theory, 231, 248

Social health, 86-87

Social research
   contexts, 80-81
   goals, 16, 75
   integrated philosophy, 78-79
   limitations, 22
   motives, 8-9
   sponsors, 40, 53, 251, 443, 470
   strengths, 21-22
   See also Literature searches

Social research question   A question about the social world that is answered through the collection and analysis of firsthand, verifiable, empirical data, 28
   descriptive, 10
   evaluating, 29-31
   explanatory, 11
   exploratory, 10-11
   feasibility, 30
   identifying, 28-29, 56-57
   pilot studies, 57
   refining, 29
   scientific relevance, 30-31
   social importance, 30
   theory and, 29

Social science   The use of scientific methods to investigate individuals, societies, and social processes; the knowledge produced by these investigations, 8

Social science approach   An orientation to evaluation research that expects researchers to emphasize the importance of researcher expertise and maintenance of autonomy from program stakeholders, 327-328

Social Security Administration, 89, 352

Social status
   definitions, 90
   voter participation and, 368-369, 369*e*, 399-401
   See also Social class

Society, as basis of social organization, 63

Sociological Abstracts Online, 32, 33*e*

Sociology
   field research, 280
   origins, 63-64

Software
   data definition, 372
   qualitative data analysis, 437-440
   statistical, 372
   See also HyperRESEARCH; SPSS

Solidarity
   mechanical, 64
   organic, 64-65

Solomon Four-Group Design, 217, 217*e*

Sonnenfeld, Jeffrey A., 210

Sosin, Michael R., 130-131

South Africa, divestment movement, 301-302

Spain, Center for Research on Social Reality [Spain] Survey, 353

Specification   A type of relationship involving three or more variables in which the association between the independent and dependent variables varies across the categories of one or more other control variables, 403-405

Spirduso, Waneen Wyrick, 40, 56, 451

Split-ballot design   Unique questions or other modifications in a survey administered to randomly selected subsets of the total survey sample, so that more questions can be included in the entire survey or so that responses to different question versions can be compared, 230, 245

Split-halves reliability   Reliability achieved when responses to the same questions by two randomly selected halves of a sample are about the same, 117

Sponsors, 40, 53, 251, 443, 470

Spouse abuse. *See* Domestic violence

SPSS (Statistical Package for the Social Sciences), 372, 508-522

Spurious relationship   A relationship between two variables that is due to variation in a third variable, 166, 188, 399, 401-402, 401*e*
   See also **Nonspuriousness**

SRI International, 311

SRL. *See* University of Illinois Survey Research Laboratory

Stack, Angela D., 181-182, 183-184, 188

Stake, Robert E., 416, 420-421, 423

Stakeholder approach   An orientation to evaluation research that expects researchers to be responsive primarily to the people involved with the program, 327

Stakeholders   Individuals and groups who have some basis of concern with the program, 314, 327-328

Standard deviation   The square root of the average squared deviation of each case from the mean, 390-391

Stanford Institute for the Quantitative Study of Society, 13, 22

Stanley, Julian C., 215

Statistical control   A method in which one variable is held constant so that the relationship between two (or more) other variables can be assessed without the influence of variation in the control variable, 185-186, 186*e*

Statistical Package for the Social Sciences. *See* SPSS

Statistical power analysis, 159

Statistical significance   The mathematical likelihood that an association is not due to chance, judged by a criterion set by the analyst (often that the probability is less than 5 out of 100, or p < .05), 398

Statistical software, 372

Statistics
   central tendency, 382-387
   descriptive, 368
   how not to lie with, 391
   inferential, 155, 368, 398
   interquartile ranges, 388-389
   mean, 383-387
   measures of association, 398

median, 383, 384-387
   mode, 382-383
   range, 387-388
   regression analysis, 405-407
   standard deviation, 390-391
   summary, 382, 387, 391
   variance, 389, 389*e*
   variation measures, 387-391

Stephens, Evelyne Huber, 348, 350, 357, 359

Stephens, John D., 348, 350, 357, 359

Stephens, Robert S., 117

Stewart, David W., 354

Stille, Alexander, 86, 87

Stratified random sampling   A method of sampling in which sample elements are selected separately from population strata that are identified in advance by the researcher, 141-143, 143*e*, 145-146
   difference from quota sampling, 149, 150*e*

Strauss, Anselm L., 290, 436

Street-level bureaucrats   Officials who serve clients and have a high degree of discretion, 268

Strunk, William, Jr., 463

Subject fatigue   Problems caused by panel members growing weary of repeated interviews and dropping out of a study or becoming so used to answering the standard questions in the survey that they start giving stock or thoughtless answers, 172-173

Substance abuse
   Addiction Severity Index, 114, 115
   Alcohol Abstinence Self-Efficacy Scale, 100, 101*e*
   alcohol use by college students, 85-86, 98, 99*e*
   binge drinking, 85, 86, 90, 91-92, 97, 112
   by adolescents, 102
   by homeless, 120
   D.A.R.E. program, 310-311, 318-319, 318*e*, 320-321
   definitions, 87-88
   effects of addiction, 180
   effects of alcohol, 88
   extent of problem, 85
   measurement of, 113-114
   prevention programs, 318*e*
   questionnaires, 116
   screening tests, 113
   self-report measures, 113-114, 117-119
   surveys, 95, 108, 108*e*, 110, 110*e*, 112
   therapeutic communities, 323-324

treatment costs, 86
treatment programs, 69, 121, 127, 323-324
Subtable Tables describing the relationship between two variables within the discrete categories of one or more other control variables, 399-401, 400*e*
Sudman, Seymour, 137, 160
Suicide
    Durkheim's study of, 64
    soap opera and actual, 206-207, 207*e*
Sullivan, William M., 298, 300-301
Summary statistics, 382, 387, 391
Summative evaluation. *See* **Impact evaluation**
Supreme Court, 107
Survey datasets, 94, 230, 353, 370
Survey research Research in which information is obtained from a sample of individuals through their responses to questions about themselves or others, 228
    advantages, 228-229
    compared to other research designs, 458
    comparison of design types, 247-248, 247*e*, 264-266, 265*e*
    costs, 229, 248
    errors in, 230-231
    ethical issues, 55, 268-269
    factorial surveys, 218-220
    fence-sitters, 236, 238
    floaters, 236-238, 237*e*
    generalizability, 229
    limitations, 408
    mixed-mode, 264, 265
    nonrespondents, 136, 230, 231
    omnibus surveys, 229-230
    presidential election polls, 137-139, 138*e*, 169, 237-238, 256
    pretesting, 120
    repeated cross-sectional designs, 169
    sample generalizability, 18
    See also **Electronic survey**; **Group-administered survey**; **In-person interview**; **Mailed survey**; **Phone survey**; **Questionnaire**
Swidler, Ann, 298, 300-301
Symbolic interaction theory Focuses on the symbolic nature of social interaction—how social interaction conveys meaning and promotes socialization, 43, 44*e*, 64, 68-69, 70
Systematic bias. *See* **Systematic sampling error**

Systematic observation A strategy that increases the reliability of observational data by using explicit rules that standardize coding practices across observers, 296-297
Systematic random sampling A method of sampling in which sample elements are selected from a list or from sequential files, with every *n*th element being selected after the first element is selected randomly within the first interval, 140-141
Systematic sampling error Overrepresentation or underrepresentation of some population characteristics in a sample due to the method used to select the sample. A sample shaped by systematic sampling error is a biased sample, 136-137, 138-139

Tacit knowledge In field research, a credible sense of understanding of social processes that reflects the researcher's awareness of participants' actions as well as their words, and of what they fail to state, feel deeply, and take for granted, 428
Taff, Gail, 86
Talley, Kathryn D., 149
Target population A set of elements larger than or different from the population sampled, to which the researcher would like to generalize study findings, 132
TARP. *See* Transitional Aid Research Project
Tavernise, Sabrina, 135
Taylor, Jerry, 310
Teenagers. *See* Adolescents
Telephone surveys. *See* **Phone survey**
Television
    medical shows, 440, 441*e*
    viewing habits and family activities, 292
Temporal A feature of narrative explanation, taking into account a related series of events that unfold over time, 340
Ten Point Coalition, 329
Tenner, Edward, 6
Termote, Marc G., 355
Test-retest reliability A measurement showing that measures of a phenomenon at two points in time are highly correlated, if the phenomenon has not changed, or have changed only as much as the phenomenon itself, 116, 120
Textual analysis. *See* **Content analysis**; Qualitative data analysis

Theoretical sampling   A sampling method recommended for field researchers by Glaser and Strauss (1967). A theoretical sample is drawn in a sequential fashion, with settings or individuals selected for study as earlier observations or interviews indicate that these settings or individuals are influential, 290-291, 292e

Theory   A logically interrelated set of propositions about empirical reality, 42
conflict theory, 64, 66-67, 70
functionalism, 64-65, 70
grounded, 436-437, 436e
paradigm change, 71-72
rational choice, 43, 44e, 64, 67-68, 70
research questions and, 29
role in social research, 41-44, 70-72
symbolic interactionism, 43, 64, 68-69, 70

Theory-driven evaluation   A program evaluation that is guided by a theory that specifies the process by which the program has an effect, 325-326

Thernstrom, Stephan A., 355

Thick description   A rich description that conveys a sense of what an experience is like, from the standpoint of the participants in it, 420-421

Thiemann, Sue, 159

Thorne, Barrie, 277, 278, 279, 284, 288, 290, 293, 296, 429-430

Time order   A criterion for establishing a causal relation between two variables. The variation in the presumed cause (the independent variable) must occur before the variation in the presumed effect (the dependent variable), 166, 181, 183-184
in cross-sectional studies, 167-169
in nonexperiments, 211
in quasi-experiments, 208
in true experiments, 203

Time series design   A quasi-experimental design consisting of many pretest and posttest observations of the same group, 207-208

Timmer, Doug A., 149

Tipton, Steven M., 298, 300-301

Toby, Jackson, 49

Tönnies, Ferdinand, 63

Toppo, Greg, 311

Toronto, Netville suburb of , 1-2, 14, 15e, 18, 19, 22, 128, 131

Tourangeau, Roger, 245

Tradition, devotion to, 7

Transitional Aid Research Project (TARP), 319, 319e

Treatment misidentification   A problem that occurs in an experiment when the treatment itself is not what causes the outcome, but rather the outcome is caused by some intervening process that the researcher has not identified and is not aware of, 212, 214-215

Trend studies. *See* **Repeated cross-sectional design**

Treno, Andrew J., 86

Triangulation   The use of multiple methods to study one research question, 15-16, 105

True experiment   Experiment in which subjects are assigned randomly to an experimental group that receives a treatment or other manipulation of the independent variable and a comparison group that does not receive the treatment or receives some other manipulation. Outcomes are measured in a posttest, 183, 195
causality, 202-203
design notation, 200, 201e
limitations, 201-202
posttests, 197
pretests, 197-198
validity, 211
See also Experimental designs

Truman, Harry S., 138

Tufte, Edward R., 377

Turabian, Kate L., 463

Turner, Charles F., 97, 230, 235, 239, 245

Turner, J. Blake, 376

Turner, Jean D. F., 210

Uchitelle, Louis, 89, 111

UCLA Center for Communication Policy, 3, 13, 22

UCLA Internet Project, 3, 14

UCR. *See* Uniform Crime Reports

Udry, J. Richard, 81

Unemployment, job-search services and depression, 196-197, 197e, 203, 213-214, 216, 221

Uniform Crime Reports (UCR), 94, 357

Unimodal   A distribution of a variable in which there is only one value that is the most frequent, 382, 383

United Nations, 353

U.S. Census Bureau, 94
advertising, 251
census reports, 104
Current Population Survey, 3, 350, 352
data available, 350-351
data quality, 354-355

geographic units, 350, 351*e*
income data, 111
international data, 353
multiracial classification, 107, 108
response rates, 134-135, 251
survey of Internet use, 9, 14
Web site, 350
U.S. Department of Commerce, 3, 9, 10, 14, 21, 261, 352
U.S. Department of Health and Human Services, 102, 332
U.S. Department of Justice, 38
U.S. Department of Labor, 352
U.S. Government Accounting Office, 320
U.S. House of Representatives, study of members, 284-285, 288, 290-291, 295, 301
U.S. Senate, Subcommittee on Problems of the Aged and Aging, 52
Units of analysis The level of social life on which a research question is focused, such as individuals, groups, towns, or nations, 174
ecological fallacy, 175, 176*e*
group, 174-175
individual, 174
reductionist fallacy, 176, 176*e*
Units of observation The cases about which measures actually are obtained in a sample, 175
Univariate distributions, 372-373
University of Chicago
Department of Sociology and Anthropology, 280
National Opinion Research Center, 230, 353
University of Illinois Survey Research Laboratory (SRL), 229, 253, 256
University of Massachusetts Medical School, 451, 456
University of Michigan. *See* Inter-University Consortium for Political and Social Research
University of Minnesota, Minnesota Population Center, 351
Unobtrusive measure A measurement based on physical traces or other data that are collected without the knowledge or participation of the individuals or groups that generated the data, 103-104
Utilization-focused evaluation, 327

Vaessen, Martin, 357
Vaillant, George E., 168
Validity The state that exists when statements or conclusions about empirical reality are correct, 16
comparison to reliability, 119*e*
concurrent, 114
improving, 117-121
of content analysis, 442, 443
of experimental designs, 211-215, 216
of quasi-experimental designs, 211
predictive, 114
See also **Causal validity**; **Measurement validity**
van de Vijver, Fons, 358
Van Maanen, John, 285, 288-289, 304, 431, 432
Van Ryn, Michelle, 196-197
Van Willigan, Marieke, 269
Van Winkle, Barrik, 439-440
Variability The extent to which cases are spread out through the distribution or clustered in just one location, 372
Variable A characteristic or property that can vary (take on different values or attributes), 44, 45
dependent, 44, 45
dichotomies, 111
extraneous, 188, 189*e*, 401-402
independent, 44, 45
intervening, 187, 188*e*, 399-401
measurement of, 92-93
operationalization, 89-92, 90*e*
Variable-oriented research Research that focuses attention on variables representing particular aspects of the units studied and then examines the relations among these variables across sets of cases, 346
Variance A statistic that measures the variability of a distribution as the average squared deviation of each case from the mean, 389, 389*e*
Verba, Sidney, 29, 178, 290, 358, 360, 369, 370
Verstehen Understanding human behavior by identifying the meaning that social actors give to their actions, 76
Victory, Nancy J., 9
Vidich Lyman, Arthur J., 280
Vinokur, Amiram D., 196-197
Voice response systems. *See* **Interactive voice response**
Voter participation
by education level, 401-402, 401*e*, 402*e*
gender and, 397, 398*e*
income and, 392-394, 393*e*, 399, 401-402, 403-405, 403*e*, 404*e*
race and, 403-404, 405*e*
social status and, 368-369, 369*e*, 399-401
trust and, 369, 397, 397*e*, 399-401, 400*e*, 404*e*

turnout rates, 346-347, 347*e*
See also Elections

W. K. Kellogg Foundation, 467
Wageman, Ruth, 204-205, 209
Waksberg, J., 253
Wallace, Michael, 67
Wallace, Walter L., 72, 73
Wallgren, Anders, 377
Walters, Pamela Barnhouse,
    357, 358
Ward, Andrew G., 210
Ware, Norma, 293
Watergate, 233
Watson, Charles G., 114
Weatherby, Norman L., 114
Web. *See* Internet
Web survey   A survey that is accessed and
    responded to on the World Wide Web, 261,
    262-263*e*
    See also **Electronic survey**
Web TV, 13
Webb, Eugene J., 103
Weber, Max, 67, 72, 75, 194, 338, 357
Weber, Robert Philip, 440, 442
Wechsler, Henry, 85, 86, 90, 97, 131
Weinberg, Darin, 121
Weis, Joseph G., 175
Weitzman, E. R., 85
Welfare programs
    evaluations, 311-312, 317, 325
    reforms, 325, 467-468
Wellman, Barry, 1, 9, 11, 12, 14, 15, 20, 128
Wells, L. Edward, 460-461
Wertz, Frederick J., 180-181
Western, Bruce, 48
Wheeler, Peter M., 352
White Americans
    attitudes toward births out of
        wedlock, 343
    political participation, 369
    poverty and juvenile delinquency, 81
    See also Race
White, Elwyn Brooks, 463
White, Michael J., 355, 356

Whyte, William Foote, 78, 285, 287-288, 289, 295,
    296, 304, 428-429
Williams, Ina, 281
Williams, Joseph M., 462-463
Williams, Kirk R., 38
Williams, Robert L., 289
Wilson, David B., 459, 460
Wilson, William Julius, 176, 470, 471
Witkin, Belle Ruth, 317
Witte, James, 11, 12, 20
Wittenbrink, Bernd, 120
Wolcott, Harry F., 278, 284, 289, 297, 299, 420
Women, attitudes toward births out of
    wedlock, 343
Work
    affective diversity in management teams, 210
    employment training programs, 323, 324*e*
    family life and, 227-228, 234-235, 240
    organization of, 194-195
    programs for poor persons, 330-331
    self-managing teams, 209-210, 209*e*
    team organization, 204-205, 206*e*
    See also Unemployment
World Bank, 311, 350
*World Handbook of Political and Social
    Indicators*, 352
Wu, Chia-ling, 269
Wunsch, Guillaume J., 355

Xerox, 204-205

Yalda, Christine, 415
Yamaguchi, Kazuo, 102
Yancey, George, 219
Yankelovich, Daniel, 329

Zaino, Jeanne, 372
Zanis, David, 117
Zaret, David, 358
Zaslow, Martha, 325
Zeller, Richard A., 91
Zetterberg, Hans L., 65
Zielbauer, Paul, 135
Zimbardo, Philip G., 54
Zitner, Aaron, 111